Lois P. Riley
966 E. Boulder Pass
Oro Valley, AZ 85737

The New Century Hymnal Companion

The New Century Hymnal Companion
A Guide to the Hymns

Edited by
Kristen L. Forman

The Pilgrim Press
Cleveland, Ohio

The Pilgrim Press, Cleveland, Ohio 44115
© 1998 by The Pilgrim Press

Biblical quotations are from the New Revised Standard Version of the Bible, © 1989 by the Division of Christian Education of the National Council of the Churches of Christ in the U.S.A., and are used by permission

Published 1998. All rights reserved. Permission is hereby granted for the "Hymn Profiles" to be reproduced in church bulletins for use in services of worship, provided that the following acknowledgment is included: From *The New Century Hymnal Companion*. Copyright © 1998 The Pilgrim Press. Used by permission.

Printed in the United States of America on acid-free paper

03   02   01   00   99   98   5   4   3   2   1

Library of Congress Cataloging-in-Publication Data
The new century hymnal companion : a guide to the hymns / edited by
   Kristen L. Forman.
     p.   cm.
   Includes bibliographical references (p.   ) and indexes.
   ISBN 0-8298-1207-5 (paper : alk. paper)
   1. United Church of Christ—Hymns—History and criticism.
2. Hymns, English—History and criticism.   I. Forman, Kristen L.
II. United Church of Christ.   III. New century hymnal.
ML3178.U56N48   1997
264'.05834023—dc21   97-34142
                                                                                                           CIP
                                                                                                            MN

Contents

Foreword   vii
    Mary Louise VanDyke
Preface   ix
    Kristen L. Forman

THE DEVELOPMENT OF THE NEW CENTURY HYMNAL

The Making of *The New Century Hymnal*   3
    James W. Crawford and Daniel L. Johnson
The Language of *The New Century Hymnal*   15
    Arthur G. Clyde

A SURVEY OF CHRISTIAN HYMNODY

Early Christian, Hebrew, Greek, and Latin Hymns in *The New Century Hymnal*   59
    Arthur G. Clyde
Hymnody from German, Scandinavian, and Finnish Sources   72
    Marilyn Kay Stulken
Sixteenth- and Seventeenth-Century Metrical Psalmody in Europe and Great Britain   83
    Emily R. Brink
Eighteenth- and Nineteenth-Century British Hymnody   95
    David W. Music
Hymnody in the United States through the Mid-Nineteenth Century   106
    Paul A. Richardson
U.S. Hymnody from the Mid-Nineteenth to Late Twentieth Centuries   125
    Mel R. Wilhoit
African American Worship Music   136
    Melva Wilson Costen
A Brief Survey of Asian Indigenous Hymnody   146
    Swee Hong Lim
A Survey of Hispanic Hymnody as Represented in *The New Century Hymnal*   154
    Raquel Mora Martínez

Twentieth-Century Hymnody in Great Britain VERNON WICKER	163
Theological Trends in Twentieth-Century Hymnody in the United States C. MICHAEL HAWN	177
A Survey of Hymn Tunes of the Late Twentieth Century JONATHAN B. MCNAIR	188
Ecumenical and Global Congregational Song in the Late Twentieth Century C. MICHAEL HAWN	199

HYMN PROFILES

Introduction to the Hymn Profiles	211
Profiles of the Hymns in *The New Century Hymnal* ROBERT L. ANDERSON	212
Bibliography to the Hymn Profiles	521
About the Contributors	525
Index to Survey of Christian Hymnody	531
Author, Composer, and Source Index	538
Tune Index	547
First Line Index	552

Foreword

The New Century Hymnal Companion clearly affirms that no hymn stands alone—each one grows out of the past, comments on the present, and embodies a hope for the future. Nor does the hymn singer sing alone—on every side stand the Old Testament psalmists, the sixteenth-century reformers, and the generations of spiritual pilgrims who search, question, affirm, and labor to share through congregational song their visions or encounters with God. Hymn singing can be uplifting, even transcending; but singing with understanding is the Christian's duty. Hence this book. A wealth of resources has been gathered here—facts that recreate for us the lives of hymns from their inspiration to the present. Here is reliable, timely information that can enrich a congregation's life, individually and corporately.

In *The New Century Hymnal* as in all collections, some of the hymns spring from joy, and others are forged in despair; some are outbursts of praise, and others confess weighty sins; some are meant to instruct for worldly life, and others share heavenly visions; some relate biblical events and paraphrase creeds while others speak in poetic metaphor. But from the perspective of these pages, they all "belong" together. Each one has a place in the journey of the Church Universal, and it is the purpose of this companion to help document their place on that journey. Here are hymnological essays and background notes on individual hymns that lend perspective on the historical origins as well as the authors, composers, and published sources of every hymn in *The New Century Hymnal*.

This volume lends itself to many uses; look upon it as a:

1. *Devotional aid.* It enriches quiet meditation or corporate worship through the stories of hymn texts by countless saints who have expressed their faithful vision through the poetry of hymns (e.g., Dietrich Bonhoeffer's "By Gracious Powers," hymn 413).
2. *Study guide.* It deepens a congregation's understanding of the events and impulses that inspired authors, composers, and folk songs throughout the centuries (e.g., "We Shall Overcome," hymn 570).
3. *History book.* It lends insight into hymns as diaries of the pilgrimages and experiences of the faithful who have tried through the centuries to live out what they believe (e.g. "We Who Would Valiant Be," hymn 494).
4. *Theological resource.* It sheds light on hymns as scriptural paraphrases, thus increasing familiarity with the Bible (e.g., "A Woman Came Who Did Not Count the Cost," hymn 206).

5. *Program builder*. It is a reference to the rich treasure of hymnody from a widening world, in which new and different translations and languages combine in exciting new ways (e.g., "O Kou Aloha No," hymn 580).

Above all, *The New Century Hymnal Companion* is an up-to-date guide that enables us to expand our understanding to match our singing. May it be used to increase our awareness of the ever-expanding community through which we experience unity in Christ as we sing God's many and varied songs.

MARY LOUISE VANDYKE

Preface

Well before the publication of *The New Century Hymnal* in 1995, worshipers and lovers of hymnody throughout the United Church of Christ and other denominations registered their hopes and visions for a companion to the new hymnal. Many expressed their appreciation for the innovative historical notes that appear at the bottom of each hymn page but clamored for yet more information specific to each hymn text and tune. Many others voiced their need for materials to better understand the origins of the hymnal and its landmark commitment to inclusive language. Still others offered numerous ideas as to what a useful companion might or might not encompass. Thus, the publication of *The New Century Hymnal Companion* became a major priority for the Pilgrim Press, and a variety of formats and means of compiling such a vast resource were explored.

The result, presented in these pages, is the work of many individuals who contributed their unique expertise, scholarship, and concern for the role of congregational song in worship. One individual, however, deserves credit for being the primary inspiration and impetus for the realization of the *Companion*, Robert L. Anderson.

In the 1980s, during his pastorate at Salem United Church of Christ in Wanatah, Indiana, Anderson and the church's organist, Isabelle Fitzsimmons, began providing the congregation with brief background notes on the hymns sung during Sunday worship. This weekly practice grew into a long-term project as Anderson decided to compile these notes and supplement them with others for future publication. He understood that busy parish pastors and church musicians do not have time to sift through the wealth of information provided in many existing companions and to develop concise, appropriate commentary for the congregation. Anderson's collection grew to include all the hymns in the three predecessor hymnals used in the United Church of Christ: *The Hymnal* of the Evangelical and Reformed Church (1941), the *Pilgrim Hymnal* (1958), and the first UCC *Hymnal* (1974). This collection and the concept of providing brief introductory sentences on the origin, author, and composer of each hymn became the basis for the hymn profiles in *The New Century Hymnal Companion*.

While that major component of the *Companion* offers immediate and specific information on every hymn, the thirteen essays that form "A Survey of Christian Hymnody" are invaluable for illuminating the historical and cultural contexts in which various genres of hymns emerged. These essays by leading hymnologists and church musicians enable individuals and church groups or congregations to identify hymns in *The New Century Hymnal* from a specific period of hymnody or a particular racial-ethnic tradition and to understand the broader movements within which they developed. Many companions offer similar hymnological essays, but all vary in the body of hymns that are discussed, because of the differing contents of the hymnals. *The New Century Hymnal*'s most noticeable difference, accentuated by these essays, is its strong multicultural emphasis. It is hoped that these essays will help to lead worshipers of all traditions to a greater appreciation of the gifts of others, and, as Raquel Mora Martínez envisions in her essay, "make the church a community where the miracle of Pentecost can be heard in the many tongues that sing of the one God."

The first section of the *Companion* fulfills the need for a documentation of the process and people that created *The New Century Hymnal*. This story, as recounted by the chairperson (James W. Crawford) and a member (Daniel L. Johnson) of the hymnal committee, outlines the mandate for a new hymnal in the United Church of Christ, the priorities established by the committee, and the theological dimensions that shaped its selection of hymns and commitment to inclusive language.

One person who was intimately involved throughout the process of hymn text revision explains how theological guidelines informed this task; he is Arthur G. Clyde, the editor of *The New Century Hymnal*. Although his thorough discussion, "The Language of *The New Century Hymnal*," was previously published in soft-cover format following the publication of the hymnal, its contents are indispensable to a full understanding of the greatest and most challenging aspect of this book. It is offered here to ensure its availability to a wider audience.

All of the aforementioned individuals and many others are to be thanked for making this *Companion* possible. Gratitude goes not only to the primary contributors, but especially to the many living hymnwriters and composers who responded to inquiries and who, through their inspired poetry and music following the legacy of earlier artists, enable us to "see God more clearly, to love God more dearly, and to follow God more nearly" in these days and in the century to come.

KRISTEN L. FORMAN

THE DEVELOPMENT OF *The New Century Hymnal*

THE MAKING OF *The New Century Hymnal*

James W. Crawford and Daniel L. Johnson

On June 29, 1995, at the Twentieth General Synod of the United Church of Christ, the United Church Board for Homeland Ministries (UCBHM) presented *The New Century Hymnal*. The hymnal expresses a hope rooted in Christ's prayer "that they may all be one" (John 17:21) and echoes the conviction of the author of the letter to the Hebrews (13:8): "Jesus Christ is the same yesterday, today, and forever." In the formation of *The New Century Hymnal*, those responsible for its preparation affirmed this prayer and conviction. One will find *The New Century Hymnal* rooted and grounded in these dual affirmations—the church's unity in Christ, and faith in the trustworthiness, everlasting reliability, and inclusiveness of divine love, revealed through Jesus Christ.

The New Century Hymnal enables Christians to immerse themselves in the music, texts, prayers, scripture readings, and orders of worship reflecting the wide horizon of Christian tradition, from the earliest to the most contemporary. The worshiper will discover some significant differences in this hymnal. The committee assembling the hymnal paid close attention to globalization: The language, meters, and music borrowed from many of the world's cultures and confessions offer new perceptions and understandings of the Triune God whom Christians worship. What worshipers gain through this hymnal will lead to a deeper appreciation for the gifts and contributions of Christians from around the world as they seek to articulate faith and express praise to the living God revealed in the life, death, and resurrection of Jesus Christ.

THE MANDATE FOR A NEW HYMNAL

The story of any hymnal, of course, cannot be pinpointed to any particular date or time. Each collection includes vast amounts of material from across the whole of the church's story. Yet now, at the junction of the centuries, we are privileged to witness a vast explosion of new hymnody. Musicians and poets collaborate on new texts and tunes, giving voice to the liberating God who calls us to new visions of justice. Congregations offer sheet music in their orders of worship as alternatives to their regular hymnals. A wide variety of instrumentation emerges alongside more traditional organ or piano accompaniment.

These developments point to a deeper, more profound story. Changes in perception wrought by the human-rights and liberation movements, the feminist revolution, the urgent cries for justice for those who are poor and marginalized, those once labeled as "handicapped," and those excluded because of sexual orientation—all these urgencies call for the recasting of familiar language. In the church there is an eagerness for inclusive metaphors to succeed the almost exclusively masculine references to God and to people used by generations of Christians. That eagerness inevitably shapes many of the texts in this hymnal. As they worked through the contents, the committee and the editorial panel believed these textual changes appropriate, necessary, and faithful to the gospel.

The story behind *The New Century Hymnal* begins, however, as the twentieth century approached its final quarter. Antecedent to the work invested in *The New Century Hymnal*, its publisher, the United Church Board for Homeland Ministries, committed itself to following the mandates of the General Synod. In 1973, for instance, the Ninth General Synod (St. Louis, Missouri) called for a "concerted effort" by conferences, associations, and local churches, "to educate the members of the United Church of Christ to the issues and sensitivities involved in the writing and using of inclusive language." It further voted: "All newly printed materials (including worship books, services, hymnals . . .) published or used officially by the agencies of the United Church of Christ will be written (or rewritten when revised) to make all language deliberately inclusive." Some four years later, in 1977, the Eleventh General Synod (Washington, D.C.) directed its executive council "to begin a process which will result in the creation of a new official hymnal which would follow the guidelines for intentionally inclusive language." *The New Century Hymnal* brings that long-insistent mandate to fruition.

In 1989, while other denominations and confessional traditions had produced or were in the midst of producing new hymnals, the Seventeenth General Synod (Fort Worth, Texas) voted affirmatively to authorize one of the United Church of Christ's instrumentalities, the United Church Board for Homeland Ministries, to "produce a new hymnal for the UCC." It also asked the United Church Board for Homeland Ministries to name an advisory hymnal committee for this purpose. The committee's members were selected in the fall of 1989, and it met for the first time at the United Church of Christ's New York offices in February 1990.

LAUNCHING THE HYMNAL COMMITTEE

The thirteen people invited to serve on the hymnal committee reflected the diversity and unity of the United Church of Christ, its historical and regional particularities, and its ethnic and cultural heterogeneity. The committee consisted of men and women, laity and clergy, African American, Latino/Latina, and Caucasian members, all of various ages. They brought an array of musical, theological, liturgical, educational, and pastoral skills. Charles Shelby Rooks, Executive Vice-President of the Homeland Board, and his successor in that position, Thomas E. Dipko, together with Ansley Coe Throckmorton, General Secretary for Education and Publication, and Dorothy Lester, of the Office for Church Life and Leadership, all served the committee ex-officio. From the very start, the committee looked forward to creating a hymnal reflective of the history and future of this still-maturing denomination.

At its first meeting in February 1990, Shelby Rooks stated clearly that while the committee would be expected to develop both the vision and many of the details of the new hymnal, final responsibility and authority for its publication lay with the UCBHM. He spoke of many denominational currents pressing for a new hymnal. He recounted the importance of hymnody in the Evangelical, Reformed, Congregational, and Christian traditions. He urged the committee to take the time necessary to do its work, yet keep its eye on a 1995 publication date.

FIVE PRIORITIES EMERGE

As the hymnal committee began its work, five priorities commanded attention. The first involved the breadth and scope of input the committee might need to fulfill its mandate. The second and third priorities called the committee to forge a theological perspective consonant with the broad diversity within the United Church of Christ and to employ that perspective in developing a vision for the hymnal. The fourth priority lay in finding the right person to edit the hymnal. And the fifth priority required an itinerary for meetings throughout the United States enabling a variety of churches and regions to make suggestions for the committee's consideration as well as to provide venues for reporting on its progress.

1. Seeking Information and Perspective

Pursuing its first priority, to gain a broad base of information and perspective for the support of its work, the committee, in collaboration with the UCBHM Research Office, developed a survey to be sent to and returned by each church in the denomination. The survey, devised and distributed, enabled the committee to discover what hymns congregations sang over the course of the year and what hymnals were used in the denomination. This process inevitably resulted in lists of most frequently sung hymns in the United Church of Christ. The survey also requested congregations to delineate the criteria they might use when the time came to choose a new hymnal. This survey circulated throughout the UCC from the summer of 1990 until the summer of 1991.

The three favorite hymns in existing UCC hymnals were "Holy, Holy, Holy," "Joyful, Joyful, We Adore Thee," and "Love Divine All Loves Excelling." The committee also discovered the favorite ten hymns from other sources, which included "How Great Thou Art," "The Old Rugged Cross," and "Great Is Thy Faithfulness." All six of these hymns, suitably altered or retranslated, are in *The New Century Hymnal*.

In identifying criteria that might determine the selection of new hymnals, the overwhelming majority of respondents favored new music and inclusive texts. To be sure, this hymnal reflects a serious effort to produce a collection aligned with the interests, needs, and visions of its churches. It seeks, however, not simply to be a mirror of the churches but also to provide a perceptual stance anticipating the twenty-first century.

Another means of gaining insight and perspective was to invite guests to share their wisdom and expertise so that the committee could better understand the cultural, historical, liturgical, and logistical elements vital to the completion of its work. These guests represented many sectors of the life and mission of the United Church of Christ and its complex theological tapestry. Editors and compilers of other hymnals told of the challenge of assembling and publishing such a compilation for our time. The committee heard social scientists refer to the rapidly shifting mindset, institutional loyalties, and personal priorities of new generations who would sing from the proposed hymnal. And finally, representatives of ethnic and cultural constituencies advocated their priorities and concerns with clarity and verve.

Pursuing those priorities and concerns was an ongoing task of the committee, realized by gathering lists of recommended hymnody from various ethnic and cultural traditions from within and outside its ranks. It received a recommended list of Hispanic hymnody from a task force assembled to provide such information and through the contributions of one of its own members, a seminary music professor from Puerto Rico. The committee's three African American members led the search to include a broad representation of the gifts of that community to religious music and to identify a "core" of hymnody vital to worship and common to nearly all traditions. The committee sought perspective from Native American sources, asking one of its members to research the literature of the United Church of Christ's Native American constituency. They sought out the hymnody of the Asian Rim, not only hearing from the churches but assigning a committee member to assemble a representative collection from the churches of the Pacific region, including the strong UCC presence in Hawaii.

The input and recommendations derived from all of these sources—the survey, the invited guests, and racial-ethnic constituencies—were indispensable to the committee in its efforts to assemble a diverse and useful collection for worship in a wide variety of settings for the present day and well into the future.

2. Theological Guidelines

The second priority of the committee, the articulation of theological guidelines for hymn selection, occupied the minds and hearts of the committee throughout much of its first year. One of the outside experts, an editor with impressive experience in hymnal making, informed the committee that it could not do its work effectively without a solid theological base. The committee worked in small task forces as well as in plenary to devise its basic approach. Furnished with a constellation of ideas and convictions, one member of the committee took the various theological considerations and molded them into a four-point outline:

1. The 1995 hymnal of the United Church of Christ enables praise of the One, Sovereign, Triune God, who in infinite mystery is always more than doctrine can describe and whose being calls forth awe, worship, love, faith, and service (Isa. 6:1–8).
2. We affirm that people of all ages, tongues, races, abilities, and both genders are created in the image and likeness of God (Gen. 1:26; 5:1–2; United Church of Christ Statement of Faith).
3. We testify to God's call to stewardship of the earth; we are not entitled to hoard, waste, or destroy what God has made, but we are called to glorify God with the earth's resources.
4. We rejoice in providing a rich variety of metaphors for singing of God and inclusive words for singing of people—words that all people can sing.

The committee presented these guidelines at a forum held during the Eighteenth General Synod (Norfolk, Virginia) in July 1991, and submitted them to the UCBHM board of directors meeting that same year, for discussion and alteration. The guidelines subsequently formed a basis for hymn selection over the course of the committee's tenure and provided the foundation for language and musical considerations.

3. Shaping a Vision of the Hymnal

Theological understandings thus developed began to shape the hymnal in view. The committee kept faith with the ecumenical church as it selected hymns with the church year in mind and compatible with the *Revised Common Lectionary*. *The New Century Hymnal* includes a lectionary index to help worship leaders locate appropriate hymns for each Sunday of the church year. Clearly, the converging traditions of the United Church of Christ sang the Psalms regularly in their early days. Therefore, a full, lectionary-based Psalter became a vital component of the book.

As the committee reflected on its United Church of Christ heritage and the church's hope for the future, it made significant decisions regarding design of the hymnal. As a result of such consideration, the committee elected to include many more hymns devoted to the sacraments and rites of the church. In order to place the liturgy into the hands of the people, the committee included portions of the United Church of Christ *Book of Worship*. In addition, another section included prayers and responses from sources across the Christian spectrum.

And of course, as the committee considered texts, particularly in consonance with its theological guidelines and the General Synod mandates for inclusiveness, it identified words, phrases, and theological implications in hymns that would need to be revised, retranslated, or, in some cases, eliminated. It proved wary of the imperial and triumphalist tendencies of nineteenth-century missionary hymnody and tended toward texts with a world-servant orientation. It selected tunes and texts from a variety of global settings as well as from racial and ethnic histories within the United Church of Christ. Male bias in reference to people, as already mentioned, so long the standard in hymn texts, could no longer be an option in UCC publications. Indeed, such limitation was unacceptable to the committee.

Expansion of the images of God beyond those inferring male identity became a central concern. This particular effort inevitably proved a most difficult and sensitive matter, and we will discuss it later in this article. But further language issues claimed the committee's theological acuity as well. Revision of language consistently equating light with good and darkness with evil compelled the committee's attention, as did terms assuming true children of God all to be heterosexual, with physical capabilities of standing, walking, running, marching, hearing, and seeing. The committee sought to affirm the full humanity of all persons and their inclusion in the family of God without figures of speech tending to separate them one from another.

Ancient and medieval cosmologies with their "flat earth," vertical dimensions, and anachronistic perceptions of the universe all found themselves vulnerable to change. The committee agreed that what children learn in church ought to be consonant with what they learn in school. The same principle applied to archaic language—the "thees" and "thous" no longer familiar in the vernacular. On this matter, the committee took the position adopted by the committees that produced the Revised Standard Version and later the New Revised Standard Version of the Bible—a position insisting that language used in religious practice keep pace with current usage generally. The committee intended this to be a "new century" hymnal.

4. Selecting a Hymnal Editor

The fourth priority undertaken by the committee lay in the selection of an editor for the hymnal project. Through a careful process of recruitment, assessment, and review, the committee selected Arthur G. Clyde, the music director of Zwingli United Church of Christ of Souderton, Pennsylvania. He began work in April 1991. In Arthur Clyde, the committee found a conscientious, diplomatic, and gifted professional, who assembled an extraordinarily able staff.

5. Conducting Hymnal Forums

The fifth priority of the committee required the scheduling of regional public hymnal forums held in conjunction with regular meetings across the country. These forums with the full committee took place primarily from 1990 through 1992, the first years of the committee's work. Additionally, when subcommittees convened around the country, more forums were held and reported to the full committee.

Predictably, the committee heard a wide diversity of opinion in these public forums. On the matter of textual revision, some urged the committee to end "sexism, ageism, racism, homophobia, and classism" in hymns. Others considered venerable texts untouchable. Some desired the highest standards of musical excellence; others clamored for "hummable" tunes and "toe-tappin' rhythms."

Serious forum participants pointed to the cultural "sea change" among those born since 1946 and the enormous implications for churches and church music inherent in that change. Others pointed to an alarming downturn in mainline church membership and worship attendance. They suggested that this decline was due partly to the failure of hymnody written decades ago for a world long gone, as well as to the persuasive voice and contemporaneity of megachurches whose souls seemed to move to the pulse of modernity. Equally serious participants reminded the committee of Christian historical continuities, urging the United Church of Christ to stay the course lest it lose its bearings in postmodern chaos. Progressive and conservative voices made themselves heard in all the forums, each claiming the authority either of tradition or of the gospel itself and each making an impact on the committee's thinking. In all cases, the committee faced a mix of opinions that needed some sorting, reviewing, and thorough discernment.

With biblical, theological, and hymnological principles established, with a full-time staff on the job and the 1995 deadline on its mind, the committee began in 1992 to meet regularly in the United Church of Christ's new offices in Cleveland and to pursue the selection of hymns.

HYMN SELECTION

The committee developed a practical process for hymn selection. It worked from a vast resource bank, consisting, first, of each of the predecessor UCC hymnals. These included: *The Hymnal* (1941) of the Evangelical and Reformed Church; the *Pilgrim Hymnal* (1957), used by primarily Congregational-Christian churches; and *The Hymnal of the United Church of Christ* (1974), used in churches of all UCC traditions. Each member of the committee reviewed every hymn in these three hymnals. Hymns that were common to all three or any two books were sung and rated by the committee to select those that would form a "core" around which the rest of the hymnal would take shape. Important hymns unique to only one predecessor book were considered individually. In addition, old and new hymnals of other Catholic and Protestant denominations, many new independent collections, and hundreds of newly composed, unpublished manuscripts lay in the committee's cache.

Because the whole committee could not manage to consider each of the prospective hymns, it divided into a number of subcommittees. These subcommittees were responsible for reviewing the hymnody of a particular season of the church year (such as Easter, for example), or for a topic (such as justice or citizenship), or for the sacraments and rites of the church. Each subcommittee met between gatherings of the whole committee, focused on the specific hymn seasons or topics assigned to it, and prepared to report on its conclusions. At subsequent meetings the committee sang every verse of every hymn recommended by the subcommittees. It then sought consensus, hymn by hymn, to accept or reject the proposed selections. From time to time, skillful advocacy could bring a rejected hymn back to the table for reconsideration. In addition, the committee simply placed some hymns on hold as it considered the enormous and varied selections before it. In total, the committee through its subcommittees considered over ten thousand hymns.

In the course of singing and selection, each hymn underwent textual and musical critique. Most texts required revision because of language issues previously described. The most frequent musical notation asked for the lowering of key signatures a half or whole step for easier singability. (The national forums had underscored this need for lower pitch.) Concerns about preferred tunes or harmonizations were also expressed at this stage.

HYMN TEXT REVIEW AND REVISION

The committee itself took little part in textual revision. A cadre of first-class wordsmiths and contemporary poets began to do the work of revision, hymn by hymn. When texts of hymns originally written in languages other than English were examined, the need for fresh new translations became a clear priority. Poets who were assigned individual hymns included Lavon Bayler, Dosia Carlson, Carl P. Daw Jr., Ruth Duck, Sylvia Dunstan, Marty Haugen, Carolyn Jennings, Madeleine Forell Marshall, Elizabeth C. Ragan, Thomas H. Troeger, and Miriam Therese Winter. A subcommittee on texts appointed from within the committee and including other poets and theologians screened these revised and newly translated texts. The work of the committee now extended to a wider network of participants.

When the text subcommittee finished its screening work, revised texts came before the full committee. Inevitably, the committee review and approval process became complicated and time-consuming. Up to this point, in the fall of 1992, most of the committee's work had proceeded in consensus. But the diversity of the denomination represented on the committee surfaced in new ways as texts were reviewed, revised, and considered one way or another for final approval. The differing perspectives among members as they considered nuances, meanings, definitions, "memory banks," and treasured texts began to consume more and more of the committee's time. As discussions continued over what textual changes might be made and what changes might not be made, for whatever valid reason, it became evident that publishing contracts drawn for a summer 1995 deadline could well be threatened. The committee was alert as well to those congregations that had clearly expressed their eagerness for the hymnal's availability.

Sensing that resolution of these differing perspectives might be possible over the long term but surely not in time to meet contractual deadlines with the printer and binder, the executive committee of the UCBHM reached a difficult strategic decision. It accepted the comprehensive work of the committee from February 1990 until April 1993 and decided to bring that portion of the hymnal development process to a close. The thirteen-member hymnal committee, over the course of three years, had reviewed thousands of hymns, designed the contents of the hymnbook, selected the repertory, and wrestled with every imaginable subtlety and challenge of the language of love, justice, and the worship of God. The UCBHM executive committee subsequently appointed a five-person editorial panel (including one member of the original hymnal committee) to carry the hymnbook to publication.

THE NINETEENTH GENERAL SYNOD

The summer of 1993 brought the Nineteenth General Synod to St. Louis, Missouri. The editorial panel and the UCBHM published a sampler of *The New Century Hymnal* to enable delegates to gain their first look at the forthcoming hymnal and to invite their comments and concerns. Among the many events at General Synod, delegates could attend informal singing sessions, discuss textual and musical changes with colleagues, and comment through the informal publications that Synod engenders. Delegates quickly depleted the supply of samplers.

The differing perspectives on changes in hymn texts that had slowed the work of the hymnal committee now extended to the caucuses, the hallways, and the floor of the Nineteenth General Synod. What seemed to some delegates to be a liberating breath of fresh air in textual revision appeared to others as rank heresy, bowdlerization, and iconoclasm. The nature of the debate encompassed a variety of issues, but one of them emerged as primary due to a formal resolution that was brought before the assembly for study and eventually a vote. The issue was the apparent elimination or replacement of the word "Lord" as a title for God and for Jesus Christ in a majority of the hymn texts as they had been revised up to that time.

Recognizing fully the historical and biblical roots of this word, the committee, in consultation with pastors and theologians beyond its ranks, had struggled to reach two conclusions: First, the acknowledged universal dominion of God and Jesus Christ could be designated by other appellations and confessional expressions; and second, this was necessary because the confessional appellation "Lord" confers a definite masculine identity to the Deity.

Delving deeper into soteriological implications, it was realized that the masculine identity inferred by the term "Lord" was not (the scandal of particularity notwithstanding) a necessary rendering of the sovereignty of God in Jesus Christ. Therefore, when referring to the sovereignty of God or Christ (a quality not necessarily contingent on masculinity), texts were amended to employ terms or phrases to address the One who rules with supreme authority, or the paradoxically servant status of the "Christ" with more-inclusive references, such as Sovereign, Ruler, or "servant of all."

The delegates to the Nineteenth General Synod wrestled with these complex theological issues just as the committee had done, though with far less time available to them. The original resolution was amended and finally approved, recommending that the UCBHM and the editorial panel "restore the word 'Lord' (with balancing metaphors where possible) to those hymns originally using it with reference to Jesus."

EDITORIAL PANEL AND THE COMPLETION OF
THE NEW CENTURY HYMNAL

Responsive to this rubric and sensitive to the theological, aesthetic, and deeply personal concerns expressed at General Synod, the editorial panel revisited all of the Christological hymn texts as it proceeded with its work over the next year. Clear-cut guidelines for evaluating the context of the use of "Lord" in each hymn were developed by the UCBHM executive committee and applied by the editorial panel. Some hymns rooted in the church's memory bank, such as "Lord, I Want to Be a Christian," went largely unaltered, while others were judged to merit revision of traditional terminology. (For a full discussion of this and other related language issues, see "The Language of *The New Century Hymnal*," immediately following this essay.)

Other aspects of the panel's work included fine-tuning sections of the book, making sure that the various topical sections and seasons of the church year had a proper balance. Every aspect of the hymnal was examined: Did each Sunday of the church year bear at least one designated lectionary hymn? How should indexes be arranged? What finally might be included in the section of miscellaneous worship resources?

The editorial panel also ultimately needed to deal with the full range of critical language issues. It became clear at this final juncture that aesthetics and tradition often stood in tension with issues of justice. When compelled to choose the language of justice, the group took responsibility for assuring the highest possible degree of aesthetics, realizing the vulnerability inherent in such a difficult choice. The editorial panel concluded its work in the fall of 1994 after having reviewed every text and the entire contents of *The New Century Hymnal* and receiving the approval of the UCBHM board of directors.

In a final phase, through the winter of 1994 to 1995, the editor Arthur Clyde and the hymnal office staff prepared the layout, edited and proofed the manuscripts, garnered the necessary copyrights, coordinated the manufacturing, and tracked down everything necessary to produce a hymn collection for the coming new century of Christian worship.

The Twentieth General Synod (Oakland, California) in July 1995 provided the occasion for the first use of *The New Century Hymnal*. The opening service of worship dedicated the new hymnal to the glory of God for use in the church, and the hymnal served as the source of worship and celebration throughout the Synod meeting. The UCBHM provided enough copies for each delegate to sing from and to take home. *The New Century Hymnal*, on that high occasion, after some five years of strenuous and joyous personal and institutional investment, made its way into the lives of Christians across the country and around the world.

ECUMENICAL REFLECTIONS ON *THE NEW CENTURY HYMNAL*

It was important for the hymnal committee, and now for the congregations, to understand the ecumenical responsibility of the making of *The New Century Hymnal*. Editors and committee heads of other churches' hymnals were consulted and heard gladly. This new hymnal, in addition to serving the congregations of the United Church of Christ, like other new hymnals becomes a contribution to the whole church from a denomination with ecumenical birthright and vision. The unitive process by which four predecessor denominations became one in 1957 brings to partial fruition the prophetic ecumenism of John Williamson Nevin and Philip Schaff, the Mercersburg theologians of the mid-nineteenth century who foresaw and worked toward the eventual healing of the divided Body of Christ.

In light of the ecumenical legacy and hope of the United Church of Christ, one must balance the hymnal committee's vision that this new hymnal would break new ground in the singing of the Christian faith with the reality that recently published hymnals of other denominations generally have retained more traditional language. Yet language experienced as traditional by repeated use is itself culturally conditioned and, for that reason, increasingly has come under serious theological analysis and criticism in most mainline churches.

Early in the process, the hymnal committee began to envision "the first hymnal on a new shelf," in the hope that with growing ecumenical recognition of the changing nature of religious language and with increasing perception of the call for justice in the ways we speak and sing of people and of God, future hymnals might come to occupy a place on this "new shelf," too. Time will tell. The century ahead can be expected to teach with new urgency the truth that while Jesus Christ is the same yesterday, today, and forever, statements about Jesus Christ are not. No new worship resource is ever fully or finally adequate. Like the United Church of Christ *Book of Worship* before it, *The New Century Hymnal* is "transitional literature." Always there is "yet more light and truth to break forth from God's holy Word" (see hymn 316).

The ecumenical imperative of Christ's prayer "that they may all be one" still disturbs remaining denominationalism. Each still-separated Christian communion knows it. Therefore those who created this new hymnal pray that, in the gracious providence of God, the coming new century will celebrate the day "when in our music God is glorified" (hymn 561); when images of God are no longer confined by anthropomorphic projections; when the ways we sing of people will embrace everyone and exclude or stereotype no one; when the hymnody of many different Christian congregations "of all ages, tongues, and races" can mingle and enrich all; when "sharing by all will mean scarcity for none"; and when the whole Church Universal, healed of its historic divisions, will sing to God a new song from one common hymnal yet to be born.

The Language of *The New Century Hymnal*

Arthur G. Clyde

THE NEW CENTURY HYMNAL AS A RESOURCE FOR OUR OWN TIME

"Every generation responds to the call of Christ in its own distinctive way. There is need for periodic revision of our hymnals, none of which can contain, in any case, more than a fraction of the great store of texts and tunes available for congregational worship gathered over the centuries." These words from the introduction to the *Pilgrim Hymnal* edition of 1958 are typical of those found in many hymnals in that they recognize that each hymnal must attempt to serve the contemporary church and at the same time function as a caretaker of the hymns of the ages. *The New Century Hymnal* is published at a time of even broader challenge as the church finds itself in an age of ecumenism and amid a revival of hymn writing.

Thus a hymnal committee at this moment is given the daunting yet joyous task of presenting not only the many hymns that have served as the core of worship in the past but also many new hymns that are in use in the ecumenical church. Moreover, this abundant list is augmented through a "hymn explosion," a great flourish of new hymns that has taken place not only in the United States, but in many other places in the world as the church enters the twenty-first century.

The New Century Hymnal is an offering to the church of a selection of past and present for the purpose of carrying us toward the future. Its contents reflect more than rootedness in reformed hymnody. A strong commitment to ancient tradition has restored many hymn texts of the early centuries of the church. In its twentieth-century choices, a conscious effort has been made to include more hymns by women and to recognize the increasingly pluralistic nature of the church. Thus, hymns of many traditions and cultures embrace the wider family that is the church today.

Throughout the ages the Psalter, which is the songbook of the Bible, has held a revered place in songs of worship. *The New Century Hymnal*, along with many denominational hymnals of this age, restores the psalms to worship in church and home and provides ways in which the psalms can be sung.

The New Century Hymnal provides more than hymns and psalms for congregational and personal worship. It also contains the traditional orders for corporate worship taken from the *Book of Worship* of the United Church of Christ. These orders not only reflect a growing ecumenical convergence of understandings on the use of liturgy in worship but also include texts that are widely accepted.

This liturgical renewal in the church at large has brought about the desire among leaders of worship in local churches to have more hymns for specific rites and sacraments. Consequently, the compilers of the hymnal have provided many hymns, traditional and new, for use at baptism, confirmation, and Holy Communion. The growing use of a common lectionary throughout many denominations has brought churches closer as the same readings are shared in Sunday worship. This has provided the opportunity for those selecting hymns to work closely with Scripture in order to find hymns related to the Bible passages that will be read in the worship service.

These are some of the main features of a book that was prepared to serve the United Church of Christ and other denominations as well. It is not only through its contents, however, that this hymnal reflects the attempt to be inclusive. One of the most distinguishing aspects of *The New Century Hymnal* is its language, which is intended to include and affirm all people as children of God. That is what this essay is about.

THE NEW CENTURY HYMNAL AND INCLUSIVE LANGUAGE

The use of inclusive language is not new to the United Church of Christ. The work that led to the publication of *The New Century Hymnal* is rooted in actions by the General Synod of the United Church of Christ. As early as 1973, the Ninth General Synod of the denomination adopted a policy to use inclusive language in all printed materials and resources,[1] and the Eleventh General Synod in 1977 directed the executive council to begin to create a hymnal using language that is inclusive. The action was accompanied by other statements that called for the development of guidelines for the use of inclusive language and their implementation.[2] In 1980 the denomination's Office for Church Life and Leadership published the *Book of Worship* in inclusive language, which received wide acceptance. The United Church Board for Homeland Ministries of the United Church of Christ (UCBHM), at the request of General Synod, set aside funds in 1989 to take responsibility for the new hymnal project, and a committee began work in 1990. This sequence gives an indication of the movement in the United Church of Christ toward the use of inclusive language in its worship life.

One of the first steps that the UCHBM took was an extensive research project among local churches that showed the inclusion of a large quantity of hymns, new hymns, worship resources, orders for worship, and good indexes to be of great importance. The response to this questionnaire was unusually high. For the majority of those interested in purchasing a new hymnal, inclusive language was a high priority. These findings gave support to the 1977 Synod action asking for an inclusive-language hymnal.

THE CONTEXT FOR THE LANGUAGE OF A NEW HYMNAL

The awareness of inclusive language in society as a whole and the experience of other denominations in dealing with worship resources, particularly hymnals, provide the starting point for the language of *The New Century Hymnal*. In society at large, people use language that attempts to show sensitivity to their neighbors. Terms such as "the deaf" and "the blind" have been replaced by "people who are deaf" and "people who are blind" in recognition that a person's humanity takes precedence over his or her ability. Change has taken place in language intended to include both women and men. The use of "man" and "mankind" to refer to all people is falling into disuse. It is common practice to use nongendered labels for roles (firefighter, salesperson) and to search for ways of not using "he, him, his" as generic pronouns, as in "everyone to their own way." This is but a sampling of the many language issues that had to be addressed in creating a book of hymns that takes cultural change and language change seriously.

The implications of all this are both simple and complex. It cannot be assumed that the reader (and in this case, the singer in worship) possesses all the background and insights to interpret the meaning of certain words and phrases the way they were intended. That would require us all to understand and agree with the following kinds of assumptions whenever we encounter these words:

- When we say "mankind" or "men," we mean "all people."
- When we sing "wash me white as snow," we are talking only about spiritual purity and not about skin color.
- Whenever we say "up in heaven," we understand that heaven is not really up but that this is an ancient understanding of the universe being arranged in three levels—a concept we know to be inconsistent with scientific knowledge.

But such language does not work in the culture of this age. All women today do not feel included in "men," even though they may be aware of its historic meaning. Many people of color are offended by the phrase "wash me white" even though they understand the symbolism. And many in the scientific community are not satisfied with the persistent use of a three-tiered view of the universe that was outmoded centuries ago. Sometimes words lose their meaning, leading to misunderstandings. A child in these times who sings about "the dumb" may well be conjuring images of people who are not smart. How might a child interpret archaic language such as "If thou but suffer God to guide thee"?

Much of the archaic language in English-language hymns was written in the period between the introduction of the King James Version of the Bible (KJV) and the first part of the twentieth century. During this time the Scriptures were read and quoted primarily in the language of the 1611 translation under King James I of Scotland; therefore, the language of worship was cast in the same style. God is referred to as "Thou" and "Thee," and auxiliary verbs such as "shalt" and "wilt" are used in prayers. But in the twentieth century, revisions of the King James translation—the Revised Standard Version (RSV) in 1952, the New Revised Standard Version (NRSV) in 1989—are being used more and more. The introduction to the RSV states that the reason for the revision is "the change since 1611 in English usage." It cites the following rationales:

- Many forms of expression have become archaic, while still generally intelligible.
- Other words are obsolete and no longer understood by the common reader.
- The greatest problem is words that are still in constant use but now convey a different meaning from that which they had in 1611.

The NRSV, acclaimed for its modern scholarship, takes into account the more recent availability of early manuscripts but also continues the process of keeping the language accessible to the reader. The NRSV introduction states that changes were made as warranted on the basis of "accuracy, clarity, euphony, and current English usage." It also recognizes "linguistic sexism arising from the inherent bias of the English language toward the masculine gender, a bias that in the case of the Bible has often restricted or obscured the meaning of the original text," and describes the guidelines by which the text was revised.

It must be kept in mind that language is always part of culture, and that language changes as culture changes. The King James Version of the Bible came from an age in which a grammarian by the name of Wilson declared that the "natural" order ought to be preserved in language. By this he meant that the "good man of the house should precede the woman, as the better Horse should precede the graye mare."[3] In 1646 another grammarian, named Poole, declared that the masculine gender is more worthy than the feminine.[4] It is clear that the societal values that have changed since the writing of the KJV have warranted the creation of new Bible translations.

The acceptance and use of these newer translations are paralleled in the language of worship. The worship books of denominations are for the most part devoid of thee's and thou's and many other archaic expressions. Although this undoubtedly has caused some pain for worshipers who had memorized liturgies, the change has been accepted overall since most people are willing to admit that clear understanding of the language of worship is basic to participants' involvement.

This digression into the change of language in Bible translation and liturgy is relevant in that it sets the stage for the appearance of a hymnal that treats language similarly. Of course, this is not to equate a hymnal with Scripture. But the reasons for the change in both instances have much in common, as do some of the methods of revision. The overall result is the possibility in worship for Scripture, liturgy, and hymns to have a feeling of being more closely linked due to a more consistent use of language.

Madeleine Forell Marshall, a scholar of languages and a hymn translator, has spoken directly to the issue of language change and the impact on hymnody.

> I think that we first should acknowledge that hymns are living texts, not historical artifacts. They are only valuable to the extent that they work for modern singers. Language changes over time. The understanding of the human condition changes over time. Varieties of religious experience familiar in one era are alien to another. Living texts must be adapted or discarded. Hymn texts are not Scripture—but if they were, we note how even Scripture is regularly retranslated, which means altered and adapted, to make sense to each era.[5]

It was within the context of cultural (and linguistic) change that the complex task was begun of finding ways to keep the stories and powerful theological teachings of our heritage of hymn poetry intact, while at the same time discovering images that communicate directly to us today and expand our understanding. How this was done in specific instances is explained later.

The New Century Hymnal is not the first hymnal to deal with the issue of inclusive language. It does, however, represent the most even and consistent approach to language of any hymnal yet published. Rather than choosing to present only new hymns in inclusive language, those responsible for the language of this hymnal took the General Synod request for an inclusive hymnal quite literally. Thus hymns of other ages are presented in ways that seek to maintain the theology and beauty of the original but without some of the biases of the time in which they were written. This hymnal also includes the ethnocultural diversity of the church and society at large, since for a hymnal to be inclusive, it must attempt to reflect the multiracial and multicultural composition of the world in which it is used.

THE PROCESS USED

The hymnal committee worked from 1990 until 1994 to accomplish this enormous task. During that time, the contents of the hymnal were selected and the way in which the book would be organized was decided. Since the majority of local churches select their scriptures according to the lectionary, a pattern of scripture readings for each Sunday, it was decided that the hymnal would be compatible with the lectionary. That is to say, hymns were selected that would be relevant to the scripture readings for each Sunday. On the basis of conversation with local church leaders, orders for worship were chosen. Hymns that were essential to large numbers of worshipers were identified from the original research that preceded the project. The various tunes commonly used for familiar hymns were reviewed and evaluated.

The next step required was revising texts to carry out the mandate of the 1977 General Synod for the creation of a hymnal for the church using intentionally inclusive language. An editorial panel completed the task of the review of each text and monitored the work of the editorial staff and the poets who were engaged to make the revisions. (For further discussion of the process, see the introduction to *The New Century Hymnal*.)

THE THEOLOGICAL DEMANDS OF REVISING HYMNS

Inclusive language is not just for the sake of clear understanding in a changing cultural context. Important theological principles are also at stake. The United Church of Christ has spoken very directly to the issue of inclusive language over a period of many years. In November 1979 *Inclusive Language Guidelines for Use and Study in the United Church of Christ* were adopted by the executive council of the denomination and published in 1980. The introduction to this document contains this statement:

> A society in which sexual or racial discrimination is traditional will employ a language in which that bias is reflected. Changes in the language to correct such bias can both reflect changes in the society and at the same time produce such changes. If women and ethnic racial groups are to be acknowledged as full human beings and partners with men and white people in the fullness of Jesus Christ, we must, as a church, confront language bias and as a church act as a continual force for human liberation, salvation, and healing. Change occurs slowly and only through the commitment of the many who begin to demonstrate new vision and new behavior. Such commitment will produce new ways of speaking about the movement of God in history as that power which has liberated and freed us all from the bondage of the past.

The premise of inclusive language has been articulated well by many within the church. But the challenge of implementing change on a large scale, particularly in the process of creating an inclusive-language hymnal, remained uncharted territory to those given the task. Brian Wren, the well-known hymnwriter, theologian, teacher, and poet, has provided what could have been a charge to the poets and editors of *The New Century Hymnal* in this passage from his book on the language of worship, *What Language Shall I Borrow?*:

> Language change is not all-important: if it were, then changing language would be all that was needed to change the world. Nor is it unimportant: if it were, we could concentrate on doing love and justice, and quit worrying about how we speak of God. To separate language from action is false. Language change is an essential part of action. If I cease using racist language I will not thereby end racism. Yet trying out new forms of speech is a necessary part of finding out what I really think. By using nonracist language I also commit myself more deeply than before, even if I can't completely live out my commitment. Language is a public medium. If I use, or abandon, racist or sexist language, or begin to name God anew, I shall open myself to comment and criticism and shall have to explain and defend my usage. It may then be easier than before to act on what I have said.[6]

The editorial panel that was given the task of overseeing the revision of texts for this new hymnal soon discovered the complexity of the task. The many considerations for each and every hymn are impossible to enumerate and describe, but suffice it to say that all hymns became a theological task. One of the reasons is that each hymn brought with it the biases of its time, and to bring a hymn into our time meant looking at it through various lenses. Considerations that were applied to each hymn included the following[7]:

- Is the hymn in the "memory bank" (that is, have many people committed its words to memory)? If so, can the changes be made "invisibly" so that the singer will not be aware of an obvious change? If not, can a poet rewrite the hymn in some way that will maintain its style, flow, and theological content?
- Does the hymn contain language that diminishes any person's full humanity as a consequence of physical ability, human stereotype, family status, or gender?
- Will language for God in this hymn be part of a balance in the final collection of nongendered, feminine, masculine, and other metaphors that build on and expand our view of God?
- Is the use of the word "Lord" integral to the meaning of the hymn?
- If the hymn speaks of the authority of God, can the paradox between authority and servanthood be maintained (the image of the God who both rules and serves) while using language that is not gender-specific?

- Does the hymn have triumphalist language—that is to say, metaphors and analogies that point toward imposing the authority of a brand of cultural Christianity on the people of the world?
- Does the hymn have coercive, militaristic language? If it does, can language be found to express the very real struggle against evil using the "weapon" of love?
- Does the hymn have archaic language, an archaic worldview, or archaic theology that can be changed?
- Will the hymns speak to the pluralities of human existence? That is to say, will the collection present, for example, exclusively rural or urban images? Will the collection present only a Eurocentric or North American point of view? Do Christmas carols include images other than those of the cold weather and the snow of the Northern Hemisphere?
- Does the hymn speak in light/dark imagery? If so, can the language be altered to keep an essential biblical or confessional theme without reinforcing racial stereotyping? In this regard, can some hymns give positive and affirming meanings to the word "dark"?
- Does the hymn present theology connected to an outmoded view of the cosmos, such as a three-tiered universe with heaven located up and hell down?
- Does the hymn present stewardship as a matter of manipulating human resources only for human benefit? If so, can it be altered to recognize the possibility of the alignment of human energies to God's purposes?
- Does the hymn promote a "domination" theology of creation in which the human species is always at the summit? Can ways be found to express a sensitivity to the place of humanity within God's design rather than in control over God's design?

This listing gives some idea of the breadth of the considerations given to texts. Although the hymnal committee had given much thought in the selection process and had developed guidelines for language (much of which is distilled in the above listing), it became the job of the editorial panel to find a way to revise texts and to apply a final review process to each hymn.

If a hymn was identified as having language difficulties and if it was considered to be in the public domain or if its authors were no longer alive, it was sent to a poet along with the panel's observations citing the language of concern; then the poet began the process of submitting drafts of revisions. If the authors were living, they were asked to make the changes themselves, or permission was sought to change the hymns.

Among the most difficult were those involving archaic language, since the change of a "thee" or "thy" might entail a considerable reworking of the text. The task would have been easier if each hymn presented only one type of problem. But in many cases, the combination of, for example, archaisms, gendered language, and triumphalism within the same hymn called for a large number of alterations.

This work probably could not have been accomplished by a "scientific" process in which each time a problematic word occurred it was methodically replaced by another. That is not possible with poetry, where each adjustment has to be true to the style and structure of the whole. Nor did it prove feasible for a committee of text revisers to work in a collaborative process around each hymn. Individual poets working on hymns one by one made the task of revision possible. That is because each hymn as a work of art needed the personal attention of a poet sympathetic to the poetical, musical, and theological integrity of the overall text. Some of the very best hymnwriters of this age contributed their skills, each being assigned lists of individual hymns. Hymnwriters who spend their lives writing hymns with the hope that they will be sung for many years understand so well the integrity that they infuse into their own work. Consequently, they respect the work of others given to them to be transformed into language that makes sense for worship today. For these reasons, such artists are best equipped to bring about changes in the hymns of their predecessors. The work was not devoid of struggle and emotion, as all the people involved in the process—poets, editorial panel, and editorial staff—realized they were working with texts that they themselves had memorized and loved.

INCLUSIVE-LANGUAGE CONSIDERATIONS IN ONE TEXT

Here is an example of the complexity of considering language revision in a single hymn text.

Joyful, joyful, we adore <u>thee</u>, God of glory, **Lord** of love;
Hearts unfold like flowers before <u>thee</u>, opening to the sun above,
Melt the clouds of sin and sadness, drive the **dark of doubt** away;
Giver of immortal gladness, fill us with the light of day.

All <u>thy</u> works with joy surround <u>thee</u>, earth and heaven reflect thy rays,
Stars and angels sing around <u>thee</u>, center of unbroken praise.
Field and forest, vale and mountain, flowery meadow, flashing sea,
Chanting bird and flowing fountain, call us to rejoice in <u>thee</u>.

<u>Thou art</u> giving and forgiving, ever blessing, ever <u>blest</u>,
Well-spring of the joy of living, ocean depth of happy rest!
<u>Thou</u> our **Father, Christ our brother,** all who live in love
   are <u>thine</u>;
Teach us how to love each other, lift us to the joy divine.

Mortals join the happy chorus which the morning stars began;
Father love is reigning <u>o'er</u> us, **brother love** binds **man to man**.
Ever singing, **march** we onward, **victors** in the midst of strife,
Joyful music leads us sunward in the **triumph** song of life.

All the words that required review according to the various "lenses" shown in the previous section, "The Theological Demands of Revising Hymns," are marked in bold type in this hymn. The underlined words indicate archaic language that needed to be changed.

"Father," "Christ our brother," and "Father love" were reviewed in regard to the use of male words for God or Christ. "Dark of doubt" was reviewed in regard to the use of dark as an negative word. "March" was reviewed in regard to the use of militaristic imagery. "Victors" and "triumph" were reviewed in regard to the use of triumphalism. Finally, "man to man" needed to be reviewed as a way of speaking of humankind. Although this task would appear to be formidable, singing through the following revision as it appears in *The New Century Hymnal* (hymn 4) should convince one that such changes are possible. The integrity and spirit of the hymn are preserved, and at the same time, the imagery is expanded.

Joyful, joyful, we adore you, God of glory, God of love;
Hearts unfold like flowers before you, opening to the sun above.
Melt the clouds of sin and sadness, drive the storms of doubt
   away;
Giver of immortal gladness, fill us with the light of day.

All your works with joy surround you, earth and heaven reflect
   your rays,
Stars and angels sing around you, center of unbroken praise.
Field and forest, vale and mountain, flowery meadow,
   flashing sea,
Chanting bird and flowing fountain, teach us what our praise
   should be.

You are giving and forgiving, ever blessing, ever blessed.
Well-spring of the joy of living, ocean depth of happy rest!
Loving Spirit, Father, Mother, all who love belong to you;
Teach us how to love each other, by that love our joy renew.

Mortals join the mighty chorus which the morning stars began;
Boundless love is reigning o'er us, reconciling race and clan.
Ever singing, move we forward, faithful in the midst of strife,
Joyful music leads us onward in the triumph song of life.

To some people the above example might exhibit some categories of language change that seem needless or that may be dismissed as "political correctness." But this hymnal is about neither "politics" nor "correctness." The language revisions in *The New Century Hymnal* were undertaken so that, as much as is humanly possible, all people would feel fully included as members of the Body of Christ, the church.

THE PRACTICE OF HYMN REVISION

It might come as a surprise to some people that revising hymns is a long-standing custom. One of the venerable hymnwriters of the eighteenth century, Isaac Watts, was quite comfortable with the practice: "Where any unpleasing word is found, he that leads worship may substitute a better; for, blessed be God, we are not confined to the words of any man in our public solemnities."[8]

The famed nineteenth-century hymnwriter James Montgomery was an ardent reviser, and speaking of a hymnal he published in 1819, he writes: "Good Mr. Cotterill and I bestowed a great deal of labor and care on the compilation of that book: clipping, interlining, and remodeling hymns of all sorts, as we thought we could correct the sentiment or improve the expression." He commented on one of the hymns that he revised: "I entirely rewrote the first verse of that favorite hymn, commencing: 'There is a fountain filled with blood,' etc. The words are objectionable as representing a fountain being filled, instead of springing up: I think my version is unexceptionable: 'From Calvary's cross a fountain flows, of water and of blood.'" Although Montgomery did not want any of his own hymns to be revised, he recognized that this was inevitable: "When I am gone my hymns will, no doubt, be altered to suit the taste of appropriators."[9]

An 1860 commentary on the use of hymns in worship observes:

[Persons] of poetic genius ought to be stimulated, rather than discouraged, by the thought that posterity will not willingly let [their] songs die; and that, even if they become antiquated in their present form, they will still live in new and fresh modifications, or become the germs of other and better songs.... Was David deterred from giving his hymns to the world, through fear that they would be modified by some future Milton or Montgomery?[10]

TYPES OF REVISIONS

Any reputable hymnal through the ages has documented changes. Usually this is indicated with the abbreviation "alt." (altered) after the text writer's name to indicate that either the present editors or perhaps some former editors changed the text. Of course, this is not a perfect process, since that would mean tracking each hymn to its original form and then observing what changes had taken place. The older the hymn, the more likely that through various editions the text has been altered. In reality, vast numbers of hymns have undergone change throughout their lifetimes. Nevertheless, good editors always try to indicate by the use of "alt." that they are aware that a change has been made. In *The New Century Hymnal,* the appearance of "alt." indicates exactly this. In many cases, it means that the text has been changed by the preparers of this book. In other cases, it indicates that it is known that the source from which it came contained alterations of the text. Sometimes the changes are extensive, and sometimes merely a single word. (The same can apply to the music of the hymn.)

Another category of change is that indicated by "adapt." (adaptation). When "adapt." appears after the writer's name, the expectation is that the text of the hymn contains considerable departures from the original meaning and content, or at least that the text is rendered in a remarkably different style.

TRANSLATION

A great number of favorite hymns sung in English are actually translations from a hymn originally written in another language. These translations often reflect the theology and outlook of the time period in which they were made as much as they reflect the style and intent of the original.

When the gendered language in "Of the Father's Love Begotten" was examined, the original fourth-century Latin text by Prudentius was consulted. The original reads "Corde natus ex parentis," which means "born from the heart of the parent." There are many existing translations of the hymn, but the one most often seen in hymnals is from 1854 by John Mason Neale, "Of the Father's love begotten." In the nineteenth century, the hymn also appeared in English as "Of the Father sole begotten," "Born of God the Father's bosom," "Of the Father's will begotten," "Son Eternal of the Father," "Yea! from the Almighty mind He sprung," and "Of the Father's heart begotten." It is interesting to note that only one of these translations uses the word "heart," and in that case designates that it is the father's heart. The doxology stanza that appears in many hymnals was not part of the original text, nor was the refrain "evermore and evermore."[11] It was the choice of the editorial panel to seek a new translation, which appears "Of the Parent's Heart Begotten" (hymn 118).

One of the most intensive pieces of translation work was "Hail, O Festal Day!," which involved examination of the Latin texts used in York, England, in the sixteenth century and the original Latin poem by Fortunatus from the sixth century, and then arranging them for use in the space of one hymn (hymn 262) to provide a festival hymn for use at Easter, Pentecost, or Ascension.

Translators were surprised to discover that a favorite hymn, traditionally listed as "Latin, fourteenth century," contained only one stanza of the original Latin hymn. A more complete description of this hymn (hymn 240), "Jesus Christ Is Risen Today," is given in Appendix B, but let it suffice at this point to say that the entire story of the women who proclaimed the good news of the Resurrection was entirely eliminated through the centuries. Through the gift of a new translation, the original story has been restored.

It is fitting that some hymns of the Reformed tradition receive new translations. The new translation from the Joachim Neander German hymn "Sing Praise to God" (hymn 22) shows how fresh, new images appear when rendered by a scholar and poet who lives and speaks in our own time.

In all, one French, fifteen German, one Greek, one Hungarian, one Japanese, one Lakota (Native American), twelve Latin, twelve Spanish, and two Swedish hymns received new translations.

Why the emphasis on new translation? We have had access to many of the hymns of earlier times through the work of such hymn translators as Catherine Winkworth, who died in 1878, and John Mason Neale, who died in 1866. These translators served their own time by giving the church the opportunity to sing the hymns in English. But they were translated into words in common use in their own day, incorporating not only the language styles of that period, but also the prevailing biases of society. Unfortunately, since then little has been offered in the way of modern translations. At best, most hymnals in the twentieth century have made alterations to the texts of the translations of the previous century. There is no intent to discredit the faithful work of these scholars, but to ignore the original texts and their authors does not pay them their due. That is to say, just as the traditional hymns of the church were rightly kept alive by way of translation in another era, so do they deserve to be freshly translated today.

CATEGORIES OF LANGUAGE CONSIDERATIONS

The remainder of this essay addresses the various categories of language that were encountered in the process of text review and revision, and some of the methods that were applied. In each category, an attempt is made to present some of the rationales for change and the ways in which the revisions were made. It is not the case that each hymn fell entirely and neatly into one of the categories. As was demonstrated in the example above, many of the hymns involved the consideration of several of the language guidelines already mentioned. It also was not the case that a formula could be applied that would solve each language problem in the same way. Finally, it is important to point out that the entire process from start to finish was one of building and learning with the human limitations that this implies, the chief of which is the possibility, indeed the probability, of inconsistencies. Having said this, what follows is an attempt to put into categories the kinds of language treatment that were generally used in the revision of texts.

Archaic Language

The shift of language from archaic expressions to contemporary usages is perhaps the most difficult of all the challenges for poets who are asked to revise hymns. It is much easier in the case of prose and other nonmetered texts. But in hymns, rhythm, meter, stress on syllables, and rhyme scheme all need to be considered when changing, for example, "thee" or "thine" at the end of a line. Archaic language is not confined to single words. There are phrases, idioms, and sometimes the entire style that inhibit clear understanding by today's singers. Take, for example, a phrase such as "If thou but suffer God to guide thee . . . He'll give thee strength, whate'er betide thee."[12] We should not be too quick to assume that a child growing up on the brink of the twenty-first century will be able to discern the meaning from the context. The same might be true for a person whose first language is not English. Or take, for instance, the phrase "Beneath the cross of Jesus I fain would take my stand," which is solved, fortunately, quite easily by "I gladly take my stand."

It must be pointed out that such changes are not uncommon in other ages. Charles Wesley originally wrote "Hark, how all the welkin rings," but this, as we know, has been altered to "Hark! the herald angels sing." This is only one of the changes made in this carol over the years.[13] (Examples of other hymns are given in Appendix A.)

The poet-revisers have often shown great creativity when faced with rhyming couplets with archaic words at the end. In "Immortal, Invisible" (hymn 1), the two lines

> We blossom and flourish as leaves on the tree,
> And wither and perish, but naught changeth thee.

are treated this way:

> We blossom and flourish as leaves and as flowers,
> then wither and perish—but naught dims your powers.

In "Jesus, the Joy of Loving Hearts" (hymn 329), the lines

> Our restless spirits yearn for thee,
> Where'er our changeful lot is cast:
> Glad when thy gracious smile we see;
> Blest when our faith can hold thee fast.

become

> For you our restless spirits yearn,
> Where'er our changing lot is cast;
> Glad when your smile on us you turn,
> blessed, when by faith we hold you fast.

Had all the challenges presented by archaic language been as easily solved, the revisions would be nearly imperceptible. That was not the case, however, and some hymns needed to be considerably reworked. As was pointed out previously, in most instances, the language difficulties that the hymn presented were multiple; that is to say, more than archaic language needed to be revised.

In the movement from archaic to contemporary language in the hymnal, it is fair to observe that sometimes more revising might have taken place than was absolutely necessary. In some instances, a poet seized the opportunity to use the basic form and text of a hymn but added some issue of more contemporary relevance. But in each and every such instance, it was sincerely hoped that these changes would expand rather than limit the imagery of the text and give the hymn more power to teach in our own time.

Gender of God

When attempting to render a text in inclusive language, one of the basic issues that needs to be considered is that of gendered words referring to God. In Scripture and throughout the ages, God has been addressed as "Father." Jesus even used the word "Abba" (which we could translate today as "Daddy"). "Father" has held an important place in the worship of the church—at baptism, in doxologies, and in private prayer. The trinitarian formula, "Father, Son, and Holy Spirit," is universally familiar in the creeds of the church. But the notion of using only these terms (two of which are male) exclusively—as the only valid names—to speak separately of the three "persons" of the one "essence" runs counter to earlier tradition. The very theologians of the early church who labored to explain the doctrine of the Trinity at the same time consistently denied that God has gender. Rather they argued that God transcends gender, and they freely used both feminine and masculine words in speaking of God.[14] The idea, then, of not using exclusively male images for God is not a modern invention; rather, it holds an important place in historic Christian theology. In Hebrew Scriptures (pre-Christian) the use of "Father" to refer to God occurs less than a dozen times; the ancient sacred name YHWH spoken by God to Moses occurs around 6,800 times, and yet its true meaning and even its pronunciation are not clear. However this name may be translated, it is not a name that means Father; it is generally transliterated as "Yahweh." It has also been rendered as "Jehovah."

"Father" is used to name the first person in the Trinity. It is a name that associates our thoughts with human attributes. And therein lies the problem of language and human thought. To accept the idea that the true nature of God is beyond human comprehension is to understand that names that stand for God do not denote or identify God literally. This is well expressed in the orthodox Jewish practice of not speaking the name of God, YHWH. This practice underscores a reverence for the awesome mystery of God, so beyond human understanding that to try to contain God's essence in a word is a sin. At issue is metaphor: Through consistent use, a metaphor comes to be thought of as a literal statement. Simply put, if a child listens to the words of worship and hears God referred to time and time again as "Father," the child may well come to believe that God is indeed a being with all the attributes that the child associates with a father. How can this learning be reconciled with the scriptural concept that we are all "created in the image of God"? If God created both male and female, does that not imply that God must have both attributes? Again, the early theologians agree to the extent that to deny "the womb of God" was considered heresy.[15]

This hymnal balances the gendered metaphors and similes for God and lessens the number of masculine pronouns and male images for God. It also strives to enrich the vocabulary of worship by using a wide diversity of metaphors from a variety of sources to refer to God. There is no end to the wealth of names to be found in Scripture and ancient hymns and that emerge from the creative minds of modern hymnwriters.

These are but a few of the names used in *The New Century Hymnal* to refer to God: Ancient of Days, Comforter, Creator, Emmanuel, Father, Mother, Father-Mother, Fashioner of spheres, Fount, God, God of Abraham and Sarah, God of mystery, God Most High, Healer, Holy One, Holy Wisdom, Love Eternal, Maker, Messiah, Mystery, Parent, Redeemer,

Rock, Root of life, Savior, Shepherd, Source and Goal, Sovereign, Triune Source, Wakantanka (Lakota language for God), Weaver, Word—and there are many more.

Thus worshipers have the opportunity to praise God with a variety of metaphors that by their diversity can expand the images of God and evoke the mystery of God that is "I AM WHO I AM"—and not limited by a single name. All of this is possible while still embracing the trinitarian name(s) of God, and at the same time giving an equally privileged place to feminine metaphor.

Use of "Father" for God

In *The New Century Hymnal*, God is not addressed exclusively as Father. The approach to language for God is to use gendered language sparingly, and in balance. Thus, although God is called Father, God is also called Mother. If it is possible to do so, balance is achieved in the same hymn. A careful look at many of the hymns that were reviewed indicated that a reference to Father was not necessarily linked to the rest of the text. In other words, "Father" was used simply as a name for God, but without relation to the metaphorical content of the rest of the text.

An example is the hymn "Great Is Your Faithfulness" (hymn 423), whose original words "O God my Father" do not have a strong relationship to the rest of the hymn, which as a whole speaks about God's creation. Nor is "Father" used as a name for God in the Lamentations passage (3:22–23) that is the origin of the hymn text. Thus, in this instance, the name "Father" is not retained and "Creator" is substituted as a name that is linked with the rest of the text. But in hymn 487 God is described as a "father, gently caring," and the rest of the text speaks of the ways in which this parenting care is shown.

"Father" is also used in some instances where it was decided to maintain the traditional words for the Trinity. (For these examples, see the section "Language about the Trinity.")

Balancing Masculine and Feminine Images

Sometimes hymns have been altered to balance male and female metaphors for God. "Father Almighty, Bless Us with Thy Blessing" (hymn 518), as revised by a twentieth-century poet, now has better-balanced metaphors by substituting "Mother of mercy" in the third verse. The poet has also expanded imagery by adding "Eternal God" and "Christ of compassion." In other cases, balance is accomplished without using words that denote gender. In a baptism hymn (325) the hymnwriter refers to "God your loving parent," making it possible to imagine God as either a mother or a father. In a benediction hymn (82) it is again up to the singer to choose to think of God as either a mother or a father (or as both), since the poet has God speaking as "I" to "my children": "Go, my children, with my blessing, you are my own." Hymn 451 uses the image "Mother and Father, you are both to me."

A similar idea is suggested by the use of "Father-Mother" as an option in the prayer of Jesus, "Our Father . . ." In the version given as option B of "Prayer of Our Savior" in "Morning Prayer" and "Evening Prayer" in the Orders for Worship, "Father-Mother" is made available as a way of addressing God. The usage of the hyphenated name "Father-Mother" may appear unusual in that no human has one parent who is both father and mother. In fact, the name may serve as a useful metaphor for God for this very reason. "Father-Mother" lets us address God with images of both fatherly and motherly attributes in mind. The hymn "Bring Many Names" (hymn 11) by Brian Wren is a good example of using gender balance and also other varied images to present the many aspects of God, who is always more than we can describe. Among the many names are not only "strong mother," "warm father," but also "old, aching God," "young, growing God," and finally "great, living God, never fully known." It might be striking for some to observe how the poet has avoided the societal stereotype of a strong father and a nurturing mother by reversing the attributes.

Use of Mother and Other Feminine Images for God

Just as some hymns use only father images for God, others refer to God only as mother, or in terms of motherhood. Although balance of gendered metaphors has not been attempted within these hymns, they balance one another in the overall book. Some of these are old, some are revised, and some are newly composed. "How Like a Gentle Spirit" (hymn 443) is a recent hymn that reflects imagery from Scripture (Deut. 32:11–12): "God like a mother eagle hovers near on mighty wings of power." "Mothering God, You Gave Me Birth" (hymn 467) is a new poem, but it is adapted from the writings of Julian of Norwich, a fourteenth-century abbess. In it God, Christ, and Spirit are expressed as a trinity that acts in mothering ways. The use of feminine images for God is not a development of modern times. It has precedents in the Bible: "As a mother comforts her child, so will I comfort you" (Isa. 66:13a). "I have kept myself still and restrained myself; now I will cry out like a woman in labor" (Isa. 42:14b). "I will fall upon them like a bear robbed of her cubs" (Hos. 13:8). And Jesus lamenting over Jerusalem employs a feminine image: "How often have I desired to gather your children together as a hen gathers her brood under her wings" (Matt. 23:37).

The use of feminine images for God is not particularly a product of female writers. In the third century, Clement of Alexandria wrote, "And God himself is love; and out of love to us became feminine. In his ineffable essence he is father; in his compassion to us he became mother." In the fourth century, Ambrose of Milan (the writer of "O Splendor of God's Glory Bright" [hymn 87]), spoke of the womb of the Father. Lists of early Christian writers cited by modern scholars make it clear that both men and women writers frequently used feminine images for God.

Masculine Pronouns for God

The same ideas that are presented in the earlier sections, "Gender of God" and "Use of Father for God," relate to pronouns referring to God. If male pronouns—"he," "him," "his"—are used consistently to refer to God, the user may begin to think of God as a male. Because it is not assumed that God is a male being, the hymnal avoids male pronouns and finds other ways to speak about God without using gender. This is done in a variety of ways, sometimes requiring a shift in the syntax, using "God" a second time, or using another word or nongendered pronoun, for example "who" or "whose." In "God Moves in a Mysterious Way" (hymn 412) the pronoun "he" gives way to adjectives or simply the word "God." Thus "his wonders to perform" becomes "great wonders to perform"; "scan his work" becomes "scan God's work"; and "God is his own interpreter, and he will make it plain" is rendered "God is God's own interpreter, whose truth shall be made plain." There is no claim that such adaptation is a perfect equivalent, but it does maintain the beauty and meaning of the original. This is an example of a process applied frequently to speak of God without giving the impression that God is a being with a specific gender.

The same principles are applied to the renditions of the psalms. Psalm 121 reads this way in the NRSV:

> My help comes from the Lord,
> who made heaven and earth.
> He will not let your foot be moved;
> he who keeps you will not slumber.
> He who keeps Israel
> will neither slumber nor sleep.

The psalter of *The New Century Hymnal* renders the word "Lord" as "God" ("Yahweh" in the Hebrew manuscripts—I AM THAT I AM) and the pronouns "he" and "him" as "God"; "his" is rendered "God's" (p. 704):

> My help comes from God,
> who made heaven and earth.

God will not let your foot be moved;
God who keeps you will not slumber.
God who keeps Israel
will neither slumber nor sleep.

The psalms thus rendered have lost neither their meaning nor sense of adoration. Yet the process has again been applied for the reasons previously cited. In the whole psalter of the NRSV, the occurrences of the pronouns "he," "him," and "his" to refer to God number over one thousand. And it may be pointed out that the use of the masculine pronouns as subjects of verbs was the result of translating the psalms into English. They do not exist in the original Hebrew texts.

It is difficult to imagine a person reading through the psalms for the first time as they appear in most English translations and concluding that God does not have male gender. The ease with which one can read and sing through the psalms in the hymnal in their gender-neutral renderings demonstrates that such a shift is possible while still maintaining the original beauty.

Gender of Jesus Christ

The hymnal occasionally retains masculine language for the historical Jesus, especially if that is essential in the storytelling sense. Thus when we sing of the baby boy in the manger, we sing "the little Lord Jesus lay down his sweet head" (hymn 124), and we sing of "Jesus our brother"(hymn 138). Male language is also retained in some other hymns that recount events in the life of Jesus:

> "What Child Is This" (hymn 148): "Nails, spear shall pierce him through..."
>
> "Hosanna, Loud Hosanna" (hymn 213): "To Jesus, who had blessed them close folded to his breast..."
>
> "Were You There?" (hymn 229): "when they nailed him to the tree..."
>
> "Jesus Took the Bread" (hymn 343): "Jesus broke the bread; then he poured the wine."
>
> "Let Us Talents and Tongues Employ" (hymn 347): "at his table he set the tone..."
>
> "Jesu, Jesu" (hymn 498) "Knelt at the feet of his friends..."

It is important to note, however, that in most cases hymns in their total message are not simply about the man Jesus of Nazareth but refer to the resurrected Jesus, the Christ, who is our Sovereign. In such cases, language has been chosen to express the divinity and sovereignty of Christ without portraying Christ in male terms. In other words, when the hymn is clearly about the resurrected Jesus, or Christ, male-oriented language is usually not used.

Likewise, in cases where the pronoun "he" appears throughout the hymn to refer to the raised Christ, the change has been effected by simply writing in "Christ," thus assuring no loss of identity but again lessening the overall bias toward the masculine identity of the second person of the Trinity. An example of this may be found in the fourth stanza of "O Spirit of the Living God" (hymn 263): "So shall we know the power of Him who came mankind to save; So shall we rise with Him to life which soars beyond the grave" has been altered to "So shall we know the power of Christ, the strength of love to save, so shall we rise with Christ to life which soars beyond the grave." And in "In Christ There Is No East or West" (hymns 394, 395), "in him no South or North" becomes "in Christ no South or North."

Also, some hymns were changed to the second person to address Christ as "you" instead of "he," which at the same time adds a more intimate expression of personal faith. An example is "We Hail You God's Anointed" (hymn 104). Phrases such as "he shall come down like showers" and "before him on the mountains" are rendered in second person as "you shall come down like showers" and "before you on the mountains."

Why should such emphasis be given to the distinction between the historical Jesus and the Christ of all humanity? The considerations are essentially the same as those regarding language about God. In the same way that male language to describe God is not emphasized, neither is male language referring to Christ. When Paul speaks of Christ in Colossians 1:15–20, he cites numerous aspects of Christ's nature: "image of the invisible God"; "firstborn of all creation, . . . before all things," and through whom "all things are held together"; "head of the body, the church"; "the beginning, the firstborn from the dead"; the one in whom "all the fullness of God was pleased to dwell," and through whom all things are reconciled to God, whether in heaven or earth, through the blood of the cross. What is not central to this description is that Christ is a male being.

Another perspective is conveyed by Paul in Galatians 3:27–29: "As many of you as were baptized into Christ have clothed yourselves with Christ. There is no longer Jew or Greek, there is no longer slave or free, there is no longer male and female; for all of you are one in Christ Jesus." Many view this passage to mean that Jesus Christ transcends gender and other social or cultural divisions, uniting us as a new body of faith, the church. The theologian Sandra Schneiders puts it simply: "Christ, in contrast to Jesus, is not male, or more exactly, not exclusively male.

Christ is quite accurately portrayed as black, old, Gentile, female, Asian, or Polish. Christ is inclusively all the baptized."[16]

The fourth-century theologian Gregory of Nazianzus says of Christ, "that which is not assumed is not redeemed."[17] Because redemption is offered to all, Christ has assumed all that we are—man, woman, rich, poor, weak, and strong. This concept parallels the creation, God's creation of humankind in God's own image, both male and female, just as Christ takes on our humanity—all of it: our riches, our poverty, our weakness, our strength, our maleness, and our femaleness. Jesus Christ has assumed all of our humanity. Rendering texts in language that does not give predominance to gender does not diminish this message.

To make sure that this central image is never lost in our worship, this theme of God taking on our humanity, the incarnation, resounds through the hymns of *The New Century Hymnal*. Hymn 209 is an old Latin hymn newly translated: "O Love, how vast . . . that God a human form should take, and mortal be for mortal's sake." An excellent modern example is "O Christ Jesus, Sent from Heaven" (hymn 47), in which all the images refer to God taking human nature. In the breadth of one hymn, Christ, the Word made flesh, is sent from heaven, lives with us, washes feet, is crucified, and feeds the church today. Hymn 208 states clearly that Christ, who was made flesh and suffered death, is the chief cornerstone, the "ground" of faith. These examples typify the great care with which the belief that Jesus Christ is God incarnate has been preserved while at the same time avoiding the repetitive use of male-gendered language.

This was considered to be the case, for example, with "O Come All You Faithful" (hymn 135). It is true that the hymn is for the event of Jesus' birth, but the refrain of praise most certainly transcends time and space so that we are singing not only to the babe in the manger, but also to the Christ of all ages, the Christ of men and women, rich and poor, weak and strong. Yet the human incarnation of God is not diminished as the hymn states: "Jesus to you shall all glory be given, Word of our God now in flesh appearing." A change such as this may give pause to many who have memorized hymns, especially carols for Christmas, and it is likely that many will continue singing these carols the way they learned them for some time to come. Still, in keeping with the language of the entire book, even these hymns were altered.

A parenthetical note here may be in order. The editorial panel that worked with poets to revise all the hymns wrestled with many texts and came to the conclusion that to a large degree the integrity of the hymnal would rest on its treatment of language, as much as is humanly possible, in a consistent way. If language is to be made inclusive, then it should be made inclusive throughout. Such consistency may not be easily accepted in cases where memorized language is at play. But the more important issue to all who worked on this hymnal was this: What language will we hand to a generation yet unborn that will guide its singing and learning of faith?

"Lord" and "Sovereign"

The word "Lord" presents a challenge when seeking to diminish the number of instances in which God is referred to in a male image. "Lord" has appeared in hymns with great frequency as a name for God and Jesus. The word implies authority, but it also is a word of gender. There was considerable debate after the word "Lord" had been eliminated temporarily from many hymns. In response to a General Synod action recommending the restoration of the word "Lord" in reference to Jesus Christ, the editorial panel reviewed the revisions that had been made in the hymns using guidelines written by the executive committee of the UCBHM's board of directors.[18]

As a result, "Lord" when referring to Jesus was retained in cases of well-known, memorized hymns, especially when it appeared in the first stanza. This can be seen in "Here, O my Lord, I see you face to face" (hymn 336); "The church's one foundation is Jesus Christ our Lord" (hymn 386); "the little Lord Jesus lay down his sweet head" (hymn 124); "Lord Jesus, who through forty days"(hymn 211); "Joy to the world! the Lord is come" (hymn 132); and "Teach me, O Lord, your holy way" (hymn 465).

In some instances, other language considerations prevailed in the decision to leave out the word "Lord." The following story gives an example of such a case. As the hymn "Fairest Lord Jesus" was being discussed, one of the African American members of the hymnal committee remarked, "to the young people in my congregation, 'fair' means fair-skinned." Knowledge that the same German hymn was translated in some hymnals as "Beautiful Savior" prompted a new translation, "Beautiful Jesus, Head of all creation" (hymn 44).

Finally, in some hymns where the word "Lord" was not used in the original language, it was not retained, such as "Joy Dawned Again on Easter Day" (hymn 241): Where Neale had translated "the apostles saw their risen Lord" ("Christ" was used in the original Latin), *The New Century Hymnal* uses "the Risen Christ to them appeared."

"I Greet You, Sure Redeemer" (hymn 251) has an interesting story of changes. "Lord" does not appear in the fifth stanza of the original French text. In Elizabeth L. Smith's translation that appears in Philip Schaff's *Christ in Song*, the words are "Comfort and give us peace, make us so strong and sure." These words were revised for *The Hymnal of the Reformed Church* (1920) as "Come give us peace, make us so strong and sure." But the 1941 *Hymnal of the Evangelical and Reformed Church* changed the text to "Lord, give us peace, and make us calm and sure." *The New Century Hymnal* uses "O dear Redeemer, make us calm and sure."

The overall result of the entire revision process is that the word "Lord" appears with less frequency than in many other hymnals. In the same way this hymnal has dealt with many other gendered words, words have been found to balance and expand images. One approach was to substitute for "Lord" "Sovereign" or some other word that keeps the idea of authority and hierarchy. This may be found in phrases such as "Jesus . . . who is God and Head of all," (hymn 145), and hymn 166, "We may not climb the heavenly steeps to bring the Sovereign down." An instance that does not represent the usual way of applying the above processes occurs in "As with Gladness Those of Old" (hymn 159). The new words are "As with joy they hailed its light, leading onward, beaming bright; so, true Morning Star, may we evermore your splendor see" ("Morning Star" replaces "Most gracious Lord").

To those for whom "Lord" is one of the main ways of addressing Jesus, all of the above changes may be unsatisfactory. But the reality is that "Lord" is respected in the hymnal as one of the many valid names used for Jesus Christ. Furthermore, the confession "Jesus Christ is Lord" is not abandoned in the hymnal but is expanded by the use of alternative images to express the sovereignty of Jesus Christ.

There is not space here even to summarize the diverse opinions about the word "Lord," but the words of the guidelines used by the editorial panel indicate the spirit in which their work of retaining the use of "Lord" was done, with "sensitivity to the fact that the term 'Lord' represents sexism and injustice for some and a historic and meaningful committed relationship for others."

Use of "Lord" for "God"

In general, "Lord" is not used in *The New Century Hymnal* as a name for God. It is only used for Jesus Christ. The same process of substitution of nongendered words was the usual way of treating this word. In the case of the Psalter, the word "Lord" as it appears in the New Revised Standard Version is often replaced with "God."

The Son of God, the Child of God

A parent would agree that there is no loss of affection in saying "you are my child" instead of saying "my daughter" or "my son." In the same way, the relationship of Jesus Christ to God as Son of God can also be expressed by saying that Christ is God's own Child. The filial relationship is affirmed, and the aspect of Christ's humanity is not diminished even though these are both expressed in a way that does not emphasize gender. The use of "Child of God" to refer to Jesus is not a modern invention. The Greek word *pais*, whose meaning is child or offspring, is used to refer to Jesus in Acts 3:13, 26; 4:27, and so on. The NRSV translates *pais* in those passages as "servant," with a footnote: "Or *child.*"

Pais is also used to refer to Jesus in the early Christian writing; see, for example, 1 Clement 59:2, 3, 4, written around 96–97 C.E. Cyril C. Richardson translated 1 Clement 59:4 as follows: "Let all the nations realize that you are the only God," That Jesus Christ is your only Child, and "that we are your people and the sheep of your pasture."[19] *Pais* is used for Jesus also in the Didache (9:3, 10:2, 3), which dates from the early second century. Didache 9:3 reads: "We thank you, our Father, for the life and knowledge which you have revealed through Jesus, your child."[20] *Pais* also is used to refer to Jesus in the communion prayer of the Liturgy of Hippolytus of the early third century: "We render thanks unto thee, O God, through Thy Beloved Child Jesus Christ, Whom in the last times Thou didst send to us [to be] a Saviour and Redeemer and the Messenger of Thy counsel."[21]

In a very few instances in *The New Century Hymnal* the name "Son" has been replaced with "Child." Hymn 209 cited above is an example. It concludes with "By Love we have been reconciled: salvation gained through God's own Child." Another example is found in hymn 198, where "Christ the Child of God" replaces "Christ the Son of God." In "O Come, O Come, Emmanuel" (hymn 116), "until the Son of God appear" becomes "until the Child of God appear."

The first line of "We Hail You God's Anointed" (hymn 104) bears comment in this regard, since "We hail you God's anointed, the long-awaited One!" is quite different from the original, "Hail to the Lord's anointed, Great David's greater Son!" From the aspect of gender language, it was apparent that three male names, "Lord," "David," and "Son" in the first line needed consideration. "Lord," in this case clearly referring to God, is changed to "God," and "Great David's greater Son" is changed to "the long-awaited One." Although it is true that the explicit allusion to Jesus' descent from David has been lost, "long-awaited One" most certainly expresses the prophecy of the Messiah, as in the words of John, "are you the one who is to come?" and the song of the triumphal entry, "the one who comes in the name of God." That same God is the God of Israel and the God of Christians.

Kings, Kingdoms, and Masters

The use of "king" as a metaphor for God has been replaced in some cases by "sovereign," or some other way has been found to eliminate the masculine gender. Hymn 248 is an example: Although the original hymn begins with the words "The King of love my shepherd is," the entire remainder of the hymn is not about a king but about shepherding. Thus, the king of love image was set aside in favor of "Such perfect love my Shepherd shows." This is not a perfect equivalent, since it could be argued that, in fact, it should have become "The sovereign of love," or the "ruler of love," or the "queen of love" in a subsequent verse for balance. But the reality is that "ruler" and "sovereign" would not work poetically (too many syllables), and balancing "king" with "queen" does not seem to achieve the desired result. The solution that was found has integrity. God still showers love, and all of the shepherd imagery of the Twenty-third Psalm is intact. In addition, five male pronouns have been removed. The end result is that the same story is told and the same wonderful metaphor for God as the caring shepherd is still powerfully portrayed, without the need to portray the shepherd as a man who is a king.

An example of the use of "sovereign" for "king" is found in "Rejoice, Give Thanks and Sing" (hymn 303). The original Charles Wesley text, "Rejoice! the Lord is King! Your Lord and King adore; mortals, give thanks and sing, and triumph evermore," now reads in *The New Century Hymnal*, "Rejoice, give thanks and sing; your Sovereign God adore! For Christ has robbed death's sting and triumphs evermore." In the original, Wesley's use of male language for God is intensified by repetition: Lord-King-Lord-King in the first line. The original phrase, "His kingdom cannot fail, he reigns o'er earth and heaven," has been changed to "Christ Jesus cannot fail to rule both earth and heaven," since in the first instance it is possible to infer that it is *we*, the heirs of the kingdom, who cannot fail, when in fact it is *Christ* who cannot fail. The revision makes clear that it is Christ who triumphs and reigns, giving us cause to rejoice. The alteration has allowed this hymn to be sung smoothly, with its images of authority and awe, but without using male language for God.

"Master" is a masculine word that for some has implications of oppression, as in the expression "master-slave." In the case of "O Master, Let Me Walk with Thee" (hymn 503), it is dealt with quite simply by the substitution of "Savior"; thus, "O Savior, let me walk with you." In another case, "You Servants of God" (hymn 305), "your Sovereign proclaim" provides a fitting replacement for "your Master proclaim."

Kingdoms of course imply kings, and predominantly male authority; but it is not necessary to use "kingdom" if "dominion" can be substituted.[22] The difficulty that arises is that "kingdom" has two syllables and "dominion" has three. Thus, in some cases the equivalent "realm" is used. In hymn 101, "Comfort, Comfort O My People," "since the realm of God is here" replaces "since the kingdom now is here." "Realm" also appears in newly written hymns: "Enter in the Realm of God" (hymn 615) and "You Are Salt for the Earth, O People" (hymn 181), for example. "Dominion" is used in "Keep Awake" (hymn 112), in the alternate version of the Nicene Creed (hymn 884), in the alternate versions of the Prayer of Our Savior in morning and evening prayer (pages 56 and 60 in the denominational edition; pages 10 and 14 in the ecumenical edition), and in Psalm 145, verses 11, 12, and 13.

Militaristic Language

Occasionally, a hymn describes the struggle against evil in purely military terms. "For All the Saints" (hymn 299) is an example of the modification of text to keep the message but "tone down" the fighting imagery. The original "O may thy soldiers, faithful, true, and bold, fight as the saints who nobly fought of old, and win with them the victor's crown of gold" has been changed to "Still may your people, faithful, true, and bold, live as the saints who nobly fought of old, and share with them a glorious crown of gold." "Thou, Lord, their captain in the well-fought fight" becomes "you, Christ, the hope that put their fears to flight." In the new rendition, the message is clear but the imagery of war is diminished. Is the message exactly the same? Probably not, but in this new language, Christ is still the leader, still struggle and warfare persist (see stanza 5), and the hope of triumph is still alive. The difference is that Christ is not symbolized as a military leader, and we are not symbolized as soldiers. It is certain that some will lament the loss of these metaphors, but others cannot sing language of such strong military tendency in a world where violence abounds. It might also be noted here that the "blest communion, fellowship divine" was indeed changed for gender reasons, and is replaced by the equally revered expression for the communion of saints, "Ringed by this cloud of witnesses divine."

Triumphalistic Language

As mentioned earlier, triumphalistic language was scrutinized in the revision process. An example is the fourth stanza of "Rejoice, Give Thanks and Sing" (hymn 303), which has usually been discarded in modern hymnals, probably because it does have truly triumphalistic overtones: "He sits at God's right hand till all his foes submit, and bow to his command, and fall beneath his feet." *The New Century Hymnal* restores this fourth verse, but in hopeful, expectant words more in keeping with the theology of the church at this time: "Rejoice in glorious hope, for Christ the Judge shall come, and take the faithful up to their eternal home. We soon shall hear a heavenly voice above the trumpet's sound, 'Rejoice!'"

Language about the Trinity

The hymnal committee developed a statement concerning the trinitarian formula: "Where a hymn is clearly trinitarian, Father, Son and Holy Spirit language may be used, but we will consult poets, theologians, and others in order to search for new ways of expressing the Triune God within orthodox parameters. We will use references to the Trinity only when they are part of the essential text." Recognizing that intense discussion about the language used to express the doctrine of the Trinity is taking place in many denominations, the approach to the use of this language is not monolithic. An examination of trinitarian language in the hymnal should help to show the result.

In the Order for Baptism (page 36 in the denominational edition), the words for the Act of Baptism are "in the name of the Father, and of the Son, and of the Holy Spirit." In hymn 324, the traditional "baptismal formula" is kept in acknowledgment of its validity in the rite of baptism: "O Father, Son, and Holy Ghost." And in what may be the most familiar of traditional Trinity hymns, the entire trinitarian formula is sung in the fourth verse: "Holy Father, Holy Son, Holy Spirit, Three we name you, while in essence truly one, undivided God we claim you." In the ancient evening hymn *Phos Hilaron* (p. 739), one of the hymns of the early church, the names of the persons of the Trinity are retained in the translation: "Immortal Father, heavenly One"; and "Father, Son, and Spirit." It should be pointed out that the first three topics by which the hymns are organized parallel the trinitarian formula: God, Jesus Christ, Holy Spirit (see the hymnal's table of contents).

Occasionally trinitarian stanzas of hymns have been omitted, especially when they were not integral or original to the hymn. "All People That on Earth Do Dwell" (hymn 7) did not contain the doxological stanza "To Father, Son, and Holy Ghost" in its original 1561 form by William Kethe. It is often the case that doxologies at the ends of a hymn are not part of the original hymn but are additions in later revisions.[23] The doxological stanza that has appeared with this hymn was composed by John Mason Neale in the nineteenth century. Of course Psalm 100, of which the hymn is a paraphrase, did not contain these trinitarian words either. In this instance, the doxological stanza is omitted in *The New Century Hymnal*.

In some cases, poets sought alternate ways of expressing the Trinity. "Now Thank We All Our God" (hymn 419) contained a trinitarian reference that read: "All praise and thanks to God the Father now be given, the Son and him who reigns with them."[24] This has been altered to: "All praise and thanks to God our Maker now be given, To Christ, and Spirit, too, our help in highest heaven, the one eternal God." It is clear that the revision does not name the Trinity in the traditional language of the Nicene formula, but it does what the guideline above suggests—namely, find alternate ways to express praise to the Triune God.

An example of this may be found in the final stanza of hymn 100, "All Praise Be Yours, My God, This Night": "Praise God who makes, sustains, sets free; one holy God in persons three." But it is not just in hymn revisions that these alternate expressions are to be found. The Easter hymn "Alleluia! Alleluia!" (hymn 243, fourth stanza) sings about the "Triune Majesty" as "God," "Savior," and "Spirit," and these exact words were penned by Christopher Wordsworth in 1872.

Some newer hymns provide excellent examples of the search for alternative language. Jane Parker Huber begins the four consecutive stanzas of her new hymn (278) with: "Creator God," "Redeemer God," "Sustainer God," and "Great Triune God." Among the many images in "O Christ Jesus, Sent from Heaven" (hymn 47), by James Crawford, there is an allusion to the Trinity in the fourth stanza, in the words "O Christ Jesus, Father-Mother, Spirit, Triune Source of all." Ruth Duck in "Womb of Life, and Source of Being" (hymn 274) provides many metaphors, including a trilogy of "Womb of life," "Word in flesh," and "Brooding Spirit." And in the "Service of the Word I" in the Orders for Worship, a benediction is provided in a trinitarian form that balances gender images: "The blessing of the God of Sarah and of Abraham; the blessing of Jesus Christ, born of Mary; the blessing of the Holy Spirit, who broods over us as a mother over her children; be with you all."

Language That Includes Women, Children, and Men

A category of language change that is familiar to most is the use of nongendered language to refer to people. As a matter of fact, this is one aspect of language change for which some groundwork had been laid in recent hymnals and the New Revised Standard Version of the Bible. Throughout *The New Century Hymnal,* poets have found creative and expansive ways to change the large volume of male-gendered language to language that includes women and children. In "Joyful, Joyful, We Adore You" (hymn 4), "reconciling race and clan" replaces "binds man to man." "O brother man, fold to thy heart thy brother" becomes "Children of God, lift hearts to one another" (hymn 533). "God of Grace and God of Glory" (hymn 436) now sings "in the fight to set us free" instead of "set men free." "Strong men and maidens meek" has become "strong souls and spirits meek" in "Rejoice, You Pure in Heart" (hymn 55). "The God of Abraham Praise" (hymn 24) has been given balance by including "The God of Sarah praise." This particular usage, by the way, appears not only in hymns but in the psalm versions, and in the orders for worship. For example, the blessing (A) in "Service of the Word I" begins, "The blessing of the God of Sarah and of Abraham." These are some of the many ways in which males and females are considered equally as children of God.

Use of the Word "Dark"

The word "dark" has appeared in hymns almost exclusively with negative meaning. Phrases like "the power of darkness" to mean "the power of evil" abound. But because "dark" and "darkness" are also associated with skin color, when we use these words in a negative sense, we also reflect upon those who have dark skin. The same is true of the association of "white" with purity. It is not surprising that Charles Wesley's stanza containing the phrase "wash the Ethiop white" was not included in the Methodist hymnal.[25] In Psalm 51:7 (p. 657), "wash me, and I shall be whiter than snow" becomes "purer than snow." The symbolism of light and dark imagery appears extensively in hymnody, and is deep-rooted in Scripture. It is possible to maintain this contrast and symbolism without using "dark" and "darkness" to denote evil. In the hymns and psalms of *The New Century Hymnal*, these words are replaced with other words to denote absence of light, words that simply state the subject of evil, or words that denote the obscuring of light. Thus in "Watcher, Tell Us of the Night" (hymn 103), "darkness takes its flight; doubt and terror are withdrawn" becomes "shadows take their flight." In "Joyful, Joyful, We Adore You" (hymn 4), "Melt the clouds of sin and sadness, drive the dark of doubt away" is changed to "storms of doubt." In "When Morning Gilds the Skies" (hymn 86), the phrase "the powers of darkness fear" is replaced by "let sin and evil fear." Brian Wren uses "darkness" in a positive sense in "Bring Many Names" (hymn 11): "Great, living God, never fully known, joyful darkness far beyond our seeing."

Language about People's Abilities

The United Church of Christ National Committee on Persons with Disabilities was consulted about the subject of sensitivity to ability. In 1992 this group met and drafted a statement that includes the following:

> As a community of persons with disabilities, we are aware of two realities. There are times when our disabilities have prevented us from being embraced by the church. Sometimes the barriers have been physical, other times they have been attitudinal. We have endeavored to remove these barriers. We are naturally concerned if the words of a hymn are clearly exclusive, implying that the ability to walk, to see, or to talk is a prerequisite to faith. Whenever a change can be made that reminds us that we are all loved and accepted by God, we affirm that change. At the same time, we are aware that the Bible and many hymns use the language of symbol. We know, for example, that when John Newton wrote in Amazing Grace that "I was blind, but now I see," he was not talking about visual ability, but about seeing with his heart. We know that when Jesus spoke of seeing, he celebrated vision but rejoiced in the perceptive heart. We believe that it would be a mistake to be overly literal, or to automatically exclude every reference to sense

or mobility. We are also aware, of course, that what is acceptable to one person is unacceptable to another. . . . We encourage the church to become as loving and accepting as it can be, and to celebrate the joys of the inclusive community in hymns.

This statement represents the starting point for the review of the many hymn texts with references to ability to be included in *The New Century Hymnal*. Throughout the process, the committee made its recommendations, and poets worked to make the necessary revisions.

Words about walking provide an example of language of ability. Hymnbooks are full of "walking" hymns. But "walk" as a metaphor was not invariably excised. In "O Savior, Let Me Walk with You" (hymn 503) the word remains, since the committee advised "that it is about spiritual walking in the context of bearing, risking, and trusting." Sometimes words about sight were changed, for example, the refrain of "Alas! and Did My Savior Bleed" (hymn 199) has been changed from "At the cross where I first saw the light" to "At the cross where I first found the light." One of the most unique additions was in the hymn "Guide My Feet" (hymn 497), where a suggested extra stanza, "Wheel with me while I run this race," was added in a note to include those in wheelchairs and as a reminder that not everyone runs races on foot.

Many more examples could be given, but these represent the basic intent of the process. It could be summed up in another quote from one of the letters sent with a group of suggestions:

> The basic point is that the context of the words have a great deal to do with their meaning. If the hymn indicates that one must walk or see in this life to participate in the faith, then a change is warranted. If the hymn indicates that walking or seeing or hearing are things that happen when one is utterly overwhelmed by finding oneself in the presence of God in the hereafter, then a change is not necessary.

The difficulty of separating shades of metaphorical usage is quite obvious. It may appear that throughout the book there are inconsistencies, and there probably are. But the work was done within the context that we live in "brokenness," and perfection is achieved only in God's realm. What does matter is that when texts were changed, it was done with the hope of avoiding stereotyping or hurt and that, as an overall result, *The New Century Hymnal* is enriched by another aspect of inclusivity.

Language That Recognizes Varied Human Experience

The hymnal committee recognized that in the past, hymns rarely spoke to some of the "dual" aspects of human existence. They wanted to assure that the collection would present, for example, not just Christmas images of cold weather and snow; not just a Eurocentric or North American point of view; and not only rural but also urban images. Some of this has been accomplished through the selection of hymns. For Christmas, "Carol Our Christmas" (hymn 141) was chosen for this very reason. The song addresses Christmas in words appropriate for summertime in the Southern Hemisphere: "Carol the summer, and welcome the Christ Child, warm in our sunshine and sweetness of air." The hymnal as a whole makes possible a more inclusive worldview and tempers the Eurocentric statement of earlier collections. Occasionally, the language of a hymn was shifted to accommodate this wider view. Hymns that referred to Asia as "the Eastern lands," for example, were altered. "The Day You Gave Us, God, Is Ended" (hymn 95) replaces "The sun that bids us rest is waking our brethren 'neath the western sky" with "waking our family members far away." And there are instances where new words mention urban life as well as rural. An example of this is in "Heaven and Earth, and Sea and Air" (hymn 566), where the new translation sings of "urban lights and canyons deep, forest, fields, with cows and sheep." A new hymn (212) begins "O Jesus Christ, may grateful hymns be rising, in every city for your love and care." It was not the intent of the committee that all the images in the book be balanced in this regard, but that there at least be reminders that not everyone's life experience is the same.

Language of Science and Technology

The Science and Technology Working Group of the UCBHM shared its insights with the hymnal committee. This affected both the selection of hymns and the development of language guidelines. Following are the main areas in which the themes of science and technology have been incorporated into *The New Century Hymnal*.

Language of a Three-tiered Universe. Often the hymns of the past, and even hymns written today, speak of our existence in a way that is separate from, if not counter to, our present view of the cosmos. For example, hymns consistently use the language of the three-tiered universe—we are in the middle, God is up, and hell is below. These are only metaphors, but as is always the case, when a single metaphor is used over and over, it becomes a reality in our minds. What is the problem with a metaphor such as God looks "down" on us? This might make sense to some, but to some from the Pacific Rim, it is upside-down. For those whose ancient culture focuses on the sea, God is in the depths. Although some of our metaphors indeed come from those whose life was spent looking at the stars, many have spent their lives pondering the depths of the oceans.

How does this relate to the language of hymns? There is a need to use a diversity of metaphors to talk about where we and God exist in the cosmos. Of course, we know that we cannot fix God in any one "spot." But we can expand our images about where God "is" in relationship to us. It is amusing to speculate that one of the reasons that so many hymns sing about "God above" is that these words rhyme conveniently with "love" and even "dove"; thus, our thoughts about God may be somewhat shaped by what rhymes. Users of *The New Century Hymnal* might notice that on occasion, the word "above" may have been changed or augmented to expand the imagery of where God is. A good example is "We Worship You, God" (hymn 26), in which "all glorious above" has been changed to "abroad, around, and above." In hymn 6, the nineteenth-century translation "Sing praise to God who reigns above" is replaced by a new translation, "Sing praise to God, our highest good." The number of times that the "location" of God is stated in older (and some newer) texts is significant. We know that hymns function as teaching instruments and that all people, especially children, learn fundamental concepts from hymns. Many of these changes simply represent replacing a medieval view of the world with images and language consistent with what children learn daily in school about the universe.

Other Language in an Age of Science and Technology. It is not only in language revision, however, that this hymnal recognizes language of science and technology. Words reflecting everyday life in an age of science and technology rightly appear in some new hymns and translations. In hymn 269, the translator Madeleine Forell Marshall has used modern images to bring alive Paul Gerhardt's seventeenth-century hymn: "Wise and careful, you [God] have counted each electron, all the sands. All-embracing you have bounded space and time in your kind hands." Herbert Stuempfle's new text (hymn 567) speaks clearly to this scientific age in which we find ourselves: "Stars and planets flung in orbit, galaxies that swirl through space, powers hid within the atom, cells that form an infant's face: these, O God, in silence praise you; by your wisdom they are made." In "Creating God, Your Fingers Trace" (hymn 462) Jeffery Rowthorn depicts celestial bodies and the elements of earth praising their creating and sustaining God.

Language of Domination. In traditional hymns about the relationship between humankind and the earth, or nature, there is a central motif. This recurrent theme is portrayed in images of earth and nature as possessions entrusted to people for their care. Human activity is often played out against a backdrop of the lovely scenery of nature. Hymns of this sort, although they may contain beautiful images, by themselves do not speak in terms large enough for a civilization that has learned the power to destroy itself. Catherine Cameron (hymn 556) raises intriguing thoughts about our existence—"[We have] probed the secrets of the atom, yielding unimagined power, facing us with life's destruction or our most triumphant hour." The Science and Technology Working Group encouraged the inclusion of hymns that would use language to expand the view of the relationship of people to their world from simply that of domination and caretaking to that of partnership with and interrelatedness to all of God's creation.

Languages Other than English

While no one book could adequately provide resources from every racial/ethnic tradition in the church or the world, *The New Century Hymnal* does offer more than one hundred hymns that are non-European in origin. The selection also represents to a large degree the diversity of cultures and ethnicities embraced within the United Church of Christ and other mainstream denominations in the United States.

One of the linguistic features of this hymnal is that it includes forty-six hymns in languages other than English. Some of these instances are English hymns translated into other languages. A large number of hymns of non-European origin appear with their original language printed first. This practice recognizes that these hymns are gifts to English-speaking culture, and that they are, first of all, hymns with their own cultural origins, made accessible through translation into English.

It was beyond the ability of the editorial panel to review and revise all of the non-English texts according to lenses of inclusive language. But due to the large number of Spanish-language hymns, a great effort was put forth to work not only with the English-language translations but with the original Spanish texts. In fact, it became clear that many of the revisions that were needed in the English translations were as a result of noninclusive language in the original text. In order to resolve this, a task force was established that included bilingual members and a poet. Working together, they sought first to revise the Spanish-language text and then to render it into English-language poetry, thus creating a higher degree of consistency between the Spanish and English texts.

NEW HYMNS AND NEW IMAGES

This overview, for the most part, has discussed the ways in which texts of older hymns have been transformed to sing in our own time with their original freshness. Much less attention has been paid to new hymns and their new images. Imagery in hymns has been expanded by modern hymnwriters not so much through the development of a new vocabulary, but in the use of everyday words of our times in new ways. One of the most striking and engaging developments is their ability to engage us in a lighthearted expression of our faith, as the following examples demonstrate.

In "When Minds and Bodies Meet as One" (hymn 399), Brian Wren uses the poetic rhythm of a jig to express the joy of community:

> When minds and bodies meet as one and find their true affinity,
> we join the dance in God begun and move within the Trinity.

and

> When teamwork serves a common aim, and players move
>   in sympathy,
> the flowing rhythm of the game is beauty in simplicity.

Shirley Erena Murray also employs playful images when writing of the Spirit in "Come, Teach Us, Spirit of Our God" (hymn 287):

> Engage our wits to dance with you, to leap from logic's base,
> to capture insight on the wing, to sense your cosmic grace.

When Ruth Duck wrote "God, We Thank You for Our People" (hymn 376), she did not hesitate to use words drawn from everyday activity: lessons learned, secrets told, hopes, memories, pranks, stories, and food by loving hands prepared.

Within the six brief stanzas of "God of the Sparrow God of the Whale" (hymn 32), Jaroslav Vajda uses a profusion of images in relation to God: sparrow, whale, swirling stars, creature, earthquake, storm, trumpet blast, rainbow, cross, grave, hungry, sick, prodigal, neighbor, foe, pruning hook, ages, loving heart, and children. Dan Damon uses images of the elephant, eagle, whale, dragonfly, spider, snail, planet, wilderness, rain forest, waterfalls, and trees to engage us in a plea for God's creation in "Pray for the Wilderness" (hymn 557). Such images from the everyday world are sure to communicate to all of us, and especially to children.

These writers can also place before us the fears and sufferings of humanity in contemporary terms. We find allusions to those who are homeless: "When bodies shiver in the night and, weary, wait for morning" (hymn 563). We are reminded of ways of serving our neighbors: "I will hold the Christ-light for you in the shadow of your fear" (hymn 539). The presence of Christ for all the victims of the world is expressed in a hymn that pictures Christ today suffering, imprisoned, scavenging for bread, and begging for crumbs (hymn 587).

Some hymns address racial issues. Hymn 585 speaks of a world in which we can be "torn and pulled apart by hate because our race, our skin is not the same." New verses inspired by "America the Beautiful" (hymn 594) remind us that our people are both "indigenous and immigrant."

Words that spring from our diverse cultures bring still other images to our worship, such as those by the Native American writers Elizabeth Haile and Cecil Corbett in "O God the Creator" (hymn 291): "the earth is our mother where all things grow" and "gentle deer and the eagle and the mighty buffalo."

Occasionally, new metaphors for God appear, as in the first stanza of hymn 398 by Dan Damon: "Shadow and substance, wonder and mystery, spellbinding spinner of atoms and earth; soul of the cosmos, person and energy, source of our being; we sing of your worth." In "By Whatever Name We Call You" (hymn 560) Dosia Carlson calls God the "Fashioner of Spheres," "Mystery," and "All-inclusive One." James Gertmanian describes God as a weaver, "The One whose thread and warp and weft are flesh and earth and air," in "The Weaver's Shuttle Swiftly Flies" (hymn 464). Herman Stuempfle employs the metaphor of a potter in "O God, as with a Potter's Hand" (hymn 550) with some very striking imagery: "And when we seized your choicest work and broke its fragile clay, your hands restored the shattered shards on earth's first Easter day."

All of these examples of new hymns should remind us that when we want to describe the sacred we draw from our own wells of diverse metaphors. In the pluralistic world in which we live, the more ways we have of speaking of ourselves and of God, the more likely we are to gain a better understanding of one another and of the many ways we have of praising God.

A WORD ABOUT PERFECT LANGUAGE

God is perfect. Human beings are not, and neither is the language that we use to speak of God. The real danger lies in making idols of the images—the words—we use to address God, thus mistaking these words for the essence of God. We all have fallen short of God's glory, and so do the words we use to speak of God. Still, in our zeal to know God and to praise God, we use the images we have been given and those we create. If we seek to expand those images, we reach toward the possibility of closer relationship. If we seek to limit our language to single formulas, we run the risk of our images of God, and thus our relationship with God, becoming static and tied only to the past. This is at the heart of the issue of language change. The tension of the language in *The New*

Century Hymnal is that it does preserve traditional expressions, at the same time allowing new expressions, and it includes both the old and the new in language free from biases that many find to be exclusive. Throughout, the goal is not to achieve the perfect or ultimate version but to make the hymns live in our own time, to be passed into the hands of coming generations for their use and adaptation.

APPENDIX A: THE WAY IT USED TO BE[26]

Texts of hymns change from time to time and age to age, even some of the most familiar. Following are some examples.

"Silent Night"

While some may assume that the English version of "Silent Night" (which is a translation from the German, "Stille Nacht") has always existed as we know it today, that is not the case. *The Evangelical Hymnal* (St. Louis, 1917) includes this version:

Holy night, peaceful night!
Through the darkness beams a light
There, where they sweet vigils keep
O'er the Babe in silent sleep,
Resting in heavenly peace,
Resting in heavenly peace.

Those brought up on *The Hymnal of the Reformed Church* (1920) will remember almost the same words (except for "yonder" instead of "there" and "the Babe who, in silent sleep, rests"). The *Pilgrim Hymnal* (1935) starts out "Silent night, holy night," but continues, "All is dark, save the light," and then proceeds the same as the Reformed version, "Yonder, where they . . ." An even earlier version from the *Christian Hymnbook* (Cincinnati, 1865) begins: "Silent night! Hallowed night, Land and deep . . ."

"Faith of Our Fathers"

This well-known hymn is no longer sung in its original form either. The author, Frederick W. Faber, was an English Roman Catholic who wrote this hymn with the political-religious mission of returning the Church of England to Roman rule. The "fathers" were the Catholic priests who were subject to persecution under Queen Elizabeth I. Two versions were published, one for Ireland and one for England.

The first stanza of the Irish version proclaims:

Faith of our fathers living still,
In spite of dungeon, fire and sword,
How Ireland's heart beats proud with joy,
Whene'er we hear that glorious word.

The third stanza of the English version is equally partisan:

Faith of our fathers! Mary's prayers
shall win our country back to thee;
and through the truth that comes from God
England shall then indeed be free.

"Hark! The Herald Angels Sing"

Charles Wesley's familiar Christmas hymn did not originally open with those seemingly timeless words. Stanza 1 began:

Hark, how all the welkin rings
"Glory to the King of kings!"

The second stanza was different as well, the last two lines of which originally appeared in Wesley's 1739 version as:

universal nature say,
"Christ the Lord is born today!"

They were changed as early as 1760 in Martin Madan's *Collection of Psalms and Hymns* to the version most know today:

With the angelic host proclaim,
"Christ is born in Bethlehem!"

"Alas! And Did My Savior Bleed"

The original version of this hymn by Isaac Watts contained several words and phrases that have been changed by editors to reflect more modern usage and sensibilities. Stanza 1, line 4 was altered from "For such a worm as I" to the more acceptable "For sinners such as I." Stanza 3, line 3 has been the object of some theological controversy: "When God, the Mighty Maker, died" was changed in some hymnals to clearly allude to the crucifixion of Jesus: "When Christ, the great Redeemer, died." Other words in this hymn that have been changed over time, include "crimes" to "sins" and "groaned upon" to "suffered on" (stanza 2).

APPENDIX B: HYMNS IN TRANSITION[27]

"Jesus Christ Is Risen Today"

The favorite Easter hymn "Jesus Christ Is Risen Today!" (hymn 240) has a history dating at least as far back as the fourteenth century. It had eleven stanzas, beginning with:

Surrexit Christus hodie humano pro solamine, Alleluia.
(Jesus Christ arose today for human solace, Alleluia.)

The familiar form that has been sung in the twentieth century is from various sources, with only the first stanza having any relationship to the original Latin. The translation of that verse comes from *Lyra Davidica* (London, 1708), a collection of new songs and translations from German and Latin:

Jesus Christ is risen today, Alleluia.
Our triumphant holy day,
Who did once upon the Cross
Suffer to redeem our loss.

The other familiar verses were added in the eighteenth century and have little, if any, relationship to the original Latin hymn:

Stanza 2, beginning: "Hymns of praise now let us sing . . ."
Stanza 3, beginning: "But the pains which he endured . . ."

These are from Arnold's *Compleat Psalmodist* (2d ed., 1749). Some hymnals carry still another stanza, created by Charles Wesley in 1740 (again, with no connection to the original Latin), beginning: "Sing we to our God above . . ."

But what of the original Latin hymn of which only one stanza survived? What was the story it told? The rest of this remarkable text tells the story of the women bearing spices to the tomb, meeting the angel, and running to tell the good news of the Resurrection. It is a drama filled with joy—a poetic narrative for Easter. It was not uncommon in the medieval church for the story to be acted out, and it is very possible that this great storytelling narrative hymn was used for just that purpose, as worshipers reenacted the scripture while they sang this hymn in a garden outside the church on Easter morning.

The decision to restore this ancient text to hymnody is an example of several such efforts in *The New Century Hymnal* whereby early hymns have been translated from German and Latin and put into fresh English poetry. *The New Century Hymnal* English version follows very closely the original Latin hymn, giving us not only a treasure intact from early church worship, but also the beautiful telling of the story of the women, which earlier revisers chose to drop.

NOTES

1. Ninth General Synod of the United Church of Christ (73-GS-41).

2. Eleventh General Synod of the United Church of Christ (77-GS-17).

3. As quoted in "Language Thought and Social Justice," The Task Force on Educational Strategies for an Inclusive Church, National Council of the Churches of Christ in the U.S.A., New York, 1986, 1.

4. Ibid.

5. Madeleine Forell Marshall, *Common Hymnsense* (Chicago: G.I.A. Publications, 1995), 10.

6. Brian Wren, *What Language Shall I Borrow? God-Talk in Worship: A Male Response to Feminist Theology* (New York: Crossroad, 1991), 82.

7. Adapted from the working guidelines for language of the hymnal committee.

8. From Watt's preface to his fourth volume of hymns, as quoted by Austin Phelps and Edward A. Park, professors at Andover, Mass., and Daniel I. Furber, pastor at Newton, Mass., in their book *Hymns and Choirs: Or, The Matter and the Manner of the Service of Song in the House of the Lord* (Andover, Mass.: Warren F. Draper, 1860), 145.

9. Ibid.

10. Ibid., 144.

11. John Julian, *A Dictionary of Hymnology* (New York: Dover Publications, rev. 1907), 1: 276.

12. For a new version, see hymn 410 in *The New Century Hymnal*.

13. Julian, *Dictionary of Hymnology*, 1: 487.

14. Jaroslav Pelikan, *Christianity and Classical Culture* (New Haven, Conn.: Yale University Press, 1993), 87, 88.

15. See Jürgen Moltmann, "The Motherly Father: Is Trinitarian Patripassionism Replacing Theological Patriarchalism?" *Concilium* 143 (1981): 51–56.

16. Sandra M. Schneiders, *Women and the Word: The Gender of God in the New Testament and the Spirituality of Women* (Mahwah, N.J.: Paulist Press, 1986), 54.

17. Ibid.

18. The following is taken from the report of the Executive Committee of the United Church Board for Homeland Ministries, Board of Directors to the Executive Council of the General Synod.

The members of the Executive Committee [of the UCBHM] reviewed the goals, history, and status of the hymnal, and the Synod action and its implications. Foremost in the discussions of the Executive Committee were:

- The covenantal responsibility of the UCBHM for a task entrusted to it by the General Synod.
- The goal of publishing for the UCC "a fully inclusive" hymnal as specified in the action of the Tenth General Synod and authorized by the Seventeenth General Synod.
- The historical and personal significance of the term "Lord" for many, as expressed in the request of the Nineteenth General Synod.
- The difficulties with the term "Lord" for many others, as expressed in the responses of UCC churches and members during the development of the hymnal and in the deliberations of the Synod.

In response to the action of General Synod on July 19, 1993, and with extraordinary sensitivity to the fact that the term "Lord" represents sexism and injustice for some and a historic and meaningful committed relationship to Jesus for others, the Executive Committee of the UCBHM Board of Directors establishes the following guidelines for the Editorial Panel in making changes in hymns in *The New Century Hymnal* where "Lord" has been replaced by "Christ."

1) That changes be made only where they will not jeopardize the 1995 publication date and budget commitments, and
2) That special consideration will be given to memory bank hymns, and
3) That consideration be given to restoring the word "Lord" if the original hymn is not compromised by other language or images, and
4) That the original language of the poets be respected when the word "Lord" was added to a hymn by translation.

19. Cyril C. Richardson, *Early Christian Fathers* (Philadelphia: Westminster Press, 1953), 71.
20. Ibid., 175.
21. See Bard Thompson, *Liturgies of the Western Church* (Philadelphia: Fortress Press, 1961), 20.
22. An excellent explanation of the semantics of the word "dominion," written by Burton H. Throckmorton Jr., may be found in *Prism* (spring 1987): 40, n. 1. In brief, it states that in the Greek scriptures

Jesus speaks of the *basileia* of God. That has been translated in English as "kingdom." Throckmorton suggests that "dominion" is more appropriate since it connotes the idea of "rule" (the exercise of authority) and "realm" (the place that is ruled) as does *basileia*, whereas "kingdom" denotes only the realm.

23. In the fourth century, Ambrose of Milan attached a doxology to the end of his hymns as a strong statement of orthodoxy in his dispute with the Arians. In the early nineteenth century, the Oxford Movement in England, which had great interest in returning to medieval hymns, resumed the practice of attaching doxologies to the ends of hymns, including preexisting hymns that did not have doxologies. For a more complete discussion, see Erik Routley, *Church Music and the Christian Faith* (Carol Stream, Ill.: Agape, 1978), 97–98.

24. In German, "Preis sei Gott, dem Vater und dem Sohne und dem, der beiden gleich."

25. *The United Methodist Hymnal* (The United Methodist Publishing House, 1989), presents nearly the entire hymn "Glory to God, and Praise, and Love," in its original form with eighteen stanzas, but rightfully omits the following stanza:

> Awake from guilty Nature's Sleep,
> And CHRIST shall give you Light,
> Cast all your Sins into the Deep,
> And wash the Ethiop white.

(It is from this original hymn that the well-known hymn "O for a Thousand Tongues" was derived by using stanzas 7, 8, 9, and 1, in that order.)

26. This appendix originally appeared as Appendix C in "Discovering *The New Century Hymnal*: A Discussion Guide for Church Musicians, Pastors, and Congregations" (Cleveland, Ohio: The Pilgrim Press, 1995).

27. This appendix appeared as Appendix A in "Discovering *The New Century Hymnal*."

A Survey of Christian Hymnody

Early Christian, Hebrew, Greek, and Latin Hymns in *The New Century Hymnal*

Arthur G. Clyde

EARLY CHRISTIAN HYMNODY

The singing of hymns and psalms was part of the earliest Christian worship. Some of the earliest hymns are from the Hebrew and Greek scriptures (Old and New Testaments) and many of them are included in *The New Century Hymnal* in the section "Canticles and Ancient Songs" (pp. 732–40). Among these beautiful, ancient texts are the Canticle of the Three in the fiery furnace (*Benedicte omnia opera*), which has been used through the ages for morning prayer and Easter vigil, the Song of Mary (the *Magnificat*), the Song of Zechariah (*Benedictus*), and the Song of Simeon (*Nunc Dimittis*). In addition to these are other songs that have been part of orders for worship throughout all of Christian history that can be found in *The New Century Hymnal* "Service Music" section (nos. 741–815)—doxologies, glorias, the tersanctus (Holy, Holy, Holy), and alleluia, for example. The trisagion, an early Greek trinitarian hymn, also appears here (nos. 745, 746, 747) and in one of its settings with the Greek text. We know that all of these songs were basic ingredients of early Christian worship, along with the psalms. The psalter of *The New Century Hymnal* is a subject unto itself, but it should be emphasized that the book of Psalms was the main songbook of the Bible, and as such, composed a large proportion of the main "hymnal" for early Christian worship.

The music to which any of these early texts were sung is not known. Thus, in *The New Century Hymnal*, they are set to a variety of tunes—traditional and new—in the "Service Music" section. In the case of the texts in the "Canticles and Ancient Songs" section and in the psalter, they are pointed for chanting to simple tunes, perhaps a style not too different from the way they were sung originally. This collection of music of the church might not at first glance be thought of as hymnody, but in fact it does represent a collection of earliest hymns of the Christian church. For the purpose of this *Companion to the Hymns of The New Century Hymnal*, the remaining commentary on these earliest Christian hymns will be limited to those that are set in the traditional form of metrical hymnody.

The New Century Hymnal contains two hymn settings of the Song of Mary in contemporary poetic form. The first ("My Heart Sings Out with Joyful Praise," hymn 106), by Ruth Duck, has been set to a Swedish folk song MARIAS LOVSÅNG (Mary's Lovesong). The second ("My Soul Gives Glory to My God," hymn 119), by Miriam Therese Winter, is set to an early American folk melody, MORNING SONG. Another Ruth Duck paraphrase of the Song of Zechariah ("Now Bless the God of Israel," hymn 110) has been set to an English melody, FOREST GREEN. The Song of Hannah, from Hebrew scripture, has been recast as an English poem by Miriam Therese Winter ("My Heart Is Overflowing," hymn 15) and is set to a twentieth-century tune by Paulette Tollefson. In addition to these, many of the Hebrew psalms have been recast as metrical hymns and will undoubtedly be mentioned in other essays in this book.

It may be appropriate here to mention two hymns in *The New Century Hymnal* that are from the Jewish tradition, although not as early as those just mentioned. The first is "Maoz Tsur Y'shuati" (hymn 10), which celebrates the feast of Hanukkah instituted in the second century B.C.E., with a text by the thirteenth-century poet called Mordechai, set to a traditional Hebrew melody. The second is "Yigdal Elohim Chai" (hymn 24), based on the Yidgal, the Jewish articles of faith set down in the twelfth century by Moses Maimonides. They are chanted in the synagogue. The tune LEONI is also from Jewish tradition.

GREEK HYMNS

In addition to the many hymns from the Greek scriptures (New Testament) already mentioned, there are four hymns in *The New Century Hymnal* that should be cited. They are from the fourth and eighth centuries.

Phos Hilaron (p. 739), one of the earliest hymns in *The New Century Hymnal*, is from the fourth century. It has been translated many ways: "O joyous light," "gracious light," and even "laughing light." The original meter of the Greek text in almost every translation is deserted in favor of a more common meter, and the tunes used are often of much later periods. *Phos Hilaron* ("O Gladsome Light") has been set in several hymnals to NUNC DIMITTIS, a tune from the sixteenth century; it also appears with a John Stainer tune. In *The New Century Hymnal*, it is set with CONDITOR ALME, an early plainsong from Sarum, England, to effect a more ancient feeling when it is sung, especially in evening prayer services, where it is associated with the lighting of the lamps. The second hymn from the fourth century, "Let All Mortal Flesh" (hymn 345), is from the Liturgy of Saint James, thought to be composed by the first bishop of Jerusalem, James. It was sung during the presentation of the bread and wine. It appears in *The New Century Hymnal* and in many hymnals to the French folk tune PICARDY.

Two other hymns are from a later time, and both are attributed to the Syrian theologian John of Damascus (c. 696–c. 754), whom John Mason Neale called the greatest of Greek poets. After retiring from the priesthood, he composed theological papers and hymns at the Lara of Sabos, between Jerusalem and Bethlehem, a center of hymnwriting. Among the most important works he completed there were canons, long poetic works made up of odes. These canons, which were intended by the monks to be a strong defense of the faith, were modeled on the canticles found in the Bible, including the songs of Moses, Hannah, Habakkuk, Isaiah, Jonah, Mary, and Zechariah, and the Song of the Three. "Come you faithful raise the strain" (hymn 230) and "The Day of Resurrection" (hymn 245) are free translations of odes from the Easter Canon made by John Mason Neale in the nineteenth century. The tunes obviously date from the period in which Neale introduced the translations. In "The Day of Resurrection," the Hebrew Scripture influence of the canticles is clear in the references to the Exodus. In the Eastern church, "The Day of Resurrection" is traditionally sung at midnight on Easter eve simultaneously with the lighting of candles to herald the arrival of Easter.

This grouping of *The New Century Hymnal* ancient Greek hymns is only a very narrow representation of all Greek hymnody, which includes the poems of Clement of Alexandria, Methodius, Gregory of Nazianzus, Synesius of Cyrene, and many more. However, it may in a small way keep before us an appreciation for the first hymnody of our Christian heritage.

THE BEGINNINGS OF LATIN HYMNODY

As in the case of Greek hymnody, Latin hymnody does not represent the output of a specific age. This category of hymnody includes hymns written in the Latin language during a span of more than fifteen centuries. Thus, rather than attempt what would seem impossible—to deal comprehensively with Latin hymns as a homogeneous genre—the following chronology will be at best an overview that incidentally cites some of the major trends of various times. This will be done on the basis of the examples contained within *The New Century Hymnal*.

The advent of Latin hymnody begins with Saint Hilary (d. 368), the bishop of Poitiers, and Saint Ambrose (d. 397), the bishop of Milan. There were others, of course, including Damascus, the bishop of Rome in 366, and Marius Victorinus (c. 360). Although only fragments of Hilary's work remain, some hymns by Ambrose have been preserved through the ages. Both these doctors of the church were avid objectors to the emperor Constantine's promotion of Arian doctrines. Hilary, exiled by the emperor to Phrygia in Greece, there learned the emerging style of metrical hymnody and brought it back to Poitiers, France. When the churches in Milan, Italy, came under siege by the Arian churches, Bishop Ambrose and his followers locked themselves in the church, where he kept their spirits up by writing hymns for their meditation. These hymns, proclaiming the divinity of Christ, were protests against

Arianism. Significantly, they were the first hymns of the church in the West. Up to this time, only the liturgies and Scriptures were sung, and composed meditations were suspect.

It was perhaps the fervor and need of the moment that caused these hymns to be accepted. They gained widespread use as congregational hymns, which was possible because of the accessible style that Ambrose developed. Classical Latin poetry was based on a quantitative (long and short syllable) scheme:

Splen-*d o r* Pa- *t e r* nae *g l o*- ri- *a e.*
(short long short long short long short long)

But these rules of quantitative poetry were rules known only to poets and the educated class. At the same time, there existed a folk style, which was in use in the main society for ballads and songs, that was rhythmic and based on accents. It was closer to the system of accents that governs the poetic meter of English-language hymns:

O **splén** - dor **óf** God's **Gló** - ry **bríght**
(alternating unaccented and accented syllables)

Ambrose and these early writers combined the two styles, making sure that the quantitative texts could also be sung rhythmically, allowing for the singing of these metered and rhyming poem-texts in a style that was familiar to many. This "Ambrosian" style was used by other poets and formed the model for much of hymnwriting in Latin for the next six hundred years. These early poets relied on simple meters such as *iambic dimeter*, but also employed more-complex and extended meters.[1] Over the centuries, there can be seen in Latin hymnody a definite movement from the quantitative to the accented rhythmic style.[2]

The tunes used for these early hymns of the church (largely a matter of conjecture) were possibly melodies from the synagogue, folk melodies, and tunes based on the Greek modes. Many scholars agree that they were probably sung syllabically—one note to a syllable—and that all the stanzas were sung to the same tune. It can be safely assumed that whatever the tunes might have been, they were uncomplicated, since in the earliest times they were for congregational use.

AN OVERVIEW OF EARLY LATIN HYMNS IN *THE NEW CENTURY HYMNAL*

Hymns in *The New Century Hymnal* from this first period of six hundred years—from 300 to 900 C.E.—include writings by Ambrose (d. 397); the Spanish theologian and poet Prudentius (d. 413); the Italian Pope Gregory I (d. 604; known as Gregory the Great); the French bishop of

Poitiers, Fortunatus (d. 609); the Venerable Bede, the English scholar, writer, and theologian (d. 735); and the German archbishop of Mainz, Rhabanus Maurus (d. 856); along with anonymous texts from the fifth, eighth, and ninth centuries. These hymns span various topics and are filled with rich metaphors.

Fourth Century

Early hymnologists attributed nearly one hundred extant hymns to Ambrose, but recent scholars narrow the list to somewhere between twelve and twenty. Only one is included in *The New Century Hymnal* and must serve as the sole representative of these first hymns of the Western church. Ambrose's *Splendor Paternae* ("O Splendor of God's Glory Bright," hymn 87) is a hymn depicting Christ as the light of the world and using other light imagery to depict the persons of the Trinity (light, sun, and radiance).

Fifth Century

Corde natus ("Of the Parent's Heart Begotten," hymn 118), by Prudentius, is from a long poem defending the faith and is the ninth of twelve long parts, one for each hour of the day. In broad strokes, it combines both creation and incarnation, using cosmic images to tell the story of the coming of Christ. The anonymous Easter hymn *Claro Paschali gaudio* (*Paschali mundo gaudium* in the Roman breviary; "Joy Dawned Again on Easter Day," hymn 241) is only the final part of a forty-two-line hymn that relates the story of Christ's rising from the grave, the women's telling of the good news, and the final prayer to the risen Christ.

Sixth and Seventh Centuries

By the early sixth century, monastic communities had been formed, and under the guidance of Saint Benedict they organized their worship around a pattern of hourly prayers called the "daily office." This transition, of course, is consistent with the "cloisterization" of church music and the beginnings of chant forms that were developed for these communities who spent life together and worshiped in song literally around the clock. New hymns were written for the daily office, and earlier ones were appropriated to certain hours. Thus, *Splendor Paternae* was established as a hymn for lauds (the beginning of the day) and *Corde natus* for compline (the close of the day). Other changes took place. It is not clear when the original long poem *Corde natus*, by Prudentius, was converted into a hymn, but in the process, the refrain *saeculorum saeculis* ("for ages of ages," or sometimes translated "evermore and evermore") was added to the original stanzas of the poem, as was a final trinitarian stanza that appears in many translations.

Nocte Surgentes ("Rising in Darkness," hymn 90) is an example of one of these daily-office hymns; it was written for lauds, the hour of the monastic day when members of the community would rise for prayer, well before dawn. As Erik Routley points out, modern translations have "suppressed that point, for fairly obvious reasons."[3] The translation in *The New Century Hymnal* returns to the original idea, with "rising in darkness" replacing translations such as Percy Dearmer's "Father we praise you, now the night is over." In fact, the original Latin does not contain the phrase "Father we praise you."

Other hymns were written for the larger, dominating cycle of worship, the church year. *Ex more docti mystico* ("Again We Keep This Solemn Fast," hymn 187), attributed to Gregory, commemorates the Lenten period of fasting and most certainly was written for a didactic purpose, as it describes the number of days, how to eat and talk, and generally how to observe this time of penitence. Fortunatus composed *Vexilla regis* ("The Royal Banners Forward Fly," hymn 221) for a service in which a church received a relic of the cross. Although *The New Century Hymnal* has only four of the original seven verses, it retains in stanza 3 one of the most exquisite expressions of theology, the image of God reigning from a tree (the cross). *Pange lingua* ("Sing, My Tongue," hymn 220), also by Fortunatus, in its original eleven stanzas traces the story of redemption from the first tree in the garden to the cross. The fourth stanza of "Sing, My Tongue" retains the beautiful and well-known meditation on the faithful cross, *crux fidelis*. *Salve festa dies* ("Hail, O Festal Day!," hymn 262) was also adapted through the ages from a longer work that uses the extended metaphor of springtime to portray the resurrection story. Originally, it was not written as a hymn to be sung but was a 110-line poem in elegiac meter written to Felix, bishop of Nantes, to commemorate the baptism of the converted Saxons. It was popularized and adapted as a hymn early in its history.

Also from this period are the well-known "O antiphons" that form the basis for *Veni Emmanuel*. Numbering seven in all (see the individual stanzas of the modern version, "O Come, O Come Emmanuel," hymn 116), one was sung on each of the evenings preceding Christmas. Two of these antiphons, *O Sapientia* and *O Oriens*, form the basis of the first two stanzas of the hymn "O Wisdom, Breathed from God" (p. 740).

Eighth Century

Bede's Ascension hymn, *Hymnum canamus gloriae* ("A Hymn of Glory Let Us Sing," hymn 259), is an example of the first Latin hymns written in England. Bede may have written more than the dozen or so that survive today; he cites a *Liber Hymnorum* in a list of his own works. *Urbs Beata Ierusalem* is a two-part anonymous text found in ninth-century manuscripts and is thought to be from as early as the seventh century. "Christ Is Made the Sure Foundation" (hymn 400) is a translation of the second part, which begins *Angularis fundamentum*. This hymn uses the city of Jerusalem as a symbol for the church and the reign of Christ, and was traditionally designated for the dedication of a church, with the first part sung at evening prayer and the second part at morning prayer.

Ninth Century

Tradition has made *Gloria, laus et honor* ("All Glory, Laud, and Honor," hymn 216), by Theodulph, bishop of Orleans, the most famous of Palm Sunday narrative hymns. It was, in fact, used in the Middle Ages for a processional from the church to the public square. The anonymous *Ubi caritas et amor* ("Where Charity and Love Prevail," hymn 396) has long been used as a prayerful meditation for the washing of feet on Maundy Thursday. The Pentecost hymn *Veni Creator Spiritus* ("Creator Spirit, Come, We Pray," hymn 268), often attributed to the famed Benedictine composer Rhabanus Maurus, has remained through the ages one of the most popular of all Latin hymns. *The New Century Hymnal* translation is fairly literal and restores many of the original metaphors (fount, paraclete, charity, fire, unction), even though three of the usual seven verses are omitted.

CONTINUED DEVELOPMENT OF LATIN HYMNODY

It should be pointed out that in most hymnals, and *The New Century Hymnal* is no exception, the Latin hymns are almost invariably set to music from a much later time. This is usually because the original music does not exist, and in cases where there are traditional chants for the texts, modern hymnals have opted for more-metrical hymn tunes. For example, *Gloria, laus et honor* (hymn 216) appears almost universally in hymnals with the seventeenth-century tune by Teschner, even though much earlier chant tunes are known. Notably, the tune CONDITOR ALME has stayed together through the ages with its text, *Conditor alme siderum* ("O Loving Founder of the Stars," hymn 111)—one of the few melodies of ancient origin to do so—and is the tune of choice in modern hymnals. The tune is very old and is found in manuscripts of the ninth and tenth centuries. It provides an excellent example of the movement toward the use of a rhythmic-accented style of composition in strict iambic dimeter. (The pattern of the English translation is identical to that of the Latin text.) The tune appears with two other texts in *The New Century Hymnal* (pp. 739 and 740).

From the Mozarabic tradition (from the Christian church in Spain before 1085 C.E.) comes *Christe lux mundi* ("Christ, Mighty Savior," hymn 93). Originally it appeared as a nine-stanza poem by an anonymous writer in the Mozarabic liturgy for vespers. Its publication in *The Hymnal 1982* (Episcopal) in a new translation by Anne K. LeCroy has fostered its great ecumenical appeal. In *The New Century Hymnal,* it is set to a remarkable twentieth-century tune by David Hurd.

Eleventh and Twelfth Centuries

O quanta qualia ("O What Their Joy and Their Glory Must Be," hymn 385) is by the famed poet-scholar and priest of the Middle Ages, Peter Abelard. He was secretly married to Héloïse, a woman also renowned for her great intellect. When her father, a canon, dissolved the marriage, Héloïse and Abelard both joined monastic orders. This hymn was written for the women of her order. Finally, Abelard was accused of heresy by the mystic Bernard of Clairvaux and tragically died on his way to defend himself. The story would take on added interest if the three hymns in *The New Century Hymnal* attributed to Bernard were really his, but that has been largely disproved by modern scholars. Nevertheless, these three hymns are of great renown and beauty. "Jesus, the Joy of Loving Hearts" (hymn 329) and "Jesus—The Very Thought to Me" (hymn 507) are both extracts from the same forty-two-line poem, translated in the nineteenth century by Ray Palmer and Edward Caswall, respectively. It could be suggested that these lovely texts are really paraphrases and that much of their beauty is owed to the poetic creativity of the translators. The third text, "O Sacred Head Now Wounded" (hymn 226), has perhaps an even more convoluted history. The base text is Latin, *Salve Caput cruentatum,* and its origins are a matter of speculation, but some scholars date it around the twelfth or thirteenth century. In 1656 Paul Gerhardt paraphrased it in German, *O Haupt voll Blut und Wunde.* James Alexander translated it from German as "O Sacred Head, Now Wounded," with the immortal phrase, "What language shall I borrow to thank you, dearest friend?" Coupled with the Hassler tune PASSION CHORALE, harmonized by Johann Sebastian Bach, this marvelous hybrid may indeed owe its ancestry to Latin hymnody, but it is much indebted to the subsequent contributors.

The twelfth century was a time of enormous intellectual activity in Europe, marked by the founding of universities and by a religious fervor culminating in the Crusades and the beginnings of the great cathedrals. Also, the quality and quantity of the hymns of this period evidence a renaissance of Latin literature. From this period emerged the major female theologian of the twelfth century, Hildegard of Bingen. Known then not only as a powerful political force in the church but as a great visionary, Hildegard has again been recognized, late in this century, for her many talents including poetry and music. Jean Janzen, a twentieth-century poet, has produced a hymn ("O Holy Spirit, Root of Life," hymn 57) that incorporates many of the rich images for God found in three of Hildegard's songs, *"De Spirito Sancto," "O Virtus Sapientiae,"* and *"O Vis Aeternitatis."*

Even though it was just stated that the hymns attributed to Bernard of Clairvaux are probably not his, this is an appropriate place to mention an aspect of his writings—the use of feminine imagery: "Bernard of Clairvaux, whose use of maternal imagery for male figures is more extensive and complex than that of any other twelfth-century figure, uses "mother" to describe Jesus, Moses, Peter, Paul, prelates in general, abbots in general, and, more frequently, himself as abbot to refer to males."[4] This is by way of providing a context for a second hymn by Jean Janzen, "Mothering God" (hymn 467), which is based on the writings of Julian of Norwich in the fourteenth century. Nonetheless, it also relates to the twelfth century in that it represents a thread of metaphorical usage—namely, the use of feminine images—that flourished during this period with Cistercian monks such as Bernard of Clairvaux, the Benedictine Anselm of Canterbury, and Hildegard of Bingen. Thus, the imagery of Julian of Norwich, writing two centuries later, should be viewed not as an isolated creation but as part of a well-established way of thinking and speaking about God.

Finally, perhaps from this period is *Finit jam sunt praelia* ("The Strife Is O'er," hymn 242). (It is often listed as a seventeenth-century creation, the date of the earliest book in which it appears.) Daniel claims it to be from the twelfth century, and John Mason Neale attributes it to the thirteenth. It must be pointed out that the hymns listed here for this century are limited to those that appear in *The New Century Hymnal*. Consequently they do not provide a full picture but merely give a taste of the richness of the age.

Thirteenth Century

If the twelfth century can be characterized as a burst of enlightenment, the next century represents its continuation, as the era produced such brilliant scholars as Thomas Aquinas, author of one of the most popular of all Latin hymns, *Adoro te devote* ("Truth Whom We Adore," hymn 339). Widely used as a communion hymn, it usually appears with the exquisitely fitting tune ADORO TE DEVOTE. Like most of the tune and Latin text pairings, this tune is a much later creation, first appearing in the seventeenth century. In the Roman tradition, the text appeared in the missal in 1570 as a Eucharistic poem for meditation. Although *The New Century Hymnal* translation is faithful to the imagery of the Latin text, it represents a selection of four of the original stanzas, which are collapsed into three. Also, this translation has deleted one metaphor for Jesus, *"pie pellicane."* The editors decided that since the symbol of Jesus as the pelican, widely understood in earlier times, has lost its metaphorical impact, and despite its being a beautiful image for those who know the legend, it was better to delete than to explain. Thus the idea is rendered simply by the phrase "Clean me spotless, Jesus *(pie pellicane)* by your blood alone."

Fourteenth Century

In Dulci Jubilo ("Good Christian Friends, Rejoice," hymn 129) is a folk carol whose origins are really not known, but it is generally assigned to this period. It appears in many hymn and carol books and with many versions of the text. The tune is thought to have a close connection with the text, and might well have been the "original" tune. *In Dulci Jubilo* probably does not belong in an essay on Latin hymnody, except that it provides an excellent example of a "macaronic" text, one in which various languages are mingled. The early versions of *In Dulci Jubilo* are a mixture of German and Latin that show the wide influence of Latin as it is playfully incorporated into folk carols composed in the vernacular. It is easy to see that the words of the carol found in *The New Century Hymnal* and other hymnals are really not translations, and much has probably been lost in the modern versions. It is interesting to note that the macaronic versions were printed in the *Marburg Hymn Book* used in colonial America. Here is one of the many early versions of the text:

In dulci jubilo
Nun singet und seid froh!
Unsers Herzens Wonne
Leit in praesepio,
Und Leuchtet als die Sonne
Matris in gremio.
Alpha es et O!

In English, similar texts were being produced during the same period, as seen in this excerpt from an anonymous hymn to Mary:

Of on that is so fair and bright
Velut maris stella,
Brighter than the day is bright
Parens et puella. . . .

In texts such as these, we can see the foundation for hymns to be written in the language of the people. But the age of writing hymns in Latin was far from over, since it was still very much the language of the church.

There is an interesting account of how another hymn from this time, the well-known Easter hymn *Christus surrexit est* ("Jesus Christ Is Risen Today," hymn 240), arrived in its present form in *The New Century Hymnal*. As with all Latin hymns, efforts were made by the editors to search for sources of the "original" text. It came as a surprise that the familiar English hymn "Jesus Christ Is Risen Today" originally appeared in a much longer form and that only the first stanza bore a strong resemblance to the Latin text, which seems to have its origins in Germany. The stanza beginning "Sing we to our God above" (the fourth stanza in many hymnals) is often correctly attributed to Charles Wesley (1740). But the stanzas not included in familiar translations, which have been restored in *The New Century Hymnal,* are those that tell the story of the women bearing spices to the tomb, meeting the angel, and running to share the good news of the resurrection. It is unfortunate that for so many years these wonderful verses lay in disuse, for as a narrative they tell of those who first recounted the Easter story as noted in the Gospels. It is very possible that in the time of its creation, this hymn was used to reenact Scripture in a garden outside the church on Easter morning, a common practice.

Fifteenth Century

The fifteenth century heralded a new era for hymns in the church. As the twelfth century is remembered for its great wave of creativity, this period is noted for making collections of hymns available for more widespread use because of the invention of the printing press. The production of church books with hymns was made possible. Consequently, many earlier hymns that were known only to one worshiping community found their way into new publications elsewhere. These books have thus provided us with a wealth of hymnody that might not otherwise have been preserved. An example is the breviary used in Salisbury, England (the Sarum breviary), in the fifteenth century, which contains the Transfiguration hymn *Caelestis [or coelestis] formam gloriae* ("O Wondrous Sight," hymn 184). It is anonymous. The music chosen for *The New Century Hymnal* setting is DEO GRACIAS, a tune also dating from the fifteenth century, composed for the victory of King Henry V at Agincourt; it, too, is anonymous. This pairing of text and tune seems to have first occurred in the Presbyterian *Hymnal* of 1933. *Salve festa dies* ("Hail, O Festal Day," hymn 262) is a text of early origin (attributed to Fortunatus, in the seventh century) that was preserved, much adapted, in a publication in England dated 1530, the York Processional.

Two more hymns of this time appear in *The New Century Hymnal*. The first, *O filii et filiae* ("O Sons and Daughters, Let Us Sing," hymn 244), is of

French origin, although it is not certain which of two people named Tisserand wrote it—Jean, a Parisian Franciscan friar who died in 1494, or Jehan, a Dominican bishop in Le Mans.[5] The text is often paired with the tune of the same name, O FILII ET FILIAE, also from France, but of the seventeenth century. The second is a fifteenth-century Italian text by Bianco da Siena ("Come Forth, O Love Divine," hymn 289) that possibly has been kept alive by its fortuitous setting to one of Vaughan Williams's most exquisite tunes, DOWN AMPNEY. Concurrent with the hymns written in Latin for the church were songs written in the vernacular, a tradition dating back to Francis of Assisi in the thirteenth century. Bianco da Siena's poem, *Discendi, amor santo*, is just such a song.

SIXTEENTH CENTURY TO THE PRESENT DAY

A few hymns in Latin have been written in the past four centuries, such as *Adeste Fidelis* ("O Come, All You Faithful," hymn 135). This carol—thought to have been written by John Francis Wade, a Latin teacher at an English school in Douay, France, in the eighteenth century—is the latest in the chronology of Latin hymns in *The New Century Hymnal*.

The main story of the development of Latin hymnody can be concluded with the sixteenth century. The Reformation, with its emphasis on vernacular language, was a major influence on subsequent hymnwriting. Protestant hymns would from this time be written in the spoken language of the country instead of the church's centuries-old language, Latin. Still, this should not be taken to suggest that Latin hymns were spurned by the reformers. As Duffield puts it,

> The first generation of Protestants, to which Luther, Melanchthon, and Zwingli belong, had been brought up on the hymns of the Breviary and of the Missal, and they did not abandon their love for these when they ceased to regard the Latin tongue as the only fit speech for public worship. They showed their relish for the old hymns, by publishing collections of them, by translating them into national languages, by writing Latin hymns in imitation of them, and even by continuing their use in public worship to a limited extent.[6]

However, the zeal for ancient hymns did not continue. From the Reformation until the early nineteenth century, there was little interest in the ancient hymns. Riding on the wave of the Romantic movement and its manifestation in the ecclesiastical realm, the Oxford movement, John Mason Neale began his life's work of restoring, through translation, the great hymns of the Western church. Others followed, both in England and America, translating the old Latin hymns for use by congregations. In this tradition, *The New Century Hymnal* has contributed to these efforts to keep the ancient hymns alive in our own time.

If we consider our rationale for preserving these songs from the distant past, we realize that they have much to offer. A glance at some of the English translations by which we know these great Latin hymns reveals the most beloved of Christian hymnody: "The Strife Is O'er," "Jesus Christ Is Risen Today," "All Glory, Laud, and Honor," "Jesus—The Very Thought to Me," "Jesus, the Joy of Loving Hearts," "Humbly We Adore You." But they contribute more than the comfort of the familiar. In an age when many metaphors have become calcified with overuse, and even many new writings disappointingly reiterate the same overworked images, the metaphors of another time come into sharp focus, especially through new translation. These words from long ago can bring freshness to worship in a technological age. Moreover, the ancient texts truly embrace us in the communion of saints, reminding us that we worship amid a cloud of witnesses whose unique telling of the story of their faith lives on in their songs.[7]

NOTES

1. In Latin poetry, one line of iambic dimeter consists of two pairs of iambs: short long short long—short long short long. In English poetry, this would be counted as four feet (not two) and would usually comprise eight syllables. Thus, most Latin poems in iambic dimeter are rendered in English as four lines of eight—that is, 8.8.8.8., or long meter (LM).

2. For an extended discussion of meter, see Matthew Britt, OSB, *The Hymns of the Breviary and Missal* (New York: Benzinger Brothers, 1922), 25–30.

3. Erik Routley, *A Panorama of Christian Hymnody* (Collegeville, Minn.: The Liturgical Press, 1979), 56b.

4. Caroline Walker Bynum, *Jesus as Mother: Studies in the Spirituality of the High Middle Ages* (Berkeley: University of California Press, 1982), 115.

5. Raymond Glover, ed., *The Hymnal 1982 Companion* (New York: The Church Hymnal Corporation, 1990), 3A: 409.

6. Samuel Willoughby Duffield, *The Latin Hymn-Writers and Their Hymns* (New York: Funk & Wagnalls, 1889), 404.

7. Also consulted in the preparation of this essay were Marilyn Kay Stulken, *Hymnal Companion to the Lutheran Book of Worship* (Philadelphia: Fortress Press, 1981), and Carlton R. Young, *Companion to the United Methodist Hymnal* (Nashville: Abingdon Press, 1993).

Hymnody from German, Scandinavian, and Finnish Sources

Marilyn Kay Stulken

Hymns as we generally understand them—rhymed vernacular verse in several stanzas, each of which can be sung to the same melody—have not always been an important part of Sunday morning worship. For centuries, the official liturgy of the Mass, the main service of the church, did not include hymns.[1] Hymns were sung during the daily offices—prayer services consisting of scripture, hymns, and prayers, conducted approximately every three hours throughout each day. Except for the Greek *Kyrie eleison,* both the Mass and the offices were in Latin. Officially, both were to be sung by clergy and choir only. Opportunities for congregational singing did exist on an unofficial level, however, in the form of occasional refrains or vernacular hymns. The practice of congregational participation was especially pronounced among the Germans,[2] who between the ninth century and the eve of the Reformation created more than fourteen hundred German vernacular hymns.[3]

Beginning in the 1300s, *cantiones,* nonliturgical sacred songs, were cultivated in the universities and monasteries. Most of these were Latin or "macaronic" (mixed Latin and vernacular) songs. "Good Christian Friends, Rejoice" (hymn 129), which is known to have existed in the 1300s, was a macaronic song in Latin and German. The tunes QUEM PASTORES (hymns 123, 510) and JOSEPH LIEBER, JOSEPH MEIN (hymn 105) are also *cantiones* from the fourteenth century.

HYMNODY OF THE LUTHERAN REFORMATION

It remained for two reformers, Martin Luther (1483–1546) and John Calvin (1509–1564)—each following a different path—to establish vernacular congregational song as an integral part of the worship service. Martin Luther was both a theologian and a skilled musician who loved music. Luther early engaged the services of his friend Johann Walther (1496–1570), a professional musician, to assist him. While it probably will never be known exactly how many early Reformation tunes are from Luther's own hand (attributions have ranged from zero to one hundred), it was certainly he who charted the course that Lutheran hymnody was to follow.

One of the tenets of Martin Luther's theology was the priesthood of all believers—the belief that each person can approach God directly, without intermediaries such as priests or saints. This doctrine had far-reaching consequences for the development of congregational song. If people were to come directly to God in the Mass, they were no longer to remain silent. They should participate, preferably in their own language. Hymn singing as developed by Luther and his followers was a liturgical act, not an embellishment. In their creation of the new hymnody, Luther, and others following his example, employed several sources.

Sources of the New Hymnody

1. *Existing Latin Texts and Plainsong Melodies.* Texts were translated to German and the melodies adapted to fit the German texts. Ambrose's (340–397) hymn "Veni Redemptor gentium" became "Nun komm der Heiden Heiland." The tune as adapted, NUN KOMM DER HEIDEN HEILAND (hymn 64), serves as the setting for a modern text in *The New Century Hymnal.* Another tune, ERHALT UNS, HERR (hymn 187), is believed to have been modeled after the same plainsong tune.

2. *Existing Vernacular Hymnody.* The texts were revised *if* necessary and *as* necessary to conform to Lutheran theology. This often involved the addition of stanzas.

3. *Secular Songs.* The words of a secular song were replaced with a sacred text, which sometimes was clearly based on the original. The process is known as "contrafactum" technique; the resulting hymn, a "contrafactum" (plural: "contrafacta"). A comparison of the first stanza of "From Heaven unto Earth I Come" (hymn 130) with a translation of the original secular stanza[4] shows how Luther's hymn was based on the secular song:

> Good news from far abroad I bring
> Glad tidings for you all I sing,
> I bring so much you'd like to know,
> Much more than I shall tell you though.

The original secular melody was later replaced with a new one, VOM HIMMEL HOCH (hymn 130), believed to have been composed by Luther himself.

Contrafactum technique continued to be used in succeeding generations. The tune NUN RUHEN ALLE WÄLDER (hymn 94), also known as INNSBRUCK, appeared in Heinrich Isaak's 1539 book with "Innsbruck, ich muss dich lassen" ("Innsbruck, I Now Must Leave Thee"), a secular song that formed the basis for John Hesse's hymn on death, "O Welt, ich muss dich lassen" ("O World, I Now Must Leave Thee"). The PASSION CHORALE (hymns 179, 202, 226) first appeared in Hans Leo Hassler's 1601 book of secular music. In 1613 it was attached to Christoph Knoll's funeral hymn, "Herzlich thut mich verlangen." In 1625 it was used with a hymn of repentance. Finally, in 1656, in Johann Crüger's (see below) *Praxis Pietatis Melica*, it was combined with "O Sacred Head, Now Wounded" (hymn 226).

In what might be considered a "latter-day contrafactum," the early seventeenth-century German folk song ES FLOG EIN KLEINS WALDVÖGELEIN ("There Flew a Little Woodbird," hymn 66) was combined with "O Day of Radiant Gladness" by George R. Woodward in 1910.

4. *Scripture Paraphrases.* Among Luther's hymns are a number of psalm paraphrases. His most famous is "A Mighty Fortress Is Our God (hymns 439, 440), for which he composed both words and music.

5. *Newly Written Hymns and Tunes.* Two of Luther's original tunes have already been mentioned. Luther's first hymn was "Nun freut euch, lieben Christen g'mein" (1523), an original text. It was associated with three different tunes in various early hymnbooks. One of those tunes, NUN FREUT EUCH (hymn 374), was reconstructed by Luther from a fifteenth-century secular tune.

Lutheran hymns of the Reformation years display a rugged confidence in the work that God has done for us and in God's protection: "Salvation unto us has come, through God's free grace and merit," "A Mighty Fortress Is Our God" (hymns 439, 440), "Dear Christians, One and All, Rejoice." Confidence in God also resounds through the melodies, many of which contain rhythmic vitality, bold leaps, and quick upbeats (as in hymn 440, for example).

THE ERA OF GERHARDT AND CRUGER (C. 1600–C. 1675)

The Hymn Texts

A number of factors shaped the hymnody of the first three quarters of the seventeenth century.

1. *Orthodoxy.* This refers to the established doctrines of the Lutheran church. The church was seen as the corporate body of Christ. Orthodox hymns were usually objective, with a "we" approach.

2. *Mysticism.* In mysticism, the individual sought to move beyond human reason and unite the soul with God through meditation and love. A frequent theme was the allegorical expression of the love of the soul for Christ, the Bridegroom.

3. *Emerging Pietism.* Both mysticism and pietism (see below) brought forth hymns with a personal—an "I"—approach.

4. *The Experiences of War.* The influences on hymnody of war and pestilence—especially the Thirty Years' War (1618–1648)—can be seen in themes of death, hell, and eternal life, of Jesus' sufferings and death on the cross, and of repentance for sin.

5. *Changes of Style in German Poetry.* These influences were not always clear-cut or mutually exclusive. Several can often be found in the works of a single hymnwriter.

The leading hymnwriter of the seventeenth century was Paul Gerhardt (1607–1676), considered second only to Luther as a writer of German hymns. Gerhardt's work blends a deeply rooted orthodoxy with more personal and mystical expressions. Of his more than one hundred hymns, many are the finest and most loved of all Christian hymns. "Now All the Woods Are Sleeping" (hymn 94), a favorite of the author himself, displays his gentler tone and his consolation in the knowledge of God's providence. Other Gerhardt hymns are "O How Shall I Receive You" (hymn 102), "Sweet Delight, Most Lovely" (hymn 269), and "Give Up Your Anxious Pains" (hymn 404). "O Sacred Head, Now Wounded" (hymn 226), a Passion hymn, is based on an earlier Latin hymn.

Also important in the transition from the objective Reformation hymn to a more personal, mystical poetry was Johann Franck (1618–1677), author of "Graced with Garments of Great Gladness" (hymn 334) and "Jesus, Priceless Treasure" (hymn 480).

Philip Nicolai's hymns stand at the head of a long line of mystical hymns of love to Christ as bridegroom of the soul. On the eve of the seventeenth century, Nicolai created two masterpieces of hymnody, both texts and tunes. His tune WACHET AUF (hymn 112) provides the basis for a new Advent text similar in focus to Nicolai's original hymn. Another hymn, WIE SCHÖN LEUCHTET, and its English translation, "O Morning Star" (hymn 158), demonstrates Nicolai's gifts as both musician and poet. Both hymns were included in his *Frewden-Spiegel dess ewigen Lebens* (*Mirror of Eternal Life*, 1599), a collection written at the time of a pestilence to comfort others and convey Nicolai's own faith and confidence.

Some hymnwriters were directly affected by the calamities of the time. When in 1613 more than two thousand people died of the plague in Fraustadt, Valerius Herberger composed a hymn for the dying, "Valet will ich dir geben." Melchior Teschner (1584–1635) wrote the tune ST. THEODULPH (VALET WILL ICH DIR GEBEN) (hymns 102, 216) for Herberger's new hymn. Martin Rinkart's (1586–1649) "Nun danket alle Gott" ("Now Thank We All Our God," hymn 419) was perhaps written in 1636, a year before the 1637 pestilence, during which Rinkart conducted burial services for as many as forty or fifty persons a day; among the victims was Rinkart's wife. Authorship of "Christ Jesus, Please Be by Our Side" (hymn 375) is attributed to Wilhelm II, Duke of Saxe-Weimar (1598–1662). Twice severely wounded during the war, then taken prisoner, Wilhelm survived and devoted himself to reconstruction efforts after the war. Georg Neumark (1621–1681) wrote both the words and the music for "If You But Trust in God to Guide You" (hymn 410). On his way to the only university not disrupted by the war, he was robbed of all his possessions. After traveling to four cities where he found no employment, he eventually became a tutor in Kiel. During this time of respite he wrote the hymn, suggested by Psalm 55:22, "Cast your burden upon the Lord and he will sustain you."

Hymnody of the period was also affected by stylistic changes in the German language. Especially influential was Martin Opitz's (1597–1639) *Buch der Deutschen Poeterey*, which set down the rules of German verse. The new poetry was more refined, more polished. One of the first hymnwriters to adopt the new style was Johann Heerman (1585–1647), author of the Passion hymn "Ah, Holy Jesus" (hymn 218) and of "O Source of All That Is" (hymn 513).

Musical Developments

Early Lutheran Reformation hymnbooks were of two types, those with text and melody line for congregational use and those with polyphonic settings of the hymns for choral use. The four-voice, note-against-note setting with melody in the top voice—the style so familiar to us today—came into existence later in the sixteenth century. Luther's musical advisor, Johann Walther, had written a few note-against-note settings early in the sixteenth century. More influential, however, were Goudimel's note-against-note settings of Genevan psalm tunes, which were carried into Germany in Ambrosius Lobwasser's German translation (1573). In all these, however, the melody was in the tenor. In 1586, Luckas Osiander took the conclusive step when he published a collection of the principal Lutheran hymns with the melody in the top voice.

Important *cantionales* (songbooks for congregational use) were created by Melchior Vulpius (c. 1560–1615), whose tune GELOBT SEI GOTT (hymn 603) was included in *Ein schön geistliche Gesangbuch* (Jena, 1609), and Michael Praetorius (1571–1621), whose *Musae Sioniae*, volume 6, contained both his adaptation of PUER NOBIS (hymns 57, 241) and his harmonization of ES IST EIN' ROS (hymn 127).

When the Lobwasser Psalter, originally prepared for the Reformed Church, became increasingly popular among Lutherans, Cornelius Becker prepared a German psalter to be sung to Lutheran hymn tunes. In 1628, Heinrich Schütz (1585–1672) composed new melodies with simple four-part settings for Becker's Psalter. One of these, PSALM 84, appears in *The New Century Hymnal* with a new paraphrase of the Psalm text "How Lovely Is Your Dwelling" (hymn 601).

Many of the hymns of Gerhardt and other poets of the period were published in the hymnbooks of Johann Crüger (1598–1662), the preeminent Lutheran composer of hymn tunes. Crüger served for forty years as *Kantor* of Saint Nicholas's Church in Berlin, the last five years with Paul Gerhardt as pastor. He composed seventy hymn tunes and published several hymnals, the most important being *Praxis Pietatis Melica*. First published in 1644, the book underwent many revisions and enlargements. The last edition, published nearly a hundred years later, contained more than thirteen hundred hymns. For Heermann's "Herzliebster Jesu," included in *Newes vollkömliches Gesangbuch Augsburgischer Confession* (1640), Crüger composed HERZLIEBSTER JESU (hymn 218). *Praxis Pietatis Melica*, (2d ed., 1647) included his NUN DANKET ALL (hymn 40), originally the setting for Gerhardt's "Nun danket all und bringet ehr" as well as NUN DANKET for Rinkart's "Nun danket alle Gott" (hymn 419). In the 1653 edition, Johann Franck's "Jesus, Priceless Treasure" appeared with Crüger's tune JESU, MEINE FREUDE (hymn 480). Franck's "Graced with Garments of Great Gladness" together with Crüger's SCHMÜCKE DICH (hymn 334) was given in *Geistliche kirchen Melodien* (1649).

Concurrent with the publication of cantionales for congregational use was the development of a new style of church music that reflected Italian opera. Much of the poetry of the time was not conceived as congregational hymnody, but as private devotional songs, which were often set to art music. Johann Rudolph Ahle (1625-1673) was a leader in this movement. His tune LIEBSTER JESU (74), originally titled a "sacred aria," was reconstructed and greatly simplified in *Das grosse Cantional* (Darmstadt, 1687), when it was associated with Clausnitzer's hymn "Liebster Jesu, wir sind hier" ("We Have Gathered, Jesus Dear," hymn 74).

Other Hymnwriters

Other hymnwriters of the Gerhardt/Crüger era include Georg Weissel (1590–1635), pastor of a newly built church at Königsberg, who wrote the hymn "Lift Up Your Heads, O Mighty Gates" (hymn 117), published in 1642. Johann Niedling (1602–1668), a teacher at Altenburg, included the hymn "O Spirit of God" (hymn 60) in his *Lutherischen Handbüchlein* (1651). Johan Rist (1607–1677) penned "Break Forth, O Beauteous Heavenly Light" (hymn 140) and his close friend, Johann Schop (d. 1671), who provided tunes for many of Rist's hymns, composed the tune ERMUNTRE DICH (hymn 140). Originally cast in triple meter, ERMUNTRE DICH received its current form in Crüger's *Praxis Pietatis Melica* (1647). The Lutheran pastor Johannes Olearius (1611–1684) wrote a commentary on the entire Bible in addition to his hymns. "Comfort, Comfort O My People" (hymn 101) was written for Saint John the Baptist's day. Samuel Rodigast (1649–1708), an educator and the son of a Lutheran pastor, wrote "God's Actions, Always Good and Just" (hymn 415) for his friend Severus Gastorius (fl. 1675) when the latter was seriously ill. Gastorius then composed the tune WAS GOTT TUT for the hymn. The tune HEINLEIN (hymn 205), bearing only the initials "M. H.," was included in the *Nurnbergisches Gesäng-Buch* (Nuremberg, 1676). The poetry of Tobias Clausnitzer (1672–1737), author of "We Have Gathered, Jesus Dear" (hymn 74), is related to that of Gerhardt.

PIETISM (C. 1675–C. 1750)

As an organized movement, pietism in Germany is often associated with the names Philip Jacob Spener (1635–1705) and August Hermann Francke (1663–1727) at Halle. Pietism sought a personal and individual relationship to God through prayer, study, and works of charity. Pietistic hymns were often personal, private, and emotional.

The function of music was seen more and more as stirring up the emotions of individuals. Hymn settings were expected to be pleasing and tuneful. Skips in the melody lines were filled in with passing tones, and triple meter was used more frequently. (Even Luther's sturdy EIN' FESTE BURG could be found cast into triple meter!) During the pietistic period, also, the trend toward smoothing out the older rhythmic chorales continued. By the turn of the century, for example, EIN' FESTE BURG (hymn 440) could be found much as it appears in hymn 439.

The most important and influential hymnbook of the pietistic era was Johann Anastasius Freylinghausen's (1670-1739) *Geistreiches Gesangbuch*. Freylinghausen, who served as unpaid assistant to August H. Francke at Halle, produced a first edition in 1704 and a second in 1714. When the two volumes were combined two years after Freylinghausen's death, the collection contained sixteen hundred hymns and more than six hundred tunes. An anonymous tune from the first edition, GOTT SEI DANK (hymn 566), was the setting for "Gott sei Dank in aller Welt."

The extremely personal poetry from this time has passed from the scene. The hymns in common use today are the more objective utterances from among the works of pietists, or hymns from orthodox hymnwriters. One of those influenced by Spener was Johann Jakob Schütz (1640–1690), a lawyer who ultimately left the Lutheran Church. He was author of "Sing Praise to God, Our Highest Good" (hymn 6). Johann Jakob Rambach (1693–1735)—educated at Halle and, for four years, successor to August Hermann Francke—wrote "Baptized into Your Name Most Holy" (hymn 324). "Ask Me What Great Thing I Know" (hymn 49) is by Johann Christoph Schwedler, friend and neighbor of Nicolaus Zinzendorf (see below).

Composers of the period include Johann Balthasar König, whose important and influential *Harmonische Lieder-Schatz* (1738) contained nearly two thousand hymns. His tune O DASS ICH TAUSEND ZUNGEN HÄTTE (hymn 324) is named for its association with a hymn of that first line from Freylinghausen's 1704 collection. Balthasar Reimann (1702–1749), who met Johann Sebastian Bach (see below) and heard him play, composed the tune O JESU (hymn 463).

JOHANN SEBASTIAN BACH

Martin Luther originated the Lutheran chorale; Johann Sebastian Bach crowned it with glory. In the two centuries between Luther and Bach, many of the hymn tunes underwent considerable change, as illustrated by the two versions of "A Mighty Fortress" (hymns 440 and 439). The pietistic versions of the chorale tunes that Bach inherited were generally isometric (made up of one basic note value) with numerous passing tones. These Bach clothed with richness of harmonic color, a profusion of nonharmonic tones, and a depth of emotion unequaled in the works of others. Bach harmonizations have found their way into hymnbooks of many denominations and have proven themselves as congregational song (see hymns 37, 60, 112, 140, 158, 179, 202, 226, 375, 404, 480).

Not all of Germany became Lutheran at the time of the Reformation. In some areas of Germany, Calvinism was established. Further, much of the country, particularly the southern areas, remained Catholic. The German-speaking country of Austria was also predominantly Catholic. From Reformation times onward, there was always some sharing of resources. The tune ST. THEODULPH (VALET WILL ICH DIR GEBEN (hymn 102) was used in Catholic as well as Lutheran churches. Following the Calvinist example, Kaspar Ulenberg created a rhyming psalter for the Catholics in 1582. The most popular psalter among the German Calvinists was prepared by Ambrosius Lobwasser (1515–1585), a Lutheran. The 1566 German language hymnbook of the Bohemian Brethren (followers of John Hus) contained MIT FREUDEN ZART (hymn 6), apparently based on Genevan Psalm 138. The Genevan psalm tune PSALM 42 (FREU DICH SEHR, hymn 101) was associated with the German Lutheran funeral hymn "Freu dich sehr, o meine Seele" in 1613, and so on.

THE MORAVIANS

The Moravians trace their heritage to John Hus, whose followers created the first vernacular (Czech) hymnbook in 1501. In 1722, the wealthy Count Nicolaus Ludwig von Zinzendorf offered the persecuted Moravians asylum on his own estates in Dresden. He ultimately became a Moravian bishop. Zinzendorf's pietism and mysticism are reflected in many of his approximately two thousand hymns. "Jesus, Still Lead On" (hymn 446) is a combination of stanzas from two hymns, one of which begins "Seelenbräutigam, O du Gottes-Lamm" ("Bridegroom of the Soul," which is reminiscent of the mysticism of Nicolai). The tune SEELENBRÄUTIGAM, by the pietist Adam Drese (1620 1701), is named for Zinzendorf's hymn.

HYMNODY OF THE REFORMED CHURCH IN GERMANY

Through the Evangelical and Reformed Church, the United Church of Christ traces some of its roots to the establishment of Calvinism in Germany. For many years, the Lobwasser Psalter was used extensively in the Reformed Church in Germany.

Germany's first important Reformed hymnwriter was Joachim Neander (1650–1680), who embraced pietism, and who by the time of his death at age thirty had created a number of immortal texts and tunes. Rare, indeed, is the hymnbook that does not contain "Praise to the Lord, the Almighty ("Sing Praise to God, Who Has Shaped," hymn 22). The tune LOBE DEN HERREN, used with Neander's hymn, is possibly a folk tune originally. Other works by Neander have also found a place in hymnals of many denominations, especially the texts "All My Hope on God Is Founded" (hymn 408) and "Heaven and Earth, and Sea and Air" (hymn 566), and the tunes UNSER HERRSCHER (hymn 67) and WUNDERBARER KÖNIG (hymn 68).

RATIONALISM (C. 1750–C. 1815)

During the last half of the eighteenth century and the early years of the nineteenth, much of hymnody was subjected to major alterations to comply with the ideals of reason, naturalism, science, and humanism. Only two items in *The New Century Hymnal* represent this period, the tunes VIENNA (hymn 448), by Justin Heinrich Knecht (1752–1817), and DIX (hymns 28, 159), by Conrad Kocher (1786–1872).

HYMNS FROM THE ROMAN CATHOLIC CHURCH

Though vernacular hymnody held a different role among Roman Catholics, numerous Catholic hymnbooks were published in Germany from the sixteenth century onward. Several books were published in Cologne. From these have come both text and tune of "Es ist ein' Ros entsprungen" ("Lo, How a Rose E'er Blooming," hymn 127), published in 1599, and LASST UNS ERFREUEN (hymns 17, 27) and O HEILIGER GEIST (hymn 60), both published in 1623. The latter hymn was associated with the Lutheran hymn "O Jesulein süss" in 1650, hence its alternate tune name. The tune WEISSE FLAGGEN (hymns 243, 542) was published in Cologne in 1741.

From other Catholic books come hymn 44, "Beautiful Jesus" (Münster, 1677), and hymn 384, OMNI DIE DIC MARIA (Trier, 1695), originally the setting for an ancient hymn encouraging daily prayers to the Virgin Mary. A melody in a 1784 collection used in the private chapel of the Duke of Würtemberg seems to have been the basis for ELLACOMBE (hymns 12, 104, 213). "When Morning Gilds the Skies" (hymn 86) comes from *Katholische Gesangbuch . . . Würzburg* (1828).

Two nearly universally known hymns are from Austria. The words and music of "Holy God, We Praise Your Name" (hymn 276) come from *Katholisches Gesangbuch* (1774), a collection published at the request of the Austrian empress Maria Theresa. A variant of the tune is called HURSLEY (hymn 96). "Silent Night" (hymn 134) had its origins in a small parish church in the Austrian Alps in 1818.

SCANDINAVIAN AND FINNISH SOURCES

The Lutheran Reformation spread quickly to Sweden and Denmark. The first small collections of Lutheran hymns appeared in Sweden in 1526 and in Denmark in 1528. Both nations have a long and fruitful hymnic history. The story of hymnody in Norway, separate from that of Denmark, begins in 1814, when Norway became an independent nation. Though Finland was likewise joined to Sweden until its independence in 1809, a number of hymns had appeared in Finnish by 1540.

The association of the tune DIVINUM MYSTERIUM (hymn 118) with "Of the Parent's Heart Begotten" comes by way of the early Finnish collection *Piae Cantiones* (1582). *Piae Cantiones*, which contained seventy-four songs of medieval origin sung in the cathedral school at Turku, was compiled by Didrik Pedersen (Theodoric Petri), a Finnish student attending the University of Rostock. In 1853, the English musician Thomas Helmore (1811–1890) copied the tune from *Piae Cantiones* and combined it with an English translation by John Mason Neale.

Also from Finland is the lovely tune NYLAND (hymn 390), which was included in the appendix to an early-twentieth-century Lutheran hymnal.

Hans Adolf Brorson (1694–1764), one of Denmark's greatest hymnwriters, wrote several collections of Danish hymns, which were later gathered into his *Troens rare Klenodie* (1739). During his last years he wrote seventy more hymns, which were published posthumously as *Svane-Sang* (1765). From the latter collection comes "Behold the Host All Robed in Light" (hymn 296).

Two Norwegians, one a poet and the other a musician, are credited with giving Norway its first truly Norwegian hymnal. The poet was Magnus Brostrup Landstad, a pastor whose interest in Norwegian folklore and songs resulted in a large collection, *Norske Folkeviser* (1853). The musician was Ludwig Lindeman (1812–1889), an organist recognized throughout Europe. He, too, was much interested in the folk materials of Norway, and in 1848 collected three volumes of folk music in the Valders, a valley northwest of Oslo. Lindeman's *Aeldre og Nyere Norske Fjeldmelodier* (*Older and Newer Norwegian Folkmelodies*, 1853) included the tune DEN STORE HVIDE FLOK (hymn 296), found here with a harmonization by the Norwegian composer Edvard Grieg (1843–1907).

The Swedish hymnody in *The New Century Hymnal* dates from the last half of the nineteenth century and has much in common with the revivalist movement in the United States of the same time. In fact, Lina Sandell (1832–1903) has been called the "Fanny Crosby of Sweden." Her "Surely No One Can Be Safer" (hymn 487) is one of some 650 hymns. The origins of TRYGGARE KAN INGEN VARA (hymn 487) are obscure. Various writers have suggested that it has English, Scandinavian, or German ancestry.

Carl Gustaf Boberg, having undergone a conversion experience at age nineteen, attended a Bible school and became a preacher in his hometown. Author of several collections of poems, he is especially remembered today for his "O Mighty God, When I Survey in Wonder" (hymn 35). The origins of O STORE GUD, the Swedish melody to which Boberg's hymn is sung, are unknown. Another hymn by Boberg, his paraphrase of the Magnificat, has given the name MARIAS LOVSANG to the tune for hymn 106.

HYMN TUNES FROM FAMOUS COMPOSERS

Several hymn tunes have been derived from larger works by well-known composers. HAYDN (hymn 91) and AUSTRIAN HYMN (hymns 307, 565) are from string quartets by the Austrian composer Franz Joseph Haydn (1732–1809). CANONBURY (hymn 531) originated in a piano piece by the German composer Robert Schumann (1810–1856). HYMN TO JOY (hymn 4) was adapted from Ludwig van Beethoven's (1770–1827) Ninth Symphony. For the four hundredth anniversary of the invention of the printing press, Felix Mendelssohn (1809–1847) composed a festival work from which MENDELSSOHN (hymn 144) was adapted. Mendelssohn also harmonized hymn tunes from earlier eras: MUNICH (hymns 272, 315) and NUN DANKET (hymn 419). FINLANDIA is from an orchestral work by the Finnish composer Jean Sibelius (1865–1957).

NOTES

1. Except in the broadest sense, such as the "Gloria in excelsis."

2. The terms "German" and "Germany" in this article will refer to German-speaking peoples and the lands in which they lived.

3. Robert L. Marshall, "Chorale," in *The New Grove Dictionary of Music and Musicians*, ed. Stanley Sadie (1980; reprint, New York: New Grove Dictionaries, 1995), 4: 313.

4. Quoted from *Luther's Works,* ed. Helmut T. Lehmann, vol. 53, *Liturgy and Hymns,* ed. Ulrich S. Leupold (Philadelphia: Fortress Press, 1965), 289.

Sixteenth- and Seventeenth-Century Metrical Psalmody in Europe and Great Britain

Emily R. Brink

The book of Psalms has always formed the heart of prayer in both Jewish and Christian traditions. There was never a time when this prayerbook of scripture disappeared from Christian worship. But there were times when the use of the psalms in worship generated a great deal of creative attention—theologically, musically, and liturgically. The sixteenth and seventeenth centuries were such times in Great Britain and on the European continent.

Now that the scriptures were translated into the language of the people, leaders like Martin Luther and John Calvin were faced with the challenge of preparing the psalms for singing. Both were committed to congregational singing in the vernacular. This movement spread quickly, resulting in an intense period of creativity, so much so that some branches of the reforming churches settled on psalmody exclusively, a practice that persists in some places to our own day.

In the first part of the sixteenth century and for hundreds of years before, the primary practice of psalmody throughout the Western world was one of Latin plainchant, also called Gregorian chant. The austere beauty of Gregorian chant was a practiced art in many monastic communities, which for centuries had chanted the psalms in a daily regimen, covering all 150 every week, or perhaps every month. In public worship, the people listened to the psalms but no longer sang them.

By 1525 Luther had introduced another, more accessible way of singing the psalms congregationally. The psalm texts were recast into various poetic meters and set to tunes designed to accommodate those meters, hence the name "metrical psalmody." The tunes were short, easily learned, and repeated for the various stanzas of text. This patterned strophic structure of texts and tunes, so familiar in popular songs of that day (and in hymnody to this day), was to become the new, dominant, and sometimes even exclusive form of congregational song for many Protestant communions. This essay deals with the rise and development of that metrical psalm tradition.

LUTHERAN BEGINNINGS

As a monk, Martin Luther (1483–1546) knew the psalms well; he no doubt had chanted them every day and perhaps knew them by heart. The psalms were deeply rooted in his spiritual life and practice.

As a musician, Luther's tendencies were conservative; even in his efforts to develop a German Mass, he wanted to preserve the chant tradition, along with choirs, instruments, and even some Latin. His desire was to honor music as one of the greatest gifts God had given to the church. The Lutherans have always been known for their high level of commitment to church music.

As a reformer, Luther was not only committed to singing psalms and hymns, he was committed to singing them congregationally in the vernacular. In 1523 in Wittenberg, he introduced a type of German chant, with daily morning and evening services, in which the psalms were chanted. But simply placing German texts over the old plainchant formulas did not begin to approach the beauty of the Gregorian tradition, since the older chant was so inextricably tied to the Latin. Luther lamented: "To translate the Latin text and retain the Latin tone or notes has my sanction, though it doesn't sound polished or well done."[1]

And so Luther began to approach the psalms the same way he and others were preparing many hymns for congregational worship. To create a body of songs for worship, writers not only composed new texts and tunes, they also turned to older German, Greek, and Latin sources for translation and adaptation into contemporary German chorales. The immediate success of congregational singing in the metrical style no doubt encouraged Luther to prepare psalms in the same way. Nine metrical psalm settings, almost a third of the collection, were included in *Geistliche Gesangbuchlein*, the first little Wittenberg hymnal of 1524. (See hymn 64 for a chorale from that collection based on chant.) More metrical psalms were included in the Wittenberg hymnal *Geistliche Lieder* (1529), including "A Mighty Fortress," based on Psalm 46 (hymns 439, 440).

Actually, "A Mighty Fortress" is more chorale than psalm. Perhaps because Luther also wanted to retain chanted psalmody sung directly from scripture, he was rather free with his metrical psalm texts. They are often more paraphrase than versification. Another example of that free approach is found in the 1641 Advent text by Lutheran pastor Georg Weissel. His chorale text "Lift Up Your Heads, O Mighty Gates" (hymn 117) is clearly a hymn text, yet also based on the second part of Psalm 24, one of the lectionary texts appointed for Advent.

Other German writers and composers contributed metrical psalters for the congregation as well as many choral compositions for the Lutheran liturgy. One simple choral setting of Psalm 84, "How Lovely Is Your Dwelling" (hymn 601), by Heinrich Schütz (1585–1672), preserves the original relationship of psalm and tune. PSALM 84 from his *Psalmen Davids, in Tuetsche Reimen gebrachte durch D. Cornelium Beckern* (1628), known as the Becker Psalter, is one of his simpler settings, freely composed (i.e., not chorale-based) to reflect the character of the psalm.

The Lutheran approach to metrical psalmody spread from Wittenberg to other German and German-speaking cities—most notably to Strasbourg, which was known for excellent tune composers. The liturgical reforms in that city by Martin Bucer included an important place for congregational psalm-singing. It was the practice at Strasbourg that influenced John Calvin to begin his work on a French metrical psalter.

THE GENEVAN PSALTER

Under the leadership of John Calvin (1509–1564), metrical psalmody was to become the virtually exclusive form of congregational song for the Reformed branch of the Reformation. Here, too, a great leader was involved from the beginning, though Calvin was a scholar and, unlike Luther, did not have a background as a monk or musician. When historians compare the two with respect to music, Calvin always comes out on the negative side of the comparison. The Reformed branch of the Reformation (in contrast to Lutherans) restricted church music to unison (no harmony) congregational singing (no choirs) of the psalms (no hymns) in meter (no chant), and sung unaccompanied (no instruments).

But that simplistic comparison doesn't begin to tell the story of the power of the tradition of metrical psalmody. Calvin's contribution and influence was also very widespread, especially in the French-, Dutch-, Hungarian-, and English-speaking areas of the Protestant Reformation. That story is rooted in the Genevan Psalter, the single great contribution to church music by the continental Calvinist movement.

While on his way to Strasbourg in 1536, just after completing his *Institutes of the Christian Religion*, Calvin passed through Geneva, where he met Guillaume Farel (1489–1565), the famous and spellbinding preacher who brought the Reformation to French-speaking Switzerland. Farel's powers of persuasion were strong enough to convince Calvin, reluctantly, to leave the life of a scholar and join him as a pastor there. The city council had just officially voted to become Protestant and suffered through an iconoclastic frenzy. The churches had already established a pattern of worship that was radical in its departure from the Roman Mass. In contrast to the conservative approach of Luther, the Genevan churches had banned all music from worship, as had Ulrich Zwingli in Zurich.

Evidently Calvin soon tried to introduce congregational singing along with other reforms. His *Articles* of 1537 include a rather hesitant attempt: "We are not able to estimate the benefit and edification which will derive from [congregational singing] until after having experienced it. Certainly at present the prayers of the faithful are so cold that we should be greatly ashamed and confused." After two difficult years, Calvin was expelled from Geneva, and he once more set out for Strasbourg.

Calvin spent three much more peaceful years in Strasbourg, a German-speaking city. He married Idelette van Buren, pastored a congregation of French refugees, and gave lectures in theology. He also heard metrical psalmody and learned firsthand of its power and the enthusiasm the people had for singing the psalms in their own language.[2] Calvin quickly determined to begin providing metrical psalm settings in French. In his systematic way, he began small but had a larger goal: to create a complete psalter. He became the guiding force behind a project that involved the best poets and musicians he could find for the next twenty-five years. The Genevan Psalter become the crowning achievement of the Calvinist contribution to church music.

Calvin's first small collection of 1539 had already been released in Strasbourg. When he returned to Geneva in 1541 he immediately sought, and this time gained, the authorities' permission to introduce congregational song. Calvin helped prepare the second collection with more than music, as the title indicates: *The Form of Prayers and Ecclesiastical Songs* (*La forme des prieres et chantz ecclesiastques*, 1542). The very title shows Calvin's concern about the place of psalmody in worship. In his prefatory "Epistle to the Reader," Calvin revealed his thinking as to the liturgical role of metrical psalmody: "As to the public prayers, there are two kinds: some are offered by means of words alone, the others with song. . . . We know by experience that song has great force and vigor to move and inflame human hearts to invoke and praise God with a more vehement and ardent zeal." The role of psalmody was one of prayer, broadly conceived.

Subsequent collections of additional psalm settings were released in Geneva in 1543 and 1551. Meanwhile, other cities also began publishing installments, and the texts were immediately translated into several languages, including Dutch, German, and Hungarian. As the installments grew in popularity, the completion of the project was eagerly awaited. In 1562 the Genevan Psalter was completed. All 150 psalms and two canticles were included, the Ten Commandments, and the Song of Simeon. Twenty-four publishers in Paris printed the complete Genevan Psalter, as did printers in Geneva, Lyons, Caen, St. Lo, and elsewhere. In the year 1562 alone, more than thirty thousand copies were sold.

The Texts of the Genevan Psalter

For texts, Calvin enlisted the help of Clement Marot (1496–1544), the most celebrated court poet in France, who at the time was entertaining the court with (of all things) French metrical settings of the psalms. Earlier, he had translated Greek and Latin verse and was now interested in Hebrew poetry. In the first collection of 1539, Calvin had contributed some of his own versifications, but he eventually withdrew his own work in favor of Marot's. Marot was a sophisticated poet, and his versifications of the psalms are stunning in their metrical variety; he used no less than 110 stanza structures and thirty-three different rhyme schemes. When Marot left Geneva before completing the project, Calvin turned to Theodore de Beza (1519–1605), who had joined him as a pastor in Geneva and eventually would succeed him as ecclesiastical leader. De Beza completed the texts.

One hymn text included in the 1545 Strasbourg edition of Marot's *Psalms* deserves special mention. "I Greet You, Sure Redeemer" (hymn 251) was long attributed to Calvin, though there is no evidence he wrote it. The text appears to be a Protestant version of the Catholic hymn "Salve Regina." The text was also included in an 1868 edition of Calvin's works (*Opera*, vol. 6).

Of course, no French texts survived in English-language psalters and hymnals. Given the Reformers' commitment to worshiping in the vernacular, the legacy of the Genevan Psalter is primarily musical. But the very essence of the tunes was born out of those metrical texts.

The Music of the Genevan Psalter

For his first collection published in Strasbourg, Calvin turned to tunes by Strasbourg composers. One of the most famous was by Matthais Greitter (1490–1550), a tune originally set to Psalm 119. That tune eventually was used with two psalms in the Genevan Psalter, 36 and 68. Two stanzas of Psalm 68 in particular became the virtual battle song of the Calvinists, the "Calvinist Marseillaise"; many French Huguenots went to their deaths singing this psalm. The tune was popular enough that two other well-known tunes are probably derived from it (at least they are closely related to it), and all three share the same opening line: OLD 113TH in the English tradition, and the German chorale LASST UNS ERFREUEN (hymns 17, 27) dating from a 1623 Cologne hymnal.

The Genevan cantor and teacher Louis Bourgeois (c. 1510–c. 1561) became the musical editor of the 1551 collection of psalms, revising some of the earlier tunes as well as adapting and composing many new tunes himself. Five tunes from the 1551 edition of the Genevan Psalter collection are included in *The New Century Hymnal*: OLD HUNDREDTH (hymn 7), PSALM 42 (hymn 101), RENDEZ A DIEU (hymn 167), TOULON (hymns 251, 358), and ST. MICHAEL (hymn 611).

All together, 125 tunes were created for the 150 psalms, falling short of Calvin's ideal of a distinct tune for every psalm. The tunes were to serve the text with "weight and majesty," unencumbered with harmony or instruments. The melodies were very straightforward: syllabic; only two note values, long and short; and a melodic range limited to an octave. The German chorale tradition was more varied, as is evident in a comparison of RENDEZ A DIEU (hymn 167) with EIN' FESTE BURG in its original rhythms (hymn 440). Yet, the strength of the Genevan tunes quickly gained the attention of composers, becoming the basis for an outpouring of choral music in the sixteenth and seventeenth centuries, such as the complete settings by Claude Goudimel (1505–1572), who actually published three complete settings of the Genevan Psalter, one in simple chordal style, one in simple motet style, and one in multi-movement, elaborate settings; Jan P. Sweelinck (1562–1621), who also wrote elaborate motets on the entire psalter; and Johann Crüger (1598–1662), who provided harmonizations with instrumental descants for the entire psalter.

The simple four-part settings usually placed the melody in the tenor, which was the prevailing custom, though the presence of women joining the men in congregational singing probably contributed to the eventual rise of the melody to the soprano voice. As Goudimel carefully indicated in the foreword to his 1565 collection, these were "not to induce you to sing them in Church, but that you may rejoice in God, particularly in your homes."

Because of the intense persecution of the French Huguenots, the Dutch Reformed churches became the primary preservers of the Genevan Psalter in Western Europe. Eventually, the tempo of congregational singing slowed down, and the sprightly rhythms of the melodies began to flatten out into all even notes. By the end of the seventeenth century, the Dutch churches permitted the use of the organ to strengthen congregational singing. Many Dutch composers began to write for the organ based on the Genevan tunes.

Some four hundred years later, after the Berlin Wall fell, Western Christians learned that the "Dutch Psalter" shares the same melodies with the "Hungarian Psalter" of the Hungarian Reformed Churches. The first 150 numbers of both the ecumenically used Dutch *Liedboek voor de kerken* (1973) and the Hungarian *Énekeskönyv: Magyat Reformátusok Használatára* (1988) include all 150 psalms, set one on one, to the Genevan psalm tunes. The tunes of the Genevan Psalter are the only unified collection of psalm tunes still in use from the days of the Reformation.

GREAT BRITAIN

There was considerable traffic between the British Isles and the continent during the turbulent days of the sixteenth-century Reformation. When the Spanish Inquisition suppressed the Reformation in the Low Countries, whole congregations moved to England. Then when "Bloody Mary" (Mary I) ascended the English throne in 1553, the traffic flowed in the other direction: Continental congregations returned home, and entire English and Scottish congregations fled to a number of European cities, including Frankfurt and Geneva. The work of crafting a liturgy in English was interrupted many times. Different leaders, working in different places under various influences from Luther, Calvin, Bucer, and others outside Great Britain, came to different conclusions about the shape and use of a prayerbook and metrical psalmody. Not only did the Church of England break away from Rome, but in subsequent years churches dissenting from the Church of England developed in different directions as well.

Even before the turbulence and "Marian Exile," a lot of traffic was generated by political interests, including intermarriage among royalty. The first printed Bible in English, translated in 1539 by Miles Coverdale (1480?–1569), was undoubtedly influenced by his knowledge of Luther's 1532 translation into German. When traveling in Germany, Coverdale heard Lutheran congregational singing and discovered the liturgical use of the Lutheran chorale and metrical psalm. In his *Goostly psalmes and spirituall songes* (London, c. 1535), Coverdale translated and published a collection of forty-one texts with their tunes, of which fifteen were metrical psalms. But within three years Henry VIII banned them, and in the volatile movements in England back and forth between Catholic and Protestant monarchies, the beginnings of cross-fertilization between the Lutheran and English liturgical traditions were squelched.[3]

The practice of casting psalms into metrical form was not new to Coverdale. What was new was the liturgical dimension: His collection included tunes. Like the Lutheran and Calvinist approaches, his texts and tunes were published together. The practice of matching texts and tunes may have entered more deeply into the English tradition of metrical psalmody had there not been another tradition already at work. Many well-educated British writers practiced their craft and their piety by translating the classics of Latin and Greek poetry as well as the psalms. The art of poetry in sixteenth-century England was an art of "imitation," involving the discipline of recasting the ideas of the great minds of earlier times into contemporary poetic form. The early metrical psalm settings were for private meditation, not for liturgical use. That practice continued into the next century, for example, in John Milton's (1608–1674) setting of Psalm 136, "Let Us with a Joyful Mind" (hymn 16).[4]

To this day, many hymnals in Great Britain are books of texts, not texts and tunes, reflecting the strength of the poetic tradition that preceded the liturgical use of psalms in meter. But the first metrical psalter that became the official psalter for the Church of England did include tunes. In practice, since changes in language throughout the centuries have resulted in successive text collections, it is the English metrical psalm tunes that have remained in use to this day. The very development of a liturgical metrical psalter that required melodies encouraged composers to set the psalm texts to music. One complete psalter, which never gained liturgical or popular use, was written by the Archbishop of Canterbury Matthew Parker, and published with nine tunes by the great English composer Thomas Tallis (c. 1505–1585). Though the texts did not become well known, some of Tallis's tunes have remained in use ever since—for example, TALLIS' CANON (hymn 100) and THE THIRD TUNE (hymns 178, 509), so named because it was the third of his nine tunes in the collection.

Beginnings of the Sternhold and Hopkins Psalter

The first English metrical psalter approved for liturgical use in the Church of England developed gradually in several places and included the work of several writers. Two names most closely associated with it were Thomas Sternhold (1500–1549) and John Hopkins (d. 1570); the psalter became known popularly as the "Sternhold and Hopkins Psalter."

The development of this psalter had many striking similarities to that of the Genevan Psalter. Both began in royal courts, came out in installments, were not completed by the writer who wrote the first settings, and became extremely popular for centuries thereafter, going through countless editions. Just as Marot and de Beza were linked as the primary poets of the Genevan Psalter, so Sternhold and Hopkins were identified with the most popular psalter in England, and both completed psalters were first published in 1652.

The beginning was modest. Sternhold, a member of the English court, prepared a small collection of nineteen psalms in ballad meter (8.6.8.6) which he dedicated in 1547 to King Henry VIII's young son and successor, Edward VI, who became king that year at age ten. That initial collection for devotional use was followed in 1549 by several more of Sternhold's texts, but he died that same year. The following year, his friend John Hopkins (d. 1570) published all thirty-seven of Sternhold's texts along with seven of his own. What tunes these texts might have been sung to is unknown; they were published without music. But they were certainly sung, and the number of reprints for the next few years indicates that they were becoming very popular. Then came the major interruption caused by Queen Mary's ascension to the throne in 1553.

Development on the Continent: The Anglo-Genevan Psalters

The relationship between the developing English and Calvinist metrical psalm traditions was very close for several years when English Protestant refugees settled in Geneva and other European cities during the "Marian Exile." The refugees took their 1552 Book of Common Prayer with them, and also their Sternhold and Hopkins Psalters. Several editions of English psalters were published in Geneva, known as the "Anglo-Genevan Psalters." But there were some tensions as well: "A division developed within the Frankfurt exiles with one party favoring Prayer Book worship and the other demanding a form more akin to the French liturgy of Calvin in Geneva. The division of opinion became a physical split. The Prayer Book party remained in Frankfurt, and the others, including Whittingham and, eventually, Knox, migrated to Geneva."[5]

Under the influence of Calvin's liturgical reforms and his (as yet incomplete) psalter, the refugees started revising the English texts to conform more strictly to the scripture. The first edition of 1556, made soon after their arrival in Geneva, was a complete metrical psalter with two title pages. The first title page clearly shows the influence of Calvin; the title of Calvin's 1555 edition (mentioned above) starts out with the same phrase. The Anglo-Genevan title of 1556 reads: *"The forme of prayers and Ministration of the Sacramentes, &c. vsed in the Englishe Congregation at Geneua: and approued, by the famous and godly learned man, Iohn Caluyn."* But then comes the second title page: *"One and fiftie Psalmes of David In English metre, whereof .37. were made by Thomas Sternholde: and the rest by others. Conferred with the hebrewe, and in certeyn places corrected as the sens of the Prophete required."* More than a third of the Sternhold and Hopkins texts were "corrected," an indication of the growing dissension among the leadership of the exiles. Some of the criticism of these texts in later years that was directed at Sternhold could as well have been directed to those who "corrected" his texts, often in a pedantic fashion.

One new development in the 1556 edition was the presence of tunes, again showing the Genevan influence. Including music was one more step toward a complete metrical psalter. The tune OLD 22ND (hymn 316) dates from that edition; its name indicates that it was set to Psalm 22.

Subsequent editions of the Anglo-Genevan Psalter included texts by a number of other writers, including the text that has been the best-known and still sung text from that century, William Kethe's setting of Psalm 100, "All People That on Earth Do Dwell" (hymn 7), sung to the Genevan tune by Bourgeois originally composed for Psalm 134. That tune happened to be set in long meter (8.8.8.8) and so was one of the shorter Genevan tunes, which is probably what commended it for English use.

Completion of the Sternhold and Hopkins Psalter

When Queen Mary died in 1558 and Elizabeth I ascended the throne, the Protestant exiles began to return home with their now considerably expanded collections of psalters developed in Strasbourg, Frankfurt, and Wesel in addition to Geneva. The complete psalter that was to become the first official psalter of the Church of England was released in

1562 by the English printer John Day (1522–1584), entitled *The Whole Booke of Psalmes, collected into Englysh metre by T. Sternhold, I. Hopkins, & others . . . with apt Notes to singe them withal* (London, 1562). An edition the following year was in four-part books, with the melody in the tenor. There is even some evidence that these psalms may have been sung in harmony in church.

The completed Sternhold and Hopkins psalter contained 131 texts in common meter (8.6.8.6), 6 in short meter (6.6.8.6), 3 in long meter (8.8.8.8), and 14 in other meters; all the psalms plus several canticles were included. Day received a monopoly from the British crown for printing it, and he eventually released thirty-six separate editions. The 1562 edition included fifty tunes. One year later he published a harmonized edition in part books with the melody in the tenor. Many of the tunes were adapted from the Genevan Psalter as well as from other continental psalters, adapted to common meter (usually double) to accommodate the English texts.

One text and one tune from the 1562 edition are found in *The New Century Hymnal*: Sternhold's version of Psalm 23, "My Shepherd Is the Living God" (hymn 247), and the tune ST. FLAVIAN (hymns 211, 318, 342) attributed to John Day. ST. FLAVIAN was originally set to Psalm 132 in eight lines with more varied rhythms; the first four lines were published and given this tune name in the 1875 edition of *Hymns Ancient and Modern*. Over the next century, many other composers wrote new tunes for the texts of this popular psalter. The anonymous tune WINCHESTER OLD (hymn 516), for example, was set to Psalm 84 in Thomas Este's *Whole Booke of Psalmes* (1592).

Scottish Psalters

Though the Sternhold and Hopkins Psalter was the official psalter of the Church of England for the next two centuries, it was not the only one in use in Britain. Under the leadership of John Knox (c. 1514–1572), who also spent time in Geneva, Scottish reformers started revising the Sternhold and Hopkins Psalter when they returned home after the Marian Exile. Already in 1560 the first Scottish Psalter was published, with many texts retained from Sternhold and Hopkins but about a third by Scottish authors. The influence of Calvin is seen even more strongly in Scotland than in England, both in the more literal approach to versifying scripture and in the greater number of tunes employed. The 105 tunes included represented greater metrical variety when compared to the 50 tunes of Sternhold and Hopkins. In a later edition, *The 150 Psalms of David* (Edinburgh, 1615), twelve "common" tunes (i.e., in common meter) were added. The common tune DUNDEE (hymn 412) dates from that 1615 edition.

Over the years the Scottish Psalter tradition has been maintained not only in Scotland, but by some Scottish Presbyterian descendants in North America. The Reformed Presbyterian Church in North America still maintains the exclusive unaccompanied metrical psalmody they brought with them from Scotland. The latest edition of their psalter is *The Book of Psalms for Singing* (Pittsburgh, 1973).

SEVENTEENTH-CENTURY DEVELOPMENTS

Just as the Genevan Psalter was to become the primary repertoire of the Reformed churches on the continent for the next centuries, so too the Sternhold and Hopkins Psalter became enormously popular as the only official psalter for the Church of England until the end of the seventeenth century. It formed the basic repertoire of congregational song for the Church of England, lasting into the nineteenth century.

No serious challenge to Sternhold and Hopkins arose until the end of the seventeenth century, when a new version was introduced by William Tate (1652–1715) and Nicolas Brady (1659–1726). They dedicated their collection to the king, who approved it for use when it was published in 1696. Both claimed connections to the king: Tate had been named poet laureate, and Brady was a royal chaplain. The very title of their work indicates their intentions: *A New Version of the Psalms of David, fitted to the tunes used in Churches.* The title "New Version" also paid homage to the enduring strength of the Sternhold and Hopkins Psalter, which became known thereafter as the "Old Version." "As Pants the Hart for Cooling Streams" (hymn 481), a setting of Psalm 42, and "Out of the Depths I Call" (hymn 483), a setting of Psalm 130, are from the New Version.

Additional tunes to the New Version were provided in the 1708 *Supplement to the New Version of Psalms by Dr. Brady and Dr. Tate*, published by the composer William Croft (1678–1727). Three tunes from that collection probably composed by him are included in *The New Century Hymnal* and in most English hymnals since they were published: HANOVER (hymn 305); ST. ANNE (hymns 25, 278, 359), originally set to Psalm 42; and ST. MATTHEW (hymns 263, 464).

Other psalm tunes that entered the British repertoire include Samuel Howard's ST. BRIDE (hymn 483), from the 1762 *Collection of Psalm Tunes in three and four parts*; the anonymous ST. THOMAS (hymns 312, 379, 588); as well as DARWALL'S 148TH (hymn 303), by John Darwall, in Aaron Williams's *New Universalist Psalmodist* (1770); and Thomas William's TRURO (hymn 117), from the 1789 *Psalmodia Evangelica*.

Despite the superior poetry of Tate and Brady, the New Version never gained the popularity of the Old Version, especially outside London. When Isaac Watts entered the scene during the eighteenth century, metrical psalmody took a large step in the direction of hymnody. The eventual development of the English hymn resulted in the weakening of the metrical psalm tradition except in those communions, like the Scottish, which continued to hold on to exclusive metrical psalmody.

NOTES

1. As given in *Luther's Works*, ed. J. Pelikan and T. H. Lehmann (St. Louis/Philadelphia, 1955), vol. 40, p. 141.

2. Charles Garside, in "The Origins of Calvin's Theology of Music: 1536–1543," *Transactions of the American Philosophical Society* 4 (1979), provides a moving description written by a young man from Antwerp who had sought refuge in Strasbourg just a few years after Calvin was there.

3. Robin Leaver provides a detailed history of those movements in his *Goostly Psalmes and Spirituall Songes: English and Dutch Metrical Psalms from Coverdale to Utenhove, 1535–1566* (Oxford: Oxford University Press, 1991).

4. His complete text, written at age fifteen, is included in Raymond F. Glover, ed., *The Hymnal 1982 Companion* (New York: The Church Hymnal Corporation, 1990), 3B: 732–33, along with this comment: "The youthful poet's stanzas have required some tidying in order to make them regular enough for singing."

5. Robin Leaver, "English Metrical Psalmody," in Glover, ed., *Hymnal 1982 Companion*, 1: 327.

Eighteenth- and Nineteenth-Century British Hymnody

David W. Music

At the beginning of the eighteenth century the congregational song repertoire of most English churches consisted of metrical psalms and other versified scripture. A few Congregational and Baptist churches had begun using hymns in the last quarter of the seventeenth century, and individuals such as William Barton, Benjamin Keach, and John Mason published collections to meet this need. However, none of these private ventures gained wide acceptance for public worship or proved sufficient to draw the churches away from more or less strict reliance on metrical psalmody.

ISAAC WATTS AND THE DEVELOPMENT OF HYMNODY

That task was left to the Congregationalist minister Isaac Watts, who almost single-handedly broke the monopoly of metrical psalmody on English religious song. Watts included a few hymns in his collection of poems titled *Horae Lyricae* (1705), in his *Divine Songs for Children* (1715; see "I Sing the Mighty Power of God," hymn 12), and with some of his published sermons. However, his most important publications of congregational song were *Hymns and Spiritual Songs* (1707) and *The Psalms of David Imitated in the Language of the New Testament* (1719). These two books together provided a complete "system of praise" incorporating all three of the forms mentioned by Paul in Colossians 3:16.

The texts of the *Hymns and Spiritual Songs* attracted attention because of their simplicity, literary quality, and practical detail, in all of which they far surpassed both the common English metrical psalms and the hymns of earlier writers such as Barton, Keach, and Mason. Watts's stated goal was to adapt the language of his hymns to the understanding of the common person. That he succeeded admirably is evident from a hymn such as "When I Survey the Wondrous Cross" (hymn 224), which out of its original total of 139 words included 120 that were composed of a single syllable. "When I Survey the Wondrous Cross" also contains such poetic devices as *chiasmus* (the crossing of words or phrases: "sorrow and love," "love and sorrow"), which serve to elevate the tone of the text and make it more memorable. Watts's practical approach is seen in his making a complete thought of each line so that the logic of the text would not be destroyed by the common practice of lining out (the leader reading or singing a line of text before it is sung by the congregation). But the most arresting feature of Watts's hymns was their emphasis on evangelical faith. In "When I Survey the Wondrous Cross," "Alas!

and Did My Savior Bleed" (hymn 200), and many other hymns, Watts gave centrality to Christ's sacrifice on the cross, an aspect of New Testament faith that could never be adequately covered by strict adherence to the Hebrew psalms.

The subtitle of Watts's *Psalms* ("imitated in the language of the New Testament") signified a new approach to psalmody, for instead of merely versifying the psalms—turning them into English poetic meter and rhyme—as earlier writers had done, he "imitated" or paraphrased the texts "to make them always speak the common Sense and Language of a Christian" (preface). Thus, for Watts the psalm served merely as a backdrop for the elaboration of New Testament ideas, and his "imitations" were essentially new hymns using psalm prooftexts. This is evident from the first word of his paraphrase of Psalm 72, "Jesus Shall Reign" (hymn 300), while his original first line for Psalm 23, "My Shepherd Will Supply My Need" (see "My Shepherd Is the Living God," hymn 247), is an allusion to Philippians 4:19 (KJV).

Watts's "system of praise" proved to be a flexible and relatively painless way for churches to make a transition from metrical psalmody to hymnody. Congregations that were ready to sing "human composures" could employ the *Hymns and Spiritual Songs*, whereas those that were content to continue using only the psalms could sing from his *Psalms of David*. The ultimate result was a breakdown of the monopoly of versified psalmody and the widespread acceptance of hymns in English-speaking churches.

JOHN AND CHARLES WESLEY AND THE RISE OF EVANGELICAL HYMNODY

The ground thus paved by Watts was quickly traveled by other hymnwriters, most notably the brothers John and Charles Wesley, the founders of Methodism. John's work in hymnody appears to have been primarily that of a translator of hymns from the German, a promoter and encourager of hymn singing, and an editor and publisher of hymns (especially those by his brother). John Wesley's earliest hymnal, *A Collection of Psalms and Hymns* (1737)—also known as the "Charlestown Collection" from its place of publication, "Charlestown" (Charleston), South Carolina—was published while he was serving as a missionary to the American colony of Georgia and was one of the earliest hymnals printed in America. This collection contained none of Charles's texts, but it did include a number of hymns by other members of the Wesley family and by Watts. The "Charlestown Collection" was but the first of at least sixty-four hymn collections published by the Wesleys, culminating in *A Collection of Hymns for the Use of the People Called Methodists* (1780).

Charles Wesley is universally acknowledged to have been the leading English hymnwriter of the eighteenth century and one of the greatest hymnists of all time. The number of hymns he wrote has been variously estimated at between 6,500 and 9,000. Even more astonishing than this large number, however, is the almost uniformly high quality of Wesley's hymns. The texts abound in scriptural allusion—see the references to Malachi 3:1 and 4:2 in "Love Divine, All Loves Excelling" (hymn 43, stanza 3) and "Hark! The Herald Angels Sing" (hymn 144, stanza 3), respectively—and in poetic devices such as *anadiplosis*, in which a word or thought at the end of one stanza is used in the first line of the next (see "O for a Thousand Tongues to Sing," hymn 42, stanzas 1–3). Like Watts, Wesley's hymns are intensely evangelical, although they reflect an Arminian rather than a Calvinistic view of salvation, as may be seen in the desire for "sinless perfection" expressed in "Love Divine, All Loves Excelling" (hymn 43).[1]

Isaac Watts and Charles Wesley stand at the very pinnacle of hymnody in English. Together they inaugurated a "golden age" of English hymnody that lasted throughout the eighteenth century. The continuing influence of these two writers is evident from the fact that *The New Century Hymnal* contains more texts by each of them than by any other author who wrote before the twentieth century.

OTHER EVANGELICAL HYMNWRITERS

The "golden age" of British hymnody inaugurated by Watts and Wesley was further enhanced by a group of writers who were, like Watts, from Independent traditions, or like the Wesleys, from the Evangelical wing of the Anglican church. This group of hymnwriters produced a number of texts that are still in common use, including "Awake, My Soul, Stretch Every Nerve" (hymn 491), by Philip Doddridge; "Rock of Ages, Cleft for Me" (hymn 596), by Augustus M. Toplady; "Angels from the Realms of Glory" (hymn 126), by James Montgomery; "Blessed Be the Tie That Binds" (hymn 393), by John Fawcett; "Come, O Fount of Every Blessing" (hymn 459), by Robert Robinson; "On River Jordan's Banks I Stand" ("On Jordan's Stormy Banks I Stand," hymn 598), by Samuel Stennett; "Guide Me, O My Great Redeemer" (hymn 18), by the Welshman William Williams; and "All Hail the Power of Jesus' Name" (hymn 304), by Edward Perronet. "All Hail the Power of Jesus' Name" was altered and a fourth stanza added in John Rippon's important *Selection of Hymns* (1787), which was also the source for "How Firm a Foundation" (hymn 407), attributed only to "K."

THE ANGLICAN EVANGELICALS AND *OLNEY HYMNS*

One of the most important British hymnals of the later eighteenth century was John Newton and William Cowper's *Olney Hymns* (1779), named for the village where Newton served as pastor and the celebrated poet Cowper, his friend and associate, also lived. As with Brady and Tate, who had published *A New Version of the Psalms* nearly one hundred years before, the compilers of the *Olney Hymns* were a combination of preacher (Newton) and outstanding literary figure (Cowper). Like most British hymnwriters of the eighteenth century, the compilers of the *Olney Hymns* represented the Evangelical wing of the Anglican church. Newton's hymns are often of a personal nature, reflecting his Calvinist wonderment at God's "amazing grace" that could convert a reprobate slave-ship captain like himself into a disciple of Christ ("Amazing Grace, How Sweet the Sound," hymn 547); but the texts are also full of scriptural allusion (see "Glorious Things of You Are Spoken," hymn 307). As might be expected from one of the leading poets of the day, Cowper's hymns are couched in elegant language ("God Moves in a Mysterious Way," hymn 412) but they also reflect his desire for a deep and intimate relationship with God (see "Listen to Your Savior Call," hymn 250, and "O for a Closer Bond with God," hymn 450).

The demand for the *Olney Hymns* was such that the collection was reissued numerous times in both England and America. The book was also influential in the large number of its texts that were reprinted in hymnals of a general character. With the publication and dissemination of Newton and Cowper's hymns, the "golden age"—one of the most productive and significant periods in British hymnwriting—may be said to have reached its zenith.[2]

EIGHTEENTH-CENTURY HYMN TUNES

When Isaac Watts published his *Psalms of David Imitated*, he observed that he had fitted the "various Measures of the verse . . . to the Tunes of the Old Psalm-Book" (preface), thus anticipating that they would be sung to tunes already familiar to the churches. Such, indeed, seems to have been the case in many congregations.

Nevertheless, eighteenth-century composers also sought to provide original tunes for the new texts of Watts, Wesley, and others, as well as for the older metrical psalms that were still in common use. Congregational singing was not a regular practice in British cathedrals or the Chapel Royal, but a number of composers who had been trained in or were employed by these institutions published new psalm and hymn tunes for use in urban parish churches, including William Croft (ST. ANNE, hymn 25) and Samuel Howard (ST. BRIDE, hymn 483). The tunes named above feature strong melodies that are similar in some respects to earlier psalm tunes. Other urban parish tunes of the time include, for example, the anonymous EASTER HYMN (hymn 233), ST. MATTHEW (hymns 263, 464, possibly by Croft), HANOVER (hymn 305, also possibly by Croft), and Felice de Giardini's ITALIAN HYMN (hymn 275). These feature more-delicate melodies that are subjected to embellishment (grace notes and trills originally found over the first notes in measures 10 and 12 of ITALIAN HYMN are now omitted), expressive "sighing" figures, and conventional functional harmony. These more secular-style tunes were designed mainly for performance by treble-dominated choirs of charity children or by the male religious societies that were attached to many urban parish churches.

Another strand of activity was represented by amateur musicians, country singing masters, and parish clerks of limited musical training who composed primarily for rural congregations. The products of such composers as John Darwall (DARWALL'S 148TH, hymn 303), William Jones (ST. STEPHEN, hymn 352), William Knapp (WAREHAM, hymn 306), Aaron Williams (ST. THOMAS, hymn 379), and Thomas Williams (TRURO, hymn 117) tended to keep the melody in the tenor (from which it has been transferred to the soprano in modern hymnals), to be more harmonically venturesome than contemporary urban tunes (the harmonies are now generally altered to more conventional ones), and to use a greater variety of rhythmic activity (the pieces listed above are among the more restrained examples in this regard). Some country parish composers favored "extended tunes," in which portions of the text could be repeated or subjected to melismatic treatment to create a longer musical piece; thus, the form of the text did not strictly determine the form of the tune. None of the British country tunes in *The New Century Hymnal* are in this "extended tune" style. However, its influence is evident in the American Oliver Holden's CORONATION (hymn 304) and especially in the repeated text and additive refrain of the English expatriate John Francis Wade's ADESTE FIDELES (hymn 135), in which the voices enter successively or in pairs. A few composers working in the country sought to provide tunes of a "higher character" for rural parishes, among whom was Edward Miller (ROCKINGHAM, hymn 208).[3]

Two special types of hymn tune came into prominence in the Methodist movement. The first consisted of adaptations from German pietist sources. An example is the tune SAVANNAH (hymn 430), which was probably adapted from a Moravian source and was published in John Wesley's first tunebook, *The Foundery Collection* (1742), where it was titled HERRNHUT. The second type included arrangements of operatic airs and new solo-style melodies in the secular art-music idiom of the time. Charles Wesley's familiar "Love Divine, All Loves Excelling" (hymn 43) was originally sung to a melody from Henry Purcell's opera *King Arthur*, "Fairest Isle, All Isles Excelling"; indeed, Wesley's hymn may have been a parody of John Dryden's text for the opera.[4]

Of course, the greatest composer living in England during the eighteenth century was G. F. Handel. While Handel did compose tunes for three Charles Wesley hymns (none of these tunes appear in *The New Century Hymnal*), most of the tunes to which his name is attached are arrangements by others of pieces from his operas and oratorios. CHRISTMAS (hymn 491) is derived from Handel's opera *Siroe*, while the source of the tune JUDAS MACCABEUS (hymn 253) is the oratorio of the same name; the tune ANTIOCH is probably a combination and adaptation of phrases from "Comfort Ye" and "Lift Up Your Heads" in *Messiah*.[5]

The most significant English collection of hymn tunes arranged from the works of eighteenth-century classical composers was William Gardiner's *Sacred Melodies from Haydn, Mozart, and Beethoven*, published in six volumes in 1812 and 1815. This book not only introduced such tunes as LYONS (hymn 26)—derived from a Sonatina for piano and violin by "G." (probably an abbreviation for "Giuseppe," i.e. Joseph Haydn)—but also served as a resource for later American compilers, including Lowell Mason. One tune by Franz Joseph Haydn that has become popular in English and American hymnody, AUSTRIAN HYMN (hymn 307), was not arranged from a larger work but was written originally as a national anthem for his native land.

THE ROMANTIC VOICE IN HYMNODY

The last decade of the eighteenth century and the early years of the nineteenth century constituted one of the great eras of English literature. Poets created a new Romantic style, in which they sought to express their own inner feelings rather than to "reflect nature" as earlier writers had done; in so doing, they created such masterpieces as William Blake's *Songs of Innocence and of Experience*, Samuel Taylor Coleridge's *The Rime of the Ancient Mariner*, Lord Byron's "She Walks in Beauty," Percy Bysshe Shelley's "Ode to the West Wind" and "To a Skylark," and John Keats's "Ode on a Grecian Urn" and "Ode to a Nightingale."

This Romantic movement also found expression in British hymnody. The chief exponent of literary hymnody was Reginald Heber, who sought to compile a hymnal that would include texts written for specific Sundays and festivals of the church year by the leading Romantic poets of the day. Only one of the poets he contacted, Henry Hart Milman (hymn 215), responded with material, and Heber was forced to provide most of the new hymns himself. Fortunately, he was well equipped for the task, and the result was such enduring hymns as "Brightest and Best" (hymns 156, 157), "Bread of the World, in Mercy Broken" (hymn 346), and especially "Holy, Holy, Holy" (hymn 277). Though not directly connected with Heber, several other British hymnists affected a higher literary style in their texts, including Sir John Bowring (hymn 193), John Keble (hymn 96), Robert Grant (hymn 26), and Henry Francis Lyte (hymn 99).

THE OXFORD MOVEMENT AND ENGLISH TRANSLATION FROM LATIN AND GERMAN SOURCES

Nineteenth-century Romanticism, which emphasized not only personal feeling but also an interest in the exotic and faraway in time and place, found further expression in the Oxford movement. The beginning of this movement is generally dated to the sermon "National Apostasy," preached at Oxford by John Keble in 1833. The adherents of the Oxford movement are sometimes known as "tractarians," from their use of a series of *Tracts for the Times* to spread their views.

In the opinion of the tractarians, the Anglican church had gone too far at the Reformation and thrown out many ancient and valuable practices that should be restored. Among these traditions were auricular confession, the use of the term "father" to designate priests, the centrality of communion, and the use of vestments, chancel choirs, and the "sung service." These customs, which emphasized the role of the church as the "ark of salvation" that had been founded by Christ, stood at the opposite end of the theological spectrum from the Evangelicals (the "Low Church"), who stressed a personal encounter with Christ. Some tractarians, such as John Newman, Frederick W. Faber (hymn 381) and Matthew Bridges (hymn 301), eventually despaired of reforming the Anglican church and became Roman Catholics; others remained within the Anglican communion, where they formed the High Church wing and continued to press for a return to ancient practice.

At first, the adherents of the Oxford movement were suspicious of hymnody because of its long association with Evangelicalism, a linkage that had begun early in the eighteenth century with Isaac Watts and Charles Wesley. However, as the tractarians researched the practices of the early church they discovered that hymns had been a significant part of both the Orthodox liturgy and the medieval Western offices. A new enthusiasm for hymnody arose in the Oxford movement, especially for translations of ancient Greek and Latin hymns.

The foremost translator of early church hymnody into English was John Mason Neale, many of whose versions have become classics, including "O Come, O Come, Emmanuel" (hymn 116) and "All Glory, Laud, and Honor" (hymns 216, 217) from the Latin, and "Come, You Faithful, Raise the Strain" (hymn 230) and "The Day of Resurrection" (hymn 245) from the Greek. Like the psalm versions of Watts, some of these works by Neale were really paraphrases of the original rather than direct translations. Second only to Neale as a translator of Latin hymns was Edward Caswall, though only one of his renderings from that language is now commonly sung: "Jesus—The Very Thought to Me" (hymn 507).

Hand in hand with the rediscovery and translation of early Latin hymn texts came an interest in the restoration of plainsong melodies.

The foremost adapter of plainsong for congregational singing was Thomas Helmore, who in association with John Mason Neale published *The Hymnal Noted* (1851 and 1854), Neale supplying the texts and Helmore the tunes. Two plainsong melodies that made their first modern appearances in this book were VENI EMMANUEL (hymn 116) and DIVINUM MYSTERIUM (hymn 118). In both cases, these tunes were set to texts other than those with which they were associated in ancient sources, but the text–tune pairings of *The Hymnal Noted* have subsequently become the standard ones.

The rendering of Greek and Latin hymns by the tractarians was paralleled by an interest in the translation of German texts from the sixteenth and seventeenth centuries. One of the finest and most prolific translators of German hymns was Catherine Winkworth, whose *Lyra Germanica* (1855) went through thirty editions and spun off several other collections containing her translations. Winkworth's versions of "O Morning Star, How Clear and Bright" (hymn 158), "If You But Trust in God to Guide You" (hymn 410), "Now Thank We All Our God" (hymn 419), "Jesus, Priceless Treasure" (hymn 480), and others have become staples of the hymnic repertory in English.[6] British hymnody was further enriched with translations from the German by Jane Laurie Borthwick (hymns 446, 488), who also wrote original texts (hymns 532, 609), Edward Caswall (hymn 86), and Robert Bridges (hymns 218, 408).

The most enduring monument to the Oxford movement was the publication of *Hymns Ancient and Modern* in 1861 and its first supplement in 1868. This collection was edited by Sir Henry W. Baker, with W. H. Monk as music editor. The "ancient" character of the book is evident from the fact that over 40 percent of the texts in the original edition were translations from the Latin. *Hymns Ancient and Modern* was far and away the most popular hymnal published in Britain during the nineteenth century, selling some sixty million copies in its first fifty years, and it became the agency for the introduction of translations by Neale, Winkworth, and others into many British churches. This significant book has continued to be issued in revised and supplemented versions to the present day.[7]

WOMEN HYMNWRITERS IN NINETEENTH-CENTURY BRITAIN

The nineteenth century in Britain witnessed a new phenomenon in hymnody, the emergence of a large number of women hymnwriters. Women had made important contributions to hymnody at least as far back as Hildegard of Bingen, not to mention the biblical figures of Deborah, Hannah, and Mary. However, the number and overall quality of women hymnwriters in nineteenth-century Britain was unparalleled by any earlier age. Many of these women were the wives, daughters, or sisters of Anglican clergymen. Most were involved in the education of children or in charitable activities.

The important work of Catherine Winkworth and Jane Borthwick as translators has been mentioned. The list of nineteenth-century British women whose original texts continue to grace hymnals includes Charlotte Elliott (hymn 207), Sarah Flower Adams (hymn 606), Cecil Frances Alexander (hymn 172), Frances Ridley Havergal (hymn 448), Elizabeth C. Clephane (hymn 190), Claudia F. I. Hernaman (hymn 211), Jeannette Threlfall (hymn 213), Katherine Hankey (hymn 522), and Christina Rossetti (hymn 128), the last-named considered one of the greatest women poets Britain ever produced.[8]

THE VICTORIAN ERA AND *HYMNS ANCIENT AND MODERN*

The late nineteenth century is often referred to as the Victorian Era, because it was bounded by the coronation of Queen Victoria in 1837 and her death in 1901. This was a period of populism and subjectivity in the arts, with emphasis given to the expression of the artist's (usually exaggerated) emotions, which the "audience" was to experience vicariously. This was the era of the "tearjerker," a tendency to which hymnwriters were not immune, sometimes adopting excessively flowery language that easily slipped into sentimentality for the mere sake of wrenching the emotions. Among the lasting hymnic products of this period that managed to escape such excesses were a number of new texts from the "modern" portion of *Hymns Ancient and Modern* and its first supplement, such as Henry Alford's "Come, O Thankful People, Come" (hymn 422), Sabine Baring-Gould's "Now the Day Is Over" (hymn 98), William C. Dix's "As with Gladness Those of Old" (hymn 159), John Ellerton's "Savior, Again to Your Dear Name" (hymn 80), Samuel J. Stone's "The Church's One Foundation" (hymn 386), and Henry W. Baker's "The King of Love My Shepherd Is" ("Such Perfect Love My Shepherd Shows," hymn 248). Other Victorian-era texts that remain in use include Christopher Wordsworth's "Alleluia! Alleluia! Hearts to Heaven" (hymn 243), Edward Plumptre's "Rejoice, You Pure in Heart" (hymn 55), William Walsham How's "For All the Saints" (hymn 299), and Folliott S. Pierpoint's "For the Beauty of the Earth" (hymn 28).

The first edition and 1868 supplement of *Hymns Ancient and Modern* also contained early indications of an emerging Victorian hymn tune style. This approach featured part-song-like writing in which the accompanying voices, though usually in note-against-note style, are sometimes more active than the tune, which is frequently static melodically and rhythmically. The melodies sometimes include "unvocal" intervals, such as diminished fifths, and often begin on the third or fifth of the chord rather than the tonic. The accompaniment is generally in a slow harmonic rhythm, with chords changing only about once a measure, but the harmonies occasionally feature liberal doses of chromaticism and usually abound with seventh and similar "added-note" chords. These features can be seen in W. H. Monk's EVENTIDE (hymn 99) and John B. Dykes's NICAEA (hymn 277), both contributed to the first edition of *Hymns Ancient and Modern*, as well as in other tunes by Dykes (ST. AGNES, hymn 281), John Goss (LAUDA ANIMA, hymn 273), Samuel S. Wesley (AURELIA, hymn 386), Henry T. Smart (LANCASHIRE, hymn 573), George J. Elvey (DIADEMATA, hymn 301), Joseph Barnby (MERRIAL, hymn 98), and Arthur Sullivan (ST. GERTRUDE, hymn 377). John Stainer, whose cantata *The Crucifixion* became the hallmark of musical Victorianism, is represented in *The New Century Hymnal* by one arrangement (hymn 129). While Victorian texts and tunes, like the Victorian era in general, are often criticized for their sentimentality, the hymns named above are like any others from previous historical eras: They have survived because they were masterfully written and rose above the culture that gave them birth.

At the opposite end of the spectrum from the frank emotionalism of many Victorian hymn tunes are the vigorous melodies from nineteenth-century Wales, where hymn singing has long been a vital part of the culture both inside and outside the church. Welsh tunes are often recognizable by their strong tunes, rhythmic vitality, and use of bar form (AAB or AABA)—features that both reflect and encourage the singing of melodies such as LLANFAIR (hymn 240), ST. DENIO (hymn 1), MEIRIONYDD (hymn 484), and BRYN CALFARIA (hymn 258) at soccer matches and other outdoor events.[9]

The death of Queen Victoria in 1901 signaled not only a change of monarchs but the end of an era in hymnody as well. Hymnwriters and composers of the early twentieth century were to react strongly against the Victorian style. Nevertheless, British hymnody of the late nineteenth century appropriately continues to have strong representation in English-language hymnals of Britain and North America.

NOTES

1. For a fine analysis of why Charles Wesley's hymns have been so durable see Timothy Dudley-Smith, "Charles Wesley—A Hymnwriter for Today," *The Hymn* 39 (October 1988): 7–15.

2. Penetrating analyses of eighteenth-century British hymnody can be found in Madeleine Forell Marshall and Janet Todd's *English Congregational Hymns in the Eighteenth Century* (Lexington: The University Press of Kentucky, 1982) and Donald Davie's *The Eighteenth-Century Hymn in England* (Cambridge: Cambridge University Press, 1993).

3. The most comprehensive study of eighteenth-century English parish church music is Nicholas Temperley, *The Music of the English Parish Church* (Cambridge: Cambridge University Press, 1979), vol. 1, chapters 5–7.

4. Fred Kimball Graham, "John Wesley's Choice of Hymn Tunes," *The Hymn* 39 (October 1988): 31.

5. John Wilson, "Handel and the Hymn Tune: II," *The Hymn* 37 (January 1986): 25–31.

6. See Robin A. Leaver, *Catherine Winkworth: The Influence of Her Translations on English Hymnody* (St. Louis: Concordia Publishing House, 1978).

7. The standard work on this important hymnal is Maurice Frost's *Historical Companion to Hymns Ancient and Modern* (London: William Clowes & Sons, 1962).

8. See Vincent A. Lenti, "Songs from the Vicarage: Hymnists among the Wives and Daughters of Nineteenth-Century Anglican Clergymen," *The Hymn* 46 (July 1995): 14–18.

9. For more information on Welsh hymnody see Alan Luff, *Welsh Hymns and Their Tunes: Their Background and Place in Welsh History and Culture* (Carol Stream, Ill.: Hope Publishing Company, 1990).

Hymnody in the United States through the Mid-Nineteenth Century

Paul A. Richardson

The early history of hymnody in North America is largely the story of traditions brought to a new environment and altered in the face of the changes encountered in this new setting. These changes—cultural, musical, theological, even political—differed from one group to another according to the tradition inherited and the particular setting in which each worshiping body found itself.

THE DOMINANCE OF PSALMODY

At first, hymnody in this hemisphere consisted almost exclusively of metrical psalmody. This limitation on repertoire reflected the dominance of Calvin's view of congregational song among the early settlers. There were two principal lines of this heritage: French, Dutch, and German traditions based on the Genevan Psalter (*Pseaumes de David mis en rime francaise*, 1562); and English traditions, using primarily Thomas Sternhold and John Hopkins's *The Whole Booke of Psalmes* (London, 1562). The earliest documented singing in the Genevan tradition occurred among Huguenots who, while exploring Florida and South Carolina in the 1560s, taught these versions to Native Americans. The party of Francis Drake, singing from the Sternhold and Hopkins Psalter during their exploration of California in 1579, seems to have been the first to bring the English tradition to North America.

In most of the colonies along the Atlantic, the English were dominant. The first permanent settlers, at Jamestown in 1607, were Anglicans who used the Sternhold and Hopkins Psalter, sung to tunes published by Thomas Este. The separatist Pilgrims who landed at Plymouth in 1620 had come from exile in Holland, where Henry Ainsworth had prepared *The Book of Psalmes: Englished both in Prose and Metre* (Amsterdam, 1612) for their use. This psalter followed Genevan models and included a wide variety of poetic meters and thirty-nine unison tunes. Though it shared tunes with the English tradition for shorter poetic meters, it also included French and Dutch tunes for the longer metric forms. OLD HUNDREDTH (hymn 7) was common to both continental and English traditions. TOULON (hymns 251, 358) is a shortened version of OLD 124TH, a Genevan tune used by Ainsworth.

The nonseparatist Puritans who settled in 1629 at Massachusetts Bay arrived with the Sternhold and Hopkins Psalter, but after only a decade they determined to prepare their own version, more faithful to the scriptures. The result was *The Whole Booke of Psalmes Faithfully Translated into English Metre* (Cambridge, 1640), commonly known as the "Bay Psalm Book." This was the first substantial English book on any subject published in the colonies. In contrast to the Ainsworth Psalter, the Bay Psalm Book had a limited range of poetic forms (112 psalms in common meter; only five other meters for the rest). Found wanting in poetic polish, it was revised in its third edition of 1651 by Henry Dunster and Richard Lyon as *The Psalms, Hymns and Spiritual Songs of the Old and New Testament Faithfully Translated into English Metre for the Use, Edification, and Comfort of the Saints*. To the psalms it added thirty-six other passages of scripture in meter. This revision was even more restricted metrically, with 125 of the psalms in common meter. The limited range of poetic forms permitted a smaller repertory of tunes. The first extant edition with music (9th, 1698) borrowed its thirteen tunes from the 1679 edition of Englishman John Playford's *A Breefe Introduction to the Skill of Musick*.

Whatever the level of musical proficiency may have been among the early English settlers (a matter of some dispute), by the late seventeenth century worshipers were singing few tunes with little vigor. To provide leadership, "lining out" was instituted. In this practice, a precentor or clerk or deacon read or sang a line to remind the congregation of the text and tune, the congregation sang what had been presented, and the pattern was repeated until the piece was completed. Lining out was begun in the Massachusetts Bay Colony by 1647 and at Plymouth in 1681. One year after the 1691 merger of the Plymouth Colony into the Massachusetts Bay Colony, the Bay Psalm Book was adopted in Plymouth to allow for the use of its shorter and simpler tunes.

The continental tradition was represented by the Dutch who, having settled New Amsterdam (New York) in 1613, used the Dutch Psalter, translated by Peter Datheen (1566) from the Genevan Psalter. Another psalter tradition was maintained among Presbyterians, who sang from the Scottish Psalter of 1650, *The Psalms of David in Meeter*. Its twelve common tunes were lined out as a regular practice.

Not only *what* to sing but *whether* to sing was still a point of controversy among Baptists. General Baptists did not sing, while most Particular Baptists, who accepted much of Calvinist theology, sang metrical psalms. Others were already singing "hymns of human composure," following the pioneering work of Benjamin Keach, a British Baptist pastor.

Instruction in psalm singing was one aspect of mission work among Native Americans. James Eliot, one of the preparers of the Bay Psalm Book, translated *Wame Ketoohomae uketoohomaongash David* (Cambridge, 1661), a metrical psalter in the Algonquin language, and bound it with his translation of the Bible.

REGULAR SINGING

By the early eighteenth century, the continuing deterioration of congregational singing among the churches in New England had become the concern of many clergy. Tempos were lethargic, melodic divergences obscured the tunes, and vitality was lacking. A number of ministers campaigned to improve psalmody through "regular singing," that is, based on the ability to read music, as opposed to the oral tradition of lining out, which was known as the "old way." Leading pastors preached and published in support of teaching worshipers to read music. Such efforts as Thomas Symmes's 1720 sermon, "The Reasonableness of Regular Singing," and Cotton Mather's 1721 pamphlet, "The Accomplished Singer, Instructions How the PIETY of SINGING with a True DEVOTION may be obtained and expressed; the Glorious GOD after an uncommon manner Glorified in it, and His PEOPLE Edified," led to the spread of singing schools. In a singing school, a leader taught participants to sing from musical notation in a series of lessons. The popularity of singing schools prompted the publication of instruction books. Two of the more prominent were produced by Congregationalist ministers: *The Grounds and Rules of Musick Explained* (Boston, 1721), by Thomas Walter, and *An Introduction to the Singing of Psalm-Tunes* (Boston, 1721), by John Tufts; the latter featured letters on a staff, rather than notes.

"Regular singing" met with considerable resistance in some quarters, particularly in rural and conservative areas, where the "old way" was considered an inherent part of the tradition, along with the texts and tunes themselves. (A similar practice persists today in some churches in the Appalachian region.)

The effort to reinvigorate congregational singing addressed singing skills and style but not repertory. The texts remained metrical psalms, and the tunes were as before. For example, Mather, though he encouraged the use of hymns for private devotion, approved only of psalms and other biblical paraphrases for worship. New psalters were being published. Mather himself produced *Psalterium Americanum* (1718) in blank verse, but it was not widely accepted. *A New Version of the Psalms of David* (London, 1696; rev., 1698; New York, 1710), the work of Anglicans Nahum Tate and Nicholas Brady supplanted Sternhold and Hopkins's collection, now more than a century old.

THE INFLUENCE OF WATTS

A new type of congregational lyric was being written in England. Isaac Watts, called by Erik Routley "the Liberator of English hymnody," was producing renovations of the psalms that not only paraphrased the biblical texts but made them Christian and contemporary. He also was writing hymns that were free expressions of scriptural ideas and personal experience. This material was included in his correspondence with his Congregationalist counterparts in the New England colonies, such as Cotton Mather. Benjamin Franklin published the first American edition of Watts's *The Psalms of David Imitated in the Language of the New Testament* (Philadelphia, 1729) but complained that it did not sell well. The time was not yet right for its acceptance, but this soon changed.

The era of religious renewal known as the Great Awakening, which began in the 1730s, opened the way for the singing of hymns rather than psalms. The profound theological changes of this period enabled, even necessitated, a change in the texts used for worship. The Great Awakening, though essentially Calvinistic in theology, elevated the importance of individual commitment. This created a need for congregational texts that permitted personal response to the preaching of repentance. The psalms and hymns of Watts, with their combination of biblical resonance, personal experience, and poetic craft, satisfied this need.

The itinerant British evangelist George Whitefield helped to make Watts's hymns popular by using them in his meetings. Jonathan Edwards defended the use of hymns alongside psalms, only to discover (to his dismay) that by the end of 1742 his congregation was inclined to dispense with psalms in favor of hymns. The psalms and hymns of Watts soon dominated the singing of the "New Lights" among Congregationalists and Presbyterians.

WESLEY'S CHARLESTOWN COLLECTION

An intriguing experiment in American hymnody was made by John Wesley. During his stay in Georgia and South Carolina as an Anglican missionary, he compiled a *Collection of Psalms and Hymns* (Charlestown [Charleston], 1737). This first American book of hymns (as distinguished from psalms) included texts of Watts and of earlier British poets, such as George Herbert, translations of German hymns, and hymns by members of the Wesley family (though none by Charles). It was not well received; indeed, Wesley's introduction of these hymns was among accusations presented against him. Though Whitefield promoted Wesleyan hymns, they did not find widespread use in America until late in the eighteenth century, after hymn singing had become more generally accepted.

HYMNODY AMONG NON-ENGLISH-SPEAKING GROUPS

The religious freedom of Pennsylvania attracted many who fled persecution in Europe. Among those who settled there in the late seventeenth and eighteenth centuries were several groups of Germans, including Lutherans, German Reformed, Mennonites, German Baptists,

Schwenkfelders, Moravians, and members of various bodies that diverged from these. They drew on Luther's freer view of hymnody, in contrast to Calvin's restriction to metrical psalms. Shortly after the establishment of their settlement in Pennsylvania, Moravians published *Hirten Lieder von Bethlehem* (Germantown, 1742). Two years later, the Brethren published their first American hymnbook, *Das kleine Davidische Psalterspiel der Kinder Zions* (Germantown, 1744).

The German Reformed were the only group who sang both metrical psalms and hymns, using a variety of collections. Their first hymnal published in America, *Neu-vermehrt-und vollständiges Gesang-Buch* (Germantown, 1753), was a reprint of a German collection, which included Ambrosius Lobwasser's translations (1565) from the Genevan Psalter and seven hundred hymns. This was used with *Kern alter und neuer* (Germantown, 1752), a reprint of a German tunebook by the same title. Lutherans and German Reformed used choirs and precentors to lead singing and introduced lining out in some locations because tunes were being forgotten.

Lutheran hymnal publication in America began with *Psalmodia Germanica* (New York, 1756), a reprint of John Christian Jacobi's 1732 London collection. The first official American Lutheran hymnbook in German was *Erbauliche Lieder-Sammlung* (Germantown, 1786). This was followed, late in the century, by two English collections edited in America, Johann C. Kunze's *A Hymn and Prayer-Book for the Use of Such Lutheran Churches as Use the English Language* (New York, 1795) and George Strebeck's *A Collection of Evangelical Hymns* (New York, 1797).

The first English psalter of the Dutch Reformed Church was *The Psalms of David . . . Translated from the Dutch* (New York, 1767). Francis Hopkinson (having taken over for Evert Byvank) prepared this book, adapting texts from Tate and Brady to fit the Genevan tunes. The companion tunebook, *A Collection of the Psalm and Hymn-Tunes* (New York, 1774), used Goudimel's settings from a 1753 Haarlem collection.

The earliest published hymns by a Native American are those of Samson Occum, a Mohegan and a friend of George Whitefield. Occum compiled *A Choice Collection of Hymns and Spiritual Songs* (New London, 1774). More than a century earlier, in the 1640s, Jean de Brébeuf, a Jesuit priest among the Canadian Hurons, had written "'Twas in the Moon of Wintertime" (hymn 151). Joseph R. Renville, a later missionary, paraphrased Jeremiah 10:12–13 in the Dakota language as "Wakantanka taku nitawa" ("Many and Great, O God," hymn 3; another translation is "Great Spirit God," hymn 341). This hymn was first published in Renville's *Dakota Dowanpi Kin* (Boston, 1842), a book used in Congregational and Presbyterian Native American churches. This was one of many hymnals in Native American languages produced in the nineteenth century.

INDEPENDENCE

Political independence brought ecclesiastical separation which often led to liturgical change. The Protestant Episcopal Church, formed in 1784, proposed a revision of the *Book of Common Prayer* in 1786. At the end of this volume was a section called "Hymns Suited to the Feasts and Fasts of the Church," which contained selections from Tate and Brady's Psalter and fifty-one hymns. For this, Francis Hopkinson edited a collection of four chants and twenty tunes. When the prayer book was adopted in 1789, the tunes had been deleted, the number of hymns reduced to twenty-seven, and the full psalter restored. Nonetheless, in this collection American Episcopalians were ahead of their British counterparts in sanctioning the use of hymns.

The Methodist Episcopal Church was founded in 1784, only twenty years after Methodism's first colonial societies (Maryland, 1764; New York, 1766). For its use, John Wesley prescribed *A Collection of Psalms and Hymns for the Lord's Day* (London, 1784), but *A Pocket Hymn Book* (New York, 1786), prepared by the American bishops, became more popular.

The first hymnal of African Americans was *A Collection of Spiritual Songs and Hymns* (Philadelphia, 1801), edited by Richard Allen, who had led in the formation of the African Methodist Episcopal Church in 1787. One distinctive feature of this hymnal was the addition of choruses to some of the hymns.

The Dutch Reformed became independent of European direction in 1787. One of the early acts of the new American Synod was the publication of *The Psalms and Hymns of the Reformed Protestant Dutch Church in North America* (New York, 1789). This collection, prepared under the leadership of John Henry Livingston, included 135 hymns along with psalms from Watts as well as Tate and Brady.

In 1788, the first General Assembly of American Presbyterians recommended that lining out be discontinued, and in *The Directory for the Worship of God* substituted "singing of psalms or hymns" for the Westminster Confession's "singing of psalms." This change was made easier by the example of Samuel Davies, a prominent Presbyterian preacher and the president of New Jersey College (Princeton University), who wrote hymns in the 1750s and 1760s.

The Synod of the German Reformed Church in the United States of America was constituted in 1793, ending its existence as a branch of the Dutch Reformed Church. Four years later, the synod issued its first official hymnbook, *Das neue und verbessert Gesangbuch* (Philadelphia, 1797). That hymnal was more commonly known as "Hendel's Gesangbuch," in reference to William Hendel, the pastor who strongly influenced its content.

THE REPERTOIRE EXPANDS

Following the Great Awakening and the reception of Watts's texts, Americans were quick to reprint the hymns of other British Evangelical writers and to incorporate these texts into their own collections. In 1742, James Davenport, the eccentric Separatist evangelist, published in Boston a "Song of Praise" without acknowledging its British author, John Mason. The first American edition of John Newton and William Cowper's *Olney Hymns* (London, 1779) was published in New York in 1792, the same year in which John Rippon's *A Selection of Hymns from the Best Authors* (London, 1787) was reprinted in New York and in Elizabethtown, New Jersey. The latter part of the eighteenth century saw the shift from psalms to hymns on a broader scale.

The freedom from metrical psalmody found in the hymns and renovated psalms of Watts encouraged the creation of a less-formal hymnody among Separatists and Particular Baptists. These spiritual songs (so-called after Col. 3:16) marked the emergence of an American folk hymnody that includes religious ballads, songs of personal experience, and invitations to the new birth. The 1742 confession of Baptists in Philadelphia endorsed hymn singing as a "holy Ordinance of Christ." Among early Baptist collections were *Hymns and Spiritual Songs* (Newport, 1766) and Joshua Smith's *Divine Hymns or Spiritual Songs* (Norwich, c. 1784; extant editions, 1793), which includes folk hymns, some with repetitive forms that foreshadowed camp-meeting songs. A Virginia Baptist book, Richard and Andrew Broaddus's *A Collection of Sacred Ballads* (Richmond [?], 1791), was the earliest to print the anonymous stanza beginning "When we've been there ten thousand years," which is now commonly associated with "Amazing Grace, How Sweet the Sound" (hymn 547).

After the Revolution, some of Watts's texts required adaptation to the circumstances in the United States. Revisions of Watts's *Psalms* were produced by John Mycall (1781), Joel Barlow (1785), and Timothy Dwight (1801). Dwight, president of Yale, wrote thirty-three new paraphrases, including "I Love Thy Kingdom, Lord," on which "We Love Your Realm, O God" (hymn 312) is based.

Reflecting both the importance and the limitations of Watts, editors sought to make his work more useful by revising, reordering, and supplementing it in volumes with such titles as "Watts and Select." In Samuel Worcester's *Christian Psalmody* (Boston, 1815), for example, the Congregationalist pastor divided the material into four "select" sections: Watts's psalms, Watts's hymns, hymns from other authors, and harmonized tunes.

AMERICAN TUNE WRITING

With the freedom to sing material beyond the psalms came a movement to compose and publish new tunes. Few Americans had published hymn tunes prior to 1770, but in the next fifty years more than five thousand tunes were written by some three hundred American composers. The texts of Watts were set more often than those from any other source, probably because many of the composers were New Light Congregationalists and Watts's works had been received favorably in their churches. Paraphrases from Tate and Brady's "New Version" were also set frequently.

Though there had been modest publications earlier, the first substantial tunebook compiled in the colonies was James Lyon's *Urania* (Philadelphia, 1761). It was followed by dozens of others, with the number surpassing 350 by 1810. The typical tunebook was oblong (wider than tall) and began with instruction in music reading (often called "rudiments" and borrowed without attribution from earlier works). Tunebooks usually had only a single stanza of text, as they were intended to support, not replace, the text-only collections.

The most famous of the "Yankee tunesmiths" was William Billings. The earliest of his six collections, *The New-England Psalm-Singer* (Boston, 1770), was the first American tunebook to consist of the works of a single composer. It included his canon, "When Jesus Wept" (hymn 192). Another of the composer-compilers was Oliver Holden, whose tune CORONATION (hymn 304), which he first published in *The Union Harmony* (Boston, 1793), is the oldest tune by an American that is still widely used.

Many of these tunebooks, beginning with *Urania*, include fuging tunes. In the fuging tune, a form from England, voices enter one at a time in imitation, typically as the tune begins the second half of the stanza. Several American composers, including Billings, adopted this style with enthusiasm and produced numerous fuging tunes in the 1780s and 1790s. Others opposed this form. Samuel Holyoke, the most prolific American composer of his time, complained that the fuging tune obscured the text.

Some compilers advocated the use of tunes borrowed or adapted from the works of prominent classical composers. Hans Gram, a German immigrant, joined with Holyoke and Holden to produce *The Massachusetts Compiler* (Boston, 1795), which featured tunes in European styles. When Jonathan Benjamin compiled *Harmonia Coelestis* (Northampton, 1799) as a tunebook for *The Hartford Selection*, he advertised its inclusion of tunes from the works of European masters. This reflected a conservative approach to providing music for revivals, the purpose for which *The Hartford Selection* (Hartford, 1799) had been compiled by Congregationalists Nathan Strong, Abel Flint, and Joseph Steward. Over the decades from 1770 to 1820, American tunebooks encompassed a wide range of styles, including psalm tunes, new compositions in chordal style, fuging tunes, folk tunes, and the florid "Methodist tunes" from England.

The earliest tunebook to include folk hymns (a folk-tune setting of a religious text) was Amos Pilsbury's *The United States' Sacred Harmony*

(1799), compiled in Charleston, South Carolina, but published in Boston. Pilsbury's collection was the first to print the anonymous tune CHARLESTOWN (hymn 78) and Elkanah Kelsay Dare's KEDRON (hymn 568). Subsequent tunebooks with folk tunes were Samuel Holyoke's *The Christian Harmonist* (Salem, 1804) and Jeremiah Ingalls's *The Christian Harmony* (Exeter, 1805). The influence of the broadening textual repertoire is revealed by the title page of *The Christian Harmonist*, which advertises that it provides tunes not only for Watts and Rippon but also for "the collection of hymns by Mr. Joshua Smith."

REVIVALISM

New waves of revivalism swept through the United States from the 1790s forward. Sometimes called the Second Great Awakening, this movement took different forms in different places. Local revivals occurred in the last decade of the eighteenth century, notably in Virginia and New England. At the turn of the century, emotional camp meetings developed in Kentucky and other areas on the western frontier, and fiery preachers like Henry Alline (who was also a hymnwriter) were active in the Northeast. Somewhat later, urban revivalism took hold in the settled areas of the Northeast and Midwest.

Participation in the camp meetings was encouraged by the use of repetitive hymnic forms that were spread easily by oral transmission. These included such elements as call-and-response patterns, tag lines, refrains, and the "traveling choruses" that were found attached to a number of traditional hymn texts. The refrain of O HOW I LOVE JESUS (hymn 52) is an example of a repetitive traveling chorus. BATTLE HYMN OF THE REPUBLIC, now linked with "My Eyes Have Seen the Glory" (hymn 610), is an anonymous tune with a form that permits easy improvisation of text.

Urban revivalism employed some of the techniques of the frontier revivals but usually with greater concern for decorum. Its most prominent figure was Congregationalist preacher Charles G. Finney, whose "new measures" were favored by some and opposed by others. Though Finney was cautious about the role of music in his services, many of his followers enlivened their meetings with tunes in popular styles.

Seeking to adapt to changing currents but to avoid what many viewed as the excessive fervor of the revival movement, Asahel Nettleton, a Congregationalist evangelist, compiled *Village Hymns* (Hartford, 1824) as a supplement to Watts. A companion tunebook, *Zion's Harp* (New Haven, 1824), edited by Nathaniel and Simeon Jocelyn, showed its conservatism by excluding folk tunes.

Joshua Leavitt, a journalist and Congregationalist minister, compiled *The Christian Lyre* (New York, 1831) and included in it not only folk tunes but secular melodies, such as "Auld Lang Syne." Leavitt intended it as a complement to Finney's work, but he apparently misread Finney and his more serious approach, for there is no evidence that Finney used Leavitt's book. *The Christian Lyre* was innovative in format, placing texts and tunes on facing pages for ease of use. The breadth of its contents is illustrated by two items that first appeared there: the folk tune PLEADING SAVIOR (hymn 397) and James Alexander's translation of "O Sacred Head, Now Wounded" (hymn 226).

Thomas Hastings (who had worked with Finney) and Lowell Mason (who had served in Lyman Beecher's congregation) countered Leavitt's book with *Spiritual Songs for Social Worship* (Utica, 1831). It borrowed the format of *The Christian Lyre* but presented a conservative, devotional style of tune alongside traditional hymn tunes. The folk tunes that were included had "improved" harmonizations. *Spiritual Songs* marked the first appearances of Hastings's TOPLADY (hymn 596) and "My Faith Looks Up to Thee," by the young Congregationalist minister Ray Palmer.

These collections were not intended to be the principal hymnbooks for worship but to supplement the standard volumes by providing less-formal material for revivals, prayer services, and "social worship."

SHAPE NOTES AND RURAL HYMNODY

An important innovation in music notation appeared in *The Easy Instructor* (Philadelphia [?], 1801) of William Little and William Smith. Note heads in different shapes were used to identify degrees of the scale. By using the same shapes for do-re-mi as for fa-sol-la, only four shapes were needed to cover the octave (fa-sol-la-fa-sol-la-mi). Though this system of notation was first employed in books edited in the North, it and the repertory associated with it were perpetuated in the collections and singing schools of the South and West. This repertoire consisted of English tunes, works of the Yankee tunesmiths, and folk hymns and camp-meeting spirituals from oral tradition.

Sixteen Tune Settings (Philadelphia, 1812), printed by Andrew Law for Virginia singing-school teacher John Logan, is the source of MORNING SONG (hymns 89, 119, 605, and 613). This tune became more widely known through John Wyeth's *Repository of Sacred Music, Part Second* (Harrisburg, 1813), which was the link between the folk tunes of the North and later Southern collections. With music edited by Elkanah Kelsay Dare, a Methodist minister, Wyeth's collection was the first shape-note book to include a substantial number of folk hymns. From this collection comes NETTLETON (hymns 59, 459).

Ananias Davisson's *Kentucky Harmony* (Harrisonburg, 1816), the first Southern shape-note tunebook, and its supplement (Harrisonburg, 1820) were important sources for later compilers. Typical of their tunebooks are several that provided first publications of tunes still in the repertoire. Among these are William Moore's *The Columbian Harmony* (Cincinnati, 1825), the source of HOLY MANNA (hymns 376, 556), and Freeman Lewis's *The Beauties of Harmony*, which included BOURBON (hymn 225) and DUNLAP'S CREEK (hymn 256) in its first issue (Pittsburgh, 1814), and CONSOLATION (hymn 247) in the enlarged edition (Pittsburgh, 1828). AMAZING GRACE (NEW BRITAIN; hymns 547, 617) was first published in Benjamin Shaw and Charles H. Spilman's *Columbian Harmony* (Cincinnati, 1829). The "corrected, enlarged, and much improved" edition of *The Christian Harp* (Pittsburgh, 1836) was the first book to include LAND OF REST (hymns 354, 378, 521).

A distinctive line of tunebooks was developed among the Mennonites in the Shenandoah Valley of Virginia. In 1816, Joseph Funk compiled *Die allgemein nützliche Choral-Music*, a German shape-note collection. His English collection, *A Compilation of Genuine Church Music* (Winchester, 1832), featured the first publication of FOUNDATION (hymn 407). BOUNDLESS MERCY (hymn 265) first appeared in the second edition of this book (1835). The earliest German shape-note book was *Der leichte Unterricht* (Harrisburg, 1810), compiled by German Reformed layman Joseph Doll and published by Wyeth. Wyeth also printed John Rothbaust's *Die Franklin Harmonie* (Harrisburg, 1821), a bilingual shape-note book.

The most widely used Southern shape-note books were William Walker's *The Southern Harmony and Musical Companion* (New Haven, 1835) and *The Sacred Harp* (Philadelphia, 1844) of Benjamin Franklin White and E. J. King. Though published in Northern cities, both were compiled in the South. These tunebooks—which are still used in some locations—helped to codify the core repertoire of shape-note hymnody. WALKER (hymn 156), DISTRESS (hymn 254), DOVE OF PEACE (hymn 349), JEFFERSON (hymn 530), and PROMISED LAND (hymn 598) first appeared in the initial edition of *Southern Harmony*; WONDROUS LOVE (hymn 223) was first published in the appendix to the second edition of 1840. *The Sacred Harp* was the first collection to include BEACH SPRING (hymn 332).

Though these shape-note books usually included one or more stanzas of a text with each tune, text anthologies continued to be published as separate volumes. "What Wondrous Love Is This" (hymn 223), an anonymous text, first appeared in two 1811 collections, Stith Mead's *A General Selection of the Newest and Most Admired Hymns and Spiritual Songs Now in Use* (Lynchburg) and Starke Dupuy's *Hymns and Spiritual Songs* (Frankfort [?], 1st edition not extant). An identifiable author of this era was James O'Kelly, the founder of the southeastern part of the Christian Church, who was also a hymnal compiler. "Unite and Join Your Cheerful Songs" (hymn 617) was included in his *Hymns and Spiritual Songs Designed for the Use of Christians* (Raleigh, 1816).

MUSICAL REFORM

In strong contrast to the shape-note collections that perpetuated the religious folk song of the United States stands the work of Lowell Mason, a leading figure in church music and music education in the nineteenth century. While a part-time church musician in Savannah, Mason edited *The Boston Handel and Haydn Society Collection of Church Music* (Boston, 1822). In its preface, he reflected on the state of church music in the United States, and commented: "Much still remains undone." Mason returned to Boston in 1827 with an agreement to lead music in three Congregational churches. He worked to elevate taste in church music following classical European models and to improve musical practice according to "scientific methods" of composition and music education. He believed that the only way to achieve lasting reform in church music was to provide a good music education for every child.

Mason's legacy is substantial. He published eighty-four collections and composed or arranged more enduring hymn tunes than any other American. Among those are ANTIOCH (hymn 132), HAMBURG (hymn 224), AZMON (hymns 383, 575), DENNIS (hymn 393), EVAN (hymn 489), and BETHANY (hymn 606). To a lesser, but significant extent, Mason established a standard for "proper" urban church music that lasted for decades.

A contemporary who shared Mason's vision and helped to shape his thought was Thomas Hastings, a writer both of texts and of tunes, including ZION (hymn 19). They influenced a number of collaborators and pupils, including George J. Webb, the composer of WEBB (hymn 609), George W. Root, Isaac Baker Woodbury, and William B. Bradbury.

HYMNS OF SUNDAY SCHOOLS AND OTHER INTERDENOMINATIONAL MINISTRIES

Sunday schools developed in the United States within a few years of the movement's founding in England in the 1780s. Building on the work of predecessor organizations, the interdenominational American Sunday School Union was constituted in 1824. The first collection from that lineage was *The Sunday School Hymn Book* (Philadelphia, c. 1818, 1st edition not extant). *Hymns for Sunday School Teachers* (New York, 1816), the earliest American publication for Sunday schools, was taken from a book by the London Sunday School Union. The first American compiler in this genre who can be identified is Hervey Wilbur, a Congregationalist, the editor of *A Sunday School Hymn Book for Youth* (Hartford, 1818).

The first tunebook for Sunday schools was E. Osburn's *The Sunday School Music Book* (Philadelphia, 1826), a companion to *The Sunday School Hymn Book*. It was printed in shape notes, though most Sunday-school books were in round notes. Thomas Hastings's *Juvenile Psalmody* (Utica,

1827) provided complete texts with music. Lowell Mason entered this field with the *Juvenile Psalmist* (with Elam Ives; Boston, 1829).

The music of the early Sunday-school collections was much like that in other tunebooks. By midcentury, a distinctive Sunday-school style developed, with simple and repetitive rhythm, melody, and harmony, all carefully following the compositional rules of Mason and his compatriots. This idiom was an important forerunner of the gospel song.

The most significant composer of Sunday-school music was William Bradbury, who produced numerous collections, beginning with *The Young Choir* (with Charles W. Sanders; New York, 1841). He set texts such as Anna B. Warner's "Jesus Loves Me" (hymn 327). Bradbury was also a leading writer of simple tunes for family and social worship, as presented in *The Devotional Hymn and Tune Book* (Philadelphia, 1864), which he edited. Among his tunes are WOODWORTH (hymn 207), BRADBURY (hymn 252), SOLID ROCK (hymn 403), and SWEET HOUR (hymn 505).

The Sunday school was but one aspect of nineteenth-century religious life that reached beyond denominational boundaries. Numerous hymnals and songbooks were published to serve the needs of other inter- and nondenominational groups, from abolitionists to missions organizations to temperance leagues to the Young Men's Christian Association. The first collection of missions texts, *Hymns and Sacred Songs for the Monthly Concert* (Andover, 1823), was compiled by Leonard Bacon while he was still a student at Andover. Later becoming a prominent Congregationalist minister and teacher, Bacon was the son of a missionary to Native Americans.

DENOMINATIONAL HYMNODY

While the number of collections for nondenominational causes was growing, many denominations were producing new anthologies for worship. These volumes were often quite large, in an effort to provide appropriate texts for every homiletic focus. The texts of Watts were still included in large numbers, but they seldom dominated collections. Rather, these hymnbooks, while focusing on a particular heritage, incorporated an increasingly wide range of material. Tunes continued to be in volumes separate from the texts.

A Selection of Hymns (New York, 1808) for Methodists was compiled by American bishops as a supplement to *A Pocket Hymn Book* and bound with it. The number of Wesleyan hymns was increased in *A Collection of Hymns for the Use of the Methodist Episcopal Church* (New York, 1821). In *Hymns for the Use of the Methodist Episcopal Church* (New York, 1849), the size of this tradition's worship book had grown to 1,148 texts.

Under the leadership of William Muhlenberg and Henry Onderdonk, the number of hymns for Episcopalian worship was enlarged considerably in *Hymns of the Protestant Episcopal Church in the United States of America* (New York, 1827) by the addition of texts from British evangelical writers. *Psalms and Hymns Adapted to Public Worship* (Philadelphia, 1831) brought together psalmody and hymnody for Presbyterians, drawing more than one-third of its contents from Watts. Following the formal division of Presbyterians into Old School and New School sides in the 1840s, several books competed for acceptance.

After the publication of a large number of local and regional collections, two large hymnbooks took hold among Baptists: in the North, *The Psalmist* (Boston, 1843), edited by Baron Stow and Samuel F. Smith, and in the South, *The Baptist Psalmody* (Charleston, 1850), by Basil Manly and Basil Manly Jr. The regional division of many denominations over slavery and other issues that led to the Civil War increased the number of hymnals, as each body sought to establish its identity by publishing a distinctive collection. *A Collection of Hymns for Public, Social, and Domestic Worship* (Nashville, 1847) of the Methodist Episcopal Church South is an example of this development.

Several new groups, such as Mormons, Shakers, and Adventists, each with its own hymnody, emerged in this era. The distinctive hymns that these sects produced had little impact outside the communities in which they developed.

Congregationalists published several significant books just after midcentury. The *Plymouth Collection of Hymns and Tunes* (New York, 1855) was prepared for Henry Ward Beecher's Brooklyn congregation. He selected the 1,374 texts, while the music was edited by his brother Charles and the church's organist, John Zundel. This hymnal is notable for its eclectic contents. The *Plymouth Collection* also established a format common for the rest of the century, with a tune at the top of each page, above a number of texts in the appropriate meter. Texts and tunes had been together in some Sunday-school books and in urban revival collections, but having them adjacent in a collection for worship was a relatively new concept. This pattern had been pioneered in *Temple Melodies* (New York, 1851), edited by Darius E. Jones, the Plymouth congregation's music director.

Elias Nason edited *The Congregational Hymn Book* (Boston, 1857) for the Connecticut Association. This was soon followed, as was the pattern, by a version with tunes, *The Congregational Hymn and Tune Book* (Boston, 1859). Two other prominent Congregationalists, Edward A. Park and Austin Phelps, compiled *The Sabbath Hymn Book* (New York, 1858), including in it fifteen hymns and translations by Ray Palmer, among them "Jesus, the Joy of Loving Hearts" (hymn 329). Lowell Mason edited the music for the edition with tunes, *The Sabbath Hymn and Tune Book* (New York, 1859), which contained the first publication of his tune BETHANY (hymn 606). By the time of the Civil War, hymnals such as these Congregationalist books had arrived at a breadth of content and a format, with text and tune adjacent, that would be typical for hymnals well into the twentieth century.

The first half of the nineteenth century saw the development of an American literary hymnody, the finest products of which equaled those of England. The accomplishment of American writers was recognized by the inclusion of two texts in the epoch-defining British collection *Hymns Ancient and Modern* (London, 1861): "You Are the Way" (hymn 40), by George Washington Doane, and "Take Up Your Cross, the Savior Said" (hymn 204), by Charles W. Everest. Other enduring American texts from this period are Edmund H. Sears's "It Came upon the Midnight Clear" (hymn 131); Elizabeth Payson Prentiss's "More Love to You, O Christ" (hymn 456); Sylvanus Dryden Phelps's "Savior, Who Dying Gave" (hymn 452; original first line, "Saviour, thy dying love"); and Frederick H. Hedge's "Sovereign and Transforming Grace" (hymn 512). Hedge also translated Luther's "A Mighty Fortress Is Our God" (hymn 439).

Unitarianism, in particular, encouraged the publication of hymns of high literary quality. Samuel Longfellow and Samuel Johnson edited *A Book of Hymns for Public and Private Devotion* (Cambridge, 1846) and *Hymns of the Spirit* (Boston, 1864). The latter included Longfellow's "Holy Spirit, Truth Divine" (hymn 63); "'Tis Winter Now; the Fallen Snow" (hymn 432); and "I Look to You in Every Need" (hymn 463); as well as texts by two renowned poets—his brother, Henry Wadsworth Longfellow, and John Greenleaf Whittier.

Among the American composers who wrote tunes in a more refined style during this period was Richard S. Willis, whose *Church Chorals and Choir Studies* (New York, 1850) contained CAROL (hymn 131) and his harmonization of SCHÖNSTER HERR JESU (hymn 44).

From midcentury on, many denominations and independent publishers issued distinct hymnals for Sunday morning worship and for other services of the church. The presence of new varieties of hymnody within the church inevitably influenced that used in worship. By this route, the hymns of urban revivalism and of social worship entered the worship of many congregations. The incorporation of these new styles into the lives of the churches occurred at different rates in different contexts. This change was encouraged by the widespread religious renewal of 1857–1858, often called the "Prayer Meeting Revival." This was the impetus for *Union Prayer Meeting Hymns* (Philadelphia, 1858), prepared by the YMCA for interdenominational midday prayer meetings. The praise services begun by Eben Tourjée in the 1850s and the song services of Edward Payson Hammond also promoted the concept of hymn singing for devotion and renewal.

HYMNODY AMONG IMMIGRANTS FROM NON-ENGLISH TRADITIONS

Immigrants from non-English cultures faced difficult decisions in a land where the English language was dominant. One solution was for these immigrants to retain their native language. For example, the joint publication by German Reformed and Lutherans of *Das Gemeinschaftliche Gesangbuch* (Baltimore, 1817) was both a sign of provision for common need for comparatively small communities and evidence of shared resistance to cultural change. German-language books continued to be produced alongside those in English through the nineteenth century.

If immigrant groups retained their linguistic heritage, they risked losing members who wanted to become part of the dominant culture. When these denominations began to use English for worship, they often borrowed materials already in English rather than translating their own, so that acculturation came at the expense of lost tradition. In the Lutheran *Hymns, Selected and Original* (Gettysburg, 1828), texts from Watts and the English evangelicals far surpassed those with German roots. In *Psalms and Hymns for the Use of the German Reformed Church in the United States of America* (Hagerstown, 1831), the first English hymnal in that tradition, much of the German heritage was omitted. Though all 150 psalms were present, most were in Watts's paraphrases, and chorales were virtually eliminated. The language problem was compounded among Lutherans, who emigrated to the United States from different countries, bringing no common language. This led to a proliferation of synods, with differing musical traditions, translations, and hymnals.

Many denominations, whatever their linguistic heritage, were divided in their response to revivalism. Persons of a more pragmatic bent were willing to abandon much that was traditional. They were opposed by those who wished to recover lost traditions and develop a more liturgical approach. The German Reformed experience illustrates this dilemma.

J. F. Berg's *The Saints' Harp* (Philadelphia, 1839) was a German Reformed collection in the revivalist tradition. *Eine Sammlung Evangelischer Lieder* (Chambersburg, 1842), though it retained the German language, was influenced by the trends of the time. It had no separate section of psalms and shifted the unique balance of psalms and pietistic chorales that the German Reformed had brought to America. In a reaction to these developments, the Mercersburg liturgical reforms led to Philip Schaff's *Deutsches Gesangbuch* (Philadelphia, 1859) and *Cantate Domino* (Boston, 1859), a service book and hymnal by Lewis Steiner and Henry Schwing. In support of this movement, Henry Harbaugh edited *Hymns and Chants for Sunday Schools* (Philadelphia, 1861), which included Harbaugh's "Jesus, I Live to You" (hymn 157). Harbaugh, a leading pastor and former singing-school teacher, set his text to I. B. Woodbury's LAKE ENON, which had appeared in Woodbury's *The Cythara* (New

York, 1854). German-speaking Sunday schools were served by Schaff's *Gesangbuch für deutsche Sonntagsschulen* (Philadelphia, 1864).

AFRICAN AMERICAN HYMNODY

Only after the Civil War were the spirituals of African Americans, certainly in use in the antebellum era, put in print. This distinctive genre featured texts rooted in biblical narrative and imagery that often emphasized themes of liberation. It utilized call-and-response forms and included musical traits that can be traced both to African heritage and American experience. Apart from the collection of Richard Allen, noted earlier, there were few books in which the African American perspective can be observed. It is clear from various accounts that a rich variety of congregational song, including distinctive stylistic treatments of Anglo-American hymns, existed in black worshiping communities.

CONCLUSION

By the 1860s, congregational song in the United States was remarkably diverse and, in many places, vital. These characteristics were the result of the complex interplay between numerous theological and musical traditions, on the one hand, and the differing social and economic contexts in which worship occurred, on the other. Particularly influential in the development of congregational singing in North America have been the periods of religious awakening and renewal. The varied traditions that emerged still live in worship, as illustrated by the citation of examples found in *The New Century Hymnal*. The hymns of our forebears continue to enrich our understanding, experience, and expression of the Christian faith.

SELECTED BIBLIOGRAPHY

Benson, Louis R. *The English Hymn: Its Development and Use in Worship*. 1915; reprint, Richmond: John Knox Press, 1962.

Brink, Emily R. "Metrical Psalmody in North America: A Story of Survival and Revival." *The Hymn* 44, no. 4 (October 1993): 20–24.

Britton, Allen Perdue, Irving Lowens, and Richard Crawford. *American Sacred Music Imprints, 1698–1810: A Bibliography*. Worcester, Mass.: American Antiquarian Society, 1990.

Brumm, James L. H. "Coming to America: RCA Hymnals in the 18th and 19th Centuries." *The Hymn* 41, no. 1 (January 1990): 27–33.

Christ-Janer, Albert, Charles W. Hughes, and Carleton Sprague Smith.

American Hymns Old and New. New York: Columbia University Press, 1980.

Crawford, Richard. "'Much Still Remains to Be Undone': Reformers of Early American Hymnody." *The Hymn* 35, no. 4 (October 1984): 204–8.

Eskew, Harry, and Hugh T. McElrath. *Sing with Understanding: An Introduction to Christian Hymnology.* 2nd ed. Nashville, Tenn.: Church Street Press, 1995.

Foote, Henry Wilder. *Three Centuries of American Hymnody.* Hamden, Conn.: Shoe String Press, 1961.

Hughes, Charles W. *American Hymns Old and New: Notes on the Hymns and Biographies of the Authors and Composers.* New York: Columbia University Press, 1980.

Kroeger, Karl. "Settings of Isaac Watts's Psalm 50 by American Psalmodists." *The Hymn* 41, no. 1 (January 1990): 19–27.

———. "William Billings and the Hymn-Tune." *The Hymn* 37, no. 3 (July 1986): 19–25.

———. "A Yankee Tunebook from the Old South: Amos Pilsbury's The United States Sacred Harmony." *The Hymn* 32, no. 3 (July 1981): 154–262.

Lowens, Irving. *Music and Musicians in Early America.* New York: W. W. Norton, 1964.

Marini, Stephen. "Rehearsal for Revival: Sacred Singing and the Great Awakening in America." In *Sacred Sound: Music in Religious Thought and Practice*, edited by Joyce Irwin. Chico, Calif.: Scholars Press, 1983.

Music, David W. "The Diary of Samuel Sewall and Congregational Singing in Early New England." *The Hymn* 41, no. 1 (January 1990): 7–15.

Owen, Barbara. "The Bay Psalm Book and Its Era." *The Hymn* 41, no. 1 (October 1990): 12–19.

Pemberton, Carol A. *Lowell Mason: His Life and Work.* Ann Arbor, Mich.: UMI Research Press, 1985.

———. "Praising God through Congregational Song: Lowell Mason's Contributions to Church Music." *The Hymn* 44, no. 2 (April 1993): 22–30.

Pratt, Waldo Selden. *The Music of the Pilgrims: A Description of the Psalmbook Brought to Plymouth in 1620.* 1921; reprint, New York: Russell & Russell, 1971.

Reynolds, William J., and Milburn Price. *A Survey of Christian Hymnody.* 3d ed. Carol Stream, Ill.: Hope Publishing Co., 1987.

Westermeyer, Paul. "Germany Reformed Hymnody in the United States." *The Hymn* 31, no. 2 (April 1980): 89–94, 96; and 31, no. 3 (July 1980): 200–204, 212.

Wilhoit, Mel R. "The Music of Urban Revivalism." *The Hymn* 35, no. 4 (October 1984): 219–23.

In addition, many handbooks and companions to various denominational hymnals provide general information on this topic; also, H. Wiley Hitchcock and Stanley Sadie, eds., *New Grove Dictionary of American Music*, 4 vols. (New York: New Grove Dictionaries, 1986), offers numerous articles on specific developments of this period in U.S. hymnody.

U.S. Hymnody from the Mid-Nineteenth to Late Twentieth Centuries

Mel R. Wilhoit

"How I long for the good old Methodist thunder. One good burst of old-fashioned music would have blown this modern singing out the window like wadding from a gun."[1] With this ardent request voiced in 1857, Congregationalist Henry Ward Beecher looked both back to a brighter past and ahead to a more glorious vision of the church's song in the face of a rapidly changing world.

HYMNS AND HYMNALS IN THE CONGREGATIONAL CHURCH

As Congregationalists entered the Civil War, they found themselves the inheritors of a hymnody influenced by the principles of Beecher's *Plymouth Collection,* containing a wide variety of hymns and tunes based on a foundation of Watts's homiletic hymns and psalm paraphrases, the Evangelical flowering of Wesley and Newton, and the contributions of American Lowell Mason and his contemporaries. In the following decades, many Congregationalists contributed to the hymnody of their denomination as well as to the larger American scene. Among these were Daniel March (author of "Hark, the Voice of Jesus Calling"), missionary and pastor Samuel Wolcott (known for "Christ for the World We Sing"), and John Zundel, organist at Beecher's Plymouth Church, whose tune BEECHER (hymns 43, 368, 495) is still widely sung.

In addition, Congregationalists were enthusiastically singing the contributions of those from outside the denomination. Unitarians were represented by Julia Ward Howe, whose abolitionistic "Mine Eyes Have Seen the Glory" (hymn 610) celebrated those values embraced by the Congregationalist college at Oberlin, Ohio, and by the pastor-poet Samuel Longfellow—brother of poet Henry Wadsworth—with "Holy Spirit, Truth Divine" (hymn 63). Quaker poet John Greenleaf Whittier produced "Immortal Love, Forever Full" (hymn 166) and "Dear Lord and Father of Mankind" ("Dear God Embracing Humankind," hymn 502), among others.

As there was no official denominational hymnal following the Civil War, autonomous Congregational churches sang from whatever book or books they found best suited to their needs. Many churches chose the works of Presbyterian pastor Charles S. Robinson, who, along with his musical editor Joseph P. Holbrook, was a prolific editor of hymnals and Sunday-school books. Their first collection was *Songs of the Church: or, Hymns and Tunes for Christian Worship* (1862), which contained nearly nine hundred hymns, primarily of the Watts-Wesley-Newton type, for the congregation (with music) and three hundred separate settings (without tunes) for the choir. A second effort resulted in the highly successful *Songs for the Sanctuary* (1865), which incorporated a greater number of modern hymns set to the popular tunes of Mason, Hastings, Bradbury, and George F. Root (the last two of whom reflected the influence of Sunday-school hymnody on regular worship practices). A third collection, *Psalms and Hymns and Spiritual Songs: A Manual of Worship for the Church of Christ* (1875), was designed solely for congregational use. This hymnal reflected a trend emanating from Beecher's *Plymouth Collection*, which sought to give prominence to the congregation in church music rather than to the choir as had been the case during the earlier part of the century.

In describing Presbyterian Robinson's contributions to Congregational hymnody, Louis F. Benson observed in *The English Hymn*: "He aimed to please the choirs by giving them a recognized choir hymn to set at will and to render; to please the ministers by giving them immense collections from which to choose sermon illustrations; and to please the people by giving them tunes they loved to sing in church and at home."[2]

This reliance on Presbyterian-derived hymnals was not so odd as it might at first seem: Congregationalists were characterized by cooperation across denominational lines and had long since entered a plan of union with the Presbyterians for home mission work. It was therefore not surprising that the Congregational Sunday School and Publication Society adopted *The Hymnal Published by Authority of the General Assembly of the Presbyterian Church in the United States of America* (1895) and reissued it two years later under the title *The Hymnal for Use in the Congregational Church* (1897) as a quasi-official hymnal.

In spite of this strong Presbyterian hymnic presence, Congregationalists had not abandoned the field, for in 1880 three new collections were issued which reflected an important shift in hymnal conception. C. H. Richards's *Christian Praise* (later *Songs of Christian Praise*) and *The Manual of Praise* (*The New Manual of Praise* in 1901), plus Hall and Lasar's *Evangelical Hymnal*, were much smaller collections of approximately six hundred hymns. These reflected a more congregationally oriented approach compared to an earlier homiletic one wherein hymnals usually contained well over one thousand entries, many of which were intended more for preaching than singing.

In addition, Hall and Lasar's *Evangelical Hymnal* and *Hymns of the Faith with Psalms* (1887), edited by George Harris, W. J. Tucker, and E. K. Glezen, reflected the English Oxford movement, with its liturgical and scholarly emphases rooted in medieval Catholicism. Only twenty-eight

American contributions appeared in *Evangelical Hymnal*, with English liturgical hymns playing a more prominent role; *Hymns of the Faith* contained a prose psalter set to Anglican chant with the hymns organized under the articles of the Apostles' Creed. Continuing even farther along the same path was *The Plymouth Hymnal*, edited by Lyman Abbott (1893), which sought to raise the supposed literary inferiority of Congregationalists toward the perceived advanced level of current Anglican worship. Perhaps not surprisingly, none of these collections was widely received, for most Congregationalists still reflected broad Evangelical convictions that valued bold, clear statements of faith over finely polished religious sentiment, and practical religious experience over historically rooted liturgical ritual. Yet Congregational hymnody was enriched by this impetus, especially in the area of older hymns translated from Latin, such as those by John Mason Neale (hymns 116, 230), Edward Caswall (hymn 86), Congregationalist Ray Palmer (hymn 329); and those translated from German sources by Catherine Winkworth (hymns 158, 410, 419).

REVIVALISM AND GOSPEL HYMNS

And then there was the influence of revivalism. From the earliest days of the Great Awakening with Jonathan Edwards, to the pious leadership of Timothy Dwight at Yale, to the "New Measures" of Charles Finney, Congregationalists had long carried the torch of religious revivalism in America. That situation remained little changed in the second half of the nineteenth century as the mantle of revivalism fell upon Dwight Lyman Moody. Converted in 1855 through the Sunday school at Boston's Mount Vernon Congregational Church, Moody embodied the religious values that characterized a significant strain of Congregationalism. Upon his move to Chicago, he joined a Congregational church but soon organized his own Sunday school and the North Market Street Mission, which ministered to both the spiritual and physical needs of the surrounding community. Although Moody's efforts were associated more with parachurch organizations than any single denomination, his personal church affiliation remained Congregationalist throughout his life.

Although Moody was untrained as a musician, he had an uncanny natural ability to sense how music influenced people. As a result of hearing a young civil servant named Ira D. Sankey sing, he invited the Methodist from Pennsylvania to join him full-time in his Chicago work. However, not until the two sailed to England in 1873 did both Moody's preaching and Sankey's musical ability take on national and eventually international importance, for there Sankey began to popularize a style of religious song that came to be called "gospel hymns" or "gospel songs." These songs became popular as both congregational song and as somewhat novel religious solos, which Sankey sang with unusual effect from behind his little pump organ placed near the pulpit. In reality, these were simply the American Sunday-school songs of William Bradbury, Fanny Crosby, and Philip P. Bliss, adapted to adult religious meetings. Demand for a collection of these songs while the men were abroad resulted in their publication in a small, words-only pamphlet, which ultimately grew to a collection of more than twelve hundred hymns with music, entitled *Gospel Hymns and Sacred Solos*. By 1875, when Moody and Sankey returned to the United States, gospel hymnody had clearly become the style of religious music most closely associated with revivalism.

Sankey immediately combined his efforts with revivalist musician and Sunday-school songwriter Philip Bliss (who had served as music director at the First Congregational Church of Chicago) to produce *Gospel Hymns and Sacred Songs by P. P. Bliss and Ira D. Sankey as Used by Them in Their Gospel Meetings* (1875). Bliss, represented by two hymns in *The New Century Hymnal* (hymns 319, 438), had already combined his gifts as hymnwriter and composer by contributing a number of successful songs to an earlier collection he edited, simply called *Gospel Songs* (1874). With Bliss's natural gifts and Sankey's immense popularity as a revival musician and hymnbook compiler, their joint effort proved a huge success, and a second volume was issued the next year. Although Bliss died in 1876, Sankey continued the series with the assistance of gospel hymnwriters James McGranahan and George C. Stebbins, running to six volumes (1875–1891, with *Gospel Hymns Nos. 1–6 Complete* in 1894). The series effectively became the bible of gospel hymnody and helped popularize many songs that have become part of an American core hymnody, such as Hawks's "I Need You Every Hour" (hymn 517) and Katherine Hankey's "I Love to Tell the Story" (hymn 522).

As Moody and Sankey continued their revival efforts, the impact was felt within almost every denomination, including Congregationalism. Many of the large and lengthy interdenominational revival campaigns were held in northeastern cities such as Boston or Hartford, where Congregationalists were actively involved in the meetings as workers or attendees. These new gospel hymns often transcended the religious sphere and became the popular music of the day, both widely sung and often parodied. It was little wonder that such popular religious song found its way into Congregational circles.

However, it often found its way in through the musical back door. For, to many of its critics, the gospel hymn was a far cry from the earlier, more stolid theological statements of Watts or the spiritually didactic expressions of Charles Wesley. These new hymns were more likely simpler statements of humankind's sinfulness and God's redeeming love, often penned from the perspective of a highly personal testimony. In addition, the music was noticeably lighter and more lively in comparison with standard fare; and most of the gospel hymns contained a chorus or refrain more characteristic of entertaining parlor songs than serious theological discourse. The songs were therefore often considered inappropriate for standard worship services and remained conspicuously absent from hymnals designed for public worship.

In spite of such concerns, the gospel hymn made significant inroads into what Congregationalists were singing, both in and out of public worship. Many of the earlier Sunday-school songs had already been accepted into the regular church hymnals. In addition, the small, inexpensive collections of gospel hymns (at about twenty-five cents each), which were issued by Sankey, Bliss, and a growing host of similar publishers, rendered these songs nearly ubiquitous in religious circles.

Undoubtedly, the best known of the gospel hymnwriters was Fanny Crosby, and one of her best-known hymns was "Blessed Assurance" (hymn 473). Beginning in 1864 as a protégé of Bradbury, she eventually produced thousands of gospel hymn texts, which were published by Biglow and Main of New York for their Sunday-school collections, later becoming popular in revival meetings. More than any other writer, she captured the spirit of nineteenth-century revivalism and became perhaps the most widely sung hymnist in the world, as American and British missionaries carried her hymns to every corner of the globe.

Crosby often collaborated with Baptist industrialist William H. Doane, who supplied her with singable tunes, as in "Jesus, Keep Me Near the Cross" (NEAR THE CROSS, hymn 197), "I Am Yours O Lord" (I AM YOURS, hymn 455), and "Pass Me Not O Gentle Savior" (PASS ME NOT, hymn 551). Doane, in turn, often worked with Baptist pastor Robert Lowry in editing Sunday-school collections. Lowry generally composed the music, as in MARCHING TO ZION (hymn 382), SOMETHING FOR JESUS (hymn 452), and NEED (hymn 517); at times he also supplied lyrics, as in "Shall We Gather at the River" (HANSON PLACE, hymn 597).

Revivalism continued unabated into the new century, with renowned preacher-musician teams such as evangelist Wilbur Chapman and his charismatic songleader Charlie Alexander. Their international preaching campaigns carried the gospel hymn tradition around the world with songs such as Charles Gabriel's "Glory Song" ("When all my labors and trials are o'er") and Congregationalist minister Jeremiah Rankin's "God Be with You till We Meet Again" (hymn 81). Alexander and his accompanist Robert Harkness also promoted use of the piano and an improvisational style of playing it. Within a few years, it had replaced the organ as the instrument most congenial to gospel music and had earned a place in many a church sanctuary.

Of even greater fame was the team of baseball-player-turned-revivalist Billy Sunday and his singer-songleader Homer Rodeheaver. Under their banner, gospel hymnody remained a strong influence, and a steady stream of new and popular songs issued from the Rodeheaver Publishing Company and its songwriters such as Charles Gabriel (HIGHER GROUND, hymn 442; SPARROW, hymn 475), George Bennard ("On a Hill Far Away," hymn 195), and C. Austin Miles ("In the Garden," hymn 237).

Revivalism influenced more than just what Congregationalists sang, however; it also influenced the actual physical orientation of hymn singing. In the nineteenth century, worshipers in some Congregationalist churches turned during the hymn and faced the rear gallery, where the choir and organ were situated. By the twentieth century, it had become more common to relocate both choir and organ to the front and center of the sanctuary, in the role of musical ministers, able to address the congregation directly—just as Sankey had modeled in his meetings. The sound of hymn singing also changed as the relatively inexpensive piano rivaled the wheezy pump organ in the Sunday school, or somber pipe organ in the sanctuary. In some churches where gospel hymnody was considered inappropriate for morning worship, it enjoyed a prominent place in Sunday evening services, given over to the spirit and forms of revivalism. Because gospel hymns were often excluded from standard hymnals, they usually were sung from separate song collections, which also occupied the hymnbook racks along with the more conservative hymnbooks.

HYMNS OF THE SOCIAL GOSPEL

Despite the strong presence of revivalism, it became clear by the turn of the century that a major shift had already taken place within Congregationalism. The earlier radical views of those such as Horace Bushnell, who had challenged the basic theological tenets of Calvinism and revivalism and had been charged with heresy, were now more widely tolerated. These new liberalizing views found their most practical application in the vision of the social gospel movement, expounded most forcefully by Walter Rauschenbusch in his *Christianity and the Social Crisis* (1907). In it the author stressed the social implications of the gospel here on earth, in contrast to the more otherworldly focus of revivalism. Instead of waiting for God to bring judgment to the end of the age, Christians were exhorted to labor earnestly within earthly social institutions to usher in God's dominion by means of spiritual warfare against the tangible enemies of poverty, greed, exploitation, and sickness. The goal was nothing less than to establish peace, justice, unity, and a complete redemption of the social order.

Whereas gospel hymns had sung about a heavenly future in the first-person singular (I), the new hymns of social conscience emphasized a present redemption of the social order in the first-person plural (we).

And where an enthusiastic but musically modest volunteer choir had helped lead congregational song in an age of gospel hymnody, a paid quartet choir of accomplished soloists became the prominent musical mainstay in many affluent urban churches where the social gospel movement found support.

Within this movement, Congregationalists played a strong role. Foremost was minister and author Washington Gladden, whose classic hymn "O Savior Let Me Walk with You" (hymn 503) emphasized sacrificial service to others; while in contrast Andover student Ernest W. Shurtleff focused on the nature of spiritual warfare with "Lead On O King Eternal" ("Lead On Eternal Sovereign," hymn 573). Non-Congregationalists also produced hymns of social concern that have become standards: Katharine Lee Bates wrote "O Beautiful for Spacious Skies" (hymn 594), Methodist Frank Mason North penned "Where Cross the Crowded Ways of Life" (hymn 543), and Presbyterian Henry Van Dyke created "Joyful, Joyful, We Adore You" (hymn 4) for Beethoven's ODE TO JOY.

Gladden also assisted editor Charles Noyes in the production of the *Pilgrim Hymnal* (1904), issued by the Congregational Sunday School and Publishing Society. Although it was not well received because of its novel content, it clearly signaled the direction Congregationalists and most other denominations would eventually take. As Louis Benson observed, the hymnal was modern in its abandonment of older terminology: Christ was viewed more as the Spirit of Love than as enthroned Majesty; there was less emphasis on Christ's atonement; the Kingdom replaced the Church, and the Christian Year was liturgically ignored; following Christ took the place of repentance; and a "pronounced humanitarianism," which emphasized the importance of this life, and broad humanitarian social service dominated its spirit.[3]

The majority of Congregational churches continued to rely on more-traditional offerings containing familiar hymnody, such as the independently published *Hymns of the Church New and Old* (1912), edited by Davis and Calkins, and *Songs of the Christian Life* (1913), edited by Charles Richards. In 1913, the *Pilgrim Hymnal* was revised with a larger inclusion of standard hymns while still retaining a strong focus on the social gospel. A second revision in 1931, which included all the stanzas of the hymns interlined between the staves of music (as opposed to setting them in poetic form below the tunes) continued the hymnal's strong social gospel emphases. Its greater reception by the churches revealed that "by the 1930s the social gospel hymn had become the marching song of liberal Protestantism in the United States," and Congregationalists had clearly joined their ranks.[4]

The year 1931 also witnessed the merger of the Congregational Church with the Christian Church. Owing to its ecumenical nature, the Christian Church had generally shared the same broad-based hymnody that characterized Congregationalist song, so that the current revision of the *Pilgrim Hymnal* served the new denomination well for a generation.

HYMNS AND HYMNALS OF THE EVANGELICAL AND THE REFORMED CHURCHES

The German heritage of the United Church of Christ, whether from the Evangelical or the Reformed wings, reflected one of three basic streams from about 1860 on:

1. A continuation of worship based on a liturgy and hymnody rooted in the Old World and the German language.
2. An enthusiastic embrace of popular American forms of worship and hymnody with a corresponding loss of the German heritage.
3. Attempts at a liturgically oriented worship and hymnody incorporating the German heritage as well as English hymnody from both the Evangelical and Oxford movements.

By midcentury, large numbers of German-speaking immigrants had swelled the ranks of those already settled throughout Pennsylvania and the Midwest. Although many brought with them their treasured *gesangbuchs*, the need for indigenous materials resulted in the Evangelical Synod's issue of *Evangelisches Gesangbuch* (1862)—a collection of 535 hymns with melodies, the whole based unapologetically on scholar Philip Schaff's earlier Reformed collection, *Deutsches Gesangbuch* (1859). The strong similarity of the two volumes clearly reflected the shared heritage of both the Evangelical and the Reformed bodies. Various tunebooks later provided the necessary musical resources. The first was *Evangelisches Choral-Buch fuer Kirke, Haus und gemischten Chor* (1877), edited by the Reverend H. Niewoehner. It included 147 chorales with florid harmonizations, preludial introductions, and interludes between stanzas. Perhaps the most popular tunebook, in circulation for over forty years, was *Liederbuch fuer Sonntagsschulen* (1882), issued by the denominational publishing house in St. Louis. The volume contained chorale tunes, folk-song melodies, and spiritual *lieder*. *Taschenbuch fuer Choralspieler* (1891) was designed for small churches with limited repertoires. It provided twenty-six popular tunes that could be employed for more than half the hymns in the 1862 *Gesangbuch*. Various official and unofficial hymn and tunebooks continued to be issued through the turn of the century, by which time the transition to English among originally German-speaking communities limited the demand for such materials.

When the demand for an English-language book finally did materialize, the result was *Hymnal of the Evangelical Church* (1899), authorized by the General Conference at Elmhurst, Illinois, and popularly known as the "Elmhurst Hymnal." The massive collection contained 888 hymns and 32 chants including 100 chorales; an appendix contained a lectionary, prayers, responses, and anthems. The hymnal set a high standard for the denomination.

The Reformed tradition had long been producing English-language hymnals and continued issuing various collections after the Civil War. The result was usually a hymnal based on a Watts-Wesley core, a strong dosage of Lowell Mason and William Bradbury, and varying degrees of revivalistic hymnody of the Fanny Crosby type. Whereas the chorale had previously held a central place in German-language hymnals, it quickly lost ground and was almost forgotten in some cases. Typical collections included J. H. A. Bomberger's *Prayers and Hymns for Sunday School* (1867) with 353 hymns and tunes; Jeremiah H. Good's *The Reformed Church Hymnal* (called "The Western Hymnal," 1878) with 631 hymns and tunes; and *The Hymnal of the Reformed Church in the United States* (called "Peace Hymnal," 1890), by James I. Good, containing 795 hymns and chants.

The popular designation of Good's efforts as "Peace Hymnal" revealed the deep rift that liturgically separated many in the Reformed camp. Since the 1850s, numerous leaders associated with the seminary at Mercersburg, Pennsylvania, had been producing liturgical and hymnic resources motivated by the principles of the Oxford movement as well as a reaction against the excesses of revivalism. In contrast to those who subscribed to the theological perspective of Mercersburg was a group sympathetic toward revivalism and calling itself the "Old Reformed"; they accused their opponents of being Romish and high church. The objects of their scorn were collections such as *Hymns and Chants* (1861), edited by Henry Harbaugh, which contained the English Evangelical hymns as well as metrical canticles, the offices of devotion, and an organization based on the church year. It also contained Harbaugh's most lasting contribution, the well-loved hymn "Jesus I Live to You" (hymn 457). Another collection in the same vein was *Hymns for the Reformed Church* (called the "Eastern Hymnal," 1874), compiled by E. E. Higbee, which offered translations of Latin, German, and Greek hymns as well as a wide representation of standard hymns. Although most of these collections received only moderate usage, they also set high standards, influencing later productions.

The twentieth century witnessed a number of cooperative efforts at hymnal publication. In 1920, the German Reformed and the Dutch Reformed (Reformed Church in America) jointly published a hymnal called *The Hymnal of the Reformed Church*. It was edited by James Good and reflected more of the "Old Reformed" posture of his earlier "Peace Hymnal." The 1934 merger of the Evangelical Synod of North America and the Reformed Church in the United States to form a new denomination also called forth the production of a new hymnal. The result was entitled simply *The Hymnal* (1941). Its compilers gave preference to Anglican hymns and German chorales while attempting to incorporate the best hymns and tunes from both their respective Germanic traditions. Social gospel hymns continued to hold a central place of importance, while standard American hymns plus new material balanced the book. Chants, responsive readings, devotional aids, and a liturgy helped to provide the relatively new denomination a sense of identity. In 1952, Armin Haeussler produced an excellent handbook to the hymnal, *The Story of Our Hymns*, which further enhanced its value and usefulness. *The Hymnal* proved a great success and has enjoyed widespread usage in Evangelical and Reformed, and later UCC, churches for over half a century.

By the mid-twentieth century, each of the two separate traditions—the Congregational Christian Church and the Evangelical and Reformed Church—had developed a broad and rich hymnody that not only reflected its own unique identity but would also soon combine to enrich the other's song in the United Church of Christ. This denomination came into being in 1957, when the two branches (each products of earlier mergers) joined to form a new Protestant communion. A new common hymnal was not forthcoming until 1974, however, when *The Hymnal of the United Church of Christ* was published to encourage the unity of the infant denomination. The book was noteworthy in three respects: ecumenical focus, organization, and number of hymns.

Ecumenical Focus. The *Hymnal of the United Church of Christ* included 90 hymns from a list of 150 identified by a Consultation on Ecumenical Hymnody (1968–1976) as being widely used in a dozen different communions. This deliberate effort was part of the committee's attempt to produce a hymnal "consonant with the ecumenical spirit of the United Church" (preface).

Organization. Departing from a traditional church year or topical format, the committee chose to organize the hymnbook around the denomination's statement of faith. This translated into six major sections ranging from "God, the Eternal Spirit" to "Blessing and Honor," and rendered a hymnbook geared to faith development.

Number of Hymns. The UCC *Hymnal* had a limited repertoire of three hundred hymns, with approximately two-thirds from one or both of the denomination's predecessor hymnals. The remaining one hundred or so hymns were new or new to the UCC traditions.

The successor to that first formal effort to provide a hymnbook for a denomination formed of various historical faith traditions and working to fulfill the mandate of its very identity—the United Church of Christ—is *The New Century Hymnal* (1995).

NOTES

1. E. S. Bucke, ed., *The History of American Methodism* (New York: Abingdon Press, 1964), 2: 341.

2. Louis F. Benson, *The English Hymn: Its Development and Use in Worship* (reprint, Richmond: John Knox Press, 1962), 479–80.

3. Ibid., 581.

3. Carlton R. Young, ed., *Companion to the United Methodist Hymnal* (Nashville: Abingdon Press, 1963), 31.

African American Worship Music

Melva Wilson Costen

Many of the forms and styles of music for worship among African Americans in a majority of Christian churches in the United States have their origins first and foremost in the music and culture of West Africa. Thus, the unique music that evolved is connected with the rich history and sociological heritage of all African Americans. An examination of this heritage is necessary since it serves as a foundation for the musical offerings included in *The New Century Hymnal*.

AFRICAN HERITAGE

One of the most noticeable attributes of African cultures was the importance they gave to music and its interrelationship with dance. Almost every activity in the life of individuals and communities included appropriate music. According to Olaudah Equiano, one of the first Africans to write a book in the English language, music and movement were integral parts of life: "We are almost a nation of dancers, musicians, and poets. Thus every great event, such as a triumphant return from battle or other cause for public rejoicing, is celebrated in public dances, which are accompanied with songs and music suited to the occasion."[1]

Appropriate music was also included in religious rites, including worship of God, lesser gods, divinities, and ancestors, as well as funerals and marriages. Among some African societies, there was a tradition of "litigation music," whereby persons engaged in a lawsuit chanted their arguments to the chief/judge with the accompaniment of drums and songs. A large portion of music-making, however, took place in less-formal, highly socialized levels that brought members of the community together to share in common experiences. There was music appropriate for celebrating the birth of children, the onset of puberty, initiation rites, and other rites of passage.

Of special importance is the poetic, picturesque, and musical language of African peoples, characterized by the use of imagery and imaginative figures of speech. In a combination of speech, poetry, dance, music (songs, chant, and recitatives), African peoples have a predilection for spontaneous and improvisational "call-and-response" performances. This allows for greater involvement of the community. African music styles serve as a means of communication and a way of sharing collective experiences.

AFRICANS IN DIASPORA

Africans transported from Africa to other places in the world retained memories of their rich cultural traditions and their understanding of the unity of sacred and secular in all aspects of life. Records from the fifteenth century (prior to the establishing of colonies in the Americas) provide evidence (when the first Africans were brought as servants to what later became the United States) to the latter half of the twentieth century. The list that follows is similar to earlier lists but without a sequencing of dates. Since many of the forms overlap, to rigidly confine forms by particular time periods might not always be helpful. A brief explanation of each form follows this list.[3]

1. *Slave verbalizations or utterances.* These include African chants, moans, field hollers, cries for deliverance, and work songs.
2. *Spirituals.* These include "folk songs of faith," sorrow songs, jubilees.
3. *Improvised hymnic forms.* These include plantation hymns, and lined-out or metered hymns ("Dr. Watts's" Hymns).
4. *From (Urban) Blues to African American Gospel Songs.* These are songs that express the faith experiences of individual composers. The performance style encourages total group participation—a practice that is basic to African American music for worship.

Slave Verbalizations or Utterances

Songs in the first category (slave utterances, moans, chants, etc.) were often described as mournful wails and expressions of sorrow evoked by the horrid conditions of slavery. These songs are the earliest evidence of "work songs" honed in connection with different occupations including domestic chores and field labor, a process clearly of African origin. Herein was the foundation for subsequent forms that allowed the community to join in with someone's single musical or textual idea and "hammer it out" until a folk song was born. In such creative communities, no one person could claim authorship.

Spirituals

According to historical records, both oral and written, spirituals are considered the first distinctive African American religious music. Some scholars have identified as many as six thousand spirituals, some of which have similar stanzas, phrases, and metaphors. In keeping with the African primal worldviews, no clear lines of demarcation between "sacred" and "secular" are drawn. We have sufficient indication by African sociologists and theologians that African peoples are by nature religious. Thus, black religious music includes what the Western tradition refers to as "secular" elements: rhythmical complexities, overlapping of leader and chorus, improvisation, percussive bodily movement (dance), and extended repetition of short phrases. The objections raised by early Euro-American observers attest to the fact that these African characteristics persisted especially during worship.

Improvised Hymnic Forms

Africans in America, both enslaved and free, listened with an improvisational ear to music they heard in worship with Euro-Americans. Historical records indicate the involvement of African Americans in the singing of "lined-out psalms" first in settings with Euro-American worshipers, and ultimately in their own worshiping space (identified later as the "Invisible Institution"). Slaves could identify with the call-and-response style of singing led by a "precentor" or song leader who lined out the song one verse at a time. This was followed by the surging-in of the congregation with a variety of slow, droning melodies, often creating a cacophony of sounds, until the precentor reentered with the line of another verse. From the beginning of this exposure, it appears that African Americans freely embellished the leader's melodies and provided new variations suitable to their own understanding of the faith. Such improvisational techniques helped create community and provided a depth of spirituality that cannot be described in words. This also accounts for the numerous hymns common to many denominational traditions that employ similar African American improvisational techniques.

Among the earliest extant records of the importance of psalm singing among early African Americans is the handwritten document, "Rules for the Society of Negroes," a society formed in 1693, with the aid of the Puritan minister Cotton Mather.[4] The lining out of psalms with characteristically slow tempos and ornamented melodic lines continued in the shaping of the metered hymns. The earlier reference to "Dr. Watts" is an indication of the preference for the psalms and hymns of Isaac Watts, which were easily accessible to the improvised "blackenized" style of African Americans. Although referred to as "meter hymns," the meter signatures were essentialy ignored and hymn tunes were modified to a free-flowing, nonmetrical, a cappella, call-and-response presentation. This helped to create a communally unified spirituality, enhanced by an emotive reflection on the text in the light of their existential situation.

From (Urban) Blues to African American Gospel Songs

Africans in America were, from the beginning, talented as instrumentalists (keyboard, string, and wind), and contributed greatly to the evolution of distinctive African American sacred forms.[5] An example is the incorporation of the keyboard techniques of ragtime and jazz with vocal urban blues. These forms helped in the shaping of African American gospel music.

Just as Euro-American gospel hymnody was created in rapidly growing urban communities during the period of the revival movement of the 1850s, black gospel was born as an urban religious form and style. African Americans not only helped shape white gospel music, with unique styles of personal testimonies in song, but they also participated in the spread of this new genre. Acknowledging the influence of hymns by Charles S. Tindley, the Methodist minister Thomas Dorsey is credited with establishing black gospel music during the 1920s. Throughout the twenties and thirties, gospel music developed further as a distinctive genre. Dorsey is also credited with being the first person to apply the term "gospel song" to this distinctive form of music and provided other elements that contributed to the development of different kinds of black gospel.

Black gospel music was, at its inception, a liturgical music, despite its seemingly secular undertones. Early in its history, gospel music was also "performed" outside of the liturgical setting in sacred-music concerts, with male and female quartet singers, with and without accompaniment. Scholars of this genre classify these songs, known as traditional gospel songs, according to their tempos or without rhythm in the tradition of the long-meter hymns. The slower the song, the more extensive the melodic embellishments; the faster the song, the greater the amount of syncopation.

During the 1950s, traditional black gospel retained its deeply emotional character but became more sophisticated with the change in the nature and quality of keyboard accompaniment. A "big gospel sound" emerged under the influence of Edwin Hawkins, with many proponents of this style still apparent. Duke Ellington affirmed the liturgical use of jazz in worship, adding a new dimension to "sacred and secular" while retaining a vital link with the African heritage. While his efforts were not totally new, Ellington facilitated the growing movement toward making music for worship relevant to the times and to the life of the faith community.

With a continual overlapping of developments, the close of the twentieth century perhaps represents the peak of what many designate as the "contemporary gospel music era." This music is strongly identified by intricate harmonies and rapid chord progressions, which provide the foundation for texts that describe encounters with the divine and hope in the midst of a computerized, instant-gratification age. Such expressions are becoming more and more at home in the liturgies of many African American congregations. While "gospel rap" emerged in the late 1980s as a relevant means of reaching youth, its association with a more "profane" means of communication has prevented it from gaining total acceptance as a liturgical form.

AFRICAN AMERICAN HERITAGE OF THE UNITED CHURCH OF CHRIST

African Americans became members of Congregational and Christian churches at varying points in their sociological journeys and continue to become part of the United Church of Christ, variously aware of their African American musical heritage. This history had its earliest beginnings in black Congregational churches in the South through the home missionary work of the American Missionary Association (AMA). We are indebted to the schools established by the AMA for helping to keep black music alive and for creating an environment in which black composers could explore their creative gifts. The first AMA school in the South for African Americans was opened near Hampton, Virginia, in 1861; it later became the world-famous Hampton Institute. Among the early teachers at Hampton was the acclaimed musician, composer, and choral director R. Nathaniel Dett. In addition to Hampton, many schools established under the leadership of AMA with music departments and/or well-known choirs still exist with the intent of keeping the African American music tradition alive; these are Howard University, Talladega College, Fisk University, LeMoyne-Owen College, Huston-Tillotson College, and Dillard University.[9] One musical prodigy of the UCC who attended these institutions and has contributed greatly to published African American musical histories is Dr. Hildred Roach, who makes this observation:

> The future of Afro American Music is supported by its past, and depends upon this heritage for its future survival. . . . Black composers have practiced their music in many types of compositions and philosophies, only now commanding the just respect which they deserve. Perhaps this knowledge of the past, this completeness of characteristic styles and a forward movement will guarantee an acceptance of individual talents, forms and ideas, and will render a new performance for tomorrow.

The New Century Hymnal takes a giant step forward in supporting African American contributions by sharing a wide sampling from the vast repertoire of songs with the whole body of Christ. There are enough selections to accommodate various parts of the liturgy throughout the church year. Following is an overview of the hymns and music with African American origins. (Two appendixes at the end of this article supplement the hymns cited in two categories with examples too numerous to cover.)

AFRICAN AMERICAN SPIRITUALS

The New Century Hymnal contains twenty-nine African American spirituals, some of which are identified as "traditional," a rather nebulous category used especially by early hymnal compilers when there was some question about a song's origin or genre. The committee's careful choices of spirituals allow for a more than adequate range of styles: from slow and somber, such as "There Is a Balm in Gilead" (hymn 553), "Over My Head" (hymn 514), and "When Israel Was in Egypt's Land" (hymn 572), to those with aggressive drive and enthusiasm, such as "Every Time I Feel the Spirit" (hymn 282) and "I'm So Glad, Jesus Lifted Me" (hymn 474).

It does not take long for worshipers to realize the hope and depth of spirituality evoked when spirituals are sung by the congregation. This should not prevent the occasional use of solo performances, but corporate a cappella singing deserves to be encouraged. This, after all, is the way that folk songs are created. Helping worshipers gain some understanding of the historical situation out of which these songs arose and their function, in many instances, as coded messages for the community can further enhance appreciation and respect for this unique song form.

The large number of spirituals included here also helps situate them as the first genre of religious music for worship. Worshipers who are not familiar with spirituals should be alerted to the fact that "clapping," "stomping," and other demonstrative physical actions are not automatically assumed to be the normative performance style of all black music. Many spirituals, for instance, evolved out of the depth of soulful experiences that may have been contemplative and deeply emotional, thus requiring a similar style of performance.

Excellent arrangements of spirituals in *The New Century Hymnal* are provided by African American musicians who served on the hymnal committee (Joyce Finch Johnson of Spelman College, Atlanta, and Jeffrey Radford of Trinity United Church of Christ, Chicago) as well as others, all of whom have life experiences and involvement with music for worship in general and African American worshiping congregations in particular. As these arrangements are used, congregations should keep in mind that "the spirituals are open to a continuing process of becoming." Thus, it is natural that they might take the shape of the local worshiping community. This concept, properly understood, will strengthen the community's faith and contribute to the unifying and bonding of the people.[1] (For a complete list of African American spirituals included in *The New Century Hymnal*, refer to Appendix A at the end of this essay.)

JUBILEE SONGS

One of the early genres of African American music is the "jubilee song," represented in *The New Century Hymnal* by "Christ Rose Up from the Dead" (hymn 239). This song is from the National Jubilee Melodies of the National Baptist Convention and is especially appropriate for Easter.

GOSPEL SONGS

The black gospel songs included in *The New Century Hymnal* provide an excellent sampling of styles from each of the gospel eras. Congregations will sing their way into the new century with examples of gospel "classics" from Charles A. Tindley, whose music inspired Thomas Dorsey, the "father of black gospel music," to Andraé Crouch and Kirk Franklin, respected representatives of contemporary gospel. (For a complete list of black gospel songs included in the hymnal, see Appendix B at the end of this essay.)

TUNES BY AFRICAN AMERICAN COMPOSERS AS SETTINGS FOR WORDS BY EURO-AMERICANS

Perhaps one of the most familiar melodies in the repertoire of congregational hymnody is MCKEE, the African American tune used for "In Christ There Is No East or West" (hymn 394). Harry T. Burleigh, the African American musician who introduced Czech composer Antonín Dvorák (1841–1904) to black spirituals, named this tune (which he arranged) "McKee," after one of his teachers at the Eastman School of Music.

The tunes by Eugene Hancock (HANCOCK, hymn 462) and David Hurd (MIGHTY SAVIOR, hymn 93; WATER OF BAPTISM, hymn 169; ST. ANDREW, hymn 171; and JULION, hymn 356) are excellent examples of contributions by late-twentieth-century American composers who have earned their reputations as fine church musicians.

HYMN TEXTS AND MUSIC BY TWENTIETH-CENTURY AFRICAN AMERICANS

Each of the songs in this category reflects the poetic and musical genius of African Americans whose faith journeys will inspire worshipers to greater spiritual depths. Most of the selections are hymns with both words and music by the same (or a related) African American writer. The musical styles range from the contemporary gospel sound of Robert J. Fryson ("Glorious Is Your Name, O Jesus," hymn 53) and Leon C. Roberts ("Jesus Is Here Right Now," hymn 348), to echoes of the spiritual tradition by Donald Swift ("See the Little Baby," hymn 147), to the jazz heritage of Duke Ellington ("Savior God Above," hymn 602). In a category by itself is "Lift Every Voice and Sing" (hymn 593), a song that speaks not only to those who will remember its significance as the "Negro National Anthem" but to all who lift their voices in praise to almighty God.

Two hymns with texts by African American writers also deserve mention here. The late Howard Thurman is one of the greatest mystic theologians and writers who ever lived. One of his poems, paraphrased and set to music by UCC minister Jim Strathdee, enables worshipers to experience Thurman's vision firsthand. That song, "I Am the Light of the World" (hymn 584), in a contemporary pop style, is already familiar to a number of UCC congregations since it previously appeared in *The Hymnal of the United Church of Christ* (1974). Another twentieth-century scholar and writer is C. Eric Lincoln, whose text "How Like a Gentle Spirit" (hymn 443) offers profound reflections on the power of God to transcend all human fears and pretensions.

ARRANGEMENT OF A TRADITIONAL EURO-AMERICAN HYMN

"Blessed Quietness" (hymn 284) provides an example of the instrumental improvisatory gift of African Americans. This setting, arranged by J. Jefferson Cleveland and Verolga Nix, is similar to many that are regularly sung in black congregations.

SONGS FROM AFRICA

Songs from the global community that are frequently used in worship around the world include the four that appear in *The New Century Hymnal* from Africa and from other African peoples in diaspora. As congregations sing these songs, they will be reminded that music from a variety of cultures helps the people of God understand the breadth of God's mercy and the graciousness of God, who incorporates all people into the body of Christ. Three songs from South Africa include "Thuma Mina" (hymn 360), "We Shall Not Give Up the Fight" (hymn 437), and "Siyahamb' ekukhanyen' kwenkhos'" (hymn 526). A Ghanaian folk song provides the melody for "Jesu, Jesu, Fill Us with Your Love" (hymn 498). A final example from the global category is the lively Jamaican tune featured with "Let Us Talents and Tongues Employ" (hymn 347).

NOTES

1. Olaudah Equiano, *The Interesting Narrative in the life of Olaudah Equiano, or Gustavus Vasa the African* (London, 1789), 105.

2. See especially the description of African singing in Portugal, c. 1445 in Gomes Eannes de Zurara, *The Chronicles of the Discovery and Conquest of Guinea*, trans. C. R. Beazley and E. Prestage (London: Hakluyt Society, 1896–1897), 1: 81.

3. For an approximate dating of these forms, see Wyatt T. Walker, *"Somebody's Calling My Name:" Black Sacred Music and Social Change* (Valley Forge, Pa.: Judson Press, 1979), 74; Melva Wilson Costen, *African American Christian Worship* (Nashville: Abingdon Press, 1993), 95. Detailed accounts are provided by Eileen Southern, *The Music of Black Americans: A History*, 2d ed. (New York: W. W. Norton, 1983), and Dena J. Epstein, *Sinful Tunes and Spirituals* (Chicago: University of Illinois Press, 1977).

4. See Costen, *African American Christian Worship*, 142–43.

5. See especially documentation provided by Southern, *The Music of Black Americans*, 27–30.

6. Ibid., 452.

7. For more details, see ibid., 461–74; Horace Clarence Boyer, *How Sweet the Sound: The Golden Age of Gospel* (Washington, D.C.: Elliot & Clark, 1995); and Bernice Johnson Reagon, *We'll Understand It Better By and By: Pioneering African American Gospel Composers* (Washington, D.C.: Smithsonian Institution Press, 1993).

8. We are indebted to the research and publications that have been helpful in this data-gathering process. See J. Stanley Taylor, *A History of Black Congregational Christian Churches of the South* (New York: United Church Press, 1978), and A. Knighton Stanley, *The Children Is Crying: Congregationalism among Black People* (New York: The Pilgrim Press, 1979).

9. Many other institutions that are now closed but which contributed greatly to the maintenance of African American music traditions include Lincoln Academy (Kings Mountain, N.C.), especially through the works and publications of Dr. Hildred Roach, a member of Peoples Congregational Church, Washington, D.C.

10. Hildred Roach, *Black American Music: Past and Present*, 2d ed. (Malabar, Fla.: Krieger, 1992), 219.

11. Costen, *African American Christian Worship*, 97.

APPENDIX A: AFRICAN AMERICAN SPIRITUALS

- 2 Glory, Glory, Hallelujah (arr. Joyce Finch Johnson)
- 75 Lord, Make Me More Holy
- 85 Jesus, Oh, What a Wonderful Child (arr. Jeffrey Radford)
- 154 Go Tell It on the Mountain
- 161 Amen, Amen, Amen [See the Baby] (arr. Nelsie Thompson)
- 229 Were You There
- 282 Every Time I Feel the Spirit
- 310 It's the Old Ship of Zion
- 322 Take Me to the Water (arr. Jeffrey Radford)
- 330 Let Us Break Bread Together (harm. David Hurd)
- 369 Keep Your Lamps Trimmed and Burning

409 I Heard My Mother Say [Give Me Jesus] (arr. Joyce Finch Johnson)
416 I Will Trust in the Lord (arr. Jeffrey Radford)
454 Lord, I Want to Be a Christian
474 I'm So Glad, Jesus Lifted Me
478 I've Got Peace Like a River
490 I Want Jesus to Go with Me (harm J. Jefferson Cleveland and Verolga Nix)
497 Guide My Feet (arr. Joyce Finch Johnson)
500 We Are Climbing Jacob's Ladder
511 I Love My God, Who Heard My Cry (arr. Richard Smallwood)
514 Over My Head (arr. J. Jefferson Cleveland and Verolga Nix)
519 Not My Brother, nor My Sister [It's Me, O Lord]
524 This Little Light of Mine / This Joy I Have (arr. Jeffrey Radford)
525 This Little Light of Mine (adapt. William Farley Smith)
553 There Is a Balm in Gilead
572 When Israel Was in Egypt's Land [Go Down, Moses]
599 Steal Away
602 We Shall Overcome (harm. J. Jefferson Cleveland)
604 Hush, Hush, Somebody's Calling My Name (arr. Jeffrey Radford)
616 I Want to Be Ready (J. Jefferson Cleveland and Verolga Nix)

APPENDIX B: BLACK GOSPEL SONGS

 14 How Can I Say Thanks [To God Be the Glory] (Andraé Crouch)
 41 I Thank You Jesus (Kenneth Morris)
188 Give Me a Clean Heart (Margaret Douroux)
288 Let It Breathe on Me (Magnolia Lewis Butts)
293 Sweet, Sweet Spirit (Doris Akers)
405 There Are Some Things [Yes, God Is Real] (Kenneth Morris)
444 We Are Often Tossed and Driven [We'll Understand It Better] (Charles Albert Tindley)
447 Beams of Heaven As I Go (Charles Albert Tindley)
472 Precious Lord (Thomas A. Dorsey)
482 I Will Lift the Cloud of Night (Charles P. Jones)
523 Someone Asked the Question [Why We Sing] (Kirk Franklin)

A Brief Survey of Asian Indigenous Hymnody

Swee Hong Lim

HISTORICAL OVERVIEW

Consisting of continental land masses as well as islands, Asia is among the most diverse and populous regions in the world. In addition, the region can claim as its own three of the five existing musical systems: the Chinese, the Indian, and the Indonesian. And if we consider the Middle East as a part of Asia, it would lay claim to the fourth musical system, the Persian.

Asia also contains diverse peoples with numerous languages, cultural traditions, and religious traditions. From the practice of animistic beliefs to that of worshiping gods and goddesses, Asia has shown itself to be a region where the people are deeply religious. Asia is the cradle of numerous world religions, among them Hinduism, Buddhism, and Taoism. Religion in Asia is not merely a set of beliefs to be embraced or discarded when it has served its purpose, but rather it is life-encompassing from birth until death and beyond. To forsake one's faith for another can often result in the severing of family ties and even the consequent loss of one's life!

The arrival of Western explorers and missionaries, from as early as 635 C.E. to as late as the 1890s, was to affect irreversibly the ways in which Asians live their lives and practice their beliefs. First, the process of colonization destroyed many of Asia's traditional practices. Second, the conquerors and their ways were seen as superior and worthy of imitation. This perception was to have profound impact on the understanding of the Christian faith and its hymnody as taught by the Western Christian missionaries. Therefore, it is not surprising that even today, many Asians resist Christianity, seeing it as a Western religion bent on wiping out their culture, indigenous religious beliefs, and practices. At the other end of the spectrum, Asians who become Christians continue to shun their own cultural tradition as being an unsuitable medium to carry the Christian gospel, preferring to hold on to what the missionaries taught them.

In most Asian churches, 90 percent of all hymns used in worship settings have their origin in the West. In countries like Singapore and Malaysia, where the use of the English language is prevalent in churches, the percentage is even higher. There are exceptions, though. Some churches in India and a few rural churches in Thailand and Indonesia have developed and are using indigenous hymnody; but these are few and far between.

What, then, is the place of indigenous Asian hymnody in the midst of this reality in Asia? In order to answer this question, we must look to the

1960s. This was a decade of great change for the world; but, more importantly, it witnessed the birth of the indigenous Asian hymnody movement.

INDIGENOUS HYMNODY MOVEMENT

In 1964, the East Asia Christian Conference (EACC) approved the publication of the first Asian hymnal. It was edited by a Sri Lankan theologian and poet, D. T. Niles, who was ably assisted by John Kelley, an American missionary. Niles's pioneering effort in promoting indigenous Asian hymnody received a cool response from the local churches in contrast to its widespread acceptance in ecumenical Christian circles. Although both good and bad have been said of this hymnal, it did succeed in bringing together indigenous Asian Christian hymns, making them accessible to the English-speaking world for the very first time.

This hymnal contained approximately 97 Asian hymns and 103 Western hymns. Many of the Asian hymns were adapted and arranged for accessibility with little regard for their indigenous musical styles or character. Despite its Western slant, the EACC hymnal failed to curb the continued thirst of Asian Christians for Western hymnody. It also failed to receive the necessary support to become a new voice for the local church. Unfortunately, Niles did not see within his lifetime a wide acceptance of his effort in Asian hymnody. On the other hand, the EACC hymnal did gain much acceptance in the ecumenical Christian quarter and thus paved the way for the development of indigenous Asian hymns.

D. T. Niles is represented in *The New Century Hymnal* by only one entry, an English translation of an original Filipino hymn, "O God in Heaven" (hymn 279).

It was not until the 1980s that the state of indigenous Asian hymnody began to improve. This came about through the work of I-to Loh. Through his untiring efforts of writing, editing, and publishing articles, making presentations at important church conferences, embarking on research trips, and recruiting students from all over Asia, the development of indigenous hymnody was advanced.

Two hymns that offer worshipers a sample of I-to Loh's wide-ranging expertise are the harmonization of the Taiwanese hymn "God Created Heaven and Earth" (hymn 33) and the phonetic transcription of the Japanese text "Sekai no Tomo" (hymn 72). Both of these are fine examples of indigenous Asian melodies adapted as tune settings.

I-to Loh's effort was further strengthened by the establishment of an institution, the Asian Institute for Liturgy and Music in the Philippines. Founded by Dr. Francisco Feliciano and Father Chandley of Saint Andrew's Seminary, Manila, it is significant in the life of the church in Asia because it provided an avenue for training musicians who could contribute significantly to the development of indigenous worship and music.

By 1989, a trial Asian hymnal edition was printed and distributed. This hymnal, *Sound the Bamboo*, published by the Christian Conference of Asia (CCA) in 1990, contains 280 hymns from twenty-two Asian and Pacific countries. This project represents a tangible effort by Asian artists to provide a voice for the Asian Church to sing its own unique praise to the one God whom all Christians worship. It is still too early to assess the success of this hymnal but in the writer's observation, the CCA hymnal has become a landmark in the development of indigenous Asian hymnody. Through its publication and forthcoming revision, it serves as an important avenue for composers and poets to express their Christian faith tangibly with local congregations. *Sound the Bamboo* has become a resource for recent denominational hymnals in the United States, including *The New Century Hymnal*, which includes eight songs from it (hymns 5, 72, 97, 141, 142, 317, 424).

By the same token, the work of the Samba Likhaan (which now includes the Asian Institute for Liturgy and Music) remains equally crucial. It is through this institution that training is made available to many who would assume positions of leadership in churches in Asia. Apart from training people for ministry, the Samba Likhaan helps further to promote the development of indigenous Asian church music through its research and publication efforts.

A composer and ethnomusicologist from the Philippines, Verne de la Peña, has contributed a number of arrangements based on indigenous musical traditions to *The New Century Hymnal*. (See especially MANGLAKAT, hymn 42; DANDANSOY, hymn 615; and the original tune EULOGIA, hymn 217.)

The move toward an indigenous hymnodic tradition is not limited to the Philippines alone. In northeastern Thailand, the Isaan Community churches were established in Udon Thani by a U.S. missionary assisted by Ruth and Inchai Srisuwan. This community is unique in its reliance on its own indigenous roots in expressing its Christian faith. It is through this community that the Institute for Faith and Culture was established. Its mission is to enable Thais to worship God within Thailand's cultural and traditional context. Inchai and Ruth Srisuwan are presently based in Bangkok and have embarked on the vision to create such faith communities all over Thailand. For now, indigenous-styled churches are being planted in northern, central, and southern Thailand. Naturally, a great number of indigenous Thai hymns have come from the efforts of the Srisuwans and their colaborers in the field.

In Indonesia, Sekolah Tinggi Teologi Jakarta is an organization similar to the Samba Likhaan. Like its counterpart, this school has been pushing actively for the development of indigenous Indonesian hymnody. Its staff creates new hymns and provides training for budding composers and poets. I am also aware of a project that is being planned by the Samba Likhaan in cooperation with Sekolah Tinggi Teologi to further the cause of indigenous Indonesian church music through a faculty exchange program. In Bali, Nyoman Darsane, a well-known artist, has done significant work in integrating the Indonesian folk-dance drama with the Christian gospel. His particular community, similar to the Isaan Community, has also begun to draw from its cultural roots to express its faith in worship.

In the countries of Japan, Taiwan, and Korea, adaptation of folk songs with Christian texts as well as the creation of new hymns have begun to bear fruit. The people are becoming more aware of using their heritage to express their worship. Two hymn tunes based on traditional Chinese melodies are TŌA-SĪA (hymn 33) and LE P'ING (hymn 470). Contributions from Japanese folk sources are SAKURA (hymn 5) and TOKYO (hymn 72).

Despite this growing acceptance of indigenous hymnody, resistance among more-conservative denominations is still strong due to the perception that indigenous hymnody draws its musical resources from "controversial" sources such as Buddhism or Confucianism. On the contrary, much of today's indigenous music has as its source traditional and folk music that are generally neutral and have no religious roots. In Taiwan, where I-to Loh is currently based, the Tainan Theological Seminary is playing an active role similar to that of the Samba Likhaan in promoting the growth of indigenous church music through training, research, and publication.

Chuang Chun Jung, a Tayal tribe member, is also a well-known personality in the Taiwanese church-music scene. Previously, it was thought that the Tayal tribe had no musical instruments. But in 1992, at the Ecumenical Seminar on Worship and Music, held in Manila, he announced the discovery of a four-note xylophone that was used in his tribe, and which he subsequently named "ta-tung." He has taught at Yu Shan Theological College in Hualien, training other indigenous people in the work of recovering their traditions to aid in transmitting the gospel.

With its use of English as the language of administration, the church in Singapore has used primarily Western hymnody, but there is a slow and steady realization that the church needs to be contextual in its expression of worship. Many hope that an indigenous hymnody movement will soon take root. This need was felt most acutely by the Methodist Church, and much of the impetus to find such a movement can be attributed to the 1991 World Methodist Conference, held in Singapore. My own efforts since then to create indigenous hymns have been viewed favorably by the pastors of the Trinity Annual Conference. With the establishment of the Methodist School of Music, the vision of having a ready pool of musicians who are skilled in both Western and Asian church music is even closer to reaching fruition.

"Down under" in New Zealand, Australia, and the Pacific Islands, there is also a move toward indigenous hymnody. Christian hymnwriters like Shirley Erena Murray (the author of numerous contemporary texts in *The New Century Hymnal*), Colin Gibson (a composer who collaborates frequently with Murray), and Jim Minchin have contributed greatly to the advancement of local hymnody.

The movement for indigenous hymnody clearly has its strongest support in the Indian subcontinent. This can be seen in the large number of indigenous Christian hymns that were composed before the 1960s. However, some Christian factions in the subcontinent are uncomfortable with the indigenous hymnody movement because it uses a musical system that is also used by Hinduism. They continue to strive for differentiation by being more "sophisticated" or Western. This attitude is most often reflected in those churches that are more urbanized or financially superior. Unfortunately, this sense of wanting to be more sophisticated is not limited to the Indian subcontinent but affects the whole of Asia. It is generally observed that churches in urban Asia tend to be more Western-oriented and less open to the development of an indigenous hymnody movement than those in rural settings.

STAGES OF DEVELOPMENT

This essay so far has attested to some form of an indigenous hymnody movement in Asia. The fundamental question that must now be addressed is whether there is one common movement with different stages or a multitude of movements. Here I would like to propose that in dealing with Asian hymnody, one must always bear in mind its diversity and the fact that any attempt to generalize would remain, at best, an attempt. But I also maintain that this movement toward an indigenous Asian hymnody is one that manifests itself in several stages. (I am indebted to I-to Loh for his classification of the four different stages of development in Asian hymnody.)

Translation and Transplantation

This stage refers to the use of hymns from outside cultures without any attempt to ensure that the hymns are relevant in the context of a particular native culture. Examples include the use of carols referring to snowfall at Christmas—which in most parts of Asia and the Pacific Rim, including Australia and New Zealand, would be quite a miraculous event.

A minimal way of accommodating the receiving culture is the translation of hymn texts into a local language. However, such attempts may fail to take into account the tonal inflection of the local language—a distinctive feature of many languages spoken in Asia. As such, it is possible to sing about Jesus as "coconut tree" or "wild animal" if one just translates the text without taking into consideration the relationship between tonal inflection and the melodic line.

It is also interesting to note that while most Asian cultures do not emphasize harmony, a great number of hymns in this genre exhibit the usual four-part Western harmonization. Alternatively, the indigenous melody is often given a major-minor tonality without due consideration of the hymn's origin and inherent idiom. One major consideration is whether the translation and subsequently transplanted hymn can be sung with integrity in that cultural context to express one's faith. Nonetheless, the bulk of Asian hymnody is of this genre. The reason for this is the perception that Asian culture cannot proclaim the Christian gospel without being syncretistic.

Acculturation

Anscar J. Chupungo, a Filipino theologian, used the term "acculturation," together with "inculturation," to discuss the adaptation of the liturgy to a particular cultural context, with special reference to the Roman Catholic liturgical tradition. In an acculturated hymn, we are concerned with how well its Western roots are adapted or modified to better carry God's message in a form that can be easily received by the Asian church. In this instance, a hymn is adapted through the process of being accepted, with modification, by the receiving host. This particular process, however, is not an academic or formal exercise instituted by a committee or an individual. Rather, it occurs naturally as the local church attempts to make a particular hymn its own, rendering it capable of expressing the community's faith in worship. Changes in this instance could be the alteration of note pitches, tonality, or even the hymn's foundational musical form.

At the same time, Asian hymns that travel out of their culture will also experience this same process of acculturation. A case in point would be the publication of Indian hymns. In the hymnals I have seen that feature hymns from the Indian subcontinent, very few have attempted to notate Indian hymns with their inherent ornamentation. There are probably many good reasons why this is not done; nevertheless, it is unfortunate, because to sing an Indian melody without its ornamentation is to neglect the inherent character of its roots. One needs to understand that it is the ornamentation that provides the distinctive sound and character of Indian music. Therefore, we at the receiving end should always try to respect the hymn and its given role as a representative from a culture different from our own. Unlike the translation and transplanting phase, acculturation is where the local church takes the first step of transforming by modifying what is not its own and then adopting it as a new song for the church's faith expression.

Inculturation

The term "inculturation" refers to the practice of adapting liturgical texts and hymns from folk tradition or writing new ones in the indigenous style. This particular development is not by any means new to the church; a precedent was set by the early German reformer Martin Luther, who sought to make the Christian faith accessible to believers of his day. Likewise, in the movement toward an indigenous Asian church music, efforts have been undertaken to blend existing traditional or folk tunes with newly composed texts. At the same time, there have also been efforts to combine traditional materials with Western-style or contemporary music-composition techniques. This results basically in hybrid hymns that reflect old traditions imbued with a new message and character through a process of recrafting. The questions that arise here are: To what degree can recrafting be carried out? And how will the uniqueness and authenticity of the given hymn be assessed after this process? In this instance, churches have begun to look deeper within to draw upon resources that better reflect their own local faith experience, while also taking into consideration their standing as modern churches with significant external influences.

Incarnation

The last level of development for an indigenous hymnody is that of an expression of faith that is developed from within.

It is quite common in Southeast Asian countries like Singapore, Malaysia, and Indonesia for people to assume that if you are a Malay, you are a Muslim, or that if you are an Indian, you are a Hindu. People often jump to such conclusions as lifestyles and cultural activities are perceived to be closely tied to religious beliefs. In short, it is believed there is almost no difference between one's race, culture, and religion.

For the Christian, it is different. When one becomes a Christian, one does not lose one's race or culture. Instead, one is transformed by the workings of the Holy Spirit and lives a life informed and guided by the teachings of Jesus Christ. The expressions of the Christian—whether in music, art, or the written word—are thus shaped by this inward transformation. The form is the same, but the essence of the Christian faith is the underlying foundation.

Incarnational hymnody is hymnody that takes the indigenous form of the people, while at the same time preserving the basic tenets of the Christian faith. As such, there will not be uniformity in the liturgy as in the Westernized churches, apart from the common beliefs of all Christians. Rather, it is a level where one's expression is as bold as one's faith in worshiping God, the amazing Creator of all cultures. Though there are very few hymns in this genre, numbers are indeed increasing as the movement toward an indigenous Asian hymnody gains strength over time.

SUMMARY

This essay has described many exciting musical developments occurring in the hymnody of different countries in Asia. One must be aware, however, that in reality these are but small efforts in the midst of an Asia that still holds on to the belief that the hymnody of the West is superior to an indigenous one. Truly, this indigenous movement is dependent on the effort of all peoples throughout this world. Although Western hymnody has been uniting various cultures in the worship of God, I firmly believe that the time has come for Asians to develop their own unique praise for the God of all creation. It is time that we exercise our responsibilities as faithful stewards in developing the gifts and talents that God has given us, so that God's people in Asia can participate more fully in the expression of praise to our Almighty God through hymns. The decision lies with the Asian church to move forward and develop its own hymnody.

What the Christian reader in the West can do is to encourage Asian Christians and the church in Asia to develop indigenous music, prayers, dramas, and dances to glorify God, and to affirm the view that it is acceptable to be different from the Western church even as we worship the same God.

SUGGESTIONS FOR FURTHER READING

Hawn, C. Michael. "Sounds of Bamboo: I-to Loh and the Development of Asian Hymns." *The Hymn*, forthcoming, 1998.

Loh, I-to. "Asian Worship." *The Complete Library of Christian Worship: Vol. 7., The Ministries of Christian Worship.* Edited by Robert Webber. Nashville: Star Song Publishing Group, 1994.

———. "Contemporary Issues in Inculturation, Arts, and Liturgy: Music." *The Hymnology Annual* 3 (1993): 47–56. (Originally published in the *Journal of the Societas Liturgica.*)

———. "Survey of Texts and Musical Styles in *Sound the Bamboo.*" *The Hymnology Annual* 4 (Kingston, N.Y.: Selah Publishing Co., 1997): 26ff. (A paper first presented at the Second WCC Ecumenical Seminar on Liturgy and Music at the Asian Institute for Liturgy and Music, Manila, 1992.)

———. "Toward Contextualization of Church Music in Asia." *The Hymnology Annual* 1 (1991): 89–114. (Originally published in the *Asia Journal of Theology* [April 1989].)

———. "Transmitting Cultural Traditions in Hymnody." *Church Music Workshop: Practical Tools for Effective Music Ministry* 4, no. 3. Edited by Gary Alan Smith. Nashville: UM Publishing, 1994.

A Survey of Hispanic Hymnody as Represented in *The New Century Hymnal*

Raquel Mora Martínez

In the United States beginning in the late 1960s, cultural renewal and reaffirmation swept through the largely Mexican American Southwest and the Caribbean communities of the Northeast and Midwest. In the Southwest, this cultural renaissance centered on the Chicano movement, which called for appreciation and use of the Spanish language along with music, drama, and folk traditions that had been neglected by Mexican Americans. Farmworkers and students organized to demand justice from employers and from schools and universities.

The churches were not exempt from these calls for using language and practices that were among the suppressed traditions, especially in poor and working-class *barrios* (neighborhoods). As clergy and laity in the churches became involved in listening to and supporting the calls for change, they realized that the church had to respond as well. A slow but steady acceptance of diverse forms of liturgy, music, instrumentation, and worship styles began to occur in predominantly Hispanic churches throughout the United States and the Caribbean. This trend has continued. One sign of it is the inclusion of original Hispanic hymnody in English-language denominational hymnals such as *The New Century Hymnal*.

Parallel developments began in the Latin American church about the same time. This is illustrated by the Brazilian theologian Rubem Alves, in talking about his upbringing in the Protestant church in Latin America: "I learned from an imported Protestant Church where I found myself that my Latin American culture was ugly and to be despised; that the true values of life were the American ones (i.e., U.S.). It took me a long time to learn to dance and enjoy the samba because the only thing I knew was how to sing American gospel songs."[1]

This was also true of many Latin American and U.S. Protestants who, because of the nineteenth-century missionary movement (however well-meaning), were encouraged to forget their songs and the use of their instruments and to worship instead with the songs taught by the missionaries. The lack of original congregational hymns and choral anthems was evident until very recently when indigenous Hispanic music began to emerge. Furthermore, the music taught to the masses was from a relatively brief period (1860–1940). It reflected a nineteenth-century pietism and a very narrow theology; there was not much by way of connecting one's faith with one's daily living.

One very important event that helped turn this around was the Second Vatican Council in 1963, convened by Pope John XXIII. Two very important decisions were taken that affected liturgical renewal: First, the people were finally allowed to worship in the vernacular, and second, the church began to identify with the poor and the oppressed. Not only was the opportunity to use the language of the people in liturgy joyously received, but composers immediately saw a need for settings of the Mass in the music of the people as well. The people began to write their own masses, drawing on their daily experiences for inspiration.

CENTRAL AMERICA

One of the more creative responses to the Second Vatican Council was the *Misa Popular Nicaragüense*—the popular mass (one of two Nicaraguan Masses) written in 1968, shortly after the close of the council. It represented members of the community writing their own theology as they understood it through their struggles and the oppression they had suffered. Now they could express their faith in their own language, with their own music; and in so doing, they were keeping their culture alive. The music of the *Misa Popular* was composed by Manuelito Dávila, Angel Cerpas, and Juan Mendoza, using Nicaraguan folk rhythms. This Mass is not to be confused with the *Misa Campesina Nicaragüense* (the Nicaraguan Peasant Mass), written in 1975, which focuses on the "God of the poor," a God who lives among the people, who laughs and suffers with them, who sides with them against their oppressors—a God of justice.

Unlike the *Misa Campesina*, which focuses largely on social justice, the *Misa Popular* hardly makes reference to social conflict. It touches on the theme of "people marching on." "Somos pueblo que camina" (hymn 340), the "canto de entrada" or "entrance song," echoes this theme in the opening line: "We are a people on a journey." The theme of "marching on" is reinforced in two other portions of the Mass as well: the communion song and the sending forth. The union of faith and daily living is another theme that appears in some of the songs in the Mass.

A favorite style of song in the Hispanic community is the *corito* or *estribillo*. Alfredo Colom M. (1904–1971) has made a contribution in this particular area. Born in Quezaltenango, Guatemala, his life was one of contrasts; now a high government official, now a drunkard. He was about to commit suicide when someone offered him a New Testament. After a few years of triumphs and defeats, Alfredo gave his life to Christ in 1940. Even though he did not read music, Alfredo composed many tunes and also wrote many texts, some of which have been translated and published in English.

"Pero queda Cristo" (hymn 88) has the elements of what is considered a *corito*. These are short, four- to six-line songs with simple folk tunes, which may be accompanied on guitar or other instruments as well as with the clapping of the hands. They reflect either praise or one's personal faith and commitment. While they are sometimes sung as the people gather for worship, they can also be an integral part of the service, used as acts of worship or during prayer.

SOUTH AMERICA

In Brazil and Argentina, as in most parts of Latin America, most Protestant churches were using primarily hymns from North America and trying to adapt them to the vernacular form. That is, they were trying to sing the hymns to the indigenous rhythms, a very difficult task for the congregation.

Pablo Sosa is another who struggled with this problem of cultural "identity crisis." Born in 1933 in Chivilcoy, Argentina, he is now an internationally recognized authority and leader in the Hispanic community. After studying theology in Argentina and music in the United States and Germany, Sosa is a professor at the Evangelical Institute of Theological Studies in Buenos Aires, as well as a composer, translator, and author of numerous hymns. He promotes Latin American religious folk songs and has led global workshops on Third World music and liturgy.

Regarding his experiences as a pioneer of indigenous Hispanic music, Sosa relates:

> During 1954, I was traveling to the United States to study music. When I arrived in the U.S., I met Joâo Wilson Faustini, a Brazilian, and together we thought a further step had to be taken in adopting that music we called "ours," Latin American music, in the worship setting. He tried to write verses to "samba" music. He got to half of the samba and said, "It cannot be done! How can we move to this rhythm in church?"[2]

Sosa explains that when he attempted to write English religious words to a *tango,* he arrived at the same conclusion as Faustini: It could not be done. At first, he thought it was impossible because of the gap between the religious and the secular; then he realized that the gap was between the culture from which he had received the gospel (Protestantism) and his own popular culture. Since then, Sosa has been writing religious texts which he has set to indigenous dance tunes, proving once again that God can be praised with the melodies and rhythms of one's own culture. Several of his songs have been published in various hymnals.

Between 1974 and 1990, Sosa edited six volumes of *Cancionero Abierto* (*Open Songster*); they were published by the School of Music at ISEDET, the theological seminary in Buenos Aires. These songbooks contain some of the best original material from different Latin American countries and reflect the folk origins of the music with a variety of dances and rhythms. Several of the songs in *Cancionero Abierto* have found their way into the more recent denominational hymnals, including *The New Century Hymnal*.

"Este es el día" (hymn 65) is one of several hymns by Sosa that first appeared in *Cancionero Abierto*. The composer explains that he wrote this song as an opening hymn for an event at ISEDET. The song consists of only four notes (C, E, F, A), which he says is intentional. Some of his other music is based on five notes (the pentatonic scale), which is used in the Andean region (north of Argentina, Bolivia, Peru, and Ecuador). The style of the refrain is that of a *baguala,* identified by the repetition of the interval of a fifth. In the original version, the left-hand accompaniment in the refrain has more movement, adding to the feeling of a dance.

"Si fui motivo de dolor, oh Dios" (hymn 544) is another of Sosa's compositions, as well as "¡Cristo Vive!" (hymn 235). The text for this latter song was written by Nicolás Martínez (1917–1972). Martínez was born in Buenos Aires, Argentina, into a Roman Catholic family. He was converted as a youth to evangelical Christianity and studied at the Evangelical Faculty of Theology in Buenos Aires, doing postgraduate work in Puerto Rico. Martínez was ordained by the Disciples of Christ in 1948 and pastored churches in Argentina and Paraguay. He also became active in ecumenical cultural efforts.

The New Century Hymnal includes another song by an Argentinean writer: "Soplo de Dios viviente" (hymn 56), by Osvaldo Catena; it is set to a Norwegian popular tune arranged by Lorraine Floríndez.

A hymn from Bolivia provides a wonderful introduction to the *cueca*, a dance with contrasting meters. "Hoy celebramos con gozo al Dios" (hymn 246) was written by Mortimer Arias, former bishop of Bolivia, and the music was composed by Antonio Auza. This happy song of celebration and thanksgiving invites the participant to dance; the use of tambourines, claves, drums, or simple body movement is most appropriate.

SOUTHWESTERN UNITED STATES AND MEXICO

The border area between the United States and Mexico has given rise to rhythms and themes that have enriched the church on both sides of the border. An influential composer in the Southwestern United States has been Carlos Rosas (b. 1939). An author and composer, Rosas was born in Linares, Mexico. He entered the Monterrey Seminary, where he studied music and liturgy for seven years. He moved to San Antonio, Texas, where for several years he worked with the Mexican American Cultural Center, teaching courses in liturgical music and Mexican culture.

Rosas has produced a repertoire of easy-to-sing authentic Mexican American music for special needs in the Hispanic community, such as weddings, funerals, baptisms, *quinceañera* celebrations, and the like, as well as music for the Christian year. He feels that music should be used in the building of God's dominion, that it should awaken us to fight the injustices committed in the community, and that it should reflect our calling to live, to share, and to serve in the community. Some of Rosas's songs reflect this struggle for justice. There are two experiences, Rosas adds, that inspire his music: biblical reflection and liturgical celebration. He says "the two go together, feeding and enhancing one another." Rosas feels that not only should liturgy be celebrated in the language of the people, it should also reflect their culture.

Rosas's "Cantemos al Creador" (hymn 39) is, according to the author, the result of years of biblical reflection. The beauty of nature, he explains, has always inspired him. Pondering over God's creation and greatness led him to write this song, one of his favorites, which has been included in several hymnals. It was first published in 1976 by Resources Publications of San Jose, California, in a collection entitled *Diez Canciones Para la Misa*. It is widely used as a meditation song after a biblical reading, and can also be very effective as a processional hymn, when performed with hand-clapping in the following manner: Swing your arms high to the left during the first 2 beats of the measure. Clap on beats 3 and 4. Lower arms on beats 5 and 6. Repeat same pattern in next measure, this time swinging your arms to the right. This may be accompanied by a guitar and a tambourine accenting on the clapped beats 3 and 4. Some of Rosas's other compositions include three collections of liturgical songs: *Con Cinco Panes* (liturgical songs selected for the Papal Mass); *Rosas del Tepeyac* (collection of songs with liturgical dance—Aztec dance during the Gloria and a Mexican dance during the offertory); and *La Semana Santa* (collection of liturgical songs for Holy Week).

Another Mexican author and composer who has left his mark in the history of Hispanic church music and liturgy is Skinner Chávez-Melo (1944–1992). Chávez-Melo was born in Mexico City on November 17, 1944. He was educated in New York City at the Union Theological Seminary, the Juilliard School, and Manhattan School of Music, and in England at the Royal School of Church Music.

Among his many responsibilities, Chávez-Melo served as organist-choirmaster at Union Theological Seminary and as music director and organist at the Church of the Intercession (Episcopal), where during his six-year tenure he built a multiple choir program and a concert series. He was the editor of *Albricias* (1987), a thirty-eight-hymn resource sponsored by the National Hispanic Office of the Episcopal Church; *Songs of Hope and Peace*, published by the United Church of Christ (1987); and the Episcopal *Spanish Altar Book* (1987).

Chávez-Melo composed the harmonizations for four Spanish hymns that appear in *The New Century Hymnal*: "Toda la tierra" (hymn 121), "Tú has venido a la orilla" (hymn 173), "Una espiga" (hymn 338), and "Sois la semilla" (hymn 528). He is also the composer of the original hymn tune RAQUEL, employed as the setting for a contemporary English text, "Hear the Voice of God, So Tender" (hymn 174).

Another Mexican author and composer is Rubén Ruiz Avila (b. 1945), who lives in Puebla, Mexico. In describing the origins of his "Mantos y ramos" (hymn 214), he simply admits that it was composed to fill a need for a song for Palm Sunday. This song has become so popular it has found its way into several mainline denominational hymnals. It makes for a festive processional hymn, especially when dramatized by children waving palm branches as the congregation sings.

"De colores" (hymn 402) is a Mexican secular folk song that has become a favorite among the religious community, especially in the Roman Catholic Church. The original version consists of several stanzas. Additional ones with a religious focus have been added in order to use this song in a worship setting. It is very effective when accompanied by a Mariachi group.

"Pues si vivimos" (hymn 499) is an anonymous folk song from Mexico, with a traditional Spanish tune. The first stanza is based on Romans 14:8 and was translated by Elise S. Eslinger. The original hymn contains three additional stanzas written by Roberto Escamilla, a United Methodist minister currently serving in Texas.

PUERTO RICO

A lively hymnody has characterized the contributions made by Puerto Rican composers. An author and composer who has contributed much to Hispanic hymnody is Pablo Fernández Badillo (b. 1919). Badillo was born in Aguadilla, Puerto Rico, and studied at the Conservatory of Music in his homeland. For several years he was professor of music in the public education department in his native city. He has composed several collections of children's songs and edited what is probably the first Puerto Rican hymnal to contain printed music, the *Himnario Criollo*. Some of Badillo's works are *Albor I* (children's songs), 1969; *Albor II* (school songs), 1972; *Himnario Criollo* (104 hymns, canticles, and responses), 1977; and *Cantar Riqueño* (choral works), 1971.

Badillo's song "Alabanza" (hymn 34), he explains, was written one afternoon in the spring of 1977. He recalls admiring the countryside when he spotted a beautiful red lily. Walking toward it, he took the lily in his hands and observed it quietly, admiring its beauty. This prompted him to take his guitar and begin writing a song inspired by the beautiful flower. As he sang, he simultaneously wrote the text and melody he was improvising. That evening, the Presbyterian church in Montaña was celebrating an anniversary. The pastor's wife, Carmen Lydia Vives, possessing a wonderful musical talent and a spirit of service in the ministry of the church, upon hearing the song, learned it quickly. Mr. Badillo and Carmen Lydia were able to sing the song as a duet that evening, Carmen holding the red lily and Mr. Badillo accompanying with his guitar.

A very important element of Puerto Rico's Christmas celebrations is the *villancico* (Christmas carol). Villancicos are lively songs that gladden the hearts of those who sing or listen to them. Some of the characteristics of a villancico include a simple melody line with few chords (usually a varied sequence of I, IV, V, I), a meter of 2/4 or 6/8, and the use of triplets and syncopation. An example of a villancico is "Los magos que llegaron a Belén" (hymn 155). The notation of the original version uses triplets at the beginning of each system in the stanzas. It may be accompanied by guitar and maracas.

This Christmas or Epiphany hymn, based on Matthew 2:1–12, is appropriate for the celebration of *Las Posadas* (literally "the inns" or "the lodgings"). Las posadas is a custom that originated in Spain but developed in Mexico. It is based on the story of Joseph and Mary attempting to find lodging in Bethlehem. It is widely celebrated in communities where there are strong Hispanic traditions. Every night between December 16 and 24, there is a procession of the "pilgrims" going from door to door seeking shelter. All this takes place through song, the outsiders singing their request for shelter, and the people inside the home singing their response. At the end of the evening, the last home approached opens its doors to the pilgrims and the fiesta begins.

"Pastores a Belén" (hymn 149) is another example of a villancico, with its simple melody line and the use of four chords throughout the song.

Another hymnwriter from Puerto Rico is William Loperena Soto (1935–1996). Father Loperena was born December 14, 1935, in Moca, Puerto Rico. He was raised in Aguadilla, Puerto Rico, where he attended the public elementary schools. He entered the Dominican seminary of San Alberto Magno in Isabela, finishing his studies in 1955. He studied philosophy in Massachusetts and theology in Holland. In addition, he studied music in Brooklyn, New York, and philosophy and law in Washington, D.C. In 1962 he was given his first assignment—the parish at Isabela.

Father Loperena loved to work among the people. Besides being their priest, he was also their friend. He learned from the wisdom of the poor and the humble, and from their culture, folklore, and music. He was a composer and a poet; liturgy attracted him from very early on. In 1968 he composed his *Misa Jíbara* (*Peasant Mass*). His contributions to church music are recognized in Puerto Rico, the United States, and Latin America, not only in Roman Catholic congregations but in Protestant settings as well.

Many of Loperena's songs reflect very lively rhythms, the folk music of his people. "En santa hermandad" (hymn 392), a song of praise to the Trinity, reflects the joy that was evident in Father Loperena's ministry. Another example of his contributions is "Un mandamiento nuevo" (hymn 389), a compelling song of Christian discipleship.

A key figure in recent Protestant sacred music in Puerto Rico is Luis Olivieri (b. 1937). Olivieri is a Baptist minister with a doctorate in sacred music from Boston University Seminary. He currently teaches at the Evangelical Seminary in Hato Rey, Puerto Rico. In 1980, Olivieri published a collection of new music for congregational singing entitled *Himnos y Coros Puertorriqueños* (*Puerto Rican Hymns and Choruses*). He has worked closely with the Puerto Rican Choral Directors Society and has contributed much to church and community through that organization. He has served as member on several hymnal committees (including *The New Century Hymnal*), often simultaneously.

"Cristo es la peña de Horeb" (hymn 45) is one of Olivieri's musical arrangements that has been included in several hymnals; it reflects the rhythms and style in which it is most often performed in his native Puerto Rico.

SPAIN

Some of the most popular Hispanic hymnody in recent years has originated in Spain. One of that country's most prolific liturgical composers was Cesáreo Gabaráin (1936–1991). He was born in Hernani (Guipúzcoa, Basque province), and following his ecclesiastical studies became a parish priest in Antzuola, a small village near his birthplace. In Madrid, Gabaráin worked in pastoral ministry in the parish of Our Lady of Sorrows, giving special attention to music and youth ministries.

Of all the Spanish religious musicians, Gabaráin was the best known internationally. He traveled to several countries including the United States in 1990, where he visited twenty-two cities and directed workshops in religious music sponsored by the Oregon Catholic Press. Gabaráin truly felt that the ministry of music is one of the noblest and most effective ministries in the life of the church. He enjoyed working with youth, causing his pastoral music styles to reflect a modern and youthful tone. Furthermore, he always sought to create texts that would enrich the faith of those who would sing them.

"Tú has venido a la orilla" (hymn 173) is Gabaráin's most famous hymn—a favorite among both Hispanic and English-speaking congregations in the United States and in other countries as well. It is based on the passage in three of the Gospels in which Jesus invites Simon and Andrew to leave their nets behind and follow him. The Spanish text is so rich that English-speaking congregations are encouraged to learn and sing it in the original language. The message is one of hope for those who are experiencing trial and suffering; it is also an invitation to "leave our nets behind" and follow Jesus into service. It is a song of commitment. One manner in which this song has been used is by having a liturgical dancer (perhaps using a fishing net) interpret the story through dance while a soloist or the congregation sings the words. The tempo should be rather slow, with a swaying motion.

Gabaráin's "Una espiga" (hymn 338), "Sois la semilla" (hymn 528), and "Camina, pueblo de Dios" (hymn 614) are also widely known in local congregations and have been included in various denominational hymnals.

CONCLUSION

The last quarter century has been a unique time in the history of Hispanic hymnody and music in the United States, Latin America, and the Caribbean. In some ways, the people who received the gospel through missionary labors are now sharing the same gospel through their melodies and rhythms for the first time. The music traditions so long submerged and unknown are now enriching the worship life of God's people throughout the world. It is refreshing to see original Spanish hymns translated into English when for so long it was the other way around! It is a new day when the Hispanic church can offer to the wider church hymnals such as *Mil Voces Para Celebrar* (United Methodist, 1996), *Cáliz de Bendiciones* (Disciples of Christ, 1996), and other denominational hymnals about to be published. It is a new day in the church!

The new Hispanic and Latin American church music is a gift that enlarges the liturgy of the universal church. It makes the church a community where the miracle of Pentecost can be heard in the many tongues that sing of the one God. As the "Credo Hispano" ("Hispanic Creed") in the Spanish United Methodist Hymnal reads, in part:

> We believe in the Reign of God, the day of the Great Fiesta
> when all the colors of creation will form a harmonious
>   rainbow,
> when all peoples will join in joyful banquet,
> when all tongues of the universe will sing the same song.
> (*Mil Voces Para Celebrar*, pp. 69–70)

May the whole church receive and enjoy this gift from Hispanic Christianity!

NOTES

1. Rubem A. Alves, *Tomorrow's Child* (New York: Harper & Row, 1972), 39.

2. Pablo D. Sosa, ed., *Todas las Voces* (San José, Costa Rica: Ediciones Sebila, 1988), 74.

Twentieth-Century Hymnody in Great Britain

Vernon Wicker

Dramatic developments in hymnody evolved during the twentieth century in Great Britain beginning with *The English Hymnal* (1906), which included the enduring musical contributions of the composer Ralph Vaughan Williams. In the latter half of the century, beginning in the 1960s, hymnwriting activities accelerated with the "hymn explosion," particularly through the work of Fred Pratt Green (b. 1903), Fred Kaan (b. 1929), and Brian Wren (b. 1936). The century has been characterized by significant works, both in texts and music, that have greatly influenced the experience of worshipers in virtually all churches and denominations to the present day.

HISTORICAL CONTEXT

In order to fully understand the sweeping changes affecting English hymnody in the twentieth century it is helpful to review the major developments of the latter part of the nineteenth century—or Victorian Era. The monumental Anglican hymnal, *Hymns Ancient and Modern* [HAM] (1860; Appendix, 1868), provided the broad backdrop for a ground swell of hymnological activity of the period, which included the Oxford movement and the work of such leaders as John Keble and John Henry Newman who reacted against the threatening influence of the Evangelicals on congregational song in the Church of England. The movement was not so much a conscious endeavor against Watts and the Wesleys as it was against the emotional excesses of many later poets and composers, from Dissenting circles as well as from those within the Church of England itself.

The complex situation was compounded when the American evangelist Dwight L. Moody and his musical associate Ira Sankey held countless evangelistic meetings for throngs of people all over Britain starting in the 1870s. Although the informal songs served the purposes of the meetings well, the Anglican Church did not greet their impact with enthusiasm.

Further, at the turn of the century there was a readiness for change—a time marked by the passing of Queen Victoria and her sixty-year reign. Many people had begun to tire of the sentimentality of some of the music in *HAM*, and large numbers were attracted to the hearty singing in evangelistic movements.

HYMNALS OF THE EARLY TWENTIETH CENTURY

At this juncture, the editors of *HAM* produced a new edition in 1904 which gave us Charles V. Stanford's ENGELBERG (hymn 561), originally composed for William W. How's "For All the Saints" and now frequently sung to Fred Pratt Green's "When in Our Music God Is Glorified." It also included a great amount of well-edited plainsong and the revision or replacement of earlier *HAM* translations of Latin hymns. Unfortunately, though, the hymnal was the product of its domineering editor, Walter Howard Frere, a leader interested in moving the Church of England and its music toward its Catholic roots while ridding it of all Victorian sentimentalism.

In the quality of its texts, it reflected the influence of the unique *Yattendon Hymnal* (1899). That earlier collection was edited by poet laureate and amateur musician Robert Seymour Bridges, a leader concerned that the village parish in Yattendon, near Oxford, sing high-quality texts and worthy music. Some of the texts were his own translations of Greek, Latin, and German hymns, and some of the music consisted of four-part, unaccompanied arrangements of old psalm tunes from Genevan and English sources edited by Oxford music professor H. E. Wooldridge.

Another hymnal contribution of this transitional time was *Songs of Syon: A Collection of Psalms, Hymns and Spiritual Songs for Public and Private Use* (1904), edited by George R. Woodward, assisted by Charles Wood. Here the orientation was similar to *HAM* 1904 regarding plainsong, the inclusion of more sixteenth-century continental European material, and the avoidance of most nineteenth-century sources. Two of Woodward's harmonizations from this collection appear in *The New Century Hymnal*: ES FLOG EIN KLEINS WALDVÖGELEIN (hymn 66) and PUER NOBIS NASCITUR (hymn 241), as well as his triumphant text "This Joyful Eastertide" (hymn 232), sung to the Dutch baroque tune VRUECHTEN (hymn 231). *Songs of Syon* received little use in congregations due to Woodward's unusual translations and the beautiful, and therefore expensive, edition. Nonetheless, it has had considerable value as a resource for hymnal editors.

The English Hymnal (1906) and Ralph Vaughan Williams

The final breakthrough of the early twentieth century was *The English Hymnal* (1906), edited by Percy Dearmer (1867–1936). The musical editor was the eminent English symphonic composer Ralph Vaughan Williams (1872–1958). The basis for the hymnal created by this team bears more significance than can be seen superficially. While Dearmer was a crusader for Anglican liturgies and aesthetic quality, he was not at all willing to sacrifice the latter for the former. Dearmer's organist, Martin Shaw (1875–1958), and others even formed the League of Arts, a movement that opposed anything tawdry or vulgar in the culture.[1]

The greatest legacy of *The English Hymnal*, however, is the unique musical contribution of Vaughan Williams. Although an agnostic, he had a respectable knowledge of church music and hymnody and a strong sense of what was singable and what sounded good when sung in unison by a congregation—a sense he nurtured while serving as a composer for the monarchy. This gift is evident in such enduring original tunes as KING'S WESTON (hymns 255, 586), DOWN AMPNEY (hymn 289), and his best known, SINE NOMINE (hymn 299), sung universally to William W. How's text "For All the Saints." Two additional Vaughan Williams hymn tunes worth noting, which are new to a UCC hymnal, are: SALVE FESTA DIES (hymn 262), a grand, sweeping melody written primarily for major Easter, Ascension, or Pentecost processionals, and THE CALL (hymn 331), a simple yet profound setting of the George Herbert text, taken from his *Five Mystical Songs* for baritone, choir, and orchestra, altered somewhat in both text and accompaniment for congregational use. Vaughan Williams also wrote classically beautiful harmonizations to two tunes frequently employed in various hymnals: LASST UNS ERFREUEN (hymns 17, 27) and HYFRYDOL (hymns 182, 257, 355), both of which have become standard settings.

Perhaps the composer's most valuable contribution to church music was his work in finding, choosing, and arranging British folk melodies for use as hymn tunes. These charming, singable melodies well exemplify what the League of Arts believed, "that there was no reason why what was popular should be degenerate." KINGSFOLD (hymn 51) has a long tradition in UCC hymnals as does FOREST GREEN (hymns 110, 434). This latter tune is frequently sung, especially in Britain, to the text "O Little Town of Bethlehem." The beautifully serene French carol melody PICARDY (hymn 345) appears in *The New Century Hymnal* in its traditional pairing with a translation of the fourth-century text from the Liturgy of Saint James, "Let All Mortal Flesh Keep Silence." DANBY (hymn 432) is coupled, as it was in the *Pilgrim Hymnal* (1931), with "'Tis Winter Now; the Fallen Snow," by Samuel Longfellow, brother of the poet Henry Wadsworth. Other hymn tunes derived from folk melodies include the German carol QUEM PASTORES (hymns 123, 510); the thirteenth-century French melody ORIENTIS PARTIBUS (hymn 138), known originally as the "donkey carol" with its folksy text depicting the story of the holy family's flight into Egypt; and KING'S LYNN (hymn 579), set in *The New Century Hymnal* with Shirley Murray's imaginative text "Great God of Earth and Heaven."

Songs of Praise

In an effort to promote the contents of *The English Hymnal*, the team of editors—Dearmer, Vaughan Williams, and Shaw—produced a new hymnal extracted from that source and designed for use in schools, *Songs of Praise* (1925; expanded version 1931). The liturgical material was omitted for that context, but the hymns gave teachers and students high-quality texts and music. Because services were an integral part of school life, young people became well acquainted with the hymns.

At the same time, *Songs of Praise* became "the hymnal used for the regular services broadcast by the BBC. So when hymnals came to be revised, especially those of the denominations least affected by this cultural revolution, their editors were pressed by the young to include what they had learned at school, and by the laity to include what they had heard broadcast."[2] In the hymns themselves as well as in the unavoidable change of purpose in *Songs of Praise*, "hymnody during the first quarter of the century [moved]: from liturgical richness towards aesthetic and intellectual liberalism."[3] This change of focus reflects Dearmer's own spiritual and intellectual journey. Although he moved entirely away from evangelical texts, such as those by Watts or Wesley, he also contributed original works, such as the hymnic gem for Holy Communion, "Draw Us in the Spirit's Tether" (hymn 337). Here, the liturgical context into which the worshiper is placed and the solidly orthodox theology represented are accessible and acceptable to Christians from virtually all denominations and traditions. Dearmer also included the work of poets otherwise unknown as hymnwriters, such as G. K. Chesterton in his "O God of Earth and Altar" (hymn 582), and excellent works by poets whom he commissioned for the occasion.

In a further effort to improve the literary quality of hymns, outstanding devotional poems from the sixteenth and seventeenth centuries were rescued for hymnody. Some examples of these "non-hymnwriters" include Samuel Crossman ("My Song Is Love Unknown," hymn 222) and George Herbert ("Come, My Way," hymn 331).

Finally, numerous respectable musical contributions came to hymnody by way of *Songs of Praise*, among them those by Martin Shaw. Three of these are represented in *The New Century Hymnal*: the adaptation of the traditional English melody, ROYAL OAK (hymn 31); the harmonization of the fifteenth-century French noel, NOËL NOUVELET (hymn 238), which he prepared for the famous *Oxford Book of Carols* (1928); and his original 1929 tune, WESTRIDGE (hymn 113).

The Church Hymnary

During the Roaring Twenties, that somewhat optimistic period between the world wars, there came *The Church Hymnary* (1927). The contributions of musical editor David Evans included the tune CHARTERHOUSE (hymns 212, 429, 527), harmonizations of the charming Finnish tune NYLAND (hymn 390), and the well-known tune SLANE (hymn 451), typically sung, as here, to the eighth-century Irish text "Be Now My Vision."

DEVELOPMENTS AT MIDCENTURY

New hymnic materials from the late 1920s until the early 1950s were rather few. The critically high standards established by Robert Bridges in the *Yattendon Hymnal* (1899) and Percy Dearmer in *The English Hymnal* (1906) and *Songs of Praise* (1925, 1931) seem to have produced in most potential textwriters either an intimidation or a sense that perhaps everything had already been said. Even those writers born at the turn of the century who did make outstanding contributions, Albert Bayly (1901–1984) and Fred Pratt Green (b. 1903), only began writing later in life—Bayly after age forty and Pratt Green after retirement.

Two composers produced new works during this time, although their output was limited. Canon Cyril Taylor (1907–1991), assistant to the head of the BBC's religious broadcasting, wrote SHELDONIAN (hymn 266) in 1951. In 1941 he wrote ABBOT'S LEIGH (hymn 70) to be sung to "Glorious Things of Thee Are Spoken" as a replacement for AUSTRIA (hymn 307), by Franz Joseph Haydn, which was at the time burdened by its association with the text "Deutschland, Deutschland, über alles." The other composer was Eric Thiman (1900–1975), whose tunes and harmonizations have seldom made it across the Atlantic until recently.

Congregational Praise and the Work of Erik Routley

Midcentury arrived with three important hymnals: *Congregational Praise* (1951), *HAM Revised* (1950), and *The BBC Hymn Book* (1951). Each made a unique contribution in the aftermath of World War II, but they contained very little new material. *Congregational Praise*, however, helped lay the groundwork in its vision and process for a good number of hymnals during the following decades.[4] Eric Thiman chaired the music committee, assuming somewhat the role that Martin Shaw had fulfilled for the Church of England, and Erik Routley (1917–1982) was committee secretary. It was here that the work of Routley emerged on a large scale.

As a discerning pastor-theologian, Routley penned vigorous, high-quality hymn texts ("New Songs of Celebration Render"), and composed creative tunes (AUGUSTINE) and inventive harmonizations (e.g., to RENDEZ À DIEU). More important was his overarching vision for a vital congregational singing that would meet the needs of contemporary worshipers while maintaining an essential integrity in theology, texts, and music. His infectiously joyful spirit contributed substantially to the editing of countless hymnals on both sides of the Atlantic, including the ecumenical, multilingual *Cantate Domino* (World Council of Churches, 1974). He wrote more material in English on hymn-related subjects than anyone in his time.[5]

Albert Bayly

A further significant contribution of *Congregational Praise* was the inclusion of texts by Albert Bayly. His practical, theologically solid, and aesthetically pleasing hymns were the product of his multidimensional background, incorporating a layperson's perspective as a shipbuilder, a pastor's sensitivity for theology, and a poet's elegant command of language. Representative texts in *The New Century Hymnal* include the Holy Spirit hymn "Fire of God, Undying Flame" (hymn 64) and the tribute to the power of music in worship "When the Morning Stars Together" (hymn 453).

Other Movements

We now come to the British sector of an international development that began in the mid-1950s and reached a high point in the 1960s. Numerous events worldwide contributed to the spirit of change, disillusionment, and rebellion. Of course, during such a time it is often difficult to discern what exactly caused a given trend, what was a part of it, or what might even have been a conscious move contrary to that trend. There was the shock that World War II had not ended war: The Korean War began and ended unresolved, and the cold war between democracy and communism became a bitter reality. The anticipation of change evolved as Queen Elizabeth II took the throne in 1952, a hopeful change away from the grim memories of the war years and away from the other aforementioned realities.

In the field of congregational singing in Great Britain, two unusual developments initially stand out: the parish communion movement and the family service movement. The parish communion movement emerged in the Anglican Church out of a concern to make the worship experience "relevant."[6] In the spirit of this endeavor, respected liturgies were often simplified, altered, and put into basic, colloquial language. In part, the music attempted "relevance" by means of imitating Broadway-type tunes of the 1930s. It was not unusual for respected, classic hymn texts to be paired with such music.

The primary driving force behind much of this activity was Geoffrey Beaumont (1905–1971) and his Twentieth Century Light Music Group. Although music like Beaumont's *Twentieth Century Folk Mass* made a large impact at that point, none of it has stood the test of time. It did, however, accomplish the gradual bankrupting of the term "folk" music. Instead of such expressions being a genuine music *from* the people, they amounted to the composing of music (in a commercialistic sense) and bringing it *to* them.

The spirit of the family service movement encompassed not only the Evangelical wing of the Anglican Church, but also many of the Dissenting churches. The songs of this movement were influenced by the Billy Graham evangelistic crusades of the 1950s and 1960s: the *Billy Graham Crusade Song Book* (1954) and the *Billy Graham London Crusade Song Book* (1966). Undoubtedly, more British people were actively singing about the gospel than before, but they most often reverted to the popular evangelistic songs of Ira Sankey and Phillip Bliss or the texts of Fanny Crosby rather than composing new evangelistic music to meet the needs of the twentieth century.[7] Some of the more "daring" music from this movement of the 1950s and 1960s came mostly in the follow-up of the campaigns themselves through more soloistic music created for evangelistic films and the popular recording industry in Hollywood.

Second Vatican Council

Also during this period a development of global scope occurred. Under the influence of the Second Vatican Council of the Roman Catholic Church (1962–1965), singing during the Mass—even hymns of non-Catholic origin—and the use of the vernacular were encouraged. The doors were opened to the use of instruments other than the pipe organ. In this context, a sort of "folk" music evolved. Amidst numerous publications, only the *New Catholic Hymnal* (compiled and edited by Anthony Petti and Geoffrey Laycock, 1971) was recognized for its substantial contributions in text and music. While the book itself did not achieve the desired impact at the time, some of its materials came into broader use later. A major contributor to this hymnal was Brian Foley (b. 1919), with fourteen entries (see "Holy Spirit, Come Confirm Us," hymn 264). Of particular note are his texts based on psalms.

Other newer Catholic congregational repertoire of that time included the Gelineau Psalms—written by Joseph Gelineau (b. 1920), a Frenchman, but translated into various languages including English; and the texts of James Quinn ("Day Is Done," hymn 92). Quinn (b. 1919), a Jesuit priest in Edinburgh, Scotland, produced a collection in 1969 with over one hundred entries, including translations and original texts. Betty Carr Pulkingham, a British Roman Catholic composer-arranger, became known in hymnody some years later (see her arrangements: hymns 364, 539).

DUNBLANE AND THE "HYMN EXPLOSION" OF THE 1960s

The major turning point in inspiring what we call the "hymn explosion" occurred with the Dunblane consultations, held at the Scottish Churches House, an ecumenical center in Dunblane, Scotland, from 1961 to 1969. Interestingly, this place was also associated with the development of *The New English Bible*.[8] The ecumenical consultations, attended by twenty-four persons (some clergy, some musicians), were a remarkably honest attempt to meet current needs while maintaining theological integrity and soundness in what was to be sung in churches. Some key persons at Dunblane were Ian Fraser, Alan Luff, and Erik Routley.

The rigorous, vulnerable process did not lead to a new hymnal but to two smaller, somewhat experimental collections: *Dunblane Praises I* (1965) and *Dunblane Praises II* (1967). The underlying principle of such supplements allowed the editors to incorporate genuinely new, perhaps even adventurous material, without the serious ramifications of including such work in the more-permanent and expensive hardcover hymnals. *Dunblane Praises I* was quite informally produced and contained only sixteen pieces, half of which were new tunes to old texts. The first printing was a mere 200 copies and priced at two shillings. It was reprinted, for a total of 1,400 copies. Most notably, it marked the first appearance of a Brian Wren text ("Lord Christ, the Father's Mighty Son").

A group of Anglican Evangelicals developed a parallel work called *Jubilate Hymns*. Michael Baughen, vicar near the University of Manchester, was its founder. They produced *Youth Praise* (1966), *Youth Praise II* (1969), and *Psalm Praise* (1973), containing works of note by such writers as Timothy Dudley-Smith, Michael Saward, Michael Perry, and Christopher Idle.

The journalist Sydney Carter (b. 1915) attempted, in an often provocative manner, to write songs perhaps best sung by a vocal soloist or group in a coffee bar to a folklike guitar accompaniment, in order to place the consumer into a desacralized worship context. Although his songs became quite popular outside the church, they were also often heard within the worship service (see "Said Judas to Mary," hymn 210). His music offended many at the time, and the vagueness of his theology was also called into question. In October 1964, Carter was invited to take part at Dunblane to present his concerns and the rationale for his approach to new congregational repertoire, but his presentation had little impact.[9]

Significant to the hymn explosion itself were two supplements to *HAM*: *100 Hymns for Today* (1969) and *More Hymns for Today* (1980), as well as *Hymns and Songs* (Methodist, 1969). The first of these, *100 Hymns for Today*, stands so close to the beginning of the explosion that merely one text each by the three best-known British hymn-text poets, Fred Pratt Green, Fred Kaan, and Brian Wren, were included. By the time *More Hymns for Today* (1980) was published, the repertoire had expanded considerably, to include eleven texts by Green, seven by Wren, and four by Kaan. These textwriters not only were associated with the hymn explosion and the three supplements, but they also dominated late twentieth-century hymnwriting in the entire English-speaking world.[10] From the start, it has been the desire of all three to articulate the classic Christian faith in contemporary language while facing issues of current or anticipated concern to the church.

PROFILES OF THREE HYMNWRITERS

Fred Pratt Green

The "senior statesman" of hymnody, Fred Pratt Green, a Methodist pastor and poet from Norwich, began seriously writing hymns in 1968 in retirement as a member of the committee compiling *Hymns and Songs*.[11] As he stated: "It was involvement in the work of the Supplement which got me busy trying to write hymns. Often we found we liked a tune but not the words set to it in other hymn books. Because I have written quite a lot of poetry in the last twenty years, I was challenged to meet the need for new words to certain tunes!"[12] This resulted in his well-known "Christ Is the World's Light" for *Hymns and Songs*. Another from this supplement was "O Christ, the Healer, We Have Come" (hymn 175). This was the beginning of his remarkably creative flow of several hundred texts, earning him the reputation as a twentieth-century Wesley. He is represented in *The New Century Hymnal* by no less than twelve texts—many of which have already achieved "classic" status in recent hymnbooks published in the United States and Great Britain.

Three hymns are noteworthy for their focus on worship and the mission of the church. "When in Our Music God Is Glorified" (hymn 561) has become something of a motto for persons involved in worship and church music on both sides of the Atlantic. Two others, "God Is Here! As We Your People" (hymn 70) and "The Church of Christ in Every Age" (hymn 306) present equally compelling reflections on the experience and meaning of the church gathered in worship and the mission of the church throughout the ages.

In "Little Children, Welcome" (hymn 323), Green demonstrates his ability to write effectively for small children while avoiding the temptation to be trite or overly simplistic. His fine harvest/thanksgiving hymn, "For the Fruit of All Creation" (hymn 425) has rightfully been included in the majority of recent U.S. hymnals. "How Blessed Are They Who Trust in Christ" (hymn 365) for good reason has become a frequently sung funeral hymn. And Green proved himself a sensitive translator in his version of Bonhoeffer's well-known text written from prison, "By Gracious Powers" (hymn 413).

Fred Kaan

Fred Kaan, born in 1929 in Haarlem, Holland, moved to England in 1952. As a minister of the United Reformed Church (Congregational) in the United Kingdom, he has held a variety of positions around the world—serving as a pastor in England, general secretary of the World Alliance of Reformed Churches, and in capacities with the World Council of Churches.[13]

Kaan's immediate purpose in writing many of his earlier hymns was for use in the next Sunday's service, which places him close to his Congregational hymnwriter forebear, Isaac Watts. Kaan may be regarded as perhaps the least musical of the three contemporary writers under consideration, and mostly chooses standard tunes and meters. Theologically, he is the most liberal. Part of that impression has stemmed from his occasional attempt to provoke the church out of its complacency or limited views. Of great importance to Fred Kaan was and is the interrelationship of the gospel and gospel-inspired action, whether in the worship service itself, in caring for others, or in caring for the environment. This concern is well expressed in one of his earlier hymns, "Sing We of the Modern City," which appeared in *The Hymnal of the United Church of Christ*, 1974.

In *The New Century Hymnal*, his rhythmically catchy text "Let Us Talents and Tongues Employ" (hymn 347) challenges the communion participant to be joyful. "God, When I Came into This Life" (hymn 354) assures the confirmand of God's sustaining presence even in times of doubt. Kaan's great concern for ecumenical thinking is well expressed in "Help Us Accept Each Other" (hymn 388) as well as in one of his best-known texts, "For the Healing of the Nations" (hymn 576).

Brian Wren

Finally, we come to the contemporary British hymnwriter more frequently represented in *The New Century Hymnal* than any other, Brian Wren.[14] As a minister of the United Reformed Church in England, he worked for several ecumenical organizations with an international outreach and then, in the early 1990s, moved to the United States, where he has been engaged as a visiting lecturer and workshop leader in numerous seminaries, colleges, and churches on subjects related to hymnwriting, creative worship, and language issues. Wren has championed the cause of inclusive language in hymnody and worship and has brought about a considerable expansion of imagery in God language—an expansion articulated in such hymns as "Bring Many Names" (hymn 11) and "May the Sending One Defend You" (hymn 79). Brian Wren has a deep concern that contemporary texts come from the real world in which we live. This includes giving voice to the experiences of those who have been neglected, rejected, abused, or divorced, as in "When Love Is Found" (hymn 362) and "This Is a Day of New Beginnings" (hymn 417), for example.

Brian Wren also brings a fresh tangibility to particular liturgies, such as the one for Ash Wednesday, "Dust and Ashes Touch Our Face" (hymn 186), or for Holy Communion, "I Come with Joy" (hymn 349). He challenges people to think anew of the creation and the environment in

"We Are Not Our Own" (hymn 564) and "Thank You, God, for Water, Soil, and Air" (hymn 559). Finally, Wren's concern for ecumenical priorities can be seen in "We Are Your People" (hymn 309), "There's a Spirit in the Air" (hymn 294), "When Minds and Bodies Meet as One" (hymn 399), "We Offer Christ" (hymn 527), "We Are Not Our Own" (hymn 564), and "Spirit of Jesus, If I Love My Neighbor" (hymn 590).

HYMN TUNE COMPOSERS

This survey of the final period of twentieth-century British hymnody has focused primarily on hymnwriters and their texts. Indeed, if the verbal message has little to say, any discussion about the music of hymns is superfluous. Fortunately for Christians living near the close of the century, textwriters have provided an enormous amount of thought-provoking, new material, thereby necessitating a discussion of music as well. Several composers have created new hymn settings for the wealth of new texts, but with mixed results. In general, it remains that it is much easier to teach a congregation a new text to a known, singable tune, than a new text to a new tune, especially if written in a new style.

Peter Cutts

One composer who has contributed a significant number of fine tunes is Peter Cutts (b. 1937).[15] Born and educated in England, Cutts has served as music director for various churches in Massachusetts, and is director of music and associate dean of chapel at Andover Newton Theological School. His 1969 tune, BRIDEGROOM (hymns 270, 552), was also previously employed in *The Hymnal of the United Church of Christ* (1974). Newer offerings in *The New Century Hymnal* are TRINITY CAROL (hymn 399) and CHATHAM (hymn 555), the latter commissioned for Fred Pratt Green's "Here, Savior, in This Quiet Place."

John Wilson

One person noted for his influence throughout the English-speaking world by means of his tunes, harmonizations, descants, and hymnal editing is John Wilson (1905–1992).[16] He studied with Ralph Vaughan Williams among other composers and held teaching positions at various institutions, including Charterhouse and the Royal College of Music. For the sake of his ecumenical activities in church music, however, it was of importance that he grew up as a Congregationalist, later joined the Anglican Church, and was also organist in the Methodist Church.

Wilson worked on the editing of numerous hymnals, from the *Clarendon Hymnal* (1936) to works published during the 1980s. In the late 1960s, Canon Ronald Jaspar asked Cyril Taylor to introduce the two new supplements of 1969—*100 Hymns for Today* and *Hymns and Songs*. Taylor, in turn, enlisted John Wilson's services to implement the successful midweek lunchtime hymn-festival series, "Come and Sing," held at Westminster Abbey each May. John Wilson can also be credited with encouraging or even challenging Fred Pratt Green to write more than twenty of his hymns. In *The New Century Hymnal*, Wilson is represented by WHITFIELD (hymn 309), composed in 1975 for Brian Wren's text "We Are Your People."

The Iona Community

Since about the mid-1980s, the folk-inspired music of the Iona Community in Scotland has become more widely known and can now be found in major denominational hymnals. This community and its strong Celtic tradition, coming from an economically depressed area, have effectively communicated concerns for the environment and social justice. The rigorous honesty of the songs written by Iona composers John Bell and Graham Maule challenge and sometimes surprise the complacency of the church, as exemplified in *The New Century Hymnal* by two Christmas pieces, "Sing a Different Song" (hymn 150) and "Who Would Think That What Was Needed" (hymn 153), as well as the prayer song "O God, My God" (hymn 515).

In spite of all the outstanding hymnody written and composed during the twentieth century in Great Britain, particularly since 1969, the century seems to be drawing to a close with the realization that the informal, often casually composed worship song receives preference over the hymn in a number of places. But, just as the superficial sometimes threatened to overcome the substantial during past centuries and was ultimately unsuccessful in doing so, future worshipers who seek a more profound avenue for expressing their praise and worship of God will probably also maintain their interest in the hymn.

NOTES

1. See Robin A. Leaver, "British Hymnody, 1900–1950," in *The Hymnal 1982 Companion*, ed. Raymond F. Glover (New York: The Church Hymnal Corporation, 1990), 1: 474–77.

2. Erik Routley, *Christian Hymns Observed* (Princeton, N.J.: Prestige Publications, 1982), 74–75.

3. Erik Routley, *A Panorama of Christian Hymnody* (Collegeville, Minn.: Liturgical Press, 1979), 175.

4. Regarding *Congregational Praise* itself, see K. L. Parry and Erik

Routley, *Companion to Congregational Praise* (London: Independent Press, 1953).

5. For a complete listing of all Routley's contributions, see Carlton R. Young, exec. ed.; Robin A. Leaver and James H. Litton, eds., *Duty & Delight: Routley Remembered* (Carol Stream, Ill.: Hope Publishing Co.; Norwich, Eng.: Canterbury Press, 1985).

6. Leaver, "British Hymnody since 1950," *The Hymnal 1982 Companion*, 1:557 ff.

7. For a discussion of evangelistic pop music in Britain, see Erik Routley, *Twentieth Century Church Music* (Carol Stream, Ill.: Agape, 1964), 196–209.

8. Leaver, "British Hymnody since 1950," 1:566–67.

9. See Paul Hammond and Joe Hall, "A Reconsideration of Sydney Carter's Incarnational Hymns," *The Hymn* 46, no. 4 (October 1995): 22–27.

10. For insight into the unique approach, style, and concerns of the three writers, see the interview/discussion moderated by Robin A. Leaver on September 6, 1983: "New Hymnody: Some Problems and Prospects" in Young, Lever, and Litton, eds., *Duty & Delight*, 217–28.

11. The authoritative sources for basic biographical information as well as the texts to all Pratt Green's hymns, ballads, and some of his poems are *The Hymns and Ballads of Fred Pratt Green* (Carol Stream, Ill.: Hope Publishing Co.; London: Stainer & Bell, 1982); and *Later Hymns & Ballads and 50 Poems of Fred Pratt Green* (Carol Stream, Ill.: Hope Publishing Co.; London: Stainer & Bell, 1989). Scrapbooks and other items of Fred Pratt Green are located in a special collection in Emory University Library and in photocopy in the library of the University of Durham (England). Further, see Vernon Wicker, "Fred Pratt Green: The Poet and His Hymns," *The Hymn* 46, no. 4 (October 1995): 12–19.

12. "Scrapbook" I, 6.

13. For more information on Fred Kaan and his hymnwriting activity, see Fred Kaan, "My Hymn-Writing Journey," *The Hymn* 47, no. 3 (July 1996): 13–20. Kaan's hymn-text collections include *Pilgrim Praise* (1972), *Break Not the Circle* (1975), *Songs and Hymns from Sweden* (1976), *The Hymn Texts of Fred Kaan* (1985), and *Planting Trees and Sowing Seeds: New Hymns by Fred Kaan* (1989), all available from Hope Publishing Co., Carol Stream, Ill.

14. An anthology of all Brian Wren's hymns to date is *Piece Together Praise—a Theological Journey* (London: Stainer & Bell; Carol Stream, Ill.: Hope Publishing Co., 1996). See also his monograph *What Language Shall I Borrow? God-Talk in Worship* (New York: Crossroads, 1989).

15. Peter Cutts's tunes appear in a number of current hymnals and in the collection *Faith Looking Forward* (Carol Stream, Ill.: Hope Publishing Co., 1983).

16. See "John Wilson—In Memoriam," "John Wilson: 'Our Generation's Most Devoted Encourager of Fine Hymnody,'" and other entries in Vernon Wicker, ed., *The Hymnology Annual: An International Forum on the Hymn and Worship* (Kingston, N.Y.: Selah Publishing Co., 1997), 111–38.

Theological Trends in Twentieth-Century Hymnody in the United States

C. Michael Hawn

The last half of the twentieth century has seen an outpouring of congregational song. Congregations have not experienced such rich diversity, quantity, and quality of hymnody since the Oxford movement. Because of the vision of John Mason Neale, the latter half of the nineteenth century resulted in a period of liturgical renewal, ranging from a revival of church architecture and research in historical liturgies to the translation of German pietistic hymns and classic Greek and Latin verse into English. Combined with the more personal piety of the gospel song and the hymns of the Evangelical wing of the Anglican Church, congregations at the turn of the twentieth century had at their disposal the widest range of sung faith known to the church. The first wave of denominational hymnals published in the United States in the late 1800s helped to secure the liturgical identities of the mainline denominations. At the turn of the century, John Julian's *Dictionary of Hymnology* (1892) set the standards for hymnological scholarship.

As the church approaches the twenty-first century, there are many parallels. Following a relatively inactive and uninteresting period of hymn writing between 1900 and 1960, congregational song not only has exploded in quantity but also prospered in quality. The liturgical reforms of the Second Vatican Council fostered a new wave of creativity that spread to Protestant churches through ecumenical consultations. Almost overnight, Roman Catholic parishes all over the world needed congregational song for the revised liturgy. Catholic musicians investigated the hymns both of their tradition and of Protestant churches. Liturgical renewal always opens up possibilities for fresh expressions of faith, and many Roman Catholic hymnwriters responded to the reforms of Vatican II with new hymns created specifically for the new rite. In many ways, Vatican II provided a seedbed for hymnological creativity similar to the productive period of the Oxford movement one hundred years earlier.

Protestant hymnwriters responded to the turmoil of the 1960s with hymns on justice and the nature of the church. They replied to the ecumenical consultations on liturgy and the sacraments with new congregational songs on the themes of the Christian year, baptism, and the Eucharist. The evangelical fervor of charismatic fellowships resulted in an outpouring of praise choruses similar in piety to nineteenth-century gospel song. Hymnals, both denominational and ecumenical, have appeared at an unprecedented rate in the United States and Canada since

1975. While there is no single work that rivals Julian's monumental *Dictionary*, The Dictionary of American Hymnology Project (an effort of the Hymn Society in the United States and Canada) and the appearance of several first-rate hymnal companions attest to a healthy level of hymnological scholarship. In many ways, hymnwriting, hymnal publication, and hymn scholarship compare favorably to the efforts in these areas at the conclusion of the preceding century.

This essay will survey the theological trends in congregational song that have affected hymnals published in the United States since 1960 with special reference to *The New Century Hymnal*. While hymnwriters from the United States will be the main focus of this analysis, we cannot escape the contributions of hymnwriters from around the world, especially those who write primarily in Spanish and those English-language hymnwriters from Great Britain, Canada, and New Zealand.

Recent hymnody develops many theological themes in fresh ways. Only a few can be discussed here. These will be examined in several broad categories: (1) The church gathered for worship; (2) the nature of the Trinity; (3) sacraments and rites of the church—baptism, communion, confirmation, ordination, marriage; (4) the mission of the church; (5) the nature and praise of God; (6) Christian unity; (7) stewardship of the environment and humanity's role in creation; and (8) the Christian year. Hymn texts cannot always be placed into a single theological niche. Many of the hymns discussed below could be included in other categories.

When appropriate, I will indicate the relative standing of a given hymn within the ecumenical community by indicating the number of times it appears in forty hymnals published in the United States and Canada since 1976. For the sake of brevity, an asterisk preceding a number in parentheses will be used to indicate the number of hymnals in which a hymn appears out of the forty surveyed; for example, (*10). The hymn must appear at least three times to receive this designation. Some hymns written during the latter half of the twentieth century are already familiar to local congregations. Others surface relatively often in hymnals (ten or more times is an excellent showing for hymns written since 1960) but have not achieved a place in congregations' preferred repertoire. Still others can be found in only one or two hymnals, while some hymns appear for the first time in *The New Century Hymnal*.[1]

THE CHURCH GATHERED FOR WORSHIP

The church gathered for worship (*ecclesia*) continues to be a subject for hymnwriters. Hymns that express the activities of the church in song, prayer, word, and sacrament reinforce the historical pattern of Service of the Word and Service of the Table (or Faithful). Among the best-known hymns that support the church at worship is Fred Pratt Green's "God Is

Here" (hymn 70), which establishes in its four stanzas an agenda for worship (*14):

Stanza 1: "to offer praise and prayer";

Stanza 2: to share in "symbols to remind us of our lifelong need of grace," including "table, font, and pulpit," as well as the cross, preaching, silence, and speech;

Stanza 3: to remind us that in our worship "our children find a welcome in the Shepherd's fold";

Stanza 4 concludes the hymn in praise of the "Sovereign God" and with the petition that God will "Keep us faithful to the gospel" and "help us work your purpose out."

A more recent hymn (1992) by Jeffery Rowthorn, "At the Font We Start Our Journey" (hymn 308), devotes a stanza to each of four symbols of Christian worship—font, pulpit, altar, and door—and reminds us that each Sunday is a celebration of our Easter faith.

Two hymns on the role of music in worship also deserve mention here. Fred Pratt Green's "When in Our Music God Is Glorified" (hymn 561), written in 1972, is one of the most widely used hymns in hymnals published since 1975 (*23). This text has given the early-twentieth-century tune ENGELBERG new life. "When the Morning Stars Together" (hymn 453), by Albert F. Bayly, is as masterful in its scope as Pratt Green's more famous hymn (*3). It traces the use of music through successive stanzas from "the angel host" and "synagogue and temple voices rais[ing] the psalmists' songs," to "Voice and instrument in union" which raised "Plainsong, tuneful hymns, and anthems" in praise of God. The final stanza is a beautiful prayer of intercession, asking God to bless those who make music and to consecrate their skills for service to God. The entire hymn addresses God in the traditional second person (you) of the Jewish *berakah* prayer form. Though less well known than Fred Pratt Green, Albert Bayly (1901–1984) is considered by many to be the first author in the British "hymn explosion" that began in the 1960s and continues through the end of the century.

THE NATURE OF THE TRINITY

The nature of the Trinity, a central doctrine of Christian orthodoxy that evolved from the Nicene Council in the fourth century, continues to be a source for hymnwriters both because of the need to search for new and vital metaphors to express this central doctrine and because the traditional formula for describing the Trinity (Father, Son, and Holy Spirit) does not express for some an inclusive vision of this central tenet. Trinitarian language permeates many hymns in *The New Century Hymnal*, even those not contained within the Trinity Sunday section of the book (hymns 273–280). Among the hymns offering new language for this traditional relationship, the most widely used include the following.

"Creating God, Your Fingers Trace" (hymn 462), by Jeffery Rowthorn, develops in successive stanzas new trinitarian language with fresh participial adjectives describing God—"Sustaining God," "Redeeming God," and "Indwelling God" (*11). "Creator God, Creating Still" (hymn 278), by Presbyterian writer Jane Parker Huber, uses perhaps the most common alternative language for the Trinity—Creator, Redeemer, and Sustainer (*4).

The New Century Hymnal includes several lesser-known but more-adventurous hymns that explore fresh trinitarian language. "May the Sending One Defend You" (hymn 79), by Brian Wren, is in the form of a benediction. Subsequent stanzas continue with "May the Given One" in the second stanza and "May the Binding One" in the third. Ruth C. Duck's "Womb of Life, and Source of Being" (hymn 274) draws upon creative metaphors for the Trinity. The final stanza offers an innovative double trinitarian formula, "Mother, Brother, holy Partner; Father, Spirit, Only Son." Jean Janzen draws upon the fourteenth-century mystic, Julian of Norwich, as an inspiration for "Mothering God, You Gave Me Birth" (hymn 467; *5). "Mothering Christ" and "Mothering Spirit" begin successive stanzas. It would appear that hymnwriters from the United States (Brian Wren is now a permanent U.S. resident) are offering hymns with the most provocative thinking on trinitarian language.

NEW HYMNS FOR THE SACRAMENTS AND RITES OF THE CHURCH

New hymns for the sacraments and rites of the church are in abundance. Hymns for Holy Communion often reflect the new communion (Eucharistic) rites that are a result of the Consultation on Church Union (COCU) in 1985. These rites encourage the reclamation of the Eucharistic theology of thanksgiving and community. "I Come with Joy" (hymn 349), by Brian Wren, is perhaps the most commonly used communion hymn written since 1960 (*17). Rather than the more traditional memorial motif, this hymn stresses joy, forgiveness, a "new community of love," and oneness in the risen Christ. Fred Kaan's "Let Us Talents and Tongues Employ" (hymn 347) also captures this spirit, not only because of the text but also because of the lively Jamaican calypso melody adapted by Doreen Potter (*5). This hymn sets the stage for a celebration of the of the Lord's Supper, especially in the refrain, "Jesus lives again, earth can breathe again, pass the Word around: loaves abound!"

Spanish-language hymns contribute both fresh metaphors and new vitality to the celebration of Holy Communion. "Una espiga" (hymn 338), by Spanish priest Cesáreo Gabaráin, is a vivid post–Vatican II text that explores agrarian images of "grapes in bunches cut down when ripe and red" and wheat "turned golden by the sun" (*8). Christian unity is expressed in the metaphor of "grains which become one same whole loaf" and "one same hope we will sing" as we gather round the table. Two Latin American hymns capture the fiesta spirit of the Eucharist as well as any of the new hymns. These are "Hoy celebramos con gozo al Dios" (hymn 246), by Bolivian Methodists Mortimer Arias and Antonio Auza, and "Somos pueblo que camina" (hymn 340), from the *Misa Popular Nicaragüense*. The spirit of these hymns almost demands that the communion elements be brought down the aisle of the church in a dancing procession.

Several hymns by U.S. writers are very significant in this category, although not as commonly used in recent hymnals. "As We Gather at Your Table" (hymn 332), by Carl P. Daw Jr., stresses the spiritual nourishment that we receive from the sacrament and our responsibility to share this feast with others (*3). The final stanza ends on an eschatological note, foreshadowing the heavenly banquet:

There no more will envy bind us
nor will pride our peace destroy,
as we join with saints and angels
to repeat the sounding joy.

Words copyright © 1989 by Hope Publishing Company, Carol Stream, IL 60188. All rights reserved. Used by permission.

"Jesus Took the Bread" (hymn 343), by Ruth Duck, captures the fourfold pattern of the Eucharist by devoting each stanza to one of Jesus' actions as he shared a meal with the disciples before his death: took, blessed, broke, and gave.

One must observe that there is considerable interest in new communion hymns in general. As the rites have moved toward themes of thanksgiving (*eucharistica*) and community, so hymns and music have developed to complement this theological emphasis.

There are also new hymns for Holy Baptism and confirmation, though not in the same abundance as those for Holy Communion. The African American spiritual "Take Me to the Water" (hymn 322) is included for what may be the first time in a mainline denominational hymnal published in the United States. UCC minister Ronald Cole-Turner wrote "Child of Blessing, Child of Promise" (hymn 325) specifically for infant baptism (*3). Canadian hymnwriter Sylvia Dunstan wrote "Crashing Waters at Creation" (hymn 326) to accompany the blessing over the water (*3). "I Was There to Hear Your Borning Cry" (hymn 351), by John Ylvisaker, recalls the experience of baptism for those receiving confirmation (*4).

The rite of ordination benefits from the inclusion of "God the Spirit, Guide and Guardian" (hymn 355), by Carl P. Daw Jr., which summarizes the vocation of ministry through the functions of the Trinity (*9). The alliterative *incipit* (opening phrase) of this hymn captures not only the attention of the singer but the spirit of dignity in this hymn.

New hymns for marriage services are represented best by Brian Wren's "When Love Is Found" (hymn 362), which has been included in a significant number of recent hymnals (*11).

THE MISSION OF THE CHURCH

The mission of the church is another area in which there has been some fresh poetic creativity. Hymns with this general theme appear throughout *The New Century Hymnal* under various topics such as "Discipleship," "Jesus Christ," "Justice and Peace," "Witness," and "The Church." Kenneth Cober's "Renew Your Church" (hymn 311), written in 1960 (*7), and "Hope of the World" (hymn 46), penned by theologian Georgia Harkness in 1954, set the agenda for hymns on this theme (*15). Harkness, the first woman ordained by the Methodist Church in the United States, wrote her hymn for the World Council of Churches General Assembly in Evanston, Illinois. More recently, Fred Pratt Green articulates this theme with "The Church of Christ in Every Age" (hymn 306). His emphasis is on a "servant church" that joins Christ in responding to injustice (*13). Fred Kaan's "For the Healing of the Nations" (hymn 576) focuses on the injustice of war and killing (*11). Three of the twenty-one hymns in the extensive "Justice and Peace" section are by New Zealand writer Shirley Erena Murray: "Great God of Earth and Heaven" (hymn 579), a warning against apathy; "O God, We Bear the Imprint of Your Face" (hymn 585), on race relations; and "Through All the World, a Hungry Christ" (hymn 587), addressing the Christian's responsibility to all who suffer in the world.

Several hymns from various cultures shed light on the mission of the church as well. These include two hymns by Spanish composer Cesáreo Gabaráin—"Camina, pueblo de Dios" (hymn 614; *5) and "Sois la semilla" (hymn 528); and "Pues si vivimos" (hymn 499), a Mexican folk hymn of Spanish origins (*5). Each of these offers a purpose for the people of God in the world. "Sois la semilla" incorporates directly into its refrain the great commission of Matthew 28 (*8).

THE NATURE AND PRAISE OF GOD

Historical hymnody attests to the many names given to God, especially as a part of the biblical witness. New hymns of the twentieth century incorporate and expand upon that witness, providing fresh and challenging ways to reflect on and praise God. This section will explore hymns not mentioned in other sections, especially "The Nature of the Trinity" and "The Stewardship of the Environment."

In Brian Wren's "Bring Many Names" (hymn 11) every stanza (beginning with the second) explores a new modifier for God based on human experiences and relationships (*4):

2. Strong mother God.
3. Warm father God.
4. Old, aching God.
5. Young, growing God.
6. Great, living God.

"God of the Sparrow God of the Whale" (hymn 32), by Jaroslav J. Vajda, is a profound hymn to all those who open themselves to its mystery (*7). Gracia Grindal's "We Sing to You, O God" (hymn 9) is firmly rooted in biblical images for God. Ruth Duck's "Colorful Creator" (hymn 30) compares God's nature to that of an artist, composer, author, and poet.

Andraé Crouch expresses praise through personal gratitude to God in "How Can I Say Thanks" (hymn 14). The refrain, "To God be the glory," echoes the simple sincerity of Fanny Crosby's nineteenth-century gospel song by the same title (*13). "God, Who Stretched the Spangled Heavens" (hymn 556), by Canadian hymnwriter Catherine Cameron, is one of the first hymns to praise God both for "the ecstasy of winging through untraveled realms of space" and for "the secrets of the atom, yielding unimagined power" (*15). Thomas H. Troeger explores the relationship between knowledge and faith in his penetrating text "Praise the Source of Faith and Learning" (hymn 411). Fred Pratt Green's translation of a poem written in 1944 by Dietrich Bonhoeffer just before his death in Nazi Germany, "By Gracious Powers" (hymn 413), is a poignant entry (*9). This profound hymn on God's providence is a worthy successor to William Cowper's "God Moves in a Mysterious Way" (hymn 412).

The Puerto Rican hymn by Pablo Fernández Badillo, "Alabanza" (hymn 34), is widely known in Latin America and now appears for the first time in a major denominational U.S. hymnal. The text expresses the integral relationship between God and all living things that characterizes Latin American cultures. Finally, *The New Century Hymnal* is to be congratulated for the new translation of Carl Boberg's "O Store Gud," "O Mighty God, When I Survey in Wonder" (hymn 35), which provides fresh insight into one of the most popular hymns in the last half of the twentieth century (*31).

CHRISTIAN UNITY

Christian unity is a significant topic of recent hymns and a prominent theme in *The New Century Hymnal*. This theme is integrated into many hymns already discussed, especially those for the Eucharist and the mission of the church. British minister John Peacey also speaks of unity within the theme of Pentecost in "Filled with the Spirit's Power" (hymn 266). Shirley Erena Murray seeks unity through service and acts of justice in "Community of Christ" (hymn 314). Fred Kaan encourages us to "accept each other as Christ accepts us" in "Help Us Accept Each Other" (hymn 388; *5). "Shadow and Substance" (hymn 398), by Dan Damon, expresses the hope for a "mystical union in prayer." Brian Wren approaches the theme comprehensively in "When Minds and Bodies Meet as One" (hymn 399). He details the agenda of unity in each stanza, acknowledging that the source of unity is the "revealing God, forever One, whose nature is Community." The Japanese hymn "Sekai no Tomo" ("Here, O God, Your Servant Gather," hymn 72) deserves to be included among the most important new hymns to express Christian unity (*9). Based on John 14:6, Tokuo Yamaguchi encourages Christians to find unity in Christ who is the Way, the Truth, and the Life. The second stanza as translated in 1958 by Everett M. Stowe captures this spirit of unity thus:

> Many are the tongues we speak,
> scattered are the lands,
> yet our hearts are one in God,
> one in love's demands.

Words copyright © 1958, renewed 1986, The United Methodist Publishing House. (Administered by The Copyright Company c/o The Copyright Company, Nashville, TN.) All rights reserved. International copyright secured. Used by permission.

THE STEWARDSHIP OF THE ENVIRONMENT AND HUMANITY'S RELATIONSHIP WITH CREATION

The stewardship of the environment and humanity's relationship with creation are also significant theological themes for hymnwriters. Some hymns speak directly to these concerns; others incorporate them into a more general text on creation or thanksgiving. These themes have assumed a role of prominence especially among the hymns written since 1960. Hymns on ecology or the stewardship of the earth may be the most significant stanza that the last half of the twentieth century will add to the church's song.

The previous emphasis in classic hymns depicted God as the omnipotent Creator of the earth and its beauty, with humankind at the pinnacle of creation, as in Watts's "I Sing the Mighty Power of God" (hymn 12) and Alexander's "All Things Bright and Beautiful" (hymn 31). The late twentieth-century orientation emphasizes not only the responsibility of humankind to protect and sustain God's creation but also the partnership or connection between God and all living things.

Brian Wren's "Thank You, God, for Water, Soil, and Air" (hymn 559) combines thankfulness to the Creator with a petition to "Help us renew the face of the earth" (*6). New Zealand hymnwriter Shirley Erena Murray contributes "Touch the Earth Lightly" (hymn 569), written in 1992 (*4). Her hymn promises to be a prophetic addition to this theme. The second stanza (which is to be sung in a minor mode) is direct in language and searing in its indictment of humanity:

> We who endanger, who create hunger,
> agents of death for all creatures that live,
> We who would foster clouds of disaster,
> God of our planet, forestall and forgive!

Words copyright © 1992 by Hope Publishing Company, Carol Stream, IL 60188. All rights reserved. Used by permission.

Another hymn by Murray, "Take My Gifts" (hymn 562), encourages us to "give away" from the abundance of those gifts that we have received. Herman G. Stuempfle Jr. is another recent voice. His "Stars and Planets, Flung in Orbit" (hymn 567) highlights the theme of partnership between the Creator and humankind in stanza four:

> Humankind, earth's deepest mystery, born of dust but touched
>   by grace,
> Torn apart by tongue and color, yet a single, striving race:
> We, in whom you trace your image, add our words to nature's song.

Words copyright © 1989, The Hymn Society. Used by permission of Hope Publishing Company, Carol Stream, IL 60188.

Ruth Duck adds her voice to this theme with "We Cannot Own the Sunlit Sky" (hymn 563). She reminds us that we do not own the gifts of creation, but are its caretakers only so "that all may have abundant life." Dan Damon takes a fresh approach in his "Pray for the Wilderness" (hymn 557). We are encouraged to "Pray for the wilderness . . . rain forest . . . waterfalls . . . [and] the planet brought down by degrees." We are to "Learn from the elephant, eagle, and whale . . . the dragonfly, spider, and snail . . . the people in neighboring lands . . . [and] children who play in the sands." This hymn expresses the interconnectedness of all of God's creation. Once again special mention must be made of a work by British hymnwriter Fred Pratt Green, "For the Fruit of All Creation" (hymn 425). Written in 1970, this hymn appears an astounding twenty two times in the forty hymnals surveyed. While its primary thrust is thanksgiving, it gently yet profoundly reminds us in the first stanza of our responsibility:

For the plowing, sowing, reaping,
silent growth while we are sleeping,
Future needs in earth's safekeeping,
thanks be to God.

Words copyright © 1970 by Hope Publishing Company, Carol Stream, IL 60188. All rights reserved. Used by permission.

Even in gratitude, there is responsibility.

THE CHRISTIAN YEAR

Various seasons and themes of the Christian year have been the topics of many new hymns. Given the available space, only those hymns reflecting broader ecumenical significance can be included in this discussion. Several hymns reflect a renewed interest in the *Magnificat,* or Mary's song (Luke 1:46–55), traditionally associated with Advent. "My Heart Sings Out with Joyful Praise" (hymn 106), by Ruth Duck, and "My Soul Gives Glory to My God" (hymn 119), by Miriam Therese Winter (*4), are two recent paraphrases of this biblical canticle. Ruth Duck also has a paraphrase of the *Benedictus,* Zechariah's song (Luke 1:68–79), "Now Bless the God of Israel" (hymn 110). Shirley Erena Murray's "Carol Our Christmas" (hymn 141) contextualizes the birth of Christ for the "upside-down" place of her native New Zealand. Geoffrey Ainger's "Born in the Night, Mary's Child" (hymn 152) has gained some prominence in recent hymnals (*3). Several Spanish-language hymns appear in recent hymnals for use during the incarnational cycle. "Toda la tierra" (hymn 121) by Spanish composer Alberto Taulé captures the anticipation of Advent (*5). "Los magos que llegaron a Belén" (hymn 155), by Puerto Rican Manuel Fernández Juncas, has been given a fresh English translation by Carolyn Jennings for *The New Century Hymnal* (*4).

The resurrection cycle begins with Ash Wednesday, and Margaret J. Douroux's "Give Me a Clean Heart" (hymn 188) captures the confessional ethos of that day of atonement (*7). UCC minister Richard Leach has contributed two hymns on Lenten lectionary texts. These include "An Outcast among Outcasts" (hymn 201) and "A Woman Came Who Did Not Count the Cost" (hymn 206). Once again Spanish-language texts and music capture the spirit of the season, as in "¡Cristo Vive!" (hymn 235), by Argentinean author Nicolás Martínez and composer Pablo Sosa. The Spanish text appears in other recent hymnals as well (*5). "Hoy celebramos con gozo al Dios" (hymn 246), by Argentineans Mortimer Arias (text) and Antonio Auza (music), is included in a major denominational hymnal for the first time. Its *cueca* rhythms are ideal for a joyful Easter communion service.

Pentecost is highlighted by several fresh hymns by U.S. hymnwriters. "Like the Murmur of the Dove's Song" (hymn 270), by Carl Daw Jr., expresses the hope for "healing of division, with the ceaseless voice of prayer" (*12). Each stanza concludes with petition, "Come, Holy Spirit, Come," anchoring the hope for unity within the spirit of Pentecost. "Wind Who Makes All Winds That Blow" (hymn 271), by Thomas Troeger, focuses on the traditional Pentecostal images of wind and flame but enlarges these metaphors (*6). Finally, Jane Parker Huber retells the Pentecost story as found in Acts 2 in "On Pentecost They Gathered" (hymn 272; *5).

Since the 1960s, political and ecumenical events have changed the face of congregational song in the United States. This essay has attempted to classify some of the theological themes that have resulted and figured most prominently in hymns written in the ensuing decades. There are undoubtedly others, but the eight described above seem to broadly encompass the concerns of writers and worshipers as we come to the turn of the millennium. One can only speculate what theological issues and concerns will find expression in twenty-first-century hymnody. But as long as hymns, songs, and spiritual songs remain central to worship in the Christian community, one can rest assured that poets will continue to find words to articulate our sung prayer and praise in new ways.

NOTE

1. The information on the hymnals comes from a report prepared by C. Michael Hawn for the Hymn Society in the United States and Canada entitled "The Tie That Binds: A List of Ecumenical Hymns in English Language Hymnals Published in Canada and the United States since 1976," *The Hymn* 48, no. 3 (July 1997): 25–37.

A Survey of Hymn Tunes of the Late Twentieth Century

Jonathan B. McNair

Composers of hymn tunes are both privileged and challenged to be working creatively in today's world. They are privileged in having ready access to fine music collected over the past one thousand years, which they may study and draw upon. This includes liturgical and nonliturgical music and various folk and popular traditions, in addition to the deep well of western "classical" music. There are, then, many resources to aid in the crafting of new, interesting tunes. One of the challenges facing composers is to make melodies that large numbers of musically untrained people can learn and sing with reasonable effort, given the liturgical settings in which these tunes will be taught and used.

The New Century Hymnal includes more than sixty hymn tunes composed during the past thirty years, mostly by active U.S. church musicians from a variety of denominational backgrounds and with a variety of stylistic orientations. Ten four-part settings were reviewed for discussion and will be addressed first. The great majority of recent tunes are to be sung in unison. In this large latter group, some accompaniments were clearly written with the organ in mind, reflecting its rich heritage of contrapuntal music. Others are more pianistic, featuring arpeggiated harmonizations. Some may work equally well for either instrument. Still others apparently were written to be accompanied by guitar, with a keyboard realization of the guitar chords being made later, perhaps for practical reasons.

There are great riches to be found in singing and playing the tunes discussed below. Individuals who plan worship services or who are active in other areas of musical leadership in the church have been provided with abundant resources of high quality in *The New Century Hymnal*. It offers music appropriate for children; tunes with roots in folk, popular, and jazz music; melodies that spring from the fertile soil of traditional hymnody; and harmonies that challenge complacent notions about church music.

FOUR-PART SETTINGS

The recent four-part settings surveyed for this article display a considerable variety of styles. TALAVERA TERRACE (hymn 562), by Colin Gibson, is youthful, attractive, and easy to learn, with its roots clearly in popular music. Displaying the influence of popular folk music is the lilting, flowing SONG OF REJOICING, by Martie McMane and Don Brandon (hymn 612), which would be very much at home in an informal setting with guitars instead of keyboard accompaniment. CONSTANTINE (hymn 20), by James Gertmenian and Ronald Huntington, is a sturdy, serious addition to traditional nineteenth-century tunes. Another very traditional four-part tune is CHATHAM, by Peter Cutts (hymn 555), commissioned by *The New Century Hymnal* for a text on healing and wholeness. As the text is a prayer, so is the tune, with clear, diatonic harmonies, smooth voice leading, and chantlike rhythm. Sally Ann Morris's melody NEW BEGINNINGS (hymn 540) is very much from the traditional English school in feeling but is "through-composed" without literal repetition, relying on related melodic gestures and a sequence for coherence. Although the harmonization is also quite traditional, it has a fresh, bright sense about it, coming in part from an occasional mild, unresolved dissonance.

The use of modes, the ancient precursors of major and minor scales, is evident in five of the four-part settings. Two tunes by William Rowan, SEED OF LIFE (hymn 83) and VERBUM DEI (hymn 353), are composed in the D mixolydian mode. Both tunes feature familiar harmonies and clear phrase construction for ease of singing and a syncopated rhythm to heighten interest. The voice leading in SEED OF LIFE is more carefully crafted than in VERBUM DEI, but the latter is more energetic. SHEPHERD'S PIPES by Annabeth McClelland Gay (hymn 320), composed much earlier than any of the other tunes included in this survey, has a very traditional, clear phrase structure. The melody and harmony are drawn (with two exceptions) from the aeolian mode on G.

Arthur Clyde's RELIANCE (hymn 280) is an interesting mixture of dorian mode on D and progressive tonality using functional chromaticisms and excellent voice leading. The melodic climax at the midpoint is balanced by the simultaneous use of the lowest bass note in the tune. The energy here is even greater because of the temporary tonicization of E-flat, a key distantly related to the main tonality of D dorian/minor. E-flat flows into a minor mode on G, which leads smoothly back to D. The use of the "Picardy third" F-sharp in the last chord (see also measure 3) adds a bit more shimmer to the prevailing minor mode. RELIANCE has a convincing dramatic shape, and should be enjoyed by choirs and congregations confident in singing in four parts.

MANTON (hymn 512), by Jane Marshall, also features a wonderfully musical flow of voice leading, demonstrative of the composer's depth of experience with choral music. It has a mystical kind of beauty about it, perhaps stemming from some modally oriented chord progressions, and the logical, yet not quite predictable, contour of the melody. MANTON begins as if it were in B-flat major, then takes a well-prepared but unexpected turn in the second phrase with a modal cadence to a C minor chord. This prepares for the surprising and satisfying A-flats in the third phrase, which is a variation of the first. The B-flat chord in this third cadence now seems quite inconclusive, not at all like the home chord ("tonic"). The fourth phrase utilizes the G-natural minor or aeolian mode, related to the B-flat scale of the first phrase, but ends with the pleasant surprise of G major with the Picardy third (B-natural).

UNISON TUNES

Influences from the English School

There are several recent unison tunes that in sound and feeling are clearly related to English-style hymn tunes of the late nineteenth and early twentieth centuries. The melodies are mostly diatonic and seem familiar due to the use of recurring motives, parallel phrase structure, or repetition. The accompaniments are generally diatonic with some functional chromaticism—functional in the sense that the chromaticisms are integral to the chord progressions rather than serving as embellishments. The part-writing is generally oriented more toward the organ, but all can be played effectively on the piano.

CAMANO (hymn 9), by Richard Proulx, proceeds in mixed meter, with measures of three and four beats, with well-proportioned rhythm. The melody has a rather Welsh character. Some modal inflections (B-naturals) occur in the accompaniment as the tonal center floats between the relative keys of D minor and F major. Particularly attractive is the second phrase, with its contour of a longer descent followed by a shorter ascent to the cadence.

SILVER SPRING (hymn 183), by Carl Schalk, could almost be sung as a four-part harmonization. There are sequences of motives in the melody but no repetition. A sense of coherence without literal repetition may also be found in AMSTEIN (hymn 559), by John Weaver. After the memorable opening gesture, this tune moves almost entirely in stepwise motion. The accompaniment features independently moving lines characteristic of organ music.

The graceful, flowing ANDERSON (hymn 61), by Jane Marshall, conveys vitality with its upward arpeggios and "short-long" rhythmic patterns. The harmony is enriched by functional chromaticisms, suspensions, appoggiaturas, and passing tones. The clear, well-proportioned, and logical phrase structure of ANNIVERSARY SONG (hymn 370), also by Marshall, help to make this very attractive melody memorable and a joy to sing. The harmonies are primarily consonant and very familiar in sound, except at the downbeat of the parallel first and third phrases, where a more dissonant voicing of the chord launches the phrase with greater energy and sense of motion.

In WINSTON-SALEM (hymn 550), by Sally Ann Morris, the pianistic accompaniment begins by moving from an inverted chord in the anacrucis to the submediant chord on the downbeat. This gentle opening also provides an appreciable harmonic contrast with the final cadence as the singer moves from stanza to stanza. The harmonies, while largely traditional, are enriched with seventh chords and added notes or nonchord tones.

Folk Song and Popular Music

The influence of authentic Celtic and U.S. folk song upon hymnody may be readily seen and heard in the various compilations of the early to mid-nineteenth century, such as *Southern Harmony, The Sacred Harp,* and other shape-note hymnals. More recently, the collection and publication of U.S. folk songs during and after the Works Progress Administration helped to make this repertoire more accessible. In the 1950s and 1960s, individuals and groups specializing in the performance of traditional and newly written folk songs attained wide popularity. The lyrics of some of these new folk songs carried political or social commentary and protest. The sociopolitical power of these songs was apparent to people who were trying to bring change and renewal to the church.

Since the 1960s considerable efforts have been made to bring folk and popular music into the church. The results have varied in quality and staying power. Some of these songs were so tied to an event or short-lived sentiment that they became "throwaway" material when the event or sentiment had passed or when popular musical styles changed enough to render them outdated. Others have remained in use, having attained popularity across denominational lines. And fortunately, some composers have absorbed useful influences from folk and popular music, responding with fresh, thoughtful, singable tunes that form a bridge between traditional hymnody and popular music.

The New Century Hymnal includes several selections that grew directly from the style of folk and protest music cultivated in the church during the 1960s and 1970s. Some of these seem more oriented toward responsorial singing, with a soloist or small group singing the stanzas and the congregation singing the refrains. A responsorial approach can make these songs more immediately accessible to congregations in cases of irregular text rhythms in successive stanzas. All of these songs work best when accompanied by piano and/or guitar and feature simple diatonic harmonies. They tend to be inextricably wed to the texts for which they were composed.

Two well-known examples are LIGHT OF THE WORLD (hymn 584), by Jim Strathdee, and SPIRIT (hymn 286), by James K. Manley. The WORLD PEACE PRAYER (hymn 581), by liturgical composer Marty Haugen, features a refrain as substantial as many entire hymn tunes but constructed with enough sequence and repetition to be easily learned. A descant is provided in the refrain. The bright, upbeat BRING FORTH (hymn 181), also by Haugen, is closer in structure to traditional hymnody and could be used, as the composer has suggested, as a processional hymn. It is, however, very much a folk song, and the frequently recurring melodic motives make it easy to learn. Somewhat more challenging is SHARE THE SPIRIT (hymn 62), by Vicki Vogel Schmidt, with its occasional irregular text rhythms. This tune is commended by its bold melody, parallel phrase construction for ease of learning, and energy more akin to rock and roll than to folk music.

A more introspective group of tunes, composed in minor modes with at least a suggestion of Celtic folk music, includes TOLLEFSON (hymn 15), by Paulette Tollefson; THROCKMORTON (hymn 302), by Dan Damon; GATHER (hymn 335), by Elaine Kirkland; and CAROL OF HOPE (hymn 435), by Annabeth McClelland Gay.

Bridging Folk and Mainstream Hymnody

There are several tunes that are part of the bridge between traditional hymnody and popular music but are more refined and more easily adaptable to a variety of texts. REJOICE, REJOICE (hymn 107), by Marty Haugen, is a modern folk carol sparkling with energy. William Rowan's AUSTIN (hymn 583) includes a recognizable fragment of the U.S. folk song "Oh, Shenandoah." TRINITY CAROL (hymn 399), by Peter Cutts, is a modern version of an old English carol with a sequential melody and a dance rhythm throughout. The two-part form is reflective of the text.

More sophisticated in the use of harmony are David Hurd's ST. ANDREW (hymn 171) and JULION (hymn 356), Emma Lou Diemer's MAUNDY THURSDAY (hymn 227), Sally Ann Morris's JOEL (hymn 269), and Jonathan McNair's BENJAMIN (hymn 590).

BENJAMIN has a gently flowing melody constructed sequentially over arpeggiated chords of mixed modes (drawn from both D major and D minor). The opening melodic gesture of JOEL is reminiscent of a slow pop-rock ballad. The rather ethereal harmonies are replete with sweet dissonances generated in part by suspensions and "sighing" figures. MAUNDY THURSDAY shares certain qualities with folk ballads in minor modes. This is especially noticeable in the melodic sequence of the last two measures, which poignantly reinforces the focus of the text. The clear, contrapuntal accompaniment is entirely diatonic with numerous attractive suspensions.

ST. ANDREW and JULION, by David Hurd, have instrumental introductions, interludes, and endings; these are brief in the former and cover an entire phrase in the latter. The rocking, wavelike melody of ST.

ANDREW, with its two-note melismas, is built on the rhythmic pattern of the first phrase of the tune GALILEE, owing perhaps to the text shared between them (see hymn 172). The harmony is considerably enriched with "added notes," many chord inversions, appoggiaturas, and suspensions. JULION, like several early U.S. folk hymns, has a pentatonic melody. The accompaniment, however, has more in common with jazz than with folk music.

Hints of Broadway and Big Bands

The mention of jazz leads to another group of tunes that hint at other popular styles. Three tunes by Carlton Young offer congregations both uplifting and calmer, more pensive music. His WESTCHASE (hymn 11), set with Brian Wren's text "Bring Many Names," became popular throughout the denomination with the use of the *"The New Century Hymnal Sampler,"* long before the hymnal was completed. This very singable and memorable tune is built sequentially on a simple melodic motive and builds to a thrilling, sustained appoggiatura in the climactic "Hail and hosanna!" HOUGHTON (hymn 30), also spun from one melodic motive, is gentle and lush with harmonies that would be at home in a jazz "standard." BEGINNINGS (hymn 417) has the simplest accompaniment of these three tunes. The considerable difference between the two endings lends an air of musical theater.

Another tune with jazz-influenced harmony is MURRAY (hymn 287), by Arthur Clyde, which flows like a happy, graceful dance. Although there are no literal repetitions or obvious melodic sequences, recurring motives reinforce its musical coherence. The use of two progressively higher melodic foci and the "blue-note" A-flat in the penultimate measure contribute to the memorability and enjoyment of this tune. The composer perhaps took delight in the last line of the fourth stanza: "new harmonies to dare."

Music Appropriate for Children

One group of tunes may be of particular interest to worship leaders and educators who are eager to include children in worship and to cultivate in younger generations a love for hymns found more often among older worshipers. These childlike tunes have simple unison melodies constructed with recurring figures and a melodic range appropriate for children, especially those seven years or more in age. The accompaniments are homophonic, with many sustained pitches and a slower harmonic rhythm than is often found in earlier hymnody. The harmonies are mostly diatonic, and in three of the tunes, guitar or autoharp could be used in addition to or in place of piano or organ, opening more possibilities for classroom or small-group settings. In addition, the texts of each of these hymns could provide ample material for exploring with children images, concepts, and issues of contemporary faith. Included in this group are two tunes by Dan Damon, STITELER (hymn 406) and TWILIGHT (hymn 398); two tunes by Colin Gibson, REVERSI (hymn 141) and TENDERNESS (hymn 569); OGONTZ (hymn 560), by Peter Niedmann; and the most widely known tune in this group, ROEDER (hymn 32), by Carl Schalk.

Dan Damon's tunes are usually tailor-made for his own texts, since he is both poet and composer. His TWILIGHT is attractive, both musically and textually, and would make a good children's choir hymn-anthem. Peter Niedmann's OGONTZ offers a more enriched harmonic palette, with somewhat more movement of inner voices and the modally inflected seventh scale step (C-natural in the key of D major). TENDERNESS, by Colin Gibson, offers an option that, although a bit obvious and theatrical, can make the singing of its text more powerful. Gibson suggests that for the second stanza, in which singers confess poor stewardship and recklessness with earth's resources, the accompanist may change from playing in the major mode to the minor mode, returning to major for the remaining stanzas. Such a change of mode is not difficult in this case, as the accompanist simply ignores the key signature for one stanza.

ROEDER, by Carl Schalk, is one of a number of more-recently composed hymn tunes that display in musical structure a strong influence of the texts for which they were written. Here, the poetry by Jaroslav Vajda is cast in stanzas of five lines, divided syntactically and conceptually into line groupings of three plus two. The tune amplifies this structure in its phrase construction. The childlike gesture opening the first phrase is used twice more in sequence, each time extending its range as it ascends convincingly to a melodic high point. Then, as the text changes from a series of addresses to God to a series of questions, the tune descends for the first time by inverting the gesture from the opening of the tune. The last phrase echoes and extends the end of the first phrase.

Renewing Classical Traditions

Among the most musically rewarding tunes in any collection are those that issue from a knowledge of the historic traditions and the more-current developments of classical music. Now, lest the reader take this as an elitist statement, note the use of the phrase "among the most." It is to be hoped that some of the newer tunes written from the perspective of folk and popular music will enter the ecumenical mainstream of treasured hymnody, for many are delightful to sing and enhance the meaning of their texts. But church musicians, clergy, and lay persons seeking to broaden, deepen, and enliven worship should peruse the more classically oriented tunes with ears, hearts, and minds wide open. This music is exalted, not pretentious, and is well worth the somewhat greater effort required to learn and sing. Two familiar precursors are CRUCIFER (hymn 198), by Sydney Hugo Nicholson, and ENGELBERG (hymn 561), by Charles V. Stanford.

One of the great discoveries by such composers as Debussy, Bartók, Copland, Hindemith, and Stravinsky is that familiar harmonies and melodic gestures can be made to sound fresh and new by employing them in a new context, reinterpreting the ways in which one sound relates to another. Several tunes in *The New Century Hymnal* share in this revitalization of traditional harmony. In DUST AND ASHES (hymn 186), composer Hal Hopson makes convincing use of progressive tonality as one means of interpreting the Ash Wednesday text, moving smoothly between closely related keys through excellent part-writing and judicious chromatic inflections. From penitent confession in E minor, the singer moves to hopeful prayer in C major. As the stanzas end, there is a compelling modulation to G major for the bright outcry of the refrain, softening again to C, with a surprise final cadence, even as the work of the Holy Spirit is often surprising. Another tune that delights the singer with the unexpected is the dancelike TOMTER (hymn 194), by Bruce Neswick. The sudden change from F major to A major at the midpoint is handled with finesse as the melody leads the singer with a note common to both keys, and proceeds in familiar parallel phrase structure. The bold, serious impression made by FORTUNATUS NEW (hymn 220), by Carl Schalk, stems in part from its entirely modal structure in both melody and harmony.

One of the numerous fine tunes composed by Peter Cutts that has become well known ecumenically is BRIDEGROOM (hymns 270, 552). The well-crafted, singable melody is constructed with a recurring rhythmic pattern in sequential phrases that build in urgency to the high point, followed by the calmer, more sustained but brief refrain.

The seemingly epic proportions of LET US HOPE (hymn 461), by Emma Lou Diemer, become easily manageable upon recognizing the repetitions and restatements. Like HYFRYDOL, the suggested alternate tune for this text, LET US HOPE flows in a winsome, dancelike manner. The contrapuntal accompaniment makes frequent use of an energetic dotted rhythm. Sequential and imitative passages also contribute to the strong sense of coherence. The harmonies are enriched by the modal D-flats, the numerous seventh chords, and the many nonharmonic tones.

ANDREW (hymn 467), by Jonathan McNair, begins as if it were in the lydian mode, but as the first phrase progresses, one realizes that the home key is G, and the opening gesture simply begins on the subdominant rather than the tonic. There are convincing modulations to the distant key of B major, then back to G through a deceptive cadence. The meter changes gracefully between groups of three, five, and six beats, following the rhythm of the text. The melodic phrases flow sequentially, and from the high point in the last phrase a descending sequence cascades down in the manner of a hemiola.

A thorough assimilation of Baroque techniques of composition may be found reinterpreted in the remarkable tune DE TAR (hymn 587). Calvin Hampton, with consummate craft, produced a short composition with considerable musical depth yet with an uncomplicated musical surface. DE TAR unfolds in three distinct layers: melody, bass line, and harmonic accompaniment. The melody has a quality not unlike an epic ballad, in that it is serious but not pompous or contrived, and is worthy of singing through numerous stanzas without "wearing thin." It is certainly within the reach of any singing congregation, with a range limited to one octave, and mostly stepwise motion. A countermelody, printed in cue-sized notes, imitates the melody canonically. Though optional, it is highly recommended, as it strengthens the reflective qualities of the melody. The bass line has a clear melodic and rhythmic shape of its own and strongly supports the melody. The harmonic layer, almost entirely consonant triads, pulsates in a syncopated figure. These three layers interact to produce a clear but seamless binary structure that allows the singer enough time at the end of each phrase to reflect a bit on what has just been sung.

Expanding Musical Parameters

Very few of the musical innovations of the twentieth century may be found in wide use by church musicians. This is unfortunate, for some of these new modes of musical thought, used with sensitivity, could make powerful impressions on worshiping congregations. It is encouraging, however, to find some well-crafted hymn tunes in which more-advanced harmonies and notions of tonality are used. These tunes appear not only in smaller, specialized, publisher's collections but in several denominational hymnals. It is hoped that these tunes are being sung—at least by soloists and choirs if not by whole congregations—for if the hymnic repertoire of the church is not refreshed and broadened, congregational singing may become stale and thoughtless.

Carol Doran has published a significant body of innovative tunes, three of which are included in *The New Century Hymnal*. CHRISTPRAISE RAY (hymn 54) is a wonderful addition to the tradition of uplifting processional hymns so treasured by the church. The attractive diatonic melody opens somewhat like a fanfare, in support of the exhortation of the text to praise Christ and the numerous attributes of Christ described therein. The second phrase draws the singer inexorably through an entire octave from the lowest melodic note upward in stepwise motion that mounts in excitement to the refrain. The refrain is also a fanfare, leaping from one to another of the structural pitches of the key, climaxing significantly on "cross." The contrapuntal accompaniment features bright, sparkling dissonances that arise largely from the voice leading and therefore seem very much a part of the texture.

AUTHORITY (hymn 176) is a name that well befits the tune, composed specifically for a text that forthrightly addresses the stories of Jesus casting out unclean spirits. In the first two phrases, the melody drives forcefully, insistently repeating pitches in a simple contour somewhat like a medieval reciting tone. The accompaniment amplifies the strange scenario with repeated chords, most of which are dissonant, even harshly so. It is difficult to specify a key or scale for these two phrases. The more hopeful sense of the third and fourth phrases is conveyed by a shapely and flowing melodic contour, a focused sense of tonality, and less dissonance in the harmony. The match of music and text is rarely as powerful as it is here, though it may be quite unfamiliar and even disturbing to some congregations.

FALCONE (hymn 271) is among the most sophisticated of recently composed hymn tunes. The musical and spiritual rewards it offers far outweigh the effort required to learn it. There is no literal repetition among phrases, but recurring rhythmic and melodic motives lend coherence. The accompaniment features a sure sense of counterpoint. The binary form of the tune reflects the poetic structure of the first two stanzas, which open with invocations to the Holy Spirit by way of evocative imagery, then state a focused prayer. The first part is more highly chromatic, with unexpected and strangely beautiful harmonies moving in a simple, mostly homorhythmic texture. The second part is more highly contrapuntal and entirely diatonic, with more motion, building powerfully to the climax in the middle of the third phrase. The urgent repeated pitches in the melody of the third phrase mirror the fervent prayer of the text.

David Hurd has also made significant contributions to church music as a composer and through his work on *The Hymnal 1982*. His tune MIGHTY SAVIOR (hymn 93) should be on the must-learn list for any congregation or worshiping group that holds evening prayer or other evening services. The melody is simple and very much like a lullaby, perhaps because the text is an evening hymn. The gently undulating melodic patterns and clear phrase structure help to make this tune memorable, and the strong but not emphatic bass and harmonic motion lend a graceful dancelike quality. Although the harmonies are basically diatonic, there are numerous chords constructed differently from traditional triadic harmonies (specifically, built up of successive and/

or adjacent perfect fourths or fifths, important intervals in medieval music theory and appropriate in setting a medieval text). These chords produce a mystical, shimmering effect. The cadences ending the first three phrases are wonderfully inconclusive, drawing the singer on through to the floating melismas of the final phrase, which fall to the lowest pitch of the tune, mirroring the nightfall.

Because of limitations of space and time, other tunes worthy of comment will simply be mentioned and commended to the reader's attention. WATER OF BAPTISM (hymn 169), another remarkable tune by David Hurd, was composed specifically for *The New Century Hymnal*. Other fine tunes, worth singing and studying, are POST STREET (hymn 201), by Dan Damon; ANNIKA'S DANCE (hymn 180), by Jane Marshall; the energetic LADUE CHAPEL (hymn 274), by Ronald Arnatt; ROSEBERRY (hymn 585), by Bruce Neswick; and the intriguing, ethereal HANCOCK (hymn 462), by Eugene Hancock.

The New Century Hymnal has made it possible for current and future generations of Christians to sing to God some of the "new songs" spoken of in the Psalms and to do so confidently, in a context of familiar tunes surrounding the newer ones. The dazzling array of musical styles may remind us all of the unimaginable vastness of the realm of God.

Ecumenical and Global Congregational Song in the Late Twentieth Century

C. Michael Hawn

Many hymnals published in the United States since 1975 reflect an awareness of global hymnody. The movement to include composed songs and folk melodies beyond European American traditions in these hymnals finds its roots in several sources. This essay will discuss three wellsprings of global hymnody: (1) Minority cultural traditions within in the United States; (2) ecumenical influences in mainline and evangelical liturgical traditions; and (3) intentional faith communities with a global perspective, most notably the communities of Taizé and Iona. The last two sections will include a discussion of an evolving core of global materials that are becoming a part of the congregational song repertoire in mainline denominational hymnals, especially as represented in *The New Century Hymnal*.

MINORITY CULTURAL TRADITIONS WITHIN THE UNITED STATES

The United States contains a world of cultural diversity within its borders. Before mainline congregations could explore the music of Asian, African, and Latin American Christians, the cultural majority needed to incorporate songs from minority neighbors into their worship. One of the major contributions of hymnals published between 1950 and 1975 was the inclusion of spirituals from both rural white and African American traditions. Most hymnals added melodies and texts from the Southern oblong tunebook heritage (also known generically as the "Sacred Harp" or Solfa tradition) and the camp-meeting revivals of the early nineteenth century. These sturdy, easy-to-sing melodies, often pentatonic, introduced churches in mainline urban America to rural religious song.[1] The Methodist *Book of Hymns* (1964) and the *Baptist Hymnal* (1975) incorporated many tunes and hymns from rural white America, especially because the piety of these denominations had roots in this tradition.

Closely related was the music of the African American spiritual. The *Pilgrim Hymnal* (1958), with seven entries, was at the vanguard of mainline hymnals from the majority culture to include African American spirituals. *The Hymnal of the United Church of Christ* (1974) records eleven "Negro melodies" in the index. Since that time, most hymnals have followed the trend of incorporating a number of African American spirituals. It is now possible to discern a core of spirituals in regular use among mainline congregations.[2] In 1976, when the Consultation on Ecumenical Hymnody (CEH) completed its list of 227 recommended hymns, the trend toward including both the tunes of the rural white tunebook tradition and African American spirituals was solidified. Eleven "Sacred Harp" tunes and four African American spirituals were on the CEH recommended list.[3]

The hymns of other minority groups within the United States now appear in recent hymnals. Spanish-language hymnals have been published increasingly in the United States since the mid-1980s by majority denominational publishers. Native American hymns, while less common, are represented in some hymnals. The best-known Native American hymn is "Wakantanka Taka Nitawa," which is provided in two English translations in *The New Century Hymnal,* including the familiar "Many and Great, O God, Are Your Works" (hymn 3), by R. Philip Frazier, and Sidney Byrd's more recent (1993) "Great Spirit God" (hymn 341). Spanish-language and Native American hymns as well as white rural and African American spirituals demonstrate the influence of songs from minority cultures on hymnals published by the majority culture.[4] The inclusion and use of these hymns prepare the way for congregations to incorporate global songs from outside the United States.

ECUMENICAL INFLUENCES IN MAINLINE AND EVANGELICAL LITURGICAL TRADITIONS

Similar to most hymnals published during the seventies, *The Hymnal of the United Church of Christ* (1974) had a paucity of global song outside of the Euro-American tradition. An Israeli folk song was employed with the Walter Jabusch text "The King of Glory" (hymn 75), and a Korean hymn tune was paired with a text by the famous Sri Lankan churchman D. T. Niles, "On a Day When Men Were Counted" (hymn 103). *The New Century Hymnal* not only rectifies this situation but is among the leaders of denominational hymnals offering a panoply of global song. The reforms of the Second Vatican Council during the 1960s opened up an ecumenical dialogue in the global liturgical community.

Among the main vehicles for ecumenical expression were the general assemblies held by the World Council of Churches (WCC) every eight years. The liturgies prepared for the assemblies are among the highlights of these ecumenical gatherings.[5] The first major hymnal of global song produced by the WCC was *Cantate Domino.* Now in its fourth edition, *Cantate Domino* was first published in 1924 (64 hymns), with revisions in 1930 (82 hymns) and in 1951 (120 hymns). The latest edition, edited by the late eminent hymnologist Erik Routley, appeared in a melody-only version in 1974 and a full-harmony version in 1980.[6] This book is a radical departure from previous editions, containing 202 selections in thirteen languages. For the first time, Roman Catholics and

Orthodox Christians participated actively in the preparation of the book. Texts appear in the original language and, usually, in English, French, and German as well. Some songs have been translated into as many as eight languages, however. Selections from *Cantate Domino* that appear in *The New Century Hymnal* include: "Ah, What a Shame I Have to Bear" (hymn 203), by Sogo Matsumoto and set to a Japanese melody; "¡Cristo Vive!" (hymn 235), by Argentineans Pablo Sosa (music) and Nicolás Martínez (text); "Jesus the Christ Says" (hymn 48), an Urdu song from Pakistan or northern India; "O Bread of Life" (hymn 333), by Chinese author Timothy Tingfang Lew and musician Yin-Lan Su; "O God in Heaven" (hymn 279), a trinitarian hymn by Filipina Elena G. Maquiso; and "Sekai no Tomo" (hymn 72), based on a Gagaku (Japanese court music of the emperor) melody with text by Tokuo Yamaguchi.

In addition to *Cantate Domino,* publications produced for the international assemblies have become a source of songs. This is especially true for the liturgies of the Sixth General Assembly in Vancouver (1983), under the theme "Jesus Christ, the Life of the World," and the Seventh General Assembly in Canberra, Australia (1991), with the theme "Come Holy Spirit, Renew the Whole Creation." From the Vancouver General Assembly, *The New Century Hymnal* includes "Many Are the Lightbeams" (hymn 163), a text based on a third-century hymn by Cyprian of Carthage; "Let Us Talents and Tongues Employ" (hymn 347), a delightful hymn for Holy Communion with a text by Fred Kaan paired with a Jamaican folk song adapted by Doreen Potter; and the "Hallelujah" refrain (hymn 766), from Zimbabwe. Music from the Canberra Assembly includes the Caribbean refrain "Halle, Halle" (hymn 236); an Argentinean prayer hymn, "Santo, santo, santo" (hymn 793); and "Praise to God" (hymn 5), a Japanese text by Nobuaki Hanoaka set to the traditional SAKURA melody. Other examples from the Taizé Community are discussed below.

Publications derived from the liturgies of the WCC assemblies continue to spread the seeds of global song. *Worshipping Ecumenically: Orders of Service from Global Meetings with Suggestions for Local Use* (1995) is a recent worship resource for use in local churches or ecumenical gatherings.[7] In addition to several of the hymns listed above, this collection of liturgies contains the following songs found in *The New Century Hymnal:* the Orthodox Trisagion "Agios O Theos" (hymn 747); Pablo Sosa's "Gloria" (hymn 758); and three South African hymns: "Masithi" (hymn 760), "Siyahamb'" (hymn 526), and "Thuma Mina" (hymn 360).

Because oral practice rather than written music establishes the performing tradition of congregational song in many parts of the world, the WCC invites musicians from around the world to teach their songs at assemblies and other gatherings and to collaborate with the WCC on its publications. The most-prominent global musicians since 1980 are I-to Loh, a Presbyterian ethnomusicologist from Taiwan; Per Harling, a Lutheran pastor from Sweden; Patrick Matsikenyiri, a Methodist composer and teacher from Zimbabwe; and Pablo Sosa, a Methodist minister and music professor from Argentina. I-to Loh has several contributions in *The New Century Hymnal*, including a harmonization of the Taiwanese hymn "God Created Heaven and Earth" (hymn 33) and the phonetic transcription of the Japanese hymn "Sekai no Tomo" (hymn 72). In addition to the "Gloria" (hymn 235) mentioned above, Pablo Sosa also composed "Si fui motivo de dolor, oh Dios" (hymn 544) and "Este es el día" (hymn 65).

Evangelical Christians, while not usually participants in the WCC, have also joined the chorus of those singing global song, largely through the preparation of special song books for specific assemblies. Both the Lausanne II assembly in Manila (1989) and the Baptist World Alliance meeting in Argentina (1995) have resulted in the publication of global collections.[8] While many of the songs used by the WCC and mentioned above are available in these collections, the gospel-song tradition of the United Sates generally plays a more significant role in these evangelical conferences. One might say that a theology of creation characterizes the WCC liturgies, and a theology of salvation guides the worship of the evangelical gatherings.[9]

INTENTIONAL FAITH COMMUNITIES WITH A GLOBAL PERSPECTIVE

The Taizé Community has become a place of pilgrimage for young people from around the world. In July 1940 Roger Louis Schutz-Marsauche, a Reformed minister, arrived in the tiny community of Taizé in the southeastern part of France, approximately one hundred miles from the Swiss border. Roger had many doubts about his faith during his seminary years at Lausanne. In response to this and to the conditions of occupied France, he cast his lot with the poor and disadvantaged. His dream was to live in community with others who would practice the essential dimensions of the gospel in a manner that would offer a response of Christian reconciliation and hope in the face of the horrors of the war. Brother Roger, as he became known, found a place for such a community in the village of Taizé, just north of Cluny. One thousand years earlier, Cluny had been the site of one of the great medieval monastic traditions of the church. The community of Taizé would draw from this heritage but expand it to fit the needs of a conquered France in search of hope.

Today, more than fifty-five years later, Brother Roger's work continues in this ecumenical community of approximately eighty brothers who, similar to their predecessors in Cluny, have taken vows of poverty and chastity.

These brothers, however, come from all over the globe and represent a wide spectrum of denominational beliefs. The community includes Reformed, Anglican, Orthodox, and Roman Catholic Christians. The overarching theme of Taizé is reconciliation through prayer. The majority of the brothers divide their time between reflection and service—a reflective life in the rolling hills of Burgundy surrounding Taizé where they greet and counsel thousands of pilgrims annually from around the globe, and a life of service in some of the poorest and most hopeless situations in the world, such as Calcutta, Haiti, and New York City.

The usual Taizé service is based on the historic Service of the Word with some variations. Singing, silence, scripture (usually read in several languages), and prayer permeate morning, noon, and evening prayer services. Daily worship at Taizé includes neither communion, except for morning prayer, nor a sermon. It draws from more contemplative roots where silence and reflection are central to worship and mantralike music allows the participants to center their thoughts on the adoration of God. To the average Protestant worshiper in the United States, prayer in the Taizé Community, with fewer words and extended periods of silence, may be at once disturbing and refreshing.

The music used in the three services of daily prayer was composed for the unique liturgical needs of the community by the brothers in the community and by Jacques Berthier, a composer and friend of Taizé who died in 1994. With young people coming to this tiny hamlet from around the world, the worship calls for a kind of music that is accessible to these global pilgrims. Through the use of chorales, ostinatos (short, repetitive refrains), acclamations, responses, and canons, worshipers with radically diverse liturgical and linguistic backgrounds are able to participate immediately. While vernacular versions of Taizé songs are available, worshipers often sing in Latin because it is a historical language of the church, unifying the singers in the mystery of prayer. After visiting Taizé, Pope John XXIII said, "Ah, Taizé—that little springtime!"[10]

The New Century Hymnal includes five selections from the Taizé Community, all found in the "Service Music" section. "Gloria" (no. 756) is a canon that can serve several functions in mainline worship within the United States. It might follow the gospel lesson or other scripture. The congregation may also sing it at the reception of tithes and offerings. During the Advent and Christmas season, it is appropriate to sing the song of the angels (Luke 2:14). With a brief rehearsal, the congregation can sing the canon in two or more parts. In the spirit of Taizé, the cantor should not prescribe the number of times the canon will be sung. Allow the chorus to swell with each repetition and then bring it to completion naturally when the time seems right. Two Taizé "Alleluias" (nos. 767, 768) are in *The New Century Hymnal*. These make excellent responses to appropriate scripture. Alleluia 768 might also be used with a suitable psalm (e.g., Psalms 100, 147, 148, 149, or 150) as a sung response by the congregation. A cantor can chant the text of the psalm freely above the humming of the choir and congregation. "Nada te turbe" (no. 772), a sixteenth-century text by Teresa de Jesús (Avila), is a popular Spanish-language refrain. As a selection to guide prayer or to prepare for silent reflection, it might be sung thirty times or more at Taizé, creating a luminous atmosphere in which the worshiper lets all other concerns fall away and communes directly with the Creator. "Eat This Bread" (no. 788) is similar in spirit to "Nada te turbe." It may be sung in preparation for Holy Communion or during the reception of the elements, either seated or in procession. All of these brief responses are easily memorized, allowing singers to reflect, listen, pray, or even move as they sing. In all cases, leaders should avoid the temptation to control, conduct, or explain how many times to sing the selections. Prepare the choir, allow them to guide the congregation in sung prayer, and wait for the movement of the Holy Spirit. While the use of an organ or other keyboard instrument can be helpful initially, encourage the congregation to sing unaccompanied at their own tempo.

The Iona Community is an ecumenical fellowship of men and women, seeking new ways of living the gospel in today's world. Iona is the island on which Saint Columba landed in 597 C.E. to begin a mission of peacemaking and evangelism, the consequences of which determined the expression of Christianity throughout the British Isles. The present Iona Community was founded in 1938 by Reverend George McLeod, initially to rebuild the ruined abbey on Iona and subsequently to be a sign of reconciliation and contradiction in the areas of politics and religion. Its spiritual home is on the small island off the west coast of Scotland, but today its two hundred members, nine hundred associates, and two thousand friends live throughout the world. Members are bound together across the geographical divides by a fivefold rule prescribing prayer, Bible study, meeting together, accountability for the use of time and money, and working for peace and justice. Each year more than two hundred thousand people visit the ancient cradle of Christianity on Iona; the community's residential centers house more than a hundred guests per week.[11]

Most worship material from the Iona Community comes from the Wild Goose Worship Group—sixteen young adults who, under the leadership of John Bell[12] and Graham Maule, discuss and develop new strategies for public worship. A core group of four is employed full-time in this liturgical ministry. They take their name from one of the ancient Celtic symbols for the Holy Spirit.[13]

The Iona Community uses an eclectic assortment of musical resources and draws on global songs from African, Asian, Latin American, and Orthodox traditions. Their own original material may take a traditional stanza form, often with a refrain, or may employ ostinato-style chorales ("wee-songs") resembling Taizé chants. Melodies are frequently of folk origin from the British nations or the United States. Others are composed by John Bell, who also adapts or reharmonizes existing tunes in the public domain.

The style of worship services encouraged by the community transcends denominational boundaries. It is highly participatory, encourages the use of symbolic action, addresses issues of social justice as well as personal spirituality, and maximizes congregational song. John Bell believes that the song of the people is paramount and encourages congregational rehearsals prior to the services, often enabling non-musicians to engage in four-part a cappella singing.[14]

The New Century Hymnal includes six hymns from the community that are more or less in the traditional form comprised of stanzas with a refrain. "Let Heaven Your Wonders Proclaim" (hymn 29) is a Filipino song arranged by Bell with a text paraphrased by the Iona Community. It first appeared in *Sent by the Lord: Songs of the World Church* (1991), one of the global collections prepared by John Bell. The melody is by Salvador Martinez, a Filipino theology professor who teaches in a Christian university in northern Thailand.

Three hymns are from the Iona collection *Heaven Shall Not Wait* (1987). "Sing a Different Song" (hymn 150) is a Christmas song that combines the joy of the birth of Christ with concern for peace and justice. Using the traditional English tune SCARLET RIBBONS, "Who Would Think That What Was Needed" (hymn 153) explores the irony of the incarnation. "Praise with Joy the World's Creator" (hymn 273) reflects on each manifestation of the Trinity within the context of justice.

The remaining two songs are from the Iona collection *Enemy of Apathy* (1988). "The Time Was Early Evening" (hymn 344) stresses that the holy meal is a place where Christ meets us. "O God, My God" (hymn 515) is a hymn based on Psalm 22 that gives voice to those who feel abandoned by God. Many of the hymns of the Iona Community express themes of justice. All hymns encourage holistic worship, where prayer and action combine, as an authentic expression of Christian faith.

CONCLUSION

In the early church, there was extreme diversity of worship practice and perspective. Much of this diversity was due to the relative isolation of individual congregations from one another and the slow process of gathering groups of churches into various strands that became the major worship traditions in the East and West. Since the Second

Vatican Council, Roman Catholics and Protestants have been engaged in liturgical dialogue around issues of lectionary and the sacraments at a level of discussion heretofore unprecedented. These discussions have resulted in some degree of unity around the lectionary readings used by many congregations and the general structure of the sacraments of baptism and communion.

At the same time, cultural diversity has come to the forefront, and liturgy consequently reflects this diversity, especially in congregational song. We should not view this diversity as negative. The early church developed regional unity around the great historical worship traditions. We may also develop a unity of spirit by sharing others' expressions of praise and prayer. As we learn one another's songs, share prayers, and compare creeds and confessions, we come closer to understanding that the image of God (*imago Dei*) is much more diverse than we had ever imagined. This cross-pollination of congregational song can only enrich those who are open to fresh winds of the Spirit. May our global singing reflect the intent of the Seventh General Assembly of the World Council of Churches, whose theme was "Come Holy Spirit, Renew the Whole Creation."

NOTES

1. For more information, see George Pullen Jackson, *White Spirituals in the Southern Uplands* (New York: Dover, 1965).

2. For the developing core of African American spirituals in mainline Protestant hymnals, see C. Michael Hawn, "A Survey of Trends in Recent Protestant Hymnody: African-American Spirituals, Hymns, and Gospel Songs," *The Hymn* 43, no. 1 (January 1992): 21–28.

3. See "Hymns and Tunes Recommended for Ecumenical Use," *The Hymn* 28, no. 4 (October 1977): 192–209, for the complete list.

4. For the general influence of global song on mainline Protestant hymnals, see C. Michael Hawn, "A Survey of Trends in Recent Protestant Hymnody: International Hymns," *The Hymn* 42, no. 4 (October 1991): 16–25.

5. See *Jesus Christ— The Life of the World: Prayers and Litanies* (Geneva: World Council of Churches, 1987) from the Vancouver Assembly (1983), and *In Spirit and in Truth: Hymns and Responses* (Geneva: WCC, 1991) from the Canberra, Australia, Assembly (1991).

6. Erik Routley, ed., *Cantate Domino: An Ecumenical Hymn Book* (New York: Oxford University Press, 1980).

7. Per Harling, ed., *Worshipping Ecumenically: Orders of Service from Global Meetings with Suggestions for Local Use* (Geneva: WCC Publications, 1995).

8. See Corean Bakke and Tony Payne, eds., *Aleluya: Let the Whole World*

Sing (Chicago: Cornerstone Press, 1994), which was the collection used in Manila for the Lausanne II gathering. See David Peacock and Geoff Weaver, eds., *World Praise* (London: HarperCollins, 1993) for the musical resource used by the Baptist World Alliance meeting in Buenos Aires in 1995.

9. For a discussion of creation versus salvation approaches, see Robert Schreiter, *Constructing Local Theologies* (Maryknoll, N.Y.: Orbis Books, 1985), 30.

10. For more information, see J. L. Gonzalez Balado, *The Story of Taizé*, 3d ed. (London: Mowbray, 1990).

11. For more information, see *What Is the Iona Community?* (Glasgow: Wild Goose Publications, 1988).

12. John Bell corresponded with the author on January 16, 1997, with comments on the material on the Iona Community for this entry.

13. For a more complete description of this creative process, see John Bell and Graham Maule, *Heaven Shall Not Wait* (Chicago: GIA Publications, 1989), 8.

14. For sample orders of worship, see *The Iona Community Worship Book*, rev. ed. (Glasgow: Wild Goose Publications, 1991).

Hymn Profiles

Introduction to the Hymn Profiles

Robert L. Anderson

The purpose of these hymn profiles is to provide information on each hymn in *The New Century Hymnal* in the form of short background notes. Thus, these profiles are designed not as an exhaustive study but as brief, inviting glances into the circumstances and sources of the words and music and the authors and composers who created them.

The format for the profiles consists of four paragraphs for each hymn within the following framework:

1. The author of the text (with birth/death dates), the reason or circumstances surrounding its creation, or the earliest source of publication.
2. General biographical information about the author or translator of the text.
3. The composer of the music (with birth/death dates), the name of the tune (in capital letters), circumstances of its creation, or the source in which it appeared.
4. General biographical information about the composer or arranger of the tune.

Obviously, because of the eclectic nature of the origins of hymns, this format cannot be followed in every case. The reader will therefore find other information such as reflections on the use or meaning of the hymn, the historical tradition or culture where it originated, or even performance suggestions. In every case, it is hoped that the information presented is relevant and even inspiring to those who seek to learn more than can be gained from the hymn page or to enhance their experience of singing a hymn in worship.

If desired, the individual background notes may be read aloud by a worship leader or reproduced in a church bulletin. (Please see copyright information on copyright page.) Since there are four notes for every hymn, a different aspect of the hymn can be featured each time it is sung. Additional notes on any given author or composer can be found by checking the index for other hymns by that person. Each of the citations is intended to provide distinct information. Taken together, they offer a fuller portrait of a writer's life and work.

1 Immortal, Invisible, God Only Wise

Walter Chalmers Smith (1824–1908) based the words of this hymn on 1 Timothy 1:17 for his 1867 Hymns of Christ and the Christian Life. It subsequently appeared with Smith's own revisions in Congregational Hymns (1884), edited by W. Garrett Horder, a Congregational minister in England.

A minister of the Free Church of Scotland, Walter C. Smith served churches in London, Milnathort, Glasgow, and Edinburgh. His interest in poetry led to the publication of a number of collections, including *The Bishop's Walk* (1860) and *A Heretic and Other Poems* (1891).

This hymn's tune, ST. DENIO, known in Wales as JOANNA, was based on an old folk melody traditionally sung with words about a cuckoo. It was modified and first used as a hymn tune by John Roberts in his *Canaidaeth y Cysegr* (1839). St. Denio is the Latin form of St. Dennis.

Many Welsh hymn tunes originated from folk songs or ballads that were already familiar in secular settings. These typically strong tunes adapted well to hymn texts and are often memorable in their predictable structure. ST. DENIO was first used with this text in *The English Hymnal* (1906)—a pairing that has proved widely successful for nearly a century.

2 Glory, Glory Hallelujah

This African American spiritual, reflecting stories of liberation in Genesis and Exodus, reminds the singer that greater health and spiritual expression can be obtained by "laying down" burdens of the temporal world. Repetition is an important element in the text.

This African American spiritual song incorporates lines from another traditional song known as "Jacob's Ladder" (hymn 500). Additional verses such as "I'm going home to live with Jesus" are often improvised but always include the response "since I laid my burdens down."

This tune, called GLORY, GLORY after the text, lends itself to a variety of performance styles. This upbeat arrangement was created for *The New Century Hymnal* by Joyce Finch Johnson, a member of the Hymnal Committee.

In her book *African American Christian Worship,* Melva Wilson Costen suggests this spiritual would be an effective song for a "ring shout" as experienced during worship at an African American "praise house" along the southeastern U.S. coast. A "ring shout" was a worship ritual involving a circular dance or shuffle.

3 Wakantanka Taku Nitawa
(Many and Great, O God, Are Your Works)

Joseph R. Renville (1779–1846) wrote this Creation hymn based on Jeremiah 10:12–13. The original seven-stanza text first appeared in the words-only hymnbook *Dakota Dowanpi Kin* (1846). It continues to hold great significance for the Dakota people and is traditionally sung slowly and with dignity.

Francis Philip Frazier (1892–1964), a Congregational minister, paraphrased the first and last stanzas of Renville's Dakota text into English for a YWCA national meeting in 1930 so that youth could understand the words. The song's popularity grew when Frazier and his wife performed it in concerts across the country.

The Dakota melody LACQUIPARLE is named for the mission established at the invitation of Joseph Renville across the Mississippi River from his trading post in western Minnesota. Renville adapted the native tune for his hymn, which appeared with the music in *Dakota Odowan* (1879).

Joseph R. Renville was the son of a French-Canadian trader and a Dakota mother. A committed Christian, he served as an interpreter for the white missionaries and Native Americans and helped translate the Bible into the Dakota language.

4 Joyful, Joyful, We Adore You

Henry van Dyke (1852–1933), a famous preacher and intellectual of his time, wrote this hymn during a visit to Williams College in Massachusetts in 1907, where he was a guest preacher. Van Dyke credited the Berkshire mountains as his inspiration and intended the hymn to be sung to Beethoven's melody.

Henry van Dyke was born November 10, 1852, in Germantown, Pennsylvania, and was educated at Princeton University. Ordained to the Presbyterian ministry, he served churches in Rhode Island and New York and later spent twenty-three years as professor of English literature at Princeton. Van Dyke died at Princeton in 1933.

Ludwig van Beethoven (1770–1827) composed this tune, called here HYMN TO JOY, as the final chorus of his Ninth Symphony. Beethoven was totally deaf when the work was first performed in 1824 in Vienna, Austria. One of the soloists had to turn him around so he could see the enthusiastic response to the music he could not hear.

Beethoven was an accomplished pianist, first playing in public at age seven. He went to Vienna to study with Haydn at the age of twenty-two and remained there for the rest of his life. Beethoven composed some of his greatest works in his last, difficult years when he struggled with deafness and poverty.

5 Praise to God

Nobuaki Hanaoka (b. 1944) wrote this hymn of praise in 1980, reminding Christians that God is known through the created order and through the community found in the church. The final stanza reflects on the triune nature of God.

Nobuaki Hanaoka was born in Saga, Japan, on Christmas Day, 1944. Following his education in Japan and the United States, he was ordained in the American Baptist Church. In 1978 Hanaoka transferred to the United Methodist Church and has served congregations in that denomination since then.

SAKURA ("cherry blossoms") is one of three hymn tunes in *The New Century Hymnal* based on traditional Japanese melodies. Although recent Asian hymn collections present the tune with melody line only, a simple accompaniment by Jonathan McNair is provided for the unison vocal line.

This hymn appears in *Sound the Bamboo* (1990), a hymnal published by the Christian Conference of Asia and the Asian Institute for Liturgy and Music. The latter institution has been instrumental in promoting the use of indigenous melodies and musical styles of Asia and the Pacific Rim in Christian hymnody.

6 Sing Praise to God, Our Highest Good

Johann Jacob Schütz (1640–1690) wrote this hymn, "Sei Lob und Ehr dem höchsten Gut," in his native German. It was published in his 1675 hymnbook, *Christliches Gedenckbüchlein*, in Frankfurt, Germany, where Schütz lived and worked as a lawyer, taking cases in both civil and canon law.

Johann J. Schütz was an early leader in the German pietistic movement. He suggested that Philipp J. Spener begin prayer meetings, which became the backbone of the movement. Schütz eventually became a separatist and turned away from the Lutheran Church.

The composer of this tune, MIT FREUDEN ZART, is unknown, but the hymn can be traced to a hymnbook of the Bohemian Brethren of 1566, where it was used with an Easter text. This melody is similar to one in the 1562 Genevan Psalter and a French secular song circa 1529.

The hymnal of the Bohemian Brethren (*Kirchengesäng*), in which this tune appeared, was one of the earliest Protestant hymnals. It was published in 1566 by Georg Vetter (1536–1599), a priest of the United Brethren (Moravian) Church who is also credited with a Czech version of the Calvinist psalms and the Kralice Bible translation.

7 All People That on Earth Do Dwell

William Kethe (d. 1593 or 1608) is usually credited with this paraphrase of Psalm 100, although some sources claim the first stanza may be the work of Thomas Sternhold. It is the oldest English psalm paraphrase still in general use, first appearing with this tune in both the Anglo-Genevan Psalter and the Scottish Psalter in 1561.

William Kethe, a native of Scotland, was forced to leave for the continent during the persecutions of Queen Mary in 1553 to 1558. He went to Frankfurt and Geneva, where he served as an envoy to fellow exiles and later as chaplain to the English troops under the Earl of Warwick.

Louis Bourgeois (c. 1510–1561), to whom OLD HUNDREDTH is attributed, was known as the music editor of *Trentre quatre Pseaumes* (or Genevan Psalter) of 1551. The tune was originally composed for Psalm 134. It is the only Genevan tune set to a psalm text in *The New Century Hymnal*.

Louis Bourgeois was born in Paris and worked closely with the Protestant Reformation leader John Calvin in Geneva, Switzerland, from 1545 to 1557. Bourgeois adapted and harmonized many French psalter tunes despite Calvin's admonition against part-singing in worship.

8 Praise to the Living God

Curtis Beach (1914–1993) wrote these words in 1966 while attending a conference concerning the "death of God" controversy. He heard the opening words, "Praise to the living God," in his head, accompanied by this tune, and wrote the words that evening, finishing at four in the morning.

Curtis Beach, born in Cambridge, Massachusetts, in 1914, was a minister of the Congregational Christian Church and later the United Church of Christ after the denomination was formed in 1957. Beach served churches in Massachusetts, California, Pennsylvania, and Maine, where he died in 1993.

George Job Elvey (1816–1893) composed DIADEMATA in 1868 for the Matthew Bridges hymn "Crown Him with Many Crowns." It has long been a favorite of hymnwriters and editors, appearing three times in *The New Century Hymnal. Diademata* is the Greek word for crowns.

George J. Elvey was born in Canterbury, England, and began his musical training as a member of the cathedral choir in that city. He continued his studies at the Royal Academy of Music and at Oxford University and served as organist and choir director for almost fifty years at St. George's Chapel, Windsor.

9 We Sing to You, O God

Gracia Grindal (b. 1943) wrote this text in 1985 at the invitation of the composer Russell Schulz-Widmar to be sung to his tune CAMANO. It is based in part on portions of the Song of Moses found in Deuteronomy 32, where God is referred to as "the Rock."

Gracia Grindal was born in Powers Lake, North Dakota, and moved with her family to Salem, Oregon, when she was twelve years old. Her poetry has appeared in a variety of magazines, including *Christian Century, College English,* and *Dialog.* From 1973 until 1978 she served on the Inter-Lutheran Commission on Worship, which produced the *Lutheran Book of Worship* (1978).

Richard Proulx (b. 1937) composed the tune CAMANO in 1979. It appeared with Gracia Grindal's text in *A New Hymnal for Colleges and Schools* (1992), for which Proulx served as musical editor. Proulx has served the Protestant Episcopal Church as organist and choir director for congregations in Seattle and Chicago.

Richard Proulx has been a consultant to many hymnal compilation committees of the late twentieth century. A composer of over 250 works for piano and organ, voice, orchestra, documentary films, and commercials, Proulx has produced two operas—*The Pilgrim* (1978) and *Beggar's Christmas* (1989).

10 Maoz Tsur Y'shuati (Rock of Ages)

This traditional Jewish hymn should not be confused with Augustus Toplady's "Rock of Ages, Cleft for Me," written in 1776. The original Hebrew text has been traced to a thirteenth-century poet known only as Mordechai.

This text, available here in Hebrew and English, is a twentieth-century translation of a very old hymn used to celebrate Hanukkah, the Jewish Festival of Lights. This celebration, mentioned in John 10:22, recalls the 165 C.E. rededication of the Temple at Jerusalem.

This melody, MAOZ TSUR, is called by its traditional Hebrew name here although it is sometimes entitled ROCK OF AGES in other hymnals. The tune, possibly a combination of two different melodies, may have roots in the German Jewish community of the fifteenth century.

This hymn tune is so popular among Jewish congregations that it has been dubbed a "synagogal musical leitmotif for the celebration of Hanukkah." It is sung with a variety of texts during that eight-day celebration, including "Rock of Ages."

11 Bring Many Names

Brian Arthur Wren (b. 1936) based this text on Genesis 1:27 and explains his interpretation in a commentary: "God gives us glimpses of the divine nature in each other, and specifically in our genderedness." Although the text offers some "glimpses" of God throughout, it concludes with the recognition that God is "never fully known."

Brian Wren published a collection of his hymns in 1989, using the name of this hymn for the title, *Bring Many Names*. He continued to work on the text, and this version is the one that appears in *Faith Renewed*—a 1995 publication of thirty-three earlier hymns presented with varying degrees of revisions.

Carlton Raymond Young (b. 1926) composed the tune WESTCHASE for this text in 1989. Young has written many articles and books on hymnody and published more than 150 compositions. He holds the distinction of having edited two major United Methodist hymnals of the twentieth century.

Carlton R. Young was born in Hamilton, Ohio, and received his education at Cincinnati College–Conservatory of Music, Boston University School of Theology, and Union Theological Seminary, New York City. In addition, he studied in Vienna, Austria, and Prague, Czechoslovakia.

12 I Sing the Mighty Power of God

Isaac Watts (1674–1748) wrote this hymn for the first hymnal published exclusively for children, *Divine Songs attempted in Easy Language for the use of Children* (1715). The hymn originally had eight stanzas. Although Watts intended "to sink the language to the level of a child's understanding," this hymn has become beloved by all ages.

Isaac Watts was born July 17, 1674, and studied at a Free School in Southampton, England. He was not allowed to attend the regular university because the Church of England would not admit Dissenters, those who disagreed with the beliefs and practices of the established church.

There are many different versions of the tune ELLACOMBE, and its composer is unknown. The tune has been traced to German Roman Catholics in the eighteenth century and may have been used first in the chapel of the Duke of Wirtemberg, Germany.

This tune is most commonly called ELLACOMBE, a place in Devonshire, England. However, it is also known as AVE MARIA, KLÄRER UND LICHTER MORGENSTERN, the title of the original German song from which it derived.

13 O My Soul, Bless Your Creator

This hymn is a paraphrase of the twenty-two verses of Psalm 103, compressed into sixteen stanzas. It was first published by the United Presbyterian Church of North America in its *Book of Psalms* (1871). That hymnbook was a revision of the Scottish Psalter of 1650, which had been in use for more than two centuries.

This metrical paraphrase of Psalm 103 omits eleven of the original stanzas. Although its origins stems from a Presbyterian hymnbook, the hymn has long been a favorite in the United Church of Christ and appeared in the hymnals that preceded *The New Century Hymnal*.

This tune is named STUTTGART, after the German city. It was first printed in Christian F. Witt's *Psalmodia Sacra* (1715), a Lutheran hymnal published in Gotha, Germany, and Witt is often credited as the composer of the tune.

Christian F. Witt (1660–1716) was trained as a church musician in Vienna, Salzburg, and Nürnberg. He served as court organist and choirmaster at Gotha and composed numerous choral and instrumental works, both sacred and secular.

14 How Can I Say Thanks

Andraé Crouch (b. 1945) wrote this hymn, both words and music, in 1971. Part of the text is derived from the opening of Psalm 115: "to your name give glory." Note that after the hymn is sung all the way through the refrain should be repeated.

Andraé Crouch grew up in a "preacher's home" and was exposed to religious music from an early age. His father became a bishop in the Church of God in Christ (COGIC) denomination. This hymn gives voice to the anxiety of not having the proper words to express gratitude to God.

Andraé Crouch (b. 1945) composed both words and music for this hymn known popularly as MY TRIBUTE. The use of rising tones on the words "To God be the glory"' increases the emotional intensity of the song. Crouch was one of the first performers to use electronic musical instruments in religious settings.

Andraé Crouch was born in Los Angeles, California, in 1945. After college he formed the concert singing ensemble Andraé Crouch and the Disciples, one of the first African American groups to receive national acceptance by Christian audiences. The group has received numerous Grammy awards.

15 My Heart Is Overflowing (The Song of Hannah)

Miriam Therese Winter (b. 1938) paraphrased 1 Samuel 2:1–10 for this text, subtitled "The Song of Hannah." Hannah was for many years childless until she bore Samuel, who became a Hebrew prophet. She, like many mothers, felt that her baby was a gift from God.

Miriam Therese Winter was invited to create a hymn setting of the biblical canticle "Song of Hannah" for *The New Century Hymnal*. She subsequently included the text in her own collection, *Songlines* (1996), set to a tune of her own composition, HANNAH.

Paulette Tollefson (b. 1950) wrote this folk-style tune in 1971 for a class on music theory at St. Olaf College in Northfield, Minnesota. She composed the tune as a setting for words by the poet Richard Wilbur. It was later accepted by the Inter-Lutheran Commission on Worship and named TOLLEFSON in her honor.

Paulette Tollefson has held various secular jobs in the Minneapolis–St. Paul, Minnesota, area, but shares her musical interests in her free time by singing in the Bethlehem Lutheran Church choir, playing in a swing band, and working with several dance groups.

16 Let Us with a Joyful Mind

John Milton (1608–1674) wrote nineteen psalm paraphrases, this one based on Psalm 136. Milton was only fifteen and a student at St. Paul's School, London, England, when he wrote this one, which originally contained twenty-four stanzas. Thomas H. Troeger adapted Milton's words for *The New Century Hymnal*, seeking to remain faithful to the spirit of the original text.

John Milton was an avid supporter of the revolution of Oliver Cromwell in England and wrote in defense of the Commonwealth and for freedom of the press. He was forced by blindness to give up other pursuits and had to dictate his greatest poetic works, including his masterwork, *Paradise Lost*.

This tune was called AN ANCIENT LITANY when first printed in the *Journal of the Society for Promotion Church Music* in 1850. It was later renamed INNOCENTS since it was composed for the Feast of the Holy Innocents, which is celebrated on December 28 in remembrance of the children martyred by Herod.

The Parish Choir was a monthly publication of the Society for Promoting Church Music that offered tunes to fit the English words in the Prayer Book. Its purpose was to improve the quality of music used in the English church of the time. Although it was published only from 1846 to 1851, it accomplished its goal.

17 To You, O God, All Creatures Sing

Saint Francis of Assisi (1182–1226) wrote this hymn in 1225, a year before he died, while suffering illness and temporary blindness during fierce summer heat. The text was inspired by the "Benedicite," an early church canticle based on verses from the Septuagint, and also known as "Canticle of the Three."

Saint Francis of Assisi is remembered as the founder of the Franciscan order. Saint Francis was a great lover of nature and a humble man. His hymns were among the earliest metrical songs in common Italian, and he was responsible for preserving the troubadour style of music in the church.

The name of this tune, LASST UNS ERFREUEN, is taken from the first line of a German Easter hymn, "Lasst uns erfreuen herzlich sehr." It has also been called ST. FRANCIS (because of its association with this text), EASTER ALLELUIA, and VIGILES ET SANCTI.

Geistliche Kirchengesäng is the title of the small Roman Catholic hymnal in which this tune first appeared in Germany in 1623. The Jesuit monks had a great influence over which of the 119 texts and ninety-three tunes were included in this work, although they did not sponsor it.

18 Guide Me, O My Great Redeemer

William Williams (1717–1791) wrote this hymn in Welsh in 1744. The hymn became popular in the United States before it was widely accepted in England. This is the only Welsh hymn to gain international favor, and it has been translated into more than seventy-five languages.

William Williams was known as "the Isaac Watts of Wales" and "the sweet singer of Wales." Although his evangelical views kept him from the ministry of the Church of England, Williams became an itinerant evangelist of the Welsh Calvinistic Methodist Church.

John Hughes (1873–1932) composed this tune, CWM RHONDDA, pronounced "koom rrhawn-tha." *Cwm* means "valley" in Welsh, and *Rhondda* is the name of a river that runs through the heart of the coal mining industry in Wales. Hughes was inspired to compose this during worship one Sunday morning.

John Hughes was born in Dowlais, Wales, in 1873 and became one of that country's most prolific hymnwriters, although he spent much of his life working for the Great Western Railway. CWM RHONDDA is by far his most famous tune, and it is even sung at football (i.e., soccer) matches in Wales.

19 Guide Me, O My Great Redeemer

William Williams (1717–1791) wrote these words in 1744, based on Psalms 104, 105, and 106. The hymn tells the story of the wanderings of the children of Israel, while mirroring the experiences of the Christian's pilgrimage of faith.

William Williams, the "sweet singer of Wales," was born February 11, 1717. He studied to be a doctor but was inspired to join the Christian ministry by a sermon he heard. Williams left the established church of Wales and became an evangelist of the Welsh Calvinistic Methodist Church.

Thomas Hastings (1784–1872) composed the tune ZION on the spur of the moment in 1830 when a new tune was needed for a hymn by Thomas Kelly. It was first published in a hymnal in 1832.

Thomas Hastings worked with Lowell Mason and William Bradbury, and they advanced church music tremendously by their partnership. A self-taught musician, Hastings published over fifty volumes of music and received an honorary doctor of music degree from New York University in 1858.

20 God of Abraham and Sarah

James Curtis Gertmenian (b. 1947) wrote this text in 1986. It was first published as a choral anthem and later revised as a hymn text for congregational singing. Some of Gertmenian's works have been published by Bread for the World, a hunger relief organization.

James C. Gertmenian was raised in South Pasadena, California. He graduated from Oberlin (Ohio) College and Union Theological Seminary in New York City. A United Church of Christ pastor, he has also served Presbyterian churches in Afton and Nineveh, New York, and Brookfield, Connecticut.

James Curtis Gertmenian (b. 1947) composed this melody, CONSTANTINE, to accompany his own text. Ronald Huntington (1929–1994) arranged it as a choral anthem, which was the basis for this four-part harmonization. Huntington was organist at Germenian's "home church" for thirty-two years.

Ronald Huntington II was born in California in 1929 and died in that state in 1994. He had served as professor of Asian religions and university organist at Chapman University in Orange, California.

21 God Reigns o'er All the Earth

Jane Parker Huber (b. 1926) wrote this text in 1981 as a study of the many realms of God's activity. Each stanza touches on a different theme, from nature to human life, to the wider universe, and finally to the revelation of Jesus Christ.

Jane Parker Huber served on the *Presbyterian Hymnal* committee from 1985 to 1989, helping her denomination select the hymns that would be included in this new worship resource. She is the author of four collections of original hymns published between 1982 and 1996.

Franklin L. Sheppard (1852–1930) adapted this traditional English melody for a text by Maltbie Babcock, "This Is My Father's World." It is named TERRA BEATA, meaning "blessed earth." Sheppard claimed to have learned the tune from his mother, although some credit him as the composer.

Franklin L. Sheppard graduated first in his class at the University of Philadelphia and joined his father's business as manager of a foundry. An elder in the Presbyterian Church, Sheppard was president of the Board of Publications and served on the committee that prepared *The Hymnal* (1911) of that denomination.

22 Sing Praise to God, Who Has Shaped

Joachim Neander (1650–1680) based this hymn of thanksgiving on Psalms 103 and 150. He wrote it at age thirty, in the last year of his life, which was cut short by tuberculosis. Neander's hymn appeared later that year in *Glaub- und Liebesübung* (1680) in Bremen.

Joachim Neander was born in Bremen, Germany, in 1650 and died there only thirty years later. A leader in the pietist movement, he has been called the "first poet of the Reformed Church in Germany." Neander sought refuge in nature, prayer, and composing and is credited with more than fifty hymn texts and tunes.

This anonymous tune, LOBE DEN HERREN, was first found in a Stralsund, Pomerania, hymnbook of 1665. Neander adapted the tune for his words in 1680, and it has long been associated with that text, which originally began "Lobe den Herren, den mächtigen König."

The 1665 version of this tune was considerably different from one that appeared with Joachim Neander's text fifteen years later. The tune as it appears here is a composite from several sources and has been sung in this form since the early eighteenth century.

23 There's a Wideness in God's Mercy

Frederick William Faber (1814–1863) wrote these words as part of a larger, thirteen-stanza poem entitled "Come to Jesus." Faber wrote his poems for private devotional use by other Roman Catholics, never intending for them to be sung in corporate worship.

Frederick W. Faber grew up a Calvinistic Protestant but converted to the Roman Catholic faith in midlife. He was rebaptized, taking a new name, Wilfred. His zeal was rewarded when he was presented with a doctor of divinity degree by Pope Pius IX in 1854.

IN BABILONE is the name of this anonymous Dutch tune, which was first transcribed for a 1710 collection of folk melodies. It was first used as a hymn tune in 1910, when Ralph Vaughan Williams paired it with "See the Conqueror Mounts in Triumph," an Ascension hymn.

Julius Röntgen (1855–1932), a renown Dutch musician, composer, and director, was asked to harmonize this simple tune for Vaughan Williams's 1906 *English Hymnal*. Röntgen lived his life in Amsterdam, where he held positions at the Amsterdam Conservatory and Society for the Advancement of Musical Art.

24 Yigdal Elohim Chai (The God of Abraham Praise)

This text is based on the "Yigdal," a Jewish Doxology used as an antiphonal song at close of services on the eve of the Sabbath or at festivals. Moses Maimonides (1130–1205) wrote the original words, which were set in metrical verse by Daniel ben Judah two centuries later.

The "Yigdal," based on Daniel, chapter 7, embodies the thirteen cardinal principles of the Jewish faith. This translation was created by Max Landsberg (1845–1928) and Newton Mann (1836–1926) in Rochester, New York. It employs the opening phrase of an earlier English version by Thomas Olivers.

This Hebrew traditional melody was first adapted by Thomas Olivers (1725–1799), a Wesleyan preacher from Wales, after he heard it sung at a synagogue in London, England. The tune, LEONI, is named for Meyer Lyon, the cantor at Duke's Place synagogue, who helped Thomas Olivers transcribe it for use in Christian worship.

Meyer Lyon (1751–1797), a Jewish cantor, began a promising career as an opera singer in London but was ultimately unsuccessful, partly because of his reluctance to perform on the Jewish Sabbath and other religious occasions. In 1787, Lyon moved to Kingston, Jamaica, to serve a new synagogue, and remained there the rest of his life.

25 O God, Our Help in Ages Past

Isaac Watts (1674–1748) based this hymn on Psalm 90. He wrote it in 1714, at a time when Queen Anne was near death and all of England was anxious about her successor. Many feared that England would be divided by civil strife upon her death. This is undoubtedly Watts's greatest hymn.

Isaac Watts, long considered the father of modern English hymnody, wrote more than six hundred hymns and paraphrases, enabling Protestantism in England and New England to free itself from line-singing the Psalms. Ill health kept Watts a semi-invalid for the last thirty-six years of his life.

William Croft (1678–1727) is thought to have written the tune ST. ANNE while he was organist at St. Anne's Church in Soho, London, England. This tune was not used with these words by Watts until 1861. Tradition holds that Anne was the mother of the virgin Mary, mother of Jesus.

William Croft was born in Ettington, England, in 1678, and greatly influenced English church music during his lifetime. He served as organist at Westminster Abbey and was buried there following his death on August 14, 1727.

26 We Worship You, God

Robert Grant (1779–1838) wrote the words to this hymn in 1833, one year before he was knighted and made governor of Bombay, India. Scholars believe that Grant's words were inspired by William Kethe's paraphrase of Psalm 104.

Robert Grant graduated from Magdalen College, Oxford, England, and became a lawyer in 1807. As a member of Parliament he authored a bill of emancipation for Jews in England, which was eventually voted into law, an early example of tolerance for other religions by a nation.

Johann Michael Haydn (1737–1806), younger brother of Franz Joseph Haydn, is believed to be the composer of this tune, named LYONS. However, it has never been found in any of his tunebooks. The tune was introduced in the United States by Lowell Mason, who discovered it in William Gardiner's *Sacred Melodies.*

William Gardiner (1770–1853), born in the same year as Beethoven, was a hosiery manufacturer who deeply loved church music. This tune was among those in his *Sacred Melodies from Haydn, Mozart, and Beethoven* (1812–1815). Gardiner was a strong admirer of Beethoven and did much to promote that composer's music in England.

27 From All That Dwell below the Skies

Isaac Watts (1674–1748) based this text on Psalm 117—the shortest psalm in the Bible, consisting of only two verses. The "alleluias" were a later addition to match the hymn tune.

Isaac Watts was an ordained minister in the Congregational Church in England, whose career as a pastor was cut short by illness. Subsequently he authored nearly sixty volumes but is best known for his hymns, which liberated worship practices from the constraints of metrical psalm-singing.

The tune LASST UNS ERFREUEN takes its name from the first three German words of the text it accompanied in a 1623 Roman Catholic hymnal from Cologne, Germany. The hymn was used during the Easter season. Like many other hymn tunes, it is believed to have its roots in a folk song.

This tune did not come into use among English-speaking Protestants until Ralph Vaughan Williams prepared this harmonization for *The English Hymnal* (1906), where it was the setting for J. Athelstan Riley's "Ye Watchers and Ye Holy Ones."

28 For the Beauty of the Earth

Folliott Sandford Pierpoint (1835–1917), an English poet, was inspired to write these words by the beauty of a spring day in his native town of Bath. He intended it to be sung as a hymn of joy for services of Holy Communion. It originally had eight stanzas.

Folliott S. Pierpoint was born in Bath, England, on October 7, 1835, and graduated from Queens' College, Cambridge. He served as headmaster at Somersetshire College, taught classics, and wrote a number of sacred poems. Pierpoint died March 10, 1917, at Newport, Monmouthshire, England.

Conrad Kocher (1786–1872), of Würtemberg, Germany, wrote this melody as part of a chorale. It was revised by William H. Monk in 1861 for William C. Dix's hymn "As with Gladness" and later was given the name DIX because of its connection with that text.

Conrad Kocher intended to be a teacher but was influenced by the music of Haydn and Mozart to become a musician. He was organist in the Stiftskirche, Stuttgart, Germany, for nearly forty years. Kocher founded a sacred choral music society and was a leader in the movement to reform German church music in the early nineteenth century.

29 Let Heaven Your Wonders Proclaim

Salvador T. Martinez (b. 1939) wrote this text based on Psalm 89, but John Bell (b. 1949) of the Iona Community reworked and adapted it for publication in *Sent by the Lord: Songs of the World Church*, volume 2 (1991). Bell learned this and another song from Martinez when the two men worked together at conferences in the United States.

The Iona Community of Scotland believes that it is important to learn and sing hymns originating in developing countries. In selecting such hymns, they pick those that are well known and "from the heart," with texts and tunes have been memorized, as proof of their authenticity.

Salvador T. Martinez (b. 1939) wrote this melody in 1989 in the style of a Philippine folk song for his paraphrase of Psalm 89. The tune has been named MARTINEZ here for him. It was arranged by members of the Iona Community for use with this English text adapted by John Bell.

Salvador T. Martinez, a native of the Philippines, has lectured in theological education around the world, primarily through the Asian Christian Council. John Bell reports that Martinez has most recently worked in Thailand.

30 Colorful Creator

Ruth C. Duck (b. 1947) wrote this hymn in 1992 for the installation service of Linda Clark as Houghton Scholar of Sacred Music at Boston University School of Theology, where Duck had also studied, earning her doctor of theology degree in 1989. The text honors the creative activity of artists, composers, and all who give expression to the holy through their work.

Ruth Duck served two local churches in Wisconsin before entering the teaching ministry. They were St. John's United Church of Christ, Hartford, where she served from 1975 to 1979, and Bethel-Bethany United Church of Christ, Milwaukee, where she was pastor from 1979 to 1984.

Carlton Raymond Young (b. 1926) composed this melody in 1992. It is named HOUGHTON for the chair to which Linda Clark was being installed at Boston University School of Theology. Young received his bachelor of sacred theology degree from that institution in 1953.

Carlton R. Young, an ordained United Methodist minister, has served the United Methodist church as director of music in Massachusetts, Ohio, Texas, and Georgia. He has received twenty-three awards from the American Society of Composers and Publishers (ASCAP) for his compositions, which number more than one hundred.

31 All Things Bright and Beautiful

Cecil Frances Alexander (1818–1895) wrote these words to illustrate the section of the Apostles' Creed that refers to God as the "Maker of heaven and earth." It was published in *Hymns for Little Children* (1848). The hymn also recalls God's declaration in Genesis that "it was very good."

Cecil F. Alexander was recognized for her poetic gifts early in life and wrote a total of four hundred hymns. Born in County Tyrone, Ireland, she married William Alexander, a leader in the Irish church, who shared her literary interests.

ROYAL OAK is a traditional English melody sung to celebrate the restoration of Charles II to the throne of England in 1660. Charles hid in an oak tree during his escape from England in 1651, and the tune was sung to words beginning "The 29th of May," the date of Charles II's restoration.

This tune was sung to two different English songs, "The Jovial Crew" and "The 29th of May." May 29, 1660, was the date that King Charles II was returned to the throne of England following the Cromwell overthrow of Charles I as king. Martin Shaw (1875–1958) adapted the traditional melody in 1915.

32 God of the Sparrow God of the Whale

Jaroslav Jan Vajda (b. 1919) wrote this hymn in 1983 at the request of Concordia Lutheran Church in Kirkwood, Missouri, for its 110th anniversary celebration. Notes by the author regarding this hymn in his collection *Now the Joyful Celebration* (1987) state that "the law of God demands perfect love from every creature."

Jaroslav J. Vajda, a Lutheran pastor, edited *This Day* magazine from 1963 until 1971. He also served three bilingual parishes whose members spoke both Slovak and English. Vajda's education and interests in his family heritage have made him one of the world's experts on Slovak hymnody.

Carl Flentge Schalk (b. 1929) collaborated with Jaroslav Vajda on many hymns, including this one. It is named ROEDER for his wife's father, Paul J. Roeder, who was a minister of the Lutheran Church, Missouri Synod.

Carl Schalk was born September 26, 1929, in Des Plaines, Illinois. He was a teacher and church musician in the Lutheran Church, serving in Wausau, Wisconsin, before becoming music director of "The International Lutheran Hour" and professor at Concordia Teachers College, Missouri.

33 God Created Heaven and Earth

This anonymous Taiwanese text is a popular Creation hymn in its original country. It is based on the opening words of Genesis, which relate one of the two Creation stories found in that book. Boris and Clare Anderson, English missionaries, translated the text into English in 1981.

This text has been traced to Amoy, China, but has received widespread use in Asian and U.S. denominational hymnals thanks to the English translation by Boris and Clare Anderson. In *Sound the Bamboo* (1990) a Taiwanese transcription is also provided.

This melody, called TŌA-SĪA, has been traced to the Pi-po tribe, which originally lived on the island of Taiwan. They were a part of the Malayo-Polynesian tribes. I-to Loh (b. 1936), a professor of church music and a hymnologist, harmonized the tune in 1963, preserving the tune's distinctiveness.

I-to Loh (b. 1936) was already active in Asian Christian hymnody before moving to California to study for his Ph.D. in music. He edited *New Songs of Asian Cities* in 1972. I-to Loh teaches at the Tianan Theological College and Asian Institute for Liturgy and Music in Manila, Philippines.

34 Alabanza (As the Rain Is Falling)

Pablo Fernández Badillo (b. 1919) wrote this Creation text one afternoon in the countryside, inspired by the beauty of a red lily. It appeared in *Himnario Criollo* (1977), possibly the first Puerto Rican hymnal to contain printed music. The text expands our awareness of God's relationship with all of creation.

Pablo Badillo was born in Aguadilla, Puerto Rico, and served as a music teacher in that city for several years. His published works include several collections for children (*Albor I, II*) as well as choral works (*Cantar Riqueño*).

Pablo Fernández Badillo (b. 1919) wrote both words and music for his hymn known as ALABANZA in the spring of 1977. Badillo improvised the melody while accompanying himself on guitar. It was first sung at a Presbyterian church in Montaña, Puerto Rico.

Pablo Badillo has contributed greatly to the repertoire of Hispanic hymnody. His *Himnario Criollo*, in which this song first appeared, included 104 hymns, canticles, and responses. The title of this song, "Alabanza," means "praise."

35 O Mighty God, When I Survey in Wonder

Carl Boberg (1859–1940) was inspired to write his nine-stanza poem "O Store Gud" after being caught in a midday thunderstorm while visiting a country estate on the southeast coast of Sweden. Years later, Boberg was surprised to hear his poetry sung to a Swedish melody.

Carl Boberg was a Swedish Lutheran pastor and one of the leading evangelical preachers of his day. In addition, he was the editor of the periodical *Sanningsvittnet*. The new translation and harmonization from Swedish sources were created especially for *The New Century Hymnal* in 1994.

O STORE GUD, an old Swedish folk melody, came to be known by this title through its association with this text by Carl Boberg. Various translations of the text have been made, accounting for the different words found in various hymnals. The tune's singability has certainly added to the hymn's popularity.

Few Swedish songs have found a permanent place in English Protestant hymnody, but this one has had a great impact. The tune was made popular by Beverly Shea, a noted gospel singer with the Graham evangelistic team. First sung in the United States in 1951, it is now among America's favorite hymns.

36 To God Compose a Song of Joy

Ruth C. Duck (b. 1947) translated Psalm 98 from the original Hebrew for a class in which she was learning that ancient biblical language; she later adapted the psalm in a metrical paraphrase for a different class. The text spoke to her of hope in God's justice.

Ruth Duck is an ordained minister of the United Church of Christ. She edited *Becoming One*, a hymn collection of the Boston (Massachusetts) School of Theology, and served on the hymnal committee for the Disciples of Christ's *Chalice Hymnal* (1995).

Thomas Haweis (1734–1820) wrote the tune RICHMOND in 1792. It was named for a friend, Leigh Richmond, who was rector at Bedfordshire Chapel in Bath, England. Haweis served as chaplain to Selina, Countess of Huntingdon, who owned the chapel.

Thomas Haweis abandoned medical studies to become an Anglican clergy. In addition to his work in ministry, he was a capable composer and hymn tune editor. Haweis served churches in Oxford and Aldwinkle, Northamptonshire, England, before becoming manager of Countess Selina's chapels.

37 Our God, to Whom We Turn

Edward Grubb (1854–1939) published this text in his volume *The Light of Life: Hymns of Faith and Consolation* (1925). Its aim was to remind a world devastated by World War I that God's eternal purposes are unchanged by human cruelties.

Edward Grubb, an English Quaker, was born October 19, 1854. He edited a monthly periodical, *The British Friend,* for many years, in addition to writing books about the Quaker religion and social issues such as prison reform. Grubb died on January 23, 1939.

This tune is an old German melody first found in a 1646 songbook. The name STEADFAST was coined by *The Hymnal 1940* to help differentiate the tune from another well-known melody harmonized by J. S. Bach.

The 1648 Appendix to the *Neu Ordentlich Gesangbuch* first included this anonymous melody. The hymnal was printed originally in Hanover, Germany, in 1646. The melody was the basis for J. S. Bach's "Chorale Parita," which presented nine variations on this tune.

38 "Lift Up Your Hearts!"

Henry Montagu Butler (1833–1918) wrote this hymn for the boys at Harrow School, England, where he served as headmaster. It became widely sung when it appeared in *The English Hymnal* (1906). The words quote the "Sursum Corda," a third-century prayer of consecration.

Henry M. Butler was born in Gayton, Northamptonshire, England, and served as headmaster at Harrow School for twenty-six years. In 1886, he became master of his alma mater, Trinity College, Cambridge. Butler's published works include collections of biographies, essays, and sermons.

Walter Greatorex (1877–1949) composed this tune in 1916 for use by the choir of Gresham's School in Norfolk, England, where he taught. He named the tune WOODLANDS for one of the residence houses on the campus. The strong unison tune should be sung with great spirit.

Walter Greatorex was born in Mansfield, Nottinghamshire, England, in 1877 and was educated at Derby School and St. John's College, Cambridge. He devoted most of his life to teaching and serving as music director at schools in England, including Uppingham and Gresham's.

39 Cantemos al Creador (Creator God We Sing)

Carlos Rosas (b. 1939) wrote this processional entitled "Alleluya" as the beginning of the second movement of "Rosas del Tepeyac." It was published in his mass setting *Díez Cançiones Para la Misa* (1976). Rosas has commented that it is one of his favorite songs.

Carlos Rosas was awarded first place in the Concurso Cancion del Papa competition with his song "San Antonio y Roman Cantan," which he performed for Pope John Paul II in 1987. Rosas has written a great deal of music, mostly for church use, and published various articles.

Carlos Rosas (b. 1939) adapted this music from his mass as a hymn tune. It was named ROSAS when used in a hymnal in 1983. In workshops, Rosas has played the tune on guitar rather than on piano or organ. The melody was specifically written as a processional, which is reflected in its steady beat.

Carlos Rosas was born in Linares, Nuevo Leon, Mexico, on November 4, 1939. Educated in Monterrey, Mexico; Mexico City; and San Antonio, Texas, he began working as music director and liturgy coordinator at San Juan de los Lagos parish in San Antonio in 1970.

40 You Are the Way

George Washington Doane (1799–1859) based this text on Jesus' words in John 14:6—"I am the way, and the truth, and the life." It was one of few hymns from the United States to be included in the enduring English hymnbook *Hymns Ancient and Modern* (1861).

George Washington Doane, an Episcopal priest, served churches in New York City, Boston, and Burlington, New Jersey. Doane was admired for his administrative skills, and his distinguished career included academic positions at Trinity College, Hartford, Connecticut, and in the founding of colleges in New Jersey.

Johann Crüger (1598–1662) composed the tune NUN DANKET ALL' in 1647 for a text by Paul Gerhardt that began with those German words. A more common name for the tune is GRÄFENBERG, although it is also known as ST. MARY MAGDALENE or EVERSLEY.

Johann Crüger was the leading composer of tunes in his time. His encouragement of congregational singing and his memorable melodies greatly influenced the spread of the Lutheran style of worship and thought. Crüger died in 1662 in Berlin, Germany, where he had worked most of his life.

41 I Thank You, Jesus

Kenneth Morris (1917–1988) wrote this song, reminiscent of an African American spiritual, in 1948. It is in the style of a "testimonial" song, in which a leader sings to express personal faith in God and the rest of those gathered affirm or echo the singer's testimony.

Kenneth Morris was born August 28, 1917, in New York City and was raised by an aunt and uncle. By age ten he was playing hymns in both Baptist and Methodist churches. He received some musical training at Manhattan Conservatory of Music and formed a jazz band that was invited to play at the 1934 World's Fair in Chicago.

Kenneth Morris (1917–1988) is believed to have written this rousing song of faith in the 1940s. Joyce Finch Johnson created her adaptation and arrangement THANK YOU, JESUS nearly half a century later for *The New Century Hymnal*, perhaps the first denominational hymnal to include it.

In 1934 at age seventeen, Kenneth Morris moved to Chicago, Illinois, and was hired by Mrs. Lillian Bowles to transcribe music for her publishing company, Bowles Music House, where he was exposed to the growing gospel style. In addition, Morris was choir director at the First Church of Deliverance, where he introduced the Hammond organ into worship.

42 O For a Thousand Tongues to Sing

Charles Wesley (1707–1788) wrote this hymn on the first anniversary of his conversion to Christ, and it has repeatedly served as the opening hymn in Wesleyan hymnals throughout the centuries. This version employs stanzas 7, 8, 9, and 1 of the original eighteen-stanza poem.

Charles Wesley and his brother John each had a mystical experience that redirected their lives in service to Christ. Together they published sixty-four hymn collections between 1738 and 1785.

Carl G. Gläser (1784–1829) wrote this tune in Germany around 1839, but it was given the title AZMON (Hebrew for "fortress") by Lowell Mason, who adapted and introduced it in the United States. It first appeared anonymously in Mason's *Modern Psalmist* (1839).

Carl G. Gläser studied law at Leipzig University in Germany but decided to follow a profession in music instead. Gläser later moved to Barmen, where he taught piano, violin, and voice in addition to composing and publishing music.

43 Love Divine, All Loves Excelling

Charles Wesley (1707–1788) first published this hymn in a 1747 pamphlet with the title "Hymns for those that seek and those that have Redemption in the Blood of Jesus Christ." Many believe his inspiration for these words stemmed from the poems of Dryden or Joseph Addison.

Charles Wesley was born in Epworth, England, on December 18, 1707, and was educated for the Anglican priesthood. He was ordained in 1735 and assisted his brother John in spreading the doctrines of the Oxford Methodists. Charles never renounced his Anglican ordination vows, however.

John Zundel (1815–1882) composed BEECHER for this text in 1870. It is named after his friend Lyman Beecher, a prominent preacher in the United States. It has also been called ZUNDEL for the composer, and LOVE DIVINE from these words by Wesley.

John Zundel was born December 10, 1815, at Hochdorf, Germany, and died at Cannstadt, Germany, in July 1882. However, he spent thirty years as a church organist in the United States, chief among them at Plymouth Congregational Church in Brooklyn, New York, where Henry Ward Beecher was the minister.

44 Beautiful Jesus

The anonymous German text "Schönster Herr Jesu" was first published in *Münsterisch Gesangbuch* (1677), a collection of hymns and tunes issued by Jesuits living in Münster, Westphalia, now part of Germany. Although it was sometimes referred to as the "Crusader's Hymn," there is no documentation that it was sung by those twelfth-century pilgrims who journeyed to the holy land.

Madeleine Forell Marshall (b. 1946) created this English translation of the divine love poem "Schönster Herr Jesu" for *The New Century Hymnal* in 1993. Earlier translations include one beginning "Beautiful Savior" by Joseph Seiss and the anonymous version "Fairest Lord Jesus" from an 1850 hymnal.

This hymn became popular in the United States only after it was published with this tune, SCHÖNSTER HERR JESU, collected from Silesia by August Heinrich Hoffmann von Fallersleben (1798–1874). It is frequently confused with the original seventeenth-century tune that is the most frequent setting for the text in Germany.

August Heinrich Hoffmann von Fallersleben (1798–1874) first published this anonymous Silesian folk song in an 1842 collection called *Schlesische Volkslieder*. The collection contained 277 secular folk songs and twenty-three spiritual folk songs from this area of Germany.

45 Cristo es la peña de Horeb
(Christ Is the Mountain of Horeb)

This Puerto Rican text uses images from the Hebrew Scriptures to speak of Christ. Mount Horeb (also called Mount Sinai) is where Moses received the Ten Commandments; the Plain of Sharon is along the coast of the Mediterranean Sea north of Tel Aviv.

This anonymous song has been widely used in Pentecostal churches in Puerto Rico. Of that island's population, 85 percent is Roman Catholic and 15 percent is Protestant.

This Puerto Rican melody is called CRISTO ES LA PEÑA after the opening words of the text. Luis Olivieri (b. 1937), a member of *The New Century Hymnal* committee, provided the arrangement of this tune in 1993, and it has been included in several other hymnals since then.

The harmonization of this Puerto Rican melody incorporates many "thirds" and supports the *pasodoble* rhythm of the song. The *pasodoble* is a light march or two-step.

46 Hope of the World

Georgia Elma Harkness (1891–1974) created this hymn to reflect the theme of the Second General Assembly of the World Council of Churches, held in Evanston, Illinois, in 1954—"Jesus Christ the Hope of the World." It was selected by the Hymn Society of America for publication in *Eleven New Ecumenical Hymns,* where it was set with two different tunes.

Georgia Harkness was ordained a Methodist minister in 1926 and had a celebrated career as a college and seminary professor. She taught at Elmira College in New York, Mt. Holyoke College in Massachusetts, Garrett Biblical Institute in Illinois, and Pacific School of Religion in California.

John Albert Jeffery (1855–1929) composed ANCIENT OF DAYS in 1886 for a text beginning with those words by William Doane. It was originally named ALBANY for the city in New York, which celebrated its bicentennial that year. The hymn was subsequently published in the Episcopal *Hymnal* (1892) for which Doane served as chair.

J. Albert Jeffery was born in Plymouth, England, on October 26, 1855, and succeeded his father as organist at St. Andrew's Cathedral in that city. He moved to the United States in 1876, taught at Albany, New York, and at the New England Conservatory of Music in Massachusetts.

47 O Christ Jesus, Sent from Heaven

James W. Crawford (b. 1936) wrote this hymn for the unity of the church as a testimony to the Johannine roots of the United Church of Christ. It was first sung at Old South Church, Boston, for its 325th anniversary in 1994. Crawford, minister at Old South for twenty-three years, has made a regular practice of writing new hymns for his congregation at Christmas and Easter.

James W. Crawford was born July 17, 1936, in Rochester, New York. Following completion of his education at Dartmouth College and Union Theological Seminary, he was ordained in 1962 to the Presbyterian ministry and has served urban churches in New Jersey, New York, and Massachusetts.

Henry Purcell (1659–1695) composed this music as part of a verse anthem, "O God, thou art my God." It was arranged as the tune BELLEVILLE for an 1843 hymnal and renamed WESTMINSTER ABBEY in 1939, when used in *Hymns Ancient and Modern.* This text may also be sung to the tune HELMSLEY, for which it was originally written.

Henry Purcell spent his boyhood as a chorister in the Chapel Royal. In 1679 he succeeded John Blow as organist of Westminster Abbey, London, England, and stayed in that position until his death sixteen years later. Purcell was buried at the abbey next to the organ.

48 Jesus the Christ Says

This anonymous text uses the "I am" sayings of Jesus as found in John's Gospel. One of the first twentieth-century hymnals to include it was *New Church Praise* (1975), which credits Dermott Monahan (1906–1957) as translator from the Urdu and includes the arrangement by Francis B. Westbrook.

This Urdu hymn makes its first appearance in a U.S. denominational hymnal after several decades of use in English collections, most recently *Rejoice and Sing* (1991), a hymnal for the United Reformed Church. That source added another stanza using the metaphor of "the vine."

This tune by an unknown composer comes from Pakistan or northern India and is believed to be an Urdu melody. It is named YISU NE KAHA, which means "Jesus says" in Urdu. Although this is the official language of Pakistan, it is the primary language of only 10 percent of the population.

Francis B. Westbrook (1903–1975), an ordained Methodist minister and church musician in England, held positions at the London College of Music and the Williams School of Church Music. He helped prepare *The School Hymn Book of the Methodist Church* (1950), in which this arrangement appeared.

49 Ask Me What Great Thing I Know

Johann Christoph Schwedler (1672–1730) wrote this hymn of Christian witness in his native German, beginning "Wollt Ihr wissen, was mein preiss." It was not published until eleven years after the author's sudden death in 1730.

Benjamin Hall Kennedy (1804–1889) created this English translation more than a century after the appearance of Schwedler's text. It was published in two collections in the United States in 1869—the Dutch Reformed *Hymns of the Church* and Philip Schaff's *Christ in Song*.

Henry Abraham César Malan (1787–1864) composed the melody HENDON in 1827. Malan spent time in England and may have selected this tune name for a village only a few miles northeast of London's St. Paul's Cathedral, in Middlesex. The tune is also called CONSECRATION.

H. A. César Malan spent most of his life in the vicinity of Geneva, Switzerland. Ordained to the Reformed ministry, Malan's controversial preaching against empty ritualism attracted people from throughout Europe to his private garden chapel where he conducted services for forty-three years.

50 I Sing the Praise of Love Almighty

Gerhard Tersteegen (1697–1769) wrote this text in 1757 as part of a longer poem. However, it was not used as a hymn until adapted for the 1825 *Choralbuch* by Johannes Gossner, who selected only those stanzas that focused primarily on Christ.

Gerhard Tersteegen is recognized as one of the most significant hymnwriters of the German Reformed Church, although he exercised his devotion most notably in prayer circles and in an ascetic lifestyle. Tersteegen wrote more than one hundred hymns; two of them appear in *The New Century Hymnal*.

Dimitri S. Bortniansky (1752–1825) may have included the melody for ST. PETERSBURG in a mass he composed in 1822. The tune was subsequently published with Tersteegen's German text in I. H. Tscherlitsky's *Choralbuch*, published in Moscow in 1825.

Dimitri S. Bortniansky was born October 28, 1752, at Gloukoff, Ukraine. He studied in Bologna, Rome, and Naples, Italy, before returning to his homeland in 1779. Bortniansky excelled at operatic composition and was widely appreciated for his work. He died September 28, 1825, at St. Petersburg, Russia.

51 O Sing a Song of Bethlehem

Louis Fitzgerald Benson (1855–1930) wrote this text to summarize the life of Jesus, from birth and ministry to death and resurrection. It appeared in *The School Hymnal* (1899) with the title "Early Life of Jesus."

Louis F. Benson was born and died in Philadelphia, Pennsylvania. He trained to be a lawyer but later attended Princeton Theological Seminary in New Jersey and was ordained in 1886. Benson's *English Hymn* of 1915 established his reputation as one of the foremost hymnologists in the United States.

Ralph Vaughan Williams harmonized this traditional English melody for *The English Hymnal* (1906). It was named KINGSFOLD for the village in Sussex, England, where the tune was documented, and first appeared with Benson's text in *The Hymnary* (1927) of the United Church of Canada.

This tune was first written down by Alfred J. Hopkins in Westminster, England, and published in an 1893 collection, *English County Songs*. It has been associated with the song "Dives and Lazarus," which Vaughan Williams employed in a setting for harp and strings for the 1939 New York World's Fair.

52 There Is a Name I Love to Hear (O How I Love Jesus)

Frederick Whitfield (1829–1904) wrote the stanzas of this hymn in 1855, and it was first distributed in leaflets in Great Britain. Whitfield later published the words, without the refrain, in his *Sacred Poems and Prose* (1861), and it appeared in the United States as early as 1864.

Frederick Whitfield was a priest in the Church of England. He served as curate at Otley, vicar at Kirby-Ravensworth, senior curate at Greenwich, and vicar at St. John's Bexley and then St. Mary's Church, Hastings, England. Whitfield published over thirty volumes of poetry and prose.

This hymn's tune is thought by some to be a traditional English melody. Most scholars, however, recognize in it the lilting simplicity typical of nineteenth-century camp-meeting songs of the United States. The tune is named O HOW I LOVE JESUS after the words of the refrain.

The refrain of this hymn has been found with numerous texts by other hymnwriters such as Isaac Watts and John Wesley dating from the 1860s. Hymnologist Ellen Jane Lorenz claims it was related to four different camp-meeting tunes of similar meter.

53 Glorious Is Your Name, O Jesus

Robert J. Fryson (1944–1994) wrote this text in 1982, and it was included in *Lead Me, Guide Me* (1987), the African American Catholic hymnal produced by G.I.A. Publications. Note that the final phrase is repeated a second time. The hymn may appropriately be sung over and over if a congregation chooses.

Robert J. Fryson, born in Raleigh, North Carolina, received an undergraduate degree in vocal music education from Virginia State University, a master's degree from Catholic University of America, and a doctorate from Howard University. He was a life member of the National Association of Negro Musicians.

Robert J. Fryson (1944–1994) composed this setting in 1982 to accompany his own text. It is named GLORIOUS IS YOUR NAME for the opening phrase. Fryson performed the song on "The First Hymnal on a New Shelf" (a video produced prior to the hymnal's publication) and died shortly thereafter.

Robert J. Fryson was director and founder of a sacred music group, the Voices Supreme. This male ensemble has released many albums. In addition, Fryson's hymns have been recorded by James Cleveland, Aretha Franklin, Albertina Walker, and the National Youth Massed Choir.

54 O Praise the Gracious Power

Thomas H. Troeger (b. 1945) was inspired by Ephesians 2:14b–16b in writing this text for the ordination of Judith Ray as a teaching elder in the Presbyterian Church (USA). Troeger was struck with the imagery of the wall of hostility being broken down, which for him sharpened the meaning of the cross.

Thomas H. Troeger grew up hearing daily Bible readings, English poetry, and the music of Bach, Handel, Haydn, and Mozart in his home. He was active in church as a youth, singing in the children's choir and attending Sunday school, and credits these influences for his later career choices.

Carol Doran (b. 1936) composed this tune, called CHRISTPRAISE RAY, in 1984 for this text by Thomas Troeger. It was one of a group of hymns developed to fit scripture readings for various Sundays on a three-year cycle as assigned in the *Revised Common Lectionary*.

Carol Doran has published two hymn collections in collaboration with Thomas Troeger, *New Hymns for the Life of the Church* (1992) and *New Hymns for the Lectionary* (1986). Doran is a member of the American Guild of Organists and the Association of Anglican Musicians.

55 Rejoice, You Pure in Heart

Edward H. Plumptre (1821–1891) wrote this text for an annual choir festival at Peterborough Cathedral, England, in 1865. The original poem contained eleven stanzas to allow for the time it would take for the choir to process into the cathedral.

Edward H. Plumptre was a distinguished English scholar, lecturer, and preacher. During his lifetime, he held posts at King's College, London, Queen's College, Oxford, St. Paul's Cathedral, and served as a professor of New Testament, all in England.

Arthur H. Messiter (1834–1916) named this tune MARION for his mother in 1883. It has long been associated with this text by Plumptre since the hymn's appearance in Episcopal hymnals of the late nineteenth century.

Arthur H. Messiter, English by birth, moved to the United States in 1863. He served briefly as organist at four different churches in Philadelphia, then moved to Trinity Church, New York City, for the next thirty-one years, where he also led a traditional English men and boys choir.

56 Soplo de Dios viviente (Breath of the Living God)

Osvaldo Catena (20th century) is the author of this text, which was first published in *Cancionero Abierto IV* (1979). The opening stanza concerns the creation of the world, the second stanza the incarnation of Christ, and the third the coming of the Holy Spirit, especially in baptism.

Argentina is a South American country, bordered by Chile on the west, Paraguay and Bolivia on the north, and the Atlantic Ocean on the east. It, like the other nations of South America, was heavily influenced by the Spanish Roman Catholic Church.

This traditional Norwegian melody is named FLORINDEZ for Lorraine Florindez, who composed this arrangement in 1991 for the Spanish Lutheran hymnal *Cantad al Señor*. Hymnwriter Osvaldo Catena frequently employs folk tunes of various cultures as settings for his new hymns.

Lorraine Florindez is a church musician in Orlando, Florida, affiliated with the Evangelical Lutheran Church in America. She served on the international editorial committee for that denomination's Spanish hymnal, *Cantad al Señor* (1991), contributing thirty arrangements to that resource.

57 O Holy Spirit, Root of Life

Jean Wiebe Janzen (b. 1933) created this hymn at the invitation of the committee for the Mennonite *Hymnal: A Worship Book* (1992), where it appeared with a different tune. It is a composite of fresh and provocative images of the Holy Spirit from the writings of Hildegard of Bingen.

Hildegard of Bingen (1098–1179), the most celebrated female musician of the middle ages, spent much of her early life with a relative at a Benedictine monastery where she received a good education. Hildegard experienced visions from an early age and documented them in her writings.

The hymn tune PUER NOBIS NASCITUR first appeared with the Latin Christmas text beginning with those words in a fifteenth-century manuscript found in Trier, Germany. The tune was adapted to this form by Michael Praetorius for "Geborn ist Gottes Söhnelein" in a 1609 collection of Protestant choral music.

Michael Praetorius (1571–1621) was born Michael Schulze in Kreutzburg, Thuringia, Germany, but latinized his name following completion of his education at the University of Frankfurt. He was a prolific composer and scholar whose major works include *Musae Sioniae* (1605–1619) and *Syntagma Musicum* (1614–1619).

58 Spirit of Love

Shirley Erena Murray (b. 1931) wrote this text in 1992 for use at the World Council of Churches Assembly at Canberra, Australia. Her original title for the hymn was "Weaver Spirit," reflecting the meeting's theme, "Come, Holy Spirit, Reconcile Your People."

Shirley Erena Murray began writing hymns in her native New Zealand but received attention in North America when five of her texts were included in *The Presbyterian Hymnal* (1990). She has published two collections of her work—*In Every Corner Sing* (1992) and *Every Day in Your Spirit* (1996).

Joseph Barnby (1838–1896) composed this music as an anthem for the 1889 wedding of the duke and duchess of Fife. Named PERFECT LOVE for its association with that occasion, the anthem was adapted for congregational use in *The Hymnal* of the Episcopal Church in 1892.

Joseph Barnby was born in York, England, on August 12, 1838. A child prodigy, he sang in the choir at age seven and was organist at Yorkminster at age twelve. Barnby became head of the Guildhall School of Music and was knighted in 1892 for his contributions to English music.

59 Holy Spirit, Ever Dwelling

Timothy Rees (1874–1939) wrote this text about the Holy Spirit in 1922 for the religious community where he lived and worked at Mirfield, Wales. The text stresses the ongoing activity of the Holy Spirit in various dimensions of existence.

Timothy Rees was born August 15, 1874, in Wales. After ordination in the Church of England in 1898, he joined the Community of the Resurrection at Mirfield. From there he went on missions to New Zealand, Canada, and Ceylon. Appointed bishop of Llandaff in 1931, Rees died on April 29, 1939.

This anonymous American folk tune carries the name NETTLETON because it was attributed to Asahel Nettleton, a nineteenth-century evangelist. He is no longer believed to be the composer, but use of his name with the tune persists. Other names for this tune are HALLELUJAH and GOOD SHEPHERD.

John Wyeth's (1770–1858) *Repository of Sacred Music*, published in 1813, is the first printed source of this anonymous U.S. tune. It has been discovered in numerous other tunebooks of the nineteenth century and appears in more denominational hymnals than nearly any other early folk tune.

60 O Spirit of God

Johann Niedling (1602–1668) included this hymn and other anonymous texts in his 1651 hymnal *Lutherische Handbüchlein*. It is now believed that Niedling was the author of the original German text, "O Heiliger Geist, o heiliger Gott," as well as many of the other texts in that collection.

Johann Niedling was a schoolteacher in Altenburg, Saxony (now a part of Germany), in addition to being a hymnwriter. His six collections of hymns used in the Lutheran tradition did much to promote hymn singing in the church, and his 1651 *Lutherische Handbüchlein* was widely used.

This tune by an unknown composer takes its name from the opening line of the hymn, O HEILIGER GEIST, meaning "O Holy Ghost." Another name used in some hymnals is O JESULEIN SÜSS, for the German Christmas text with which it is more frequently sung.

The *Geistliche Kirchengesäng* was a German hymnal printed in Cologne in 1623. This particular tune was reprinted in a number of other hymnals and included by J. S. Bach in *Musikalisches Gesangbuch* (1736), which he edited for Georg Christian Schemelli in Leipzig.

61 Gracious Spirit, Holy Ghost

Christopher Wordsworth (1807–1885) based this text on Paul's treatise on love in 1 Corinthians 13. The text serves as a paraphrase or reflection on the meaning of the biblical passage. Wordsworth wrote the original poem in 1862.

Christopher Wordsworth inherited his love of scholarship from his father and his love of poetry from his uncle, the poet William Wordsworth. In his lifetime, he served as a school headmaster, church vicar, and bishop of the Church of England. He also wrote a Bible commentary.

Jane Manton Marshall (b. 1924) composed the tune ANDERSON in 1985 as a new setting for the poem by Christopher Wordsworth. By providing new tunes for older texts, composers help to breathe new life into texts that have fallen into disuse but are still meaningful.

Jane Marshall was born in Dallas, Texas, on December 5, 1924. She is recognized as an outstanding author, composer, and conductor of church music. She was awarded, among other honors, the Woman of Achievement award from Southern Methodist University, her alma mater, in 1965.

62 Come, Share the Spirit

Vicki Vogel Schmidt (b. 1945) was inspired to write this hymn to reflect on the theme of a meeting of the Northwest Minnesota Synod of the Evangelical Lutheran Church in America. The original version included a refrain to be sung as a round.

Vicki Vogel Schmidt was born on May 8, 1945, in Fargo, North Dakota, and grew up there, becoming active in the Lutheran ministry. She began writing hymns and poetry in high school but did not continue in this work until twenty years later, when her church needed a seventy-fifth anniversary hymn.

Vicki Vogel Schmidt (b. 1945) wrote both the words and music for this Spirit song in 1987. The tune takes its name, SHARE THE SPIRIT, from the text. It was first published in a Bread for the World worship resource, *Banquet of Praise* (1990).

Vicki Vogel Schmidt has worked as director of refugee resettlement for the North Dakota Episcopal Diocese and Lutheran Social Services. She is also the North America coordinator of Sister Parish, Inc., a program seeking to link churches globally for mutual ministry and sharing.

63 Holy Spirit, Truth Divine

Samuel Longfellow (1819–1892) intended this text to be a "prayer for inspiration." The original six-stanza poem was published in a Unitarian collection, *Hymns of the Spirit* (1864), which Longfellow edited with Samuel Johnson.

Samuel Longfellow was born and died in Portland, Maine. He was as well known as his now famous poet brother Henry Wadsworth during his lifetime. He served three parishes as a Unitarian minister and then retired to write a biography of his brother.

Louis Moreau Gottschalk (1829–1869) composed the popular and sentimental piano piece "The Last Hope." Although it was greatly inferior to some of his earlier works, it was adapted as a hymn by Edwin P. Parker (1836–1925). The tune is termed variously as MERCY, GOTTSCHALK, and LAST HOPE.

Louis M. Gottschalk, a child prodigy at the piano, was the son of an English Jew of German descent and a Creole mother of aristocratic French background. He was one of few recitalists from the United States to enjoy success on European concert stages in the nineteenth century.

64 Fire of God, Undying Flame

Albert Frederick Bayly (1901–1984) used various aspects of the Holy Spirit to frame this hymn. The text recalls that the Spirit is manifest as fire, breath, strength, truth, and love. The exact date when this text was written is unknown.

Albert F. Bayly was trained as a shipwright at the Royal Dockyard School in Portsmouth, England, but later chose to enter the Congregational ministry. He served seven churches in a forty-four-year career. Bayly also wrote librettos for cantatas by W. L. Lloyd Webber.

This old Latin medieval plainsong is entitled NUN KOMM DER HEIDEN HEILAND for the German text by Martin Luther with which it has long been associated. One of the earliest sources is a 1524 Wittenberg, Germany, songbook edited by Johann Walther.

Johann Walther (1496–1570) edited and prepared much of his 1524 *Geistliches Gesangbuchlein* while a guest in the home of his friend Martin Luther. It was less a hymnal than a collection of polyphonic motets based on Lutheran chorales, designed for choral rather than congregational use.

65 Este es el día (This Is the Day)

Pablo D. Sosa (b. 1933) based this song of praise on Psalm 118:24: "This is the day that God has made; let us rejoice and be glad in it." In writing and composing the refrain, Sosa tried to recreate the effect that he heard as Argentinian cowboys greeted one another in the morning while riding out to their work.

Pablo Sosa has an international reputation as a church music leader, having shared his talents at the United Methodist Global Gathering in Louisville, Kentucky, in 1988; the United Methodist Women's Assembly in Kansas City, Missouri, in 1990; and at the World Council of Churches meeting in 1983.

Pablo D. Sosa (b. 1933) composed both the words and the tune for this hymn, ESTE ES EL DIA. The music reflects the rhythms of his native Argentina, conveying an exuberance and joy appropriate to Psalm 118.

Pablo Sosa was born in Chivilcoy, Argentina, the son of a Methodist pastor. He studied theology and music in Argentina, Germany, and the United States. Sosa has served as professor of music at the National Conservatory of Music in Buenos Aires, Argentina.

66 O Day of Radiant Gladness

Christopher Wordsworth (1807–1885) presented this text in six stanzas as the opening hymn in his collection *The Holy Year* (1862). In the version provided in *The New Century Hymnal*, only the first two stanzas are from Wordsworth's original; the third and fourth were created for *The Hymnal 1982*.

Christopher Wordsworth spent fourteen years as public orator at Cambridge University and headmaster of Harrow School. Later he was rector for nineteen years at a quiet country parish where he had time for study and writing. A Greek scholar, Wordsworth often wrote about Greek culture.

This old German tune is named ES FLOG EIN KLEINS WALDVÖGELEIN after the first line of a folk song translated as "There flew a little forest bird." It was first paired with Wordsworth's text in George R. Woodward's *Songs of Syon* (London, 1904).

George Ratcliffe Woodward (1848–1934) harmonized this tune found in a seventeenth-century manuscript. His *Songs of Syon* (1904) was a supplemental collection of plainsong and metrical melodies, Lutheran tunes, and psalm tunes from various countries.

67 Let Me Enter God's Own Dwelling

E. Benjamin Schmolck (1672–1737) wrote the original German words for this hymn in 1732. The text was popular with both the Reformed and Evangelical German immigrants to America, although they sang these words to different tunes. Madeleine Forell Marshall's translation provides all but one of the original seven stanzas.

Benjamin Schmolck, a German Lutheran pastor, is credited with more than a thousand hymns of varied quality. Schmolck faithfully served the few Lutheran churches in a wide area of Germany that had been virtually taken over by the Roman Catholic Church according to the terms of the Peace of Westphalia.

Joachim Neander (1650–1680) composed this tune and published it in his *Glaub- und Liebesübung* (1680) with his text beginning UNSER HERRSCHER. The tune is often called NEANDER for the composer.

Joachim Neander, following his conversion, was a leader of the pietist movement. He was headmaster of the Reformed grammar school at Düsseldorf, Germany. An ancient skeleton was discovered in 1856 in a valley near Düssel named for his family, hence Neanderthal Man.

68 God Is Truly with Us

Gerhard Tersteegen (1697–1769), a German mystic, published this hymn in 1729. He translated the words of Labadie from French to German and paraphrased some of the Frenchman's thoughts for the text. The English translation is a composite from many sources.

Gerhard Tersteegen gave up a career as a silk weaver to devote his life to his religious calling. Each year, he traveled to Holland to hold preaching services and help the unfortunate. Tersteegen held large prayer meetings in his home and encouraged the practice of congregational singing.

Joachim Neander (1650–1680) composed WUNDERBARER KÖNIG as the setting for a text he had written, and both were published in 1680. The tune is sometimes called ARNSBERG. The melody has undergone many changes from its original form and would hardly be recognized by Neander.

Joachim Neander enjoyed the carefree life of a student while a youth in Bremen, Germany. He was greatly moved by the preaching of Theodore Undereyck and became a follower of the pietist movement. Neander was an independent thinker and made his living primarily as a teacher in a grammar school.

69 Come, God, Creator, Be Our Shield

Marion M. Meyer (b. 1923) wrote this hymn to provide a grace for use by residents at their assisted living center. The grace is based on a German prayer Meyer knew from childhood and is the basis for the second stanza of this hymn; the other stanzas are modeled on it.

Marion M. Meyer served the United Church of Christ on the publications staff of the Board for Homeland Ministries from 1958 until 1988. She promoted the use of inclusive-language texts and encouraged Ruth Duck's early work in *Bread for the Journey* (1981) and *Everflowing Streams* (1981).

Marion M. Meyer (b. 1923) wrote this tune before adding the text. She named it OLD FIRST for Old First Reformed Church, UCC, in Philadelphia, Pennsylvania, where she is a member. It served as the opening hymn when the church dedicated its new hymnals in a service on September 17, 1995.

Marion M. Meyer was born July 14, 1923 in Sheboygan, Wisconsin, and learned music from her mother, a church soloist. Educated at Lakeland College nearby and at New York University, she taught English, athletics, and religion at the American School for Girls in Baghdad, Iraq, from 1950 to 1956.

70 God Is Here! As We Your People Meet

Fred Pratt Green (b.1903) wrote this text in 1979 at the request of Russell Schulz-Widmar, director of music at University United Methodist Church of Austin, Texas. The director sought a new hymn for the closing service of a festival of worship, music, and the arts to help introduce this tune to the congregation.

Fred Pratt Green wanted to devote his retirement years to art and working in pastels. However, beginning in 1969, his work with the Methodist hymnal committee postponed these plans as he was asked to provide hymns on various topics for which the committee could find no appropriate texts.

Cyril Vincent Taylor (1907–1992) wrote this tune in the spring of 1941 for the text "Glorious Things of Thee Are Spoken." At the time he was working at the wartime headquarters of the religious broadcasting department of the British Broadcasting Company in ABBOT'S LEIGH, hence the tune's name.

Cyril Vincent Taylor was born in Wigan, Lancashire, England, and following his education was ordained to the Anglican priesthood. He held a number of positions in his career, serving finally as precentor and canon at Salisbury Cathedral from 1969 to 1975.

71 Rejoice, You Pure in Heart

Edward Hayes Plumptre (1821–1891) wrote this text in eleven stanzas for an annual choir festival at Peterborough Cathedral, England, in 1865. This hymn is used often for processionals and recessionals and has endured despite criticism of the text by hymnologists.

Edward H. Plumptre was a distinguished English scholar, theologian, and author. He was a member of the Old Testament revision team for the Authorized Version of the Bible. In addition, his translations of classics of literature were widely used in England.

Richard Wayne Dirksen (b. 1921) was commissioned to compose a setting for this text for an installation service held at Washington Cathedral on June 11, 1974. The tune necessitated the addition of the words "Hosanna" to the refrain. VINEYARD HAVEN is a town in Martha's Vineyard, Massachusetts.

Richard W. Dirksen is a respected Episcopal church musician and composer of operettas, anthems, and an oratorio. Dirksen has received honorary degrees from George Washington University (Washington, D.C.) in 1980 and Mount Union College (Alliance, Ohio) in 1986.

72 Sekai no Tomo (Here, O God, Your Servants Gather)

Tokuo Yamaguchi (b. 1900) wrote this text for a 1958 World Council of Christian Education convention, calling on the church to lead the way in seeking unity and world peace through Jesus Christ. The hymn was first printed in *Hymns of the Church* (1963), published by the United Church of Christ in Japan.

Tokuo Yamaguchi is a Methodist minister who served a number of different churches during his career from 1924 to 1979. His longest pastorate (more than forty years) was at Toyohashi Church, Aichi Prefecture, which became the United Church of Christ in Toyohashi in 1941.

Isao Koizumi (b. 1907) created this traditional Japanese tune, TOKYO, in the Gagaku mode, which can be traced from China and the traditional court music of Japan. The arrangement demonstrates the use of parallel harmonies characteristic of some composers in post–World War II Japan.

Isao Koizumi is a prominent Japanese church musician and hymnal editor. Trained as an economist, he served as minister of music at the United State Far East Air Force Chapel Center in Tokyo, Japan. He became director of the Christian Music Seminary in Tokyo in 1967.

73 Enter, Rejoice, and Come In

Louise Ruspini (20th century) based this text on Psalm 100. It grew in popularity in the United States during the 1970s. The opening stanza is based on Psalm 100:4, and the rest of the stanzas invite a willingness to be open to the leading of the Spirit in worship.

Louise Ruspini has published her work in *Journey to Freedom*. This hymn appears with a harmonization by Betty A. Wylder (1923–1994) in *Singing the Living Tradition,* a hymnal published by the Unitarian Universalist Association in 1993.

Louise Ruspini (20th century) composed the tune ENTER, REJOICE to accompany her text based on Psalm 100. The simple tune is meant to be sung in unison. Guitar chords are provided for congregations wishing to experiment with a different accompaniment.

In the 1960s and 1970s many congregations experienced a wave of new music and contemporary worship services. In the Roman Catholic Church this included the use of the vernacular in worship. Songs like this one by Louise Ruspini in a popular style were frequently used as gathering songs during this time.

74 We Have Gathered, Jesus Dear

Tobias Clausnitzer (1619–1684) wrote these words in German in 1663 as a *predigtlied,* or sermon hymn. It was the tradition in German churches to sing part of a hymn before the sermon and the rest as the minister descended from the pulpit at the conclusion of the sermon.

Tobias Clausnitzer was a German Lutheran pastor who served as chaplain to the Swedish army at Leipzig. As such, he preached the thanksgiving sermon in St. Thomas' Church, Leipzig, when Queen Christina assumed the throne of Sweden. Later he served churches at Weiden and Pergstein.

Johann Rudolph Ahle (1625–1673) called this tune LIEBSTER JESU after the first words of the German text. When the tune was brought to the United States the name was changed to NUREMBERG or DESSAU, which was a city important to the Lutheran religious movement.

Johann R. Ahle was born on Christmas Eve Day, 1625, at Mühlhausen in Thuringia (now part of Germany). He was a distinguished German church organist influenced by Heinrich Schütz and the Italian school of music. Ahle's career also included terms as city council member and mayor.

75 Lord, Make Me More Holy

This spiritual has been traced to coastal areas near Charleston, South Carolina, where it was used as the closing hymn at religious services and camp meetings. Although personal in nature, when sung by a congregation it serves as a corporate prayer for the highest Christian virtues.

The benediction in this song, "until we meet again," makes it a popular hymn of parting. The attributes being requested can easily be changed to adapt the hymn for various occasions. "Loving," "patient," "giving," and "prayerful" are but a few suggestions. The word "us" may be substituted for "me."

This African American spiritual melody is one of the few to have a regular meter. It is here entitled LORD, MAKE ME MORE HOLY for the words of the text. The 6/8 meter is less common in the spiritual tradition and contributes to the drawn-out feeling of the song, as in an extended "goodbye."

This anonymous arrangement lends itself to a call-and-response performance of this spiritual, with a leader singing the opening phrase (and deciding which attribute to implore of God) and the congregation responding in harmony.

76 Sent Forth by God's Blessing

Omer Westendorf (b. 1916) published this hymn under the pseudonym J. Clifford Evers in the *People's Mass Book* (1964). It was the first vernacular hymnbook to implement the changes in Roman Catholic liturgy ordered by the Second Vatican Council.

Omer Westendorf was born on February 24, 1916, at Cincinnati, Ohio. He became a church organist at the age of twenty and served at St. Bonaventure Church, Cincinnati, for over forty years. The church's choir has recorded religious music and performed on television, radio, and in live concerts.

This Welsh folk melody, THE ASH GROVE, was traditionally sung to a tragic ballad recounting a hunting accident, entitled "Llwyn Onn." Another ballad sung to this tune in England was a happier tale of a country lover.

Leland Bernhard Sateren (b. 1913) harmonized this tune in 1972 when it was included in the Lutheran supplement *Contemporary Worship–4: Hymns for Baptism and Holy Communion*. Sateren has served on the music faculty of Augsburg College and has composed more than three hundred choral works.

77 Lord, Dismiss Us with Your Blessing

John Fawcett (1739/40–1817) was only sixteen years old when he was inspired to enter the ministry by the preaching of George Whitfield. It has been reported that Fawcett wrote a hymn for every sermon he preached. This text appeared anonymously in a 1773 hymnbook, but is widely attributed to Fawcett.

John Fawcett was a Baptist minister and served his entire ministry in two small rural churches, rejecting opportunities for larger and more important parishes. Besides writing hymns, he also published theological works, devotional books, and volumes of poetry.

This melody of unknown origin has many names, including SICILIAN MARINERS, or SICILY (although no Sicilian folk melody like this has been found); DISMISSAL or DISMISSION, because of the words now sung with it; and O SANCTISSIMA, because of Latin words used with it at one time.

This tune first appeared in the United States in 1794 with a Latin hymn to the virgin Mary called "Prayer of the Sicilian Mariner," from which the present tune name comes. The Latin words began "O sanctissima, O piissima."

78 Part in Peace

Sarah Fuller Flower Adams (1805–1848) wrote this text for use in evening worship. Many of her poems originally appeared in the *Unitarian Monthly Repository* and in a collection published in 1840 or 1841, *Hymns and Anthems*.

Sarah Adams is usually remembered for another hymn, "Nearer, My God, to Thee." Born into a literary family in England, Adams became a poet and Shakespearean actress. She received enthusiastic reviews for her portrayal of Lady Macbeth, but poor health kept her from continuing that artistic path.

This tune, named CHARLESTOWN, may come from Charleston, South Carolina, the birthplace of Amos Pilsbury. He first printed this music in *The United States Sacred Harmony* in 1799, but the version found here is from a different hymnal, *Southern Harmony*, published in 1835.

William (Singin' Billy) Walker (1806–1875) was an evangelist who traveled throughout the southern United States teaching singing. He published a number of tunes he had collected in two influential books—*Southern Harmony and Musical Companion* (1835) and *Christian Harmony* (1867).

79 May the Sending One Defend You

Brian Arthur Wren (b. 1936) was inspired to write this hymn upon hearing the tune played by the composer Mikkel Thompson at his home in March 1989. Wren wrote this text in the style of a Celtic trinitarian blessing in less than twenty-four hours, completing it on March 14.

Brian Wren began attending church at Upminster Congregational Church in his hometown of Essex, England, when he was fourteen. He was baptized by confession of faith at nineteen and felt called by God to enter full-time Christian service at about this same time in his life.

Mikkel Thompson (b. 1948) composed the tune ROLLINGBAY to experiment with the effect of alternating meters from 3/4 to 4/4 every measure. It is named for Rollingbay, Bainbridge Island, Washington, where Thompson lived at the time he wrote the tune.

Mikkel Thompson was born in Sioux Falls, South Dakota, on June 4, 1948, and grew up in a Lutheran parsonage in Tacoma, Washington. A trained musician and ordained Lutheran minister, he has served parishes in Moscow, Idaho, as well as Bainbridge Island and Aberdeen, Washington.

80 Savior, Again to Your Dear Name

John Ellerton (1826–1893) wrote these words as the concluding hymn for an 1866 choir festival in Nantwich, Cheshire, England. Originally it had six stanzas but was shortened to four by Ellerton for the Appendix to *Hymns Ancient and Modern* (1868).

John Ellerton was an Anglican minister and respected hymnologist, editor, and translator. He wrote two volumes of prose and fifty original hymns, which were published in a collection of his work in 1888.

Edward John Hopkins (1818–1901) composed ELLERS as a unison tune in 1869 for Ellerton's text and later created the four-part setting. Hopkins was one of the founders of the Royal College of Organists, England, and had a long and distinguished career in church music.

Edward J. Hopkins was one of the greatest organists of his time. He was widely known for his skill in improvisation and service playing; he served as the accompanist for many Jenny Lind concerts. Hopkins was organist at Temple Church in London, England, for fifty-five years.

81 God Be with You

Jeremiah Eames Rankin (1828–1904) based this hymn on the familiar words of parting "God be with you," often contracted into the term "goodbye." After completing the first stanza, Rankin sent it to two musician friends. He added the other stanzas later after selecting the tune by William Tomer.

Jeremiah E. Rankin was a Congregational minister who served churches in New York and New England before being called to First Congregational Church in Washington, D.C. This hymn was written during his fifteen-year tenure as pastor at that church.

William Gould Tomer (1833–1896) wrote the tune GOD BE WITH YOU at the invitation of his friend Jeremiah Rankin. Tomer was minister of music at Grace Methodist Episcopal Church in Washington, D.C., at the time, although he had little formal training as a musician.

William G. Tomer served on the staff of General Oliver O. Howard (for whom Howard University is named) in the Civil War. Later he taught school in New Jersey and worked for the government and as a newspaper reporter. Tomer was editor of the Hunterdon (New Jersey) *Gazette* at the time of his death in 1896.

82 Go, My Children, with My Blessing

Jaroslav Jan Vajda (b. 1919) wrote this text in 1983 for Concordia Publishing, which was seeking an alternative to the hymn "God Who Made the Earth and Heaven," traditionally sung with this popular Welsh tune. Vajda conceived of the text as a "hymn of dismissal" by God.

Jaroslav J. Vajda was born in Lorain, Ohio, on April 28, 1919. He began his education for the ministry at age thirteen at Concordia College in Fort Wayne, Indiana. Vajda has translated over one hundred Slovak and Czech poems, along with parts of Slovakia's classic literature.

This traditional Welsh melody is named AR HYD Y NOS, which means "The Livelong Night." The tune was first printed by Edward Jones in *Musical Relicks of the Welsh Bards* (1784) in Dublin, Ireland. There it was scored for solo voice, chorus, and harp.

This Welsh ballad by an unknown composer was traditionally sung with the secular texts "The Livelong Night" in Welsh and "Here Beneath a Willow, Weepeth Poor Mary Anne" in English. It made its appearance as a hymn tune in the United States when it was printed in *The Christian Lyre* (1831).

83 I Sing As I Arise Today

Saint Patrick (c. 372–466) is believed to be the writer of the words on which this hymn is based. An eleventh-century manuscript says that the hymn, called a "Breastplate," was written to protect Patrick and his monks from their deadly enemies.

Saint Patrick of Ireland was born in Britain of Christian parents. After being taken captive and made a slave in Ireland at age sixteen, he escaped and was ordained to the ministry. He then returned to Ireland as a missionary, converted the nation, and was consecrated bishop in 432 C.E.

William Patrick Rowan (b. 1951) included the tune SEED OF LIFE in his 1993 collection *Together Met, Together Bound*, where it appeared with a text by Herbert O'Driscoll, "Before the World Had Yet Begun." This is its first publication as a setting for the hymn of Saint Patrick.

William P. Rowan holds degrees from Southern Illinois University and the University of Michigan. He has served as director of music ministries at St. Mary Cathedral in Lansing, Michigan, and written many hymns and anthems for use in the Roman Catholic Church and the wider ecumenical community.

84 This Is the Day

Leslie Norman Garrett (b. 1943) paraphrased Psalm 118:24 for the first stanza of this hymn, which is a traditional opening sentence for worship. The other two stanzas, which are anonymous, reflect on the events celebrated in two major Christian festivals, Easter and Pentecost.

Les Garrett served as pastor of the Christian Family Center in Maddington, Western Australia. He is the author of two published books, *Which Bible Can We Trust?* and *Best of All, God Is with Us*, as well as a 1967 hymnbook, *Scripture in Song*.

Leslie Norman Garrett (b. 1944) composed this tune, called THIS IS THE DAY, to accompany his paraphrase of Psalm 118. The hymn is effective when sung antiphonally, with one group starting and another echoing the phrases. All join together in singing the last eight measures.

Les Garrett was born on July 15, 1943, at Matamata, North Island, New Zealand, and received his formal education at Word of Faith Bible School. He has lectured at Hebron Bible College and traveled the world speaking at conventions and church gatherings.

85 I Woke Up This Morning

This African American spiritual song is in the traditional leader-response format. The leader would start a song, and others would join in when they recognized it. The text is a reminder to keep Jesus as one's focus during both good and bad times.

In the 1981 collection of African American music *Songs of Zion*, this spiritual appears with several different stanzas, two of which begin "Can't hate your neighbor in your mind, if you keep it stayed on Jesus" and "The devil can't catch you in your mind, if you keep it stayed on Jesus."

This tune, long used with these words, is named WOKE UP THIS MORNING for the opening line of the text. The "Hallelujah" at the end of the hymn was a possible addition and would often be improvised and sung over and over again with great energy and emotion.

Jeffrey Radford (b. 1953), music director for Trinity United Church of Christ in Chicago, Illinois, contributed arrangements for eight African American spirituals in *The New Century Hymnal*, including this one. His contemporary gospel style lends a fresh sound to these timeless songs of discipleship.

86 When Morning Gilds the Skies

This anonymous hymn has been traced to two German Roman Catholic hymnals of the nineteenth century. The translation by Edward Caswall (1814–1878) first appeared in *Catholic Hymns* (1854). Additional stanzas were added four years later for Caswall's publication *Masque of Mary and Other Poems*.

Edward Caswall (1814–1878) translated this and many other German hymns into English. He was ordained to the Church of England but converted to Catholicism during a visit to Rome in 1847. Two years later, he published *Lyra Catholic,* a translation from the Roman Breviary.

Joseph Barnby (1838–1896) composed the tune LAUDES DOMINI for this text for the Appendix to *Hymns Ancient and Modern* (1868). Barnby, a leading musician of the Victorian era, wrote a variety of church music, including choral anthems and vocal solos.

Joseph Barnby, son of an organist and an organist himself since age twelve, lost the first Mendelssohn scholarship competition to Arthur Sullivan in 1856. He nevertheless had a distinguished career as an organist in various English churches and was an authority on the music of Bach.

87 O Splendor of God's Glory Bright

Saint Ambrose (340–397), one of the most significant figures in the history of hymnody, was bishop of Milan, Italy. He wrote this Latin text for lauds, one of the early morning services held in monastic orders. This English translation is a composite made from a variety of sources for *The New Century Hymnal*.

Saint Ambrose was one of the great "fathers" of the early church. He converted Saint Augustine to Christianity and defended the faith from domination by the Roman government. Ambrose created the first hymns for congregational singing, and many others quickly adopted his style.

This plainsong tune, SPLENDOR PATERNAE, derives its title from the first words of Ambrose's Latin text with which it was traditionally sung in the Sarum liturgy of Salisbury, England. It appears in a 1518 source from Paris, *Hymnorum cum notis,* and a thirteenth-century manuscript at Worcester Cathedral.

The early hymns of the church are often sung to plainsong melodies from later times when a system of notes was invented. It is doubtful that any of those melodies are from the time of Ambrose, the writer of this text. However, since the early hymns were written in verses in strophic form, it is likely that all the verses were sung to the same melody, just as they are today.

88 Pero Queda Cristo (My Soul Overflows with Praise)

Alfredo Colom M. (1904–1971) wrote this text in Spanish in 1954. Both keyboard and guitar accompaniment are provided here so that congregations may experiment with a variety of instrumentation. Carolyn Jennings (b. 1936) provided this English version of Colom's text for *The New Century Hymnal*.

Carolyn Jennings is professor of music and chair of the Music Department at St. Olaf College in Northfield, Minnesota. She also serves as music coordinator for St. John's Lutheran Church.

Alfredo Colom M. (1904–1971) composed the tune POR LA MAÑANA in 1954 to accompany his Spanish text. It reflects elements of a *corito*—a song with a simple folk-like melody and a text that expresses one's praise or commitment to God.

Alfredo Colom M. was born in Quezaltenango, Guatemala. He served as a government official for a time, but alcohol dependency hindered that career. After his conversion to Christ in 1940, he began writing religious songs, which have since appeared in some hymn collections in English.

89 Awake, Awake to Love and Work

Geoffrey A. Studdert-Kennedy (1883–1929) wrote these words as the last three stanzas of a poem, "At a Harvest Festival." It appeared in his book *The Sorrows of God and Other Poems* published in 1921. In addition to his poetry, Studdert-Kennedy was known for his original and eloquent preaching.

Geoffrey A. Studdert-Kennedy was a famed British chaplain in World War I, known to thousands of soldiers as "Woodbine Willie." He was later appointed chaplain to the king of England and was a well-known preacher in both that country and the United States.

This tune appears as CONSOLATION in *Kentucky Harmony* (1816) and other early shape-note tunebooks in a variety of arrangements. The title MORNING SONG derives from the morning text by Isaac Watts which it often accompanied.

Kentucky Harmony (1816) was a hymnal developed for Presbyterian churches in that state. It used notes of various shapes to help beginning musicians distinguish one tone of the scale from another. This hymnal was edited and published by Ananias Davisson, a singing master in Harrisonburg, Virginia.

90 Rising in Darkness

Gregory the Great (540–604) is believed to have written the words to this Latin office hymn for matins, although some scholars believe that it may be the work of the poet Alcuin (735–804). It was the practice of monastic communities to hold services at appointed hours throughout the day and night.

Gregory the Great was a celebrated early pope of the Roman Catholic church—a post which he held from 590 until his death in 604. He was responsible for sending Augustine of Canterbury as the first Christian missionary to England and had a great influence on liturgy and music.

This anonymous French church melody, CHRISTE SANCTORUM, has been traced to a 1681 *Paris Antiphoner*. The name is taken from the first line of a different medieval Latin hymn text. The musical style reflects the French preference for metered psalm tunes of the English.

La Feillée's *Méthode de plain-chant* was an instructional book for choral directors that provided music and addressed the performance not only of traditional plainsong but of newer forms of church music. It was published in a number of editions.

91 Wake, My Soul

Friedrich Rudolph Ludwig von Canitz (1654–1699) wrote the original German text "Seele, du musst munter werden" in fourteen stanzas; it was published posthumously in the early eighteenth century. The hymn was not translated into English until 1838. *The New Century Hymnal* provides a new translation by Madeleine Forell Marshall.

Friedrich R. L. von Canitz was born in Berlin, Germany, on November 27, 1654. He traveled throughout Europe as a kind of roving ambassador and was made baron by Emperor Leopold I in 1698. This hymn is a testimony to his devout faith and positive outlook, which he maintained until his death.

Franz Joseph Haydn (1732–1809) wrote this melody as part of one of his symphonies around 1794. It now bears his name, HAYDN. It has also been called LUX PRIMA, Latin for "first light," because of these words. Other names ascribed to the tune are EDNA and HALLE.

Franz Joseph Haydn composed four oratorios, twenty-two operas, forty-four sonatas, 120 symphonies, and eighty-three instrumental quartets. Each composition was prefaced with the words "In nomine Domini" (in the name of God!).

92 Day Is Done

James Quinn, S.J. (b. 1919), wrote this evening hymn in 1969 and included it in *New Hymns for All Seasons,* published that year. As a consultant for the International Commission on English in the Liturgy, Quinn has extended his influence on the changing Catholic liturgies.

James Quinn was born in Glasgow, Scotland, and educated in that city. He was ordained as a Roman Catholic priest in 1950 and joined the British province of the Society of Jesus (Jesuits). His hymns have been accepted in the wider Christian community and appear in a number of Protestant hymnals.

The title of this Welsh tune, AR HYD Y NOS, comes from the refrain of a text with which it was commonly sung, known as "The Livelong Night." It was previously familiar in the church as an evening hymn melody through its association with Reginald Heber's "God That Madest Earth and Heaven."

This anonymous Welsh ballad is known as "The Livelong Night" in Wales and "Here Beneath a Willow, Weepeth Poor Mary Anne" in England. Because of these secular uses, the tune was not utilized as a hymn melody until it appeared as such in *The English Hymnal* (1906).

93 Christ, Mighty Savior

The source of this ancient text is a tenth-century Mozarabic evening hymn for the third Sunday after Epiphany. The 1916 translation by Alan McDougall was intended as a devotional poem. Anne LeCroy (b. 1930) created this version for *The Hymnal 1982*, in which the hymn appears with three different settings.

Anne Kingsbury LeCroy, born in Summit, New Jersey, is an English scholar who has served the Protestant Episcopal Church in numerous capacities. She was a member and secretary of the Standing Liturgical Commission and a consultant to the Text Committee for *The Hymnal 1982*, contributing hymn alterations and translations.

David Hurd (b. 1950) composed this tune for *The Hymnal 1982* of the Protestant Episcopal Church to provide a serene setting for this modern English translation of an ancient text. The tune is named MIGHTY SAVIOR from the opening words of the text.

David Hurd was born in Brooklyn, New York, on January 27, 1950. In 1976 he became professor of music and organist at General Theological Seminary and in 1985 the director of music for All Saints Episcopal Church, New York City. He has also served on the faculty of the Manhattan School of Music.

94 Now All the Woods Are Sleeping

Paul Gerhardt (1607–1676), a German Lutheran preacher, published his text "Nun ruhen alle Wälder" in 1648. It was criticized by Frederick the Great as "silly and stupid," but Germany's great poet Schiller spoke well of it. This translation from the *Lutheran Book of Worship* (1978) incorporates the opening line of an earlier version by Catherine Winkworth.

Paul Gerhardt is considered by many to be the greatest German hymnwriter after Martin Luther. His 132 hymns reflect a transition from the confessional style of Luther to a more subjective orientation that stresses the singer's personal relationship with God.

Heinrich Isaak (1455–1517), a Flemish musician, is credited as the composer of this tune. Originally named O WELT, ICH MUSS DICH LASSEN, it is now better known as NUN RUHEN ALLE WÄLDER. It has also appeared as INNSBRUCK from a secular song about a homesick German artisan.

This tune has had a tremendous influence on later musicians. J. S. Bach used it in "St. Matthew's Passion." Johannes Brahms utilized it for a chorale prelude he wrote on his death bed. This tune was sung on November 25, 1963, as part of a requiem mass in Washington D.C. for John F. Kennedy.

95 The Day You Gave Us, God, Is Ended

John Ellerton (1826–1893) wrote this evening hymn and published it in 1870 in "A Liturgy for Missionary Meetings." Queen Victoria asked that this hymn be sung throughout the British Empire in 1887 in services marking her Diamond Jubilee as queen of England.

John Ellerton, an Anglican minister, was author of many books and an expert on hymns. He translated hymns into English and introduced them to the English-speaking world. However, he is now remembered primarily as a hymnwriter.

Clement Cotterill Scholefield (1839–1904) composed this melody for Ellerton's text. It was first published in *Church Hymns with Tunes,* edited by Arthur Sullivan, who created the title ST. CLEMENT by adding "St." to the composer's name. This was not an unusual practice for Sullivan.

Clement Cotterill Scholefield was an Anglican minister and served as chaplain at Eton College (England); vicar at Holy Trinity Church, Knightsbridge, London; and curate at St. Peter's Church, South Kensington, London. His organist there was Arthur Sullivan, who also wrote light operas with W. S. Gilbert.

96 Sun of My Soul, O Savior Dear

John Keble (1792–1866) based this text on Luke 24:29: "Stay with us, because it is almost evening, and the day is now nearly over." He included it in the hymnal he published anonymously in 1827 to provide hymns for use throughout the Christian year. The original hymn had fourteen stanzas.

John Keble was a brilliant student at Oxford University, England, earning double first class honors, a rare achievement. His volume of poetry, *The Christian Year* (1827), was recognized as a literary masterpiece and published in ninety-six editions.

This tune from an unknown composer was named HURSLEY by the editors of an 1861 hymnal, for the village where John Keble was pastor. It is a variation of an eighteenth-century Catholic hymn tune, GROSSER GOTT, WIR LOBEN DICH, but has also been called STILLORGAN, PASCAL, and FRAMINGHAM.

This melody is a variation of a Roman Catholic tune from Vienna, Austria. It was first printed in the 1774 Catholic hymnbook *Katholisches Gesangbuch* as a setting for a German text that began GROSSER GOTT, WIR LOBEN DICH. The tune was a favorite of Empress Maria Theresa, who was the mother of Marie Antoinette.

97 Salup na ang Adlaw (Now the Sun Is Setting)

Elena G. Maquiso (b. 1914) wrote this evening hymn in 1970. The text was meant to reflect on the day's activities, seeking God's direction and forgiveness, and anticipating a peaceful rest. It reminds Christians of the need to begin and end each day in prayer and praise to God.

Elena G. Maquiso studied the music and folklore of the Ulahingan region in the southern Philippines for many years and directed the Ulahingan Research Project at Silliman University. In 1992 she published her research and findings in *Ulahingan: Epic of the Southern Philippines.*

Elena G. Maquiso (b. 1914) composed this tune for her original text. She named it MONING to recognize a classmate at the Divinity School at Silliman University in Dumaguete, Philippines, where she has taught Christian education and served as acting dean.

Elena G. Maquiso was named professor emeritus by Silliman University in 1994 for her many years of service and for her accomplishments as an educator, composer, and researcher of indigenous music and culture.

98 Now the Day Is Over

Sabine Baring-Gould (1834–1924) wrote this hymn while serving as the curate of Horbury parish, Yorkshire, England. This was his first church as an ordained minister, and he wrote the text for the children of the town. It was first published in 1868.

Sabine Baring-Gould was an Anglican minister and a man of wide-ranging interests. He published over eighty-five books on a variety of subjects, and it is said that he had more book titles listed after his name in the literary catalog of the British Museum than any author of his day.

Joseph Barnby (1838–1896) composed this tune, which appeared with Baring-Gould's words in an 1869 collection. Although this tune is not used in England, it is the popular setting in the United States. The title MERRIAL was created by an American, who combined his daughter's first name and middle initial, "Mary L."

Joseph Barnby, son of a church organist, sang in the York Minster, England, choir at age seven and directed it at twelve. He was a student at the Royal Academy of Music at sixteen. Barnby had a successful career as a choral conductor in churches and promoted interest in the works of Bach.

99 Abide with Me

Henry Francis Lyte (1793–1847) wrote these words in his last year of life, knowing that he was dying. The hymn is appropriate for memorial or evening services. It was introduced in the United States in Henry Ward Beecher's *Plymouth Collection* (1855).

Henry F. Lyte served parishes in Ireland and in Hampshire and Devonshire, England, where he stayed for the last twenty-four years of his life. Lyte published three collections of verse from 1826 to 1834.

William Henry Monk (1823–1889) wrote EVENTIDE for these words, and after it appeared in *Hymns Ancient and Modern* (1861) it received greater acceptance than a tune composed by the author, Henry Lyte. The hymn has been traditionally sung at "the Cup"—a national football (i.e., soccer) match in England.

William H. Monk was editor of the landmark collection *Hymns Ancient and Modern,* published in England in 1861, and was responsible for its timeless title. This is the best known of the nearly fifty tunes he contributed to various editions of that hymnal.

100 All Praise Be Yours, My God, This Night

Thomas Ken (1637–1711) wrote this evening hymn for his *Manual of Prayers* in 1692. Originally the hymn had twelve stanzas and was sung by schoolboys at Winchester College, England, for the evening vespers service. The new fourth stanza was added by Carl P. Daw Jr. in 1992.

Thomas Ken was a devout English bishop. When King Charles II visited Winchester with his mistress Nell Gwynne, Ken refused the king's demand to allow Gwynne to stay in his home. Later he refused to take a loyalty oath to King William III and was fired for it.

Thomas Tallis (c. 1505–1585) wrote TALLIS' CANON for a version of Psalm 67 in Matthew Parker's *Whole Psalter* (1561). The tune, which was number eight in that volume, was described by Tallis as "milde: in modest pace."

Thomas Tallis was a contemporary of other celebrated English church musicians such as Orlando Gibbons, William Byrd, and Christopher Tye. He served four monarchs as organist and choirmaster at such famous sites as Waltham Abbey, Canterbury, and Chapel Royal.

101 Comfort, Comfort O My People

Johannes Olearius (1611–1684) wrote this hymn based on Isaiah 40:1–8 for use on St. John the Baptist's Day, June 24. The hymn is now more often used during Advent. Catherine Winkworth (1827–1878) provided this translation from German to English in her *Chorale Book for England* (1863).

Johannes Olearius was born in Halle, Germany, educated at the University of Wittenberg, and rose to positions of power and authority in the church of his day. He published *Geistliche Singe-Kunst* (1671), an influential hymnbook which contained twelve hundred hymns, one-fourth of them by Olearius.

This tune, perhaps adapted from a French folk song by Louis Bourgeois (c. 1510–c. 1561), was first printed in the Genevan Psalter of 1551 as a setting for a version of Psalm 42 by Theodore de Beze. It was from this association that the tune is named PSALM 42, although it is also known as FREU DICH SEHR for another text.

Trente Quatre Pseaumes (1551), commonly known as the Genevan Psalter, was developed at the insistence of John Calvin, the Reformed theologian, who believed that only the psalms should be sung in worship. His great influence on the church kept Reformed churches singing only psalms for centuries.

102 O How Shall I Receive You

Paul Gerhardt (1607–1676) based this hymn on Matthew 21:1–9 for the first Sunday in Advent, but it is often used for Palm Sunday when called for by the lectionary readings. The translation is a compilation from several sources, including Catherine Winkworth (1827–1878).

Paul Gerhardt, in addition to his pastoral duties, composed many hymns. His work marked the transition from the old style confessional hymns used in the Lutheran church to more devotional hymns. Gerhardt stressed the God of love rather than the wrathful God that Luther wrote about.

Melchior Teschner (1584–1635) composed this and another melody for a hymn by Valerius Herberger in the early seventeenth century. This tune name, VALET WILL ICH DER GEBEN, is from the opening of that text. ST. THEODULPH derives from the tune's association with a different Latin hymn.

Melchior Teschner studied philosophy and theology in addition to music at the University of Frankfurt-an-der-Ober. This training served him well in a career that included positions as cantor, teacher, and pastor. Teschner died in 1635 as a result of an attack by the Cossacks.

103 Watcher, Tell Us of the Night

John Bowring (1792–1872), a politician, poet, and master of languages, served as counsel and governor of Hong Kong. His time spent in that Eastern commonwealth is said to have influenced the imagery in this text based on Isaiah 21:11–12.

John Bowring published two volumes of sacred verse and more than thirty other books on a wide array of subjects. Highly regarded for his immense intellect, facility with languages, and diplomatic skills, Bowring served in the British parliament for two separate terms, totaling ten years.

Joseph Parry (1841–1903) composed the tune ABERYSTWYTH in 1879 in the Welsh seaside town of that name, where he was born. The tune was first set with Bowring's poetry in *The Hymnal 1940* with effective results. The words and music continued to be paired in hymnals throughout the twentieth century.

Joseph Parry dropped out of school at the age of ten to help support his family. They moved to the United States in 1854 and settled in Danville, Pennsylvania, where Parry received his first music lessons. He returned to England in 1868 to study at the Royal Academy of Music, London, and he eventually completed a doctor of music degree at Cambridge University.

104 We Hail You God's Anointed

James Montgomery (1771–1854) wrote this text for use at a Moravian settlement Christmas service in 1821 and later included it at the close of a speech delivered at a Liverpool, England, missionary meeting. Adam Clark, who was present at the meeting, was so impressed that he published it in his Bible commentary of 1822.

James Montgomery was one of England's greatest hymnwriters, ranking with John Wesley, Isaac Watts, John Newton, and William Cowper. He wrote and published more than four hundred hymns in over ten volumes; he also worked as a newspaper editor and teacher of poetry.

This anonymous tune is named ELLACOMBE, an Anglo-Saxon word meaning island or coastal area (*combe*) of elves (*ella*). It first appeared in a Roman Catholic hymnal from Wirtemberg, Germany, in 1784. The tune name was supplied by an English hymnal editor.

This anonymous tune was first published in *Gesangbuch der herzoglichen Wirtembergischen katholischen Hofkappelle* (1784). It appeared a century later in England in the Appendix to *Hymns Ancient and Modern* (1868), where it was the setting for a children's hymn that began "Come, sing with holy gladness."

105 Gentle Joseph, Joseph Dear

Carol Birkland (b. 1946) wrote this paraphrase of a fifteenth-century German carol to make the words more accessible to today's generation of children. In other translations, the text consists of Mary's words to Joseph. The paraphrase altered this style to make the words a dialogue between the couple.

Carol Birkland has served several churches as director of Christian Education and has written and edited curriculum for Friendship Press and United Church Press. She has also been an active singer in professional and church music groups, where she nurtures a lifelong interest in hymnody.

The tune JOSEPH LIEBER, JOSEPH MEIN takes its title from the original German text with which it was traditionally sung. A fifteenth-century German melody from a mystery play, it is arranged as a simple lullaby by Arthur G. Clyde, editor of *The New Century Hymnal*.

This tune is also known as RESONET IN LAUDIBUS. In its original form, it was sung as a lullaby around the manger as part of a medieval Nativity mystery play held in the church. Mystery plays were like little operas that brought biblical stories to life.

106 My Heart Sings Out with Joyful Praise

Ruth C. Duck (b. 1947) paraphrased the "Song of Mary" for this text so that it could be used in Protestant churches for evening prayer services. The canticle known as the *Magnificat* is found in Luke 1:46–55 and is an expression of faithfulness by Mary, the mother of Jesus.

Ruth Duck was appointed to the faculty of Garrett-Evangelical Theological Seminary in Evanston, Illinois, in 1989. She serves as associate professor of worship and dean of the chapel. She is also a member of the North American Academy of Liturgy.

This Swedish folk melody is called MARIAS LOVSÅNG. It appeared in *The Covenant Hymnal* (1973) as a setting for another paraphrase of the *Magnificat* by Swedish pastor Carl Boberg, "My Soul Now Magnifies the Lord," and thus seemed a fitting tune for Ruth Duck's new version of that canticle.

This Swedish folk melody appears in two hymnals of the Evangelical Covenant Church of America, including the denomination's most recent, *The Covenant Hymnal* (1996). However, the arranger of the tune is not cited in either case.

107 Awake! Awake, and Greet the New Morn

Marty Haugen (b. 1950) used the imagery of various chapters from the books of Isaiah and Matthew for this Advent hymn, written in 1983. These are traditional texts for the Advent season, and Haugen wanted to provide them in a format that was easy for church congregations to sing.

Marty Haugen served on the editorial team for the Roman Catholic hymnal *Gather,* a collection of hymns and songs in contemporary folk style. He has contributed his work to more than ten other denominational and independent hymnals and has written articles for a number of journals.

Marty Haugen (b. 1950) composed this tune for his own text, calling it REJOICE, REJOICE, from the opening words of the last stanza. Haugen has recorded sixteen collections of music, including a communion service for Lutheran congregations, *Now the Feast and Celebration.*

Marty Haugen has written and recorded a performance work based on the words of Western church leaders such as Martin Luther King Jr., Dorothy Day, and Oscar Romero. The work, called "Agape," premiered at the 1993 National Pastoral Musicians convention held at St. Louis, Missouri.

108 Isaiah the Prophet Has Written of Old

Joy Forster Patterson (b. 1931) wrote this text in 1981, based on the vision of the peaceable dominion in Isaiah 11. It was one of the winning hymns in a 1982 contest sponsored by the Hymn Society and was published in *New Hymns for Children* that same year.

Joy F. Patterson was born in Lansing, Michigan, and grew up in LaGrange, Illinois. A Fulbright scholar at the University of Strasbourg, France, she taught French and worked as a Social Security claims representative. As a musician, she is mostly self-taught and has six published choral pieces.

Sydney Bertram Carter (b. 1915) wrote this music in 1964 for his song known as JUDAS AND MARY. Carter composed church music largely in a folk-song style, and his work quickly became popular with youth during the 1970s in England and the United States.

Sydney B. Carter, born in Camden, England, was a schoolmaster at Frensham Heights School and served with the Quaker Ambulance Unit during World War II. His two collections of songs are *9 Ballads or Carols* (1962?) and *Green Print for Song* (1973).

109 With Joy Draw Water

Anne McKinstry (b. 1937) was inspired by the joy conveyed in the Isaiah text to write this hymn in honor of a member of the church in Canaan, New York, where her husband served as pastor. The church missions committee published thirty of McKinstry's hymns in *Our Arms Have Held Thy Gifts* (1986).

Anne McKinstry was born on December 13, 1937, in Peabody, Massachusetts, and grew up there. She was educated at the University of Massachusetts and married a United Church of Christ minister. While supporting his work in the ministry, she developed her gifts in writing hymns and teaching piano.

This traditional Irish melody, ST. COLUMBA, is by an unknown composer. Saint Columba is highly revered in Northern Ireland, and even a Protestant Cathedral in Londonderry is dedicated to him. Saint Columba lived from 521 to 597 and took Christianity to Scotland from Ireland.

Charles Villiers Stanford (1852–1924) first included this tune in his *Complete Collection of Irish Music as Noted by George Petrie* (1902). The harmonization appeared a few years later in *The English Hymnal* (1906) as the setting for a paraphrase of Psalm 23 by Henry W. Baker.

110 Now Bless the God of Israel

Ruth C. Duck (b. 1947) paraphrased the *Benedictus* found in Luke 1:68–79 for this text. The biblical passage is also known as the "Canticle of Zechariah," who was the father of John the Baptizer. Duck's hymn was first sung in 1985 at an annual meeting of the UCC Massachusetts Conference for a morning prayer service.

Ruth Duck was an early advocate for using inclusive language in hymns and decided to use her gifts for artistic rather than political expression through writing hymn adaptations and new texts for the Ecumenical Women's Center in Chicago, Illinois. She coedited *Because We Are One People* for that organization in 1974.

FOREST GREEN is the name given this traditional English tune by Ralph Vaughan Williams, who first heard it in Surrey, England. The song was an old narrative ballad called "The Ploughboy's Dream." The harmonization is one of many that Vaughan Williams composed for *The English Hymnal* (1906).

Traditional English melodies are used as settings for at least seventeen hymns in *The New Century Hymnal*. FOREST GREEN is a particular favorite, appearing twice, with this hymn and with "All Beautiful the March of Days."

111 O Loving Founder of the Stars

A ninth-century manuscript found at Bern, Switzerland, is the basis for this hymn, although the text may be much older than that. Beginning with the Latin words "Conditor alme siderum," the text was sung during Advent at daily vespers services in monasteries.

This new English translation provides five of the original seven Latin stanzas. Earlier versions include John Mason Neale's "Creator of the Stars of Night" from the mid-nineteenth century when there was a renewed interest in hymns of the early church as part of the Oxford movement in England.

This simple melody with a range of only six notes is an example of syllabic chant. The melody was named AMBROSE by Lowell Mason, on the assumption that Saint Ambrose had written the text, but it is more often called CONDITOR ALME after the Latin text with which it has traditionally been associated.

This ancient plainsong melody was sung by Protestants after the Reformation with a variety of German texts, including two by Michael Weisse, a leader of Bohemian Brethren communities. J. S. Bach later used the melody in some of his organ works.

112 Keep Awake, Be Always Ready

Arthur G. Clyde (b. 1940) wrote this text in 1993 after finding no appropriate hymn using the newly revised lectionary readings for the first Sunday in Advent. He was inspired by the hymn "Wake, Awake" and wanted to maintain the flavor of that older text and its traditional tune.

Arthur G. Clyde served as music director at Zwingli United Church of Christ in Souderton, Pennsylvania, for twenty years. Subsequently he was editor of *The New Century Hymnal* (1995); he now leads workshops and develops educational resources on music and worship for the United Church of Christ.

Philipp Nicolai (1556–1608) composed this melody, often called the "king of chorales," for his German text after which the tune is named, WAUCHET AUF. It is possible that he followed a common sixteenth-century practice and adapted the tune from older material. The harmonization is by J. S. Bach.

Philipp Nicolai was the son of a German Lutheran pastor and was himself ordained in 1576. Always loyal to Lutheran theology, he often became involved in controversies, whether with Catholics, Calvinists, or Sacramentarians. He died of fever on October 26, 1608.

113 Little Bethlehem of Judah

Calvin George Seerveld (b. 1930) based this text on Micah 5, which recounts King Herod's answer to the Magi's question about the location of the Savior's birth. He wrote this metrical paraphrase for the *Psalter Hymnal* (1987) of the Dutch Reformed Church.

Calvin Seerveld was born August 18, 1930, at Bayshore, New York. He received his Ph.D. degree from the Free University of Amsterdam, Holland. Fluent in biblical and modern languages, he has published widely in the areas of biblical studies, philosophy, and Christian aesthetics.

Martin Edward Fallas Shaw (1875–1958) composed the tune WESTRIDGE in 1929 for a children's hymn that began "Jesus, friend of little children." Shaw served as organist at various London, England, churches beginning in 1908; from 1935 to 1945 he was director of music for the diocese of Chelmsford.

Martin F. Shaw was born in London, England, on March 9, 1875, and studied at the Royal College of Music. He founded the Purcell Society to promote the music of that early composer. Shaw collaborated with Percy Dearmer, with whom he worked at St. Mary's Church, Primrose Hill, London, on hymnals.

114 Return, My People

James F. D. Martin (b. 1953) wrote this Advent hymn in 1981 while in his second year as an ordained minister in the United Church of Christ. He and his wife, Jenny Dawson, were expecting their first child, and the season of obedient and patient waiting took on special meaning for them, reflected in this text.

James F. D. Martin was born on June 8, 1953, in Elmhurst, Illinois, and grew up in nearby Villa Park. His grandfather was a United Church of Christ minister in Wisconsin, Illinois, and Oregon. When Martin was age five he announced, "I'm going to be a minister like Grandpa." Martin was ordained in 1980.

Charles Hubert Hastings Parry (1848–1918) composed this music for use in his oratorio *Judith* in 1888. It was later adapted as a hymn tune and named REPTON. Parry spent his life teaching and composing and was knighted in 1898 for his contributions to English music.

C. Hubert H. Parry was born in Bournemouth, England, and grew to be expert in music of all kinds. He became director of the Royal College of Music in 1894 and was professor of music at Oxford University from 1900 until 1908. Parry died at Rustington, England, in 1918.

115 The Baptist Shouts on Jordan's Shore

Charles Coffin (1676–1749) wrote this hymn in Latin for use in lauds during the season of Advent. It was simultaneously published in his *Hymni sacri* and in a Paris breviary (worshipbook) in 1736. All six of the original stanzas are provided here in a new translation.

Charles Coffin served as rector at the University of Paris and later as principal of the College at Beauvais. Coffin is one of only a few French poets and Roman Catholic clerics whose hymns have been used in English Protestant churches. This is perhaps the most widely sung of his more than one hundred hymns.

This tune, WINCHESTER NEW, was first found in a German songbook published in 1690. It was discovered and adapted by editors of eighteenth-century English hymnals such as John Wesley and George Whitefield. William Havergal published the version closest to the present one in 1847.

English hymnal editors are responsible for the title of this tune, WINCHESTER NEW, since the melody originally came from Germany. The modifier "new" differentiates it from an earlier and unrelated one called WINCHESTER OLD.

116 O Come, O Come, Emmanuel

This metrical hymn based on the "O antiphons" of the medieval church may date from the twelfth century, although the source for the translation is the version found in a French Roman Catholic hymnal of 1710.

John Mason Neale translated the original five stanzas of this text beginning "Draw nigh, draw nigh, Emmanuel" for his *Mediaeval Hymns and Sequences* (1851). He later altered the first line to the present "O come, O come." The other two stanzas (2 and 7) are the work of Henry Sloane Coffin from his *Hymns of the Kingdom of God* (1916 ed.)

This metrical hymn tune, VENI EMMANUEL, was likely derived from phrases of plainsong settings. It first appeared in plainsong notation on a four-line staff in Thomas Helmore's *The Hymnal Noted* (1854) with the heading "From a French Missal in the National Library, Lisbon."

Thomas Helmore compiled and edited his *Hymnal Noted* in 1852, which provided musical settings of John Mason Neale's translations of Latin hymns. Both men were leaders in the Oxford movement in England and sought to restore ancient plainsong in the Anglican Church.

117 Lift Up Your Heads, O Mighty Gates

Georg Weissel (1590–1635) created this German hymn, "Macht hoch die Tür," for the first Sunday of Advent. The English text by Catherine Winkworth (1827–1878) is from her *Lyra Germanica* (1855), the first of two successful volumes of German hymn translations.

Georg Weissel was a Prussian pastor who served a church at Königsberg for most of his career. Of his twenty hymns, this is the only one to endure. In addition to her hymn translations, Catherine Winkworth also published a biography of German hymnwriters.

This anonymous tune, TRURO, was first published in the second part of Thomas Williams's *Psalmodia Evangelica* (1789) with a text by Isaac Watts. The tune name refers to an ancient town in the extreme southwestern part of Cornwall, England.

Psalmodia Evangelica was a hymnal published by an English musician, Thomas Williams, in 1789. This collection of tunes was intended for use by "churches, chapels and dissenting meetings in England, Scotland and Ireland," meaning those churches that had broken away from the Church of England.

118 Of the Parent's Heart Begotten

Marcus Aurelius Clemens Prudentius (348–413) wrote this Latin text as part of his sacred ode *Cathemerinon,* which provided a reflection on Christ's life for every hour of the day. The work consisted of twelve poems varying in length from 80 to 220 lines. This hymn is taken from the ninth poem.

Marcus Aurelius Clemens Prudentius was born into a distinguished Spanish family in 348 C.E. After serving as a judge for most of his life, he joined a monastery at age fifty-seven and began writing religious verse, from which many Christian hymns have been derived.

This ancient plainsong tune dates from as early as the tenth century. It was first found in print in Petri's *Piae Cantiones* (1582), where it was paired with the Latin text DIVINUM MYSTERIUM. In *Hymnal Noted* (1854), it was the setting for Neale's translation of the present Latin text by Prudentius.

DIVINUM MYSTERIUM is a plainsong melody that was utilized for a "trope" on the word "Sanctus" in the Middle Ages. Tropes were words not found in the authorized liturgical texts, which were sung to florid musical phrases during this period.

119 My Soul Gives Glory to My God

Miriam Therese Winter (b. 1938) paraphrased the "Canticle of Mary" (also known as the *Magnificat*) while she was a doctoral candidate at Princeton Theological Seminary in 1978. She later created a new fifth stanza and recorded the hymn with this tune on the album "Woman Song" in 1987.

Miriam Therese Winter is a Medical Mission sister who has been writing religious songs since Vatican II, a council that greatly liberated worship and hymnody in the church. Her most recent publication, *Songlines* (1996), presents one hundred of her songs from several decades of hymnwriting.

MORNING SONG has been traced to John Logan's *Sixteen Tune Settings* (1812), where it was called CONSOLATION. Since then, it has been reprinted in a large number of nineteenth-century hymnals and is one of few American tunes to be included in recent British hymnals.

Kentucky Harmony was a local hymnbook published in 1816, combining the work of a number of other hymnals. It was produced by Ananias Davisson for use in Presbyterian churches. The hymnal used shape notes, a method of musical notation developed to help untrained singers.

120 There's a Voice in the Wilderness

James Lewis Milligan (1876–1961) wrote this hymn in 1925 to celebrate the formation of the United Church of Canada through the merger of the Congregational, Methodist, and Presbyterian denominations in that country. The text was consequently published in the church's hymnal *The Hymnary* (1930).

J. Lewis Milligan was born in Liverpool, England, and received his education there. In 1911 he moved to Canada, became a lay pastor in the Methodist Church, and was a successful journalist writing for various Canadian papers. His interest in poetry led to hymnwriting.

Henry Hugh Bancroft (1904–1988) composed this tune, ASCENSION, in 1938. It appeared as the musical setting for Milligan's text in the United Church of Christ *Hymnal* (1974).

H. Hugh Bancroft was born February 29 (leap day), 1904, at Lincolnshire, England, and moved to Winnipeg, Canada, in 1929. He served as organist and choir director for Anglican churches in various provinces. In 1977 Bancroft was awarded a Lambeth doctorate in recognition of his musical contributions to the Anglican community.

121 Toda la Tierra (All Earth Is Waiting)

Alberto Viñas Taulé (b. 1932) wrote this text for the season of Advent. It utilizes images of promise from the Hebrew Scriptures and those of fulfillment through Christ's birth from the New Testament. This, Taulé's first hymn to be published in the United States, originally appeared in *The United Methodist Hymnal* (1989).

Alberto Taulé, a Roman Catholic priest, has served a small parish in Barcelona, Spain, and worked for the national offices on liturgical issues related to music. He received his education at Pontificio Istituto di Musica Sacra S. Pio X. Roma, also in Spain.

Alberto Viñas Taulé (b. 1932) composed this tune for his own text, and it was named TAULE in U.S. hymnals to honor him. Much of Taule's music has been recorded and continues to grow in popularity far beyond his native Spain.

Alberto Taulé was born December 2, 1932, at Sabadell, Spain. Many of his thirty-five hymns have been included in *Cantoral Litúrgico Naçional*, the official Roman Catholic hymnal used in Spain. He serves as the director of music publications in Centre de Pastoral Liturgica in Barcelona, Spain.

122 Come, O Long-Expected Jesus

Charles Wesley (1707–1788) first published this hymn in two stanzas of eight lines in his *Hymns for the Nativity of Our Lord* (1744). It is a favorite Advent hymn in every Protestant denomination but was not included in a Wesleyan hymnal until 1875, nearly one hundred years after the author's death.

Charles Wesley used the language of Scripture for his poetry and hymns. He cites all but four books of the Bible in his texts, which number more than 6,500. An Anglican deacon and elder, he traded the parish ministry for an itinerant one, traveling and preaching throughout England with his brother John.

Christian F. Witt (1660–1716) is believed to be the composer of this old German chorale, although it was printed anonymously in the 1715 hymnal *Psalmodia Sacra.* Most chorales are referred to by their German texts, but this one is unusual, being named STUTTGART for the city in Germany.

Christian F. Witt, the son of the court organist at Altenberg, Germany, received a fine musical education and was appointed court organist at Gotha, Germany, in 1686 and *kapellmeister* in 1713, serving with distinction for the rest of his life.

123 Mary, Woman of the Promise

Mary Frances Fleischaker (b. 1945) submitted this text, written in 1988, to a competition that was seeking new hymns about Mary, the mother of Jesus. The hymn reflects on the role of Mary in the Gospel stories and offers new and creative understandings of this woman of faith.

Mary Frances Fleischaker is a member of the Adrian Dominican order of the Roman Catholic Church. Her knowledge of "Marialogy" is reflected in this hymn. The text aids in understanding Mary's significance even though she has not been venerated within Protestant traditions.

This German carol from the fourteenth century first appeared in print in Valentinum Triller's *Ein Schlesich Singebüchlein* (1555). It was later used with other texts, including QUEM PASTORES LAUDAVERE, translated as "He Whom Shepherds Once Came Praising."

The word "quem" in the tune's name has an interesting history. It is a shortened form of "quempas," which by the sixteenth century had come to mean Christmas carols. Martin Luther even participated in "quempas singen" (Christmas carol singing) with his Latin School students.

124 Away in a Manger

Although this hymn has been attributed to Martin Luther, the great German reformer, modern hymnodists now know that he was not the author. Actually, this hymn originated in the United States and was first published in Philadelphia in 1885.

"A Lutheran author in Pennsylvania in the nineteenth century" is about as close as scholars have come to identifying the writer of these words. Scattered facts have traced the song's use to Pennsylvania's Lutheran churches. Many historians have labored to discover more, but without success.

This tune for "Away in a Manger" was written by an anonymous United States composer, although others have been given credit for it. The familiar title is AWAY IN A MANGER for the opening words, but it has also been called MÜLLER.

This tune is only one of more than forty tunes that have been used with this familiar cradle song. Some believe that James R. Murray may have been the composer, as the initials J.R.M. are found with this tune in an 1887 songbook for children.

125 Angels We Have Heard on High

This traditional French carol probably came from the eighteenth century. It was first published in France in *Nouveau reçueil de cantiques* (1855) with words beginning "Les anges dans nos campagnes." The Latin refrain quotes the song of the angels: "Glory to God in the Highest."

There are various English translations of this original French text. The translation of the first three stanzas is from *Crown of Jesus Music II* of 1862, and the last stanza appeared in *Carols Old and Carols New,* published in Boston, Massachusetts, in 1916.

This traditional French carol is named GLORIA for the words of the refrain. The composer is unknown. Other names for this tune are LES ANGES DANS NOS CAMPAGNES, taken from the first line of the hymn in French, and IRIS, from its association with James Montgomery's "Angels from the Realms of Glory."

This harmonization was used in *Carols Old and Carols New* (1916), edited by Charles L. Hutchins. No composer or arranger was cited for this hymn. However, the English musician S. S. Greatheed was listed as the arranger of the tune when it appeared as the setting for another hymn in that collection.

126 Angels, from the Realms of Glory

James Montgomery (1771–1854) published this poem under the title "Nativity" in the Christmas Eve, 1816, issue of his newspaper, *The Sheffield Iris*. It received little attention until revised and reprinted in 1825 in another paper he published called the *Christian Psalmist.*

James Montgomery was born November 4, 1771, in Ayrshire, Scotland, the son of a Moravian minister. After trying various jobs, he became editor of the *Sheffield Register* and held that post for thirty-one years. He died at Sheffield, England, on April 30, 1854, and hundreds of people attended his funeral.

Henry Thomas Smart (1813–1879) composed this tune, but it was named REGENT SQUARE in 1867 by the editor of the *English Presbyterian Hymnbook,* James Hamilton. Hamilton was the pastor of Regent Square Presbyterian Church in London, England, at the time.

Henry T. Smart, son of a well-known violinist, gave up his study of law to study music. Mostly self-taught, Smart served as organist and choirmaster at various Anglican churches in Blackburn and London, England. He continued playing even when blind during his last fifteen years of life.

127 Es ist ein' Ros entsprungen
(Lo, How a Rose E'er Blooming)

This hymn was in use at least by the time of Martin Luther. The earliest printed source is a manuscript from St. Alban's Carthusian monastery in Trier and dates from between 1582 and 1588. In its original form, the twenty-three stanzas of the Latin hymn told of the events recorded in Luke 1 and 2 and Matthew 2.

Theodore Baker (1851–1934) author of this English translation, was an editor for G. Schirmer, Inc., in New York City. Perhaps his greatest accomplishment was the *Biographical Dictionary of Music and Musicians* (1900), which continues to be published to the present day.

EST IST EIN' ROS is the name of this hymn tune, taken from the first line of the carol in German. Also called ROSA MYSTICA, this tune is believed to have its roots in Germany. For many years it was used primarily as a choral anthem because of its irregular meter.

This is a traditional German tune, thought to be from the sixteenth century. Michael Praetorius (1571–1621) arranged the tune for inclusion in the fourth volume of his *Musae Sionae* in 1609. Born on February 15, 1571, Praetorius died exactly fifty years later, on his birthday.

128 In the Bleak Midwinter

Christina Georgina Rossetti (1830–1894) wrote this poem, entitled "A Christmas Carol," and it was first printed in *Scribner's Monthly* in January 1872. *The English Hymnal* (1906) introduced it as a hymn with the new, plaintive setting by Gustav Holst, with which it has been associated ever since.

Christina G. Rossetti was the daughter of an Italian refugee to England. Like her father and brother, she was a gifted writer, and produced several volumes of poetry. She was also strikingly beautiful and posed as the virgin Mary for a painting by her brother Dante Gabriel, a noted artist.

Gustav T. Holst (1874–1934) wrote this melody, CRANHAM, which refers to his birthplace, Cranham Woods, near Cheltenham, England. Of Swedish heritage, Holst was one of England's leading composers and a contemporary of Charles V. Stanford and Ralph Vaughan Williams.

Gustav Holst was unable to realize his dream of becoming a concert pianist due to poor eyesight, weak lungs, and neuritis. His spirit was not diminished, however, and he achieved international acclaim as a composer and earned great respect for his service as music director at the prestigious St. Paul's School in London.

129 Good Christian Friends, Rejoice

The earliest manuscript of this old medieval carol at Leipzig University dates from around 1400. That version appeared in Klug's *Geistliche Lieder* (1533) and became widely used in both Protestant and Roman Catholic collections.

John Mason Neale (1818–1866) included this English translation in his *Carols for Christmas-tide* (1853), which he edited with Thomas Helmore (1811–1890). That inexpensive volume contained a dozen carols for use by church choirs.

This German melody from the fourteenth century is named IN DULCI JUBILO, for the Latin words of the refrain. The tune has always been used with this text and appeared in an early Lutheran hymnal, *Geistliche Lieder,* published in Wittenberg, Germany, in 1533 by Joseph Klug.

This tune was first used in Protestant services in 1529, and Martin Luther included it in his hymnal of the same year. J. S. Bach utilized the tune in two different organ pieces, and at least twenty-five other uses of the melody were documented by G. R. Woodward in *Piae Cantiones* (1910).

130 From Heaven unto Earth I Come

Martin Luther (1483–1546) wrote this fifteen-stanza hymn in 1535 for his son Hans. On Christmas Eve, one person representing an angel sang the first seven stanzas, and the children responded with the other eight. This is a form of a garland song, a popular singing game of Luther's day.

Martin Luther loved children and often played his flute for them. Yet even in his children's hymns, he never missed an opportunity to teach about the doctrine of the church and interpret Holy Scripture. The Christmas season was always an important one for songs and games in German families.

Martin Luther (1483–1546) is believed to have adapted or composed this tune which appeared with his Christmas hymn in Valentin Schumann's 1539 hymnal *Geistliche Lieder* from Leipzig, Germany. The tune is named VOM HIMMEL HOCH for the first words of the original German text.

Martin Luther is remembered as a Roman Catholic priest who left his order and began the Protestant Reformation. It is sometimes forgotten that he was a family man who married a former nun and helped to raise their eight children, six of whom grew to maturity.

131 It Came upon the Midnight Clear

Edmund Hamilton Sears (1810–1876) is now remembered for this hymn alone, published in the *Christian Register* (1850) in Boston. It was one of the earliest hymns in the United States to stress the social justice aspects of the Christian message.

Edmund H. Sears was born April 6, 1810, at Sandisfield, Massachusetts. In 1839 he was ordained in the Unitarian Church, although he continued to preach Christ throughout his ministry in the Boston area. This Christian commitment was reflected in his hymns and writings. He died on January 16, 1876.

Richard Storrs Willis (1819–1900), composer of the tune CAROL, adapted it from an earlier melody for another familiar Christmas text. The tune received widespread acceptance when published in various editions in the United States as the setting for Sears's text "It Came upon the Midnight Clear."

Richard S. Willis graduated from Yale University and studied music with Mendelssohn in Germany. He subsequently became a journalist, serving as music critic for the *New York Tribune* and other newspapers. Willis arranged a number of chorales and psalm tunes and wrote original compositions.

132 Joy to the World!

Isaac Watts (1674–1748) created this text by "Christianizing" the last five lines of Psalm 98. The original poem was entitled "The Messiah's Coming and Kingdom" in Watts's *Psalms of David, Imitated in the Language of the New Testament* (1719).

Isaac Watts first served the Protestant Church as assistant pastor under Isaac Chauncy at Mark Lane Independent (Congregational) Church, in London, England, where he preached his first sermon in 1699. Chauncy was the son of the president of Harvard College, Massachusetts.

Lowell Mason (1792–1872) is credited as the composer of the hymn ANTIOCH, as he first published it in a hymnal in 1836, marked "arr. from Handel." He or another composer or arranger utilized melodic fragments from George F. Handel's (1685–1759) *Messiah* in the tune.

ANTIOCH was the Syrian city where the disciples of Jesus were first called Christians, according to the book of Acts. Although closely associated with this text in the United States, the melody is not used with these words in English hymnals.

133 O Little Town of Bethlehem

Phillips Brooks (1835–1893) based this text on his trip to the holy land in 1865. On Christmas Eve he sat in the field where the angels appeared to the shepherds and attended services at the Church of the Nativity. Two years later he wrote this hymn about his experiences.

Phillips Brooks was an eloquent preacher, renowned in both the United States and England. Ordained in the Episcopal Church in 1859, he rose to the position of bishop of Massachusetts. A statue of Brooks by Augustus Saint-Gaudens stands next to Trinity Church in Copley Square, Boston, where he served for twenty-seven years.

Lewis Henry Redner (1831–1908) may have been the driving force behind the creation of this beloved Christmas hymn. He had suggested to Phillips Brooks the possibility of a collaboration, and on Christmas Eve Redner produced this tune, entitled ST. LOUIS, completing the harmonization the next morning before services.

Lewis H. Redner was born in Philadelphia, Pennsylvania, in 1831. He was a highly successful real estate agent in that city, beginning his career at age sixteen. He played the organ at four different Philadelphia churches during his lifetime and died in 1908 in Atlantic City, New Jersey.

134 Silent Night, Holy Night

Joseph Mohr (1792–1848) was assistant priest at Oberndorf an der Salzbach, Austria, when he wrote this text on Christmas Eve, 1818, after the organ had broken down. The repairman, Karl Mauracher, helped to circulate the hymn throughout Tyrol as a "Tyrolian folk song." Its origins were not clarified until 1854 when Gruber sent a letter to Berlin with a detailed account of the song.

Joseph Mohr was born December 11, 1792, in Salzburg, Austria. His father was an army mercenary and was often away from home. Joseph was helped by a kind priest and joined the Roman Catholic priesthood in 1815. He died December 4, 1848, after serving various parishes.

Franz Gruber (1787–1863) quickly composed the tune STILLE NACHT in 1818 and played it on the guitar for the Christmas Eve service at St. Nikolaus Church. Gruber and the pastor, Joseph Mohr, sang the stanzas, and a choir repeated the last two lines in four-part harmony.

Franz Gruber, son of a linen weaver, secretly studied violin and, later, the organ. When he substituted for a sick organist, his father recognized his talents and allowed him to continue his musical training. Although he wrote more than ninety compositions, he is remembered for this one hymn tune.

135 Adeste Fideles (O Come, All You Faithful)

John Francis Wade (1711–1786) is believed to be the writer of this Latin text. Six manuscripts of the hymn exist, all in Wade's handwriting—the earliest and most likely original dating from 1743. The English version is based on a translation by Frederick Oakeley beginning "Ye faithful, approach ye."

John F. Wade was an Englishman who worked in Douay, France, a center for Catholic refugees from England following the abdication of King James II. Hymns that he wrote and transcribed from Latin were published in 1751. Wade was born in 1711 and died in 1786.

ADESTE FIDELES is a Roman Catholic tune that has found wide acceptance in Protestant churches. When the tune was first printed in 1782, no composer's name was indicated. It has served as a setting for many other hymns since the nineteenth century.

This Roman Catholic tune is now found in practically every Christian hymnal in the world. John F. Wade (1711–1786) is credited as the composer, but it is not known if the melody is original or copied from an earlier source. Wade was born in England but fled to France during the Jacobean rebellion of 1745.

136 Jesus, Jesus, Oh, What a Wonderful Child

This song from the African American tradition demonstrates the strong rhythmic characteristics of the spiritual genre. The rhythmic feeling is further enhanced by an additional keyboard arrangement by Jeffrey Radford (b. 1953) found in the accompanist edition of *The New Century Hymnal*.

This traditional African American Christmas song or chorus can be effectively performed without accompaniment. The single stanza may be sung over and over and could support a Christmas reading of Scripture or a tableau depiction of the manger scene.

WONDERFUL CHILD is the name given to this African American song. Singing it in a soft, hushed tone reinforces the power of the words, giving the feeling that the singers have approached the manger to see the new-born baby, much as the shepherds and Magi did in the biblical accounts.

Jeffrey Radford (b. 1953) arranged this tune and several others for use in *The New Century Hymnal*. Radford has served as music director at Trinity United Church of Christ in Chicago, Illinois, the largest congregation of that denomination in the United States.

137 Hitsuji wa nemureri (Sheep Fast Asleep)

Genzō Miwa (b. 19th century) wrote this Christmas hymn in 1907, and it has become a favorite in Japan. It was first published in the Japanese hymnal *Kyodan Sambika* (1954). In short phrases, the text tells of visits from the shepherds and the Magi to worship the baby Jesus.

John Moss (b. 1925) served as a missionary for the United Church of Christ, stationed in Niigata, Japan. In 1957 he translated this Christmas carol by Genzō Miwa in order to share it with English-speaking people.

Chūgorō Torii (b. 1898) wrote the tune KŌRIN in 1941, and it was first used with this text in *Kyodan Sambika* (1954), a Japanese hymnal. The hymn was introduced in English in *Hymns of the Church* (1963), an English-language hymnal published by the United Church of Christ in Japan.

The story of Christianity in Japan reflects the strong influence of the U.S. missionary movement of the nineteenth century. Much of the church music of Japan bears the obvious imprint of Western harmony while maintaining its unique Japanese flavor. This hymn is one example.

138 Jesus, Our Brother, Strong and Good

This traditional French carol has been traced to the twelfth century. It has often been referred to as "The Friendly Beasts" and may have been used as part of a Nativity play. In the United States it was used in Clarence Dickinson's 1920 cantata, *The Coming of the Prince of Peace.*

It is easy to imagine individuals dressing up as the animals mentioned in this text and singing the appropriate stanza. For people who could not read the Scriptures for themselves in medieval times, such plays portrayed an understanding of the Christmas event, even if not entirely biblical.

This French melody is called ORIENTIS PARTIBUS, from the beginning of a medieval Latin and old French text meaning "from the Eastern regions the donkey is now come." It was part of a church festival begun at Rouen, France, in the tenth century which celebrated the donkey that carried Mary.

Pierre de Corbeil (d. 1222?), who became archbishop of Sens in 1200, wrote a liturgy for the Office of Circumcision and included this tune from a familiar church festival. The festival paid tribute to the role of the donkey that carried Mary to Bethlehem and later to Egypt to escape persecution.

139 The First Nowell

This traditional English carol was first published in 1823 in *Some Ancient Christmas Carols,* although its actual origin is unknown. The hymn consisted of nine stanzas in its original form. The word "Nowell" is a joyous expression of greeting to celebrate the birth of Christ.

It is difficult to trace the origins of this anonymous English carol. While some scholars believe that it cannot be older than the seventeenth century, others feel the text suggests it may have originated earlier than that.

This traditional English melody is named THE FIRST NOWELL for the first words of the carol. It was published with this text in 1833 by William Sandys (1792–1874), a British amateur musician who did much to preserve traditional carols and interest people in using them.

This anonymous tune may have been a descant or portion of the melody of one or more other hymns. Examples of these included Jeremiah Clark's "An Hymn for Christmas Day," "Rejoice and Be Merry," and "Hark, Hark, What News the Angels Bring."

140 Break Forth, O Beauteous Heavenly Light

Johann Rist (1607–1667) based this Christmas hymn on Isaiah 9:2–7, and it appeared in his *Himlische Lieder* (1641) in eleven stanzas. His ninth stanza is found here as the first. The second is a new translation that Fred Pratt Green (b. 1903) made in collaboration with German pastor Friedrich Hofmann.

Johann Rist wrote 680 hymns but, strangely, none of them was sung during his lifetime at the church in Wedel, Germany, where he was pastor for more than thirty years. In addition, he served as the town's physician and was a prodigious writer as well as an expert in horticultural science.

Johann Schop (c. 1595–1667) composed ERMUNTRE DICH as a setting for the words by his friend Johann Rist, whose hymnal he edited. The name is taken from the original German text and means "Bestir thyself." J. S. Bach composed the harmonization in 1734 and used it in his *Christmas Oratorio* of 1737.

Johann Schop was an accomplished teacher and performer on the organ, violin, lute, trumpet, and zinke. He composed both religious and secular music. Born in Hamburg, Germany, he served as director of music and organist of the town council. He was also violinist at the Danish court for a short time.

141 Carol Our Christmas

Shirley Erena Murray (b. 1931) experiences Christmas not in the winter but in the heat of summer in her native New Zealand. This carol, called "Upside-Down Christmas," raises awareness of that contrasting perspective for those living in the northern hemisphere.

Shirley Erena Murray, following her education at Otago University, New Zealand, became a teacher, specializing in foreign languages. She also served as a church organist and pianist. Murray later began writing hymn texts and has produced many poems and satirical songs.

Colin Gibson (b. 1933) composed this tune in 1986 for Shirley Erena Murray's Christmas text. It is named REVERSI in reference to the contrast in climate between the southern hemisphere, where it is summer at Christmas time, and the northern hemisphere, where snow and cold often prevail.

Colin Gibson began composing tunes for hymns in 1972 and has completed more than two hundred for texts by writers that include Bob Dylan, Richard Wilbur, John Bennett, and Shirley Erena Murray. His compositions have been recorded and broadcast on all the continents of the world.

142 Manglakat na Kita sa Belen (Let Us Even Now Go to Bethlehem)

Angel Sotto (b. 1885) wrote the opening stanza of this Philippine carol, and in 1981 Lois Bello expanded it with two additional stanzas. It is an example of one of the songs used in an annual Christmas ritual that takes place on the streets of villages in the Philippines.

Angel Sotto was born in Cebu City, Philippines, and trained as a reporter at his uncle's newspaper. He was one of the earliest Protestant converts in Cebu Island and studied at Manila Theological School. Sotto, an outspoken writer and preacher, established seven Protestant churches in his native country.

Angel Sotto (b. 1885) composed this tune for his text in 1981, and it is named MANGLAKAT for the opening words of the carol in the Philippine language. Verne de la Peña (b. 1959) provided the unison arrangement in a lowland folk-dance style appropriate to the cultural origins of the song.

Angel Sotto was a popular and controversial writer, publisher, and minister in the Philippines. He also pioneered in composing original hymns and in translating Spanish songs into Cebuano-Visayan dialect. Sotto published the first Visayan hymnal, *Mga Alawiton*.

143 On Christmas Night All Christians Sing

This traditional carol from the area of Sussex, England, was transcribed and published with a collection of texts and tunes by Ralph Vaughan Williams (1872–1958) in 1919. The hymn is effective when sung antiphonally, with two groups singing alternate phrases of the text.

Ralph Vaughan Williams spent much of his career working to preserve the folk songs of England. His work gave the world many texts and tunes that otherwise would have been lost and that are now standard parts of the repertoire of English church music.

Ralph Vaughan Williams (1872–1958) first discovered this melody in his research on traditional tunes in Sussex, England—thus the title SUSSEX CAROL. Jonathan B. McNair (b. 1959), assistant editor for *The New Century Hymnal*, created the new four-part harmonization of the tune in 1993.

Jonathan B. McNair holds music degrees from Appalachian State University, Southern Methodist University, and the Cleveland Institute of Music. A composer and teacher, he currently serves as director of music at Signal Crest United Methodist Church in Chattanooga, Tennessee.

144 Hark! The Herald Angels Sing

Charles Wesley (1707–1788) wrote this text less than one year after his conversion experience. The hymn is a condensed course in biblical doctrine in ten stanzas, using a variety of terms for the newborn Christ. Wesley published it in his 1739 hymnal, and many consider it his finest hymn.

Charles Wesley was already active in the church and an ordained clergyman when he wrote that he was converted and "found peace with God and rejoiced in the hope of a living Christ" on Whitsunday, May 20, 1738. He saw this conversion as the beginning of his Christian life.

Felix Mendelssohn-Bartholdy (1809–1847) composed the tune MENDELSSOHN in 1840, but it was not set to Wesley's Christmas words until fifteen years later. Mendelssohn's cantata, *Festgesang*, in which the melody appeared, was composed for the Gutenberg Festival at Leipzig to celebrate the four-hundredth anniversary of the invention of printing.

Felix Mendelssohn-Bartholdy was a child prodigy, playing the piano publicly at the age of nine. A prolific composer, he was deeply sensitive to criticism. Mendelssohn died November 4, 1847, at Leipzig, Germany, shortly after hearing of the death of his sister Fanny.

145 Once in Royal David's City

Cecil Frances Alexander (1818–1895) wrote this text in 1848 as part of a series of hymns based on the Apostles' Creed. This one taught children the meaning of the phrase "born of the virgin Mary." The hymn is now a standard at the Festival of Carols at King's College, England.

Cecil Frances Alexander established a school for the deaf with her sister before marrying William Alexander, a minister of the Anglican Church, who rose to be archbishop of Armagh and primate of all Ireland. Her most important volume was *Hymns for Little Children* (1848).

Henry John Gauntlett (1805–1876) composed the tune IRBY in 1849 for this text. It was originally scored for solo voice and piano and published in *Christmas Carols* (1849). The composer later rearranged it as a hymn for inclusion in the Appendix to *Hymns Ancient and Modern* (1868).

Henry J. Gauntlett is believed to have written more than ten thousand hymn tunes, but only a few of them survive to this day—IRBY and HOUGHTON being the best known. Gauntlett began working as a church organist at age nine but entered the law profession at the insistence of his father.

146 Nu Oli (Glad Tidings)

Fanny Jane Crosby (1820–1915) is the author of this hymn, which was not one of her most popular in the mainland United States. However, when translated by missionary Lorenzo Lyons (1807–1886) into the Hawaiian language, it became a favorite there. Only one of the original English stanzas is included here.

Lorenzo Lyons (1807–1886) wrote and translated so many hymns that he became known as the "Isaac Watts of Hawaii." His most famous hymn, "Hawaii Aloha," is widely sung in both religious and secular settings. His name in Hawaiian was "Laiana."

Robert Lowry (1826–1899) wrote this tune called GLAD TIDINGS in 1873 for Fanny Crosby's words. The hymn was later named NU OLI as presented here, when it appeared in Hawaiian hymnals with the translation by Lorenzo Lyons.

"Nu Oli" appears as the third hymn in *Na Himeni Haipule Hawaii* (1972), the sesquicentennial edition of the *Hawaiian Hymnbook*, published by the Hawaii Conference of the United Church of Christ. This early placement in the book attests to the widespread popularity of the song.

147 See the Little Baby

Donald Swift (b. 1952) paraphrased the traditional Christmas story from Luke's Gospel for this text. Published in 1990, this was the first choral composition by Swift to be accepted for distribution. Note that the refrain is to be sung following each stanza, including the second and final one.

Donald Swift was born in Atlanta, Georgia, and first received musical training at Luther Judson Price High School. He studied at Morehouse College, graduating cum laude in 1974. Swift then pursued further education at Candler School of Theology at Emory University in Atlanta.

Donald Swift (b. 1952) composed the tune LITTLE BABY along with his own words. The song was first performed at Sisters' Chapel of Spelman College, sung as a four-part choral arrangement by the Spelman-Morehouse College Glee Clubs for their annual Christmas concert in 1985.

Donald Swift attended Zion Hill Baptist Church in Atlanta, Georgia, as a child. As he grew up in this congregation, he sang in the choir, taught Sunday school, and served as assistant Boy Scout master. From 1984 until 1992 he lived in Chattanooga, Tennessee, and was a church pianist there.

148 What Child Is This

William Chatterton Dix (1837–1898) wrote a longer Christmas poem, "The Manger Throne," from which this hymn was derived. It appeared in this form with the tune GREENSLEEVES in *Christmas Carols New and Old* (1871).

William C. Dix, son of a famous Bristol, England, surgeon and author, enjoyed writing and translating hymn texts, although it was not his career. As a scholar of Greek and Abyssinian hymns, he translated many of them into metrical English texts.

This old English tune has been traced to 1580. It was used in *The Beggar's Opera* and was mentioned in works by Shakespeare. Now called GREENSLEEVES, it had been known as "The Blacksmith" or "The Brewer." The first license for the printed use of the tune was issued in 1580.

William Shakespeare mentioned the tune GREENSLEEVES in his play *The Merry Wives of Windsor*. There Shakespeare joked that it could not be used as a tune for singing Psalm 100. However, from its earliest reference in history, it has been used with both sacred and secular words.

149 Pastores a Belén (As Shepherds Filled with Joy)

This traditional Puerto Rican carol is written in the first person. It reflects the thoughts of the shepherds as they hurry to see the baby lying in a manger; it captures the urgency and eagerness experienced by them and by modern day Christians when singing this bright carol.

Christmas in Puerto Rico and in other warm climates offers the opportunity to celebrate at outdoor festivals. The holy days bring people out of their homes and into village and town centers to sing together and share in fellowship, dancing, and feasting.

The tune of this traditional Christmas carol is named here for the opening Spanish words, PASTORES A BELEN. The tune reflects the sense of urgency conveyed by the text, with the running notes being a reminder not only to hurry to see this miracle but to bring a gift as an offering.

This traditional Puerto Rican carol is an example of a *villancico* with its simple melody, limited chords, and 6/8 meter. It should be sung lightly with the feel of a dance.

150 Sing a Different Song

John L. Bell (b. 1949) and Graham Maule (b. 1958) collaborated on this text in 1987 for the Iona Community's Wild Goose worship group. This aspect of the Iona Community develops new liturgical and worship materials to help share the gospel message in a new form.

The Iona Community in Scotland is situated on an island west of the mainland. It is believed that this holy site holds the graves of sixty kings—forty-eight Scottish, eight Norwegian, and four Irish. Legend holds that Macbeth and Duncan were both buried at this site.

John L. Bell (b. 1949) wanted to create a robust bouncy tune as an antidote to the "mushy baby festival melodies" often used with Christmas hymns when he composed this music in 1987. It has been named DIFFERENT SONG after the words of the text.

John Bell was born on November 20, 1949, in Kilmarnock, Scotland. His mother was a devoted Christian and his father an agnostic until late in life. Bell was ordained to the Presbyterian ministry in 1978 and worked as a youth coordinator in Glasgow and at the Iona Community from 1978 to 1986.

151 'Twas in the Moon of Wintertime

Jean de Brébeuf (1593–1649) put the story of Christ's birth into language that made sense to the native Huron people in Canada for this, the earliest known Canadian carol. A Jesuit priest, de Brébeuf left his native France to serve as a missionary in the region around Quebec, Canada.

Jean de Brébeuf was born in Condé-sur-Vire, France, and ordained a Jesuit priest. From 1626 to 1633 he traveled by canoe from Quebec, Canada, to live with the Bear tribe. He died a horrible death at Saint-Ignace, Quebec, on March 16, 1649, during an Iroquois massacre.

This melody is an old French folk song entitled UNE JEUNE PUCELLE, also known as JESOUS AHATONHIA. It is a Christmas carol brought to North America by French missionaries or fur trappers and traders. The tune was used as the setting for both de Brébeuf's original French words and for the English translation.

This French "noël," or Christmas carol, is from the late sixteenth century. A number of French baroque composers used it as the theme for organ compositions. In addition, there is evidence that it may be related to the German chorale "Von Gott Will Ich Nicht Lassen."

152 Born in the Night, Mary's Child

Geoffrey Ainger (b. 1925) wrote this text in 1964. It begins as a Christmas song, but the third stanza is about Jesus' crucifixion, and the fourth reflects on the second coming at the end of time. The hymn is a reminder that Christmas is only the beginning of the gospel story of salvation through Christ.

Geoffrey Ainger, a former schoolteacher and Methodist circuit minister in southeast London, has retired and lives in that city. In the 1960s, he served in London's Notting Hill area, a community of many Caribbean immigrants, and where a group of hymnwriters collaborated on new music for the church.

Geoffrey Ainger (b. 1925) composed the melody MARY'S CHILD to be accompanied by guitar when sung with this text. He wrote the song for a drama, set in modern times, presented by the youth of his church in Loughton, England. The carol has become popular around the world.

English Methodist minister Geoffrey Ainger's sweet blues-like setting is part of his effort to make the Christmas story relevant to people today, especially youth. Richard D. Wetzel (b. 1935) arranged Ainger's tune in 1972 when it appeared in *The Worshipbook* of the Presbyterian Church.

153 Who Would Think That What Was Needed

John Bell (b. 1949) and Graham Maule (b. 1957) wrote this text in an attempt to "undomesticate" Christmas. They sought to remind Christians of the surprise that Christmas brings, rather than the mundane repetition that often comes with each year's routine celebration.

John Bell and Graham Maule have worked as colleagues in youth ministry and in worship and spirituality for more than fifteen years. Maule earned a degree in architecture from Glasgow University but left this work for the ministry. He is the first person Bell turns to for editing of his musical work.

Evelyn Danzig (b. 1902) should be credited as the composer of the tune SCARLET RIBBONS. It became popular in the United States and England when recorded by singer Harry Belafonte, with words written by Jack Segal about a young girl's birthday desire for hair ribbons.

Evelyn Danzig was born in Waco, Texas, on January 16, 1902, and began her musical career playing piano for radio shows. Among her popular tunes that became successful on the pop charts were "Warm-Hearted Woman," "Teddy Bear," and "We're All Kids at Christmas."

154 Go Tell It on the Mountain

John Wesley Work Jr. (c. 1871–1925) included these three stanzas of this African American spiritual in his collection *American Negro Songs and Spirituals* (1940). Another stanza sung prior to Work's version began "When I was a seeker," but utilized the same refrain.

John W. Work Jr. received his education at Fisk University, Nashville, Tennessee, where he was born. Although his primary area of study was classical languages, he became increasingly involved in research and the performance of African American spirituals with his brother, Frederick Jerome Work.

Hymnologists have noted similarities between the melody of this spiritual and other traditional songs, such as Stephen Foster's "Oh, Susanna." It was first published by R. Nathaniel Dett in his *Religious Folk Songs of the Negro* (1927).

John W. Work Jr. was a leader in arranging spirituals such as this one. He brought them to wider audiences through his publications and performances by the Fisk Jubilee Singers, whom he directed. Joyce Finch Johnson (b. 1935), of Spelman College, created this arrangement for *The New Century Hymnal*.

155 Los magos que llegaron a Belén
(The Magi Who to Bethlehem Did Go)

Manuel Fernández Juncos (1846–1928) based this story on the visit of the Magi to the manger as told in Matthew 2. The text is well suited for Christmas pageants, with a trio singing the first stanza and a person representing each of the Magi singing the second, third, and fourth.

Carolyn Jennings (b. 1936) translated this traditional Epiphany carol in 1993 for *The New Century Hymnal*. The English translation is closely matched to the original Spanish text, and it is quite acceptable for congregations to sing both languages at the same time.

This traditional Puerto Rican carol is called LOS MAGOS here, meaning "The Magi," but is named ISLA DEL ENCANTO ("Enchanted Island") in other denominational hymnals. It is in a popular dance form called a "danza" and reflects the feeling of people on a journey.

The Epiphany story of the visit of the Magi and the star that led them to the baby Jesus is set to a stately dance reflecting the graceful regal procession. The narrative stanzas contrast with the faster, more rhythmic introduction which helps to set the scene.

156 Brightest and Best

Reginald Heber (1783–1826) wrote this text in a small composition book in which his daughters practiced their geometry problems. The booklet is now in the British Museum. He first published this poem in the November 1811 issue of *The Christian Observer* magazine.

Reginald Heber was a widely known Anglican priest who served churches in England. He was eager to learn about congregational singing from the Methodists and Independents and introduced this practice in Anglican churches, which previously had discouraged congregational singing.

Southern Harmony was a collection of tunes collected by William Walker, and this tune bears the name WALKER to honor him. The composer, however, is unknown. The tune may have been a familiar folk tune in the southern United States.

William Walker (1806–1875) traveled extensively in the southern United States, teaching singing to all who wished to learn. He published a collection of melodies he had heard in his *Southern Harmony* (1835), and it became an important source of pre–Civil War tunes.

157 Brightest and Best

Reginald Heber (1783–1826) pioneered the concept of arranging hymnals according to the church year in his collection published posthumously in 1827. This hymn appeared there but was written earlier for a series in *The Christian Observer*, which Heber prepared to be "appropriate to the Sundays and principal Holy days of the year."

Reginald Heber was appointed bishop of Calcutta in 1823 and spent the next three years traveling extensively in India. His busy schedule precluded him from writing any poetry during this time. Heber died unexpectedly on April 3, 1826—a day on which he had baptized forty-three persons.

James P. Harding (1850–1911) composed this tune as a choral anthem in 1892 for the Gifford Hall Mission in Islington, North London. It is named MORNING STAR for the reference in Heber's text to the Epiphany star that led the Magi to the Christ child.

James P. Harding worked as a civil servant in London, England, most of his life. Church music was his avocation. He played the organ at St. Andrew's Church, Islington, for twenty-five years, and composed many hymn tunes and children's festival music.

158 O Morning Star, How Clear and Bright

Philipp Nicolai (1556–1608) wrote this text, based on Psalm 45, in seven ten-line stanzas and published it in 1599. The beginning letters of each stanza formed an acrostic, which referred to one of Nicolai's students. Catherine Winkworth translated the German text "Wie schön leuchtet der Morgenstern" in 1863.

Philipp Nicolai was born in Waldeck (now part of Germany) on August 10, 1556, and was an outstanding Lutheran preacher of his time. He served parishes in Herdecke in the Rhineland, Cologne, Unna in Westphalia, and Hamburg, where he died October 26, 1608.

Philipp Nicolai (1556–1608) composed this tune, WIE SCHÖN LEUCHTET, during a time of plague while he was a minister in Westphalia. It became widely popular throughout Germany and was used for many occasions, especially weddings.

Philipp Nicolai changed his surname from Rafflenboel to Nicolai, using a form of his father Nicolas's first name. As a child, he anticipated his life's work by "playing church" and officiating at funerals for pets who died. When Nicolai was ordained to the ministry he was only twenty years old.

159 As with Gladness Those of Old

William Chatterton Dix (1837–1898) wrote this Epiphany hymn during an illness sometime around 1860. Having read Matthew 2 as his morning devotional, he lay in bed trying to put the words into a metrical form. By evening, the text had been created.

William C. Dix wrote hymns and devotional materials as a hobby, and many of his works were published. This one was included in his *Hymns of Love and Joy* (1861). Dix worked as manager of a marine insurance firm in Glasgow, Scotland.

Conrad Kocher (1786–1872) composed this melody as a chorale tune for "Treuer Heiland." It was adapted by William Henry Monk in 1861 and named DIX for the author of the words. Kocher was an editor of chorale books in Germany and popularized four-part singing in Württemberg.

Conrad Kocher left Germany for Russia to prepare for the teaching profession but returned with a dedication to music. His friend Muzio Clementi encouraged him, and he went to Rome to pursue his studies. Kocher was influenced by the works of Palestrina and founded a school of sacred song.

160 Hark! The Herald Angels Sing (Jesus, the Light of the World)

Charles Wesley (1707–1788) wrote the popular Christmas text on which this hymn is based. It was adapted by George D. Elderkin, who added the phrase "Jesus, the light of the world" to Wesley's text. Elderkin's adaptation was first published in his collection *The Finest of the Wheat* (1890).

Charles Wesley arrived in Savannah, Georgia, with his brother John in 1736 and served as secretary to General Oglethorpe for that year. He returned to Oxford, England, where he dedicated his life to preaching the gospel; he later traveled on various evangelistic trips with his brother.

George D. Elderkin (dates unknown) wrote the tune that now bears his name, ELDERKIN, adapting Wesley's words for the music. The refrain uses additional text written by Elderkin, providing a personal affirmation and promise to follow "Jesus, the light of the world."

Jeffrey Radford (b 1953) arranged this tune, which is especially popular among African American congregations. Radford has been active in the United Church of Christ as a worship leader for gatherings such as FaithWorks and National Youth Event. He has also served as music director for meetings of the denomination's United Black Christians.

161 Amen, Amen

This spiritual song grew in popularity when it was included in the motion picture *Lilies of the Field*. It was sung by Sidney Poitier, who starred in the film. The text, preferably sung by a solo voice, charts the course of the life of Christ from birth to resurrection.

This spiritual is typical of the narrative-response style. The events of the story are told by a solo voice, with the congregation providing an affirmation of the story by repeating the word "Amen."

Nelsie T. Johnson (b. 1912) arranged this traditional African American melody for *The Presbyterian Hymnal* (1990). A South Carolina native, Johnson taught school and was choral director, organist, and pianist for churches around Greenville and Spartanburg, South Carolina.

This African American spiritual presents a variety of performance options, such as singing antiphonally (back and forth) between a leader and congregation, with hand clapping, or with movement.

162 In a Lowly Manger Born

Kō Yūki (b. 1896) wrote this text in 1923 in the second year of his fifty-year pastorate at Tokyo Futaba Independent Church, later named Kyodan Higashi Nakono Church, and part of the United Church of Christ in Japan. It was first published as a prologue in his *Poems on the Life of Jesus* (1929) and has proven extremely popular throughout Japan.

Kō Yūki was born April 16, 1896, at Sakaiminato, Tottori Prefecture, Japan. He studied biblical science, theology, and French literature at Kwansei Gakuin University in Osaka, earning a doctoral degree. Yūki is the author or translator of more than five hundred hymns.

Seigi Abe (1890–1974) composed the tune MABUNE, which means "manger," in 1930. In Japan, this tune has become one of the best loved and most widely sung hymns of the Japanese Christian community. The tune was first published in *Sambika,* a 1931 collection.

Seigi Abe was born May 18, 1890, in Sendai, Japan. He studied piano, voice, sacred music, and composition at the New England Conservatory of Music in Boston, Massachusetts, from 1913 to 1926. Abe returned to Japan and taught music at Meiji Gakuim, a Presbyterian boys' school, from 1927 until 1948.

163 Many Are the Lightbeams

Cyprian of Carthage (d. 258) wrote the Latin work *De unitate ecclesiae* (meaning "of church union"), on which this hymn is based, in 252 C.E. That work was paraphrased into Swedish by Anders Frostenson (b. 1906), and subsequently translated into English by David Lewis (b. 1916) to form this hymn.

Anders Frostenson served as pastor of the Isle Lovi beyond Stockholm, which included service at the Drottningholm Royal Castle. There he preached for three Swedish kings. Frostenson became a leader of the movement to revive Swedish hymnody since he resumed hymn writing in 1960.

Olle Widestrand (b. 1906) composed this tune for the Swedish paraphrase by Anders Frostenson, and it is named LIGHTBEAMS from the English text. Frostenson sought to modernize the hymns used in Sweden and looked for new tunes, such as this one, for his translations, paraphrases, and adaptations.

This tune appeared with Swedish, English, German, and Spanish versions of the text in *Jesus Christ—The Life of the World,* the worshipbook for the Sixth Assembly of the World Council of Churches, held in Vancouver in 1983. The original source of the hymn is *Psalmer och Visor 76*, a Swedish supplement.

164 Arise, Your Light Is Come

Ruth C. Duck (b. 1947) was working on a revision of the traditional text "Rise Up, O Men of God" when this adaptation came to her in 1973. It marked the beginning of her involvement in hymnwriting. This was her first text to be accepted for publication in a denominational hymnal.

Ruth Duck was deeply influenced by the evangelical faith and music of her family in Tennessee. She was nurtured by such groups as Youth for Christ and made her confession of faith at the age of thirteen at a Methodist church in Annapolis, Maryland.

William Henry Walter (1825–1893) composed the tune FESTAL SONG in 1872 for the hymn "Awake and Sing the Song." It was probably from this connection that the tune received its name. The hymn appeared in an Episcopal hymnal edited by John Ireland Tucker and in an 1894 revision.

William Walter, born in Newark, New Jersey, showed musical talent at an early age. While only a boy, he played the organ for two churches in Newark. He later served as organist at various churches in New York City and was appointed organist at Columbia University in 1865.

165 Love Came Down at Christmas

Christina Georgina Rossetti (1830–1894) wrote this poem for *Time Flies: A Reading Diary* (1885) under the date December 29. Obviously reflecting on her Christmas celebration, she used the word "love" twelve times in the text, seeing Christmas as the birthplace of love.

Christina G. Rossetti was so beautiful that her brother Dante Gabriel and the artist Millais asked her to sit as a model for their portraits of the Madonna. Ill health from the age of sixteen kept her in seclusion and contributed to her deep religious faith, expressed in poetry and prose.

Maurice C. Whitney (1909–1984) composed this tune as an anthem setting for Christina Rossetti's text in 1962. This is its first appearance as a four-part hymn tune, named WHITNEY for the composer.

This relatively obscure hymn is a welcome addition to the repertoire for Christmas and Epiphany. Other tunes with which this text have been associated include the Irish melody GARTAN (in *The Hymnal 1982*) and R. O. Morris's HERMITAGE (in *Rejoice and Sing*, 1991).

166 Immortal Love, Forever Full

John Greenleaf Whittier (1807–1892) wrote this text as part of a thirty-eight-stanza poem, "Our Master," first printed in *The Tent on the Beach and Other Poems* (1866). He never intended his words to be used as a hymn, but others saw merit in adapting it for congregational singing.

John Greenleaf Whittier believed deeply in the antislavery movement and risked his career, financial future, and well-being to fight for that cause when others around him, including the church in New England, were reticent.

William Vincent Wallace (1812–1865) composed this music for "Ye Winds That Waft," a secular love song. The first section was arranged as a hymn tune in 1869 by Uzziah C. Burnap (1834–1900), a Brooklyn, New York, church organist. It is named SERENITY after the sentiment of Whittier's poem.

William V. Wallace was born in Waterford, Ireland, of Scottish parents and became a professional musician at fifteen. He traveled widely, spending time in Australia and New Zealand, South and North America, and India, giving concerts and living an adventuresome life. In addition, he wrote piano music and seven operas.

167 Mark How the Lamb of God's Self-Offering

Carl Pickens Daw Jr. (b. 1944) wrote this hymn for the first Sunday after Epiphany, a day when churches celebrate the baptism of Jesus. The text recalls Jesus' temptations in the wilderness, which occurred following his baptism, and calls on Christians to renew their baptismal vows.

Carl P. Daw Jr. was the oldest of four brothers, and his father was a Baptist pastor and Navy chaplain. During his childhood, Daw studied both cello and piano. He received bachelor's and master's degrees in English; his dissertation was "An Annotated Edition of Five Sermons by Jonathan Swift."

Louis Bourgeois (c. 1510–c. 1561) may have written this melody, which appeared in the Genevan Psalter (1551) as well as the Scottish Psalter (1564). The tune name, RENDEZ À DIEU, is derived from a French paraphrase of Psalm 118 beginning with those words.

Louis Bourgeois was born in Paris, France. He was serving as cantor and choirmaster at St. Peter's Church in Geneva, Switzerland, at the time John Calvin was preaching there. Calvin gave him the job of editing the Genevan Psalter, a psalmbook that set the course of music in the Reformed Church.

168 O Radiant Christ, Incarnate Word

Ruth C. Duck (b. 1947) was commissioned in 1991 by the Lutheran School of Theology in Chicago, Illinois, to write this Epiphany text for a project led by Mark Bangert, a teacher at the school. Duck chose to make the hymn a prayer addressed to Christ and incorporated numerous references to "light."

Ruth Duck received an honorary degree from Chicago Theological Seminary in 1983 for her work in developing innovative worship resources and hymns. Her texts have served to awaken the church to be sensitive to include all people in the words used in song and liturgy.

Lee Hastings Bristol Jr. (1923–1979) adapted this hymn tune from a larger anthem he wrote in 1962 as a setting for "Lord of All Being Throned Afar." It is named DICKINSON COLLEGE for Bristol's alma mater in Carlisle, Pennsylvania, which presented him with an honorary doctorate in 1959.

Lee H. Bristol Jr. was born in Brooklyn, New York. A man of many talents, he received eleven honorary degrees during his lifetime. Bristol was active in the Protestant Episcopal Church, serving as president of Westminster Choir College, Princeton, New Jersey, from 1962 to 1969.

169 What Ruler Wades through Murky Streams

Thomas H. Troeger (b. 1945) was inspired to write this text in 1984 after seeing a picture of the Jordan River. Instead of being the pure river pictured in many works of art, it was muddy. It served to remind Troeger of the scope of Jesus' humility to walk into such a muddy river.

Thomas H. Troeger was born in Suffern, New York, and educated at Yale University and Colgate Rochester Divinity School in Rochester, New York. His first book, *Meditation: Escape to Reality,* studied the relationship of Hatha yoga to Christian prayer forms.

David Hurd (b. 1950), a highly respected church musician and composer, was asked to provide this tune for *The New Century Hymnal.* It is named WATER OF BAPTISM for the topic of the text by Thomas H. Troeger, who suggested that a new tune should capture the mystery of Christ's baptism.

David Hurd serves on the Standing Commission on Church Music for the Protestant Episcopal Church. He is a composer of organ, choral, and instrumental works, and his liturgical compositions and arrangements have appeared in several hymnals.

170 Your Ways Are Not Our Own

Lavon Bayler (b. 1933) wrote this text in 1988 for her collection of lectionary aids called *Refreshing Rains of the Living Word.* She based it on Luke 6:27–38, a Gospel reading for Epiphany 7 in year C of the lectionary. Bayler originally suggested FESTAL SONG as the setting for the hymn.

Lavon Bayler was ordained in 1959 to the ministry of the United Church of Christ after finishing her studies at Lancaster Theological School and Eden Theological Seminary. Her father, Emil Burrichter, was also a minister and served churches in Ohio, Indiana, and Iowa when she was growing up.

Robert Schumann (1810–1856) is credited as the composer of this tune in *Cantica Laudis,* an 1850 music collection edited by Lowell Mason and George Webb. The purpose of the collection was to provide great melodies adapted for choir and congregational use. The tune is named SCHUMANN here.

Although Robert Schumann is credited as the composer of this tune published by Lowell Mason and George Webb in their 1850 collection *Cantica Laudis,* music scholars have been unable to find it in any known Schumann compositions.

171 Jesus Calls Us, o'er the Tumult

Cecil Frances Alexander (1818–1895) wrote this text for use at a St. Andrew's Day celebration in 1852. She based the text on Matthew 4, which tells of the calling of the first disciples. It was Andrew who first responded to Jesus' call, and brought his brother Simon Peter to Jesus.

Cecil F. Alexander was a gifted Irish poet who lived in County Tyrone with her husband, a pastor in a remote parish at the time this hymn was written. She and her sister later established a school for the deaf in that same area.

David Hurd (b. 1950) composed the tune ST. ANDREW in 1980 for this text by Cecil F. Alexander. It is a folk-like melody based on the pentatonic scale and was published in *The David Hurd Hymnary* (1983). The tune's name refers to the disciple of Jesus mentioned in the second stanza.

David Hurd, a concert organist and composer, has received honorary doctorates for his work from Berkeley Divinity School in New Haven, Connecticut, the Church Divinity School of the Pacific, Berkeley, California, and Seabury-Western Theological Seminary, Evanston, Illinois.

172 Jesus Calls Us, o'er the Tumult

Cecil Frances Alexander (1818–1895) intended this hymn, based on Matthew 4:18–20, for use by children. It was first published under the title "Follow Me/For St. Andrew's Day" in *Hymns for Public Worship* (1852) and has since received widespread use in worship settings by people of all ages.

Cecil F. Alexander, daughter of a major in the Royal Marines, was born at Miltoun House in County Tyrone, Ireland. She dedicated her life to writing sacred verse; many of her poems have been used for hymns. Her major project was a series of hymns based on the Apostles' Creed.

William Herbert Jude (1851–1922) composed the tune GALILEE for this text by Cecil Alexander in 1874. The tune name was inspired by the scriptural reference to the lakeshore where Jesus ministered in the region of Galilee and which is cited in the second stanza of the hymn.

William H. Jude was born in Westleton, Suffolk, England, in September 1851, and was one of the first English composers to travel to Australia as a lecturer on musical subjects. His particular expertise was the music of Henry Purcell. Jude died in London, England, on August 7, 1922.

173 Tú has venido a la orilla
(You Have Come down to the Lakeshore)

Cesáreo Gabaráin (1936–1991) based this text on the calling of Peter and Andrew as recorded in the Gospels. The hymn was first printed in a small booklet and has since been translated into more than eighty languages.

Cesáreo Gabaráin was born in Hernani, Spain, on May 16, 1936. He studied theology and was ordained to the Roman Catholic priesthood. In addition to serving as a parish priest, he was Spanish chaplain to Pope Paul VI. Gabaráin died on April 30, 1991, at Mondragon, Spain.

Cesáreo Gabaráin (1936–1991) wrote this melody to accompany his text. The name of the tune, PESCADOR DE HOMBRES, was the original title by which the song was known in Spain. Skinner Chávez-Melo (1944–1992) provided the harmonization in *Albricias* (1987), a songbook he edited for the Protestant Episcopal Church.

Cesáreo Gabaráin spent his life as a Roman Catholic priest in Spain, serving various parishes. In addition, he became a leading composer of congregational music and served as president of a Spanish liturgical music association.

174 Hear the Voice of God, So Tender

Lavon Bayler (b. 1933) wrote this text in 1987 for *Whispers of God,* a book of liturgical resources for Year B of the Common Lectionary. She suggested the hymn for use on the Eighth Sunday after Epiphany. Her book provides a new hymn text for each Sunday of the year.

Lavon Bayler served as copastor at a four-point charge in Central Ohio with her husband, Robert Bayler, whom she met at seminary. She had previously spent a year as the national youth associate for the Evangelical and Reformed Church.

Skinner Chávez-Melo (1944–1992) wrote this tune as a setting for "Sing of Mary, Pure and Lowly" in *The Hymnal 1982,* for which he was a consultant. It is named RAQUEL for Raquel Gutierrez-Achon, another consultant to the Standing Commission on Music at the time.

Skinner Chávez-Melo was born in Mexico City but studied music in the United States and England. He served as choral director and instructor at the Manhattan School of Music and Mannes College of Music; he was organist and choirmaster at Union Theological Seminary in New York City.

175 O Christ, the Healer, We Have Come

Fred Pratt Green (b. 1903) wrote the first draft of this hymn overnight when the committee for *Hymns and Songs* (1969) could not find a suitable hymn on the subject of the healing ministry of Jesus. Originally entitled "A Prayer for Wholeness," it was one of the first modern texts to deal with mental and physical health.

Fred Pratt Green is the son of a leather manufacturer, and he worked beside his father in this business for four years. At one time, Green planned to become an architect. At Didsbury Theological College in Manchester, England, he wrote his first play, *Farley Goes Out*, as well as his first hymn.

Richard W. Gieseke (b. 1952) composed the tune KENTRIDGE in 1988. At the time, he was serving as a teacher and director of music at Word of Life Lutheran School in St. Louis, Missouri. In addition, he has worked as minister of music for various churches in the St. Louis area.

Richard Gieseke was born May 15, 1952, in Elgin, Illinois. He attended Concordia University in River Forest, Illinois, where he studied with Richard Hillert and Carl Schalk, earning both bachelor's and master's degrees. In 1989, he joined the editorial services department of the Concordia Publishing House.

176 "Silence! Frenzied, Unclean Spirit"

Thomas H. Troeger (b. 1945) based this text, written in 1984, on the story of Jesus exorcising a demon. Troeger goes beyond the biblical story to explore a modern-day understanding of demons, ending with a prayer for wholeness for all people.

Thomas H. Troeger seeks in many of his hymn texts to vividly portray a biblical story, then to explore the story's implications for the present day. This type of biblical exegesis is enabled by Troeger's experience as an ordained minister and his gift for poetic expression.

Carol Doran (b. 1936) composed this melody to convey the two contrasting moods presented by the text. The first half exhibits the struggle of the demon and the strength that Christ brought to its exorcism, while the second section suggests Christ's assurance of healing. The tune is called AUTHORITY.

Carol Doran serves as associate professor of worship and pastoral music at Colgate Rochester Divinity School, Bexley Hall, Crozer Theological Seminary in Rochester, New York. There, she has developed a Master of Arts in Pastoral Music program to train professional church musicians.

177 God of Change and Glory

Alvin Allison Carmines Jr. (b. 1936) was commissioned to write this hymn in 1973 for the Assembly of the Women's Division, General Board of Global Ministries of the United Methodist Church. The text expresses the diversity and acceptability of all human gifts.

Al Carmines was ordained to the United Church of Christ ministry in 1960. He was pastor at Judson Memorial Church in New York's Greenwich Village for twenty years before moving to Rauschenbusch United Church of Christ, also in New York City.

Alvin Allison Carmines Jr. (b. 1936) wrote this tune to accompany his own words and named it KATHERINE after his mother. The hymn often appears in hymnals under its familiar title "Many Gifts, One Spirit."

Al Carmines has served as adjunct professor of musical theater at Columbia University. He is the recipient of five Obie Awards, the Drama Desk Award, and the Vernon Rice Award for his work in the theater, which includes musical plays, an opera, and a dance oratorio.

178 We Have the Strength to Lift and Bear

Thomas H. Troeger (b. 1945) based this text on Mark 2:1–12, the story of the healing of a paralyzed man. After contemplating the work of nurses who care for stroke patients, he incorporated that imagery to help develop the biblical story in a more meaningful way.

Thomas H. Troeger grew up in Cooperstown, New York. While in high school, he decided to become a professional flutist but changed his mind due to the power of his pastor's preaching. This led him to study theology and, ultimately, to ordination in the Presbyterian Church.

Thomas Tallis (c. 1505–1585) composed the melody now called TALLIS' THIRD TUNE for Psalm 2 in Matthew Parker's *The Whole Psalter* (1567–1568). The "third" referred to was the "third" or "Phrygian" mode, used to convey the anger of the psalm text. Originally, Tallis put the melody in the tenor line.

Thomas Tallis was one of the preeminent musicians of sixteenth-century England. Cited as the "father of English cathedral music," Tallis managed to survive political changes in church and state through the reigns of King Henry VIII, King Edward VI, Queen Mary, and Queen Elizabeth I.

179 We Yearn, O Christ, for Wholeness

M. Dosia Carlson (b.1930) was inspired to write this text after the respected minister Harold Wilke visited the Church of the Beatitudes in Phoenix, Arizona. Wilke, born without arms, encourages churches to be barrier-free to persons with handicaps, through the work of his "Healing Community."

Dosia Carlson expresses her faith through writing hymns. While preparing for ordination in the United Church of Christ in 1979, she used some of these hymn faith statements as part of her ordination presentation, and others encouraged her to make her words available through publication.

Hans Leo Hassler (1564–1612) wrote the tune PASSION CHORALE in 1601. Originally it was named HERZLICH TUT MICH VERLANGEN after the opening words of the German love song with which it appeared. J. S. Bach harmonized the tune more than one hundred years later.

Hans Leo Hassler was born in 1564, the same year that marked the birth of William Shakespeare and the deaths of John Calvin and Michelangelo. Hassler was the leading composer of his time and was in demand among some of the most powerful and influential families in Germany.

180 Blessed Are the Poor in Spirit

Howard M. Edwards III (b. 1955) paraphrased this text from the Beatitudes, the familiar "blessings" delivered by Jesus on the Mount of Olives. *The New Century Hymnal* marks the hymn's first publication in a denominational hymnal. It is especially appropriate for use on Epiphany 4, year A, as well as on All Saints' Day.

Rusty Edwards was born in Dixon, Illinois, in 1955. He was ordained to the Lutheran ministry in 1985 and has since served two Illinois churches, most recently as senior pastor at Gloria Dei Lutheran Church, in Rockford, Illinois.

Jane Manton Marshall (b. 1924) composed this tune in 1993 for Rusty Edwards's paraphrase of the Beatitudes. It is named ANNIKA'S DANCE in honor of liturgical dancer Annika Gustafson, who first interpreted the hymn through that art form.

Jane M. Marshall is a well-known educator, composer, and conductor in the United Methodist Church. She chaired the hymnal supplement task force for her denomination and contributed a great deal of liturgical music to *The United Methodist Hymnal* (1989).

181 You Are Salt for the Earth, O People

Marty Haugen (b. 1950) based this text on Matthew 5:13–15, the passage that immediately follows the Beatitudes in Jesus' Sermon on the Mount. The first and second stanzas are paraphrases of the text, while the third and fourth are Haugen's original reflections on the passage.

Marty Haugen has composed and recorded a new communion service for use by Lutheran congregations called *Now the Feast and Celebration*. His ecumenical work is demonstrated by his contributions to the *Book of Worship* for the Canadian Roman Catholic Church and the Anglican Church in England.

Marty Haugen (b. 1950) wrote the tune BRING FORTH for his own words. The tune's name indicates the processional nature of the music. He wrote it at the Holden Village Retreat Center in Chelan, Washington, for use during outdoor worship.

Marty Haugen has traveled throughout the United States, Canada, Europe, Australia, and Central America teaching, leading workshops, and presenting concerts of his music. He has published more than two hundred pieces of religious music for a wide variety of settings.

182 We Have Come at Christ's Own Bidding

Carl Pickens Daw Jr. (b. 1944) based this text on the Gospel story of the Transfiguration. The poem juxtaposes the responses of the disciples Peter, James, and John with those of modern-day Christians as they approach the worship experience.

Carl P. Daw Jr. was ordained to the ministry of the Episcopal Church in 1982 and was assigned as vicar-chaplain of St. Mark's Chapel at the University of Connecticut at Storrs. During his chaplaincy at that institution, he also served as a lecturer in English from 1988 to 1989.

Rowland Hugh Prichard (1811–1887) composed this tune and included it in his *Cyfaill y Cantorion* (*The Singer's Friend*), which was published in 1844 to provide more-appropriate music for Sunday-school songs. The tune HYFRYDOL means "pleasant" and "melodious" in Welsh.

Rowland H. Prichard worked in the textile industry but enjoyed composing church music as his hobby. His simple yet powerful tunes were typical of his native Wales. The churches in Wales encourage singing, often a capella, and Welsh choirs produce a sound unlike any found elsewhere.

183 Jesus, Take Us to the Mountain

Jaroslav Jan Vajda (b. 1919) wrote this Transfiguration hymn in 1991 for St. Luke Lutheran Church in Silver Spring, Maryland. The church members wanted a new hymn to help commemorate their fiftieth anniversary as a congregation. The text tells the story of the Transfiguration in verse.

Jaroslav J. Vajda began writing poetry at the age of eighteen. This interest led to his work on the Commission on Worship for the Lutheran Church, serving from 1960 until 1978. He has been a popular workshop leader and has published several collections of his works, including *Now the Joyful Celebration* (1987).

Carl Flentge Schalk (b. 1929) composed SILVER SPRING in 1991 for this text by Jaroslav Vajda, naming it for the Maryland city where St. Luke Lutheran Church is located. A frequent collaborator with Vajda, both men served on the Inter-Lutheran Commission on Worship in the 1960s and 1970s.

Carl F. Schalk has composed more than fifty hymn tunes in his long career as music director, professor, and editor. He has edited *Church Music* magazine since 1966 and is the author of *Luther on Music: Paradigms of Praise* (1988), a book on Martin Luther's influences on church music.

184 O Wondrous Sight, O Vision Fair

This text is translated from the Sarum Breviary, a Latin service book that has been traced to 1495. The hymn was part of the liturgy for the Feast of the Transfiguration when this festival became widely celebrated. John Mason Neale provided the English translation in 1851.

The Sarum Breviary was a worship book used in Salisbury, England, which contained services for daily worship in the church. It was written in Latin, as was all sacred literature of the time. The particular version of the breviary referred to here was printed in 1495.

This tune is called DEO GRACIAS ("Thanks to God"). Although the composer's name has been lost to history, it was originally a setting for a ballad about the victory of King Henry V of England over the French at Agincourt in 1415. The king attributed this victory to God's graciousness.

The Hymnal (1933) of the Presbyterian Church was the first publication to pair this fifteenth-century text and tune together. *The New Century Hymnal* is the first UCC hymnal to include this Transfiguration hymn. Another tune with which it has been associated is WAREHAM (hymn 306), by William Knapp.

185 Savior, When in Tears and Dust

Robert Grant (1779–1838) wrote this text, which first appeared as a poem entitled "Litany" in the English magazine *Christian Observer* in 1815. The text has been altered frequently by hymnal editors and was even translated into Latin in 1871 as "Quando genua flectentis."

Robert Grant, like his father, Charles, was an important English statesman, serving as a member of Parliament, judge advocate, and governor to India. His hymns were collected and published by his older brother after Grant's death in India on July 9, 1838.

Benjamin Carr (1768–1831) published an arrangement for solo, quartet, and full chorus, based on an "Air from an Ancient Spanish Melody" in 1826. A metrical version known as SPANISH HYMN was published by Montague Burgoyne the following year. Despite its title, the tune has never actually been traced to Spain.

Benjamin Carr, born in England, was a music student of Samuel Arnold (publisher of Handel) and Charles Wesley. After moving to Philadelphia in 1793, he opened one of the first music stores in the United States and published some early patriotic music, including "The Star-Spangled Banner."

186 Dust and Ashes Touch Our Face

Brian Arthur Wren (b. 1936) wrote this lenten text for the choir of the United Church, Hyde Park, in Chicago, Illinois, for use on Ash Wednesday. The imposition of ashes serves as a reminder of our human sin and failure and increasingly is practiced in Protestant churches at the beginning of Lent.

Brian Wren, in addition to writing hymn texts, at one time developed liturgical materials for worship. In 1967, he wrote and published *Contemporary Prayers for Public Worship*. Wren leads workshops around the world to share his ideas about worship and hymnody.

Hal H. Hopson (b. 1933) composed the tune DUST AND ASHES for this text after Brian Wren shared it with him in 1989. Hopson works as a freelance church music composer and has served on the music faculties of Westminster Choir College in Princeton, New Jersey, and Scarritt Graduate School, Nashville, Tennessee.

Hal H. Hopson was born in White Mound, Texas, on June 12, 1933. A Presbyterian, Hopson conducts choral festivals and workshops throughout the world. His cantata *God with Us* was selected by a Kennedy Center panel to be included in a time capsule during the American Bicentennial in 1976.

187 Again We Keep This Solemn Fast

Gregory the Great (540–604) is often credited as the author of this Latin text beginning with the phrase "Ex more docti mystico." The text has been found in various manuscripts, the earliest dating from the tenth century. The English translation was made by Peter J. Scagnelli (b. 1949).

Gregory the Great was born in Rome, Italy, in 540 C.E. and died there in 604. Although he was a member of a wealthy family, he gave up his riches for the monastic life. Elected pope in 590, Gregory urged the spread of Christianity to England through the work of Augustine at Canterbury.

This tune, ERHALT UNS, HERR, was adapted from another piece of music, called "Jesu, dulce cordium," found in the 1543 edition of *Geistliche Lieder*, a music book published by Joseph Klug. An earlier edition of this hymnal (1529) was edited by Martin Luther.

Joseph Klug was one of four publishers in Wittenberg, Germany, who supplied literature, tracts, hymnals, and books for the Lutheran Reformation. Evidence has been found of his printing work beginning in 1523 and ending in 1552.

188 Give Me a Clean Heart

Margaret J. Douroux (b. 1941) wrote this hymn as the refrain of a gospel song in 1970, using Psalm 51:10 as her inspiration: "Create in me a clean heart, O God, and put a new and right spirit within me." Douroux's entire song, including the two stanzas, can be found in *Songs of Zion* (1981).

Margaret J. Douroux is the daughter of a Baptist minister. Her religious songs have achieved great popularity through recordings by singer James Cleveland. One of her best-known songs is "God Is Not Dead"; it was recorded by Cleveland, who has been called the "crown prince of gospel."

Margaret J. Douroux (b. 1941) wrote this tune for her own words, and it bears the name DOUROUX to honor her. Like much music from the modern gospel tradition, it can easily be sung over and over again as a prayer response. It is especially appropriate during the penitential season of Lent.

Margaret J. Douroux has written many gospel songs, and they have been accepted by a wide audience. James Cleveland, who popularized much of her work, organized the "Gospel Music Workshop in America" to help promote the work of artists such as Douroux.

189 Down at the Cross

Elisha Albright Hoffman (1839–1929) wrote this text, which first appeared in the 1878 hymnal *Joy to the World*, printed in Cleveland, Ohio. The text speaks of the cleansing power of Christ to forgive sins. The inspiration that prompted Hoffman to write these words is not known.

Elisha A. Hoffman was born in Pennsylvania and attended Union Bible Seminary of the Evangelical Association. For eleven years he was associated with the Board of Publication and served as a pastor of the Evangelical Association. His last parish was First Presbyterian Church in Benton Harbor, Michigan.

John Hart Stockton (1813–1877) composed this tune. It is called DOWN AT THE CROSS here, after the song's title, although it is also known as GLORY TO HIS NAME in some hymnals. Stockton wrote hymn tunes for use at the evangelistic meetings that were popular in his day.

John H. Stockton was born in New Hope, Pennsylvania. He became a licensed preacher in the Methodist Episcopal Church in 1857 but was forced from active ministry by ill health. He remained in evangelical work, helping with Moody-Sankey meetings held in Philadelphia, Pennsylvania.

190 Beneath the Cross of Jesus

Elizabeth Cecilia Clephane (1830–1869) wrote this hymn at a young age with the knowledge that she was dying. Three years after her death in 1872, it was published in *Family Treasury*, a Scottish Presbyterian magazine. Even then, it was introduced anonymously.

Elizabeth C. Clephane was born June 18, 1930, in Edinburgh, Scotland, and died in Melrose on February 19, 1869, at the age of thirty-nine. She was a generous contributor to humanitarian causes and earned the nickname "Sunbeam" from those whom she helped.

Frederick Charles Maker (1844–1927) wrote this melody for these words, and they appeared together in a supplement to *The Bristol Tune Book* (1881). The name ST. CHRISTOPHER seems to have no relevance to the hymn. Christopher is the patron saint of travelers and travel.

Frederick C. Maker was born and died in Bristol, England. He was one of the most eminent organists of the Nonconformist churches (Congregational) in England and a composer of anthems, cantatas, and piano pieces. He retired from serving as a church organist in 1910 and died in 1927 at the age of eighty-three.

191 Before Your Cross, O Jesus

Ferdinand Quincy Blanchard (1876–1968) wrote this hymn in 1928 for use in his own congregation in Cleveland, Ohio. It was provided as an alternative to the text by Elizabeth Clephane ("Beneath the Cross of Jesus," hymn 190) to "have modern appeal."

Ferdinand Q. Blanchard, born in Jersey City, New Jersey, was educated at Amherst College and Yale Divinity School and entered the Congregational ministry. He served as a trustee at Fisk University and supported educational ministries among blacks through the American Missionary Association.

Frederick Charles Maker (1844–1927) composed the tune ST. CHRISTOPHER for an earlier text by Elizabeth Clephane. It was retained by Ferdinand Blanchard when he wrote a similar hymn focusing on the cross for his Cleveland, Ohio, congregation.

Frederick C. Maker, in addition to being a church organist, accompanied the Bristol, England, Festival choirs for many years. The director of this music festival was Alfred Stone, who had been Maker's organ instructor early in his life and who later published Maker's hymns in *The Bristol Tune Book*.

192 When Jesus Wept

William Billings (1746–1800) based the simple yet profound words of this canon text on John 11:35, "Jesus began to weep" at the death of Lazarus. Billings often employed passages from Scripture or the Anglican Prayer Book for his anthems and hymns, sometimes taking liberty with the texts to reflect contemporary or patriotic issues.

William Billings was trained as a tanner and never received any musical education. Yet, as one of the earliest composers of religious music in the United States, he set high standards for church music and enjoyed wide popularity. Billings published six tunebooks in his lifetime.

William Billings (1746–1800) composed WHEN JESUS WEPT as a canon or round. It was one of 120 original tunes and anthems in the *New England Psalm Singer* (1770)—the first tunebook by a single composer to be published in the United States.

William Billings lived through the American Revolutionary War, and his tune CHESTER was one of the most popular melodies to come from that time. Billings's fuguing tunes offered a contrast to the austere psalm tunes used exclusively in New England churches in his day.

193 In the Cross of Christ I Glory

John Bowring (1792–1872) based this text on Paul's letter to the Galatians 6:14, and the opening line appears on his tombstone. This hymn alone has assured Bowring a place of distinction forever in the history of Christian hymnody.

John Bowring was a Christian Unitarian who had a distinguished diplomatic career, holding positions in France and Hong Kong. Bowring was fluent in more than one hundred languages and was knighted by Queen Victoria in 1854 for his service to his nation of Great Britain.

Ithamar Conkey (1815–1867) composed this tune in 1849 and named it RATHBUN for the last name of the leading soprano in his church choir. At the time, he was organist and choir director at Central Baptist Church, Norwich, Connecticut. The tune was first published in 1851 but did not appear with Bowring's text until 1865.

Ithamar Conkey was born in Shutesbury, Massachusetts, on May 5, 1815. After working in Norwich, Connecticut, he moved to New York City, where he had a successful career as a church and oratorio singer. One of his positions was at Calvary Episcopal Church, where Walter Greatorex served as music director.

194 In the Cross of Christ I Glory

John Bowring's (1792–1872) enduring text first appeared in *Hymns: As a Sequel to Matins*, published in London in 1825. The version given here is nearly identical to the original in which the first stanza was also repeated as the fifth.

John Bowring at one time wished to become a Unitarian minister, but his father dissuaded him from that calling. In addition to editing and translating anthologies of poetry, Bowring composed original hymns as an expression of his deep faith.

Bruce Neswick (b. 1956) wrote this tune by request, to provide an alternate melody for the text by John Bowring. He named the music TOMTER for Patrick Tomter, an Episcopal priest with whom Neswick worked while an undergraduate at Pacific Lutheran University in Tacoma, Washington.

Bruce Neswick served as organist and choirmaster at St. Paul's Episcopal Church, Buffalo, New York, from 1983 until 1991. After studying for a year in Switzerland, he accepted a similar position at Christ Church Cathedral in Lexington, Kentucky.

195 On a Hill Far Away (The Old Rugged Cross)

George Bennard (1873–1958) began writing this hymn in 1912 but did not complete it until the following year during an evangelistic mission in Sturgeon Bay, Wisconsin. After being introduced by Homer Rodeheaver, the song became widely popular in the United States.

George Bennard was born in Youngstown, Ohio, on February 4, 1873, the son of a coal miner. His father died when George was sixteen, leaving him as the sole source of support for his mother and four sisters. He was converted to Christianity at a Salvation Army meeting in Lucas, Iowa.

George Bennard (1873–1958) wrote both the words and music for this song, THE OLD RUGGED CROSS, but another gospel-song composer, Charles H. Gabriel, helped him complete the harmonization. Bennard composed more than three hundred hymns, but this is clearly his best known.

George Bennard joined the Salvation Army immediately after his conversion and later traveled throughout the Midwest and Canada as an evangelist with the Methodist Episcopal Church. Bennard died on October 10, 1958, in Reed City, Michigan, at the age of eighty-five.

196 When, like the Woman at the Well

Edith Sinclair Downing (b. 1922) was inspired to write this hymn for a contest seeking new texts on the gospel story of Jesus meeting the woman at the well. She felt a personal need to affirm the role of women in the church and in religious service.

Edith Sinclair Downing did not begin writing hymn texts until she was in her sixties. She started while leading a poetry-sharing group at a home for the elderly. Downing was trained in religious education and music and served various churches as organist and children's choir director.

Celene Welch (b. 1949) was inspired to compose this tune in 1990 during Minister's Week at Brite Divinity School, Texas Christian University, for "A Woman in a World of Men," by Brian Wren, who was a guest on campus. The tune name, CRAVEN, honors Toni Craven, a professor of Hebrew and Hebrew Bible at the school.

Celene Welch was born and raised in Texas and knew from an early age that she wanted to pursue a career in church music. She earned master's degrees in music and divinity and is an ordained Lutheran minister, serving as associate pastor at Trinity Lutheran Church in Fort Worth, Texas.

197 Jesus, Keep Me near the Cross

Fanny Jane Crosby (1820–1915) wrote these words for a tune given to her by William Howard Doane. This is the reverse of the more common course of hymn composition, wherein a text is written first and the tune composed to accompany it.

Fanny J. Crosby, born in Putnam County, New York, on March 24, 1820, lost her eyesight in infancy as a result of improper medical treatment. She married Alexander Van Alstyne, a blind musician, when she was thirty-eight years old. She died on February 12, 1915, a month before her ninety-fifth birthday.

William Howard Doane (1832–1915) first composed this tune and then asked Fanny Crosby to provide words for it. The hymn was published in 1869 in William Bradbury's *Bright Jewels*. The tune name, NEAR THE CROSS, derives from Fanny Crosby's text.

William H. Doane, born February 3, 1832, at Preston, Connecticut, was a successful industrialist and inventor. A committed Christian, he enjoyed writing religious music. He did his first composing at age fourteen but began writing hymns only after a serious illness when he was thirty.

198 Lift High the Cross

George William Kitchin (1827–1912) wrote the text on which this hymn is based in 1887 for the festival of the Society for the Propagation of the Gospel in Winchester Cathedral, England. Emperor Constantine's vision "In this sign, thou shalt conquer" may have been the author's inspiration.

Michael Robert Newbolt (1874–1956) revised George Kitchin's text in 1916, making it less militaristic. The hymn was not printed in a U.S. hymnal until 1974, when it appeared in *Hymns for the Living Church*. It has since been included in numerous denominational hymnals.

Sydney Hugo Nicholson (1875–1947) wrote this melody for the text by Kitchin and Newbolt, and they were printed together in *Hymns Ancient and Modern*, the 1916 second supplement. The tune, named CRUCIFER, literally means "cross-bearer."

Sydney Hugo Nicholson was knighted in 1938 for his contributions to English church music. He served as organist in some of the most prestigious churches in England until 1927, when he resigned to found the School of English Church Music at St. Nicholas College.

199 Alas! and Did My Savior Bleed (At the Cross)

Isaac Watts (1674–1748) titled this Passion text in six stanzas "Godly Sorrow Arising from the Sufferings of Christ" when it appeared in Book Two of his *Hymns and Spiritual Songs* (1707). It has enjoyed wide acceptance in the United States, perhaps because of the countless editorial changes made to it over the years.

Isaac Watts was not allowed to attend public schools in England because his family belonged to the Independent Church movement. His father even spent time in jail for his beliefs. Unwilling to deny his religious heritage and join the Church of England, Watts completed his education at the Nonconformist Academy at Stoke Newington.

Ralph E. Hudson (1843–1901) composed this tune, which includes a refrain not found in other versions of the hymn. It appeared in his *Songs of Peace, Love, and Joy* (1885) and bears his last name, HUDSON. The refrain most likely was appended from a familiar camp-meeting chorus of the time.

Ralph E. Hudson was a volunteer Union soldier and nurse during the Civil War. He later taught music at Mount Union College, Alliance, Ohio, and established a music-publishing company. An active prohibitionist, many of Hudson's works were temperance songs.

200 Alas! and Did My Savior Bleed

Isaac Watts (1674–1748) produced this hymn during a two-year period following his academy education, when he was devoted to writing. The fruits of his labors took the form of three books comprising his *Hymns and Spiritual Songs*: "I. Collected from the Scriptures"; "II. Composed on Divine Subjects"; "III. Prepared for the Lord's Supper."

Isaac Watts lived and served as tutor at the home of John Hartopp for six years until 1702, when he was ordained as a Nonconformist minister and accepted a call to Mark Lane Independent Church. The church grew significantly during his tenure there, and Watts became highly regarded in London.

Hugh Wilson (1764–1824) won a copyright suit concerning this tune in the 1800s, although its origins have been traced to a Scottish folk melody. It has been published under many different titles, including MARTYRDOM and AVON (for one of the twenty rivers in Scotland and England).

Hugh Wilson was born in Fenwick, Ayrshire, Scotland, in 1764 and trained as a shoemaker. In addition, he was manager of the village church and helped found the church's Sunday school. Wilson died August 14, 1824, and was buried in the graveyard at Old Kilpatrick Church.

201 An Outcast among Outcasts

Richard Dole Leach (b. 1953) sought to write a hymn attentive to members of minority groups or oppressed peoples following a presentation by Jon Michael Spencer at the 1992 conference of the Hymn Society. The image in Luke 17 of the healed leper, an outcast by ethnic identity and religious uncleanness due to illness, was the starting point.

Richard D. Leach began producing hymn texts in 1987 to interpret particular Bible passages and tell their stories in new ways. Selah Publishing has made his texts available in three collections, and several appear in recent denominational hymnals.

Daniel Charles Damon (b. 1955) composed POST STREET in 1994, when Richard Leach presented him with this text at the Hymn Society's annual conference. The hymn received its premiere at the 1995 conference of that organization during a festival presentation on *The New Century Hymnal*.

Dan Damon usually composes tunes for his own texts, letting his words dictate the nature of the melodies. He has said that his goal in hymn composition is to keep things "simple and singable while, at the same time, exploring the edges of the spoken and sung faith."

202 O God, How We Have Wandered

Kevin Francis Nichols (b. 1929) combines ideas from Luke 15 (the story of the lost son) and 2 Corinthians 5 (becoming new beings in Christ) for this text, written in 1980. Wandering from God's will and being called back and forgiven are important themes for the Lenten season.

Kevin Nichols was born in Newcastle-upon-Tyne, England, in 1929. Following his education at Cambridge and the University of Liverpool, he was a lecturer in education and then became national advisor for religious education. More recently, he has served as a parish priest in County Durham.

Hans Leo Hassler (1564–1612) composed the tune HERZLICH TUT MICH VERLANGEN as an air for a love song in 1601. The tune was later used with religious words and named PASSION CHORALE. It appears five times in J. S. Bach's *St. Matthew's Passion*, among other works.

Hans Leo Hassler studied music with his father, who was the official town musician and organist in Nürnberg, Bavaria, and then became a student of Andrea Gabrielli in Venice. He was the first famous German musician to receive his education in Italy.

203 Ah, What Shame I Have to Bear

Sogo Matsumoto (1840–1903) wrote this text in 1895 from the point of view of the lost son in Jesus' parable in Luke 15. The text imagines the thoughts and emotions of the son as he sits and contemplates the errors of his life and his resolve to return to seek forgiveness.

Esther Hibbard (b. 1903) translated this text from Japanese in 1962. Since retiring from her work as a United Church of Christ missionary, she has lived at Pilgrim Place in Claremont, California. This hymn was submitted to the committee by Janelle Landis, another retired missionary, who served in Sendai, Japan.

This twelfth-century Japanese melody is called IMAYO. It has been used here for a Christian text, although Christianity did not come to Japan until the sixteenth century. The use of indigenous music to convey new texts of the Christian faith is part of a growing movement around the world.

The arrangement of the Japanese melody, IMAYO, alternates phrases in unison octaves with those in four-part harmony. The setting may be performed with a solo voice singing the unison phrases and the choir or congregation joining in only on the harmonized sections.

204 "Take Up Your Cross," the Savior Said

Charles William Everest (1814–1877) was only nineteen when he wrote this text based on Jesus' response to the disciple Peter's rebuke of him found in Mark 8. Everest published it that same year along with other poems in *Visions of Death and Other Poems* (1833).

Charles W. Everest was born in East Windsor, Connecticut, and was ordained to the Episcopal priesthood in 1842. He served only one church in his career—at Hampton, Connecticut, beginning in 1842. Everest retired to Waterbury, Connecticut, in 1873 and died four years later.

This tune, from *The Grenoble Antiphoner*, a French work published in 1753, is called DEUS TUORUM MILITUM. It was a musical setting for a hymn for martyrs in the liturgy of the Latin office. The opening line of that text can be translated "God, the portion, the crown and reward of your soldiers."

The Grenoble Antiphoner of 1753 was a transitional work that helped move French church music from plainchant to more-modern music. Some of the tunes included in this worshipbook came from secular sources, others from plainsongs. Many of these hymns were introduced to England in 1851.

205 Forty Days and Forty Nights

George Hunt Smyttan (1822–1870) wrote three poems for Lent, one of which became this hymn. It was published in the March 1856 edition of *The Penny Post* and was revised five years later in *Hymns Fitted to the Order of Common Prayer* (1861), by Francis Pott.

George H. Smyttan was an Anglican clergyman who published three collections of verse. Smyttan moved in 1859 to Germany, where he died at Frankfurt-on-the-Main, unknown and friendless. He was buried in a pauper's grave, and his name was entered in the burial registry only as "Smyttan, England."

Martin Herbst (1654–1681) is believed to have written this tune, but it is named HEINLEIN after Paul Heinlein (1626–1686), another German composer to whom it was attributed in the past. The tune also has been called AUS DER TIEFE, for the German text with which it appeared in a 1676 hymnbook.

Martin Herbst was born in Nürnberg, Germany, and became a Lutheran pastor. He served as rector for the school and pastor of the church at Eisleben in 1680 but died of the plague the following year, at age twenty-seven. This is one of three tunes attributed to Herbst.

206 A Woman Came Who Did Not Count the Cost

Richard Dole Leach (b. 1953) wrote this text for use at an ecumenical service preceding a Palm Sunday breakfast. He knew that people would hear the Palm Sunday scriptures later in the day and chose the story of the anointing at Bethany as the focus for a sermon and this hymn.

Richard D. Leach was born in Maine on August 7, 1953, and attended Holden (Maine) Congregational Church as a youth. He received his education at Bowdoin College, Brunswick, Maine, and Princeton Theological Seminary in New Jersey. In 1979, he was ordained to the ministry of the United Church of Christ.

This traditional Irish folk song WEXFORD CAROL, originally a Christmas carol sung by the people outside the church, was handed down orally. The tune was appropriated for use with the poignant story of the woman and the jar and was arranged for *The New Century Hymnal* by editor Arthur G. Clyde.

Irish melodies, like those of England, Scotland, and Wales, have been popular sources of hymn tunes. Usually the tunes were handed down from one generation to another, and those that remained popular did so because their tunes were memorable and easy to sing.

207 Just as I Am

Charlotte Elliott (1789–1871) was forty-five years old and in ill health when she wrote this hymn, a resolute expression of her understanding of Christ's atonement and its impact on her life. She remained an invalid for the last fifty years of her life but still wrote many poems.

Charlotte Elliott was born in Clapham, England, on March 18, 1789, and wrote light verse in the early years of her life. After meeting evangelist César Malan of Geneva, Switzerland, she dedicated herself to religious poetry, writing more than 150 hymns. She died in Brighton, England, on September 22, 1871.

William Batchelder Bradbury (1816–1868) wrote and published this tune, WOODWORTH, in his *Third Book of Psalmody* in 1849. Originally it was used with other words, but when combined with Charlotte Elliott's poem, it became a popular gospel hymn in the United States.

William B. Bradbury was born October 6, 1816, at York, Maine. He moved to Boston at the age of seventeen and studied with Lowell Mason and George J. Webb. Bradbury taught piano and voice for a time, then moved to New York, where he served as organist at the Baptist Temple.

208 God Loved the World

This text was translated into English by August Crull from an anonymous German hymn which appeared in *Heiliges Lippen und Herzens Opfer*, a 1778 hymnal from Stettin, Germany. The hymn is a paraphrase of John 3:16–17, one of the most frequently quoted scriptures.

August Crull (1845–1923) was born in Rostock, Germany, but moved to the United States with his family after his father's death. Crull completed his education, was ordained to the Lutheran ministry, and served as a pastor in Milwaukee, Wisconsin, and Grand Rapids, Michigan.

This anonymous tune by an unknown composer originally was called TUNBRIDGE. In 1790, Edward Miller (1731–1807) adapted it and named it ROCKINGHAM for the Marquis of Rockingham, a patron and friend who was also prime minister of Great Britain.

Edward Miller (1731–1807) worked for his father as a paver until he ran away to study music. He became a flute player in G. F. Handel's orchestra and later organist at Doncaster (England) Parish Church. Miller was also a harpsichordist.

209 O Love, How Vast, How Flowing Free

This anonymous fifteenth-century Latin hymn is not the work of Thomas à Kempis, as was once assumed. The poem on the incarnation from which this text was taken consisted of twenty-three stanzas. The translation begins with the original second stanza, "O amor quam exstaticus."

This text appears in a new translation developed for *The New Century Hymnal* as an alternative to an earlier one by Benjamin Webb. In the only surviving manuscript of the original Latin text, it is a Nativity hymn of great piety.

This anonymous tune is known by two names. It received the name AGINCOURT because the melody was a folk song recounting King Henry V's victory at Agincourt in 1415. However, Henry ordered that this secular song not be sung and that God receive the thanks and praise; hence the second title, DEO GRACIAS.

This folk tune, DEO GRACIAS, dates from the first half of the fifteenth century in manuscripts now at Trinity College, Cambridge. It was a ballad commemorating King Henry V's victory over the French, and it has made the transition from a secular to a sacred song.

210 Said Judas to Mary

Sydney Bertram Carter (b. 1915) wrote this text as a conversation to relate the incident reported in John 12:1–8, Mary of Bethany's anointing of Jesus with expensive perfume. Jesus answered Judas' criticism of this act of devotion by replying, "you always have the poor with you."

Sydney Carter was a schoolmaster at Frensham Heights School, England. When World War II began, he joined the Friends' Ambulance Unit and served from 1940 until 1945. Although not a Quaker, he believed in their message of peace and nonviolence and often wrote to promote such ideas.

Sydney Bertram Carter (b. 1915) was inspired by traditional English carols when he wrote this hymn in 1964. Called JUDAS AND MARY after the opening words, it recounts the confrontation between those two followers of Jesus, paraphrasing the biblical account in John 12.

Sydney Carter wrote many religious songs in popular style during the 1950s and 1960s to provide an alternative to traditional hymns. His best-known such song is "Lord of the Dance," which made use of the nineteenth-century Shaker tune "Simple Gifts."

211 Lord Jesus, Who through Forty Days

Claudia Frances I. Hernaman (1838–1898) wrote this lenten hymn specifically for children. It was published with thirty-six other original hymns and translations from Latin in *The Child's Book of Praise* (1873). A year later, Hernaman produced *Christmas Carols for Children*.

Claudia F. I. Hernaman, the daughter of an Anglican priest, was born in Surrey, England, on October 19, 1838. She married a minister who was a school inspector. Most of her 150 hymns and her hymn collections were written for children. She died October 10, 1898, nine days short of her sixtieth birthday.

This anonymous tune has been printed with a variety of names since its first appearance in Day's *Whole Booke of Psalms* in 1562. It was called REDHEAD NO. 29 when published in *Hymns Ancient and Modern* (1861) but was renamed ST. FLAVIAN when that hymnal was revised in 1875.

John Day's *Whole Booke of Psalms* (1562), from which this tune is taken, was named for its London, England, printer rather than for the editors of the work. It was the first English psalter to contain all 150 of the psalms in metered verse and was the hymnal of choice in England for more than a century.

212 O Jesus Christ, May Grateful Hymns

Bradford Gray Webster (1898–1991) wrote this text in response to the Hymn Society's search for new hymns about the city. It was selected for use at the Convocation of Urban Life in America in 1954, sponsored by the Council of Bishops of the Methodist Church, and was subsequently published.

Bradford Gray Webster was born in Syracuse, New York, attended Amherst (Massachusetts) College, and served in World War I. Ordained to the Methodist ministry following graduation from Boston University School of Theology, he served churches in New York state for forty years.

David Evans (1874–1948) composed CHARTERHOUSE for a different text in *Revised Church Hymnary* (1927). Evans was the editor and a member of the revision committee for this work, representing his native Wales. The hymnbook sought to update church music in use in Great Britain.

David Evans served from 1903 until 1939 as professor of music at University College in Cardiff, Wales, where he also received his education. In addition, he was senior professor at the University of Wales. He died shortly after conducting a Gymanfa Ganu (singing festival) near Wrexham in 1948.

213 "Hosanna, Loud Hosanna"

Jennette Threlfall (1821–1880) is the author of this hymn recalling the triumphal parade and the exhilaration of Jesus' followers as they entered the city of Jerusalem on Palm Sunday. It appeared in her collection of poetry, *Sunshine and Shadow* (1873).

Jennette Threlfall was a child of misfortune. She was orphaned at an early age and was left mutilated and completely helpless from two different accidents. Yet she maintained a cheerful outlook on life. She was cared for by relatives and died at a cousin's home on November 30, 1880.

ELLACOMBE is the name of this anonymous tune traced to eighteenth-century German Roman Catholic hymnbooks. Its earliest known use was in 1784 in Wirtemberg, Germany. The tune has long been a popular choice for this text; it appears three times in *The New Century Hymnal*.

ELLACOMBE was first found in *Gesangbuch der Herzoglichen Wirtembergischen Katholischen Hofkapell*, a Roman Catholic hymnbook published at Wirtemberg, Germany, in 1784. What is most unusual about this Roman Catholic hymnbook is that most of the hymns were by Protestants.

214 Mantos y Ramos (Filled with Excitement)

Rubén Ruíz Avila (b. 1945), a native of Mexico, wrote this Palm Sunday processional hymn for the choir of the United Methodist Church in Covington, Virginia. His first and presumably only composition, it received a warm reception when sung at a choral festival in Mexico City in 1980.

Gertrude Suppe (b. 1911) prepared the English translation for *Celebremos II*, published in 1983 by the United Methodist Church. The song subsequently appeared in *The United Methodist Hymnal* (1989) with slight alterations.

Rubén Ruíz Avila (b. 1945) composed this tune setting, called HOSANNA, for his own text. The word "Hosanna" used in the Palm Sunday biblical texts is an exclamation of praise to God that means "Pray, Save us." Alvin Schumaat's (b. 1921) arrangement was published in *Canciones de Fe y Compromiso* (1978).

The Palm Sunday processional march is traditional in Christian nations around the world, whether held in church buildings or outdoors. The use of a donkey and palm branches adds to the excitement as Christians recreate this biblical event.

215 Ride On! Ride On in Majesty

Henry Hart Milman (1791–1868) was an Anglican minister and a newly appointed professor of poetry at Oxford University, England, when he wrote this Palm Sunday text at age thirty. It was published by his friend, Reginald Heber, six years later in a hymnbook organized by the church year.

Henry H. Milman, an English scholar and priest, rose to positions of prominence in the Anglican Church, finally serving as dean of St. Paul's Cathedral. After writing plays in his early years, he concentrated on historical work, including *History of the Jews* (1862), which drew loud criticism.

John Bacchus Dykes (1823–1876) composed ST. DROSTANE for Milman's text for *Congregational Hymn and Tune Book* (1862). It was named for Saint Drostane, a nephew of Saint Columba, who, like his uncle, also founded churches in Ireland and Christian communities in Scotland.

John B. Dykes is the best known of the Victorian hymn-tune writers, and three hundred of his works remain in use. In addition, he published sermons, anthems, and service music. Dykes served as Anglican precentor at Durham (England) Cathedral and later as vicar of St. Oswald's Church, Durham.

216 All Glory, Laud, and Honor

Theodulph of Orléans (d. 821) wrote this processional hymn while imprisoned by King Louis I, son of Charlemagne. The original Latin poem comprised thirty-nine couplets. In medieval and modern England and France, clergy and choirs paraded through their towns on Palm Sunday singing this hymn.

Theodulph of Orléans was a leading intellectual in Charlemagne's court and was appointed Bishop of Orléans. When Charlemagne's son, Louis I (called Louis the Pious) became Emperor in 818, he accused Theodulph of plotting against him. Theodulph spent his last years of life in prison, where he died in 821.

Melchior Teschner (1584–1635) composed this and another tune for a German hymn of consolation, VALET WILL ICH DIR GEBEN, for which it was first named. It was given the title ST. THEODULPH when it appeared with this text in *Hymns Ancient and Modern* (1861).

Melchior Teschner, born in Fraustaut, Silesia, in 1584, served as Lutheran pastor in the village of Oberpritschen, Posen, during a period of the plague. It was his only parish, and he remained there until his death on December 1, 1635. His son and then grandson followed him as pastors in this same church.

217 All Glory, Laud, and Honor

Theodulph of Orléans (d. 821) wrote these words while imprisoned by King Louis I, son of Charlemagne. John Mason Neale first translated the seventy-two-line Latin poem in 1851. This version derives from a second that appeared slightly altered in *Hymns Ancient and Modern* (1861).

John Mason Neale translated more than two hundred early Greek and Latin hymns that appeared in six volumes. In addition, Neale published collections of hymns for children and carols for Christmas and Easter. He founded one of the first nursing homes in England, the Sisterhood of St. Margaret.

Verne de la Peña (b. 1959) composed the tune EULOGIA in 1994 and an expanded anthem arrangement of it for Pilgrim Press a year later. It is reminiscent of a gong-orchestra melody (gamelan, kulintang) of Southeast Asia, reflecting the composer's Philippine origins.

Verne de la Peña received his master's degree in music composition from the University of the Philippines and served there as an assistant professor for six years. In addition, he has worked as a minister of music at various Christian congregations in the Philippines and, more recently, in Hawaii.

218 Ah, Holy Jesus

Johann Heermann (1585–1647) based this German hymn on a portion of the Latin work *Meditationes,* perhaps written by Jean de Fécamp (d. 1078). Heermann's fifteen stanzas first appeared in a book he published in 1630. This English paraphrase was created in 1899 by Robert Bridges (1844–1930).

Johann Heermann was a pastor, but poor eyesight forced him to give up teaching and throat trouble forced him to abandon preaching in 1634. His difficulties during the Thirty Years' War were the basis for some of his greatest hymns concerning hardship and God's loving care.

Johann Crüger (1598–1662) has been credited with the tune HERZLIEBSTER JESU, and it has been used with Heermann's Passion hymn since 1640. It appears to be an adaptation of a 1543 tune for Psalm 23 from the Genevan Psalter and Johann Schein's tune GELIEBEN FREUND in his *Cantional* (1627).

Johann Crüger was born on April 9, 1598, near Güben, Prussia. He left theological studies to become cantor at St. Nicholas Church in Berlin, Germany, and to teach. He remained a teacher until his death on February 23, 1662. Crüger was one of the most important chorale composers of his time.

219 Journey to Gethsemane

James Montgomery (1771–1854) wrote this hymn twice. In 1820 he published one version in Thomas Cotterill's *Selection of Psalms and Hymns*, and in 1825 he greatly revised it for another collection. The revised text was more popular with the English Nonconformists and churches in North America and is the basis for the version here.

James Montgomery was a journalist and editor of the *Sheffield Iris* for thirty-one years. His views did not always please the Tory government, and he was imprisoned twice for printing unfavorable material. Montgomery is recognized as one of England's greatest hymnwriters.

Richard Redhead (1820–1901) composed this tune in 1853, calling it REDHEAD NO. 76 since it was the seventy-sixth tune he had written. Others renamed it GETHSEMANE when it was used with the text by Montgomery. Still other names for the tune are AJALON, HAZEN, and PETRA.

Richard Redhead was born in Harrow, Middlesex, England, on March 1, 1820. He passionately supported the Oxford movement in favor of Roman Catholic renewal. He was organist at St. Mary Magdalene Church, Paddington, England, for thirty years. Redhead died April 27, 1907, at Hellingly, Sussex, England.

220 Sing, My Tongue

Venantius Honorius Fortunatus (c. 530–609) wrote this text as a ten-stanza poem, beginning "Pange, lingua, gloriosi proelium." In the Latin daily office, five stanzas were sung at midnight matins and the other five at sunrise lauds. It was used daily in the week from Passion Sunday until Maundy Thursday.

Venantius Honorius Fortunatus is the subject of legend; he is said to have been healed of an eye disease by oil from a lamp burning at the altar of St. Martin of Tours in a church in Ravenna, Italy. In gratitude, he took a pilgrimage to the shrine of St. Martin at Tours, France, in 565 C.E., where he met Queen Rhadegunda, who became his patron.

Carl Flentge Schalk (b. 1929) composed this tune as an alternative to a 1872 tune by Arthur Sullivan. Because the original tune was named FORTUNATUS, Schalk named his composition FORTUNATUS NEW. It was first published in *Spirit* (1967) and then included in a Lutheran supplement.

Carl Schalk was the musical director of "The International Lutheran Hour," a radio show originating in St. Louis, Missouri, from 1958 until 1965. He then began a teaching career at Concordia (Illinois) Teachers College, where he had received his bachelor of science degree in 1952.

221 The Royal Banners Forward Fly

Venantius Honorius Fortunatus (c. 530–609) wrote this processional hymn, "Vexilla Regis prodeunt," for the November 19, 568 C.E., service when the relics of the cross were brought to Queen Rhadegunda's new monastery at Poitiers. This hymn traditionally has been sung at vespers during Holy Week.

Venantius Honorius Fortunatus was encouraged by Queen Rhadegunda to take his holy orders, and he entered the Abbey of St. Croix at Poitiers, Gaul. He was appointed Bishop of Poitiers in 599 C.E. and remained at this post until his death in 609.

Percy Carter Buck (1871–1947) composed GONFALON ROYAL in 1918 for use by the students of Harrow School, England, for a translation of the Fortunatus text by John Mason Neale. The boys would often sing this hymn as they marched to their classes. "Gonfalon" is an old Norman-English word meaning "banner."

Percy C. Buck served as director of music at Harrow School, England, for twenty-six years. During this time he also taught at Dublin University, then at the University of London. Buck was honored as a fellow of Worcester College, Oxford, and of the Royal College of Music. He was knighted in 1936.

222 My Song Is Love Unknown

Samuel Crossman (c. 1624–1684) first published this text in seven stanzas in *The Young Man's Meditation* (1664), a book of nine poems, but not until the nineteenth century did the text receive acceptance as a hymn. Some scholars have speculated that the phrase "love unknown" is derived from a poem by George Herbert.

Samuel Crossman was one of the first English authors to write hymns that were not based on the psalms. He was dismissed from the Anglican ministry because of his support of the Puritans, but later reversed himself, was reinstated, and was appointed as chaplain to the king.

John David Edwards (1806–1885) named this tune LOVELY when it was first published in 1838. However, it appeared as RHOSYMEDRE with Crossman's text in *Songs of Praise Enlarged* (1931) to commemorate the town in Wales where Edwards served as rector for many years.

John D. Edwards, ordained an Anglican priest in 1832, was vicar for many years at Rhosymedre, Ruabon, North Wales. In addition to his parish duties, he composed liturgical music for use during worship. In 1836, he published his major work, *Original Sacred Music,* in two volumes.

223 What Wondrous Love Is This

This old U.S. folk hymn can be traced to an 1811 camp-meeting songbook entitled *A General Selection of the Newest and Most Admired Hymns and Spiritual Songs Now in Use*, published at Lynchburg, Virginia. By 1843, the text was published with this accompanying tune.

Camp meetings were religious revival services held throughout the United States in the nineteenth century. They were marked by lively singing and spirited preaching meant to convert those living sinful lives. Often the meetings were held in tents or outdoors.

The early U.S. tune WONDROUS LOVE appeared as the setting for this text and was attributed to "Christopher" in Walker's Appendix to *The Southern Harmony* (1843). In a later tunebook, *Christian Harmony*, that individual was further identified as James Christopher of Spartanburg, South Carolina.

William Walker (1806–1875), a Baptist minister and singing teacher, spent much of his life in the area of Spartanburg, South Carolina. He traveled throughout the South, gathering tunes which were published in his collections: *Southern Harmony* (1835), its Appendix (1843), and *Christian Harmony* (1867).

224 When I Survey the Wondrous Cross

Isaac Watts (1674–1748) based this hymn on Galatians 6:14 and intended it as a hymn for Holy Communion, giving it the title "Crucifixion to the World by the Cross of Christ." Many hymnologists believe this to be one of the finest hymns ever written in the English language.

Isaac Watts became severely ill in 1712 and was invited to live at the home of Thomas Abney, a former lord mayor of London and a member of Watts's congregation. Watts's health never fully improved, and he remained there for the last thirty-six years of his life.

Lowell Mason (1792–1872) arranged this melody in 1825 from a Gregorian chant (tone I) and named it HAMBURG. It was first published in his *Boston Handel and Haydn Society Collection of Church Music* (1825), the highly successful collection that allowed Mason to devote the rest of his career to music.

Lowell Mason, a sixth-generation New Englander, was descended from English forebears who landed in Salem, Massachusetts, in 1630. Like his father and grandfather, he was born in Medfield, Massachusetts, and he spent the first twenty years of his life there.

225 It Was a Sad and Solemn Night

Isaac Watts (1674–1748) wrote this Maundy Thursday text as a hymn for Holy Communion. It appeared in Book III of Watts's *Hymns and Spiritual Songs* (1709). The hymn has not been widely used in U.S. hymnals but is familiar in the United Church of Christ through the *Pilgrim Hymnal* (1958).

Isaac Watts was the author of other works and poetry in addition to his six hundred hymns. He wrote some sixty volumes on a variety of subjects, including a logic textbook that was long used at Oxford, a book on the improvement of the mind, and several catechisms.

Freeman Lewis (1780–1859) is credited with the tune BOURBON, which appeared with Watts's text in *Columbian Harmony*, an 1825 collection assembled by William Moore in Wilson County, Tennessee. The twentieth-century harmonization is by Louise McAllister.

Freeman Lewis was born in Uniontown, Pennsylvania. He trained as a surveyor but also composed a number of pieces of music. He is little known as a composer, and few of his works have remained in use to the present day. In 1813, he published a tunebook, *The Beauties of Harmony*.

226 O Sacred Head, Now Wounded

Bernard of Clairvaux (1091–1153) has been previously cited as the author of the Latin text on which this hymn is based, although it has also been credited to Arnulf Von Loewen (1200–1250). The original poem had seven sections, each addressed to a part of Christ's body on the cross. Paul Gerhardt paraphrased the last one, focusing on the head, as this metrical hymn.

Translator James W. Alexander (1804–1859) was born in Hopewell, Virginia, of Scottish heritage. He attended Princeton Theological Seminary and ministered to several Presbyterian churches in Virginia, New Jersey, and New York. Alexander also held several teaching positions and was the author of more than thirty books.

Hans Leo Hassler (1564–1612) composed PASSION CHORALE in 1601 as the setting for a secular text. It was subsequently used with a funeral hymn and finally became associated with these words in Johann Crüger's *Praxis Pietatis Melica* (1656). The tune was used by J. S. Bach in numerous works.

Hans Leo Hassler was born in 1564 and was the first German musician to be educated in Italy. He served as music director at Nürnberg, Germany, and then as organist at Ulm and Dresden, Germany. He died June 8, 1612, while traveling to the imperial election at Frankfurt with the Elector of Saxony.

227 Christ at Table There with Friends

Anabel Schlosser Miller (b. 1921) wrote this communion poem during Lent in 1982. A lifelong reader of the Bible, she used various references to the cup, as found in the four Gospels, for this text. It was first sung on Maundy Thursday at First Presbyterian Church in Santa Barbara, California.

Anabel S. Miller was born in China of missionary parents from the United States. She received her bachelor's degree from Greenville College in Illinois. She met Emma Lou Diemer when she was a member of the choir at First Presbyterian Church, Santa Barbara, California, and Diemer was the church's organist.

Emma Lou Diemer (b. 1927) was given this text by the author Anabel Miller in 1992 and asked to compose a melody for it. The women submitted the new hymn to the committee preparing *The New Century Hymnal*, and it was selected for publication. The tune is named MAUNDY THURSDAY.

Emma Lou Diemer is the daughter of educators; her mother was a Christian-education director and her father a college president. Diemer was granted a Fulbright scholarship to study in Belgium. Her numerous compositions include music for orchestra, band, chorus, solo instruments, voice, and organ.

228 Ruler of Life, We Crown You Now

Jennie Evelyn Hussey (1874–1958) wrote this Holy Week hymn in 1921. It speaks not only of the agony of Gethsemane but also of the victory of the resurrection. The hymn recognizes that there cannot be adequate appreciation of the Easter event without the trials of Holy Week.

Jennie Evelyn Hussey was born in Henniker, New Hampshire, on February 8, 1874, where her family had lived for four generations. She spent most of her life caring for an invalid sister. In later life, she was crippled by arthritis in her fingers. Hussey died at Concord, New Hampshire, in 1958.

William James Kirkpatrick (1838–1921) wrote the tune DUNCANNON in 1921, the last year of his life. It is named for a town in Pennsylvania where he lived as a boy after emigrating from Ireland. He was a prolific composer of gospel music for the church.

William J. Kirkpatrick served as a fife major in the Civil War and was in the furniture business until his wife's death in 1878. He then opened the Praise Publishing Company, which published over one hundred collections of gospel songs from 1880 until his death in Philadelphia, Pennsylvania, in 1921.

229 Were You There?

This African American spiritual was born in the adversity of slavery in the southern United States. The first printed version of the song is found in William E. Barton's *Old Plantation Hymns* (1899). The original text, as recorded in that source, included a final stanza referring to Christ's ascension.

John Lovell Jr. in his book *Black Song* (1972) reflects on the indicting aspect of this song, which implies "If you were there, what were you doing? How . . . could you have let it [the Crucifixion] happen?"

It is nearly impossible to document definite versions of African American spirituals, which were the products of an oral tradition and varied from one region to another. Scholars have identified similarities between some songs of the African American tradition and white spiritual songs, suggesting the possibility of cross-influences.

This arrangement, by Joyce Finch Johnson, is only one of numerous versions of this melody that seems to convey perfectly the tragedy of the Crucifixion. It was often sung by contralto Marian Anderson to great acclaim in her concert tours around the world.

230 Come, You Faithful, Raise the Strain

John of Damascus (c. 696–c. 754), one of the most significant poets of the Greek church, based this hymn for the Sunday after Easter on the Song of Moses in Exodus 15. In it, the poet compares the deliverance by Moses to that of Christ on the cross. Some hymnals have eliminated the comparison.

John of Damascus spent most of his life in the monastery of St. Sabas, overlooking the Dead Sea. One of the most learned men of the eighth century, John of Damascus had an important role in the documentation of Byzantine chant and promoted a new musical form, the canon.

Arthur Seymour Sullivan (1842–1900) composed ST. KEVIN, named for an Irish saint, for this Easter text. Although Sullivan wrote more than fifty hymn tunes and was a church organist, he is better known for the light operas he created with William S. Gilbert.

Arthur S. Sullivan, a child prodigy of extraordinary gifts, was the son of an Irish musician. By age twelve he was chorister in the Chapel Royal, and at fourteen he won the first Mendelssohn Scholarship contest in England. He was knighted by Queen Victoria in 1883 as one of England's greatest musicians.

231 Because You Live, O Christ

Shirley Erena Murray (b. 1931) presented this Easter text as the opening hymn in her collection *In Every Corner Sing* (1992). Her commentary in that source explains the poem's origins: "The creative irritant to write this came from the outdated words in our parish hymnbook and my love of this great tune."

Shirley Erena Murray was born in Invarcargill, New Zealand—at one time the southernmost city of the British Empire. Her forebears had come there from Scotland to settle. She married a Presbyterian pastor and now lives and writes in the inner city of Wellington.

This seventeenth-century Dutch folk melody was first used with the harvest song "De Liefde Voortgebracht." It was named VRUECHTEN for the hymn with which it appeared in *David's Psalmen*, published by Joachim Oudaen in 1685. The Dutch text began: "Hoe groot de Vruechten zijn."

Joachim Oudaen published his *David's Psalmen* in 1683 in Amsterdam, Holland. It was a collection of Dutch music for use in singing the 150 psalms of the Bible. Worship during the seventeenth century allowed the singing of only the psalms. No other texts were permitted to be sung.

232 This Joyful Eastertide

George Ratcliffe Woodward (1848–1934) edited the *Cowley Carol Book* to provide music for Christmas, Easter, and Ascension. The book was published in three different volumes. This Easter text appeared in the second (1902) edition, with the Dutch tune.

George R. Woodward was an Anglican priest who served various parishes in England. In addition, he translated a large number of hymns from Greek, Latin, and German and introduced them to English-speaking churches in a number of volumes.

This seventeenth-century Dutch folk melody is called VRUECHTEN, from a text with which it was used in Joachim Oudaen's *David's Psalmen*, published in 1685 in Amsterdam, Holland. The earliest use of the tune was with a popular harvest song.

George R. Woodward created this combination of text and tune early in the twentieth century in England. *The New Century Hymnal* marks its first appearance in a hymnal of the United Church of Christ. The single stanza makes it useful as a canticle or choral introit for Easter.

233 Christ the Lord Is Risen Today

Charles Wesley (1707–1788) published this Easter hymn in 1739 in eleven stanzas. With his brother John, Wesley was the power behind one of the greatest religious revivals in English history and one of the founders of the Methodist Church.

Charles Wesley, known as the "sweet singer" of Methodism, traveled hundreds of miles in the United States on horseback, preaching to crowds of thousands, often in open fields or on city streets. Although critical of the established church, he remained a lifelong Anglican clergyman.

EASTER HYMN, the name of this anonymous tune, was originally the setting for another Easter hymn, "Jesus Christ Is Risen Today." Around 1753, the name was changed to CHRISTMAS DAY when it was paired with a Christmas text by Charles Wesley, but it is now reestablished as an Easter tune.

Lyra Davidica, the source of this tune, was a hymnal printed in London, England, in 1708 by J. Walsh. It contained a total of twenty-five tunes: nine German chorales, two Latin melodies, and fourteen of English origin, including this one.

234 I'll Shout the Name of Christ Who Lives

Vivincio L. Vinluan (b. 1937) used the apostle Paul's comments about dying and rising with Christ in Romans 6 as the basis for this text, adding a sense of exhilaration not found in Paul, with the use of the word "shout." The Easter event is not something to be quietly pondered but loudly exclaimed.

I-to Loh included this hymn in *Hymns from the Four Winds*, which he edited in 1983. Born in Tamsui, Taipei, Taiwan, on September 28, 1936, Loh was educated at Tainan Theological College and Union Theological Seminary in New York City. Since the 1960s he has researched indigenous Asian Christian hymnody.

Wesley Tactay Tabayoyong (b. 1925) based this 1981 tune, BAHAY KUBO, on a contemporary Filipino folk melody, although the four-part harmonization suggests Western influences. The source of this hymn does not provide any further information concerning the origin of the tune or the arranger.

I-to Loh (b. 1936) collected hymns from throughout Asian Christianity for his 1983 collection, *Hymns from the Four Winds*, a supplement to *The Methodist Hymnal* of 1966. This hymnal brought together music from China, the Philippines, Japan, Korea, and Taiwan.

235 ¡Cristo Vive! (Christ Is Living)

Nicolás Martínez (1917–1972) paraphrased 1 Corinthians 15:12–23 for the text of this Easter hymn. He wrote it for *Cantico Nuevo* (1962), a hymnal produced to introduce new music into the liturgy of the Roman Catholic Church in South America.

Nicolás Martínez was raised as a Roman Catholic in his native Argentina but converted to evangelical Christianity as a youth. Ordained to the ministry of the Disciples of Christ in 1948, he served churches in Argentina and Paraguay until his death in 1972.

Pablo D. Sosa (b. 1933) composed this tune for Martínez's text in 1960 and named it CENTRAL for Central Methodist Church in Buenos Aires, Argentina. The music and words were first published together in *Cantico Nuevo* in 1962 and later included in *Cantate Domino* (1974), an ecumenical hymnal produced by the World Council of Churches.

Pablo Sosa is an active church music composer and authority on issues of Hispanic music and worship. He has been a professor in Buenos Aires and led international workshops.

236 Halleluja

This text merely repeats the word "Halleluja." The word comes from Hebrew roots, "hallelu," meaning "praise" and "Jah" for Jehovah or Yahweh, the name for God. It has become associated in Christian theology as an exclamation of joy relative to Jesus' resurrection.

"Halleluja," an exclamation of joy, forms the basis of this text. Congregations can be creative in finding ways to incorporate this response into a resurrection celebration on Easter Day or the Sundays following Easter.

This Caribbean melody is called HALLELUJA after the text. The tune's origins are not known. Like much music of the Caribbean, it conveys an exuberance that is contagious and may inspire movement and dancing. A repeat sign invites unlimited repetition.

Caribbean island music, often accompanied only by guitar, steel drums, or other percussion instruments, has a feel all its own. However, this genre can be traced to the same roots that also gave birth to African American jazz, spirituals, and gospel music.

237 I Come to the Garden Alone (In the Garden)

C. Austin Miles (1868–1946) experienced a vision of Mary Magdalene meeting the risen Christ in the garden (John 20) and wrote this hymn interpretation of that encounter. It was published in *The Gospel Message No. 2* (1912).

C. Austin Miles studied at Philadelphia College of Pharmacy and the University of Pennsylvania to become a pharmacist but left this work to pursue a career in music publishing after the success of his first gospel song. Miles worked for Hall-Mack Publishing Company in Philadelphia for thirty-seven years.

C. Austin Miles (1868–1946) wrote this tune the same evening he wrote the text of the poem, in 1912. It has become one of the most popular gospel hymns of all time and was used by Homer Rodeheaver, who led singing at the Billy Sunday rallies and services. It is named GARDEN.

C. Austin Miles was born in Lakehurst, New Jersey, in 1868 and made his debut as an organist when he was only twelve, playing for a funeral at a Methodist Church. He was a popular music director for church conventions and camp meetings. Miles died in Pitman, New Jersey, in 1946.

238 Now the Green Blade Rises

John MacLeod Campbell Crum (1872–1958) wrote this Easter text specifically for this old French carol tune. They were printed together in *The Oxford Book of Carols* (1928). Crum appropriated the image of seeds, which appear dead in winter but return to life in spring, as a metaphor for the resurrection.

John M. C. Crum was ordained a priest in the Anglican Church in 1900 and rose to be canon of Canterbury, where he served from 1929 to 1943. Earlier in his career, he had been chaplain to the Bishop of Oxford, Francis Paget, and later wrote a biography about him.

This fifteenth-century French carol is entitled NOËL NOUVELET for the original text. This melody was the inspiration for Marcel Dupré when composing his "Variations on a Noël." The harmonization was created by Martin F. Shaw (1875–1958) for *The Oxford Book of Carols* (1928).

Martin F. Shaw coedited two of the most significant hymn collections of twentieth-century England: *Songs of Praise* (1925, 1931) and *The Oxford Book of Carols* (1928). At the Royal College of Music, Shaw studied under such distinguished composers as Charles V. Stanford, C. H. H. Parry, and Walford Davies.

239 Christ Rose Up from the Dead

This traditional Easter song is a simple retelling of the resurrection event, except that the final line makes it a personal affirmation. The text is not only a historical account but a personal witness to the power of the resurrected Christ.

This hymn is a standard in predominately African American churches and is used often for the opening of Easter Sunday services. The text reviews the events of Good Friday, Holy Saturday, and Easter Day. William Farley Smith suggests that it should be sung with unrestrained joy.

This tune was named ASCENSIUS by William Farley Smith, whose arrangement appears in *The United Methodist Hymnal* (1989). The word is derived from *ascensus*, meaning to climb or rise. The sense of uplift is present not only in the words but also in the music.

George Pullen Jackson discovered two similar stanzas to those given here in a Southern white hymn tunebook, *The Sacred Harp* (1844). The arrangement of this traditional Easter song by Phil V. S. Lindsley is from *The New National Baptist Hymnal* (1977).

240 Jesus Christ Is Risen Today

This classic Easter hymn is a translation from the Latin text, "Surrexit Christus hodie," found in three manuscripts dating from the fourteenth century from Prague, Engelberg, and Munich. It came into English usage in 1708 with *Lyra Davidica*. The first stanza is from that version; the rest are newly translated for *The New Century Hymnal*.

The original Latin text on which this hymn is based consisted of nine two-line stanzas. It may have originated as a trope on the "Benedicamus Domino," which was sung at the conclusion of the Easter services. The hymn was especially popular in the Bohemian Brethren churches of the fifteenth century.

Robert Williams (c. 1781–1821) is believed to be the composer of this Welsh tune, which appears in his notebook with the date July 14, 1817. Although the composer named it BETHEL, the present title, LLANFAIR, refers to the village in Montgomery County where Williams was born.

Robert Williams was a Welsh musician who was blind and who lived his entire life on the island of Anglesey in North Wales. He worked as a basket weaver but more importantly preserved many folk tunes from his native country. Williams was able to write down a tune after hearing it only once.

241 Joy Dawned Again on Easter Day

This ancient Latin text comes from a longer poem called "Aurora lucis rutilat," which was sung at lauds on the Sundays following Easter. It is one of the earliest hymns to be found in a medieval breviary for use during a special season. This translation is by John Mason Neale (1818–1866).

John Mason Neale was stricken by lung disease early in his career. However, this allowed more time for hymn translating. He was fluent in twenty-one languages and was the first to translate Greek hymns into English. Many of Neale's translations are still in common use.

PUER NOBIS NASCITUR was adapted by Michael Praetorius (1571–1621) from an older carol. It was the setting for "Begorn ist Gottes Söhnelein" in the fourth volume of his *Musae Sioniae* (1609). The twelve volumes of that massive work included twelve hundred choral arrangements in a variety of styles.

Michael Praetorius was born February 15, 1571, in Saxe-Weimar and died on his fiftieth birthday at Wolfenbüttel, Germany. Largely self-taught, Praetorius became a prolific author and composer and an innovator in using both harmony and counterpoint.

242 The Strife Is O'er

The origin of this Latin hymn is unknown, although its earliest source is a 1695 Jesuit hymnbook from Cologne, Germany—*Hymnodia Sacra*. John Mason Neale made an English translation for his *Medieval Hymns and Sequences* (1851), but the version by Francis Pott, which appears here, has been more widely used.

Francis Pott (1832–1909) translated this Latin text in 1861 for his *Hymns Fitted to the Order of Common Prayer*. An altered version of it appeared that same year in *Hymns Ancient and Modern*, for which Pott was a member of the committee.

Giovanni Perluigi Sante da Palestrina (1525–1594) composed the melody from which this tune was adapted for his "Magnificat Tertii Toni" (1591). It was arranged for this text and entitled VICTORY by William Henry Monk for *Hymns Ancient and Modern* (1861).

Giovanni P. S. da Palestrina is believed to have been born in 1525 in Palestrina, Italy, and received his musical training in Rome. Palestrina served six popes and set new musical standards for the church. He died in Rome on February 2, 1594, and was buried in St. Peter's Cathedral there.

243 Alleluia! Alleluia! Hearts to Heaven

Christopher Wordsworth (1807–1885), an English clergyman of great renown in his time, wrote this Easter hymn with numerous scriptural allusions as part of a collection of hymns for the church year, *The Holy Year* (1862). Many of his hymns were written on scraps of paper as he traveled around England as bishop of Lincoln.

Christopher Wordsworth, the nephew of the poet William Wordsworth, served as lecturer at Cambridge University and headmaster of Harrow, one of England's finest preparatory schools. He then had a career as a clergyman, serving as a canon, vicar, parish priest, archdeacon, and finally bishop of Lincoln.

This anonymous hymn, WEISSE FLAGGEN, has been traced to a number of German Catholic hymnals, including *Tochter Sion* (1741), published in Cologne. Scholars believe that the tune may have roots in a popular folk song.

In *Tochter Sion* (1741), this melody appeared with the words "Lasst die weissen Flaggen wehen," from which the present tune name is derived. The pairing of this tune with Wordsworth's text follows from the *Pilgrim Hymnal* (1958). Other tunes with which it is sung include HYFRYDOL and LUX EOI.

244 O Sons and Daughters, Let Us Sing

Jean Tisserand (d. 1494) wrote this hymn, which was used on the evening before Easter Day in French Roman Catholic churches, as the salutation of the Blessed Sacrament. The booklet in which the text was found is now in the collection of the Bibliothèque Nationale in Paris, France.

Jean Tisserand was a Franciscan Minorite friar in Paris, France. He was widely known and respected during his lifetime and is recognized for founding an order of "penitent" women. He is believed to be the author of a history of Minorites martyred in Morocco in 1220.

This traditional French melody was first found in printed form in a 1623 Parisian hymnal. It is known as O FILII ET FILIAE from the opening words of the Latin text with which it was sung. An altered version of the tune is called EASTERTIDE. It is clearly a Roman Catholic melody.

Airs sur les hymnes sacrez, odes et noels was a 1623 hymnal printed in Paris, France. This source is the earliest yet found to contain this music, although the tune most likely is much older. It is believed that the tune was the original one used with Tisserand's Latin text.

245 The Day of Resurrection

John of Damascus (c. 696–c. 754), an eighth-century monk and poet, wrote the "Golden Canon for Easter," from which this hymn is derived. John Mason Neale translated the entire canon, but the present hymn is only a portion of it, from Ode I. In Greek churches, the hymn traditionally is sung at a midnight service on Easter Eve as worshipers light candles.

The Greek "canon" consisted of nine "odes" based on the Canticles from Scripture, which were sung at the daily office. Each ode was made up of three or more stanzas. These odes were sung to a corresponding number of modal melodies, or *"echoi,"* known as Byzantine chant.

Henry Thomas Smart (1813–1879) composed the tune LANCASHIRE for a text by Reginald Heber in 1836. It is named for the English county in which Smart served as organist. The tune was popular in Nonconformist (Congregational) churches but was not used widely until published in a 1867 Presbyterian hymnal.

Henry T. Smart followed in the footsteps of his father and his grandfather to become a noted church musician. He was one of England's most eminent organists in the nineteenth century and continued to play, compose, and even design organs late in life, despite being blind for his last fifteen years.

246 Hoy celebramos con gozo al Dios (Come, Celebrate with Thanksgiving)

Mortimer Arias (b. 1924), a Methodist from Uruguay, wrote this text as a hymn of celebration appropriate for services on Easter, Thanksgiving, communion Sundays, or Pentecost. It was first sung in Sucre, Bolivia, in a Methodist church, "El Vive," and published in the hymnal *Canta-Canta* (1973).

Mortimer Arias was born in Uruguay on January 15, 1924, but became a Bolivian citizen in 1968, the year he wrote this hymn. He is now retired from the United Methodist ministry in his native Uruguay. His notes on the hymn state: "The *cueca* rhythm is very alive and popular in Bolivia, and people accompany it by clapping and dancing at the refrain."

Antonio Auza (1915–1981) composed the tune CHUQUISACA, named for the province in Bolivia where he was born and worked all his life. It is in the style of Andean folk music.

Antonio Auza was born June 13, 1915, in Sucre, Chuquisaca, Bolivia, and died there on March 19, 1981. He composed several tune settings for texts by Mortimer Arias, which have been published in Hispanic and U.S. hymnals.

247 My Shepherd Is the Living God

Isaac Watts (1674–1748) created three metrical paraphrases of the beloved Psalm 23. This version includes most of the stanzas from the one that originally began "My Shepherd will supply my need" but substitutes the first two lines from Thomas Sternhold's paraphrase of 1549 in the first stanza.

Isaac Watts published the fourth and final collection of his hymn texts in 1719, *The Psalms of David, Imitated in the Language of the New Testament*. It provided metered versions of the psalms that went far beyond the bounds of paraphrase, many of them reinterpreted from a Christian perspective.

This tune, CONSOLATION, first appeared in the shape-note tunebook *The Beauties of Harmony*, published by Freeman Lewis in Pittsburgh, Pennsylvania. There it was called HOPEWELL and was the setting for "Come Humble Sinner in Whose Breast." Other early sources called it RESIGNATION.

In William Walker's *Southern Harmony* (1854), a Baptist hymnbook used primarily in the Southeastern United States, this tune was matched with Isaac Watts's text and bore the present name, CONSOLATION.

248 Such Perfect Love My Shepherd Shows

Henry Williams Baker (1821–1877) paraphrased Psalm 23 for this text and, in the spirit of Watts, included several New Testament references. It appeared in the Appendix to *Hymns Ancient and Modern* (1868), the landmark English hymnal for which Baker chaired the committee.

Henry W. Baker, born in London England, received his education at Trinity College, Cambridge. He was ordained a priest of the Church of England in 1844. Baker spent twenty years working on *Hymns Ancient and Modern*, which became the unofficial hymnal of the Anglican Church.

John Bacchus Dykes (1823–1876) composed this melody in 1868 for Baker's text. The tune name, DOMINUS REGIT ME, is the Latin version of the opening phrase of Psalm 23, on which the hymn is based.

John B. Dykes was recognized as one of the great church musicians of the Victorian era, and in 1861 he received a doctorate in music from the University of Durham, England. Dykes composed only in his spare time when not occupied by his duties as precentor at Durham Cathedral.

249 Peace I Leave with You, My Friends

Ray Repp (b. 1942) based the text of this hymn on Jesus' words in John 14. This lectionary text is the appointed Gospel reading for the sixth Sunday of Easter. The hymn is also appropriate for the close of worship. "Shalom" is the Hebrew word for peace.

Ray Repp's music has been translated into twenty-eight languages and can be heard around the world. He is a founder of K & R Music, Incorporated, located in Trumansburg, New York. Repp continues to work at this music production company and lives in that vicinity.

Ray Repp (b. 1942) composed this tune to accompany his own words. It has been named PEACE, MY FRIENDS, from the text's title. Use of guitar accompaniment for this hymn is appropriate. It was newly arranged for congregational singing in *The New Century Hymnal*.

Ray Repp has composed and recorded more than eleven albums of songs, including his *Mass for Young Americans*, written in 1965. Much of his music is best accompanied by guitar. Repp believes that music is an effective medium for encouraging a change in attitude or direction for Christians.

250 Listen to Your Savior Call

William Cowper (1731–1800) was considered one of the finest poets of his day. He based this text on John 21, a conversation between the resurrected Jesus and the apostle Peter. The first three stanzas are meant to be the words of Jesus, with the final stanza providing an opportunity to reply to Jesus' command.

William Cowper, the son of an English clergyman, was trained as a lawyer, although he never worked in that field. Throughout his life, he fought severe depression and found his greatest peace when working with John Newton at the Olney, England, parish. They published a hymnal together in 1779.

This French melody, ORIENTIS PARTIBUS, takes its name from a text for the Feast of the Circumcision, which combined medieval Latin and Old French. Pierre de Corbeil (d. 1221) is believed to have written the Office of the Circumcision, in which this tune was sung. The words mean "from the Eastern regions the donkey is now come." This festival celebrates the donkey that carried Mary on the flight to Egypt.

Richard Redhead (1820–1901) adapted this ancient French melody in 1853, when it appeared in his *Church Hymn Tunes*. Redhead served as organist at two English churches and favored the ideals of the Oxford movement.

251 I Greet You, Sure Redeemer

This anonymous French text, "Je te salue, mon certain Redempteur," appeared in the Strasbourg edition of Clement Marot's *Psalms* (1545). In 1868 it was included in the sixth volume of John Calvin's *Opera*, which led some scholars to erroneously assume that Calvin was the original author.

Elizabeth Lee Smith (1817–1898) prepared her English translation of this hymn in the same meter as the original French text, and it appeared in Philip Schaff's *Christ in Song* (1870). Smith's version was later adapted to the meter of the Genevan psalm tune TOULON.

TOULON is a shortened version of the tune that appeared with Psalm 124 in the 1551 Genevan Psalter. That tune, OLD 124TH, was one of the most universally known in the sixteenth-century Reformed churches and appeared with eight psalms in the Ainsworth Psalter, which was brought to the American colonies by the Pilgrims.

The Genevan Psalter of 1551 provided metrical versions of the psalms in French for use by Reformed congregations that were greatly influenced by John Calvin. Calvin did not approve of the singing of any hymn texts except those based on the 150 psalms of the Hebrew Scriptures.

252 Savior, Like a Shepherd Lead Us

Dorothy Ann Thrupp (1779–1847) is believed to have written these words, although they were originally published without an author's name. The hymn was first printed in 1836 in a volume Thrupp compiled called *Hymns for the Young*.

Dorothy A. Thrupp was born in London, England, on June 20, 1779. Although she never married, she had a great love for infants and children and wrote many hymns especially for them, sometimes using the pseudonym "Iota." Thrupp died in London on December 14, 1847.

William Batchelder Bradbury (1816–1868) wrote this tune in 1859, and it appeared in his collection entitled *Oriola*. It was given the name BRADBURY by a hymnal editor and is used almost exclusively with this text. The tune has also been called SHEPHERD from the first line of the hymn.

William B. Bradbury served as a church organist in Maine; New Brunswick, Canada; Boston, Massachusetts; Brooklyn, New York; and New York City. At this final site, he was instrumental in introducing music instruction into the public school curriculum.

253 A toi la gloire, ô Ressuscité!
(Yours Is the Glory, Resurrected One!)

Edmond L. Budry (1854–1932) wrote this hymn in French in 1884, and it was published in a Lausanne hymnal the following year. His inspiration may have been a German Advent poem. The hymn won fame when sung at the First Assembly of the World Council of Churches in Amsterdam, Holland, in 1948.

Edmond L. Budry was born August 30, 1854, and studied theology in Lausanne, Switzerland. He served as pastor in Cully, France, and then at the Free Church in Vevey, Switzerland. Budry was a sought-after translator for German, English, and Latin hymns and often adapted and improved upon the original in his resulting French texts.

George Frideric Handel (1685–1759) composed this melody as part of a chorus in his oratorio *Joshua* and later transferred it to another, with the same title as this tune, JUDAS MACCABEUS. The tune has been used as a hymn setting since 1760, when it appeared with another Easter text, "Christ the Lord Is Risen Today."

George Frideric Handel was born February 23, 1685, in Halle, Germany, the son of a barber-surgeon. He gave up studying law and took up the violin after his father died. Handel was considered a musical genius even in his own day. He died April 14, 1759, and was buried at Westminster Abbey, London.

254 These Things Did Thomas Count

Thomas H. Troeger (b. 1945) based this 1984 text on the doubt expressed by the apostle Thomas and mirrored in the twentieth-century rational enlightenment. Troeger reminds those who sing this hymn that belief must transcend "reasoned certainties."

Thomas H. Troeger, a Presbyterian seminary professor, has described the audience for his hymns as "thinking persons of faith who have a passion for beauty." Troeger's collected works were published in *Borrowed Light: Hymn Texts, Prayers, and Poems* (1994).

This tune, called DISTRESS, appeared in a number of early shape-note collections, such as *The Sacred Harp* (1844) and *Southern Harmony* (1835), where it was set to Anne Steele's "So Fades the Lovely Blooming Flower," a song about Jesus' parable of the prodigal son.

The Sacred Harp, one of a number of Baptist shape-note tunebooks, was compiled in 1844 by B. F. White, the brother-in-law of another tunebook compiler, William Walker. Many of the tunes in these books derived from folk melodies of the British Isles. This one may be a variation of the Scottish folk tune "Laird O' Cockpen."

255 Jesus, Sovereign, Savior

Patrick Miller Kirkland (1857–1943) incorporated in this text references to Jesus' crucifixion, the Emmaus road experience, and the upper-room appearance of the resurrected Christ. It was published only after Kirkland's death, in the *Trinity Hymnal* (1961) of the Orthodox Presbyterian Church.

Patrick M. Kirkland was an English Presbyterian. Although Presbyterianism is more closely associated with Scotland, the Reformed Church spread throughout the world much as did Lutheranism, and Reformed Churches are now found around the globe.

Ralph Vaughan Williams (1872–1958) composed KING'S WESTON as a setting for Caroline Noel's "At the Name of Jesus" in *Songs of Praise*, 1925. The tune's name honors the country home of Philip Napier Miles overlooking the Bristol Channel in England, where Vaughan Williams spent many weekends.

Ralph Vaughan Williams was a leading twentieth-century composer in England. He was influenced by the music of the Tudor composers, especially Thomas Tallis and Henry Purcell. Vaughan Williams composed operas, symphonies, ballets, and film scores in addition to church music.

256 We Live by Faith and Not by Sight

Henry Alford (1810–1871) included this hymn in an 1844 hymnal he edited called *Psalms and Hymns, adapted for the Sundays and Holidays throughout the Year*. In this work, Alford sought to provide resources for the church year, much as lectionary aids do today.

Henry Alford was ordained in the Church of England in 1833 and served as curate to his father at three charges. He was vicar at Leicestershire for eighteen years and in 1857 was appointed dean of Canterbury. Alford was a Greek scholar and assisted in a New Testament revision.

Samuel McFarland (dates unknown) is credited in the second edition of *Beauties of Harmony* (1816) as the composer of the tune DUNLAP'S CREEK. In the nineteenth century, this tune was included in more denominational hymnals than any other.

Freeman Lewis (dates unknown) compiled *Beauties of Harmony* in 1814, with a second edition in 1816. This was a shape-note hymnbook, which used notes of four different shapes to help the musically untrained to recognize various pitches. It was published in Pittsburgh, Pennsylvania.

257 Alleluia! Gracious Jesus!

William Chatterton Dix (1837–1898) called this poem "Redemption by the Precious Blood" and intended it to fill the need for communion hymns in the Anglican Church. It is rich in scriptural allusions and has been appropriated for use on Ascension Day, which occurs forty days after the resurrection.

William C. Dix enjoyed studying languages and poetry. He translated works from Greek and Ethiopian and published his poetry in four volumes, including *Hymns of Love and Joy* (1861) and *Altar Songs, Verses on the Holy Eucharist* (1867).

Rowland Hugh Prichard (1811–1887) composed HYFRYDOL before the age of twenty and included it in his *Cyfaill y Cantorium* (1844). It came into use with English hymns when it appeared with this text in *The English Hymnal* (1906).

Rowland H. Prichard felt strongly about the music used during worship and often wrote tunes to replace those he viewed as inappropriate. His tunes were easy to sing but conveyed a sense of power and majesty. Most were first published in Welsh periodicals.

258 Christ, Enthroned in Heavenly Splendor

George Hugh Bourne (1840–1925) wrote this text for use at the chapel of St. Edmund's College in Salisbury, England, where he was serving as warden. This hymn was one of seven postcommunion hymns that he wrote and had printed privately in 1874.

George H. Bourne, born in Kent, England, received his education at Christ Church College, Oxford, England, and received three degrees there. He was ordained in the Church of England in 1863 and served as headmaster and warden at Chardstock College. He died on December 1, 1925.

William Owen (1814–1893) wrote this powerful tune, BRYN CALFARIA (which means "Hill of Calvary" in Welsh), for a Welsh hymn about Christ and the cross. The melody was used in the 1941 movie about Welsh coal miners, "How Green Was My Valley," and as a result became widely known.

William Owen was a Welsh composer who worked in the slate quarries as a youth with his father. In 1886, he published *Y Perl Cerddorol* (*The Pearl of Music*), a compilation of his hymn tunes and anthems, including BRYN CALFARIA.

259 A Hymn of Glory Let Us Sing

The Venerable Bede (673–735) is believed to have written this early Latin hymn, "Hymnum canamus Domino," in eleven stanzas. The earliest known copy of the hymn is an eleventh-century manuscript in the British Museum. Two English translations from the mid-1800s were combined for this version.

The Venerable Bede was educated at the monasteries of Wearmouth and Jarrow in England. He was ordained a deacon at age nineteen and a priest ten years later. He was given the title "Venerable" to indicate the high regard shown him by his and succeeding generations for his numerous scholarly achievements.

This tune, called DEO GRACIAS here, is from "The Agincourt Song," which originated in England to celebrate King Henry V's victory over the French at Agincourt on October 25, 1415. The Latin words literally mean "thanks be to God."

Edward George Power Biggs (1906–1977), who emigrated to the United States from England in 1930, utilized "The Agincourt Song" in an organ fantasia in his *Treasury of Early Organ Music* (1947). This piece provided the basis for Richard Proulx's hymn adaptation of 1985.

260 Hail the Day That Sees Christ Rise

Charles Wesley (1707–1788) wrote the original ten stanzas of this hymn, but they were greatly revised in 1820 by Thomas Cotterill (1779–1823), an Anglican minister. The alleluias were added by yet another hymnbook editor, G. C. White, in 1852.

Charles Wesley spent most of the year of 1736 in Georgia as secretary to General James Oglethorpe. His brother James had convinced him to travel to the colonies as a missionary, but he became disillusioned and decided to return to England, stopping in Boston where he preached at Old South Church.

GWALCHMAI is from an 1868 collection of Welsh hymns by Joseph David Jones (1827–1870). Whether he wrote the tune or transcribed it is unknown. It appeared with a poem by George Herbert in *The English Hymnal* (1906). GWALCHMAI is the name of a Welsh town and also a famous Welsh singer.

Joseph D. Jones (1827–1870) included GWALCHMAI in an 1868 hymn collection. As a child of poor parents, Jones had only one year of schooling yet taught himself to play cello and became a renowned hymnwriter. One of his sons was a celebrated Congregational minister and another was elected to Parliament.

261 Let Every Christian Pray

Fred Pratt Green (b. 1903) wrote this text at the request of John Wilson for use on Whitsunday (Pentecost), when the coming of the Holy Spirit to the church is celebrated. Written in 1970, it is an early example of the three hundred hymns this poet has generated since his retirement from the ministry in 1969.

Fred Pratt Green was encouraged to write poetry by a parishioner, the poet Fallon Webb. For twenty years, he and Webb wrote and critiqued each other's work during regular meetings. Green had first visited Webb in 1944, when Webb's child was in the Sunday school where Green served as pastor.

Joseph Barnby (1838–1896) composed LAUDES DOMINI in the style of Victorian part-songs popular during his lifetime. It first appeared in the Appendix to *Hymns Ancient and Modern* (1868) with the hymn "When Morning Gilds the Skies," to which it is still frequently sung.

Joseph Barnby was born in York, England, and became organist at Yorkminster Cathedral at age twelve. He later became principal of Guildhall School of Music and was a prolific composer of oratorios, service music, motets, anthems, organ, and piano pieces. He died in London, England, in 1896.

262 Hail, O Festal Day

Venantius Honorius Fortunatus (c. 530–609) composed the 110-line poem from which this hymn is drawn as early as 582 C.E. Portions of it, beginning at line 39, were widely used during the Middle Ages for processionals on festival days. They were combined as one hymn in *Songs of Praise* (1931), as in this version.

Venantius Honorius Fortunatus was born near Treviso, Italy, and educated at Ravenna and Milan, Italy. He moved to Gaul (now France), became a monk of the Abbey of St. Croix, and was active in the court of Queen Rhadegunda. He was appointed bishop of Poitiers in 599.

Ralph Vaughan Williams (1872–1958) composed this tune for another translation of the Fortunatus poem in *The English Hymnal* (1906), although it was published anonymously there. The tune's name, SALVE FESTA DIES, comes from the opening phrase of the original Latin text.

Ralph Vaughan Williams is considered by some to be the greatest English composer since Purcell and was greatly influenced by that composer and Thomas Tallis. Vaughan Williams served as musical editor of several significant hymnals of the early twentieth century, most notably *The English Hymnal* (1906).

263 O Spirit of the Living God

Henry Hallam Tweedy (1868–1953) wrote this hymn in 1933 to help people of his generation understand the story of Pentecost, as recorded in Acts 2. It first appeared in the *Methodist Hymnal* (1935) and later in *The Hymnal of the Evangelical and Reformed Church* (1941).

Henry H. Tweedy was born in Binghamton, New York, on August 5, 1868, and was ordained in the Congregational Church in his thirtieth year. He served as professor of practical theology at Yale Divinity School from 1909 to 1937 and wrote a number of books concerning the Christian life.

William Croft (1678–1721) has long been identified as the composer of the tune known as ST. MATTHEW. However, it was anonymous when printed in early sources, such as *A Supplement to the New Version of the Psalms* (1708). A later hymnbook published by one of Croft's students credited it to him because of a manuscript in Croft's handwriting.

William Croft served as church organist at the Chapel Royal and later at Westminster Abbey, London, England, where he is buried. He wrote not only church music but also music for the theater and various instrumental pieces. Three of his hymns are among those considered the best English hymn tunes.

264 Holy Spirit, Come, Confirm Us

William Brian Foley (b. 1919) used the letters of the apostle Paul to the churches at Corinth, Rome, and Ephesus as the basis for this text about the Holy Spirit. The text was one of fourteen of his hymns included in the *New Catholic Hymnal* (1971).

Brian Foley was born near Liverpool, England, in 1919 and ordained a Roman Catholic priest in 1945 following an education at Christian Brothers' School in Crosby and Upholland Diocesan Roman Catholic Seminary. He has served as a parish priest in addition to writing hymns.

Vicar Earle Copes (b. 1921) wrote this tune for a communion text by Louis F. Benson. It was first sung at the National Convocation of Methodist Youth in 1960. Originally the hymn was named KINGDOM but was retitled FOR THE BREAD by the composer in 1989 when he prepared this new harmonization.

V. Earle Copes served as music editor of the General Board of Education of the Methodist Church from 1958 to 1967. He developed the first Methodist Sunday-school music curriculum, wrote many hymn studies, and edited *Music Ministry*, a monthly periodical.

265 Come, O Spirit, with Your Sound

John A. Dalles (b. 1954) based this hymn on Acts 2:1–4, the story of the birth of the church at Pentecost. He wrote the text for the anniversary celebration of the Wabash Valley (Indiana) Presbytery. The service at which it premiered was held on Pentecost Sunday in 1983.

John A. Dalles, an ordained Presbyterian minister, won the 1985 Hymn Society's "Hymns for World Peace" contest and has written more than two hundred hymn texts. A native of Pittsburgh, Pennsylvania, Dalles has served pastorates in that state as well as in Indiana and Florida.

This tune, BOUNDLESS MERCY, first appeared in William Caldwell's *Union Harmony*, published in 1837 in Maryville, Tennessee. It is not known whether Caldwell wrote the tune or copied it from unpublished sources in circulation at that time.

William Caldwell collected many tunes used in Methodist, Baptist, and Presbyterian churches in the mountain regions of Tennessee and surrounding areas. Caldwell added harmony to these airs and published them in his 1837 collection *Union Harmony*.

266 Filled with the Spirit's Power

John Raphael Peacey (1896–1971) turned his attention to writing hymns after his retirement from the parish ministry in 1967. This text was a product of that productive time and appeared in his *100 Hymns for Today* (1969). Peacey was active in the union of the Church of England and the Methodist Church.

John R. Peacey received the Military Cross during his service with the British Army in France in World War I. After ordination, he was headmaster at Bishop Cotton School in Simla, India, from 1927 to 1945. After returning to England, Peacey served as canon at Bristol Cathedral until 1966.

Cyril Vincent Taylor (1907–1992) named this hymn SHELDONIAN for a theater next door to the University Music School in Oxford, England, where Taylor often met with the hymnal committee that prepared the *BBC Hymn Book* (1951). The tune was often played on British radio during World War II.

Cyril Vincent Taylor was educated at Oxford and Cambridge, was ordained to the Anglican priesthood in 1932, and served at Bristol Cathedral, Cerne, Abbas, and Salisbury Cathedral, all in England. In addition, he was a respected hymnal editor and chair of the Hymn Society of Great Britain and Ireland from 1975 to 1980.

267 Come, O Spirit, Dwell among Us

Janie Alford (1887–1986) wrote this text in 1979 when she was ninety-two years old, although she had written poetry all her life. Hal Hopson encouraged Alford to write hymns based on the seasons of the church year. This hymn was included in *Nine Hymns for the Church Year* in response to that request.

Janie Alford was born in Nashville, Tennessee, and worked for over forty years as a medical secretary. She briefly studied library science in college and helped start the library at Westminster Presbyterian Church in Nashville, where she was a charter member. She died in 1986 at the age of ninety-nine.

Thomas John Williams (1869–1944) included this melody as part of an anthem he composed around 1890, "Golen yn y glyn" ("Light in the Valley"). Called EBENEZER for a chapel he attended, the tune is alternately known as TON-Y-BOTEL (Welsh for "tone in a bottle"), after a fanciful but untrue story that it washed ashore in a bottle.

Thomas J. Williams was born in the Swansea Valley, Glamorganshire, Wales, in 1869. He was a student of David Evans and served as organist at two churches in Llanelly, Wales, beginning in 1913 and continuing until his death in 1944. Williams composed a number of anthems for church choirs.

268 Creator Spirit, Come, We Pray

Rhabanus Maurus (d. 856) is usually credited as the author of this ninth-century Latin text, "Veni Creator Spiritus." It was used as part of the daily office during the season of Pentecost and is sung at ordination services to this day. The hymn has also been sung in the English coronation rite since 1307.

Rhabanus Maurus was born in Mainz and educated at Fulda, both in Germany. He then entered the Benedictine order as a Roman Catholic monk. A respected teacher, Maurus served as head of the school at Fulda and later its abbot. He wrote important biblical commentaries and a Latin-German glossary on the Bible.

Lee Hastings Bristol Jr. (1923–1979) composed DICKINSON COLLEGE in 1962 as part of a hymn-anthem. It is named for the Pennsylvania institution from which he received one of his eleven honorary doctoral degrees. Bristol was an active Episcopal lay reader and was licensed to preach in that denomination.

Lee Hastings Bristol Jr. began his career as director of public relations in his family's business, Bristol-Myers. He left this work to serve as president of Westminster Choir College in Princeton, New Jersey, from 1962 to 1969. Bristol was honored as a fellow of the Royal School of Church Music and the Hymn Society of America.

269 Sweet Delight, Most Lovely

Paul Gerhardt (1607–1676) wrote this text in German in 1648. At that time, he was serving as tutor to Anna Maria Barthold in Berlin, Germany. Three years later he was ordained a minister, and seven years later he married Anna Maria. The text has been newly translated here by Madeleine Forell Marshall.

Paul Gerhardt is considered one of Germany's greatest hymnwriters. Born in Saxony in 1607, he lived during the Thirty Years' War, a time when political and religious persecution was commonplace. Gerhardt wrote 132 hymns.

Sally Ann Morris (b. 1952) composed the tune JOEL in 1991 for a text by Alan Luff beginning with a quotation from the popular songwriter, Billy Joel. This was one of six tunes Morris submitted to a contest seeking new hymns for a Lutheran retirement home's centennial anniversary.

Sally Ann Morris was born in Winston-Salem, North Carolina, on September 16, 1952. She began composing hymn tunes in 1990 and now has more than fifty to her credit. She created a four-part anthem setting of this hymn for The New Century Anthem Series, published by the Pilgrim Press in 1995.

270 Like the Murmur of the Dove's Song

Carl Pickens Daw Jr. (b. 1944) wrote this text for the tune BRIDEGROOM, by Peter Cutts. Daw explained that this hymn study of the Holy Spirit conveys in the first stanza "how" the spirit comes; in the second, "where" and "to whom" the Spirit comes; and in the final stanza, "why" the Spirit comes to the church.

Carl P. Daw Jr. received his bachelor's degree from Rice University, his master's and doctorate from the University of Virginia, and his theological degree from the University of the South, in Sewanee, Tennessee. Daw was ordained to the Episcopal ministry in 1982.

Peter Warwick Cutts (b. 1937) was asked in 1968 by Erik Routley to compose this tune for "As the Bridegroom to His Chosen"; hence the tune name, BRIDEGROOM. It is one of Cutts's most successful tunes and has been used with a number of new texts, such as this one.

Peter Cutts was born in Birmingham, England, and received his education there. He taught music at three schools in Wakefield, England, before moving to the United States. Cutts was encouraged by Erik Routley to write hymn tunes and collaborated with Brian Wren on *Faith Looking Forward* (1983).

271 Wind Who Makes All Winds That Blow

Thomas H. Troeger (b. 1945) wrote this text in 1983 for Father Sebastian Falcone, dean of St. Bernard Institute in Rochester, New York, for a mass celebrating the gift of the Holy Spirit. One of Troeger's most highly acclaimed hymns, it appears in many denominational hymnals of the late twentieth century.

Thomas H. Troeger was appointed the Peck Professor of Preaching and Communications at Iliff School of Theology in Denver, Colorado, in 1991. An ordained Presbyterian minister, he served as president of the Academy of Homiletics. His most recent work is an opera libretto, *An Island of Sand*.

Carol Doran, who often collaborates with the hymnwriter Thomas Troeger, provided this setting, called FALCONE. The tune name honors Father Sebastian Falcone, a Roman Catholic priest for whom the hymn was written. Although challenging, the tune is an effective vehicle for these words.

Carol Doran was born in Philadelphia, Pennsylvania. She attended West Chester University in Pennsylvania and studied music at the Eastman School of Music and the University of Rochester. She holds a doctoral degree and teaches worship and pastoral music in a multidenominational seminary.

272 On Pentecost They Gathered

Jane Parker Huber (b. 1926) wrote this text for use at Pentecost. The first two stanzas tell the story from Acts 2, and the final two stanzas apply the lessons of Pentecost to the modern-day church. Like this one, many of Huber's hymns were written to be sung to familiar or traditional tunes.

Jane Parker Huber has worked with the Social Justice and Peacemaking Ministry Unit of the Presbyterian Church (U.S.A.), visiting with women in local churches, leading workshops on women's issues, and helping to make women more aware of their great potential to change the world.

MUNICH is an old German chorale tune first recorded in *Neuvermehrtes Meiningisches Gesangbuch* (1693) with the text "O Gott, du Frommer Gott." The tune was adapted and harmonized by Felix Mendelssohn in 1847 for his oratorio *Elijah*, with the opening words "Cast thy burden upon the Lord."

The third edition of the *Neuvermehrtes Gesangbuch* was published in Meininger, Germany, in 1693. It contained 647 hymns, 169 of which had melodies and figured bass. The book included hymns by the wife and father-in-law of Duke Bernhard of Saxony, who had requested the collection.

273 Praise with Joy the World's Creator

The Iona Community contributed this hymn for an international, ecumenical gathering of young people in 1985. It was first sung at the opening worship at Giles Cathedral in Edinburgh, Scotland. This conference celebrated the seventy-fifth anniversary of the Edinburgh Mission Conference, birthplace of the contemporary ecumenical movement.

The Iona Community conducts retreats throughout the year for people seeking a deeper religious experience. It also hosts an annual youth retreat entitled "Experiencing Easter," in which people from all over Britain are encouraged to reflect on the meaning of Holy Week.

John Goss (1800–1880) composed LAUDA ANIMA, Latin for "Praise my soul," in 1869 for H. F. Lyte's hymn beginning with those English words. It became one of the most popular of the Victorian tunes in Great Britain and is frequently sung at weddings.

John Goss, the son of an organist, became one of the greatest organists to serve at St. Paul's Cathedral, London, England, in the nineteenth century. It was said that he never began a composition without first asking for God's blessing upon his work. Goss was knighted in 1872.

274 Womb of Life, and Source of Being

Ruth C. Duck (b. 1947) created this 1986 text as an exploration of trinitarian theology, by which the church has sought to understand God for centuries. It was developed during a class taught by Linda Clark and revised with help from Brian Wren in 1990. The text includes both new and old names for God.

Ruth Duck, a seminary professor, has lectured and led workshops throughout North America on the subjects of worship and hymnody. She has spoken before denominational and ecumenical groups, sharing what she has learned about the importance of liturgy and song for a vital and modern church.

Ronald Arnatt (b. 1930) composed the tune LADUE CHAPEL in 1986. Arnatt founded the Washington, D.C., Cantata Chorus; in St. Louis, Missouri, he served as organist at Christ Church Cathedral, director of music at Mary Institute, and associate professor at the University of Missouri.

Ronald Arnatt was born in London, England, on January 16, 1930. He came to the United States at age seventeen to continue his musical education and has become widely known as a concert organist, composer, and conductor. Arnatt founded the St. Louis (Missouri) Chamber Orchestra and Chorus.

275 Come Now, Almighty God

This anonymous hymn was written as a parody of the British national anthem, "God Save Our Lord the King." The author feared reprisal when the text appeared in a leaf inserted in George Whitefield's *Collection of Hymns for Social Worship* (1757).

This anonymous rewriting of the British national anthem replaced words usually reserved for the monarch with words of praise to God. During the Revolutionary War, British soldiers broke into a Long Island church, ordering the worshipers to sing the national anthem. They did so but substituted this text instead.

Felice de Giardini (1716–1769) wrote this tune for these words, and they have been sung together since 1769. First called TRINITY, since the text is a hymn to the Trinity, the tune is here named ITALIAN HYMN for de Giardini's birthplace. It is also sometimes called MOSCOW, for the city where he died.

Felice de Giardini was an Italian virtuoso violinist and harpsichordist. He moved to England in 1750 and was highly successful for a time. In 1787, he moved to Russia in hopes of finding new opportunities but died in Moscow in 1769, in poverty and disappointment.

276 Holy God, We Praise Your Name

Ignaz Franz (1719–1790) may have written this German version of the "Te Deum," an ancient prayer. Here it is listed as anonymous. It is known that Franz included this text in *Katholisches Gesangbuch* (1774), which he published in Vienna, Austria, without indicating an author.

Clarence Alphonsus Walworth (1820–1900) provided this English translation dated 1853 in the *Evangelical Hymnal* (1880), published in New York. Walworth moved from the Presbyterian to the Episcopal Church during his theological studies and eventually became a Roman Catholic priest. He was a founding member of the Order of Paulists in the United States.

The tune GROSSER GOTT, WIR LOBEN DICH appeared with that German text in *Katholisches Gesangbuch*, a 1774 Roman Catholic hymnbook in Vienna, Austria. Other names for this tune and its variants are HURSLEY, FRAMINGHAM, HALLE, HUNGARIAN MELODY, and LAUDAMUS.

Ignaz Franz, a Roman Catholic priest, published *Katholisches Gesangbuch* in Vienna, Austria, in 1774. He compiled this hymnal by order of the empress Maria Theresa, a devout Roman Catholic, in order to make tunes and words available to the people in the churches of Austria and Hungary.

277 Holy, Holy, Holy

Reginald Heber (1783–1826) wrote this hymn of pure adoration to God, based on Revelation 4:8–11, for use on Trinity Sunday. This tribute to the triune God was first published in the year Heber died, 1826, and has become the most widely sung of all his hymns.

Reginald Heber showed himself to be a genius at age seven, when he translated one of Plato's dialogues into versified English. A bishop of the Anglican Church, he did much to introduce congregational singing in the Church of England, which was previously contemptuous of that practice.

John Bacchus Dykes (1823–1876) composed the tune NICAEA in 1861 and named it for the site of the 325 C.E. Christian church council which developed the Nicene Creed. It appeared with this text in *Hymns Ancient and Modern* and has been described as the "archetypal Victorian hymn tune."

Scholars have noted similarities between Dykes's tune and several others, including the German chorale WACHET AUF, John Hopkins's TRINITY, and a tune by Lowell Mason for the same text. None of these, however, have been identified as the true source of Dykes's melody.

278 Creator God, Creating Still

Jane Parker Huber (b. 1926) wrote this, her second hymn text, in 1977. In it, she experimented with the use of fresh images for the persons of the Trinity. The hymn appeared in her collection *Joy in Singing* (1983) with this common meter tune, ST. ANNE.

Jane Parker Huber has frequently written new texts for specific tunes that she knows are popular with congregations of Reformed theological backgrounds. Her technique has met with widespread acceptance, as congregations can more easily sing new words to a familiar tune.

William Croft (1678–1727) is thought to have composed ST. ANNE while he was organist at St. Anne's Church in London. The tune first accompanied Psalm 42 in Tate and Brady's *New Version of the Psalms* (1708). The opening measures were used by both G. F. Handel and J. S. Bach in later compositions.

William Croft published the two-volume *Musica Sacra* in 1724. This was the first church music to be engraved in scores on plates. Although he wrote music for the theater and other genres, Croft was best known for his church music compositions, especially psalm tunes.

279 O God in Heaven

Elena G. Maquiso (b. 1914) explores the three persons of the Trinity in this hymn. The first stanza concerns God as Creator; the second, God as Redeemer; and the third, God as Spirit. She wrote the text in 1961, and it was first published in *E.A.C.C. Hymnal* (1964) in a translation by D. T. Niles.

Daniel Thambyrajah Niles was born in Ceylon in 1908 and was inspired to change his course of study from law to the Christian ministry. He was ordained in the United Methodist Church in 1932 and rose to become a leader in that denomination and in the World Council of Churches, serving as president of the East Asia Christian Conference.

Elena G. Maquiso (b. 1914) composed the tune HALAD. It was originally used with a text in Cebuano that began "Panalangini ang mong halad," meaning "Bless our offering" in *Awitan Ta Ang Dyos* (1962), the first Protestant Cebuano hymnbook.

Elena G. Maquiso, a composer and conductor, has been recognized by Silliman University as the "primary and moving spirit behind a movement in the United Church of Christ in the Philippines to create and popularize religious music and hymns in Cebuano." For many years, she led "Banikanhong Mag-aawit," a Cebuano choral group.

280 O Trinity, Your Face We See

Douglas C. Eschbach (b. 1960) wrote this text after a theology professor had commented that there were few good hymns available dealing with the Trinity. In it he portrays in rich imagery the work and relationships of the persons of the Trinity, while also affirming God's essential unity.

Douglas C. Eschbach was born on the Feast of the Epiphany, January 6, 1960, in Columbus, Ohio. He grew up in Dayton, Ohio, was ordained to the Lutheran ministry, and served churches in Telford and Quakertown, Pennsylvania, before moving to social ministry with senior citizens.

Arthur G. Clyde (b. 1940) composed this melody in 1988, at a time when he and the text's author, Douglas Eschbach, were working at nearby churches in Pennsylvania. They often met in Souderton to work on their collaboration. RELIANCE is a local place name.

Before joining the United Church Board for Homeland Ministries staff in 1991 as editor of *The New Century Hymnal*, Arthur G. Clyde worked as a church musician, conductor, and composer. His compositions include choral works, musicals, and an opera.

281 Come, Holy Spirit, Heavenly Dove

Isaac Watts (1674–1748) published this text in his 1707 collection, *Hymns and Spiritual Songs*. John Wesley objected to one stanza for overstressing human frailty and another because it referred to God in familiar terms. Those two stanzas do not appear in this rendition.

Isaac Watts learned Greek, Latin, French, and Hebrew early in his education and was offered a university education by a sponsor who agreed to pay his way. However, his ties with the Nonconformist movement prevented him from attending any of the universities, which were affiliated with the Church of England.

John Bacchus Dykes (1823–1876) wrote the tune ST. AGNES in 1866 for a different text. The name honors a Roman maiden who was executed in 304 C.E. at the age of thirteen for her Christian allegiances. Her feast day is celebrated on January 21.

John B. Dykes was born in Hull, England, in 1823. His father was a banker, and one of his grandfathers was an Evangelical clergyman. Dykes was ordained a priest in 1848 and served churches in Durham, England, including the city's cathedral and St. Oswald's.

282 Every Time I Feel the Spirit

This spiritual was written by a slave-poet unknown to us today. The first stanza of the text recalls Moses' experience on the mountaintop when he received the Ten Commandments, and the second stanza alludes to baptism in the Jordan River and the "heavenly train."

This is one of a group of African American spirituals that capture the power of the Spirit to strengthen and invigorate each individual. The theme may derive in part from African beliefs in spirit possession which were reinterpreted in a Christian context by the enslaved brought to North America.

This spiritual was sung for President Abraham Lincoln during the Civil War by a group under the direction of Aunt Mary Dines, a former White House employee. Their singing of this song brought tears to the president's eyes. Reports say that on one occasion the president even sang along during a concert.

Notice that each stanza in this tune has two lines, after which the refrain is sung again. The arrangement is one of eight contributed to *The New Century Hymnal* by Joyce Finch Johnson, a member of the hymnal committee.

283 Spirit of the Living God

Daniel Iverson (1890–1977) was inspired to write this hymn after hearing a sermon at the George T. Stephans evangelistic revival meeting held at Orlando, Florida, in 1926. After it was printed without his permission in *Revival Songs* (1929), it took years to restore his name as the author.

Daniel Iverson was born in Brunswick, Georgia, in 1890. Ordained as a Presbyterian minister, he served churches in Georgia, South Carolina, and North Carolina before founding Shenandoah Presbyterian Church in Miami, Florida. He served there from 1927 until his retirement in 1951.

Daniel Iverson (1890–1977) wrote this tune and text together in 1926, and it was used later that evening at a George T. Stephans revival meeting in Orlando, Florida. The song was taught to the congregation by rote, as was the practice at such meetings. It is named IVERSON here for the composer.

Daniel Iverson received his education at the University of Georgia in Athens; the Moody Bible Institute in Chicago, Illinois; Columbia Theological Seminary in Decatur, Georgia; and the University of South Carolina. He died in Asheville, North Carolina, twenty-six years after his retirement.

284 Joys Are Flowing like a River (Blessed Quietness)

Manie Payne Ferguson (b. 1850) wrote this text circa 1900 following a feeling of holiness or "entire sanctification," as it was called in her denomination, the Wesleyans. The text speaks of the transforming power of the Holy Spirit.

Manie P. Ferguson was born in Carlow, Ireland. She married a Wesleyan evangelist who worked on the west coast of England, and together they founded Peniel Missions, with branches in Egypt, China, and the United States. Ferguson lived in Los Angeles, California, in the early 1900s.

W. S. Marshall (dates unknown) provided this setting of Ferguson's text. It is called BLESSED QUIETNESS for the opening words of the refrain. The tune has been arranged in a variety of styles in the twentieth century and is effective when performed slowly with a swaying motion or in a more upbeat tempo.

This arrangement by J. Jefferson Cleveland (b. 1937) and Verolga Nix (b. 1933) appears in *Songs of Zion*, a collection of African American songs and arrangements that they edited in 1981.

285 O Holy Dove of God Descending

Bryan Jeffery Leech (b. 1931) wrote this text for *Hymns for the Family of God*, for which he was associate editor. This popular hymnal was published by Paragon in 1976. Leech won a hymnwriting contest in 1973 for an ecumenical hymn to be used with the "Key 73" evangelistic effort.

Bryan Jeffery Leech was born on May 14, 1931, at Buckhurst Hill, Essex, England. He moved to the United States in 1955 and became associated with the Evangelical Covenant denomination. Ordained in 1959, he served churches in Massachusetts, New Jersey, and California.

Bryan Jeffery Leech (b. 1931) created this tune, O HOLY DOVE, for the text he wrote in 1976. Leech had first called the tune LOIS for the wife of the editor of *Hymns for the Family of God*, the 1976 hymnal in which the words and music first appeared.

Bryan Jeffery Leech has written a musical play, *Ebenezer*, coauthored a novel, edited a church hymnal, and worked as a freelance writer and religious broadcaster. He has also written hymn texts and tunes that have been included in various contemporary hymnals.

286 Spirit, Spirit of Gentleness

James Keith Manley (b. 1940) felt the urging of the Holy Spirit to write this hymn after he had completed the rough draft of his Doctor of Ministry thesis. Manley added a fourth stanza at a later time. The hymn was first sung at Waiokeola Congregational Church in Honolulu, Hawaii.

James K. Manley was born in 1940 at Holyoke, Massachusetts, and received his education at Whittier College, Pacific School of Religion, and Claremont School of Theology, all in California. He was ordained to the ministry of the United Church of Christ in 1966.

James Keith Manley (b. 1940) wrote the tune SPIRIT for his text of 1978, and it appeared in his collection *After Eden* (1990) with an arrangement by Jim Strathdee. A new arrangement was created for *The New Century Hymnal*. Note that the refrain is to be sung over following each stanza.

James Manley served as pastor of Congregational United Church of Christ in San Marino, California, from 1978 to 1988 and then moved to Foothills United Church of Christ in Los Altos, California. This new congregation was gathered in 1960.

287 Come, Teach Us, Spirit of Our God

Shirley Erena Murray (b. 1931) wrote this text for a contest sponsored by an educational institution. Because of this, she used images of teaching and learning, reminding those who sing the hymn that learning is both the acquisition of facts and the creativity to use them.

Shirley Erena Murray has served as affairs coordinator for Amnesty International in New Zealand. Amnesty International is an organization that tracks civil rights abuses in the world's nations and seeks more-humane treatment for the poor, prisoners, and refugees.

Arthur G. Clyde (b. 1940) composed this tune in 1993 when Shirley Erena Murray's text was selected for inclusion in *The New Century Hymnal*. Clyde named the tune MURRAY in honor of the author. It was subsequently published in Murray's newest collection *Every Day in Your Spirit* (1996).

Arthur G. Clyde is a graduate of Muhlenberg College in Allentown, Pennsylvania, and studied further at Temple College of Music in Philadelphia. In addition, he studied conducting under Robert Page. Clyde was responsible for editing *The New Century Hymnal*.

288 Let It Breathe on Me

Magnolia Lewis-Butts (d. 1949) wrote this gospel hymn for the Metropolitan Community Gospel Church of Chicago, Illinois, where she worked as a secretary. It quickly became the regular sung response after the prayer of invocation at Metropolitan Church.

Magnolia Lewis-Butts was born in Kansas City, Missouri, but her exact date of birth is unknown. She taught bookkeeping in Kansas City and moved to Chicago, where she became a church secretary and private secretary to the church's minister of music. She died in Chicago, Illinois, in 1949.

Magnolia Lewis-Butts (d. 1949) wrote both the words and music for BREATHE ON ME. In the original song, stanza 1 serves as the chorus for the verses (stanzas 2 and 3 here). Lewis-Butts, in addition to her own writing and composing, arranged many African American spirituals and gospel songs for use by church choirs.

Magnolia Lewis-Butts was a founder of the National Convention of Gospel Choirs and Choruses, Inc., along with Thomas A. Dorsey ("the father of gospel music") and Theodore R. Frey. This group, founded in 1932, became the model for all other gospel-music conventions.

289 Come Forth, O Love Divine

Bianco da Siena (d. c. 1434) wrote these words as part of a sixty-line poem that began "Discendi, amor santi" in the people's Latin of the thirteenth century. The translation from the *People's Hymnal* (1867) is by Richard F. Littledale (1833–1890), an Anglican clergyman and scholar who published some fifty works.

Bianco da Siena joined a newly founded religious order of men in 1367 to follow the rule of Saint Augustine. He lived in Venice, Italy, and probably died there in 1434. His hymns were published four hundred years after his death in *Laudi Spirituali*, meaning "spiritual songs."

Ralph Vaughan Williams (1872–1958) wrote the tune DOWN AMPNEY in 1906 for *The English Hymnal*. The title refers to the composer's birthplace in Gloucestershire, England. It has been praised as "perhaps the most beautiful tune composed since OLD HUNDREDTH."

Ralph Vaughan Williams enlisted at age forty-one as an orderly in the Royal Army Medical Corps when World War I began and served the entire war. During World War II, he contributed greatly to relief projects and organized musical concerts for service personnel.

290 Spirit of God, Descend upon My Heart

George Croly (1780–1860) is believed to be the writer of these words, first printed in *Britannica* (1866), a hymnal for the Church of England. The hymn was inspired by Galatians 5:25: "If we live by the Spirit, let us also be guided by the Spirit."

George Croly, born in Dublin, Ireland, on August 17, 1780, moved to London, England, at the age of thirty. He became a successful conservative minister and author of dramas, novels, and historical and theological works. Croly died while walking down the street in Holborn, England, on November 24, 1860.

Frederick Cook Atkinson (1841–1897) composed this tune in 1870 for Henry F. Lyte's hymn "Abide with Me." Although first entitled HELLESPONT, it is more often called MORECAMBE for a bay in western England, not far from a church where Atkinson served as organist. It is widely sung with this text in the United States.

Frederick C. Atkinson was born in Norwich, England, on August 21, 1841, and served as assistant choirmaster and organist there prior to his studies at Cambridge. Atkinson returned to Norwich to serve at the cathedral there from 1881 to 1885. He died at East Dereham, England, in 1897 at age fifty-six.

291 O God the Creator

Elizabeth Bess Haile (b. 20th century) and Cecil Corbett (b. 20th century) wrote this text as the theme song for the 1977 Indian Youth Conference held in Tulsa, Oklahoma. It first appeared in *Indian Quest*, published by Charles Cook Theological School in 1977.

Elizabeth Haile and Cecil Corbett are both Native Americans. Haile lives on the Shinnecock reservation, Southampton, Long Island, New York, and Corbett served a number of Native American congregations before being named president of Charles Cook Theological School in Tempe, Arizona.

Joy F. Patterson (b. 1931) composed the tune KASTAAK in 1989 at the request of the *Presbyterian Hymnal* committee. KASTAAK is the Americanized form of Sofia Porter's birth name. Porter, a Native American born in Sitka, Alaska, was also a member of the Presbyterian hymnal committee.

Joy F. Patterson has written more than thirty hymns, giving credit to her maternal grandmother, Ella Blachly Andrews, who sat in the choir loft with her mother as she grew up during the Civil War. Patterson continues a long line of poets in her family.

292 Breathe on Me, Breath of God

Edwin Hatch (1835–1899) wrote only a few hymns, and this has been recognized as his best. The text was printed on a leaflet in 1878 entitled "Between Doubt and Prayer" but was not used in a hymnbook until eight years later, when it appeared in Henry Allon's *Congregational Psalmist Hymnal* (1886).

Edwin Hatch was born September 4, 1835, in Derby, England. He was a professor at Oxford University, and then at Trinity College in Toronto, Canada, for eight years. He subsequently returned to Oxford, where he served a parish and continued to teach until his death on November 10, 1889.

Robert Jackson (1842–1914) wrote the tune TRENTHAM in 1894 for a different hymn. Jackson succeeded his father as organist at St. Peter's Church, Oldham, Lancashire, England, where the two served in the same position for a total of ninety-four years.

Robert Jackson was a well-known English organist, teacher, and church-music composer. He studied at the Royal Academy of Music and was organist and choirmaster of St. Mark's Church in Grosvenor Square, London, England, for a time. In 1868, he returned to his birthplace of Oldham, Lancashire, and spent most of his career there.

293 Sweet, Sweet Spirit

Doris Mae Akers (b. 1922) wrote these opening words after her choir prayed before entering a worship service. The words of the prayer stayed with her throughout the day. On Monday, she wrote this gospel song, both words and music, to praise the goodness of the Holy Spirit.

Doris Akers, with no formal musical training, wrote her first gospel song at the age of ten. She has served as the choir director for the Sky Pilot Radio Church, one of the first racially mixed choirs in Los Angeles. This song and "Lead Me, Guide Me" are her two most popular compositions.

Doris Mae Akers (b. 1922) wrote this musical setting for her own text, and the tune name reflects the opening phrase, SWEET, SWEET SPIRIT. This hymn, created in 1962, has become one of the most popular gospel songs of the "golden age of gospel" (1930–1969) and appears in numerous hymnals.

Doris Akers was born in Brookfield, Missouri, on May 21, 1922, one of ten children. She moved to California and joined the Sallie Martin Singers of the Martin and Morris Music Studio. This studio published her first songs. Akers has composed over three hundred gospel songs.

294 There's a Spirit in the Air

Brian Arthur Wren (b. 1936) wrote this text for use on Pentecost Sunday at Hockley Church, England, where he was serving as pastor. In a recent collection, *Faith Renewed* (1995), Wren explains that he "aimed for simple language, suitable for all ages."

Brian Wren was born on June 3, 1936, at Romford, Essex, England, and was educated at New College and Mansfield College, both of Oxford University in England. He was ordained to the Congregational Church ministry in 1965 and served two churches before turning to full-time work writing hymns.

This medieval French melody is called ORIENTIS PARTIBUS, which means "from the Eastern regions." It was sung during the Middle Ages for a church festival that commemorated the holy family's escape to Egypt. During the festival, a young woman rides a donkey through town.

This harmonization of ORIENTIS PARTIBUS is from Richard Redhead's *Church Hymn Tunes, Ancient and Modern* (1853). Another tune that is often paired with this text in contemporary hymnals is LAUDS, by John W. Wilson (1905–1992).

295 I Sing a Song of the Saints of God

Lesbia Scott (1898–1986) wrote this hymn for her own three children; like all her texts, it was never intended to be published. It was meant to be used on saints' days as a reminder that sainthood is a possibility even in the context of our daily lives.

Lesbia Scott was born in London and educated at Raven's Croft School in Sussex, England. She took a great interest in amateur theatrical productions and wrote a number of religious dramas. She was married to John Mortimer Scott, a British naval officer.

John Henry Hopkins (1861–1945) named this tune GRAND ISLE for a town in Vermont on Lake Champlain, where he lived in retirement from 1929 until his death in 1945. Hopkins wrote the tune for this text in *The Episcopal Hymnal* (1940) and was a member of the committee for that hymnal.

John Henry Hopkins, son of a clergyman and grandson of the second Episcopal bishop of Vermont, was ordained in 1891 and served several churches in the Midwest. He became rector of the Church of the Redeemer in Chicago, Illinois, before returning to Vermont, where he died in 1945.

296 Behold the Host All Robed in Light

Hans Adolf Brorson (1694–1764) wrote seventy hymns, including this one, at the age of seventy—the last year of his life. His son published those hymns the year after his death in *Svane-Sang*. This hymn was popularized in the United States by the St. Olaf College Choir.

Hans A. Brorson, known as one of Denmark's greatest hymnwriters, began writing hymns to provide native-language texts for the Tonder parish in Denmark, which previously had sung only German hymns. He was pastor there from 1729 until 1737 and later rose to bishop of Ribe, Denmark, where died on June 3, 1764.

This anonymous Norwegian folk tune is called DEN STORE HVIDE FLOK, which means "behold a host" or "great white host." Of nineteen tunes used with this text in Denmark, this one has found acceptance in the United States. The tune has been traced to a folk song from Heddal, Denmark.

Edvard Grieg (1843–1907) used folk tunes of his native Norway in many compositions. This arrangement is from his Opus 30, no. 10, for four-part male chorus with baritone solo. Grieg was conductor of the Bergen Harmonic Society and established the Norwegian Academy of Music.

297 Give Thanks for Life

Shirley Erena Murray (b. 1931) wrote this hymn in 1986 as a funeral meditation and included it a year later in her collection *In Every Corner Sing* (1987). The text celebrates a full life well lived and ends with an "Alleluia," usually found only in hymns of exuberant celebration.

Shirley Erena Murray is well known in her native New Zealand as a hymnwriter, and her reputation is spreading around the world. Her work was first introduced to North American churches in *The Presbyterian Hymnal*, (1990), and it has been gaining in popularity since that time.

Nancy M. René (b. 1942) dedicated this tune, ROBINSON, to her grandmother, Georgia Ann Robinson, who, in 1915, became the first African American woman hired by a police force. Her career with the Los Angeles Police Department ended when she was blinded in the line of duty in 1928, but she continued her social ministry helping women.

Nancy M. René was born in Los Angeles, California, on June 29, 1942. She received her bachelor's degree at U.C.L.A., sang with the Roger Wagner Chorale, and taught in the Los Angeles Unified School District. A member of the Church of Christian Fellowship (UCC), she is principal of Dorsey High School.

298 O Savior, for the Saints

Richard Mant (1776–1848) included this hymn and several other original texts in *Ancient Hymns from the Roman Breviary, for Domestic Use*, compiled in 1837. At that time, Mant was serving as bishop of Killaloe, Kilfenoragh, Down, and Conner, Ireland.

Richard Mant, the son of a Church of England rector, was also ordained to that church's ministry in 1803. He traveled as a lecturer before beginning his career as a parish priest. Mant wrote several volumes of sacred poetry, *The Book of Psalms in an English Metrical Version* (1824), and the *History of the Church in Ireland*.

William Henry Walter (1825–1893) composed FESTAL SONG, which was first printed in *The Hymnal with Tunes Old and New* (1872) as the setting for "Awake and Sing the Song." John Ireland Tucker was the editor of that volume.

William Walter, born in Newark, New Jersey, began playing the organ for church services in his youth. After completing his education, he moved to New York City, where, over a period of twenty-five years, he was organist for four different Manhattan churches.

299 For All the Saints

William Walsham How (1823–1897) wrote this hymn in eleven stanzas, which was published in the 1864 collection *Hymns for Saints' Days and Other Hymns by a Layman*. The "layman" referred to in the title was Earl Nelson, a relative of England's famous Admiral Nelson.

William W. How was born December 13, 1823, in Shrewsbury, England, and rose in the Church of England to be suffragan bishop of Bedford, East London. A plain, unassuming man, he often turned down appointments to more-prestigious positions without even consulting his family.

Ralph Vaughan Williams (1872–1958) composed this tune for *The English Hymnal* (1906) as an alternative to SARUM, with which this text had been associated for many years. The title, SINE NOMINE (or "without a name"), may refer to the saints whose names are known only to God.

Ralph Vaughan Williams's name became connected with religious music when he was asked to help edit *The English Hymnal* (1906). This work had a great influence on the standards of music in churches in England and the United States. The hymnal remained in use for over sixty years.

300 Jesus Shall Reign

Isaac Watts (1674–1748) paraphrased the second half of Psalm 72 as the basis for this hymn. It is a classic example of Watts's practice of adding Christian concepts to psalm texts, yielding a new form of congregational song. As was the practice in his time, only the psalms were sung during worship.

Isaac Watts was known as the "father of modern hymnody." The ill health he suffered because of intensive periods of study in his early years gave him more time to write some six hundred hymns. This text appeared in his *Psalms of David, Imitated in the Language of the New Testament* (1719).

John Hatton (c. 1710–1793) was first credited as the composer of this tune in Dixon's *Euphonia* (1805). It had been published anonymously in 1793 with a text called "Addison's 19th Psalm." Here the tune is named DUKE STREET, which is where Hatton lived in St. Helen's, England.

John Hatton's life is mostly a mystery to hymnologists. He was born in Warrington, England, and is believed to have died when accidentally thrown from a stagecoach. Hatton's funeral was December 13, 1793, at the Presbyterian Chapel at St. Helen's, a township in Windle, England.

301 Crown with Your Richest Crowns

Matthew Bridges (1800–1894) in 1851 wrote the text that is the foundation for this hymn based on Revelation 19:12. Godfrey Thring (1823–1903) wrote an adaptation of Bridges's text, which appeared in *Hymns and Sacred Lyrics* (1874). Hymnal editors combined the two versions in the early 1900s.

Matthew Bridges was trained as an Anglican priest and wrote against the Roman Catholic Church. However, influenced by John Henry Newman and the Oxford movement, he later converted to Catholicism. He died in Quebec, Canada. Godfrey Thring served as an Anglican priest his entire career.

George Job Elvey (1816–1893) composed this tune for Matthew Bridges's text seventeen years after it was written. He gave it the Greek name for "crown," DIADEMATA. It was included in the Appendix to the original edition of *Hymns Ancient and Modern* (1868).

George Job Elvey (1816–1893) was knighted by Queen Victoria in 1871 for his contributions to church music. Born in Canterbury, England, he was a skilled organist by age seventeen and was appointed organist to St. George's Chapel, Windsor, England, at age nineteen. Elvey held the post for forty-seven years.

302 Eternal Christ, You Rule

Daniel Charles Damon (b. 1955) was inspired to write this text after hearing a sermon delivered by Ansley Coe Throckmorton for the Earl Lectures at the Pacific School of Religion. To the question, "How does Christ rule?" she answered, "By keeping company with pain." That phrase became the opening line of the hymn.

Dan Damon worked in his father's bicycle repair shop in Rapid City, South Dakota. This training was put to good use when he became a bicycle delivery messenger in downtown San Francisco, California, during a time when musical work was difficult to find.

Daniel Charles Damon (b. 1955) honored the preacher who inspired this hymn by naming the tune THROCKMORTON. Ansley Coe Throckmorton was general secretary of the UCBHM Division of Education and Publication and the key staff person responsible for the production of *The New Century Hymnal*.

Dan Damon supported himself for many years playing piano in the theater district of San Francisco, California, and in some of the city's great hotels. Now a United Methodist minister, Damon is one of the few hymnwriters who create both words and music.

303 Rejoice, Give Thanks and Sing

Charles Wesley (1707–1788) published this hymn in his 1746 collection, *Hymns for Our Lord's Resurrection*. The text includes references to numerous scriptural passages as well as the "Great Thanksgiving" from the Eucharist, cited as the end of stanzas 1, 2, and 3.

Charles Wesley wrote primarily positive and uplifting hymns, usually expressing his own strong faith. The author of some 6,500 hymns, he was ten times more prolific than Isaac Watts, who was also one of the greatest hymnwriters of the English language.

John Darwall (1731–1789) composed this tune for a 1773 recital celebrating the installation of a new organ at the church in England where he had recently begun his ministry as the new vicar. It is known as DARWALL'S 148TH because it was used as a setting for a paraphrase of Psalm 148.

John Darwall was a clergyman, poet, and amateur musician. In 1761, he began his work at St. Matthew's Parish Church in Walsall, Staffordshire, England, where he remained for the rest of his life. Darwall composed tunes for each of the 150 psalms in the *New Version* (1696).

304 All Hail the Power of Jesus' Name

Edward Perronet (1726–1792) published the first stanza of this hymn in *Gospel Magazine* (1779) and the other seven the next year. Three of these stanzas are presented here. The fourth was added by John Rippon, a Baptist minister from London, in his *Selection of Hymns* (1787).

Edward Perronet's family came to England in 1680 as Huguenot refugees from Switzerland and became acquainted with the Wesleys. When John Wesley once asked Edward to preach, he felt inadequate to the task and instead read Jesus' Sermon on the Mount aloud.

Oliver Holden (1765–1844) composed CORONATION for Edward Perronet's text in 1793, and it appeared in *The Union Harmony*. It is the only eighteenth-century American hymn tune still in general use. The small pipe organ on which Holden composed it is in the Old State House museum in Boston, Massachusetts.

Oliver Holden became a successful businessman in real estate and construction. He helped to rebuild Charlestown, Massachusetts, after the British burned it in the battle of Bunker Hill during the Revolutionary War. Holden generously used his own money to build churches and publish music.

305 You Servants of God, Your Sovereign Proclaim

Charles Wesley (1707–1788) wrote this hymn as encouragement to Methodists, who were being persecuted for their beliefs in England. He published the hymn in a 1744 collection entitled *Hymns for Times of Trouble and Persecution*, and it has become a favorite in many denominations.

Charles Wesley and his brother John published fifty-six hymnbooks and hymn tracts in a period of fifty-three years. Charles was one of the most widely sung authors in the English language, writing over 6,500 hymns in his lifetime.

William Croft (1678–1727) has long been credited as the composer of HANOVER, which appeared anonymously in *A Supplement to the New Version* (1708). His authorship, however, has never been proven. The tune has a longevity of use unsurpassed in hymn singing—appearing in nearly every major hymnal published since 1750.

William Croft was organist of the Chapel Royal in England, working with Jeremiah Clarke and succeeding him on his death. Croft had been trained by John Blow, whom he followed as organist at Westminster Abbey when Blow retired in 1708. Croft was one of England's greatest musicians.

306 The Church of Christ, in Every Age

Fred Pratt Green (b. 1903) wrote this text in six stanzas, entitled "The Caring Church," at the request of the committee compiling *Hymns and Songs* (1969), a British Methodist collection. The author subsequently altered it for the *Lutheran Book of Worship* (1978), and it has been widely used since.

Fred Pratt Green, the leader of the twentieth-century "hymn explosion" in England, has enjoyed many opportunities to contribute hymns for special occasions. His ability to translate a local church experience to a wider audience has made his hymns modern statements of the work of the Christian church.

William Knapp (1698–1768) composed this tune, named WAREHAM for his birthplace in England although it was called ALL SAINTS in early sources. It was first published in Knapp's *Set of New Psalm Tunes and Anthems in Four Parts* (1738) as a setting for Psalm 36:8–10. The original version of the tune was more florid.

William Knapp was known during his lifetime as an eccentric. He served as clerk at St. James Church in Poole, England, for thirty-nine years and was buried there after his death in 1768. This tune is the only one of his compositions to endure. It is believed that Knapp was of German descent.

307 Glorious Things of You Are Spoken

John Newton (1725–1807) based this text on Psalm 87:3, "Glorious things are spoken of you, O City of God," as well as other passages from the Hebrew Scriptures. It was first published in *Olney Hymns* (1779) and has been judged by many to be Newton's finest hymn.

John Newton was born in London, England, on July 24, 1725, and at an early age he went to sea with his father. He disliked the discipline of the navy and ended up selling slaves. Converted to Christianity, he became a priest in the Church of England. Newton died December 21, 1807, in London, England.

Franz Joseph Haydn (1732–1809) composed AUSTRIAN HYMN as the setting for a newly commissioned Austrian national hymn by the poet Lorenz Leopold Hauschka. It was first sung on the emperor's birthday, February 12, 1797, at the National Theater in Vienna. It may contain portions of a Croatian folk song.

Franz Joseph Haydn was born in Rohrau, Austria, near the Hungarian border, on March 31, 1732. After struggling early in his life, his genius was recognized, and he served as court composer for Prince Esterhazy of Hungary for thirty years. Haydn died in Vienna, Austria, on May 31, 1809.

308 At the Font We Start Our Journey

Jeffery Rowthorn (b. 1934) wrote this hymn as a gift to St. John's Episcopal Church of Waterbury, Connecticut. Rowthorn visited the congregation on April 7, 1991, to help them rededicate their church organ, which had been damaged by a tornado in 1989.

Jeffery Rowthorn was ordained to the Episcopal priesthood in 1963 and, after serving two parishes in England, was appointed dean of instruction and chaplain at Union Theological Seminary, New York City. From 1973 to 1987, he served as chapel minister and professor at Yale University Divinity School.

Henry Purcell (1659–1695) composed this melody around 1680 for an anthem. It was later adapted as a hymn tune and named WESTMINSTER ABBEY to honor the London church where Purcell was organist from 1679 until his death in 1695. The tune was used at the 1960 wedding service of England's Princess Margaret.

Henry Purcell was the greatest English composer of the seventeenth century and perhaps of all time. He began composing music at the age of eight and wrote operas, stage works, and chamber music, in addition to a variety of church music.

309 We Are Your People

Brian Arthur Wren (b. 1936) wrote this text for the 1973 hymnal of the United Reformed Church of England and Wales, *New Church Praise*. As revised by the author in 1993, the text is in the form of a corporate prayer to the Holy Spirit by the church, which is Christ's body.

Brian Wren was ordained a minister of the Congregational Church of Britain and Wales in 1965. This denomination later merged with others to become the United Reformed Church in Great Britain. Since 1983, Wren has devoted himself to a "freelance" ministry, which is realized through writing hymns and leading workshops.

John Whitridge Wilson (1905–1992) composed the tune WHITFIELD in 1975 and named it in memory of his wife, Mary Whitfield, whose father chaired the Congregational Union of England and Wales. The hymn was premiered in 1977 at Westminster Abbey, where Wilson founded an annual hymn festival, "Come and Sing."

John Wilson studied mathematics and physics but chose a career in music instead. A respected scholar and teacher, he served on the editorial committees of eight hymnals. Wilson was also treasurer of the Hymn Society of Great Britain and Ireland.

310 It's the Old Ship of Zion

Researchers have found that this spiritual has roots in both the African American spiritual tradition and the white shape-note songbooks of the singing schools of the South. This common heritage may come from an English seafaring song heard during long ocean voyages.

This text may have developed from "occupational singing," in which work was made to pass more quickly when accompanied by song. The ship imagery may indicate occupations such as loading and unloading ships at various harbors and river ports.

This tune, OLD SHIP OF ZION, is named for the text, which may have had a double meaning. One reference may have been the passage from earthly life to eternal life, with Jesus as captain; the other may have been a code calling escapees for the trip to freedom via escape routes using water travel.

The tune for this hymn is similar to that for "Old Time Religion," and the two are often interchanged or even intermixed. George Pullen Jackson wrote that he heard the tune sung at camp meetings of both African slaves and whites in the rural southern United States.

311 Renew Your Church

Kenneth L. Cober (b. 1902) wrote this text in 1960 for year two of a Baptist Jubilee Advance five-year program to encourage evangelism in the local church. At the time, Cober was traveling around the United States doing denominational work for the American Baptist Church.

Kenneth L. Cober served as executive director of the Division of Christian Education of the American Baptist Church from 1953 to 1970. Before taking on this position, he had been pastor at Baptist churches in Canandaigua and Buffalo, New York.

This old English melody takes its name, ALL IS WELL, from the concluding part of the text that it originally accompanied. This same tune was used for a famous Mormon hymn, "Come, Come Ye Saints," which was written during the Mormons' thousand-mile journey to Utah.

Some doubt that this tune, ALL IS WELL, is English and instead claim it may have originated in the United States. It was found in *Songs of Zion*, published in 1842 in Boston, Massachusetts, attributed to C. Dingley, and began with the words "What's this that steals upon my frame."

312 We Love Your Realm, O God

Timothy Dwight (1752–1817) based this text on Psalm 137:5, 6. He supplied thirty-three metrical versions of psalms that Isaac Watts had not versified in his famous psalter and published them in 1801 along with other texts. This version is an adaptation made by Lavon Bayler in 1992.

Timothy Dwight, a grandson of Jonathan Edwards, assumed the presidency of Yale University in 1795. A Congregational minister, he prepared a revision of Watts's *Psalms of David* for the Presbyterian Church, adding thirty-three of his own hymns; the revision came to be known as "Dwight's Watts." This hymn is a paraphrase of Psalm 137 from that volume.

Aaron Williams (1731–1776) either composed this tune or included it from an anonymous source in his 1763 edition of *The Universal Psalmist*. It was later abridged to this form and named ST. THOMAS in his subsequent collection of 1770, *New Universal Psalmist*.

Aaron Williams was born and died in London, England. In his lifetime, he published a number of books of music for use in singing the psalms, the only acceptable texts for use in worship during his lifetime. In addition, he worked as a teacher and music engraver.

313 Like a Tree beside the Waters

James F. D. Martin (b. 1953) wrote this text and a tune he named CAMPBELLSPORT for a church anniversary. The pastor had been requested to provide a text based on Jeremiah 17. It was first sung on the opening Sunday of the church's celebration in January and then throughout the year of 1993.

James F. D. Martin, a minister of the United Church of Christ, received his theological education at United Theological Seminary of the Twin Cities, Minnesota. After serving at two other churches, he joined his wife as copastor of Saron UCC in Sheboygan Falls, Wisconsin, in 1983.

Roy Hopp (b. 1951) composed this tune on December 18, 1989, while visiting the SILVER CREEK resort in the Colorado mountains and so named the tune for that area. It first appeared in *The Roy Hopp Hymnary* (1990) as the setting for Michael Perry's "God Whose Love We Cannot Measure."

Roy Hopp received his undergraduate education at Calvin College, in Grand Rapids, Michigan, a master's degree in choral conducting at Michigan State University, and a master's degree in church music composition at Concordia University in River Forest, Illinois.

314 Community of Christ

Shirley Erena Murray (b. 1931) wrote this text for use at the 1995 General Assembly meeting of the Presbyterian Church of New Zealand. The text lays out the work of the church, often referred to as the "body of Christ" but here termed the "Community of Christ."

Shirley Erena Murray once worked in the Labour Party Research Unit in the New Zealand Parliament. She has been actively involved in political matters during her career, including work with Amnesty International in New Zealand.

Meyer Lyon (1751–1797) was a London concert singer and cantor at various synagogues, including the one where Thomas Olivers heard him sing this Hebrew melody. Lyon transcribed the tune for Olivers around 1770, and it is named LEONI in his honor.

This Hebrew melody has been found in many places around the world, including the Spanish Basque region and Russia. It may have been carried by Jews during times of immigration to other lands. The tune LEONI was also used in Bedřich Smetana's 1874 orchestral piece, *Vltava*.

315 O Word of God Incarnate

William Walsham How (1823–1897) wrote this text, which was published in a supplement to an English Congregational hymnal in 1867, although How was an active Anglican pastor. He spent most of his ministry working with the downtrodden in depressed areas of East London, England.

William W. How was known as the "poor man's bishop" for spending his ministry with the dispossessed in East London. He turned down appointments as bishop at two other districts without even telling his family. These posts would have more than doubled his salary.

Felix Mendelssohn (1809–1847) borrowed this tune from a 1693 hymnbook used in Meiningen, Germany, and used it in his oratorio *Elijah*. The tune, known as MUNICH, is generally sung with William How's words in U.S. churches. This combination is not popular in England, however.

The *Neuvermehrtes Meiningisches Gesangbuch* of 1693 contained 647 hymns with 169 melodies, 22 of them new. As was the practice in earlier times, many hymns were sung to the same tune. The hymnbooks indicated the meter of the words so they could be matched with an appropriate tune.

316 We Limit Not the Truth of God

George Rawson (1807–1889) based this text on pastor John Robinson's farewell sermon to the Pilgrims as they left Leyden, Holland, for England and then for America on two ships, the *Speedwell* and the *Mayflower*. Only the *Mayflower* eventually made the voyage to America, in 1619 to 1620.

George Rawson was a lawyer in his hometown of Leeds, England, where he was born on June 5, 1807. Yet he contributed greatly as a layperson to the English Congregational Church. He even published three hymnals, including the *Leeds Hymn Book* of 1853, in which this text first appeared.

This traditional psalm tune was found in the 1556 Anglo-Genevan Psalter. First used with Psalm 16, it was more commonly associated with Psalm 22, the source of the name, OLD 22ND. In 1621, the tune was harmonized in four parts and used with Psalm 38 in Ravenscroft's Psalter.

The Anglo-Genevan Psalters of 1556, 1560, and 1561 were created to provide worship books for the English and Scottish refugees who escaped from Queen Mary's persecutions. They settled in Frankfurt-on-the-Main, Germany, and Geneva, Switzerland. With the accession of Elizabeth I, they were able to return home, bringing these books back to Great Britain with them.

317 Mikotoba o kudasai (Make a Gift of Your Holy Word)

Yasushige Imakoma (b. 1926) submitted this text for a new hymnal being compiled for the United Church of Christ in Japan in 1967. Paul Gregory, former East and Southeast Asia Secretary of the United Church Board for World Ministries, provided the new English translation in 1994.

Yasushige Imakoma was born March 10, 1926, in Tokyo, Japan, and, after completing his education in 1957, was ordained to the ministry of the United Church of Christ in Japan. He ministered in Japan until his retirement in 1989.

Shōzō Koyama (b. 1930) composed this tune, MIKOTOBA, in 1965 when a suitable setting was being sought for this text to be included in *Sambika* (*Hymns of Praise,* 1967). The name derives from the opening words of the text.

Shōzō Koyama was born in Nagano-ken, Japan, in 1930 and educated at Kunitachi College of Music, where he later served as professor. In 1965, Koyama was awarded the Westminster Choir College prize. He has published a number of books and musical compositions.

318 Almighty God, Your Word Is Cast

John Cawood (1775–1852) wrote this text in 1815 in the second year of his ministry as perpetual curate at St. Ann's Chapel of Ease, Bewdley, in Worcestershire, England. He remained at this post until his death on November 7, 1852, at age seventy-seven.

John Cawood was the son of poor farmers and received limited education as a child. However, he was hired by a Nottinghamshire, England, clergyman and was tutored by the Reverend Edward Spencer before attending St. Edmund Hall, Oxford University. He was ordained to the Anglican ministry in 1801.

This tune from John Day's *Whole Booke of Psalms* is called ST. FLAVIAN. In that tunebook, it was part of a longer melody set to Psalm 132. Revised by Richard Redhead in *Church Hymn Tunes* (1853), it was given the name ST. FLAVIAN in the 1875 revised edition of *Hymns Ancient and Modern*.

John Day (1522–1584) published *The Whole Booke of Psalms* (or English Psalter) in 1562. He was responsible for the first church-music book in English, *Certain Notes Set Forth in Four and Three Parts to Be Sung,* printed in 1560. Day's printed works were often illustrated with woodcuts.

319 Sing Them Over Again to Me (Wonderful Words of Life)

Philip Paul Bliss (1838–1876) wrote this Bible hymn, and it appeared in a Sunday-school paper published by Fleming H. Revell. The hymn became a favorite closing song at George Pentecost's revivals, when sung by George C. Stebbins.

Philip P. Bliss, born in Clearfield County, Pennsylvania, was raised in extreme poverty. Although he lacked musical training, he became a fine musician and at age twenty-six was hired by the Root and Cady Music Company of Chicago, Illinois. He later was associated with Dwight L. Moody as a gospel song leader.

Philip Paul Bliss (1838–1876) composed both the words and the tune WORDS OF LIFE to create this gospel hymn. It appeared in the first issue of a Sunday-school paper of the same name, published in 1874. Sung as a duet by Bliss and his wife during an evangelistic campaign in Connecticut, the hymn immediately became popular.

Philip P. Bliss met Dwight L. Moody in Chicago, Illinois, in 1869 and became his song leader and a gospel hymnwriter. He was killed at age thirty-eight when a train bridge near Ashtabula, Ohio, collapsed. Bliss survived the sixty-foot drop but died trying to rescue his wife from the fire.

320 Deep in the Shadows of the Past

Brian Arthur Wren (b. 1936) developed the idea for this text after reading James Barr's *The Bible in the Modern World*. It respects a variety of perspectives on the authority and inspiration of Holy Scripture and is one of few modern texts to deal with this topic.

Brian Wren first wrote this text in 1973 and revised it more than twenty years later in 1994 for his collection *Faith Renewed* (1996). In that source (with regard to I AM WHAT I WILL BE), Wren refers the reader to Exodus 3:13–15, in which "the Hebrew denotes an incomplete action."

Annabeth McClelland Gay (b. 1925) composed this music as the setting for an original Christmas song in 1952. As she sat at the piano composing one evening, this tune "dropped out of the blue." Its name was born when her husband said it sounded like "SHEPHERDS' PIPES."

Annabeth McClelland Gay met her husband, a United Church of Christ minister, while both were studying at Union Theological Seminary in New York City. She earned a master's degree in sacred music from this institution and has served various churches as choir director, with her husband serving as pastor.

321 Break Now the Bread of Life

Mary Artemisia Lathbury (1841–1913) was asked to write this "study hymn" by John H. Vincent, one of the founders of the Chautauqua, New York, Literary and Scientific Circle. The hymn prayer has been a standard part of the Chautauqua Institution's Sunday evening vespers services for over a century.

Mary A. Lathbury was born on August 10, 1841, in Manchester, New York. She was a leader in the Chautauqua movement, becoming the unofficial poet laureate of that group. An active Methodist layperson and artist, she was at one time the editor of the Methodist Sunday School Union publications.

William Fiske Sherwin (1826–1888) wrote the tune BREAD OF LIFE for this text in 1877, and they have been together ever since. Sherwin, a Baptist, was music director of the Chautauqua Methodist Assembly in the summer of 1877.

William F. Sherwin was considered a "genial tyrant" as a choral conductor. One newspaper writer described him as one "who would scold his chorus until they cried and then heal all their hearts with his 'Day Is Dying in the West.'" Sherwin studied with Lowell Mason and was on the faculty at the New England Conservatory of Music, in Boston.

322 Take Me to the Water

This African American spiritual may have been a "marching song," sung as a congregation moved from their worship site, whether in the woods, a schoolhouse, barn, or small church, to the nearest river, where immersion baptisms were performed. New words most likely were improvised during the walk to the river.

A baptism was an occasion of great joy in early African American communities, as it was a sign of the conversion and salvation of another soul and the continuing of their religious traditions. Baptisms were generally not performed with infants, except in some Episcopal and Roman Catholic congregations.

This African American spiritual is not frequently found in U.S. denominational hymnals. Its appearance in *The New Century Hymnal* provides a choral or congregational song appropriate for adult baptisms.

Jeffrey Radford (b. 1953), arranger of this African American spiritual, has served on the faculty of the Gospel Music Workshop of America, which was founded by the late James Cleveland in 1968. Radford is music director at Trinity United Church of Christ in Chicago, Illinois.

323 Little Children, Welcome

Fred Pratt Green (b. 1903) wrote this baptism text in 1973. The opening words can be adapted to "Little sister" or "Little brother," for example, as the specific occasion warrants. The hymn might be sung in two parts—as the family comes forward and as they leave the baptismal area.

Fred Pratt Green was born in a suburb of Liverpool, England, and educated in English schools. He was ordained to the Wesleyan Methodist ministry in 1928 and served various congregations throughout England in his twenty-two year career as a parish pastor. He retired in 1969.

Roy Hopp (b. 1951) wrote this simple tune on April 21, 1988, so that even the youngest of singers could participate. It was composed for Fred Pratt Green's text and named SAIPAN in honor of Hopp's nephew, who had recently been born on that island near Guam and west of the Philippines.

Roy Hopp, a member of the Christian Reformed Church, serves that denomination through the work of the Board of Publications. Hopp is also director of music at Woodlawn Christian Reformed Church of Grand Rapids, Michigan.

324 Baptized into Your Name Most Holy

Johann Jakob Rambach (1694–1735) wrote this baptism text, and it was published in 1734—a year before he died of a fever. Rambach had just become director of the Paedogogium at Giessen, Germany, after moving there to serve as the first professor of theology and superintendent of that institution.

Johann J. Rambach was the son of a cabinetmaker and first studied medicine. His interest soon turned to theology, however, and he joined the faculty of the University of Halle, Germany, after completing his education there. Rambach was a prolific scholar and also wrote some 180 hymns.

This tune is named from the opening line of the German text O DASS ICH TAUSEND ZUNGEN HÄTTE, with which it was once paired. Many believe that Johann König, the editor of *Harmonischer Liederschatz*, composed the tune but failed to give himself credit in his 1738 hymnal.

Johann Balthasar König (1691–1758) published the *Harmonischer Liederschatz* (1738), which contained nearly two thousand tunes and was among the largest and most influential collections of the eighteenth century. König was both a church organist in Frankfurt, Germany, and the city music director.

325 Child of Blessing, Child of Promise

Ronald Stephen Cole-Turner (b. 1948) used this text written in 1981 for the 1982 baptism of his daughter, Rachel Elizabeth. It first appeared in the hymn supplement *Everflowing Streams*, published by the Pilgrim Press in 1980, and has since been included in numerous denominational hymnals.

Ronald S. Cole-Turner was born in Logansport, Indiana, three days before Christmas, 1948. Ordained to the United Church of Christ ministry in 1974, Cole-Turner has been a professor of theology at Memphis Theological Seminary in Tennessee and at Pittsburgh Theological Seminary in Pennsylvania.

Christian Friedrich Witt (1660–1716) is believed to have composed this tune, named STUTTGART for the German city. It was found in *Psalmodia sacra* (1716), which included 774 chorales and 356 melodies—over 100 of them new and most likely composed by Witt.

Christian Friedrich Witt was born and died in Altenburg (Gotha), Germany. He began his musical studies with his father, a court organist in that city, and later trained with Georg Kaspar Wecker in Nuremberg. In 1686, he became organist at the Gotha court and in 1713 was appointed *kapellmeister*.

326 Crashing Waters at Creation

Sylvia G. Dunstan (1955–1993) wrote this text to accompany a prayer for blessing of the water in the baptismal rite of the United Church of Canada. She undertook this task as part of her work as an editor of liturgies on baptism and renewal of baptism for her denomination.

Sylvia G. Dunstan was raised by her grandparents, whose religious roots were Methodist and Salvation Army. She was ordained in the United Church of Canada in 1980 and served a two-point charge in Alma-Albert, New Brunswick. Later, she became chaplain at an Ontario maximum-security prison.

Christian Friedrich Witt (1660–1716) compiled an important German hymnal, *Psalmodia sacra*, in 1716. This volume contained a large number of church tunes. In addition, there were one hundred new tunes, most of them likely composed by Witt himself.

Christian F. Witt was born in Altenburg, Germany, where his father was the court organist. Following training by his father and others, he became organist at the court of Gotha, Germany, in 1686. He continued there until his death in 1716.

327 Jesus Loves Me

Anna Bartlett Warner (1820–1915) collaborated with her sister Susan to write these simple words, which are often the first religious song children learn. The text appeared in an 1860 novel entitled *Say and Seal*, also written by Susan, and the words and music were published in *Golden Shower* (1862).

Anna B. Warner lived with her sister at Good Crag on Constitution Island in the Hudson River, near West Point, New York. They conducted Sunday-school classes for the cadets for many years. Warner died at age ninety-five and was accorded military honors. Her home is now a national shrine.

William Batchelder Bradbury (1816–1868), "the father of Sunday-school music," composed this melody. It is named JESUS LOVES ME here but called CHINA in other hymnals because missionaries reported that it was a favorite of Chinese children. Bradbury wrote the tune for Warner's text and added the refrain.

William B. Bradbury, a native of York, Maine, served as organist for churches in Boston, Massachusetts, Brooklyn, and New York City and composed many lively tunes that were easy to sing. Bradbury, with his brother, established a family business known as the Bradbury Piano Company in 1854.

328 Wonder of Wonders, Here Revealed

Jane Parker Huber (b.1926) wrote this text in 1980 for use during baptisms. She had realized how few hymns there were for use during the sacraments in Reformed churches, and she dedicated herself to filling the need. This hymn, in stanza 4, stresses the worldwide bond of baptism.

Jane Parker married William A. Huber, a Presbyterian minister, in 1947. He served as pastor of St. Andrew Presbyterian Church in Indianapolis, Indiana, for thirty-three years. She also served that congregation as an elder, choir member, and editor of the church's newsletter, *The Channel*.

William Boyd (1847–1928) composed PENTECOST in 1864 as a setting for "Come, Holy Ghost, Our Souls Inspire" at the request of Sabine Baring-Gould for a Pentecost service he had organized for coal miners in Yorkshire, England. The tune incorporates Boyd's wife's first name, "Pen."

William Boyd was born in Montego Bay, Jamaica, but received his education in England under the influence of Sabine Baring-Gould and E. Power Biggs. Boyd was ordained a priest in the Anglican Church and served for twenty-seven years as vicar at All Saints, Norfolk Square, London, England.

329 Jesus, the Joy of Loving Hearts

Bernard of Clairvaux (1090–1153) has previously been credited with the long Latin poem from which this hymn was taken, beginning "Jesu dulcis memoria," but his authorship is dubious. The oldest manuscript, dating from the twelfth century, may be seen in the Bodleian Library at Oxford University.

Ray Palmer (1808–1887) selected and translated cantos from a twelfth-century Latin poem, and the resulting hymn was published in *The Sabbath Hymn Book* (1859). A graduate of Yale University, Palmer served Congregational churches in Maine and New York and later was corresponding secretary of the American Congregational Union.

Henry Williams Baker (1821–1877) composed the tune HESPERUS (also known as QUEBEC, among other names) in 1854 when he was a student at Oxford University. His tune was submitted anonymously to the London *Penny Post* in 1861 when the newspaper was searching for a tune to accompany "Sun of My Soul."

Henry W. Baker served only one church in his career, at Monkland, near Leominster, England. He was ordained into the Anglican Church in 1844 after completing his education at Trinity College, Cambridge. Baker wrote hymn texts and translations in addition to musical settings.

330 Let Us Break Bread Together

This spiritual developed its communion emphasis after the Civil War. Some believe it attests to the attendance of African Americans at liturgical services of the Roman Catholic or Episcopal Church, in which the Eucharist was celebrated. Traditionally, Anglican churches were situated so that early morning communion was received facing east, "into the sun."

Other traditional stanzas for this spiritual include those that begin "Let us all pray together" and "Let us face the cross together." The petition for mercy in the final line may echo the words of persons in Scripture who sought and received healing by Jesus.

This melody, by an unknown composer, is named LET US BREAK BREAD for the text. The melody has a relatively broad range compared to other songs of this genre (an eleventh). It first appeared in John W. and Frederick J. Work's *Folk Songs of the American Negro* (1907) and has become part of the standard repertoire of most mainline hymnals.

David Hurd (b. 1950) prepared this harmonization for *The Hymnal 1982* of the Protestant Episcopal Church. Hurd, an active organist and composer, was a member of the Standing Commission on Church Music of that denomination from 1976 to 1985.

331 Come, My Way, My Truth, My Life

George Herbert (1593–1633) wrote this highly crafted poem, entitled "The Call," shortly before his death in 1633. It was included in a collection of his work, *The Temple*, published the following year by a friend. Rich in biblical allusions, each stanza elaborates on the metaphors presented in the opening phrases.

George Herbert served as an Anglican priest in England but is now better known as a poet. His work was largely ignored after his death until it was rediscovered by John Wesley, who often used Herbert's texts in his own hymnals.

Ralph Vaughan Williams (1872–1958), one of England's greatest modern composers, wrote this musical setting of Herbert's poem in 1911 as the fourth of five mystical songs for baritone, chorus, and orchestra. The song was adapted into a unison hymn version for *Hymnal for Colleges and Schools* (1956) and assigned the poem's original title, THE CALL, as a tune name.

Ralph Vaughan Williams was educated at the Royal College of Music and Trinity College, Cambridge. He studied with Max Bruch in Berlin, Germany, and with Maurice Ravel in Paris, France. His compositions include six symphonies, string fantasias, ballets, operas, music for film, and choral works.

332 As We Gather at Your Table

Carl Pickens Daw Jr. (b. 1944) wrote this text in 1989 for the tercentenary celebration of Eastern Shore Chapel (Episcopal) in Virginia Beach. In stanza 2, Daw utilized references to postcommunion prayers of the Eucharist. Stanza 3 reflects on the parable of the banquet.

Carl P. Daw Jr. was a member of the Standing Commission on Church Music for *The Hymnal 1982* of the Episcopal Church when he was inspired to begin writing hymns. Soon, Daw began to receive commissions to write hymns for particular occasions, such as this one.

Benjamin Franklin White (1800–1879) may have written or adapted this tune, BEACH SPRING. It was first found in a tunebook called *The Sacred Harp* (1844), which White edited with Elisha James King. This book contained tunes collected from the southern United States.

B. F. White was the youngest of fourteen children and had fourteen children of his own. A self-taught musician, he traveled the southern United States as a singing-school teacher. He and his brother-in-law William Walker, editor of *Southern Harmony*, collected hymns together.

333 O Bread of Life

Timothy Tingfang Lew (1892–1947) wrote this text, "Jiu shi zhe shen," in his native Chinese, incorporating both Christian and Buddhist imagery. It was subsequently included in *Hymns of Universal Praise* (1936) and was used by Chinese Christians imprisoned in Japanese prison camps before and during World War II.

Timothy Tingfang Lew was a leading Chinese educator and author. He studied in China and the United States, represented China at three sessions of the World Council of Churches, and chaired the commission that prepared *Hymns of Universal Praise* (1936), the Chinese Union hymnbook.

Su Yin-Lan (1915–1937) composed this distinctively Chinese tune based on a pentatonic scale, SHENG EN, in 1934. The tune has been presented in a variety of arrangements in United States hymnals; this one is by Darryl Nixon from *Songs for a Gospel People* (1987), a Canadian hymnal supplement.

Su Yin-Lan was born in Tientsin, China, and earned a music degree at Yenching University. She died at the age of twenty-two immediately after of giving birth to her son as the advancing Japanese army was bombing the city. The sound of the bombs literally frightened her to death.

334 Graced with Garments of Great Gladness

Johann Franck (1618–1677) wrote this German text around 1649, and it has been sung at Holy Communion services in Germany for over three hundred years. The text was translated into English many times. This translation is adapted from one by Catherine Winkworth, in her *Chorale Book for England* (1863).

Johann Franck was a Lutheran layperson who was active in politics in his native Güben, Germany. His hymns are extremely subjective in nature and introduced a mysticism that was previously unknown in Lutheran and Reformed hymnbooks. He died in 1677 in his birthplace, Güben.

Johann Crüger (1598–1662) composed this melody in 1649 for this text by Johann Franck, and the two have been paired together ever since appearing in Crüger's *Geistliche Kirchen Melodien*. The tune is named SCHMÜCKE DICH after the opening words of Franck's German text.

Johann Crüger was one of the most creative musical talents of the seventeenth century. However, the adversities of the Thirty Years' War sapped much of his strength, keeping him from composing any music during that time. Nonetheless, his output includes five major collections of hymns.

335 Come, Gather in This Special Place

Philip A. Porter (b. 1953) began this text with the idea of a table large enough to seat everyone who wished to commune. He wrote the hymn to fill a need for more communion texts, and it was first sung at Peace United Church of Christ in Oakland, California, where Porter worshiped for seven years.

Phil Porter was born in Bloomington, Indiana, on March 16, 1953, and attended the Methodist Church there. For over twenty years he has been interpreting theology through the arts. In 1977 he joined First Congregational Church (UCC) in Berkeley, California, where he is artist-in-residence.

Elaine Kirkland (b. 1946) composed the tune GATHER in 1991 for this text by Phil Porter. The hymn was introduced to the wider church at a Northern California conference women's retreat, where Kirkland was serving as music director. She met Porter at a United Church of Christ Fellowship and the Arts event in 1977.

Elaine Kirkland was born in Charleston, South Carolina, the daughter of a Methodist minister. In addition to music degrees, she earned a master of divinity degree at Pacific School of Religion in Berkeley, California. She is a teacher, conductor, composer, and organist, and leads music workshops.

336 Here, O My Lord, I See You Face to Face

Horatius Bonar (1808–1889) wrote this communion text at the request of his older brother, who was also a Scottish minister. It was first read after communion at the author's church in October, 1855. Originally, the hymn had ten stanzas and was published in *Hymns of Faith and Hope* (1857).

Horatius Bonar, known as the "prince of Scottish hymnwriters," wrote many of his hymns hurriedly, often for children and often while riding on trains. He seldom revised the hymns further, and therefore many of them seem unpolished. Several, like this one, have endured.

Frederick Cook Atkinson (1841–1897) composed this tune for another hymn, "Abide with Me," with which it appeared in *Congregational Church Hymnal* (1887). It was named MORECAMBE for a bay in western England. The bay was not far from Bradford, England, where Atkinson served as a church organist.

Frederick C. Atkinson served as organist and choirmaster at churches in Bradford, Norwich, and Lewisham, England, after receiving his bachelor of music degree from Cambridge University. In addition, he composed a number of piano pieces, songs, and church anthems. Atkinson died in 1897.

337 Draw Us in the Spirit's Tether

Percy Dearmer (1867–1936) wrote these stanzas to supplement another postcommunion text and included them in *Songs of Praise Enlarged* (1931), which he edited. Dearmer's stanzas now stand on their own and provide a fitting hymn for Holy Communion, especially in the contemporary setting by Harold Friedell.

Percy Dearmer was educated at Christ Church, Oxford, England, receiving his bachelor of arts degree in 1892 and his master of arts degree in 1896. He was ordained as a deacon in the Anglican Church in 1891 and as a priest in 1892. During his career, he edited many important hymnals.

Harold W. Friedell (1905–1958) composed a choral setting for Dearmer's text in 1957. Ten years later, Jet E. Turner extracted a portion and adapted it as a hymn tune. The title, UNION SEMINARY, refers to the theological school in New York City where Friedell taught and Turner was a student.

Harold W. Friedell was born in Jamaica, New York, in 1905 and served most of his career as organist in New York City churches. A fellow of the American Guild of Organists, he also taught at the Guilmant Organ School, Juilliard School of Music, and Union Theological Seminary School of Sacred Music.

338 Una Espiga (Sheaves of Summer)

Cesáreo Gabaráin (1936–1991) wrote this communion hymn to remind Christians of their unity expressed around the table. It was first published in *Alabemos al Señor* (1976) by Seminario Regional de Veracruz.

George F. Lockwood IV (b. 1946) provided this English translation of "Una Espiga" and eight other Spanish hymns for *The United Methodist Hymnal* (1989). Lockwood, a Methodist minister, became interested in Hispanic music after serving as a missionary to Costa Rica and attending a church-music workshop there.

Cesáreo Gabaráin (1936–1991) composed this tune to accompany his own words. It is called UNA ESPIGA (which means "sheaves of summer") after the opening words of the text. The tune sings much like a "dance tune," and is reminiscent of the folk dances of Gabaráin's native Spain.

Skinner Chávez-Melo (1944–1992) provided the accompaniment for this communion song by Cesáreo Gabaráin, a Spanish church musician and composer. Chávez-Melo was editor of *Albricias* (1987), in which the arrangement first appeared, and served as chair of the National Hispanic Music Committee of the Protestant Episcopal Church.

339 Adoro te devote (Truth Whom We Adore)

Thomas Aquinas (c. 1225–1274) used simple and straightforward language for this Latin text. It may have been written around 1260 when he was preparing the office and mass for the festival of Corpus Christi. Its earliest use was as a poem of devotion rather than as a hymn to be sung.

Thomas Aquinas was the son of Landulph, Count of Aquino, and a nephew of Emperor Frederick I. Thomas's decision to join the Dominican order so displeased his mother that she had him imprisoned for two years. He was released only when the pope influenced Emperor Frederick to do so.

This plainsong melody found in a 1697 Paris, France, tunebook, *Processionale*, is called ADORO TE DEVOTE after the opening words of the Latin text. The new translation and harmonization provided here enable modern worshipers to experience this mystical and meditative hymn of earlier centuries.

The ancient plainsong melodies were "modernized" in the sixteenth and seventeenth centuries in France as part of an effort to update the breviaries. Many of these reworked tunes were introduced to English churches by La Feillée's *Méthode de plain-chant*, published in 1750, 1782, and 1808.

340 Somos pueblo que camina (We Are People on a Journey)

This hymn is the "canto de entrada," or entrance song, for the *Misa Popular Nicaragüense* (or "popular mass"). The text of the mass focuses on the theme of "people marching on," one that is particularly evident in the opening line of this song.

The *Misa Popular Nicaragüense* was created in response to the reforms of the Second Vatican Council, providing an authentic reflection of the faith experience of the local Nicaraguan community in which it was created.

This tune, entitled SOMOS PUEBLO here, was written to accompany the opening song in the *Misa Popular Nicaragüense*, a contemporary setting of the Roman Catholic mass in Nicaragua. It was well received, and its popularity spread to other Latin American nations and churches.

The music for *Misa Popular Nicaragüense* was composed by Manuelito Dávila, Angel Cerpas, and Juan Mendoza. The composers incorporated Nicaraguan folk rhythms in the settings of various components of the mass.

341 Great Spirit God

Joseph R. Renville's (1779–1846) Dakota hymn was translated in 1993 by Sidney Byrd (b. 1918), a Presbyterian minister and member of the Dakota tribe. Byrd and others have testified to the significance of this song as a legacy of the faith demonstrated by the thirty-eight Dakota prisoners executed in 1862.

Immediately following the Dakota uprising of 1862, more than three hundred Indians were sentenced to death by a white military court at Mankato. After reviewing their records and impressed by the appeals of missionaries, President Lincoln released all but thirty-eight. As the condemned men marched to their execution on December 26, they sang this hymn of praise to God, which many mistakenly thought to be a death chant.

This hymn tune from the Dakota nation is called LACQUIPARLE, a Dakota phrase that means "lake that speaks." The name also refers to the mission on the banks of the Mississippi River that operated a church and school from 1835 to 1854 and taught the Dakota people weaving and modern agricultural methods.

James R. Murray's harmonization of this Native American tune is from the 1879 edition of *Dakota odowan*, the hymnbook published by the Dakota Mission of the American Missionary Association and the Presbyterian Board of Foreign Missions.

342 Be Known to Us in Breaking Bread

James Montgomery (1771–1854) recalled the revelation of the resurrected Christ to travelers on the road to Emmaus in this hymn text, first published in his *Christian Psalmist* (1825). There it was entitled "The Family Table," suggesting its use for grace before meals.

James Montgomery, the son of Moravian missionary parents, was one of the greatest and most prolific of English hymnwriters. Although he made his living as a journalist, he published more than four hundred hymns in various volumes during his lifetime.

This anonymous tune is called ST. FLAVIAN here, although it was previously known as REDHEAD NO. 29 or OLD 132ND. There was a Saint Flavian, the bishop of Constantinople, who died in 499 C.E. This tune was first set to Psalm 132 in Day's Psalter of 1562.

Day's Psalter of 1562 was the first to contain the entire Book of Psalms in English meter. Although the work was done by Sternhold and Hopkins, the psalter is named for John Day, who printed it. As a young man, Day moved to London, England, where he learned the printing trade.

343 Jesus Took the Bread

Ruth C. Duck (b. 1947) completed a summer study on liturgy at the University of Notre Dame in South Bend, Indiana, in 1980. This hymn grew out of her reflections on the actions involved in giving and receiving Holy Communion during that time. It was first sung at New Hope United Church of Christ in Milwaukee, Wisconsin.

Ruth Duck's first collection of original texts was *Dancing in the Universe* (1993), in which this hymn appeared. A second collection, *Circles of Care*, is due for publication by the Pilgrim Press in 1998. It will contain forty-six new texts set to music, many on themes of healing and reconciliation.

Ruth C. Duck (b. 1947) composed this melody to accompany her own words, written in 1982. Duck has become well known for innovative and enlightened texts, but few are aware that she also has musical gifts. The tune, NEW HOPE, is named for the church in Wisconsin where it was first sung.

Randall Sensmeier (b. 1948) provided the arrangement for Ruth Duck's original tune in her collection of new hymns, *Dancing in the Universe* (1992). Sensmeier is an associate editor for G.I.A. Publications in Chicago, Illinois, and serves as cantor for Ascension Lutheran Church in Riverside, Illinois.

344 The Time Was Early Evening

The Iona Community created this text to be sung during "house communion" in the dining room of Iona Abbey during an "Experiencing Easter" retreat. The hymn was part of a service seeking to recreate the secular location of the supper rather than using the community's chapel.

Iona is an ecumenical Christian community founded in 1938 by the Very Reverend George MacLeod. Committed to finding new ways of living the gospel in the modern world, MacLeod was inspired to create this community while working in the poorest areas of Glasgow, Scotland, during the Great Depression.

This traditional Scottish melody is named AFTON WATER. John Bell (b. 1949), as a child, heard his parents sing this folk tune to accompany a poem by Robert Burns, "Flow Gently Sweet Afton." The Iona Community often uses folk tunes because of their memorable and easy-to-sing melodies.

John Knox founded of the Church of Scotland, also known as the Presbyterian Church, during the time of the Protestant Reformation. Although this is the official church of Scotland, people are free to worship as they choose. About one million of the nation's five million people are Presbyterians.

345 Let All Mortal Flesh Keep Silence

This ancient Greek hymn is known as the "Prayer of the Cherubic Hymn" from the liturgy of St. James and was sung while carrying the bread and wine to the communion table. The liturgy is commonly ascribed to Saint James the Less, the first Bishop of Jerusalem.

Gerald Moultrie (1829–1885), an Anglican priest, contributed this translation of the Greek liturgical prayer to the second edition of *Lyra Eucharistica* (1864). Moultrie also translated Latin and German hymns and wrote some original hymn texts.

This traditional French carol is named PICARDY for one of the oldest provinces in northern France. The tune has been traced to a seventeenth-century carol, "Jesus Christ s'habille en pauvre," which paraphrases the story of the rich man and Lazarus. Its first use in an English hymnal was in 1906.

Ralph Vaughan Williams (1872–1958) harmonized this French melody for *The English Hymnal* (1906) to form a lasting association with this text. Gustav Holst's anthem setting of the hymn has further contributed to its popularity among British and North American churches.

346 Bread of the World, in Mercy Broken

Reginald Heber (1783–1826) intended this text to be sung before the sacrament, as its title suggests. It was not made public until the year after his death in 1826, when his hymns were collected and published as *Hymns Written and Adapted to the Weekly Church Service of the Year*.

Reginald Heber was appointed bishop of Calcutta, India, but refused the call until 1822. He brought great energy to his new job, ordaining the first native Indian to the Christian ministry. But the demands of long hours and travel took their toll, and Heber died on a visit to Trichnopoly in 1826.

John Sebastian Bach Hodges (1830–1915) composed the tune EUCHARISTIC HYMN for Reginald Heber's text. The name was given to this tune by the hymnal editor of *Book of Common Praise* (1869). Other hymnals call the tune PANIS, Latin for "bread" or "loaf of bread."

John S. B. Hodges was born in England and immigrated to the United States when he was fifteen years old. As an Episcopal priest, he served churches in Pennsylvania, Illinois, and New Jersey, finally serving thirty-five years at St. Paul's in Baltimore, Maryland, where he reinstituted the men and boy's choir.

347 Let Us Talents and Tongues Employ

Frederik Herman Kaan (b. 1929) wrote this text in 1975 to fit this music. Doreen Potter had heard this Jamaican folk melody and envisioned the possibility of using it as a hymn tune. The combination was first sung together at the World Council of Churches Assembly in Nairobi, Africa, in 1975.

Fred Kaan was born in Haarlem, Holland, on July 27, 1929, and endured as a youth the Nazi occupation of his native country. His father was a member of the Dutch Resistance; his family hid a Jew and a political prisoner in their home; and three of his grandparents starved to death during this time.

Doreen Potter adapted this Jamaican folk song, now called LINSTEAD. Singers should remember that the refrain is repeated after each verse, the first time being sung softly and the second time loudly. The tune uses syncopation by altering quarter and eighth notes and moves at a brisk tempo.

The music of the Caribbean islands is not often associated with hymn tunes. Yet the religious heritage of these islands is rich, having been influenced by the Europeans of various nations who claimed these islands and settled them and by individuals who worked there as slaves.

348 Jesus Is Here Right Now

Leon C. Roberts wrote this text and musical setting in 1986. At the time, he was choir director of Sts. Paul and Augustine Parish of Washington, D.C. His "Mass of St. Augustine" celebrated the first African American parish in the city, founded by freed slaves with the help of President Abraham Lincoln.

Leon C. Roberts was born in Coatsville, Pennsylvania, and studied music at West Chester State College, Pennsylvania, and at Howard University, Washington, D.C. He converted to Catholicism and has been a leader in blending the African American gospel form with Catholic liturgy.

Leon C. Roberts composed this tune in 1986, and it is named JESUS IS HERE after the opening words of the text. His gospel compositions have been widely used in Roman Catholic liturgies in African American congregations. This was written as a sung response during the communion portion of the mass.

Leon C. Roberts has published over 125 gospel songs and two complete theater pieces for stage and television. In addition, he leads a professional group of singers known as "Roberts' Revival" and has conducted a wide variety of gospel choirs.

349 I Come with Joy

Brian Arthur Wren (b. 1936) wrote this hymn in 1968, one of his earliest, for the congregation he was serving at Hockley, England. It served as a summary of a series of sermons on the meaning of communion. The author suggests that the hymn be sung in three parts, for gathering, sharing, and departing.

Brian Wren was ordained to the Congregational ministry in England in 1965 and served at Hockley and Hawkwell, Essex, England from 1965 to 1970. He had discovered his interest in hymnwriting while a student at Mansfield College in Oxford, England, and now makes it a primary focus of his ministry.

DOVE OF PEACE is the name of this tune, first found in *Southern Harmony*, an 1835 tunebook. There it was set to words that began "O tell me where the Dove has flown," a hymn about the search for inner peace. Austin C. Lovelace (b. 1919) arranged the tune for this text in *Ecumenical Praise* (1977).

Austin C. Lovelace is an organist, teacher, and composer who has held positions of leadership in the National Fellowship of Methodist Musicians, the Hymn Society in the United States and Canada, and the Choristers Guild. His book, *The Anatomy of Hymnody* (1965), is regarded as a classic text for students in this field.

350 Now in the Days of Youth

Walter John Mathams (1853–1932) wrote this hymn for use at Christian Endeavor meetings at the English church he served. It was brought to North America in the 1913 Sunday-school hymnal *Worship and Song*. Sylvia Dunstan adapted Mathams's words to reflect the challenges youth face at the dawn of the twenty-first century.

Walter J. Mathams began his pastoral ministry as an English Baptist but joined the Church of Scotland in 1905. Many of his hymns and poems were directed toward youth. In his early years, he had run away to sea, been shipwrecked, and later impressed into the Brazilian army.

George Job Elvey (1816–1893) composed this tune for the hymn "Crown Him with Many Crowns," and it is known by the Greek name for crown, DIADEMATA. The tune was first published in the Appendix to *Hymns Ancient and Modern* (1868) and has been used with a variety of texts ever since.

George J. Elvey was knighted by Queen Victoria of England in 1871 for his contributions to English music. He composed music for many state occasions in addition to many anthems, service music, and oratorios for the church. Elvey's lasting fame, however, rests with his hymn tunes.

351 I Was There to Hear Your Borning Cry

John Ylvisaker (b. 1937) wrote this text, his best known, in 1985. It was the signature song of his collection of five hundred hymns and songs, *Borning Cry* (1992). The text is written in the first person as though the singer is the voice of God speaking to confirmands.

John Ylvisaker was born September 17, 1937. He soon moved with his family to Morehead, Minnesota, where his father, a Lutheran pastor, had accepted a position on the Concordia College faculty. His father died when John was only nine, and his mother supported the family as the college librarian.

John Ylvisaker (b. 1937) wrote both the words and the tune, BORNING CRY, for this popular song, which is beginning to appear in denominational hymnals and larger supplements such as *With One Voice*, where the tune bears the name WATERLIFE.

John Ylvisaker is able to play most musical instruments. He is especially versatile on keyboard instruments but also plays flute and guitar regularly. During his workshops throughout the United States, he also performs on historic instruments and African drums.

352 My God, Accept My Heart This Day

Matthew Bridges (1800–1894) wrote this text in 1848, the year he left the Anglican Church to follow John Henry Newman into the Roman Catholic Church. It appeared in Bridges's *Hymns of the Heart* under the title "Confirmation." The text reflects the motto of John Calvin of the Reformed Church: "My heart I offer as a sacrifice devoted to God."

Matthew Bridges was born July 4, 1800, in Essex, England, and was raised in the Anglican Church. He published works critical of the Roman Catholic Church, only to be converted to Catholicism by the influence of the Oxford movement.

William Jones (1726–1800) first published this tune, with the title ST. STEPHEN, on the last page of a 1789 collection, where it was set with a paraphrase of Psalm 23 by Thomas Sternhold. He later made a few harmonic changes and called it NAYLAND for the community where he worked.

William Jones was a prolific writer as well as an Anglican clergyman. He became known as "Jones of Nayland" after being appointed the perpetual curate of Nayland, Suffolk, England, in 1777. Jones was the author of a dozen volumes, including *A Treatise on the Art of Music* (1784).

353 Great Work Has God Begun in You

Carol Birkland (b. 1946) wrote this text to express to confirmands the love and support they might expect from God, who is present in their lives both at the confirmation of their faith and throughout their faith journeys. Trained as a Christian educator, Birkland has spent many years as a confirmation teacher.

Carol Birkland incorporated in this text three Bible verses that have been significant to her. Colossians 2:6 was written on the inside cover of her first Bible. The references to Philippians 1:6 and Ephesians 5:1 are passages she has used in her teachings to reinforce the idea that all are called to respond to God's call to discipleship.

William Patrick Rowan (b. 1951) wrote the tune VERBUM DEI (Latin for "Word of God"), and it was first published in his 1993 collection of original tunes, *Together Met, Together Bound*. Rowan serves as a liturgical consultant for the Roman Catholic diocese of Lansing, Michigan.

William Rowan was born in San Diego, California, on November 30, 1951. He has composed more than thirty-five hymn tunes, organ works, and anthems that are in current use. Rowan's hymn tunes have been sung at music festivals throughout Europe, Great Britain, and the United States.

354 God, When I Came into This Life

Frederik Herman Kaan (b. 1929) wrote this text in 1979. This confirmation hymn is a reminder that God's claim on our lives exists from our birth and that confirmation is our opportunity to publicly recognize this claim.

Fred Kaan received his undergraduate education at the University of Utrecht; the Western College of Bristol, England; and the University of Bristol. With a dissertation titled "Emerging Language in Hymnody," he received a Ph.D. degree from the Geneva Theological College in 1984.

This tune, possibly of British origin, can be traced to *The Christian Harp* (1832), a small collection of Appalachian folk tunes. It is called LAND OF REST because Annabel Morris Buchanan (1888–1983), who provided the harmony, recalled her grandmother singing "O land of rest, for thee I sigh" to this melody.

Annabel Morris Buchanan was born and received her early musical training in Texas. She continued her studies in piano, organ, and composition in New York, then returned to the South to teach music in Texas, Oklahoma, and Virginia. She was a highly regarded scholar of folk music in the United States.

355 God the Spirit, Guide and Guardian

Carl Pickens Daw Jr. (b. 1944) wrote this hymn for the consecration of Jeffery Rowthorn as bishop suffragan for the Episcopal diocese of Connecticut on September 19, 1987. The hymn is trinitarian in structure and opens with a petition to the Third Person because ordination prayers are traditionally addressed to the Spirit.

Carl P. Daw Jr. is a minister of the Episcopal Church. Inspired to try his hand at hymnwriting as a seminarian, Daw has become increasingly involved in the field of congregational song. He became executive director of the Hymn Society in the United States and Canada in 1997.

Rowland Hugh Prichard (1811–1887) wrote the tune HYFRYDOL in 1844 to provide more-fulfilling hymn tunes for use in Sunday schools. It was harmonized by Ralph Vaughan Williams for *The English Hymnal* (1906) and was the basis for one of his "Three Preludes on Welsh Hymn Tunes" (1920).

Rowland H. Prichard worked as a loom tender most of his life. At the age of sixty-nine, he was given a small promotion to assistant loom tender by the Welsh Flannel Manufacturing Company. Although undistinguished in his primary vocation, Prichard was successful as a hymn composer.

356 God, Who Summons through All Ages

Edith Sinclair Downing (b. 1922) wrote this text to fill a void in ordination hymns addressed to women in ministry. This text meets that need but is equally appropriate for any service at which people are commissioned for service to the church in Christ's name

Edith S. Downing was born in Aromas, California, to Scottish parents who had moved to North America in their twenties. Her father served as a American Baptist minister, but moved to the Presbyterian Church later on. Downing holds master's degrees in religious education and theology.

David Hurd (b. 1950) composed this tune in 1974 as a "generic tune," meaning he had no specific text or circumstance in mind for it. The tune is named JULION for John Julion Mann, a friend of the composer. The introduction serves as an interlude between each stanza and is mirrored by the final coda.

David Hurd, born in Brooklyn, New York, received his education at the High School of Music and Art of the Juilliard School, New York City; Oberlin (Ohio) College; and the University of North Carolina at Chapel Hill. In addition to composing, Hurd has spent much of his life teaching.

357 You Are Called to Tell the Story

Ruth C. Duck (b. 1947) wrote this text for the ordination of her longtime friend Elizabeth Caldwell. The service was conducted by the Chicago, Illinois, Presbytery in January 1991. Duck and Caldwell graduated together in 1969 from Southwestern at Memphis (now Rhodes) College, Tennessee.

Ruth Duck received her bachelor's degree at Southwestern University in Memphis, Tennessee, in 1969. The school is now Rhodes College. Having felt the call to the ordained ministry, she attended Chicago Theological Seminary and was awarded a master of divinity degree in 1973.

David Hurd (b. 1950) wrote this as a "generic tune" for use with any number of texts that match its 8.7.8.7.8.7. meter. It was first published in *The David Hurd Hymnary* (1983). It is named JULION in honor of Hurd's friend, John Julion Mann.

David Hurd is an internationally known concert organist as well as a composer. In 1977, he received first prize for playing and improvisation from the International Congress of Organists and in 1981 a diploma for improvisation from Siching International Organconcours.

358 God of the Prophets

Denis Wortman (1835–1922) wrote this poem in October 1884 on behalf of his class of 1860 for the centennial of the New Brunswick (New Jersey) Theological Seminary of the Reformed Church in America (Dutch Reformed). Wortman's original seven-stanza poem was titled "A Prayer for Young Ministers."

Denis Wortman, a leader of the Dutch Reformed Church in America, was born in Hopewell, New York, on April 30, 1835. After serving four parishes, he became head of his denomination's Ministerial Relief Fund and, in 1901, president of General Synod. Wortman died on August 28, 1922.

This anonymous tune is named TOULON, after the French city. The original melody was the setting for Psalm 124 in the 1551 Genevan Psalter and was later abridged to fit other texts. A nearly identical version, called MONTAGUE, appeared in *The National Psalmist* (1848), edited by Lowell Mason and George Webb.

The Genevan Psalter of 1551 was developed at the insistence of John Calvin, the theologian of the Reformed Church movement. Calvin felt that nonbiblical words should not be used in singing, as to do so would cause errors and legends to creep into the church's theology.

359 O God, Who Teaches Us to Live

Thomas Merrell Hunter (b. 1946) created this hymn text to honor teachers, those in both Sunday schools and secular schools. After acknowledging God's role as teacher, the text offers "thanks and praise" for the contributions of all teachers and for those who participate in the learning process.

Tom Hunter was ordained as a United Church of Christ minister in 1972. His ministry is realized through sharing music with students in schools, following the model of "minstrels" of old. Hunter works from his home base in Bellingham, Washington.

William Croft (1678–1727) is believed to have written this tune, ST. ANNE, in 1708 while serving as organist at St. Anne's Church, Soho, London, England. Tradition holds that Anne was the mother of the virgin Mary, the mother of Jesus.

William Croft was one of the outstanding organists and composers of the eighteenth century. Early in his career he wrote music for the theater, but his true genius did not emerge until he began writing religious music. Croft composed the earliest examples of the English psalm tune, which have endured for nearly three centuries.

360 Thuma Mina (Send Me, Lord)

This prayer song from South Africa opens with a leader introducing the prayer and the congregation responding. A suggestion from the first published source of the song, *Freedom Is Coming*, is for the congregation to hum a stanza while a prayer is being read aloud. Improvisation is encouraged.

This African song was collected by Anders Nyberg of the Church of Sweden mission and published in *Freedom Is Coming; Songs of Protest and Praise from South Africa* (1984). Nyberg made this music available to the United States after it received an enthusiastic response in his native Sweden.

This South African traditional song is called THUMA MINA after the opening words. It was originally sung in the language of Nguni, spoken by the Zulu and Xhosa people. According to Anders Nyberg, this music "demands" movement, either a rocking motion or a small step from side to side.

South African freedom songs come from an oral tradition that had never been formally recorded until 1980. Anders Nyberg, a Swedish missionary, collected some examples of these songs and published them, first in Sweden and four years later in the United States.

361 Your Love, O God, Has Called Us Here

Russell Schulz-Widmar (b. 1944) wrote this text in 1981 for *The Hymnal 1982*, for which he chaired the music committee. Schulz-Widmar intended that the hymn be used not only for weddings but for marriage-renewal services and services with a family emphasis.

Russell Schulz-Widmar has published over one hundred compositions in addition to teaching in Episcopal and Presbyterian seminaries and serving as director of music in a local church. He was president of the Hymn Society in the United States and Canada from 1988 to 1990.

This tune is known as both GERMANY and GARDINER. William Gardiner, a tunebook editor, in his 1838 memoirs attributed the tune to Beethoven but could not specify which work. Some believe it was from Beethoven's Piano Trio, op. 70, no. 2. Others recognize melodic fragments from Mozart's *The Magic Flute* in it.

William Gardiner (1770–1853) published *Sacred Melodies* in 1815. In this collection, he adapted many classical eighteenth-century melodies as hymn tunes. Gardiner is largely responsible for introducing the works of Mozart, Haydn, and Beethoven to England.

362 When Love Is Found

Brian Arthur Wren (b. 1936) wrote this text for two weddings that he was unable to attend in 1978, specifically for the English folk melody presented here. Wren preferred the tune for its short lines, which lend themselves to the text's "simplicity and directness."

Brian Wren wrote many hymns during his "early period," from 1968 to 1978. They were subsequently published in his first collection, *Faith Looking Forward* (1983), many with tunes by Peter Cutts. Wren later revised a number of those texts and published them in a new collection, *Faith Renewed* (1995).

Cecil Sharp (1859–1924) called this anonymous tune O WALY WALY in his five-volume collection of traditional English melodies, *Folk Songs from Somerset, Series 3* (1906). The tune has become very popular for use at weddings in England and Australia.

Cecil Sharp (1859–1924) collected nearly five thousand English folk tunes. His work renewed the nation's interest in its musical heritage and inspired English composers such as Ralph Vaughan Williams to further research this important area of musical history.

363 O God of Love

William Vaughan Jenkins (1868–1920) wrote this text for his own wedding. However, it was not published until nine years later in *The Fellowship Book* (1909). The hymn is in the form of a prayer and can be sung appropriately as a response to the prayers of the marriage liturgy.

William Vaughan Jenkins was born in Bristol, England, in 1868. An accountant by trade, he was a leader in the National Adult School movement in England and encouraged the establishment of schools in many churches. He died at Bitton, Somerset, in 1920.

This anonymous English folk tune collected by Cecil Sharp (1859–1924) is called O WALY WALY. With a varied meter, it has been named GIFT OF LOVE in other hymnals. The new arrangement was composed by Jonathan McNair, assistant editor of *The New Century Hymnal*.

Cecil Sharp (1859–1924) lived in the United States during World War I and gathered American tunes of English origin. His work *English Folk Songs from the Southern Appalachians* was published after his death. He was also an authority on folk dance in England and the United States.

364 God, Today Bless This New Marriage

Marie J. Tuinstra Post (1919–1990) wrote this text in 1966 for her son's wedding. Post served on the revision committee of the *Psalter Hymnal* (1987) of the Dutch Reformed Church and was a respected poet. Her works were published in several church magazines and the *Grand Rapids* (Michigan) *Press*.

Marie J. Post was born on February 8, 1919, in Jenison, Michigan. She attended Calvin College and taught junior high school. A collection of her poetry called *I Had Never Visited an Artist Before* was published in 1977 and another, *Sandals, Sails, and Saints* (1993), was published posthumously. Post died on Ascension Day, May 24, 1990.

Richard Gillard (b. 1953) composed the tune SERVANT SONG for a text he had written in 1977, "Won't You Let Me Be Your Servant?" When the editors of *The New Century Hymnal* were looking for a suitable setting for Marie Post's wedding hymn, this melody seemed just the perfect fit.

Richard Gillard was born in Malmesbury, Wiltshire, England, but moved with his family to North Island, New Zealand, at age three. Gillard works in a warehouse that distributes plumbing goods and worships at the Brethren Assembly Church. He enjoys playing guitar, mandolin, and electric bass.

365 How Blessed Are They Who Trust in Christ

Fred Pratt Green (b. 1903) wrote this text of strength for the grieving by drawing on his forty years in the pastoral ministry. This was one of four new texts accepted by the Hymn Society of America in a 1980 contest for hymns on Christian living.

Fred Pratt Green became the leader of an "explosion" of new hymnwriting that began in England in the twentieth century. The author's extensive repertoire now includes more than three hundred hymns, published in three volumes.

Henry Percy Smith (1825–1898) wrote this tune in 1874 for John Keble's "Sun of My Soul" at the request of Arthur Sullivan, music editor for *Church Hymns with Tunes* (1874). It has proven to be Smith's most enduring hymn tune. MARYTON is the name of a farm or manor home.

H. Percy Smith was born in Malta but educated in England. Ordained by the Anglican Church, his ministry took him to three charges in England and one in Cannes, France. Finally, he was appointed canon of the cathedral of Gibraltar.

366 God of Our Life

Hugh Thompson Kerr (1872–1950) wrote this text for the fiftieth anniversary of Shadyside Presbyterian Church in Pittsburgh, Pennsylvania, where he was serving as pastor in 1916. The hymn recalls the past and then looks to the future, invoking God's leadership for the church.

Hugh T. Kerr was born in Canada in 1872. He was ordained to the Presbyterian ministry and served churches in Kansas and Illinois before moving to Shadyside Presbyterian Church in Pittsburgh, Pennsylvania. In 1930, he was elected moderator of the General Assembly of his denomination.

Charles Henry Purday (1799–1885) composed this tune in 1860 for John Henry Newman's "Lead, Kindly Light" and named it LANDON. The name was changed later by a hymnbook editor to SANDON. The change may have been a mistake or may refer to the name of an old English residence.

Charles H. Purday belonged to a music publishing family in London, England. A vocalist who sang at Queen Victoria's coronation, he lectured on musical subjects and advocated revision of copyright laws for musical works. Purday was one of the first to use program notes at concerts.

367 Christ the Victorious

Carl Pickens Daw Jr. (b. 1944) wrote this text for use at memorial services, incorporating biblical allusions and phrases from the Order for Burial in the Book of Common Prayer. Daw cites the "Christus Victor view of atonement" from a book by Gustav Allen as the source of the word "Victorious" in the opening line.

Carl P. Daw Jr. was an associate professor at the College of William and Mary for eight years following completion of his master's and doctoral degrees at the University of Virginia. In 1978, he left his teaching career to return to school to study for the Episcopal priesthood.

Alexis Feodorovich Lvov (1798–1870) composed RUSSIAN HYMN at the decree of Emperor Nicholas of Russia, who wanted a new national anthem. Lvov sought to compose something "majestic, powerful, full of sentiment and comprehensible to all." RUSSIAN HYMN was first performed in 1833.

Alexis F. Lvov was born in Reval, Estonia, and died near Kovno, Lithuania. After serving in the Russian army, he followed his father as director of the imperial court chapel at St. Petersburg. Lvov was a violin virtuoso and performed with a string quartet but retired from musical pursuits in 1867 because of deafness.

368 Sheltered by God's Loving Spirit

Deborah Lynn Patterson (b. 1956) wrote this text as a gift to Dorothy Weber for the funeral of her husband, who had died suddenly. Dorothy was herself dying of cancer at the time. Patterson used phrases from the UCC *Book of Worship* Memorial Service as the inspiration for her text.

Deborah Patterson grew up in Canada and was a member of Josephberg United Church of Christ in Alberta, one of only two UCC churches located in Canada as part of the Northern Plains conference. Ordained to the ministry in 1991, she is minister of religion and health at Deaconess Incarnate Word Health Systems in St. Louis, Missouri.

John Zundel (1815–1882) composed BEECHER for *Christian Heart Songs*, published in 1870. The tune name honors Zundel's friend Henry Ward Beecher, who was pastor at Plymouth Church in Brooklyn, New York, where Zundel served as organist at the time.

John Zundel was raised in Germany and worked there as a church organist and bandmaster. In 1847, he emigrated to the United States, where he served as an organist at various Brooklyn, New York, churches. After retiring, he returned to Germany, where he died in 1882.

369 Keep Your Lamps Trimmed and Burning

Many African American spirituals are based on themes from the Hebrew Scriptures. This one, however, is based on the New Testament parable of the bridesmaids, found in Matthew 25:1–13.

The text of this African American spiritual incorporates stanzas from another, better-known spiritual, "Jacob's Ladder," which add to the sense of anticipation and hope for future rewards in God's realm.

The tune for this spiritual is called KEEP YOUR LAMPS, and the new four-part harmonization was created especially for *The New Century Hymnal*. As the performance note indicates, other names and people may be substituted in the refrain.

This spiritual combines texts from two different songs, "Keep Your Lamps Trimmed and Burning" and "Jacob's Ladder." The tune is more often used with the first text than the second, but both fit well.

370 What Gift Can We Bring?

Jane Manton Marshall (b. 1924) wrote this text in three stanzas in 1980 for the twenty-fifth anniversary of Northaven United Methodist Church in Dallas, Texas, where she is a member. Two years later, Marshall adapted stanza 1 to create stanza 4, in reply to the questions the hymn raises.

Jane M. Marshall received an award in 1974 for distinguished service to church music from the Southern Baptist Church Music Conference. Marshall was the chairperson of the task force that prepared the 1982 *Supplement to the Book of Hymns* of the United Methodist Church.

Jane Manton Marshall (b. 1924) composed the tune ANNIVERSARY SONG for her own text, and the hymn was sung for the anniversary celebration of Northaven United Methodist Church in Dallas, Texas, in 1980. It was later included in a supplement to the *Book of Hymns* (1982).

Jane M. Marshall received her education at Southern Methodist University and later returned there to teach church music. A frequent contributor to church-music journals, she has published many anthems for church choirs.

371 God, Creation's Great Designer

Jane Parker Huber (b. 1926) in this text set out to expand on the idea of God as Creator by appropriating new titles or functions for God, such as architect, artisan, dreamer, builder, and refiner. She hoped her text would help worshipers acknowledge that the church is more than a building.

Jane Parker Huber received an honorary doctorate in humane letters from Hanover (Indiana) College in 1988, was named a "valiant woman" in 1991 by Church Women United at their Jubilee Celebration, and was named an honorary life member by Presbyterian Women in 1992.

J. T. Morrow (1911–1982) wrote this tune, called NEW REFORMATION, for use with a text by Roger K. Powell. It was first sung at an ecumenical conference. NEW REFORMATION is an invitation for the church to continue the task begun by the Protestant reformers in the sixteenth century.

J. T. Morrow (his actual name; the initials are not abbreviations) graduated from Trinity University in Texas and continued his education at McCormick Theological Seminary in Chicago, Illinois. His career was spent working with ecumenical groups related to the National Council of Churches.

372 God, You Have Set Us

Jane Parker Huber (b. 1926) was asked to provide a hymn to celebrate two events in the life of the Church of St. Andrew in Roswell, Georgia—the dedication of a remodeled sanctuary and the congregation's twenty-fifth anniversary. This text was her offering for those two occasions.

Jane Parker Huber has published a number of collections of inclusive-language hymns. These include *Fresh Words to Familiar Tunes* (1982) *and A Singing Faith* (1987), each of which offered seventy-three new hymn texts for congregational worship.

George William Warren (1828–1902) composed this tune for New York City's celebration of the centennial of the United States Constitution. It was first printed in the 1892 Protestant Episcopal *Hymnal* with "God of the Ages." The tune is called NATIONAL HYMN from its association with that text.

George W. Warren was born in Albany, New York. After completing his education, he served as organist at churches in Albany and later in New York City. No music was played at his funeral service in 1902 as a sign of respect for the deceased, the one who had directed the music at St. Thomas's Church.

373 They Did Not Build in Vain

Alan Luff (b. 1928) used various references from the Epistles and Acts of the Apostles as the basis for this hymn praising those who have taken part in planning and constructing new church congregations and buildings. This often unrecognized work is an important part of church growth and evangelism.

Alan Luff served as precentor of Westminster Abbey, London, England, from 1979 until 1992 and then was called as residentiary at Birmingham Cathedral, England. He also serves as the international consultant for the Hymn Society of Great Britain and Ireland. Luff was born at Bristol, England, in 1928.

This traditional Yigdal melody is called LEONI. Thomas Olivers was so taken with this Jewish tune when he first heard it sung by Cantor Meyer Lyon that he decided to adapt it for use in Christian worship. He stipulated that the tune should be called LEONI in honor of Lyon.

Meyer Lyon (1751–1797) was an opera singer in England, but his unwillingness to sing on Friday evenings or on Jewish religious festivals hampered his success as a performer. He became a cantor in Kingston, Jamaica, in 1787, serving at a new synagogue there until his death in 1797.

374 O God of All Your People Past

Thomas Hornblower Gill (1819–1906) wrote this text based on Psalm 90 on November 22, 1868. He recalled that day to be "almost the most delightful day in my life." The hymn, in seven stanzas, appeared in his *Golden Chain of Praise*.

Thomas H. Gill, an English Unitarian, became increasingly dissatisfied with his church in his later years and eventually turned to the Evangelical branch of the Anglican Church instead. A great admirer of the work of Isaac Watts, Gill wrote some two hundred hymns.

This tune, NUN FREUT EUCH, is known by the first line of Martin Luther's first congregational hymn, beginning with those German words. Although the melody bears some resemblance to a fifteenth-century secular folk song, many scholars credit Martin Luther as the composer.

Geistliche Lieder was a hymnal printed by Joseph Klug in Wittenberg, Germany, in 1535. Martin Luther edited the collection, which contained fifty-two hymns in musical settings, most reprinted from a 1529 version, plus two new ones contributed by Luther.

375 Christ Jesus, Please Be by Our Side

Wilhelm August II, Duke of Saxe-Weimar (1598–1662), is believed to have written this poem, although others doubt his authorship. This German hymn was intended for use before the sermon to help worshipers prepare their hearts and minds to be open to the word of God.

Wilhelm August II, a nobleman born on April 11, 1598, was wounded during the Thirty Years' War and taken prisoner. Following his release, he became a leader in the Weimar government and was one of the signers of the Peace of Prague in 1625. He died at Wiemar on May 17, 1662.

This tune is named HERR JESU CHRIST, DICH ZU UNS WEND for the first words of the German text with which it was sung in 1651. The tune had appeared earlier without a text in the *Pensum Sacrum* (1648).

Some researchers have traced the melody to John Huss, an early reformer. The *Pensum Sacrum* was a collection of Latin odes that was first published in 1648. Most of the material in this collection of eighty hymn tunes was written by Hauschkonius and others at the University of Prague, Czechoslovakia.

376 God, We Thank You for Our People

Ruth C. Duck (b. 1947) listened to the stories of the McSwain family before creating this text for use at their family reunion in 1986. She had the tune HOLY MANNA in mind when writing, as both McSwain and Duck trace their family histories to the southern United States, where the tune originated.

Ruth Duck is the author of two books about the language of Christian worship: *Gender and the Name of God: The Trinitarian Baptismal Formula* (1991) and *Finding Words for Worship* (1995). In addition, she has published books of worship resources and original hymn texts.

William Moore (19th century) is credited as the composer of this tune called HOLY MANNA. It was included in a collection Moore edited in 1825, *The Columbian Harmony*, as well as in a number of hymnals published in the southern United States during the period of Reconstruction.

William Moore was credited as the composer of eighteen tunes in *The Columbian Harmony*, a four-shape shape-note tune book that he published in 1825. Little is known about Moore's life or religious history except that he lived in Wilson County and the District of West Tennessee.

377 Forward through the Ages

Frederick Lucian Hosmer (1840–1929) wrote this hymn in 1908, the same year he delivered a major series of lectures on hymnody at Harvard Divinity School. The hymn was one of fifty-six of his own texts that were included in *The Thought of God in Hymns and Poems* (1918).

Frederick L. Hosmer not only wrote hymns, he was also a scholar of church hymnody and gave lectures on this subject at various seminaries. Hosmer was an ordained Unitarian minister and served churches across the United States until his death in Berkeley, California, in 1929.

Arthur Seymour Sullivan (1842–1900) composed the tune called ST. GERTRUDE in 1871 while visiting a friend named Gertrude Clay-Ker-Seymour in Dorsetshire, England. Sullivan had a habit of giving his friends the title "Saint" when used as the name for a hymn tune.

Arthur S. Sullivan, best remembered for his collaborations with W. S. Gilbert on light operas, is also recognized in the church for his many fine hymn tunes. Queen Victoria knighted Sullivan in 1883, and he received honorary doctorates from both Oxford University and Cambridge University.

378 Jerusalem, My Happy Home

This hymn is possibly based on the Latin *Liber Meditationum* (1553), which some have attributed to Saint Augustine. A person known only as F.B.P. created the metrical form of the text for a song of the late sixteenth century. An original manuscript of that twenty-six-stanza hymn is in the British Museum.

For centuries, the practice in hymnbooks was to omit references to the author or composer of hymns. Later, it became traditional to indicate the source by giving only the initials of the author's name, as with this hymn. Eventually, hymnbook editors began to credit authors and composers by name.

The original melody for this tune came from Scotland or North England. Named LAND OF REST, it was first found in *The Christian Harp* (1832), a hymnal from the Appalachian region of the southern United States. It was reintroduced to U.S. churches by Annabel Morris Buchanan in this harmonization.

The Christian Harp was a hymnal published in 1832. Annabel Morris Buchanan (1888–1983) adapted some of the tunes from it for her *Folk Hymns of America* (1938). Born in Groesbeck, Texas, Buchanan became a specialist in Anglo-American folk music and early U.S. hymnody.

379 Come, We Who Love God's Name

Isaac Watts (1674–1748) originally composed this hymn in ten stanzas; it appeared in his first collection of 1707 under the title "Heavenly Joy on Earth." John Wesley selected stanzas from two versions of Watts's text for his 1737 Charleston *Collection* and revised the title as "Heaven Begun on Earth."

Isaac Watts never married, but he was a friend to children and concerned with their well-being. Although he is most widely remembered for his three hymn collections, Watts also published *Divine and Moral Songs for Children*, which was commonly found in households throughout England.

Aaron Williams (1731–1776) either composed this tune or included it in his hymn collection from another source. ST. THOMAS, as given here, is only a portion of an extended tune setting for "Soldiers of Christ, Arise." It was known as HOLBORN when it first appeared in 1763.

Aaron Williams was a music teacher in London, England, as well as a publisher and clerk of the Scottish Church in London Wall. His 1770 compilation was the fifth edition of his *Universal Psalmist*. It provided many new tunes, some of which he composed.

380 O Saints in Splendor Sing

Sylvia G. Dunstan (1955–1993) was inspired by Revelation 7 in this hymn of hope for struggling congregations. The Revelation passage identifies those who have "come out of the great ordeal," giving hope and encouragement to those who question the value of their faith efforts.

Sylvia G. Dunstan had written poetry since her school days, but a professor at Emmanuel College at the University of Toronto, Canada, encouraged her to write hymn texts. Dunstan received master of divinity and master of theology degrees from that institution.

ST. THOMAS was published in Aaron William's *New Universal Psalmist* in 1770. It was adapted from a longer tune called HOLBORN, which was the setting for "Soldiers of Christ, Arise" in *The Universal Psalmist* (1763 ed.). The shortened form of the tune was also used as a setting for Psalm 48 in Isaac Smith's *Psalm Tunes* (1770).

Aaron Williams (1731–1776) edited and compiled *The Universal Psalmist*, which was printed in London, England, in 1763. The work was issued in a number of editions, with the fifth edition being released in 1770 as the *New Universal Psalmist*.

381 Faith of the Martyrs

Frederick William Faber (1814–1863) wrote this poem for a collection of hymns published in 1849. A recent convert to Roman Catholicism, he provided this hymn in two versions—one for Ireland, which was predominately Catholic, and one for England, which was Anglican.

Frederick W. Faber was raised a Huguenot Calvinist but converted to Roman Catholicism after coming under the influence of John Henry Newman at Oxford University in England. For years, Faber headed a society of secular priests and published devotional books as well as hymns.

Henri Frederick Hemy (1818–1888), in his *Crown of Jesus Music* (1865), published this tune, ST. CATHERINE, for a hymn honoring the saint. It has also been known as TYNEMOUTH, FINBAR, and PRINCE. The last eight measures, now the refrain, were added in 1874 by James G. Walton (1821–1905).

Henri F. Hemy, born in England of German parents, was a Roman Catholic musician who served for many years as organist at St. Andrew's Church in Newcastle, England. Hemy was also professor of music at Tynemouth, England, and wrote *Royal Modern Tutor for the Pianoforte* (1858).

382 Come, We Who Love God's Name

This hymn is an interesting combination of beloved texts from the eighteenth and nineteenth centuries. Isaac Watts (1674–1748) wrote the stanzas in 1707, Robert Lowry (1826–1899) added the refrain more than a century later. Watt's text can also be found in another setting in hymn 379.

Isaac Watts's father was in prison for Nonconformist views when Watts, the first of nine children, was born on July 17, 1674. A clothier by trade, Watts's father was a deacon at Above Bar Congregational Church in Southampton, England. In addition, he and his wife ran a boarding school.

Robert Lowry (1826–1899) composed the refrain to Isaac Watts's classic text in 1867 and called his tune MARCHING TO ZION after the words he had added. He included the combination in *Silver Spray* (1868), a collection of Sunday-school songs published by Biglow and Main of New York City.

Robert Lowry developed his capabilities as a hymnwriter while serving as pastor at a Baptist church in Brooklyn, New York. Although he was successful as a composer and hymnal editor, Lowry's greatest desired was to be remembered for his preaching.

383 Come, Let Us Join with Faithful Souls

William George Tarrant (1853–1928) wrote this text for a supplement to the *Essex Hall Hymnal* (1892). Tarrant often contributed poetry and hymns to a weekly Unitarian newspaper, *The Inquirer*, which he edited from 1887 to 1897. He was also the author of *The Story and Significance of the Unitarian Movement* (1910).

William G. Tarrant grew up in the Church of England but left it for the Unitarian Church because of the influence of George Dawson, an eminent preacher from Birmingham, England. Tarrant served as a Unitarian minister at Wandsworth, London, for a term of thirty-seven years, from 1883 to 1920.

Carl Gotthelf Gläser's (1784–1829) melody is called AZMON, after a place mentioned in Joshua 15 and Numbers 34. The name was given by Lowell Mason, a hymnal editor, who often named tunes after places in the Hebrew Scriptures. Other names for the tune are GASTON and DENFIELD.

Carl G. Gläser was a music professional at Barmen, Germany. There he taught piano, violin, and voice. In addition, he was a music dealer, publishing chorales and school songs. Gläser received his education at Leipzig (Germany) University, in music and law.

384 For the Faithful Who Have Answered

Sylvia G. Dunstan (1955–1993) wrote this text to celebrate the fiftieth anniversary of the ordination of women in the United Church of Canada. Her denomination commissioned her to write the hymn in 1986, the same year in which she received her master of theology degree.

Sylvia G. Dunstan began by writing metrical versions of the 150 psalms in modern language. She had completed about half of them before her untimely death from liver cancer at age thirty-eight. Dunstan learned that she had this disease on March 21, 1993, and died on July 25 of the same year.

OMNI DIE is a German hymn tune that can be traced to 1625. First set to words beginning "Omni die dic Mariae," it was a "Marienlieder," or song about the virgin Mary. These songs were very popular among Roman Catholics in Germany.

David Gregor Corner (1585–1648) compiled the *Gross Catolisch Gesangbuch*, which was published in Nürnberg, Germany, in a number of editions beginning in 1625. In his career, Corner served as a parish priest, a Benedictine prior, and rector of the University of Vienna, Austria.

385 O What Their Joy and Their Glory Must Be

Peter Abelard (1079–1142) wrote this text, "O quanta qualia," for use at vespers services. It was one of ninety-three hymns included in his hymnbook, *Hymnarius Paraclitensis*, for the Nunnery of Héloïse. Abelard was secretly married and had a child with Héloïse before her uncle, canon Fulbert of Notre Dame, forced their separation.

Peter Abelard was a famed teacher and priest who attracted great throngs of followers. He was tried for heresy twice (in 1121 and 1141) and condemned through the efforts of another twelfth-century poet-scholar, Bernard of Clairvaux.

O QUANTA QUALIA is the name of this French tune, although it is called REGNATOR ORBIS in other hymnals. It first appeared in the *Paris Antiphoner* (1681) and was reused by La Feillée in *Nouvelle Méthode de Plain Chant* (1808). This later printing is the source of this version of the tune.

La Feillée's 1808 collection *Nouvelle Méthode de Plain Chant* did much to introduce French hymn tunes into English-speaking nations. Brought to England, the tunes were warmly welcomed and incorporated into English hymnbooks, such as John Mason Neale's *The Hymnal Noted* (1851).

386 The Church's One Foundation

Samuel John Stone (1839–1900) based this 1866 hymn on Article Nine of the Apostles' Creed, to defend accepted church dogma against the attacks of Bishop John William Colenso. This was one of twelve hymns that Stone wrote to explain the High Church position in this controversy.

Samuel J. Stone was born April 25, 1839, at Staffordshire, England, while his father was priest to the poorest parish in England. After completing his education, he succeeded his father at St. Paul's, Haggerston, London, where he remained for twenty years. Stone died on November 19, 1900.

Samuel Sebastian Wesley (1810–1876) composed the tune AURELIA in 1864 as the setting for a wedding hymn by John Keble. It appeared with a variety of texts that same year, including the canto "Jerusalem the Golden" from a long Latin hymn by Saint Bernard. The tune has been closely associated with Stone's text since appearing together in *Hymns Ancient and Modern* (1868).

Samuel S. Wesley was devoted to improving the level of compensation and respect for church musicians of his day. His innovative ideas were developed in *A Few Words on Cathedral Music and the Musical System of the Church, with a Plan of Reform* (1849). He was the greatest musical genius of the gifted Wesley family.

387 O Christ, the Great Foundation

Timothy Tingfang Lew (1892–1947) wrote this hymn while teaching at Yenching University in Peking. At the time, he was head of a commission to prepare a Chinese Union hymnal. He later edited the *Union Book of Common Prayer*, which was used by four different Protestant Chinese groups.

Timothy Tingfang Lew, born in China, received his advanced education in the United States at Yale, Columbia University, Union Theological Seminary, and Oberlin College. He worked in China from 1932 until 1941, then returned to the United States and was teaching at the University of New Mexico when he died in 1947.

Samuel Sebastian Wesley (1810–1876) composed the tune AURELIA in 1864, and it appeared with a variety of texts including the canto "Jerusalem the Golden," translated from the Latin by John Mason Neale. The tune name derives from that association, since "golden" in Latin is *aureus*.

Samuel S. Wesley was the son of a musical genius also named Samuel and was therefore the grandson of Charles Wesley, the brother of John Wesley, the founder of Methodism. He was one of the first cathedral organists to demand a full pedal-board on the organs that he played.

388 Help Us Accept Each Other

Frederik Herman Kaan (b. 1929) wrote this hymn on acceptance in 1974 after reading a Bible-study article written by Jacki Mattonen, a member of the executive committee of the World Alliance of Reformed Churches. It was published in the World Council of Churches hymnbook, *Cantate Domino* (1974), and has become widely used in Christian ecumenical services.

Fred Kaan, born in the Netherlands, was drawn to England by a long correspondence with a pen pal in London and an article by Karl Barth on congregationalism. Although he first considered becoming a painter, Kaan began his study of theology in 1949 and was ordained in 1955 by the Congregational Union of England and Wales.

Samuel Sebastian Wesley (1810–1876) wrote this music for a translation of a Latin text that began "Jerusalem the Golden." The tune name AURELIA was supplied by Wesley's wife. It derived from the Latin word for golden, *aureus*, from which the chemical symbol for gold, Au, also comes.

Samuel S. Wesley was known for his adventuresome spirit in seeking reform of church music in nineteenth-century England. Wesley was a professor of organ at the Royal Academy of Music in England and published *European Psalmist*, a collection of over 700 hymn tunes, 130 of them original.

389 Un mandamiento nuevo
(Jesus a New Commandment)

William Loperena (1935–1996) wrote this text as a summation of Jesus' teachings on love. The hymn's last two stanzas form a trinitarian Doxology that is traditionally used to conclude many church hymns. The refrain should be sung following each pair of stanzas.

William Loperena was born December 14, 1935, in Moca, Puerto Rico. He attended the Dominican Seminary San Alberto Magno in Isabela, Puerto Rico, graduating in 1955. He continued his studies in Massachusetts and Holland and entered the parish priesthood in 1962.

William Loperena (1935–1996) wrote this tune in 1965 to accompany his original words. It is named LOPERENA in his honor. Loperena frequently employed rhythms and folk song melodies from his native Puerto Rico in his work. Such devices made his songs easy to learn and to sing.

William Loperena composed numerous folk-style songs for worship including the popular "Un mandamiento nuevo." Loperena felt a strong affinity for the Roman Catholic liturgy. He composed a peasant mass in 1968—*Misa Jíbara*.

390 Eternal Christ, Who, Kneeling

William Watkins Reid Jr. (b. 1923) found inspiration for this text in the image of Jesus kneeling in prayer at the Mount of Olives. The first stanza of the hymn quotes the motto of the United Church of Christ, "That They May All Be One," from the Gospel of John.

William W. Reid Jr. served in the United States Army Medical Corps during World War II. He was a German prisoner of war for eight months and earned three battle stars during his military service. A United Methodist minister, he has served congregations in North Dakota and Pennsylvania.

This tune, by an anonymous composer, is named NYLAND after a province in Finland where it was found. It was first published in an appendix to *Suomen Evankelis Luterilaisen Kirken Koraalikirja* (1909). The tune was introduced to the English-speaking world by David Evans, who adapted it in 1927.

David Evans (1874–1948) sought out a variety of new tunes for *Revised Church Hymnary*, a 1927 hymnal for which he was musical advisor. From 1903 until 1939, he was professor of music at University College in Cardiff, Wales, and a leading scholar on music of many nations.

391 In the Midst of New Dimensions

Julian Rush (b. 1936) sought to incorporate Native American spiritual imagery with Hebrew imagery in this text, written in 1985. He had learned about native spirituality from a friend in Colorado. The text and the tune were created simultaneously.

Julian Rush was born on August 24, 1936, in Meridian, Mississippi, and grew up there. He was educated at Perkins School of Theology, Southern Methodist University (Texas), and the University of Denver, where he earned a master's degree in drama.

Julian Rush (b. 1936) composed the tune NEW DIMENSIONS for his own words. The hymn was sung four times at a 1985 church conference and was played in a different musical style each time, including Asian, African American, Latin American, and European American, for services reflecting these four cultural traditions.

Julian Rush was named the founding director of the Colorado AIDS Project in 1983. Ordained to the United Methodist ministry in 1964, he served as youth minister at Forth Worth, Texas, and Colorado Springs, Colorado, and as minister of education at Boulder, Colorado, before joining the AIDS Project.

392 En santa hermandad (United by God's Love)

William Loperena (1935–1996) wrote this hymn in a trinitarian format. Stanzas 1 and 2 concern God as Creator, stanza 3 focuses on Christ the Redeemer, and stanza 4 offers praise to the Holy Spirit. This common formula has been used in hymnwriting for centuries.

William Loperena, a member of the Dominican Roman Catholic Order, lived and worked in Puerto Rico. His ministry took him close to the people but was cut short by his untimely death in 1996. Loperena had served as a member of the task force that recommended a body of Hispanic hymnody for *The New Century Hymnal*.

William Loperena (b. 1935) composed the tune EN SANTA HERMANDAD, named here for the opening words of his text. Loperena's songs have become very popular in his native Puerto Rico and are gaining a following elsewhere in the world. His recurring theme is the ecumenical ministry of the church.

William Loperena was a Dominican Roman Catholic priest who worked in Puerto Rico. The Dominican Order, also called the Order of Preachers, was founded by Dominic in the early thirteenth century. It is dedicated to teaching and scholarship as well as preaching.

393 Blessed Be the Tie That Binds

John Fawcett (1740–1817) was inspired to write this text after having refused a call to move his family from a small Baptist church in Yorkshire, England, to accept a charge in London. Even with the household goods packed, he decided not to leave the church and the people he loved.

John Fawcett was born January 17, 1740, in Yorkshire, England. As a teenager he was influenced by George Whitefield and converted to Methodism. However, he was later ordained in the Baptist Church. Fawcett was the author of more than 160 hymns, written primarily to reflect on his sermons.

Johann Georg Nägeli (1773–1836) wrote the music from which this tune was adapted by Lowell Mason in *The Psaltery* (1845). There, it was the setting for Philip Doddridge's "How Gentle God's Commands" and was given the name DENNIS for a town in Cape Cod, Massachusetts.

J. G. Nägeli, a Swiss music educator, began a music periodical in 1803 to publish new piano works by contemporary composers. This periodical included three new Beethoven sonatas. Nägeli lectured on music appreciation and founded choral societies throughout Switzerland.

394 In Christ There Is No East or West

John Oxenham (1852–1941) wrote this hymn as part of "The Pageant of Darkness and Light," which was presented at the London Missionary Exhibition in 1905. The pageant was a major attraction of that monthlong event and later toured Europe and the United States.

John Oxenham was born as William Arthur Dunkerley in Manchester, England, on November 12, 1852. He used a pen name because he was a successful businessman in England and France. Oxenham eventually turned to writing full-time, producing over forty novels and twenty other works of poetry and prose.

Harry T. Burleigh (1866–1949) adapted this tune from a spiritual, "I Know the Angel's Done Changed My Name," for use with Oxenham's text. It is named MCKEE for the minister of St. George's Protestant Episcopal Church in New York City. Burleigh, grandson of a Maryland slave, was baritone soloist at this church for fifty-two years.

Harry T. Burleigh was born in Erie, Pennsylvania, and began his musical career as a chorister at St. Paul's Cathedral there. He rose to be one of the greatest singers of his day, accompanying Booker T. Washington on his fund-raising trips and singing for King Edward VII. Burleigh was the composer of songs and anthems, including "Deep River," and a founder of ASCAP.

395 In Christ There Is No East or West

John Oxenham (1852–1941) wrote this hymn as part of the libretto for the "Pageant of Darkness and Light," which was performed during a missionary exhibition in London, England, in 1905. Oxenham had been asked to contribute music for the show by its organizer, who was his nephew.

John Oxenham was the pen name of an English businessman named William A. Dunkerley. His success in writing novels and religious works brought his other career to an end, and, beginning in 1913, he devoted all his time to his literary pursuits. He also wrote under the name Julian Ross.

Alexander Robert Reinagle (1799–1877) composed this tune as a solo setting for Psalm 118 when he was organist at St. Peter-in-the-East Church in Oxford, England. The tune appeared with the name ST. PETER in a collection published by the composer in 1840. It is also called OXFORD or CHRIST CHURCH.

Alexander R. Reinagle was born at Brighton, England, on August 21, 1799, to parents who were part of a famous musical family. For thirty-one years he served as organist at St. Peter-in-the-East Church, Oxford, England, and gave organ lessons to the likes of John Stainer. Reinagle published two collections of hymn tunes and other sacred music.

396 Where Charity and Love Prevail

This early ninth-century Latin hymn began "Ubi caritas et amor." It was traditionally sung during the Maundy Thursday foot-washing service, at which the ranking church official washed the feet of lower-ranking individuals, recalling Jesus' act of washing the feet of the disciples in John 13.

Omer Westendorf (b. 1916) created this paraphrase of the traditional Latin liturgical text in 1961. Westendorf, a lifelong resident of Cincinnati, Ohio, has compiled several hymnals including the *People's Mass Book* (1964), which met the need for new Roman Catholic liturgies and hymns following the Second Vatican Council (1962–1965), called by Pope John XXIII.

Paul Benoit (1893–1979) composed this tune, named CHRISTIAN LOVE after the topic of the text. The melody, to be sung freely and in unison, is reminiscent of the chant style used in the ninth century when the Latin text was written. Benoit composed many organ works during his ministry.

Paul Benoit was a Benedictine monk of the Roman Catholic Church. As a Benedictine, he followed strict rules of the order established by Saint Benedict of Nursia around 500 C.E. The main emphasis of the order was seven daily celebrations of the Divine Office.

397 Thank Our God for Sisters, Brothers

Roger Kingsley Powell (b. 1914) wrote this hymn for a 1948 union Thanksgiving service in Camillus, New York. It was later used in 1952 for the first gathering of the National Council of Churches of Christ. This association enables mutual ministry among a number of different denominations.

Roger Powell was born August 4, 1914, in Kingston, New York. An ordained American Baptist minister, he served two New York churches before being appointed registrar and instructor in speech at Colgate Rochester (New York) Divinity School in 1952.

This anonymous tune, called PLEADING SAVIOR, was first printed in *The Christian Lyre* (1831). There, it appeared with a text beginning "Now the Savior Stands A-pleading," hence the tune name. When the tune was used in England, it was renamed SALTASH.

Joshua Leavitt edited *The Christian Lyre*, which was published in New York City in 1830. This collection was considered a landmark in American hymnals, although it received severe criticism from Lowell Mason and Thomas Hastings, leading musical scholars of the time.

398 Shadow and Substance

Daniel Charles Damon (b. 1955) produced this text in 1989, inspired by the opening of the television series *The Twilight Zone*. The narrator's invitation to "enter a world of shadow and substance" struck Damon as an excellent metaphor for God. Brian Wren helped in revising the text.

Dan Damon produces his hymn texts by listening in silence. When he hears a word or phrase that excites him, he writes them in his prayer journal and allows the creative power of God to help him develop a first draft of a number of stanzas. Several revisions of the text generally follow.

Daniel Charles Damon (b. 1955) wrote this tune for his own text and named it TWILIGHT, for the television series *The Twilight Zone*, which inspired the text. He first used the tune for another hymn, "Strong, Gentle Children," which appeared in his collection *Faith Will Sing* (1993).

Dan Damon was pursuing a career as a jazz pianist before he felt called to enter Pacific School of Religion, Berkeley, California. There he rediscovered his faith, completed his academic work, and was ordained to the ministry of the United Methodist Church.

399 When Minds and Bodies Meet as One

Brian Arthur Wren (b. 1936) included this text among those he revised in *Faith Renewed* (1995). In his notes to that collection, Wren asks rhetorically, "Why shouldn't the Trinity have a carol—especially with Peter Cutts's lively tune?"

Brian Wren was born in Romford, Essex, England, in 1936 and attended Royal Liberty Grammar School. He grew up during World War II, remembering air raid sirens, bombs, and anti-aircraft fire. His father served in the army and was absent from home for seven years of Wren's early life.

Peter Warwick Cutts (b. 1937) composed this melody for Brian Wren's words and named it TRINITY CAROL: "Trinity" for the focus of the first verse and "Carol" for the style of music, which moves along briskly. The tune was written in 1980 and published three years later in *Faith Looking Forward*.

Peter Cutts received his bachelor's and master's degrees at Clare College, Cambridge, and read theology at Mansfield College, Oxford. Cutts served as organist at several United Reformed churches in England and taught music at three different schools before moving to the United States.

400 Christ Is Made the Sure Foundation

The original Latin hymn on which this translation is based consisted of eight stanzas. It has been used for services of dedication of churches since the Middle Ages, traditionally in two parts: one for vespers and one for lauds. This version begins with stanza 5, "Angularis fundamentum."

John Mason Neale (1816–1866) included this hymn in his *Medieval Hymns* and *The Hymnal Noted*, both published in 1851. The other half of his translation of this Latin text, "Urbs beata Jerusalem," is the hymn "Blessed City, Heavenly Salem."

Henry Thomas Smart (1813–1879) composed this tune, but it was not named REGENT SQUARE until James Hamilton chose it for inclusion in an 1867 English Presbyterian hymnbook. Hamilton was serving as minister at Regent Square Presbyterian Church, London, England, at the time.

Henry T. Smart was the son of an English violin and piano manufacturer and nephew of one of England's greatest conductors, Sir George Thomas Smart. Although largely self-taught, Smart became a celebrated organist and designer of that instrument.

401 O God in Whom All Life Begins

Carl Pickens Daw Jr. (b. 1944) wrote this text for the installation service of Susan Huizenga as pastor of the Rochester Reformed Church in Accord, New York. It appeared in his collection *New Psalms and Hymns and Spiritual Songs* (1996) with two settings, ACCORD by Roy Hopp and RITTER by Kevin R. Hackett.

Carl P. Daw Jr. was assistant rector at Christ and Grace Church, Petersburg, Virginia, from 1981 to 1984. During this time he served as a delegate to the Virginia Council of Churches. Born in Louisville, Kentucky, he grew up there and in Nashville and Murfreesboro, Tennessee.

This traditional English melody was expanded and arranged by Arthur S. Sullivan (1842–1900) for use with the Christmas hymn "It Came upon the Midnight Clear." The tune NOEL is still the primary one sung with that text in England. It may have derived from the carol "Dives and Lazarus."

Arthur S. Sullivan is better remembered for the operas he created in collaboration with W. S. Gilbert, although he did compose a number of hymn tunes and edited *The Hymnary* (1872) and *Church Hymns with Tunes* (1874). This arrangement appeared in the latter collection.

402 De colores (Sing of Colors)

This Mexican folk song promotes racial understanding and cooperation. The first stanza speaks of the colors of nature, and the second of the different colors of the people of the earth. The song, originally written in Spanish, has become a rally song for the United Farm Workers movement.

Mexican music continues to reflect the Spanish cultural heritage of the nation. Primarily Roman Catholic, Mexico was heavily evangelized beginning in the sixteenth century by various orders of Roman Catholic priests, on orders from the Spanish crown.

This Mexican tune takes its name from the text, DE COLORES. It is commonly performed with guitars and trumpets in Mariachi style. This arrangement, by Alfredo Morales, incorporates repeated use of thirds in the treble part as is characteristic of Mexican folk music.

Recent years have witnessed the use of secular musical styles in the churches of Mexico, including the Mariachi mass, with guitars and trumpets. "De Colores" has become a popular song adapted for use in Mexican and Mexican American churches.

403 My Hope Is Built on Nothing Less

Edward Mote (1797–1874) wrote this text on the "Gracious Experience of a Christian" during 1834, while he was working as a cabinetmaker in a suburb of London, England. It appears in his collection *Hymns of Praise, A New Selection of Gospel Hymns* (1836). The refrain was added in 1863.

Edward Mote spent his professional life as a cabinetmaker, but at age fifty-five he constructed a church building for a Baptist congregation in Horsham, England. He then became their pastor and served the church for the next twenty-one years until ill health forced him to resign his pulpit in 1873.

William Batchelder Bradbury (1816–1868) wrote the tune SOLID ROCK for Mote's text in 1863 and added the refrain at that time. It was published in *The Devotional Hymn and Tune Book* (1864) in Philadelphia. This was the only Baptist hymnal to be published during the Civil War.

William B. Bradbury was one of the foremost composers of early gospel music in the United States. Encouraged by Lowell Mason, another prolific gospel tune writer, he not only served as church organist but organized many music festivals at Baptist Tabernacle in New York City.

404 Give Up Your Anxious Pains

Paul Gerhardt (1607–1676) wrote this hymn of assurance and hope based on Martin Luther's translation of Psalm 37:5. Originally the hymn had twelve stanzas, beginning "Befiehl du deine Wege." John Wesley was the first to translate this text into English.

Paul Gerhardt, second only to Martin Luther as Germany's greatest hymnwriter, was born on March 12, 1607, near Wittenberg, Germany. He was educated at the university there, and his life was influenced by the Thirty Years' War, which disrupted the normal course of existence for that entire area of Germany.

Johann Sebastian Bach (1685–1750) included this tune in a songbook he edited in 1736, and authorities believe it to be his work. The tune name, ICH HALTE TREULICH STILL (or "I Remain Ever Faithful"), comes from the German text with which it appeared.

J. S. Bach composed a vast repertoire of church music during his career as organist and director for Lutheran churches in Leipzig. This tune, however, was more likely intended as a personal song of devotion for use in a private setting.

405 There Are Some Things I May Not Know (Yes, God Is Real)

Kenneth Morris (1917–1988) wrote this text in 1942 and used it at the National Baptist Convention. For a number of years, his songs were great hits at the convention, and he gained financial success by selling large amounts of music through his mail-order music publishing company.

Kenneth Morris was successful as both a composer and a music publisher. He cofounded Morris and Martin Music, Inc., with Sallie Martin, to publish the work of independent gospel songwriters. Morris transcribed the compositions that the company purchased for as little as fifteen dollars.

Kenneth Morris (1917–1988) wrote this tune for his own text, and it is named YES, GOD IS REAL after the words in the refrain. This song was his most successful composition, written shortly after he opened the Martin and Morris Music Studio and Teaching School in Chicago.

Kenneth Morris realized that many of those who appreciated his gospel music had limited education and musical training, so he wrote and arranged his songs for the ability level of the people who would use it. Although he was criticized by some for this practice, his sheet music sold extremely well.

406 Not with Naked Eye, Not with Human Sense

Daniel Charles Damon (b. 1955) explores the senses by which human beings perceive the world and God's presence, naming four of the five senses in the text of this hymn. Stanza 1 is based on John 1:18 and stanza 4 on John 20:26–29, the story of the disciple who doubts Christ's resurrection.

Dan Damon's life is evidence that the path to God is not always a straight one. He began his career as a high school music teacher, and worked as a truck driver, bakery dishwasher, bicycle delivery messenger, and jazz pianist before he became a minister in the United Methodist Church and a hymnwriter.

Daniel Charles Damon (b. 1955) wrote this tune for his own text. It is named STITELER for Valerie C. Jones Stiteler, a United Church of Christ minister who was ordained in 1988. The melody is meant to be sung in unison, and guitar chords are provided as one means of accompaniment.

Dan Damon published twenty-four of his new hymns in *Faith Will Sing*, a 1993 collection. As an ordained United Methodist minister, he has served a number of churches in northern California, most recently at Point Richmond United Methodist Church.

407 How Firm a Foundation

The unknown author of this hymn is identified only by the initial "K," although later editions of Rippon's *Selections* credit "Kn" and "Keen." This has led many to speculate that it may have been written by R. Keene, the precentor in Rippon's church who wrote the tune with which the hymn first appeared.

John Rippon (1751–1836) published *A Selection of Hymns from the Best Authors* (1787), a hymnbook of collected works by Watts and others. The hymnal became a standard for English Baptist churches and was very successful in the United States as well.

FOUNDATION is an anonymous early American melody that appeared with this text in several tune collections from the southern United States. The earliest of these sources is *A Compilation of Genuine Church Music* (1832), published by Joseph Funk (1778–1862), a singing-school teacher in Virginia.

Joseph Funk, a descendant of German Mennonite immigrants, constructed a log schoolhouse on his farm near Harrisonburg, Virginia, and later converted it to a printshop for his publications. Funk led singing schools and established a monthly music journal.

408 All My Hope on God Is Founded

Joachim Neander (1650–1680) based this German text, "Meine Hoffnung stehet feste," on 1 Timothy 6:17: "to set their hopes . . . on God who richly provides us with everything for our enjoyment." He intended the hymn to be used as a prayer following the evening meal. The English paraphrase was made by Robert S. Bridges in 1899.

Joachim Neander was born in Bremen, Germany, in 1650, and his family may have been of Jewish heritage. Neander worked as headmaster of a Reformed grammar school at Düsseldorf, Germany, but was fired for making changes in the school without permission of the school's ministers.

Herbert Norman Howells (1892–1983) wrote this music at the breakfast table after receiving a request in the morning mail for a new tune from Thomas Feilden, the director of music of the Charterhouse School, England. Howells named the tune MICHAEL to honor a son who had died in childhood.

Herbert Howells was a professor of composition at the Royal College of Music in London, England, for over fifty years. In addition, he succeeded Gustav Holst in 1936 as director of music at St. Paul's Girls School in London, remaining in that position until 1962.

409 I Heard My Mother Say

This African American spiritual expresses our need for Jesus in every circumstance of life. Each stanza recalls a different stage of development, from childhood at one's mother's knee, to times of crisis, to dying, and finally to new life in Christ.

The theme of finding comfort and liberation through the person of Jesus Christ is a prevalent one in African American spirituals. This text conveys the slave-poet's affirmation of Jesus as the slave's closest, most reliable friend and the assurance of eventual escape from the travails of this life to new life with Jesus in heaven.

This tune takes its name, GIVE ME JESUS, from the opening words of the refrain. This new arrangement of the music was created by Joyce Finch Johnson for *The New Century Hymnal*. Note that the refrain should be repeated after singing each stanza.

Joyce Finch Johnson's harmonization of this very old traditional song combines two styles: first, a unison melody reminiscent of a solo singer; and second, a refrain cast in harmonies that recall a rich tradition of group singing. It might be performed in this way or sung entirely in unison.

410 If You But Trust in God to Guide You

Georg Neumark (1621–1681) wrote this German hymn, "Wer nur den lieben Gott," in 1640. It was first used at Kiel that winter and at the funeral of King Frederick William I of Prussia a century later. Catherine Winkworth (1829–1878) included the translation in her *Chorale Book for England* (1863).

Georg Neumark was born at Langensalza, Thuringia, in what is now Germany. The victim of many misfortunes as the result of the Thirty Years' War, Neumark enjoyed some security as a tutor and later librarian and court poet to the Duke of Saxe-Weimar.

Georg Neumark (1621–1681) composed the tune NEUMARK, which was named for him by later hymnal editors, as the setting for his hymn text. The tune has also been called AUGSBURG and BREMEN. J. S. Bach borrowed it for eight of his cantatas and a number of other works.

Georg Neumark was born on March 16, 1621, in Langensalza, Thuringia. He was robbed while on the way to study law at Königsberg and left destitute. Neumark turned to teaching to raise tuition money and finally was able to continue his studies in law and poetry. He died in Thuringia on July 18, 1681.

411 Praise the Source of Faith and Learning

Thomas H. Troeger (b. 1945) was commissioned to write this text in 1987 by Duke University in honor of retired professor of ethics Waldo Beach. It is based on the school's motto, "Faith and Learning," and first appeared with William Albright's tune in *Singing the Living Tradition* (1993).

Thomas H. Troeger studied African American preaching and worship styles while he was a student at Colgate Rochester Divinity School. This awakened his interest in discovering how different cultures worship and use music. These ideas continue to influence Troeger's work.

William Hugh Albright (b. 1944) was commissioned to compose the tune PROCESSION in 1992 by the First Unitarian Universalist Church of Ann Arbor, Michigan for its 125th anniversary in 1990. Albright has taught at the University of Michigan since 1970 and also served as associate director of the electronic music studio there.

William H. Albright was born in Gary, Indiana. Following completion of his musical education in Michigan and Paris, France, he entered the teaching profession. His honors include two Koussevitzky composition awards, a Fulbright Fellowship, and an American Academy of Arts and Letters award.

412 God Moves in a Mysterious Way

William Cowper (1731–1800) may have written this, the last of his sixty-seven hymns, as early as 1772, according to correspondence with John Newton. It was included in the famous *Olney Hymns* along with sixty-seven other original texts.

William Cowper, considered one of the finest poets of his day, lived a sad life of ill health and mental instability. Twice he was engaged to be married, but both times his mental illness interfered. Cowper was appointed a clerk in the House of Lords but so feared the formal hearings that he was committed to an asylum for a year.

The tune DUNDEE first appeared in *The 150 Psalms of David* (1615), published by Andro Hart. There it was called FRENCH TUNE. This was the first psalter to identify hymns by meter, and it contained twelve tunes in common meter (C.M.)—a designation for a text in four lines with eight syllables in the first and six in the next, with the pattern repeated.

Andro Hart's (d. 1621) *The 150 Psalms of David* helped define the meter of standard melodies for singing psalms. Hart, a well-known publisher in Edinburgh, Scotland, printed Bibles, hymnbooks, and many foreign works. He was imprisoned in 1596 for a disagreement with the political powers.

413 By Gracious Powers

Dietrich Bonhoeffer (1906–1945), a renowned German theologian, wrote this text as a poem entitled "Powers of Good" for New Year's Day 1945. It was smuggled out of a Nazi prison where he was being held for his part in an assassination attempt on the life of Adolf Hitler.

Dietrich Bonhoeffer, son of a noted physician, spoke out against Adolf Hitler's rise to political power in Germany in 1933. Arrested following an unsuccessful attempt to assassinate Hitler, he died by hanging on April 9, 1945, after being imprisoned for two years at Tegel, Germany.

Herbert G. Hobbs (b. 1934) composed the melody BONHOEFFER for this hymn for a service of worship based on the life of Dietrich Bonhoeffer. The service was held on January 25, 1976, at Ferrum College, Virginia, where Hobbs was serving as chaplain.

Jan Helmut Wubbena (b. 1947) harmonized this tune for Herbert Hobbs and later developed it into an anthem. Originally from Dover, Delaware, Wubbena was on the faculty of Ferrum College, Virginia, with Hobbs. He later moved to John Brown University, Siloam Springs, Arkansas.

414 Incarnate God, Immortal Love

Alfred Tennyson (1809–1892) wrote a long poem, "In Memoriam," as a tribute to his deceased friend, Arthur Hallam. Although Hallam died in 1833, Tennyson did not publish the poem until 1850, when he had recently married and come to terms with his grief. The hymn is from the poem's prologue.

Alfred Tennyson was born at Somerset, England, on August 6, 1809, and became one of England's greatest poets, named poet laureate in 1850. He married at age forty-one and died on October 6, 1892, at Aldworth, England. Tennyson was affected by melancholy throughout his life.

Edward Miller (1731–1807) adapted this tune in 1790 from a shorter melody called TUNBRIDGE. It is named ROCKINGHAM for Miller's patron and friend, the Marquis of Rockingham, who was prime minister for two terms. The tune was called MAYHEW in collections edited by Lowell Mason.

Edward Miller edited *The Psalms of David for Use of Parish Churches* (1790), the source of this tune and one of the most successful hymn collections printed in England. Miller served as organist at Doncaster Parish Church for fifty-one years and was also an accomplished player on the flute and harpsichord.

415 God's Actions, Always Good and Just

Samuel Rodigast (1649–1708) wrote and read this German poem, "Was Gott tut, das ist wohlgetan," as his good friend Severus Gastorius lay ill. Gastorius was greatly comforted by this gesture and, when he recovered his health, set the words to the tune with which it is still sung.

Samuel Rodigast was born at Gröben, Germany, on October 19, 1649, the son of a Lutheran pastor. A fine scholar, he turned to teaching and spent most of his career as rector of a school in Berlin. Rodigast turned down numerous offers from other universities. He died in Berlin on March 29, 1708.

Severus Gastorius (fl. 1675) first heard this poem, written on his behalf during an illness, in 1675. When he recovered, he composed the tune setting, named WAS GOTT TUT for the first line of the German text. J. S. Bach later used the tune in a number of cantatas.

Severus Gastorius was cantor in a small Saxon city about 1675 and a friend of Samuel Rodigast, who was on the faculty at the University of Jena. Little more is known about him, and no other music by him has survived in common church use.

416 I Will Trust in the Lord

This spiritual is in the form of a sung testimonial. Sometimes the first stanza is recast in the form of a question: "Sister . . . , Brother . . . , Preacher, will you trust in the Lord?" Individuals are then given the opportunity to affirm their own faith as they respond to the inquiry by singing "I will trust . . . till I die."

Researchers have found this hymn used in camp meetings led by both African Americans and whites. Many camp meetings in the southern United States allowed interracial attendance, as the need to hear God's word far outweighed the racial restrictions imposed by unfair laws.

This tune, TRUST IN THE LORD, is tied to the text. Tunes often were varied as new stanzas were added. Songs were passed on orally and not sung exactly the same from place to place. Researchers have observed that this hymn is properly sung slowly with "dignified swaying body motion."

African American spiritual melodies and texts are invariably linked. They generally developed together and, unlike European hymn tunes, are not easily interchanged with other tunes because of the irregular meter of many texts.

417 This Is a Day of New Beginnings

Brian Arthur Wren (b. 1936) wrote this text for a 1978 New Year's Day service at Holy Family Church, Blackbird Leys, Oxford, England. Originally the text was a series of questions and answers, beginning "Is this a day of new beginnings?" Wren later revised the text to this form for the United Methodist hymnal revision committee.

Brian Wren published this hymn in *Faith Looking Forward* (1983) and in his recent revision of that collection, *Faith Renewed* (1995). In addition to hymnody, Wren is the author of prose volumes that reflect his theological work, including *What Language Shall I Borrow?* (1989).

Carlton Raymond Young (b. 1926) composed the tune BEGINNINGS for this text in 1987. As the text was originally a series of questions and answers, the music reflected this format, ending all but the last line on the dominant fifth. The harmonies are in the style of a 1930s Broadway ballad.

Carlton R. Young, as a music educator, has taught at various seminaries in the United States and in Europe. He is an ordained elder in the United Methodist Church and has served that denomination as director of music for local churches in Massachusetts, Ohio, Texas, and Georgia.

418 My Faith, It Is an Oaken Staff

Thomas Toke Lynch (1818–1871) wrote this text, which many believe to be his best, for inclusion in his collection *The Rivulet* (1855). The text uses the traveler's staff as a metaphor for the strength of faith, which not only supports and guides but also defends the Christian traveling along life's journey.

Thomas T. Lynch edited a hymnal in 1855 that split the English Congregational Church. The hymnal, called *The Rivulet, Hymns for Heart and Voice*, was opposed by Charles Haddon Spurgeon, who claimed that Lynch's theology was negative and nondoctrinal.

This anonymous Swiss melody was used as a folk song long before it was appropriated as a hymn tune. The tune, named for this text, is THE STAFF OF FAITH. Its structure is AABA, a form that makes it easily learned. The hymn with this setting appeared in *The Pilgrim Hymnal* (1958).

Few Swiss melodies are found in modern hymnals in the United States. The Swiss culture historically has encompassed aspects of French, German, and Italian cultures, and all three languages are spoken in various sections of Switzerland.

419 Nun danket alle Gott (Now Thank We All Our God)

Martin Rinkart (1586–1649) wrote this hymn of thanks to be sung by his family as a table grace during the Thirty Years' War. He based the first two stanzas on Ecclesiasticus 50 and added the third as a Doxology later. This hymn is now sung for all days of national thanksgiving in Germany.

Martin Rinkart served as a pastor in Eilenburg, Saxony, the town of his birth. The walled city was a refuge for many fleeing war and pestilence. Left as the only clergyman in town, he often buried as many as forty or fifty persons in one day. Although his wife died of the pestilence, Rinkart survived.

Johann Crüger (1598–1662) introduced NUN DANKET, his best-known tune, in his *Praxis Pietatis Melica* (1647 edition) with this text by Rinkart. It was used by J. S. Bach in his Reformation cantata. The tune has also been called GRATITUDE and WITTENBERG.

Johann Crüger, son of a prosperous innkeeper, grew up in Prussia. After being educated as a musician, he moved to Berlin, Germany, where he lived the rest of his life. He served as cantor at the Church of St. Nicolai, Berlin, for forty years.

420 We Praise You, O God

Julia Bulkley Cady Cory (1882–1963) was commissioned to write this hymn in 1902 to replace older words sung to the tune KREMSER, which were thought too militaristic by the organist at Brick Presbyterian Church in New York City. The earlier text celebrated a Dutch victory over Spain.

Julia B. C. Cory, the daughter of one of New York City's most distinguished architects, was a Presbyterian all her life. She began writing hymns at her father's urging when she was only seventeen years old. Cory spent most of her life in New York City and Englewood, New Jersey.

This anonymous tune was a secular song in Holland and dates from 1626. Lost for two centuries, it was rediscovered by an Austrian composer, Edward Kremser (1838–1914), in 1877 and used for a work based on six old Dutch melodies. The tune is named KREMSER for him.

Edward Kremser (1838–1914) was born in Vienna, Austria, on April 10, 1838, and died in that city seventy-six years later on November 26, 1914. He served as the conductor of the Vienna Mannergesangverein and used a number of forgotten Dutch patriotic songs for a men's chorus in 1877.

421 We Gather Together

An anonymous Dutch patriot wrote this text to celebrate his nation's freedom from the Spanish after a century of occupation and oppression. It was first published in a 1626 collection, *Nederlandtsche Gedenckclanck*. The English translation is by Theodore Baker (1851–1934).

Theodore Baker (1851–1934) was born in New York City on June 3, 1851, and received his Ph.D. from Leipzig University in 1882. His *Biographical Dictionary of Music and Musicians*, first published in 1900, has remained a standard reference. Baker also studied the music of Native Americans.

This anonymous tune, named KREMSER, comes from a collection first published in 1626 in Holland. It had been used with a patriotic song before falling into disuse for two centuries. The tune's name honors the man who arranged it, Edward Kremser.

Edward Kremser (1838–1914), a Viennese choral director and composer, rediscovered a number of Dutch tunes from Adrian Valerius's collection of 1626, *Nederlandtsche Gedenckclanck*. The tunes became popular with soldiers fighting in World War I.

422 Come, O Thankful People, Come

Henry Alford (1810–1871) wrote this hymn as "After Harvest," with an eschatological emphasis reflecting Jesus' parable in Matthew 13. However, this composite version, with stanza 2 by Anna Laetitia Aiken Barbauld (1743–1825), eliminates that focus and renders it primarily a hymn of thanksgiving.

Henry Alford was dean of Canterbury Cathedral, England, from 1857 until his death in 1871. He always wanted to visit the holy land, but never realized his ambition. His tombstone reads "The inn of a pilgrim traveling to Jerusalem," reflecting that dream.

George Job Elvey (1816–1893) composed this tune for different words. It was first combined with Alford's text in *Hymns Ancient and Modern* (1861), and the two have remained together since. The name, ST. GEORGE'S WINDSOR, honors the chapel where Elvey worked as organist for forty-seven years.

George J. Elvey was a skilled church organist by the time he was seventeen years old but nonetheless continued to improve his playing and knowledge through study and practice. Elvey composed hymn tunes, anthems, service music, and oratorios.

423 Great Is Your Faithfulness

Thomas Obediah Chisholm (1866–1960) wrote this hymn as a religious poem in 1923 while living in Vineland, New Jersey. His longtime friend, the composer and Methodist minister William Runyan, provided the tune. An additional scripture reference for the text is James 1:17c.

Thomas O. Chisholm wrote more than twelve hundred poems, many of which were published in religious magazines. In his lifetime, Chisholm was a newspaper and magazine editor, Methodist minister, and life insurance agent. Poor health kept him from serving in the ministry longer than a single year.

William Marion Runyan (1870–1957), a friend of the author, wrote tunes for many of Chisholm's poems, including this one. Composed in 1923 in Baldwin, Kansas, it was named FAITHFULNESS, for the theme of the text, and was included in Runyan's *Songs of Salvation and Service* (1923).

William M. Runyan was playing the organ at his church at the age of twelve. After being ordained to the Methodist ministry, he served as pastor and the evangelist for the Central Kansas Methodist Conference. He was associated with the Moody Bible Institute in Chicago, Illinois, during his retirement.

424 Praise Our God Above

Tzu-chen Chao (1888–1979) wrote this text as a harvest song for use by Christian congregations in China. It was first printed in *Hymns of Universal Praise* (1936), a collection of Western hymns translated into Chinese for use in Chinese churches.

T. C. Chao was one of China's leading Christian theologians. After Maoist Communists took over the government, he suffered persecution but was allowed to continue teaching at Yenching Union Theological Seminary, where he served as dean from 1928 until 1953.

This Chinese melody was used as a Confucian temple chant before being adapted to accompany a Christian text. The tune name, HSUAN P'ING, conveys a proclamation of peace. It may be familiar to some UCC congregations as this hymn was included in the *Pilgrim Hymnal* (1958).

W. H. Wong (b. 1917) arranged this ancient Confucian chant for use as a Christian hymn tune, and it appeared in a 1977 revised edition of *Hymns of Universal Praise*. This hymnal, originally released in 1936 by T. C. Chao, provided hymns for various Protestant churches in China.

425 For the Fruit of All Creation

Fred Pratt Green (b. 1903) was asked to write a harvest hymn by English composer John Wilson, and this text is the result. The two men were together at a meeting of the Methodist Music Society of Great Britain. The text was originally written for a contemporary English tune, EAST ACKLAM.

Fred Pratt Green served as an ordained minister of the English Methodist Church in parishes in northern and southern England. He began his ministry in 1927 and retired in 1969. During those years, he wrote hymn texts as time permitted, but after retirement he devoted all his time to hymnwriting.

This traditional Welsh melody is named AR HYD Y NOS, which means "The Livelong Night." The harmonization found here was done in 1906 by Luther Orlando Emerson (1820–1915), who gave up a promising medical career to study music with I. B. Woodbury.

A copy of this widely known Welsh melody was first found in printed form in Edward Jones's *Musical Relicks of the Welsh Bards*, a 1784 work. In that version, the ballad was sung accompanied by a harp. A soloist would sing a verse and the chorus join on the refrain, "Ar hyd y nos."

426 O God, Whose Steadfast Love

James Lewis Haddix (b. 1946) wrote this text to honor his mother, Margaret Ann Lewis Haddix, on the occasion of her retirement from a thirty-year career as an elementary-school teacher. The hymn has broad applications as it celebrates the love of God exemplified by mothers and women of the Bible.

James L. Haddix was ordained in the United Church of Christ in 1971. He served at the Congregational Church in Temple, New Hampshire, from 1969 to 1990 and since 1990 at All Souls Congregational Church (UCC), Bangor, Maine. He is also adjunct professor at Bangor Theological Seminary.

John David Edwards (1806–1885) composed this tune around 1838, and it was named LOVELY when it appeared in his *Original Sacred Music* (1840). However, a later hymnal editor renamed it RHOSYMEDRE for the town in North Wales where Edwards served as an Anglican vicar and minister.

John D. Edwards was born in Cardiganshire, Wales, in 1806 and educated at Oxford University. He was ordained to the ministry of the Church of England in 1832. In addition to his parish work, Edwards composed a large amount of music. He died in North Wales at the rectory in 1885.

427 God Made from One Blood

Thomas H. Troeger (b. 1945) was asked to write this text to recognize the variety of family units represented at Yale University chapel services. The hymn was included in *A New Hymnal for Colleges and Schools* (Yale University Press, 1992) set to the Basque carol NORMANDY.

Thomas H. Troeger, a Presbyterian minister, has spent much of his career as a professor at theological schools. He served for seven years at Colgate Rochester Divinity, Bexley Hall, Crozer Theological Seminary in Rochester, New York, and then moved to Iliff School of Theology, Denver, Colorado, in 1991.

This Welsh ballad is called ST. DENIO. The tune was adapted from a melody published by John Roberts in *Caniadaeth y Cysegr* (1839). Many different words have been used with this tune, including a song about a cuckoo and another beginning "A hundred years from now."

John Roberts (1822–1887), known in his native Wales as Ieuan Gwyllt, published this Welsh ballad in *Caniadaeth y Cysegr*, an 1839 collection. He founded the Welsh singing festivals called Gymanfa Ganu. Roberts spent his career as a Calvinistic Methodist minister in Wales, retiring in 1869.

428 Malipayong Adlaw'ng Natawhan (What a Glad Day)

Grace R. Tabada (b. 1942) wrote this song in 1992 to increase the selection of songs available to church members for use in birthday celebrations. According to a local custom in the Visayas provinces of the Philippines, church members visit the birthday celebrant at dawn and awake him or her by singing this song.

Fé R. Nebres (b. 1938) created this English translation for inclusion in *The New Century Hymnal*. It is an appropriate replacement for the traditional "Happy Birthday to You" sung in the United States. Fé Nebres is an associate conference minister for the United Church of Christ in Hawaii.

Grace R. Tabada (b. 1942) composed this melody for her own words, and it was titled TABADA in her honor. Tabada is a teacher of music and director of the Divinity School publication center at Silliman University in the Philippines, and the sister of translator Fé Nebres.

Vérne de la Peña (b. 1959) arranged this tune to reflect the style of a Philippine lowland folk dance or serenade. A composer of music for chorus, chamber ensembles, theater, and dance, de la Peña is completing his Ph.D. in ethnomusicology at the University of Hawaii and the East-West Center.

429 God, Bless Our Homes

Frank von Christierson (b. 1900) wrote this hymn in 1957, and it was first printed in *Monday Morning, April 28, 1958*. In the text, the author recognizes that values are learned at home; it is those same values that Christians bring to their churches and their missionary work.

Frank von Christierson received his education in California public schools, at Stanford University, and at San Francisco Theological Seminary. A United Presbyterian minister for more than fifty years, he served churches in Berkeley, North Hollywood, and Sacramento, California.

David Evans (1874–1948) composed CHARTERHOUSE in 1924 for use at Charterhouse School in England. It was published in *The Revised Church Hymnary* (1927), a hymnal of the Presbyterian Church for which Evans represented Wales and served as musical advisor in chief.

David Evans was one of Wales's most outstanding modern musicians. He was made a member of the Royal College of Musicians and promoted the creation and use of Welsh music throughout his country. Evans died in 1948 after conducting a choir of four thousand voices at a music festival.

430 Praise to God, Your Praises Bring

William Channing Gannett (1840–1923) was serving as pastor for a Unitarian church in St. Paul, Minnesota, when he wrote this "harvest festival" text in 1872. It was not published until the 1885 edition of *The Thought of God in Hymns*, which Gannett helped edit.

William C. Gannett was a gifted poet and hymnwriter in addition to serving Unitarian and Congregational churches in five different states. In 1908, he delivered a series of lectures on hymnody at Harvard Divinity School (Massachusetts).

This old Moravian tune was titled HERRNHUT by John Wesley in his 1742 tunebook. In a later printing, it was called SAVANNAH for the city in Georgia Wesley visited on a missionary trip. In yet another edition, it was called IRENE for the name of the ship on which Moravian settlers traveled to Savannah.

Tobias Friedrich compiled the chorales for the oldest "choralbuch" of the Moravian Brethren from 1735 to 1744. It was used by the Moravians at Herrnhut, Saxony. Many of its tunes were also included by John Wesley in his early Methodist tunebook, *The Foundery Collection* (1742).

431 Now Greet the Swiftly Changing Year

This Slovak hymn from the seventeenth century appeared in a 1636 collection, *Tranoscius,* edited by Juraj Transovsky (1591–1637). The original text had seventeen stanzas, which Jaroslav Vajda compressed to seven in his translation.

Jaroslav J. Vajda (b. 1919), a Missouri Synod Lutheran pastor, translated this hymn for *Worship Supplement, 1969* of the *Lutheran Hymnal.* The original Czech text traditionally is sung by Slovak Lutherans as a hymn for New Year's and the Feast of the Holy Name of Jesus.

Alfred V. Fedak (b. 1953) composed the tune SIXTH NIGHT as a setting for Jaroslav Vajda's text in *The Hymnal 1982.* The tune name makes reference to New Year's Eve as the "sixth night" in the observation of the "twelve days of Christmas."

Alfred V. Fedak was born in Elizabeth, New Jersey, in 1953. He attended Hope College and Montclair State University in Montclair, New Jersey, and has most recently served as director of music at Pompton Reformed Church in his home state.

432 'Tis Winter Now; the Fallen Snow

Samuel Longfellow (1819–1892) wrote this poem, which captures the beautiful aspects of winter, and included it in his *Hymns of the Spirit* (1864). Longfellow had a firsthand knowledge of winter, having served churches in Massachusetts, Pennsylvania, and New York state.

Samuel Longfellow, who was born and died in Portland, Maine, was educated at Harvard College and Harvard Divinity School and then ordained for a career in the Unitarian ministry. Along with his pastoral duties, he wrote hymns on a wide range of subjects.

This traditional tune, DANBY, is believed to have originated as an English ballad. Ralph Vaughan Williams prepared a four-part setting of it for this text in *The English Hymnal* (1906) and later developed this unison version for *Songs of Praise* (1925).

This English melody was first paired with the seasonal text by Longfellow in *The English Hymnal* (1906) but is perhaps more familiar to some congregations of the United Church of Christ as part of the repertoire of the *Pilgrim Hymnal* (1958).

433 In the Bulb There Is a Flower

Natalie Allyn Wakeley Sleeth (1930–1992) was inspired by a phrase from a poem by T. S. Eliot for this text, written in Denver, Colorado. She had been contemplating the change of seasons from winter to spring and even purchased a potted yellow tulip plant to help her in writing these words.

Natalie Sleeth was born in Evanston, Illinois, on October 29, 1930. She began piano lessons at age four and majored in music theory at Wellesley College. Her first work, "Canon of Praise," was not published until 1969, but her choral works have received wide acceptance since that time.

Natalie Allyn Wakeley Sleeth (1930–1992) composed the tune PROMISE for her own words, and the song was first performed in anthem form at Pasadena Community Church, St. Petersburg, Florida, at a March 1985 concert. Her husband, dying of a malignancy, requested that this hymn be played at his funeral service.

Natalie Sleeth, the wife of a Methodist minister and professor of homiletics, spent most of her life in university communities in Nashville, Tennessee; Dallas, Texas; Evanston, Illinois; and Denver, Colorado. Sleeth received two honorary degrees for her work in church music.

434 All Beautiful the March of Days

Frances Whitmarsh Wile (1878–1939) was requested to write this hymn by William Channing Gannett, her pastor at First Unitarian Church of Rochester, New York. The two of them worked for about two years revising the text to provide a winter hymn for that congregation.

Frances W. Wile educated herself by reading. With her husband, she moved to Rochester, New York, and was active in the Unitarian Church, women's suffrage, and the study of theosophy. Wile died in Rochester on July 31, 1939.

This melody is known as FOREST GREEN because that was the place in Surrey, England, where Ralph Vaughan Williams first heard it sung to a ballad called "The Ploughboy's Dream." The tune has become a popular setting for many different hymn texts.

Ralph Vaughan Williams (1872–1958) contributed greatly to church hymnody with his adaptations and harmonizations of traditional English tunes. He enjoyed finding and studying the folk music of Great Britain and adapted much of it for use as hymn tunes in the early twentieth century.

435 Each Winter As the Year Grows Older

William Gay (b. 1920) wrote these words in 1969 for a Christmas letter he and his wife sent to friends. The Vietnam War was causing great consternation not only for the Gays but for the nation, as is reflected in the text and tune.

William Gay, a minister in the United Church of Christ, was ordained in 1949. During his career, he served at four Ohio churches and was active in the wider ministry of the denomination. Since retirement, he has lived in Lincoln, Nebraska.

Annabeth McClelland Gay (b. 1925) composed this tune, which was first printed in *A New Song, 3* along with this text by her husband. The melody is titled CAROL OF HOPE for the theme of the text that celebrates new birth out of the bleakness of winter, death, and warfare.

Annabeth McClelland Gay was born in Ottawa, Illinois, the daughter of a Presbyterian minister. Educated at Knox College and Union Seminary, New York City, she has served as organist for a number of United Church of Christ congregations in Ohio and has been involved with denominational ministries.

436 God of Grace and God of Glory

Harry Emerson Fosdick (1878–1969) wrote this stirring hymn in 1930 while vacationing at his home in Boothbay Harbor, Maine. It was sung at the opening service of Riverside Church in New York City on October 5, 1930, and also for the church's dedication on February 8, 1931.

Harry Emerson Fosdick, an American Baptist minister, was one of the most influential preachers of his time. Through his seminary teaching and writing, he touched generations of Christians with his social gospel message. Fosdick was the founding minister of Riverside Church in New York.

John Hughes (1873–1932) composed the tune CWM RHONDDA for a Gymanfa Ganu (a Baptist song gathering). The title refers to an area of Wales. *Cwm* means valley, and *Rhondda* is a river. Fosdick's original tune choice for this text was REGENT SQUARE.

John Hughes was an active church layman at Salem Baptist Church at Llantuit Fardre, Wales. He composed music as an avocation, writing many hymns that are easily identified by their Welsh titles. In addition, Hughes wrote Sunday-school marches and two anthems.

437 We Shall Not Give Up the Fight

This South African freedom song reflects the willingness of people to stand together for hours or days for their rights. In Pretoria Central Prison, singing went on day and night, and even the condemned sang on the way to their executions. Preferably, no instrumentation should be used with this hymn.

South African music was sung without accompaniment, and, contrary to popular opinion, drums were not a part of the Nguni (Zulu and Xhosa) tradition. It was said that a song never was sung the same way twice and that there is no way to "sing wrong."

This South African tune is called ONLY STARTED. It came to Europe by way of Tanzania, but the original text was lost. New words were added, changed, and edited again. Syncopation and pauses are an important part of the music. It is best sung with no accompaniment, not even a piano.

Modern South African music played a central part in the liberation of that country from an apartheid form of government to a majority democracy. Three of these freedom songs have been included in *The New Century Hymnal*, the first denominational hymnal to include examples of this genre.

438 When Peace, like a River (It Is Well with My Soul)

Horatio G. Spafford (1828–1888) wrote this text as a source of comfort after learning that his four daughters had been drowned when the ship *Ville du Havre* collided with another ship en route to England in 1873. Spafford's wife was the only family member on board to survive.

Horatio G. Spafford was a Chicago, Illinois, attorney who lost all his holdings in the Chicago fire of 1871. Yet he helped evangelist Dwight L. Moody rebuild the North Side Tabernacle, the first building reconstructed after this terrible fire.

Philip Paul Bliss (1838–1876) was given this text by Horatio Spafford, his neighbor on May Street in Chicago, Illinois. Spafford asked him to provide a melody for it. The resulting song was included in *Gospel Hymns No. 2* (1876), compiled by Bliss and Ira Sankey. The tune is named VILLE DU HAVRE after the ship on which Spafford's daughters died.

Philip P. Bliss was born in Clearfield County, Pennsylvania, on July 9, 1838. In Chicago, Illinois, he joined the evangelical ministry of Dwight L. Moody and Ira Sankey. Bliss became one of the most prolific songwriters of his generation. He and his wife died in 1876 in a train accident in Ohio.

439 A Mighty Fortress Is Our God

Martin Luther (1483–1546) based this hymn on Psalm 46 in response to King Charles V, who in 1529 had demanded that evangelical cities reintroduce the Roman mass and disown Luther's thinking. When these cities defied the king, the term "Protestant" was used for the first time.

Martin Luther's great hymn spread throughout Germany, rallying many to the Reformation cause. Singing it was considered to be in defiance of the rule of the Roman Catholic Church. This hymn did not become well known in the English-speaking world until the mid-nineteenth century.

Martin Luther (1483–1546) in about 1529 wrote this tune, now titled EIN' FESTE BURG for the opening line in German. The tune, somewhat refined here, has also been called WORMS and LUTHER. Mendelssohn, Meyerbeer, Wagner, Nicolai, and Bach all used the tune in various compositions.

Martin Luther became dismayed by the corruption in the Roman Catholic Church and in 1517 nailed his "ninety-five theses" on the church door at Wittenberg to begin a debate. Instead, his tract brought about a permanent break with the Roman church that was to become the Protestant Reformation.

440 A Mighty Fortress Is Our God

Martin Luther (1483–1546) based this text on Psalm 46. He wanted the psalm to come alive for the church of his time, which was struggling with the meaning of faithfulness to Christ's gospel. A new translation by Madeleine Forell Marshall provides a fresh interpretation of Luther's paraphrase.

Martin Luther's anger with his church erupted into action in 1517, when Tetzel, a Dominican monk, tried to sell indulgences to Luther's poor students at Wittenberg, Germany. The money was being collected to build St. Peter's Church in Rome and to finance projects of Albert of Brandenburg.

Martin Luther (1483–1546) wrote both words and melody for this hymn. This version of the tune, known as EIN' FESTE BURG, is close to Luther's original. Other names include LUTHER and WORMS. The Diet of Worms was a 1521 meeting where Luther refused to recant his beliefs.

Martin Luther translated the Bible into German over a period of years, from 1521 to 1534, enabling people to read the Scriptures for themselves. Previously, the Bible was available only in Latin, a language few German people could read during this time in history.

441 Jesus, Savior, Pilot Me

Edward Hopper (1818–1888) wrote this poem, which first appeared anonymously in *The Sailor's Magazine* in 1871. Hopper did not take credit for his work until 1878, when it was published in *Spiritual Songs*. The hymn historically has been used by missionary groups ministering to sailors.

Edward Hopper was born in New York City on February 17, 1818, and was an ordained Presbyterian minister. He served at the Church of Sea and Land in New York, where many worshipers were sailors. Hopper published all his hymns anonymously and died unexpectedly on April 23, 1888, while writing poetry.

John Edgar Gould (1822–1875) composed this tune in 1871 for Edward Hopper's text the night before he left on a trip to southern Europe and Africa. Although seeking to improve his health, Gould died on the trip, making this his last work. The tune is now called PILOT for the first line of the text.

John E. Gould was born in Bangor, Maine, in 1822 and began composing music early in life. He was a merchant in New York City but moved to Philadelphia around 1868 to form a music company with another hymnwriter, William Fischer. He died on March 4, 1875, while on a trip to Algiers.

442 I'm Pressing on the Upward Way (Higher Ground)

Johnson Oatman Jr. (1856–1922) wrote the words of this hymn in 1892 and sent it to Charles Gabriel, a noted composer, for a tune to be added. The hymn was published in *Songs of Love and Praise No. 5* (1898) and became a favorite of camp-meeting revival crusades.

Johnson Oatman Jr. spent his career working as an insurance agent in Mount Holly, New Jersey, but wrote the words for over five thousand gospel hymns as his spiritual discipline. Although ordained by the Methodist Episcopal Church, he never took a pastoral assignment.

Charles Hutchinson Gabriel (1956–1932) composed this tune, called HIGHER GROUND after the words of the refrain, when he returned to Chicago from a trip. He sold it to a songbook compiler for five dollars. The words and tune were published together in 1898.

Charles H. Gabriel was born in Iowa but spent much of his life in Chicago. He taught singing schools as he traveled from town to town and collected and compiled many collections of gospel and Sunday-school songs. Gabriel composed some seven thousand gospel hymns, anthems, and cantatas.

443 How Like a Gentle Spirit

Charles Eric Lincoln (b. 1924) submitted this text and two others at the invitation of the United Methodist Hymnal Committee, which was seeking hymns using alternative metaphors in reference to God. This hymn was finally selected for that denomination's 1989 hymnal.

C. Eric Lincoln was born in Athens, Alabama, on June 23, 1924. He holds numerous degrees, including an M.Ed. and a Ph.D. from Boston University and thirteen honorary doctorates. Lincoln has served as a college and seminary professor for most of his career and has written extensively on the African American religious experience.

Alfred Morton Smith (1879–1971) submitted this tune anonymously for the text "Lift Up Your Hearts." It was first used in the 1940 hymnal of the Episcopal Church and is named SURSUM CORDA. The name is Latin for "Lift Up Your Hearts."

Alfred M. Smith was born at Jenkintown, Pennsylvania, on May 20, 1879, and educated in Pennsylvania. He was ordained an Episcopal priest in 1906, served as a hospital chaplain following World War I, and held positions at churches in Pennsylvania and California. Smith died at Brigantine, New Jersey, on February 26, 1971.

444 We Are Often Tossed and Driven
(We'll Understand It Better By and By)

Charles Albert Tindley (1851–1933) published this gospel song in 1905, and the refrain quickly became a favorite funeral hymn when sung without the stanzas. Although the hymn is widely known, many may not be aware that the author was a legendary preacher in Philadelphia, Pennsylvania.

Charles A. Tindley was called as the pastor of Bainbridge Street Methodist Church in Philadelphia, Pennsylvania, in 1902. When he died in 1933, the church's membership had grown to over ten thousand, and it was renamed Tindley Temple in his honor.

Charles Albert Tindley (1851–1933) composed the tune BY AND BY for his own words. Tindley was recognized as a pioneer of the gospel style, and several of his songs appeared in *Gospel Pearls* (1921), the first hymnal to utilize the term "gospel" in relation to this music.

Charles A. Tindley was born on July 7, 1851, in Berlin, Maryland, an African American community on the Eastern Shore of the Chesapeake Bay. After a spectacular career as a Methodist Episcopal church minister, he died at the Frederick Douglass Hospital in Philadelphia, Pennsylvania, on July 26, 1933.

445 Lift Your Heads, O Martyrs, Weeping

Károly Jeszensky (1851–1927), a Protestant pastor in Hungary, based this 1890 hymn on one that Pauli Joachim (1636–1708) wrote when Protestant pastors were imprisoned and tortured in attempts to force them to convert to Catholicism. The text pays tribute to forty-two who were sold as galley slaves and eventually ransomed by the Dutch government in 1676.

William Tóth, a minister of the Hungarian Reformed Church, created this English translation in 1938 so that U.S. congregations could sing this hymn of the Hungarian Reformation. Theodore S. Horvath adapted the text for *The New Century Hymnal* to preserve its use for future generations of Christians.

The history of the hymn tune MAGYAR ("Hungarian") is difficult to document, as the composer and source are unknown. The repetitive rhythm and plaintive melody are reminiscent of the monotony and suffering endured by the galley slaves. In Hungarian Reformed churches it is sung slowly and with great dignity.

Gustav Julius Neumann, who has been credited as the adapter and harmonizer of this tune, was the poet responsible for creating the metrical version of William Tóth's English text that appeared in *The Hymnal* (1941) of the Evangelical and Reformed Church.

446 Jesus, Still Lead On

Nicolaus Ludwig von Zinzendorf (1700–1760) wrote two hymns in 1721, which were combined by Christian Gregor for his 1778 hymnal. Jane Borthwick translated that version into English in 1846. Zinzendorf wrote these hymns before his conversion to the United Brethren Church.

Nicolaus Ludwig von Zinzendorf was a founder of the United Brethren Church, a group that grew from Moravian roots. Banned by the government of Saxony, Zinzendorf traveled widely in Germany, Holland, England, the United States, and the West Indies, spreading his church's doctrines.

Adam Drese (1620–1701) composed the tune SEELENBRÄUTIGAM for a text he wrote beginning with this German word. It first appeared in his hymnal of 1698, *Geistreiches Gesangbuch*, published in Darmstadt, Germany. Drese was serving as *kapellmeister* at Arnstadt at the time.

Adam Drese was born in December 1620 in Darmstadt, Germany. He was sponsored by Duke Wilhelm IV of Weimar to study in Warsaw, Poland, and became *kapellmeister* to the duke upon his return. After the duke died, Drese was taken to Jena by the duke's son and later became mayor of that town.

447 Beams of Heaven As I Go

Charles Albert Tindley (1851–1933) published this gospel song (also known as "Some Day") in 1905. During his preaching, Tindley would often begin singing one of his newly written hymns and after he had sung a few stanzas, the congregation would naturally join in.

Charles A. Tindley studied for the Christian ministry at a Pennsylvania seminary and through a correspondence course. His song texts employed biblical imagery and were intended especially to speak to African Americans who had been freed from slavery not long before.

Charles Albert Tindley (1851–1933) composed the tune SOME DAY for his own words. He nurtured the work of Thomas Andrew Dorsey, who has become known as the "father of gospel music" and who claimed his mission was to "further what Tindley started."

Charles A. Tindley composed a total of forty-five gospel hymns and was recognized as the first composer of that genre. He was the founding pastor of what is now called Tindley Methodist Church on the corner of Broad and Fitzwater Streets in Philadelphia, Pennsylvania.

448 Take My Life, God, Let It Be

Frances Ridley Havergal (1836–1879) wrote this poem following a prayer meeting in 1874. It has been translated into many languages, including French, German, Swedish, Russian, and some African and Asian languages. Havergal's gratitude and Christian commitment are reflected in the text.

Frances R. Havergal spoke English, French, and German fluently and wrote verse in these languages, as well as in Greek, Latin, and Hebrew. Although her delicate health kept her from traveling extensively, she kept in touch with friends through letters.

Justin Heinrich Knecht (1752–1817) was an accomplished organist and wrote many compositions for the church and theater. He was born in Biberach, Würtemberg, and spent most of his life there. This tune, called VIENNA or RAVENNA, was included in a collection of ninety-six other original tunes in 1799.

Justin Heinrich Knecht had a classical education and learned to play a number of orchestral instruments as well as the organ. In 1790, Knecht introduced the use of program notes in his concert programs, to provide the audience with background information on the music being performed.

449 Softly and Tenderly

Will Lamartine Thompson (1847–1909) wrote these words, which became one of the favorite hymns of the evangelist Dwight L. Moody. It was often used as a hymn of invitation at Moody's evangelistic meetings in the United States and Great Britain.

Will L. Thompson was born in East Liverpool, Ohio, on November 7, 1847. He attended the New England Conservatory of Music and later studied in Germany. His life's ambition was to write music for the general public, and after a successful secular career he was able to compose gospel hymns full-time.

Will Lamartine Thompson (1847–1909) composed both words and music for this popular gospel hymn, SOFTLY AND TENDERLY. It was first published in *Sparkling Gems* (1880), by J. Calvin Bushey.

Will L. Thompson established a music publishing business late in life in his hometown of East Liverpool, Ohio, with a branch in Chicago, Illinois. He would often travel by horse and buggy from town to town in Ohio, singing his gospel songs to introduce people to his new hymns.

450 O for a Closer Bond with God

William Cowper (1731–1800) cited Genesis 5:24 ("Enoch walked with God") as a reference for this text when it appeared in *Olney Hymns* (1779). Cowper wrote the poem on December 9, 1769, as a friend, Mary Unwin, lay critically ill.

William Cowper has been described as one of the most popular poets of his generation in England, and his hymns are among the finest in the English language. Cowper wrote during times of health, although much of his life was spent in mental and physical anguish and illness.

John Bacchus Dykes (1823–1876) composed BEATITUDO in 1875 for a text by Isaac Watts. The word, coined by Cicero, means "the condition of blessedness." It was first published in the second edition of *Hymns Ancient and Modern* (1875) and has been used with Cowper's hymn since 1892.

John B. Dykes was the best known of the English Victorian hymnwriters and one of the most prolific. In addition, he published many sermons and articles on theology and liturgics, and wrote anthems and service music. His greatest legacy, however, consists of his hymn tunes.

451 Be Now My Vision

This ancient Irish poem, which dates from the eighth century, began "Rop tu mo bhoile, a Comdi cride." It was translated into English prose by Mary E. Byrne (1880–1931) and then into verse form by Eleanor H. Hull (1860–1935). It is an example of a Celtic *lorica*, a prayer for physical and spiritual protection.

Early Gaelic culture might never have been uncovered in the twentieth century had it not been for the work of Eleanor H. Hull (1860–1935). She was founder of the Irish Text Society and president of the Irish Literary Society of London, England. Her work reawakened interest in Irish culture.

This traditional Irish tune accompanied a folk song that began "With my love on the road." SLANE refers to a hill outside of the community of Tara, County Meath, Ireland. It was on this hill that Saint Patrick lit the Paschal fire and challenged the authority of the pagan king.

This Irish folk song was adapted and arranged by David Evans (1874–1948) for use with these words, bringing together two Irish sources into one hymn. Evans was one of Wales's most distinguished musicians. He spent a great deal of time researching folk tunes of the British Isles.

452 Savior, Who Dying Gave

Sylvanus Dryden Phelps (1816–1895) submitted this text to Robert Lowry, who was seeking new hymns for his collection, *Pure Gold* (1871). Lowry wrote to the author on his seventieth birthday: "Happy is the man who can produce one song which the world will keep on singing after its author shall have passed away."

S. Dryden Phelps was born in Suffield, Connecticut, on May 15, 1816. He served Baptist churches in Bristol and New Haven, Connecticut, and Providence, Rhode Island, before becoming editor of *The Christian Secretary*, a religious journal. He died in New Haven on November 23, 1895.

Robert Lowry (1826–1899) composed the tune SOMETHING FOR JESUS for Phelps's text, employing the final phrase for the tune name. The hymn was published in a volume called *Pure Gold* in 1871. This hymnbook was extremely popular, generating sales of over a million copies.

Robert Lowry did not begin to write hymns until he was forty years old. He served as a Baptist minister and college professor at Bucknell University in Pennsylvania. Lowry's final post was the Baptist Church of Plainfield, New Jersey, which he served as pastor until his death in 1899.

453 When the Morning Stars Together

Albert Frederick Bayly (1901–1984) wrote this text in praise of music in 1969, and it appeared in *Rejoice Always* (1971) prior to its publication in several denominational hymnals with the tune WEISSE FLAGGEN. The text surveys the role of music in worship from the dawn of time to the modern era.

Albert Bayly was born on Bexhill-on-Sea, Sussex, England, on September 6, 1901. He studied for the ministry at Mansfield College, Oxford, and was ordained in the English Congregational Church in 1928. Bayly was honored in 1978 at a special service at Westminster Abbey.

Jean Slates Hawk (b. 1925) wrote this tune, OFFERING, for a different text as part of an assignment for a 1991 hymnwriting workshop at St. Olaf College in Northfield, Minnesota. Having already written a centennial hymn for the State College Presbyterian Church, Pennsylvania, she took the course to develop her skill further.

Jean Slates Hawk was born November 10, 1925, in Tremont, in the anthracite coal region of Pennsylvania. She learned to play the organ while sitting beside her mother, a church organist. She studied piano, clarinet, and oboe and played in the Nashville (Tennessee) Symphony Orchestra from 1950 to 1963.

454 Lord, I Want to Be a Christian

This African American spiritual is an example of a mask-and-symbol song, which can be understood on two levels. The mask is that it is a simple song of longing for the Christian faith. The underlying symbol of "in my heart" is a commentary on insincere people who treat others with brutality.

R. Nathaniel Dett (1882–1943) transcribed this hymn for his *Religious Folk-Songs of the Negro* in 1927. It was sung by the Hampton Institute student chorus, which Dett organized in 1930. The chorus toured extensively in the United States and Europe.

This anonymous tune is named I WANT TO BE A CHRISTIAN after the first line of the text. It was written in the pentatonic mode, meaning that it can be played using only the black keys on the piano if started on G-flat. This pentatonic mode was frequently used in African American melodies.

The tunes of the spiritual tradition were "forged of sorrow in the heat of religious fervor" according to one expert in the field, James Weldon Johnson. By use of repetition and sustained high notes, the tunes reinforced the emotions of the words for the singers.

455 I Am Yours, O Lord

Fanny Jane Crosby (1820–1915) was inspired to write this hymn one night after conversing about God's presence with her host, William H. Doane. Hebrews 10:22 ("Let us approach with a true heart") was given as a scriptural reference for the hymn when it was first published.

Fanny J. Crosby lost her eyesight as an infant when a doctor's remedy for inflammation did not work. Crosby attended the New York City School for the Blind and taught school for eleven years after her graduation. She collaborated frequently with the composer William H. Doane.

William Howard Doane (1832–1915) composed the tune I AM YOURS for this text after Fanny Crosby created it during a visit to his Cincinnati, Ohio, home. The hymn was first printed in *Brightest and Best*, a Sunday-school songbook that Doane edited with Robert Lowry in 1875.

William H. Doane grew up in Preston, Connecticut, and directed the school choir at Woodstock Academy at age fourteen. In his final year there, he was converted to Christianity. Doane worked for a woodworking-machine manufacturer in Cincinnati, Ohio, for most of his career.

456 More Love to You, O Christ

Elizabeth Payson Prentiss (1818–1878) wrote this hymn hurriedly in 1856 during a stressful time. She did not share it with her husband until thirteen years later. Published in 1870, it was adopted by the revival movement in the United States and was sung throughout the country.

Elizabeth P. Prentiss was born in Portland, Maine, on October 26, 1818. She taught school before marrying a Presbyterian minister and seminary professor. Her talent as a writer was evident early in life, and her work was published when she was only sixteen.

William Howard Doane (1832–1915) included this tune with Elizabeth Prentiss's text in his 1870 hymnal, *Songs of Devotion for Christian Associations*. The tune name, MORE LOVE TO YOU, derives from the opening line. The text and tune are now considered inseparable.

William H. Doane's first cantata was entitled "Santa Claus," and many others were based on this theme, even though Doane was a sincere Christian. He wrote more than 2,200 compositions and published some forty songbooks. He died in South Orange, New Jersey, on Christmas Eve, 1915.

457 Jesus, I Live to You

Henry Harbaugh (1817–1867) wrote this poem, known affectionately as the "Mercersburg Hymn," around 1860 while serving as a pastor in Pennsylvania. It may have been inspired by a famous German confirmation hymn, "Jesu, Dir leb'ich." The hymn was first published in Harbaugh's *Hymns and Chants for Sunday Schools* (1861).

Henry Harbaugh was born October 28, 1817, in Waynesboro, Pennsylvania, and was ordained to the Reformed Church ministry after training with John W. Nevin. Harbaugh served as a church pastor before teaching theology at Mercersburg (Pennsylvania) Seminary, where he died on December 28, 1867.

Isaac Baker Woodbury (1819–1858) wrote this melody, named LAKE ENON, in 1854 for a hymn by Ann Steele, "While My Redeemer's Near." "Enon" is a scriptural word meaning "an abundance of water," although a specific location is unclear. The tune is also called MERCERSBURG, since the hymn has long been sung at that Pennsylvania academy.

Isaac B. Woodbury was born in Beverly, Massachusetts, on October 23, 1819. At the age of nineteen, he gave up his job as a blacksmith to study violin and voice, traveling to England for training. Woodbury returned to the United States to teach music. He died in Columbia, South Carolina, at age thirty-nine.

458 I've Got a Feeling

This text, like most traditional African American religious songs, was passed along by oral tradition. It most likely was used in worship as a response to a spoken need by an individual, with the community singing its support, using a leader-response style.

Nineteenth-century African American music was practical music. There was a song for every occasion and every need. Most worship settings had a song leader in addition to a preacher. The song leader would begin a song in response to his or her feelings about a sermon or situation.

This African American tune takes its name from the opening words of the text, I'VE GOT A FEELING. Note that the response is provided in harmony for stanzas 2 and 3 after an initial phrase is introduced by a solo leader or the congregation singing in unison voice.

Jeffrey Radford arranged this traditional African American song in a swing style for *The New Century Hymnal*. To "swing" the rhythm, the pairs of eighth notes in the accompaniment should be played as parts of a triplet: long note, short note.

459 Come, O Fount of Every Blessing

Robert Robinson (1735–1790) is believed to be the author of this hymn, although the original manuscript has not been found. Robinson noted in his diary that a Mr. Wheatly of Norwich had published his hymn in 1758. It only appeared with Robinson's name in later collections.

Robert Robinson was born September 17, 1735, at Norfolk, England. He was influenced by George Whitefield, John Wesley, and other evangelical preachers and converted to Christianity at the age of twenty. Robinson entered the ministry, but his unstable nature caused him to move from one denomination to another. He was a friend of the scientist Dr. Joseph Priestley.

This anonymous American folk tune is named NETTLETON because it was attributed to Asahel Nettleton, a nineteenth-century evangelist. Although he is not believed to be the composer, his name continues to be used with this tune.

John Wyeth's (1770–1858) *Repository of Sacred Music* (1813) marks the first printed use of this anonymous American tune. It may be an old tune that was sung with "Go tell Aunt Tabby her old gray goose is dead." A similar melody exists in the African American spiritual tradition.

460 Be Not Dismayed (God Will Take Care of You)

Civilla Durfee Martin (1869–1948) wrote this hymn while confined to bed because of illness in 1904. At the time, she and her husband, a Baptist minister, were working at the Practical Bible Training School, Lestershire, New York, to compile a songbook for the school's president.

Civilla D. Martin was born in Jordan, Nova Scotia, Canada, on August 21, 1869. She began her career as a schoolteacher in her native country and contributed her musical abilities to her husband's traveling evangelistic campaigns. Martin died in Atlanta, Georgia, on March 9, 1948.

Walter Stillman Martin (1862–1935) was given this poem by his wife when he returned home from a preaching assignment. He immediately sat down and composed this tune for it one Sunday afternoon. It is named MARTIN here but appears as GOD CARES in some sources.

W. Stillman Martin was born in Massachusetts and educated at Harvard University. He was ordained to the Baptist ministry but later moved to the Christian Church, Disciples of Christ. Martin was professor of Bible at Atlantic Christian College, North Carolina, until the end of his life.

461 Let Us Hope When Hope Seems Hopeless

David Beebe (b. 1931) wrote this hymn of hope for a worship service at the close of a creative-writing course he was teaching in 1989. Beebe had recently begun his work with the United Church of Christ Stewardship Council as associate for stewardship education.

David Beebe was born in Arkansas and ordained to the United Church of Christ ministry in 1959. He served churches in northern California and Chattanooga, Tennessee, before entering denominational work. Beebe also served as a college chaplain for six years.

Emma Lou Diemer (b. 1927) composed the tune LET US HOPE for David Beebe's text expressly for *The New Century Hymnal*. She also created an anthem setting of the tune for a new anthem series published by the Pilgrim Press in conjunction with the hymnal in 1995.

Emma Lou Diemer grew up in Kansas City and Warrensburg, Missouri. She began her study of the piano at the age of five or six and started composing music shortly thereafter. Diemer became the organist at her home church (Christian—Disciples of Christ) in her early teens and since then has devoted her life to music and composing.

462 Creating God, Your Fingers Trace

Jeffery Rowthorn (b. 1934) assigned his students at Yale University's Institute of Sacred Music the task of paraphrasing a psalm in modern language. Never having done this himself, he decided to complete the assignment as well. This text was the result of that exercise and has appeared in many hymnals.

Jeffery Rowthorn was born in Wales, educated and ordained in England, worked as a seminary professor and dean in the United States, and in 1987 was consecrated bishop suffragan of Connecticut. In 1993, he moved to Paris, France, to serve as bishop of the American Convocation of Churches in Europe.

Eugene W. Hancock (b. 1929) composed this tune, now titled HANCOCK in his honor, in 1989. It was played at an organist guild meeting and later brought to the attention of the committee for the *Presbyterian Hymnal* (1990), in which it was published.

Eugene W. Hancock was born in St. Louis, Missouri, but raised in Detroit, Michigan. Since 1970, he has served as professor of music at the Borough of Manhattan (New York) Community College. Hancock also served as director of music at West End Presbyterian Church in New York.

463 I Look to You in Every Need

Samuel Longfellow (1819–1892) wrote this text for a hymnal he edited in 1864. Theistic in nature, the hymnal gives evidence of Longfellow's move away from Unitarian Christianity. This was one of the earliest American hymns to connect faith with physical and spiritual well-being.

Samuel Longfellow was the younger brother of poet Henry Wadsworth Longfellow. During his education at Harvard University (Massachusetts), he and a friend edited *A Book of Hymns for Public and Private Devotions*. In 1864, they edited a second hymnal, *Hymns of the Spirit*.

This tune, O JESU, was first found as the setting for a German hymn that began "O Jesu, warum legst du mir," from which its name derives. Longfellow's text was first paired with this German tune in *The English Hymnal* (1906).

J. Balthasar Reimann (1702–1749) published a songbook in 1747 entitled *Sammlung Alter und Neuer Melodien Evangel*. The collection was unique in that it contained two of only a few chorale melodies thought to be written by J. S. Bach. Reimann once met Bach and modeled his own life after that composer.

464 The Weaver's Shuttle Swiftly Flies

James Curtis Gertmenian (b. 1947) used imagery from Job 7:6 ("My days are swifter than a weaver's shuttle, and come to their end without hope") for this text written in 1990. *The New Century Hymnal* marks the hymn's first publication in a denominational collection.

James Gertmenian, the grandson of Armenian immigrants to the United States, is a United Church of Christ minister, ordained in 1972. He has served churches in Weston, Connecticut, and Minneapolis, Minnesota.

William Croft (1678–1721) composed the tune ST. MATTHEW in 1708 for a paraphrase of Psalm 33. The name honors one of the twelve disciples, although it had no significance in relation to the text. This tune has been cited as one of the greatest English hymn tunes ever written.

William Croft served as church organist at the Chapel Royal, England, and later at Westminster Abbey, where he is buried. In addition to church music, he wrote music for the theater and various instrumental pieces. Croft was one of England's most important composers.

465 Teach Me, O Lord, Your Holy Way

William Tidd Matson (1833–1906) wrote the poem "The Inner Life" in 1866, in 321 four-line stanzas. This hymn utilizes only a portion of that work. It appeared in the *Evangelical Hymnal* (1917) with a tune different from the setting provided here.

William T. Matson was born October 17, 1833, in England. He grew up in the Church of England but left to join the Methodist New Connection and eventually became a Congregationalist minister. Matson published numerous collections of poetry, and some of his hymns were well known.

Edward Miller (1731–1807) adapted this tune in 1790 and named it ROCKINGHAM after his patron, the Marquis of Rockingham. Other names for this tune include BISHOP, CATON, COMMUNION, and MAYHEW.

Edward Miller was a composer as well as a church organist. Trained as an apprentice bricklayer, he soon ran away from this job to study music. Miller received a doctor of music degree from Cambridge University in 1786 and served as organist at Doncaster, England, for fifty-one years.

466 Unto the Hills We Lift Our Longing Eyes

John Douglas Sutherland Campbell, Duke of Argyll (1845–1914), wrote this metrical version of Psalm 121, the "traveler's psalm." An Englishman, he traveled frequently, making trips to India and Canada, which at the time were part of the British Commonwealth.

John Campbell, Duke of Argyll, was governor-general of Canada and son-in-law of England's Queen Victoria. He was active in public life in England and served as a member of Parliament and governor of Windsor Castle, among other posts. Campbell published a *Book of Psalms* in 1877.

Charles Henry Purday (1799–1885) composed the tune SANDON for John Newman's hymn "Lead, Kindly Light." Purday named the hymn LANDON, but the name was changed to SANDON, perhaps because of a typographical error. Purday was a well-known vocal soloist in his time.

Charles Henry Purday came from a family of music publishers and wrote many tunes himself. He fought for copyright protection for musical publications, was among the first to use concert program notes, and avidly promoted congregational singing through music education.

467 Mothering God, You Gave Me Birth

Julian (d. c. 1417) was born in 1342 and lived in Norwich, England, serving as an "anchoress" at St. Julian at Conisford. She was a sort of spiritual advisor who remained cloistered near the church, devoted to prayer. At the age of thirty, Julian experienced "showings" or revelations of Christ's suffering on the cross. This hymn incorporates ideas from her writings on that experience.

Jean Wiebe Janzen (b. 1933), a lifelong member of the Mennonite Church, returned to school for a graduate degree in creative writing at Fresno State University in California after her children were grown. She has since taught poetry-writing in colleges and public schools.

Jonathan McNair (b. 1959) composed his setting of Jean Janzen's text in 1994 after reflecting on the writings of Julian of Norwich. It is named ANDREW for McNair's second son. The hymn was first sung in 1995 at the annual conference of the Hymn Society in the United States and Canada, held in San Diego, California.

Jonathan McNair was born on March 15, 1959, in Villa Rica, Georgia, the son of a Presbyterian minister. During his childhood, the family lived in Georgia, North Carolina, and Missouri, finally settling in Asheville, North Carolina, where McNair first developed his interest in music and the church.

468 The Care the Eagle Gives Her Young

R. Deane Postlethwaite (1925–1980) based this text on the imagery of Deuteronomy 32, the eagle pushing her young from the nest. This was one of the earliest hymns to experiment with feminine imagery for God; it led to further research into scripture in search of other feminine references.

R. Deane Postlethwaite was a minister of the United Methodist Church who served churches in Kansas, New York, and Minnesota. His hymns were written as modern expressions of faith for use in his own congregations and were published in *Eight Hymns in Context* in 1980, the year of his death.

Jesse Seymour Irvine (1836–1887) has been recognized as the composer of CRIMOND only since 1950, when hymnologists discovered a letter from her sister citing its origins. There are some who still believe it is the work of David Grant, an Aberdeen tobacconist, who was credited as the composer when it first appeared in *Northern Psalter* (1872).

Jesse Seymour Irvine was born in Kincardineshire, Scotland, in 1836, the daughter of a minister. Her father served parishes in Dunnottar, Peterhead, and Crimond, all in Scotland. She remained at her father's last charge, Crimond, and died there in 1887 at the age of fifty-one.

469 O Grant Us Light

Lawrence Tuttiett (1825–1897) wrote this poem in six stanzas. It appeared with the heading "Divine Guidance" in *Germs of Thought on the Sunday Services* (1864). It was also included with slight alterations in Horder's *Congregational Hymn Book*, published twenty years later.

Lawrence Tuttiett was born in Devonshire, England, in 1825. He abandoned his studies in medicine to train for the Christian ministry and was ordained in the Anglican Church in 1848. Tuttiett served three different parishes and published several collections of hymns.

Henry W. Baker (1821–1877) composed this tune, HESPERUS, for John Keble's "Sun of My Soul" in 1854 while he was a student. It was published anonymously in the *Penny Post* in 1861 and in an English hymnal five years later. Baker eventually claimed it as his own.

Henry W. Baker edited the most successful English hymnal ever published, *Hymns Ancient and Modern* (1861). It sold more than sixty million copies over the next fifty years and was considered the hymnal of choice in the Church of England. In 1859, Baker was knighted for his work.

470 Golden Breaks the Dawn

Tzu-chen Chao (1888–1979) is the author of this morning hymn, which was included in *Hymns of Universal Praise* (1936), a landmark Chinese Christian hymnal. Frank W. Price (b. 1895) included this English translation along with twenty-two other indigenous hymns in *Chinese Christian Hymns* (1953).

T. C. Chao was born February 14, 1888, in Hso-tsun, China, and educated at Soochow University. He received his master's and divinity degrees at Vanderbilt University in Nashville, Tennessee. Chao published over fifty indigenous Chinese Christian hymns in *Hymns of the People* (1931).

This Chinese folk song is named LE P'ING, which means "Happy Peace." The hexatonic melody was adapted by Te-ngai Hu (b. circa 1900). It was one of seventy-two authentic Chinese tunes included in *Hymns of Universal Praise* (1936) and later in *Chinese Christian Hymns* (1953).

Hymns of Universal Praise was a 1936 project undertaken by six major denominations to translate and publish four hundred western hymns into the Chinese language. It also included sixty-two hymns written by Chinese Christians and seventy-two tunes with Chinese folk origins.

471 What a Covenant

Elisha Albright Hoffman (1839–1929) wrote this hymn in 1887 at the suggestion of A. J. Showalter, a music publisher. It has been published in more than one thousand music books and translated into nearly every language of the world where Christianity is practiced.

Elisha A. Hoffman was born May 7, 1837, in Orwigsburg, Pennsylvania. He was an ordained Evangelical minister and served churches of several denominations in the Midwest. Hoffman was an editor for the Evangelical Association Publishing House in Cleveland, Ohio, for more than a decade.

Anthony Johnson Showalter (1858–1924) composed the tune LEANING in 1887 and the refrain in 1888. The tune was inspired in part by letters from two friends, both of whom had been recently widowed. In his sympathy notes to them, he quoted Deuteronomy 33:27, and he based this gospel song on that verse.

A. J. Showalter was born in Rockingham County, Virginia, in 1858. A composer and music teacher, he formed his own publishing company with branches in Georgia, Texas, and Tennessee and published over one hundred books on music during his life. He died in Chattanooga, Tennessee, in 1924.

472 Precious Lord, Take My Hand

Thomas A. Dorsey (1899–1965) wrote this prayer hymn in 1932 after hearing of the death of his wife and newborn son. Consoling himself at the piano with the familiar Protestant hymn "Must Jesus Bear the Cross Alone," Dorsey forged his own text affirming the presence of Jesus in times of extreme grief.

Thomas A. Dorsey experienced a "definite spiritual change" and began writing gospel songs to express his feelings. Already an accomplished and successful performing musician in the jazz and blues field, Dorsey eventually became known as the "father of gospel music."

Thomas A. Dorsey (1899–1965) developed PRECIOUS LORD from an old Sunday-school tune called MAITLAND. The hymn was first sung in 1932 at Ebenezer Baptist Church on the south side of Chicago, Illinois, by the choir director, Theodore Frye, with Dorsey serving as accompanist.

Thomas A. Dorsey was born in Villa Rica, Georgia, and was influenced by the blues pianists of Atlanta, Georgia. In 1923, he formed the Wildcat's Jazz Band, with whom Ma Rainey performed. For forty years, Dorsey was choir director at Pilgrim Baptist Church in Chicago, Illinois.

473 Blessed Assurance

Fanny Jane Crosby (1820–1915) demonstrated her God-given talent by providing just the right words for a tune with this hymn. She wrote it in 1873, immediately after hearing the tune played by its composer, Phoebe Knapp, and it became the single most popular song of the 8,500 Crosby wrote.

Fanny Crosby lived to be ninety-four years old. She was born in Putnam County, New York, but spent most of her life in New York City. Crosby provided texts for all the major gospel songwriters of her days, including several for Phoebe Knapp, the composer of this hymn.

Phoebe Palmer Knapp (1839–1908) visited her friend Fanny Crosby in 1873 and asked her to provide a text for this tune, now called ASSURANCE for Crosby's words. They were published together by John R. Sweney in *Gems of Praise* for the Methodist Episcopal Church.

Phoebe Knapp composed more than five hundred gospel hymns and songs for children. Her father, William Palmer, was a Christian evangelist. She married Fairfield Knapp, the founder of the Metropolitan Life Insurance Company, and after his death in 1891 gave much of her fortune to various charities.

474 I'm So Glad, Jesus Lifted Me

This text is an expression of thankfulness in response to a religious experience. The feeling of transcendence brought on by a lifting of the burdens of sin evokes a response of joy such as that expressed in this text. It is an appropriate response to an assurance of pardon.

African American spirituals must be interpreted in light of the experience of slavery in which they were born. Although on the surface many would appear to be a reflection on the slaves' religious experience or conversion, they can also be interpreted to refer to the anticipation of freedom through Jesus' intervention in this life or the eternal life to come.

This African American melody takes its name, I'M SO GLAD, from the text. The style is repetitive, consisting of short, syncopated phrases sung several times. Each repetition starts on a higher note, helping to convey the message of liberation and happiness.

Written notation often cannot convey the excitement of a piece of music as it would have been performed. Subtleties of rhythm are often a matter of "feel." Jeffrey Radford has attempted to capture the mood of this song in an arrangement in the accompanist edition of *The New Century Hymnal*.

475 God's Eye Is on the Sparrow

Civilla Durfee Martin (1866–1948) was inspired to write this poem while visiting a friend in Elmira, New York, who endured chronic illness. The friend said she never became discouraged because "my Heavenly Father watches over each little sparrow and I know he loves and cares for me."

Civilla D. Martin, born in Nova Scotia, Canada, wrote poetry only as a hobby until her husband, W. Stillman Martin, encouraged her to write hymn texts. He composed the music for many of her songs and served as a professor at a Bible College in Johnson City, New York.

Charles Hutchinson Gabriel (1856–1932) was asked to write this tune when W. Stillman Martin, the textwriter's husband, was dissatisfied with his own attempts. This combination was first sung at Royal Albert Hall, London, England, during the 1905 Torrey-Alexander revival meeting.

Charles H. Gabriel, born in Wilton, Iowa, became one of the most prolific early twentieth-century gospel songwriters. Without ever having a formal music lesson, he edited more than 150 religious songbooks. Gabriel often used the pseudonym Charlotte G. Homer for his hymn texts.

476 My Life Flows On in Endless Song (How Can I Keep from Singing)

This text appeared in the songbook *Bright Jewels for the Sunday School* without identifying the writer of the words. It is known that Robert Lowry (1826–1899) was the editor of that 1869 hymnal. The third stanza is a twentieth-century addition by Doris Plenn.

Robert Lowry (1826–1899) was a preacher for Baptist churches in Pennsylvania, New York City, Brooklyn, and Plainfield, New Jersey. In addition, he succeeded William B. Bradbury as music editor for songbooks published by Biglow and Main, New York. Lowry edited twelve Sunday-school collections.

Robert Lowry (1826–1899) is believed to have composed the tune ENDLESS SONG for these words, contrary to earlier sources that implied it was a Quaker melody. The tune's name is taken from words in the opening line of the text.

Robert Lowry was a prolific composer of gospel hymns. He worked with William H. Doane on a dozen collections and was the music editor for New York publishers Biglow and Main, succeeding William B. Bradbury in that position. Lowry was also a Baptist preacher.

477 Though Falsely Some Revile or Hate Me

Chi-pi Ni (b. 1909) wrote this text for a hymnal of indigenous Chinese Christian hymns. It reflects the difficulty of living in a nation where Christianity is a minority religion and where its followers are often reviled and ridiculed by others for their faith.

Frank W. Price (1895–1974) translated this text from the original Chinese as one of twenty-three hymns in *Chinese Christian Hymns* (1953). A Presbyterian missionary to China for three decades, Price was kept in detention by the Communists for three years and was released in 1952.

Maryette H. Lum (dates unknown) wrote this tune, named THE BROOK CHERITH, in 1934. The name comes from the fourth stanza, which relates a drought predicted by the prophet Elijah (1 Kings 17). God ordered him to stay for some time at the "Wadi Cherith," where he was fed by ravens bringing bread.

Maryette H. Lum is the composer of two tunes in the Chinese Union hymnbook *Hymns of Universal Praise* (1936, rev. ed. 1971)—this one and a setting of "O Christ, Our Great Foundation" by Timothy Tingfang Lew.

478 I've Got Peace like a River

The Hebrew prophet Isaiah's imagery of "peace like a river" (66:12) is thought to be the basis for this spiritual's text. Other nautical references might imply that this was a seacoast or riverboat song. The Mississippi River, for instance, was a major trade route.

The references to peace, joy, love, and faith include four of the nine "fruits of the spirit" mentioned in Galatians 5:22. This is one of very few hymns to use water similes to describe the attributes of faith—like a river, fountain, ocean, and anchor.

This tune, named PEACE LIKE A RIVER from words in the text, has its roots in the African American spirituals that sustained people in poverty and captivity. The tranquil images contrast with the stressful life and demands of life as a slave.

Note that each stanza of this spiritual is sung twice, once with the first ending and once with the second ending. The editorial note in the hymnal invites congregations to invent other similes to describe what other "fruits of the spirit" might be like. Water is the connecting theme here.

479 God Is My Shepherd

Lavon Bayler (b. 1933) created this modern adaptation of one of the best-loved psalm paraphrases for *The New Century Hymnal*. The original version, found in *The Psalms of David in Meeter* (or the Scottish Psalter, 1650), is actually a composite of several earlier texts.

The Scottish Psalter of 1650 was created in response to a desire by the English Parliament to create a common hymnal for England and Scotland. Dissatisfied with the approved 1646 work, the Scottish church developed the 1650 version, which became the standard Scottish hymnal.

James Leith Macbeth Bain (c. 1840–1925) was known as Brother James. This tune, called BROTHER JAMES' AIR, is one of several melodies he composed and no doubt sang in his healing ministry. Gordon Jacob (1895–1984) arranged the tune for an anthem published in London in 1934.

James L. M. Bain was born in Scotland around 1840. After reaffirming his faith following a period of agnosticism, he formed a "brotherhood of healers" for treating both physical and spiritual illness. Late in life, he worked in the slums of Liverpool, England. He died September 19, 1925.

480 Jesus, Priceless Treasure

Johann Franck (1618–1677) composed this song of devotion to Jesus following the example of a secular love song. The text was first published in Crüger's *Praxis Pietatas Melica* (1653) and has been translated into many languages. This English version is by Catherine Winkworth from her *Chorale Book for England* (1863).

Johann Franck, a lawyer and public official, was born June 1, 1618, at Güben, Germany. A Lutheran layman, he wrote 110 hymns, many filled with a deep mystical sense that was new to Protestant hymns of that time and anticipated the pietist movement to come. He died on June 18, 1677, at Güben.

Johann Crüger (1598–1662) is believed to have composed this tune in 1653, but he may have based it on a traditional German melody. The arrangement used here is by J. S. Bach, from his motet JESUS, MEINE FREUDE, the first phrase of the German text and the tune's name.

Johann Crüger was knowledgeable about various forms of composition of his time and was able to use them to great advantage. He was greatly influenced by the science of harmony brought to Germany by Italian masters, and employed this new approach to music.

481 As Pants the Hart for Cooling Streams

This anonymous text is a free paraphrase of Psalm 42 in English. The original work, first published in Tate and Brady's *New Version of the Psalms of David* (1696), contained thirteen stanzas. This version uses stanzas 1, 6, 10, and 12.

The *New Version of the Psalms of David* was published by Nahum Tate (1652–1715) and Nicholas Brady (1659–1726), two Irishmen who spent most of their lives in England. This work replaced the first English psalmbook, published in 1562, which subsequently became known as the "Old Version."

Hugh Wilson (1764–1824) is credited as the composer of this classic Scottish tune, MARTYRDOM. It was originally titled FENWICK for the village where Wilson was born but has also been called ALL SAINTS, AVON, BOSTAL, DRUMCLOG, and INVERNESS.

Hugh Wilson was a shoemaker by trade but eventually became a calculator and draftsman for a mill. Wilson was a member and founder of a Sunday school in the Secession Church and sometimes led the psalm singing.

482 I Will Lift the Cloud of Night

Charles Price Jones (1865–1949) wrote this text, which originally began with the phrase "I will make the darkness light." Although Jones wrote some thousand hymns, most are relatively unknown because of their distinct theological emphasis on perfectionism and separatism.

Charles P. Jones founded a new denomination, the Church of Christ (Holiness) USA, in the late nineteenth century because the Baptist and Methodist denominations had rejected his ideas. The Holiness movement produced its own music, which has not been widely used in other churches.

Charles Price Jones (1865–1949) wrote and edited many hymnbooks, including *Jesus Only Songs and Hymns Standard Hymnal*, the first official denominational hymnal of the Holiness Church, published in the 1940s. Jones's own works constitute about half of the hymns in that resource. This tune, JONES, is named for him.

Charles P. Jones, of Jackson, Mississippi, was a follower of the Holiness movement, marked by a dissatisfaction with the spiritual condition of the black Protestant churches. Jones's songs, which he published in several volumes from 1899 to 1928, were among the earliest in the emerging gospel-music style.

483 Out of the Depths I Call

This metrical version of Psalm 130 was first published in *A New Version of the Psalms of David*, edited by Nahum Tate (1652–1715) and Nicholas Brady (1659–1726). This publication provided two-part music by John Darwall, an English minister and composer, for each of the 150 Psalms.

Naham Tate and Nicholas Brady collaborated on a new collection of the 150 Psalms for use in English churches, *A New Version of the Psalms of David* (1696). Since the old Sternhold and Hopkins Psalter had been in use for 130 years, this "new version" was only gradually accepted.

Samuel Howard (1710–1782) wrote this melody as a setting for Psalm 130. It is named ST. BRIDE for Howard's church near St. Bridget's (or St. Bride's) well, a spring whose water was thought to have healing powers. Although Anglican in origin, the tune became widely used in Nonconformist churches.

Samuel Howard was a chorister in the Chapel Royal and sang tenor for G. F. Handel. Although he composed primarily for the English theater, he also worked on a three-volume collection called *Cathedral Music*. Howard lived his entire life (1710–1782) in London, England.

484 O Come to Me, You Weary

William Chatterton Dix (1837–1898) wrote this hymn during a time of illness. Later he felt that writing it had been the turning point in his recovery to health. The words were first published in *The People's Hymnal* (1867).

William C. Dix, the son of a Bristol surgeon and author, spent his career as a manager at a marine insurance company in Glasgow, Scotland. His hobby, however, was writing poetry, and many of his poems were published and incorporated as hymns.

MEIRIONYDD is a remote western county in Wales. The tune was named by William Lloyd (1786–1852), who had arranged it as a hymn after being given the tune in manuscript form. Lloyd lived in Meirionydd County, Wales, at the time he arranged the tune.

William Lloyd was a Welsh cattleman and farmer who conducted singing schools in his home and throughout the region. Lloyd was born in 1786 in Carnarvonshire, Wales, and died there in 1852.

485 O Love That Will Not Let Me Go

George Matheson (1842–1906) wrote this hymn in a fraction of an hour during a time of "extreme mental distress" in 1882 when the rest of the family had gone out of town to attend his sister's wedding. Some believe it was written when his fiancée had called off their marriage due to Matheson's blindness.

George Matheson was born in Glasgow, Scotland, on March 27, 1842. Hindered by poor eyesight, which left him virtually blind by age eighteen, he nevertheless completed his education at the University of Glasgow and served with distinction as minister to three different parishes. He died August 28, 1906.

Albert Lister Peace (1844–1912) composed this tune to provide a setting for George Matheson's text for *The Scottish Hymnal* (1884). The tune is named ST. MARGARET for the Scottish Queen Margaret (1046–1093), who encouraged reform in the church of her day. She was canonized in 1249.

Albert L. Peace was born January 26, 1844, at Huddersfield, Yorkshire, England, and was a child prodigy in music. He could identify any note or chord played on the piano at the age of five and became the foremost organist of his day in England. Peace died in Liverpool, England, on March 14, 1912.

486 I Must Tell Jesus

Elisha Albright Hoffman wrote this hymn for *Pentecostal Hymns* (1894), which he helped edit. He also included it in another hymnal released the same year, *Christian Endeavor Hymnal*. The text is an invitation to prayer and deeper sharing of life's problems with the Savior.

Elisha A. Hoffman received his theological education at Union Bible Seminary of the Evangelical Association in New Berlin, Pennsylvania. He worked for the denomination's publishing house in Cleveland, Ohio, for eleven years and was the first music editor of Hope Publishing Company.

Elisha Albright Hoffman (1839–1929) wrote both words and music for this hymn. The Baptist hymnal committee named the tune ORWIGSBURG for the Pennsylvania town where Hoffman was born. In performing this song in 9/8, it is helpful to think of each measure as having three beats, with the eighth notes sung as triplets.

Elisha A. Hoffman was born in Orwigsburg, Pennsylvania, on May 7, 1839, and educated in Philadelphia's public schools. He was ordained an Evangelical minister, served churches in three different denominations, and wrote the texts or music for more than one thousand gospel hymns.

487 Surely No One Can Be Safer

Karolina Wilhelmina Sandell (1832–1903) wrote this text while still in her teens and published it in 1855. It later appeared in *Sionstoner*, a publication of the Swedish Evangelical National Association, where she worked on the editorial staff.

Lina Sandell, the daughter of a Swedish Lutheran pastor, wrote 650 poems during her lifetime and worked on the editorial staff of the Evangelical National Foundation. There, she became acquainted with Carl Rosenius, a leader in the pietist movement in Sweden. She also assisted her husband, C. O. Berg, in his literary pursuits.

This melody is called TRYGGARE KAN INGEN VARA for the opening words of the Swedish text. The tune may date as far back as the seventeenth century and may be an adaptation of a Swedish folk song or a song from Germany or England. It was first paired with this hymn in an 1873 songbook.

In the middle of the nineteenth century, Sweden experienced a wave of revivalism similar to movements in England and the United States of the same time. This gave rise to the need for evangelical hymns and songbooks. In addition to popular U.S. gospel songs, these books contained new hymns by Swedish writers such as Lina Sandell and composer Oskar Ahnfelt.

488 Be Still, My Soul

Katharina Amalia Dorotheo von Schlegel (b. 1697) wrote this German text, "Stille, mein Wille! Dein Jesus hilft siegen," one of twenty-six hymns by her that survive. Jane L. Borthwick translated five of the original six stanzas for her *Hymns from the Land of Luther* (second series, 1855).

Katharina A. D. von Schlegel was born October 22, 1697. She may have been a canoness of an Evangelical Lutheran women's seminary at Cöthen or one of the ladies of the court of the Duke of Cöthen. From her writings, it is known that she was from the eighteenth-century pietist school.

Jean Sibelius (1865–1957) created the tone poem from which this melody, FINLANDIA, is taken. It was composed in 1899 in reaction to repressive measures imposed on the Finnish people by Russian forces. The melody was adapted for this text in a 1933 hymnal of the Presbyterian Church, USA.

Jean Sibelius was raised by his grandparents in Finland and trained for a legal career. But music called him, and he became Finland's greatest composer of large-scale symphonic works, songs, sacred music, and choral pieces. Sibelius received a government pension, which allowed him to devote his time to composing.

489 I Heard the Voice of Jesus Say

Horatius Bonar (1808–1889) wrote this text in a notebook he always carried with him when walking or traveling. It was written while he was at his first charge, North Parish at Kelso, Scotland, and appeared in his *Hymns Original and Selected* (1846).

Horatius Bonar received his education at the University of Edinburgh, Scotland. An 1855 visit to the holy land influenced his preaching and writing, in which he explored the concept of the second coming of Christ and the fulfillment of Hebrew scriptural prophecy.

William Henry Havergal's (1793–1870) tune EVAN was composed in 1847 as a setting of a poem by Robert Burns. Lowell Mason (1792–1872) arranged the tune for his *New Carmina Sacra* (1850). Havergal greatly disliked Mason's arrangement, and there is evidence that Mason tried to claim ownership of it for himself.

William H. Havergal was ordained to ministry in 1816 but was forced into early retirement by a serious accident. During this time of recuperation he began studying music. He was the father of hymnwriter Frances Havergal, author of "Take My Life, God, Let It Be" (hymn 448), and "God, Speak to Me, That I May Speak" (hymn 531).

490 I Want Jesus to Go with Me

This text is categorized as a "sorrow song," meant for individual rather than group singing. It may have been used as a response during a time of prayer and has a meditative quality to it. The hymn easily could be used as a prayer response during corporate worship.

This song may have roots similar to a white spiritual, which "thrived in rural Appalachian culture for more than 200 years," according to Don Hustad in *Dictionary Handbook to Hymns for the Living Church*. It may have been sung in nineteenth-century camp meetings that welcomed all races.

This melody, although not titled here, is called SOJOURNER in the 1989 *United Methodist Hymnal*. It was named by William Farley Smith for Sojourner Truth, a courageous freed slave woman who preached the abolition of slavery and equality for all people.

This spiritual is a "journey song" similar to "Jesus Walked This Lonesome Valley" and "We Shall Walk through the Valley." This type of spiritual spoke of a journey, in which the singer asks for or affirms the presence of others traveling along with him or her.

491 Awake, My Soul, Stretch Every Nerve

Philip Doddridge (1702–1751) wrote this hymn to be sung after a sermon. It appeared under the title "Pressing On in the Christian Race" in a collection of his works published posthumously in 1755.

Philip Doddridge was a contemporary of Isaac Watts and the Wesley brothers in England. He served as minister for the Nonconformist chapel at Castle Hill, Northampton, and also established an academy there. It attracted students from England, Scotland, and Holland, many of whom became Independent (Congregational) ministers.

George Frideric Handel (1685–1759) composed the melody on which this tune is based for an aria in his opera *Siroe*. The tune is now called CHRISTMAS because of its close association with Nahum Tate's text "While Shepherds Watched Their Flocks by Night."

George Frideric Handel's greatest musical achievement was the oratorio *Messiah*, which he composed in twenty-four days in 1741. It was first performed in Dublin, Ireland, in 1742. Handel's last public appearance was at a performance of that work on April 6, 1759. He died eight days later.

492 I Would Be True

Howard Arnold Walter (1883–1918) sent this poem in a letter to his mother while he was teaching English at Waseda University in Tokyo, Japan, in 1906. She submitted it to *Harper's Magazine*, which published it the following year. Walter titled his original poem "My Creed."

Howard A. Walter was born in New Britain, Connecticut, on August 19, 1883. A Congregational minister, he served in Hartford before volunteering with the YMCA for work in India and Ceylon. Walter took a position at a college in Lahore even though he knew that he had a heart condition. He died suddenly in 1918.

Joseph Yates Peek (1843–1911) became acquainted with Howard Walter one summer while the young minister was substituting at Peek's church in Brooklyn, New York. Although Peek was not a trained musician, he felt that Walter's poem would be an inspiring hymn and composed this melody, now known as PEEK. An organist harmonized it from Peek's whistled version.

Joseph Y. Peek, born in Schenectady, New York, on February 27, 1843, was a florist for over twenty years. He left this work to become a lay preacher in the Methodist-Episcopal Church. Peek's dream of being ordained was realized only two months before his death, on March 17, 1911, in Brooklyn, New York.

493 O Jesus, I Have Promised

John Ernest Bode (1816–1874) wrote this hymn in 1855 for the confirmation of his daughter and two sons at the English church where he was rector. It was first published in a leaflet in 1868 by the Society for the Promotion of Christian Knowledge.

John E. Bode, an English rector, received his education at Eton, Charterhouse, and Christ Church, Oxford, England. He served churches in Oxfordshire and Cambridgeshire, England, after working as a tutor for seven years. Bode wrote two volumes of verse, but this is his only enduring hymn.

Arthur Henry Mann (1850–1929) composed the tune ANGEL'S STORY in 1881 for the hymn "I Love to Hear the Story Which Angel Voices Tell." A Fellow of the Royal College of Organists in England, he played at King's College, Cambridge, for fifty-three years.

Arthur H. Mann received his early musical training as a chorister and played the organ for a cathedral service at the age of eight. When his voice changed, he abandoned singing but continued his studies and earned a doctor of music degree in 1882. Mann spent most of his career at King's College, Cambridge.

494 We Who Would Valiant Be

John Bunyan (1628–1688) included this hymn in his *Pilgrim's Progress*, a Christian allegory he wrote while imprisoned for practicing his Baptist faith in England. The hymn was intended as a summary of Bunyan's message following a conversation between Mr. Great-heart and Mr. Valiant-for-truth.

John Bunyan, author of *The Pilgrim's Progress* and some sixty other books, was a leading Nonconformist minister in England. He was imprisoned twice for preaching without conforming to established church doctrines. During one of these terms, Bunyan wrote his autobiography, *Grace Abounding to the Chief of Sinners* (1666).

Charles Winfred Douglas (1867–1944) composed ST. DUNSTAN'S in 1917 while riding on a train from New York City to his home, St. Dunstan's Cottage in Peekskill, New York. Douglas had long admired Bunyan's *Pilgrim's Progress* and wanted the tune to convey the necessary "strength and vigor."

C. Winfred Douglas was born on February 15, 1867, at Oswego, New York. He was ordained into the Protestant Episcopal Church and was the greatest Protestant authority on Gregorian music during his lifetime. A tireless teacher and lecturer, Douglas was music editor of two Episcopal hymnals.

495 Called as Partners in Christ's Service

Jane Parker Huber (b. 1926) wrote this text in 1981 for the women's breakfast held when two Presbyterian denominations convened joint General Assemblies in Houston, Texas. The partnership she wrote about was that of women and men in ministry, but the hymn's meaning has now expanded.

Jane Parker Huber inherited her love for service through the Presbyterian Church from both her father and mother. Her father was president of Hanover College in Indiana, and her mother served on two national Presbyterian bodies.

John Zundel (1815–1882) composed BEECHER in 1855, and it was published in *Christian Heart Songs* (1870). The tune's name is for Henry Ward Beecher, pastor of Plymouth Church in Brooklyn, New York, where Zundel served as organist for thirty years. The two men collaborated on *The Plymouth Collection* (1855).

John Zundel was born and educated in Hochdorf, Germany, but immigrated to the United States. He served different churches in New York and in 1850 began a thirty-year ministry of music at Plymouth Church, Brooklyn, where he became friends with the pastor, Henry Ward Beecher.

496 Ekolu Mea Nui (Three Greatest Things)

Robert Nawahine (1868–1951) based this text on 1 Corinthians 13:13, which celebrates as the three greatest things "faith, hope, and love." Written in Hawaiian, this text can easily be sung by people who do not speak Hawaiian, as the language has only twelve letters, and every word ends with a vowel.

This hymn appears in *The New Century Hymnal* at the request of representatives of the Hawaii Conference of the United Church of Christ, which published *Na Himeni Haipule Hawaii* in 1972. "Ekolu Mea Nui" is a favorite hymn from that hymnbook.

Robert Nawahine (1868–1951) composed this melody for his own words, and it is named NAWAHINE in his honor. The tune was arranged by Martha Hohu (b. 1907), a Hawaiian church musician, translator, and composer who chaired the Hawaiian hymnbook committee (1969–1972).

A biography of Robert J. K. Nawahine in the Hawaiian hymnal *Maipule Hawaii* describes him as an "outstanding Christian musician and leader among the central Maui churches. Many of his compositions won prizes at song contests among the church choirs."

497 Guide My Feet

Hebrews 12:1–2 may be the inspiration for this African American spiritual based on Paul's metaphor that compares the life of discipleship to "running the race." It may have another meaning as well, referring to the race to elude capture while seeking freedom from slavery.

Many African American spirituals trace their inspiration to biblical texts. Singing was one way of passing on religious tradition, since in many places it was illegal to teach African American slaves to read and write.

This tune, GUIDE MY FEET, was one of many spiritual tunes preserved by Willis Laurence James in his 1900 collection. Most spirituals were freely passed from place to place, and different song leaders would alter the words to suit various situations.

Joyce Finch Johnson arranged this tune in 1992 for use in *The New Century Hymnal* while she was a member of the hymnal committee. Johnson serves on the music faculty of Spelman College in Atlanta, Georgia.

498 Jesu, Jesu, Fill Us with Your Love

Thomas Stevenson Colvin (b. 1925) wrote this text for new church members in village churches in multilingual districts around Tamale. Colvin suggests that the opening words be pronounced "Jey-soo," as is the custom in most African languages.

Tom Colvin was born in Glasgow, Scotland. He left engineering to study for the ministry and was ordained by the Church of Scotland in 1954. Colvin worked as a missionary in northern Ghana and Malawi from 1954 to 1974 and later returned as a training consultant to the Zimbabwe Christian Council.

This Ghanaian folk song was one of many that Tom Colvin (b. 1925) collected while serving as a missionary in northern Ghana. He adapted it for this original text and named it CHEREPONI to honor a church in Chereponi, northern Ghana. This hymn was used to help dedicate a new church there.

Tom Colvin was a lieutenant for the Royal Indian Engineers in Burma and Singapore before entering church work as a missionary. Many of the songs he collected when serving in Africa were published in *Free to Serve* (1976), *Leap my Soul* (1976), and *Fill Us with Your Love* (1983).

499 Pues si vivimos (In All Our Living)

This Mexican folk hymn was tape-recorded by Gertrude C. Suppe (b. 1911) when she asked two Mexican women to sing it in Los Angeles at La Trinidad United Methodist Church. The opening stanza is based on Romans 14:7–8 and is appropriate for baptisms, weddings, and graveside committals.

Elise S. Eslinger (b. 1942) added the second stanza to this hymn in 1983. She was serving as music editor of *Celebremos II* at the time and felt the hymn would be more useful with another stanza. In the *United Methodist Hymnal*, the text was printed with two more stanzas which are not included here.

This anonymous tune is named PUES SI VIVIMOS (In All Our Living), from the opening words of the original Spanish text. The tune was called SOMOS DEL SEÑOR in *The United Methodist Hymnal*, the first denominational hymnal in the United States to include it.

This hymn was shared with the committee compiling *Celebremos II*, a Spanish-language supplemental hymnal of the United Methodist Church. Gertrude C. Suppe (b. 1911) had collected this hymn in 1980 as part of her research as a hymnologist.

500 We Are Climbing Jacob's Ladder

This anonymous text was based on Genesis 28:10–17, which tells of Jacob's dream at Bethel. However, the biblical story is only the starting point for the text, which becomes one of persevering in faith, rung by rung and stanza by stanza.

In *Black Song: The Forge and the Flame,* John Lovell Jr. explains the significance of climbing to the slave-poet, who "felt that he had been kept down for too long." Lovell suggests that Jacob's story is only a metaphor for the slave-poet's desire to "rise from his [or her] low estate and to progress up the material and spiritual ladder."

This music is beautifully suited for these words, as the rhythmic pattern suggests climbing a rung on a ladder and then pausing for breath before taking the next step. The anonymous tune is called JACOB'S LADDER after the text's subject matter.

Many African American melodies contain a refrain and stanzas meant to be sung by a lead singer or various lead singers, but this one is different because it has no refrain. In addition, whereas most spiritual tunes have irregular meter, this one has a standard meter, 8.8.8.5.

501 We Are Dancing Sarah's Circle

Carole A. Etzler (b. 1944) was inspired by feminist theologian Nelle Morton to create this alternate text to "Jacob's Ladder," using the story of Sarah, found in Genesis 17 and 18. The circle dance is an ancient traditional dance, involving an entire community.

Carole A. Etzler works as a performing artist, writer, and composer. A member of the Unitarian Universalist Church, she attends Champlain Valley Unitarian Universalist Society in Middlebury, Vermont, and expresses her faith through her use of music.

This anonymous African American tune is called JACOB'S LADDER, after the other text with which it is associated. The tune moves up and down the scale, much as Jacob moved up and down the ladder in his vision, found in Genesis 28.

A frequent topic of debate concerning African American music is whether it was imported from the African continent, is a unique new form of music that originated in the Americas, or represents a blend of the two. Most authorities accept the last possibility as the best answer.

502 Dear God, Embracing Humankind

John Greenleaf Whittier (1807–1892), a Quaker poet and newspaper editor, published his polemical seventeen-stanza poem "The Brewing of Soma," in the April 1872 issue of *Atlantic Monthly*. The English editor W. Garrett Horder adapted the later stanzas to form this prayer-hymn and included it in his *Worship Song* (1884).

John Greenleaf Whittier was born in Massachusetts to a farming family. By working as a shoemaker and teacher, he finally earned enough money to pursue studies briefly at Haverhill Academy. Whittier was inspired by the poetry of Scottish nationalist Robert Burns and began writing his own verse at the age of fourteen.

Frederick Charles Maker's (1844–1927) tune REST (sometimes called ELTON) is his best-known hymn tune. It appeared with this text in the *Congregational Church Hymnal* (1887), published in London, and was previously included in a small collection of eighteen tunes by Maker with the hymn "There Is an Hour of Peaceful Rest."

Frederick C. Maker was a British church organist in Nonconformist churches. Maker spent his life in Bristol, England, the city of his birth. He was active in the Bristol Church Choir Association, a group of church choirs that united for special musical services throughout the year.

503 O Savior, Let Me Walk with You

Washington Gladden (1836–1911) wrote this poem for a devotional column, "The Still Hour," and published it in his magazine *Sunday Afternoon* (1879). He never intended that this poem be converted into a hymn, but it was first published as such one year later in Charles H. Richards's *Songs of Christian Praise*.

Washington Gladden, an outspoken minister and writer on social-justice issues, served churches in New York, Massachusetts, and finally in Columbus, Ohio. He was moderator of the National Council of Congregational Churches from 1904 to 1907 and associate editor of *The Pilgrim Hymnal* (1904).

H. Percy Smith (1825–1898) composed the tune MARYTON in 1874 for the hymn "Sun of My Soul," by John Keble, with which it appeared in *Church Hymns with Tunes*, edited by Arthur Sullivan. It was Washington Gladden's preferred tune for his hymn.

H. Percy Smith was born in December 1825 on the island of Malta. A minister in the Anglican Church, he served churches in England until he was appointed chaplain at Cannes, France, and, in 1892, canon of Gibraltar. Smith died at Bournemouth, Hampshire, England, on January 28, 1898.

504 You Walk along Our Shoreline

Sylvia G. Dunstan (1955–1993) wrote this text in 1984 after reading an article in which fishing was used as a metaphor for ministry. She drew upon a number of stories from the Gospels to speak of Jesus' invitation to the disciples that they follow him and become fishers of a different type.

Sylvia G. Dunstan was born in Simcoe, Ontario, Canada, and attended high school there. She received a baccalaureate degree in history from York University in Toronto. A minister in the United Church of Canada, Dunstan accumulated an extensive collection of hymnals, works by women poets, and the writings of Søren Kierkegaard.

This traditional Irish melody, SALLEY GARDENS, was newly harmonized as a setting for this text in *The New Century Hymnal* by assistant music editor Jonathan McNair. Traditional Irish melodies often accompanied ballads or dances and were sung with great emotion whenever people gathered for communal activities and fun.

The poignant Irish melody SALLEY GARDENS is typical of other Irish ballads with a nearly pentatonic melody. One can imagine it being played simply by a fiddle and a flute in its country of origin.

505 Sweet Hour of Prayer

William W. Walford (1772–1850) wrote this text in 1842 by dictating it to a friend, since he was blind. The friend took the poem to the *New York Observer*, where it was published in 1845. It first appeared as a hymn in the *Baptist Hymnal* (1859).

William W. Walford was an English lay preacher in Coleshill, Warwickshire, England. He made his living by carving figures from ivory and selling them at his trinket shop. He preached the gospel at various churches for his minister friends, undeterred by his blindness.

William Batchelder Bradbury (1816–1868) composed the tune SWEET HOUR fourteen years after this text appeared. The addition of Bradbury's melody increased the song's popularity around the world. This hymn is an encouragement to all to find strength and comfort in prayer.

William B. Bradbury, born in York, Maine, was one of America's most prolific hymnwriters, producing lively and popular songs that were easy to sing and easy to learn. His works were especially popular with Sunday-school children and traveling evangelists.

506 What a Friend We Have in Jesus

Joseph Scriven (1819–1886) wrote this hymn to comfort his mother in a time of sorrow, never imagining that it would come to public attention. A friend found it during Scriven's last illness, in 1886. When asked about this hymn, he said, "The Lord and I did it between us."

Joseph Scriven's life was changed by the drowning death of his fiancée in Ireland on the eve of their wedding. He moved to Canada at age twenty-five and went from house to house living with friends. Scriven spent his time doing menial chores for people with illnesses or disabilities.

Charles Crozat Converse (1832–1918) published this tune in 1870 in *Silver Wings*, a book of Sunday-school hymns. He named the hymn ERIE, probably because Converse practiced law in Erie, Pennsylvania, from 1875 until his retirement to Highwood, New Jersey.

Charles C. Converse was born and raised in Massachusetts. He studied in Germany under the great musicians at Leipzig Conservatory, where he became friends with Franz Liszt. His music includes solos, chorales, hymns, and chamber works. He also held a law degree, earned in 1861.

507 Jesus—The Very Thought to Me

This twelfth-century Latin poem, "Jesu dulcis memoria," has been traditionally attributed to Bernard of Clairvaux, although his authorship is questionable. It was translated into English in 1849 by Edward B. Caswall (1814–1878), a convert to Roman Catholicism. Another part of the poem is "Jesus, the Joy of Loving Hearts" (hymn 329).

Bernard of Clairvaux (1090–1153) was the son of a knight who died during the First Crusade. Bernard became a Cistercian monk and in 1115 founded the monastery at Clairvaux, France, where he stayed for the rest of his life. He was the greatest religious presence of his age.

John Bacchus Dykes (1823–1876) composed this tune in 1866 for these words. He named the tune ST. AGNES to honor the thirteen-year-old Roman girl who was executed in 304 C.E. for refusing to marry a nobleman. She is considered the patroness of purity and innocence.

John B. Dykes was an outstanding musician of the mid-Victorian era and contributed many new tunes that have endured to the present day. He served as a clergyman in the Church of England and was a somewhat controversial figure because of his high-church views.

508 Prayer Is the Soul's Sincere Desire

James Montgomery (1771–1854) was asked to write this hymn by a friend in 1818. It was first distributed on individual sheets, and Montgomery used the hymn for his Sunday-school classes in Sheffield, England. It was published the next year in *Treatise on Prayer*.

James Montgomery's parents expected him to enter the Moravian ministry. They were missionaries in the West Indies and died there when he was only nineteen. Montgomery was expelled from school because he spent his time writing poetry rather than attending to his studies.

John Bacchus Dykes (1823–1876) is the composer of ST. AGNES, which was first printed in John Grey's *Hymnal for Use in the English Church* (1866) with a translation of the Latin hymn "Jesu dulcis memoria." Saint Agnes was martyred in 304 C.E. at age thirteen for refusing to marry a nobleman.

John B. Dykes, a priest in the Anglican Church, composed three hundred hymn tunes, eight of which appear in *The New Century Hymnal*. Even though he died at age fifty-two, his tunes have an enduring quality and remain popular more than a century after his death.

509 How Deep the Silence of the Soul

Sylvia G. Dunstan (1955–1993) wrote this two-stanza text as a reflection on her experience of meditating in her mother's garden in Mill Valley, California. It appeared in the author's first collection of original hymns, *In Search of Hope and Grace* (1991).

Sylvia G. Dunstan began experimenting with music in the church with the St. James United Church of Canada youth choir of Simcoe, Canada. That choir sang secular pop music and the music of Ray Repp, with Dunstan accompanying them on guitar. She grew up in this congregation.

Thomas Tallis (c. 1505–1585) composed this melody, his THIRD TUNE, sometime around 1557 while serving as organist of Waltham Abbey, England. In 1577, he and William Byrd were appointed joint organists at the Chapel Royal.

Thomas Tallis was one of Tudor England's leading musicians. Queen Elizabeth I granted him and his partner, William Byrd, the sole right to print music in England. His music included masses, magnificats, motets, and other church music. Tallis died at Greenwich, England, in 1585.

510 Grant Us Wisdom to Perceive You

Rae E. Phillips Whitney (b. 1927) was inspired by a prayer of Saint Benedict of Nursia (480–543) to write this adaptation. Benedict founded the Benedictine monastic order around 529 C.E. and established his principal monastery (of twelve) at Monte Cassino, midway between Rome and Naples.

Rae Whitney (b. 1927), an Episcopalian, was born and raised in England and received her education at the University of Bristol. Whitney's hymns have been published in a number of hymnals, supplements, and a single-author collection, *With Joy Our Spirits Sing* (1995).

This anonymous German tune is called QUEM PASTORES and comes from the fourteenth century. In 1555, it appeared in print in Valentinum Triller's *Ein Schlesich Singebüchlein aus Göttlicher Schrifft*. By the sixteenth century, "quempas" had become a generic term for Christmas carols.

The German tradition of singing Christmas carols was called "quempas singen." Martin Luther reported singing in such groups with his students in Latin School. The term had come from a carol published in 1555.

511 I Love My God, Who Heard My Cry

Isaac Watts (1674–1748) is the author of this hymn, a paraphrase of the first two verses of Psalm 116. His original text included the entire psalm and appeared in his *Psalms of David Imitated in the Language of the New Testament*, which was published in 1719.

Isaac Watts, although burdened by ill health beginning in 1712 when he was thirty-two, continued to promote the interests of the Dissenting churches of England by his writing and by corresponding with the Congregational churches in the New England colonies.

This anonymous tune has been named SMALLWOOD in honor of the arranger, Richard Smallwood (b. 1948). This hymn is an interesting combination of an eighteenth-century English metrical psalm text and a modern rendition of an African American gospel tune.

Richard Smallwood (b. 1948) was one of three men who began the first black gospel choir on a college campus in the United States. All were music majors at Howard University and initially were forbidden to play gospel music in the school's practice rooms. Their efforts ultimately changed the music curriculum.

512 Sovereign and Transforming Grace

Frederick Henry Hedge (1805–1890) wrote this text in 1829 for the ordination of a friend. This was also the year in which he was ordained to the Unitarian ministry, at age twenty-four. Hedge served churches in Bangor, Maine, Providence, Rhode Island, and Brookline, Massachusetts.

Frederick H. Hedge was accepted at Harvard College when he was twelve years old, but his parents sent him to Germany to study with George Bancroft for five years instead. Eventually educated at Harvard, he ended his career there as professor of German. He was an important leader of the Transcendentalists.

Jane Manton Marshall (b. 1924) was commissioned to compose this tune in 1992 as a new setting for Hedge's text. The request came from the Hymnbook Resources Commission, which prepared *Singing the Living Tradition* for the Unitarian Universalist Association. It is called MANTON for her middle name.

Jane Marshall was educated at Southern Methodist University, where she earned a bachelor's degree in music in 1945 and a master's degree in 1968. Since 1969, she has served on the faculty of church music at SMU's Perkins School of Theology of the United Methodist Church.

513 O Source of All That Is

Johann Heermann (1585–1647) included this text, "O Gott, du Frommer Gott," in his *Devoti musica cordis*, published in Breslau in 1630. There he called it "A Daily Prayer." The hymn may have been written between 1623 and 1630, when Heermann was suffering from extreme illness and distress.

Johann Heermann lost all he had living during the Thirty Years' War. Esteemed as the most important German hymnwriter between Martin Luther and Paul Gerhardt, his hymns express a deep faith in the midst of social turmoil, personal ill health, and a number of close calls with death.

This chorale named O GOTT, DU FROMMER GOTT from the opening words of Johann Heermann's German text, probably was developed from a Thuringian melody. Its earliest publication was in a 1672 appendix to a hymnal by George Falk, but the tune was altered slightly for the 1693 *Gesangbuch*.

The *Neuvermehrtes Gesangbuch* of 1693 was the third edition of a hymnal ordered by Duke Bernhard of Saxony. It contained 647 hymns and 169 melodies, many by members of the duke's family. Nicolaus Hassert published the hymnal from his printshop in Meiningen, Germany.

514 Over My Head

This African American text affirms the existence of God with a healthy pessimism that recalls the writing of Ecclesiastes. Although God is not always felt to be near, there is solace in knowing that God is somewhere, even if it is "over my head."

This old spiritual was one of many adapted for use in the civil-rights marches of the 1960s. As a freedom song, the words were often changed to meet changing circumstances. The text alludes to Jesus' ascension: "Over my head, I see Jesus in the air."

This unnamed tune is practically identical in each of the four lines of music, mirroring the repetition in the text. Small variations keep the tune interesting, however. Many versions of the tune existed; this arrangement was made in 1981 by J. Jefferson Cleveland and Verolga Nix for *Songs of Zion*.

This spiritual has been cited as one that was sung in slave communities as a coded means of communicating that a worship service was about to take place. These secretive worship practices for purposes of avoiding slaveholders and overseers came to be known as the "Invisible Institution."

515 O God, My God

John L. Bell (b. 1949) and Graham Maule (b. 1958) created this 1988 text on the theme of abandonment by paraphrasing Psalm 22. They had found few contemporary songs dealing with this theme and wrote it for use at a Monday-evening house liturgy for an Iona Community worship group.

The Iona Community, situated on a small island west of Scotland, was the first base for Saint Columba when he left Ireland for a mission to the Scots. The present cathedral of this religious community was rebuilt on the site of Saint Columba's original monastery.

John Bell (b. 1949) composed this tune called O GOD MY GOD while he and Graham Maule were revising their original text based on Psalm 22. The words and music of the refrain came together simultaneously. Remember to sing the refrain one last time after singing the fourth stanza.

John Bell became a member of the Iona Community in 1982, when he served as youth coordinator. Since 1986, he has been a resource worker in worship and spirituality for the community. As such, he works with "The Wild Goose Worship Group," developing music and liturgy resources in a collaborative process.

516 O Grant Us, God, a Little Space

John Ellerton (1826–1893) wrote this hymn for use at a midday service in a city church in London, England. This is one of the first hymns to recognize science and art as part of God's creation and work. The text was first published in *Church Hymns* (1870).

John Ellerton was born in London, England, on December 16, 1826. Ordained to priesthood in the Church of England in 1850, he served various parishes. In addition, he wrote literature and hymns, edited hymnals, and worked for various welfare programs. He died at Torquay, England, on June 15, 1893.

This melody by Thomas Este WINCHESTER OLD, first appeared in his *Whole Booke of Psalms* (1592), where it was a setting for Psalm 84 and was harmonized by George Kirbye. The tune may be derived from Christopher Tye's *Actes of the Apostles* (1553), four-part settings of the early chapters of Acts.

Thomas Este's *The Whole Booke of Psalmes* (1592) contained many "short tunes," meaning they consisted of four lines rather than the usual eight. In addition, this was the first hymnal to provide names for tunes and to present music in full score.

517 I Need You Every Hour

Annie Sherwood Hawks (1835–1918) was doing her housework one day when she felt very near to God. This hymn came into her mind, and she wrote it down. It was first sung publicly at the National Baptist Sunday School Association meeting in Cincinnati, Ohio, in 1872.

Annie S. Hawks was born in Hoosick, New York, on May 28, 1835, and spent most of her life in Brooklyn, where she attended Hanson Place Baptist Church. After her husband's death, she lived with one of her three daughters in Bennington, Vermont, where she died on January 3, 1918.

Robert Lowry (1826–1899) composed NEED for this text by Annie Hawks in 1873. Hawks was a parishioner in the Brooklyn church where Lowry was serving as pastor. Lowry's widow preferred the full first line of the text as the tune name, but it was shortened to NEED by later hymnal editors.

Robert Lowry was a Baptist minister who would have preferred to be remembered for his preaching. He developed his interest in hymnwriting while serving as pastor at a Baptist church in Brooklyn, New York, where he met the author of this hymn.

518 Father Almighty, Bless Us

The writer of this text is known only by the initials L.J.W. The hymn was first found in a Unitarian hymnal, *The Sunny Side*, printed in England in 1875. As revised, each stanza of this prayer seeking God's blessings for our lives begins and ends with a different name for God.

The Unitarian movement gained momentum in England and the United States in the early eighteenth century. Rejecting the doctrine of the Trinity, Unitarian hymns omitted references to the deity of Jesus Christ and instead concentrated on the unity of God.

Friedrich Ferdinand Flemming (1778–1813), a German physician, composed this tune in 1811 for a Latin poem, Horace's Ode XXII, which began INTEGER VITAE; hence the tune name. The tune is also called FLEMMING for the composer. It appeared in several German Roman Catholic hymnals in the nineteenth century.

Friedrich F. Flemming, a physician by trade, practiced medicine in Berlin, Germany. He was active in musical circles and composed many songs for a male vocal ensemble, Liedertafel. Born in Neuhausen, Saxony, on February 28, 1778, Flemming died in Berlin, Germany, on May 27, 1813.

519 Not My Brother, nor My Sister
(Standing in the Need of Prayer)

In this African American spiritual, the singer takes full responsibility for recognizing his or her personal need for prayer. This text served to stress the need for strong individual character on the part of the enslaved in order to endure such difficult circumstances.

This song is appropriate for use during an altar call or a call to personal repentance. Like many spirituals, it is in the literary form of a prayer and appropriately stresses the need for that faith discipline.

This tune, called NEED OF PRAYER for that catch phrase in the text, was preserved by James Weldon Johnson in his 1925 collection of African American spirituals. Without his work, many of these traditional songs may well have been lost.

This spiritual is a perfect example of those created in call-and-response style, in which solo passages sung by a leader alternate with a response sung by the congregation. The refrain is to be sung by all.

520 Eternal Spirit of the Living Christ

Frank von Christierson (b. 1900) submitted this text to the Hymn Society of America for a collection of new texts being compiled and published in 1974. Von Christierson was honored as a fellow of the Hymn Society in 1982 for his significant contributions to church music.

Frank von Christierson was born on Christmas Day 1900 in Lovisa, Finland. During his early years, he lived in a house that had formerly belonged to Finnish composer Jean Sibelius. Christierson emigrated to the United States with his family at the age of five and has lived in California for most of the twentieth century.

Alfred Morton Smith (1879–1971) submitted this tune anonymously to the committee for *The Hymnal 1940* of the Episcopal Church. There it was paired with the text "Lift Up Your Hearts!" It is named SURSUM CORDA for the Latin title of that liturgical text. There is also another tune by that name.

Alfred M. Smith graduated from the University of Pennsylvania and Philadelphia Divinity School before being ordained to the Episcopal ministry in 1906. He joined the U.S. Army and served as a chaplain in France and Germany in World War I. Smith composed two masses, as well as hymn and carol tunes.

521 In Solitude

Ruth C. Duck (b. 1947) felt as if these words came from deep within the collective unconscious of her evangelical roots in the southern United States. Although an extremely personal statement, this text speaks of all Christians' deep yearning for spiritual contact with God.

Ruth Duck edited three collections of liturgical resources between 1980 and 1990: *Bread for the Journey* (1981), *Flames of the Spirit* (1985), and *Touch Holiness* (1990). All of these resources for worship were published by the Pilgrim Press of the United Church of Christ, now based in Cleveland, Ohio.

LAND OF REST has been traced to an 1836 appendix to *The Christian Harp*, which was a four-shape shape-note hymnbook compiled by Samuel Wakefield, a Methodist minister. The tune appeared in numerous tunebooks of the nineteenth century in two-, three-, and four-part arrangements.

Annabel Morris Buchanan (1888–1983) collected tunes for her *Folk Hymns of America* (1938) and wrote a number of compositions based on some of them. Buchanan donated her extensive collection of books, photos, recordings, and papers to the University of North Carolina at Chapel Hill in 1978.

522 I Love to Tell the Story

Katherine Arabella Hankey (1834–1911) in 1866 wrote a long, two-part poem on the life of Christ. The first half, written in January, was captioned "The Story Wanted," and the second half, penned in November, was titled "The Story Told." This hymn is from the second half of the poem.

Katherine Hankey, daughter of a London banker, was born in Clapham, England. Early in life she joined a group of Anglican Evangelicals headed by William Wilberforce. She promoted Bible study among young working women and traveled to South Africa to learn of missionary efforts there.

William Gustavus Fischer (1835–1912) in 1869 composed I LOVE TO TELL THE STORY, also named HANKEY after the text's author. He may have been asked to write this music by Charles McCabe, later a bishop of the Episcopal Church. The hymn became a favorite Sunday-school song.

William G. Fischer was born in Baltimore, Maryland, of German descent. He worked as a bookbinder in Philadelphia, Pennsylvania, taught at Girard College in that city, and was a favorite song leader for revival meetings. With John E. Gould, he began a successful music and piano business.

523 Someone Asked the Question (Why We Sing)

Kirk Franklin (b. 1970) released a recording of this song in June 1994, and within a month, it was one of the five best-selling gospel albums in the United States. It was his first release, recorded with his group Kirk Franklin and the Family.

Kirk Franklin, born in Fort Worth, Texas, was abandoned by his teen-aged parents when he was three. He was raised by a distant aunt, Gertrude Franklin. He began playing piano at age four and at age seven was offered a recording contract, which his aunt refused.

Kirk Franklin (b. 1970) loosely based this popular song on "God's Eye Is on the Sparrow" (hymn 475), a gospel hymn by Civilla D. Martin (1869–1948). Franklin provided the arrangement found here and entitled the song WHY WE SING. The hymn is in a contemporary gospel style.

Kirk Franklin began writing and arranging Christian music at age eleven, when appointed music minister at Mt. Rose Baptist Church, Fort Worth, Texas. His first triumph was turning pop musician Elton John's "Bennie and the Jets" into a gospel tune. He describes his compositions as "Christian love music."

524 This Little Light / This Joy I Have

This hymn is actually two different texts which may be sung to the same tune. "This Joy I Have" is a proclamation that no adversity, including slavery, can keep the true believer from experiencing the joy that only God can give. (See also "This Little Light of Mine," hymn 525.)

Worshiping communities are encouraged to improvise in substituting different words for "joy" in this text, although the music necessitates that they be only one syllable. Some common variations are provided in stanzas 2 through 5: "love," "hope," "faith," and "peace."

THIS JOY is the name of this tune, taken from the opening phrase. It was arranged by Jeffrey Radford in 1993. As with much African American music, great latitude can be taken in the singing of the melody, and improvisation is encouraged.

Jeffrey Radford (b. 1953), a member of *The New Century Hymnal* committee, arranged this tune for congregational singing from an African American tune of unknown origin. Radford was responsible for arranging eight different spirituals for *The New Century Hymnal* and for several keyboard arrangements in the accompanist edition.

525 This Little Light of Mine

This was a traditional parting hymn in African American worship and perhaps took the evening sky as its inspiration, as many services were held outdoors in the evening hours. The text includes many biblical references to light, especially Jesus' admonition to "let your light shine."

Although this text most likely developed over a period of time, the motif of light and stars is a familiar one in African American hymns. The God who created the stars and light is capable of giving each life purpose; and every individual, no matter how downtrodden, has "the gift of shining."

William Farley Smith (b. 1941) adapted this traditional African American melody in 1987 and named it LATTIMER for Louis Lattimer, who worked with Thomas Edison in developing the incandescent light bulb. Lattimer was an American scientist of African descent.

William Farley Smith received his music and education degrees from the Manhattan School of Music and Columbia University. He has taught in the New York City public schools, at Montclair State College, and at Drew University. Smith was a consultant for *The United Methodist Hymnal* (1989).

526 Siyahamb' ekukhanyen' kwenkhos' (We Are Marching in the Light of God)

This South African freedom song was a reminder that the Christian national government did not monopolize religious faith in the nation. The people's "Amandla" (Zulu for "power") came from the desire for rights and freedoms being expressed by the black majority of the nation.

South African racial strife gave birth to freedom songs for racial equality and justice. Singing naturally accompanied protest marches as large groups of people voiced their commitment to a more just world in Christ's name. The hymn is best sung without accompaniment.

This South African song is named SIYAHAMBA here for the first word of the text. The melody is in a march tempo, as it was frequently sung by large groups of demonstrators marching or walking to protest the actions of a government that denied them participation.

South African freedom music played a central role in the overthrow of a minority white government. *The New Century Hymnal* is the first major denominational hymnal to include this song. It is best learned as it was learned in South Africa, from a singer who teaches it to others.

527 We Offer Christ

Brian Arthur Wren (b. 1936) was commissioned by St. Paul's United Methodist Church, Orangeburg, South Carolina, to write this hymn for its 150th anniversary, celebrated in 1986. The second verse recalls John Wesley's conversion ("strangely warmed") and the Protestant Reformation.

Brian Wren included this hymn in his earliest collection, *Bring Many Names* (1989), with a tune by Hal Hopson, ORANGEBURG. It is helpful to read and contemplate the text in order to fully appreciate its message and use of language.

David Evans (1874–1948) composed the melody CHARTERHOUSE for a text with which it appeared in *Revised Church Hymnary* (1927). The name honors Charterhouse School, where Evans served as headmaster. He composed it, perhaps as early as 1924, for use by the students at the school.

David Evans was a professor of music at University College, Cardiff, Wales, from 1930 until 1939. Prior to that, he was editor of a Welsh music periodical and *The Church Hymnary* (1927), to which he contributed many lasting harmonizations and original tunes.

528 Sois la Semilla (You Are the Seed)

Cesáreo Gabaráin (1936–1991) wrote this text in the 1970s, and it was first printed in a small booklet in Madrid, Spain. The English translation was prepared for *The United Methodist Hymnal* (1989), which brought many of Gabaráin's hymns to the attention of North American churches.

Cesáreo Gabaráin held postgraduate degrees in theology, journalism, and musicology from the University of Madrid, Spain. He served as a Roman Catholic parish priest as well as a composer of modern church music.

Cesáreo Gabaráin (1936–1991) wrote both the music and words for this hymn, probably for use in his parish church. Named ID Y ENSEÑAD (meaning "Go and Teach"), this work was arranged by Skinner Chávez-Melo, a Mexican organist and choral director.

Cesáreo Gabaráin was born at Hernani, Spain, in May 1936. A Roman Catholic priest, he served as the Spanish chaplain to Pope Paul VI and was named emeritus shortly before his death at Mondragon, Spain, on April 30, 1991.

529 Now Let Us All, in Hymns of Praise

Fred Pratt Green (b. 1903) wrote this text in 1982 as a reminder of the work the church on earth has to do. Many recognize the church hymnal as being second in importance only to the Bible as a book of faith, and often Christians remember words of hymns more easily than scripture texts.

Fred Pratt Green wrote plays and poetry during his years as a Methodist minister in England. These works were published in *This Unlikely Earth* (1952), *The Skating Parson* (1963), and *The Odd Couple* (1976). His writing became even more prolific after his retirement.

Roy Hopp (b. 1951) composed this tune on May 21, 1990, and included it in *The Roy Hopp Hymnary*, a collection of thirty-five new hymn tunes for use with contemporary texts. The tune is called OPEN DOOR from the concluding words of the second stanza.

Roy Hopp has used his musical talents not only as a composer but also as a conductor. He holds degrees in choral conducting and composition and has worked as a director of music in Michigan. Many of his hymn tunes have been included in recently published hymnal collections.

530 God Our Author and Creator

Carl Pickens Daw Jr. entered this text in a hymn contest on the theme of missionary work as part of daily living. The competition was held for the centennial of the Southern Baptist Convention's Women's Missionary Union in 1985. Daw's entry won the contest.

Carl P. Daw Jr. succeeded Thomas Smith as executive director of the Hymn Society in the United States and Canada in 1997. Prior to his appointment, Daw conducted workshops on hymnody, liturgy, and music, and consulted on those topics for the Protestant Episcopal Church.

This tune, named JEFFERSON, was first printed in *Southern Harmony* (1835), a tunebook published by William Walker. Although Walker compiled the tune collection with the aid of his brother-in-law, Benjamin Franklin White, only Walker's name appeared in the book, published in New Haven, Connecticut.

William Walker (1806–1875) was a Baptist music teacher who lived in the area of Spartanburg, South Carolina. He traveled throughout the southern United States, teaching singing and sharing tunes. He published the tunes he compiled in two major volumes: *The Southern Harmony* (1835) and *Christian Harmony* (1867).

531 God, Speak to Me, That I May Speak

Frances R. Havergal (1836–1879), despite lifelong infirmity, wrote this text as a poem entitled "Worker's Prayer," based on Romans 14:7. The poem consisted of seven stanzas and was published in *Under the Surface* (1874).

Frances R. Havergal, the youngest child of an Anglican clergyman, was a person of frail health all her life. Even so, she began to write verse at age seven, had a religious experience as a young girl, learned several languages, and also composed music. She died at age forty-two.

Robert Alexander Schumann (1810–1856) composed the melody on which this tune is based as a piano piece, Nachtstücke in F, op. 23, no. 4 (1839). It was adapted later for use as a hymn tune known as CANONBURY and published in J. Ireland Tucker's *Hymnal with Tunes, Old and New* (1872).

Robert Schumann longed for a career as a concert pianist, but a crippling injury to his hand forced him to turn to composition instead. His wife, Clara, was one of the greatest pianists of her time and did much to make her husband's music known. Schumann suffered from depression and spent the end of his life in an asylum.

532 Come, Labor On

Jane Laurie Borthwick (1813–1897) based this text on two Gospel passages in which Jesus employs the metaphor of the harvest (Matthew 9:37–38 and John 4:35–37). She first included it in her *Thoughts for Thoughtful Hours* (1859) and then revised it for the 1863 edition of that work.

Jane L. Borthwick is better remembered for translating hymns from German into English than for her own poetry. A member of the Free Church of Scotland, she supported various missionary projects, including work in Singapore, Labrador, and in her native Edinburgh, Scotland.

Thomas Tertius Noble (1867–1953) wrote the tune ORA LABORA for this text, and they were first published together in *The New Hymnal* (1918). Noble lived in the United States, but his works have been compared favorably to some of the great English unison tunes by Charles Villiers Stanford and C. Hubert H. Parry.

T. Tertius Noble was an English organist of note, and his wife was the daughter of an Anglican bishop. They moved to the United States in 1913 when he accepted a position at St. Thomas Episcopal Church, New York City, where he served for thirty years.

533 Children of God

John Greenleaf Whittier (1807–1892) wrote these stanzas in 1848 as part of his longer poem "Worship" to articulate his Quaker views on that subject. The poem included a biblical reference to James 1:27 when it was published in Whittier's *Labor and Other Poems* (1850).

John Greenleaf Whittier was born near Haverhill, Massachusetts, on December 17, 1807. He began writing poetry as a teenager and became friends with William Lloyd Garrison, whose abolitionist views he shared. Whittier was not a hymnwriter, but at least seventy-five cantos from his poems have been used in various hymnals.

Alfred Scott-Gatty (1847–1918) named this tune WELWYN after a model suburb being built near London, England. He composed the tune in 1902, and it was published that year in *Arundel Hymns*. It found wider acceptance, however, after appearing in *The Church Hymnary* (1927).

Alfred Scott-Gatty had two passions in life: writing children's songs and heraldry. He wrote hundreds of songs, many of which were published by his mother in *Aunt Judy's Magazine*. Scott-Gatty founded the Magpie Madrigal Society in 1886 and published an operetta, *Tattercoats*, in 1900.

534 O God of Strength

Shepherd Knapp (1873–1946) wrote this hymn for a meeting of the men's association at the Brick Presbyterian Church, New York City, in 1907. Knapp was serving the church as assistant pastor at the time. The hymn is a reminder of the importance of obedience to God's call.

Shepherd Knapp was born September 8, 1873, and ordained to the Congregational ministry. He was a descendant of Jonathan Edwards, the Puritan New England preacher. Knapp served Central Congregational Church in Worcester, Massachusetts, for the last twenty-eight years of his ministry.

Alfred Scott-Gatty (1847–1918) composed WELWYN in 1902, and it was first published in part 4 of *Arundel Hymns* (1902). That Roman Catholic collection was edited by the Duke of Norfolk and Charles T. Gatty, the composer's uncle.

Alfred Scott-Gatty was born on April 26, 1847, at Ecclesfield, Yorkshire, England. The son of a dean at York Cathedral, he was knighted in 1904 after being appointed Garter Principal King-of-Arms by the College of Heralds. Scott-Gatty died in London, England, on December 18, 1918.

535 O Holy God, Whose Gracious Power

Jane Parker Huber's (b. 1926) focus in this text is the stewardship of human resources as it relates to the church's mission. It seeks to emphasize "giving and receiving mission in a global church unified in Christ." The hymn employs a traditional trinitarian outline while avoiding use of gender-exclusive language.

Jane Parker Huber was educated in the Hanover, Indiana, public schools and in Northfield School for Girls in East Northfield, Massachusetts. She attended Wellesley College in Massachusetts and received a bachelor of arts degree in 1948 from Hanover College, Indiana.

Alfred Scott-Gatty (1847–1918) composed WELWYN in 1902 and named it for a model suburb being constructed near London, England. The tune, first published in *Arundel Hymns* in 1902, became even more popular when included in *The Church Hymnary* (1927).

Alfred Scott-Gatty was born on April 26, 1847, at Ecclesfield, Yorkshire, England. The son of a dean of York Cathedral, he had two overpowering interests in life: composing music for children and heraldry. He was knighted in 1904 and died in London on December 18, 1918.

536 Savior, an Offering Costly and Sweet

Edwin Pond Parker (1836–1925) wrote this hymn to accompany a particular sermon he preached for Center Church in Hartford, Connecticut, where he was pastor and choir director. It was first published in *The Christian Hymnal* (1889).

Edwin P. Parker wrote more than two hundred hymns, most of them after the age of fifty-five. Born in Castine, Maine, he attended Bowdoin College and Bangor Theological Seminary. Parker served three Congregational churches, spending most of his career at Center Church in Hartford, Connecticut.

Edwin Pond Parker (1836–1925) composed this tune for his text in 1888 and gave it the name LOVE'S OFFERING for the sentiment of the words. The hymn first appeared in *The Christian Hymnal* (1889) and was later included in both the *Pilgrim Hymnal* (1958) and *The Hymnal* (1941).

Edwin P. Parker served as the pastor of Center Church (Congregational) in Hartford, Connecticut, for fifty years. In addition to his pastoral duties, he wrote hymn texts and tunes and helped to compile several hymnals. He died in Hartford, Connecticut, on May 28, 1925.

537 Christian, Rise and Act Your Creed

Francis Albert Rollo Russell (1849–1914) included this hymn in *Break of Day*, a hymnal he published in London in 1893. After appearing in the *Pilgrim Hymnal* (1904), the hymn became popular in Congregational churches but never gained wide acceptance in other denominations.

Francis A. R. Russell was an English Unitarian who received his education at Christ Church, Oxford. A fellow of the Royal Meteorological Society, Russell's hymns are a reminder that the Christian faith and the pursuit of scientific truth can be compatible.

INNOCENTS is the name of this anonymous tune, so named because it was used originally with a hymn for the Feast of the Holy Innocents, traditionally observed on December 28. This day recalls the killing of all baby boys by the order of King Herod, as told in Matthew 2:16.

The Parish Choir was a monthly music journal published in England from 1846 to 1851 for an organization of Anglican musicians affiliated with the Oxford movement. The journal sought to improve the level of music in the liturgy, especially those portions sung by the choir.

538 Standing at the Future's Threshold

Paul R. Gregory (b. 1922) wrote this hymn for the final service of the 175th anniversary meeting of the United Church Board for World Ministries, held in 1985. The text serves as a reminder of the many forms of missionary work needed to heal the world and as a call to continue in that ministry.

Paul R. Gregory was ordained as a minister of the United Church of Christ in 1944. He served as East and Southeast Asia secretary of the United Church Board for World Ministries from 1957, when the denomination was formed, until his retirement in 1986.

Arthur Seymour Sullivan (1842–1900) composed the tune LUX EOI for the text "Hark! A Thrilling Voice Is Sounding." It first appeared in his *Church Hymns with Tunes* (1874) and then in *Hymns for the Church of England* (1875). The Latin word *lux* means "light."

Arthur S. Sullivan was the son of a British Army bandmaster and professor of clarinet. A child prodigy, Sullivan had learned to play most woodwind instruments by age eight, wrote an anthem at age thirteen, and won the Mendelssohn Scholarship at the Royal Academy of Music at age fourteen.

539 Won't You Let Me Be Your Servant?

Richard Gillard (b. 1953) wrote this text in 1977, and it was first released on a record album the following year by Scripture in Song, an Auckland, New Zealand, publishing company. It was later sung on *New Harvest*, an album recorded by the St. Paul's Anglican Church Singers.

Richard Gillard was born in England on May 22, 1953, the oldest of six children. When he was three years old, his family emigrated to New Zealand, and he has lived on the north side of North Island since that time. Gillard is a member of a local Brethren Assembly.

Richard Gillard (b. 1953) composed SERVANT SONG in 1977, and it is named for the topic of the text. A self-taught musician, he prefers to play by ear and allows others to transcribe his songs into manuscript form. Gillard has almost no formal musical training.

Betty Carr Pulkingham (b. 1928) arranged and adapted this tune. Born in Burlington, North Carolina, she has been a high-school music teacher, church choir director, and published composer. Pulkingham is a founding member of the Community of Celebration, based in Berkshire, England.

540 We Plant a Grain of Mustard Seed

Mary Bryan Matney (b. 1955) wrote this text as a wedding present for her friends Agnus French and John Kunkel. It was first sung by an ensemble at their wedding, with the congregation joining in singing the last stanza. This is the first text by Matney accepted for publication.

Mary Bryan Matney was born May 3, 1955, in Atlanta, Georgia. Her father was a Presbyterian minister, and the family lived in Florida and North Carolina. Matney has earned her living as a bakery owner, as a water-bed salesperson, and in the recycling business.

Sally Ann Morris (b. 1952) named this tune NEW BEGINNINGS from a phrase in the fifth stanza of Matney's text. This was only Morris's second hymn tune. Agnus French Kunkel, for whose wedding it was written, urged her to submit it to a hymn contest in Charlotte, North Carolina.

Sally Ann Morris met Mary Bryan Matney when both were attending St. Andrew's Presbyterian College in Laurinburg, North Carolina. Morris graduated from that institution with a bachelor's degree in music in 1975. The two women have remained close friends since college days.

541 They Asked, "Who's My Neighbor?"

Ruth Jannelle Smith Wesson (b. 1925) used Jesus' parable of the man who fell among thieves in Luke 10 as her inspiration for this text. The format is that of a metrical paraphrase, a style popularly used with the psalms in the eighteenth century. The fourth stanza presents the moral behind Jesus' story.

Jan Wesson was born April 25, 1925, in Greenville, Illinois, and graduated with honors from St. Louis High School in 1942. She is a soprano who also writes texts for hymns and songs. Wesson's family includes four children and ten grandchildren.

Jan Wesson (b. 1925) created this musical setting, titled NEIGHBOR, for her own words, and it was first published in *New Hymns for Children* (1982) by the Hymn Society in the United States and Canada. The hymn subsequently appeared in *Holding in Trust*, a retrospective collection of hymns from seven decades, published by that same organization in 1991.

Jan Wesson's hymn has begun to appear in recent hymnals, such as *The Worshiping Church* (1990) and *The New Century Hymnal* (1995), to fill a need for more narrative hymns that are especially appealing and educational for children and youth.

542 Born of God, Eternal Savior

Somerset Thomas Corry Lowry (1855–1932) titled this hymn "For Unity" when he first published it in a magazine called *Good Will* in 1894. The next year it was included in the *Christian Social Union Hymn Book*. Lowry was serving at North Holmwood, England, when he wrote the hymn.

Somerset T. C. Lowry was born in Dublin, Ireland, on March 21, 1855, and spent his life as a priest in the Anglican Church. In addition, he wrote sixty hymns and several devotional books. He died at Torquay, England, on January 29, 1932.

This anonymous tune was first printed in a Roman Catholic hymnal in Cologne, Germany, in 1741. The tune's name, WEISSE FLAGGEN, is taken from the German text with which it appeared, "Lasst die weissen Flaggen wehen." The hymn may have originated as a popular folk song.

Tochter Sion was a Roman Catholic hymnal printed in Cologne, Germany, in 1741. It was one of more than thirty hymnals printed in that region of Germany for Roman Catholic churches. Many of these hymnals contained variations on tunes popular with German congregations.

543 Where Cross the Crowded Ways of Life

Frank Mason North (1850–1935) was challenged by one of the editors of the 1905 *Methodist Hymnal* to provide a contemporary missionary hymn. Based on Matthew 22:9, the opening line may have been inspired by the view of crowded New York City streets from North's office window.

Frank M. North was born in New York City on December 3, 1850. A Methodist minister, he served churches in three states before joining the staff of the New York Missionary Society of the Methodist Episcopal Church and subsequently the Methodist Board of Foreign Missions. North also served as editor of *The Christian City*.

William Gardiner (1770–1853) harmonized the tune GERMANY for his 1815 hymnal, *Sacred Melodies*, citing Beethoven as the source. This connection, however, has never been proven. GERMANY has served as the setting for North's text since they were first paired in *The Methodist Hymnal* (1905).

William Gardiner was influential in bringing the music of Beethoven, Haydn, and Mozart to England. Music was his hobby, and he made many trips to the European continent. Gardiner wrote about his experiences in *Music and Friends* (1838–1853). When he was not traveling, Gardiner lived in Leicester, England.

544 Si fui motivo de dolor, oh Dios
(If I Have Been the Source of Pain, O God)

C. Maud Battersby (19th–20th centuries) was the author of the gospel hymn "If I Have Wounded Any Soul Today," which appears here both in a Spanish translation by Sara M. de Hall and in an English translation from the Spanish version by Janet W. May.

C. Maud Battersby's original hymn on which this version is based can be found in the *New National Baptist Hymnal* (1977) under the title "An Evening Prayer" and set with a popular gospel tune by Charles H. Gabriel.

Pablo D. Sosa (b. 1933) composed the tune CAMACUA as a new setting for an old gospel song that had been translated into Spanish by Sara M. de Hall. Sosa's modal melody has received widespread use not only in South America but also among Hispanic Christians around the world.

Pablo Sosa is a leading Argentinean composer and conductor. He was coleader of music for the Sixth Assembly of the World Council of Churches in Vancouver, Canada, in 1983 and has held workshops on Hispanic religious folk music around the world.

545 There Was Jesus by the Water

Gracia Grindal (b. 1943) used the story of Jesus' healing of the little girl as found in the Synoptic Gospels (Matthew, Mark, and Luke) for this narrative text. She wrote it in 1983 when she was trying to "break out of a rhythmic metrical straitjacket."

Gracia Grindal received her education at Augsburg College, Minnesota, and the University of Arkansas, where she received a master of fine arts degree in 1969. She also studied for a year in Oslo, Norway. Grindal wrote the libretto for the cantata *Dream of Shalom* in 1976 and has published numerous hymn texts and translations.

Howard M. (Rusty) Edwards III (b. 1955) composed the tune TALITHA CUMI in 1983 for Gracia Grindal's text while he was a student in her hymnwriting class at Luther Northwest Theological Seminary in Minnesota. The hymn was included in a booklet, *Singing the Story* (1983), along with others from the class.

Rusty Edwards, an ordained minister of the Lutheran Church, is senior pastor at Gloria Dei Lutheran Church in Rockford, Illinois. He has published a collection of original hymns, *Faith Is the Yes of the Heart*. Edwards earned his doctorate degree in creative ministry.

546 Jesus, Lover of My Soul

Charles Wesley (1707–1788) wrote this simple hymn shortly after his conversion in 1738. (Of its 137 words, 109 are monosyllables.) It was so intensely intimate that it was not published in John Wesley's *Collection* until the 1797 edition, eight years after Charles's death.

Charles Wesley, the "sweet singer of Methodism," was the youngest son in a family of fifteen. He traveled to the Georgia colony with his brother John, where they came into contact with Moravians, who would have a lasting influence on the two men.

Simeon Butler Marsh (1798–1875) wrote the tune MARTYN for an Easter hymn during a trip by horseback from Amsterdam, New York, to Johnston, New York, while he was working as a singing-school teacher. This tune was first used with Charles Wesley's text in 1851.

Simeon B. Marsh, born in Sherburne, New York, was singing in a choir at age seven. While teaching music in his spare time, he founded and edited two newspapers in New York state, the *Amsterdam Intelligencer* and the *Sherburne News*. Marsh was a friend of composer Thomas Hastings.

547 Amazing Grace, How Sweet the Sound

John Newton (1725–1807) wrote this autobiographical yet universal hymn some time prior to its publication in *Olney Hymns* (1779), a collection named for the English church and town where Newton served as pastor from 1764 to 1779. The final stanza, common to a number of nineteenth-century hymns, was added later and has become the standard conclusion for Newton's text.

John Newton, along with William Cowper, published *Olney Hymns* (1779), which consisted of three books on varied topics, as opposed to following the church year. It became an important resource among Evangelicals within the Anglican Church.

AMAZING GRACE is an early melody from the United States that takes its name from the first line of Newton's text. This old Southern tune once was sung to "Loving Lambs." It has also been called NEW BRITAIN, HARMONY GROVE, SYMPHONY, SOLON, and REDEMPTION. It was first published in *Columbian Harmony* (1829).

Edwin Othello Excell (1851–1921) arranged the tune AMAZING GRACE in its present form for his hymnal *Make His Praise Glorious*, published in Chicago, Illinois, in 1900. Excell had moved to Chicago in 1883 to begin his gospel-song publishing business.

548 Onuniyan tehanl waun
(Amazing Grace, How Sweet the Sound)

John Newton (1725–1807) was not ordained to the ministry of the Church of England until age forty, in 1765. He wrote this hymn, now known throughout the world, around 1779 as a reflection on his earlier life. At that time, he was traveling in Switzerland and Italy seeking to recover his health.

Stephen W. Holmes (b. 20th century) translated John Newton's English-language text into the Lakota tongue in 1987 with the help of members of his congregation. The hymn was popular among the Dakota people, but it had never before been translated into their language.

This tune, known most widely as AMAZING GRACE or NEW BRITAIN, has been traced to *Columbian Harmony*, an 1829 hymnal, and *Virginia Harmony*, an 1831 collection. It was first used as a setting for Newton's hymn in *Southern Harmony* (1835).

Edwin O. Excell (1851–1921) was the son of a German Reformed Church minister. He became a popular song leader for Sunday school conventions and revival meetings. Excell composed more than two thousand gospel songs and published fifty songbooks.

549 Bless God, O My Soul

Russell E. Sonafrank II (b. 1947) wrote this paraphrase of Psalm 103 in 1987 in collaboration with his longtime friend Stephen Morris. Sonafrank was drawn to that particular psalm text "for its rich, accessible imagery depicting the absoluteness of God's grace."

Russell E. Sonafrank II was born on January 11, 1947, in Peru, Indiana, and completed three degrees at Indiana University in Bloomington. He has worked as an English teacher for more than twenty-five years and has also served as an organist and choral director in the United Methodist Church.

Stephen J. Morris (b. 1956) composed this tune as a setting for the paraphrase of Psalm 103 by his friend Russell E. Sonafrank. It is named SPRING WOODS for the United Methodist Church in Houston, Texas, where Morris was serving as organist and choir director at the time.

Stephen J. Morris was born August 23, 1956, in Angola, Indiana. He holds degrees from DePauw University (Indiana) and Southern Methodist University (Texas). Morris has worked as a high-school and college music director, a church organist, and, more recently, as a freelance musician in Houston.

550 O God, as with a Potter's Hand

Herman G. Stuempfle Jr. (b. 1923) watched his son David work at his potter's wheel and was reminded of various biblical texts referring to God as a potter. Stuempfle subsequently developed these memories and metaphors as the basis for this text, which appeared in his *The Words Goes Forth* (1993).

Herman G. Stuempfle Jr. was born April 2, 1923, in Clarion, Pennsylvania. An ordained Lutheran pastor, he served various churches before joining the staff of the Board of Social Missions. Stuempfle served as president of Lutheran Theological Seminary in Gettysburg, Pennsylvania, from 1976 to 1989.

Sally Ann Morris (b. 1952) matched this tune, an earlier composition of hers, with Herman Stuempfle's text. It proved to be a winning combination when the hymn received a prize in a Hymn Society contest. Morris named the tune WINSTON-SALEM to honor her North Carolina hometown.

Sally Ann Morris grew up in Winston-Salem, North Carolina, in a musical family. She began piano lessons at age six and continued to study voice and piano through college. Morris sells pianos for a living and is also a trained choral conductor.

551 Pass Me Not, O Gentle Savior

Fanny Jane Crosby (1820–1915) wrote this text in 1868 after visiting a Manhattan, New York, prison. One prisoner shouted, "Good Lord! Do not pass me by." That evening, Crosby incorporated the first line as suggested by William H. Doane, who then composed the tune for it.

Fanny Crosby was a famous person in her lifetime, meeting U.S. presidents John Quincy Adams, Martin Van Buren, James Polk, James Buchanan, and Andrew Johnson. Yet she never lost touch with average people and through her life supported causes that helped those who were less fortunate.

William Howard Doane (1832–1915) composed PASS ME NOT for his 1870 hymnbook, *Songs of Devotion for Christian Associations*. Doane collaborated with Crosby on many of her hymns and was associated with the publishing house that was a major distributor of her gospel songs.

William H. Doane, the composer of more than 2,200 tunes, received an honorary doctor of music degree from Denison University in Granville, Ohio, in recognition of his philanthropy. Doane supported numerous charitable and educational causes with donations.

552 From the Crush of Wealth and Power

Kendyl L. R. Gibbons (b. 1955) wrote this text to be sung to the melody BRIDEGROOM. It was commissioned by the Unitarian Universalist Association for the 1993 hymnal *Singing the Living Tradition*. The text deals with the stresses of life in modern times.

Kendyl L. R. Gibbons is a Unitarian Universalist minister and has contributed hymn texts to her denomination to help widen the use of female imagery for the Divine. She has served churches in Illinois, including DuPage Unitarian Church in Naperville, for more than ten years.

Peter Warwick Cutts (b. 1937) composed the tune BRIDEGROOM for the text "As the Bridegroom to His Chosen" at the suggestion of Erik Routley. The tune and text were first used in *One Hundred Hymns for Today*, published in 1969.

Peter Cutts was born in Birmingham, England, and was educated in that country. He later moved to the United States and has served as music director at churches in Massachusetts and as a faculty member at Andover Newton Theological School.

553 There Is a Balm in Gilead

This spiritual is based on the writings of the Hebrew prophet Jeremiah. The text provides an answer to Jeremiah's question, "Is there no balm in Gilead?" (Jer. 8:22). The balm referred to was resin from the styrax tree, which was used in Gilead for healing purposes. This song interprets the question figuratively.

In a commentary on this spiritual, Melva W. Costen speculates that since it is based on a specific biblical text, it may have been sung originally in response to a sermon on that passage from Jeremiah.

This melody, BALM IN GILEAD, was derived in conjunction with these words. The refrain is best sung at a comfortable (not dragging) tempo, and the stanzas are best performed a little faster to maintain the hopeful tone of the text.

Frederick J. Work Jr. included this spiritual in his *Folk Songs of the American Negro* (1907). A later choral arrangement by William L. Dawson in 1939 made the song more accessible to worshiping congregations and helped to increase its popularity.

554 Out of the Depths, O God, We Call

Ruth C. Duck (b. 1947) based this hymn on Psalm 130:1–8, a text traditionally called the "De Profundis." The hymn was commissioned in 1988 for the Women and the Word Conference at the Anna Howard Shaw Center of Boston University School of Theology in Massachusetts.

Ruth Duck was born in Washington, D.C., on November 21, 1947, and grew up there, although her family's roots are in Tennessee. In 1974, she was ordained to the United Church of Christ ministry by the Chicago Metropolitan Association, where she still holds her ministerial standing.

Robert J. Batastini (b. 1942) composed this tune for Ruth Duck's text in 1994. He was at his summer retreat home in Fennville, Michigan, and named the tune FENNVILE for this small town situated midway between the shore of Lake Michigan and the Kalamazoo River in Allegan County.

Robert J. Batastini was born on New Year's Day 1942 and has been active in Roman Catholic music ministry his entire career. Educated at DePaul University, he has served several parishes and the archdiocese of Chicago. Batastini is senior editor of G.I.A. Publications, Inc.

555 Here, Savior, in This Quiet Place

Fred Pratt Green (b. 1903) wrote this text specifically for use in healing services. The Protestant church in the late twentieth century has rediscovered a need for services of healing, and the body of hymns on this topic is growing to meet the need for more resources.

Fred Pratt Green was born in Roby, near Liverpool, England, on September 2, 1903. He attended Wallasey Grammar School, Rydal School, Huyton High School, and Didsbury College, Manchester. During his career as a Methodist minister he served circuits throughout England.

Peter Warwick Cutts (b. 1937) provided this tune for Fred Pratt Green's text at the request of the *New Century Hymnal* editors, who were not satisfied with other settings currently in use. It is named CHATHAM for a town in Massachusetts. At the time of composing this work, Cutts was serving as an organist in Watertown, Massachusetts.

Peter Cutts was born in Birmingham, England, and was educated in that nation. At the prodding of Erik Routley, he began writing hymn tunes and became successful both in England and in the United States. Cutts moved to Massachusetts and joined the faculty of Andover Newton Theological School.

556 God, Who Stretched the Spangled Heavens

Catherine Arnott Cameron (b. 1927) wrote this text in 1967 over a period of months while she was experiencing a renewed sense of creativity and growth in her life. She wrote the hymn to reflect the human community's obligation to be sure that its creativity complements that of God.

Catherine Cameron was born in St. John, New Brunswick, Canada, the daughter of Presbyterian minister John Sutherland Bonnell. She has written poetry since childhood, and her hymns have appeared in a number of major American hymnals. She is now a U.S. citizen.

William Moore (19th century) included HOLY MANNA and seventeen other original tunes in his shape-note collection, *Columbian Harmony*, (1825). This four-part harmonization most likely dates from the twentieth century.

William Moore compiled a four-shape shape-note tunebook called *The Columbian Harmony* in Wilson County, Tennessee, in 1825, although it was published in Cincinnati, Ohio. Shape-note tunebooks provided an easy way for singers to learn tunes by providing different shapes for various notes.

557 Pray for the Wilderness

Daniel Charles Damon (b. 1955) struggled for many months to write a hymn about ecological issues and the stewardship of God's creation. After viewing a movie about the depletion of the world's rain forests, he produced this text in August of 1989.

Dan Damon was born in Rapid City, South Dakota, on July 2, 1955, and grew up immersed in the gospel-hymn tradition of the Evangelical Free Church. He received a bachelor's degree in music education from Greenville (Illinois) College and used it in teaching high-school band and choir.

Lee Yu San (dates unknown) composed this tune in 1967. The editors of *The New Century Hymnal* named it WILDERNESS when they selected it as the setting for Dan Damon's text. The tune is based on a Korean song.

Dan Damon originally set this hymn text with the Irish tune SLANE in his collection of twenty-four new texts, *Faith Will Sing* (1993). That familiar tune enhanced the hymn's use at several conferences.

558 O How Glorious, Full of Wonder

Curtis Beach (1914–1993) was inspired to write this text when looking at a World War II photograph of Cologne Cathedral in Germany. American bombers had been instructed to destroy railroad yards nearby but not to hurt the cathedral, giving the picture an aura of both destruction and beauty.

Curtis Beach was educated at Harvard University and Boston University School of Theology and earned his Ph.D. at the University of Southern California. Beach was ordained at the Neighborhood Church in Pasadena and served that congregation from 1943 to 1959.

This traditional Dutch melody, IN BABILONE, was first printed in 1710 in a collection of old and new Dutch peasant songs and country dances. As three of the four phrases are the same, this simple melody is quite easily learned and must have been popular even with untrained singers.

Julius Röntgen (1855–1932) arranged this hymn for *The English Hymnal* (1906). Röntgen was a distinguished Dutch pianist and composer. He went to Amsterdam in 1877 and spent most of his career there working for musical institutions as a conductor and director.

559 Thank You, God

Brian Arthur Wren (b. 1936) wrote this text in 1973 and revised it in 1988. This ecological hymn is a reminder that all of nature is God's gift and our stewardship of that gift is to allow nature's renewal. Wren has praised John Weaver's tune AMSTEIN as the "ideal musical partner" for his text.

Brian Wren was educated at New College, Oxford, England, and Mansfield College, Oxford. He completed his doctoral work in theology at Oxford University in 1968. His thesis was on the language of prophetic eschatology in the Hebrew Scriptures.

John Weaver (b. 1937) composed this setting for Brian Wren's text when it was selected to appear in *The Presbyterian Hymnal* (1990). It is named AMSTEIN for the associate pastor of Madison Avenue Presbyterian Church, New York City, where Weaver served as music director.

John Weaver was born in Jim Thorpe, Pennsylvania, when it was still called Mauch Chunk. During military service, Weaver was organist at West Point Academy, New York. He teaches organ at two world-renowned music institutes.

560 By Whatever Name We Call You

M. Dosia Carlson (b. 1930) wrote this hymn in 1990, inspired by the preaching of the senior pastor at the Church of the Beatitudes, Phoenix, Arizona, where she served on the ministerial staff. The hymn recognizes that humans cannot fully comprehend the nature of God or totally respond to God's love.

Dosia Carlson was ordained to the ministry of the United Church of Christ in 1979 and used that opportunity to incorporate examples of hymns she had written into her faith statement. Her autobiographical collection, *God's Glory*, was published in 1986 by the Beatitudes Center for Developing Older Adult Resources.

Peter Niedmann (b. 1960) was commissioned by *The New Century Hymnal* committee to compose this musical setting for Dosia Carlson's text. He named it OGONTZ for a lake in Lyman, New Hampshire, the site of a summer choir camp he attended as a youth.

Peter Niedmann was born on October 12, 1960, in New London, Connecticut, and graduated from that state's university. He serves as organist and choirmaster at Trinity Episcopal Church, Tariffville, Connecticut. He has published various anthems and received an award for organ improvisation.

561 When in Our Music God Is Glorified

Fred Pratt Green (b. 1903) titled this hymn, written as a celebration of music, "Let the People Sing!" It has appeared in the British supplement *New Church Praise* (1975) and nearly all major hymnals and smaller collections since.

Fred Pratt Green has been called the most important hymnist in Methodism since Charles Wesley, but he personally rejects the comparison. He is considered the leader of a twentieth-century "hymnic explosion" in England and has encouraged the production of new hymns for use by the entire church.

Charles Villiers Stanford (1852–1924) composed ENGELBERG for William How's "For All the Saints" in a 1904 English hymnal, but Ralph Vaughan Williams's tune SINE NOMINE eclipsed its popularity. ENGELBERG is a strong tune in its own right and has grown in popularity since being paired with this text.

Charles V. Stanford was born in Dublin, Ireland, and died in London, England, seventy-two years later. He taught composition at the Royal College of Music and at Cambridge University and counted Ralph Vaughan Williams and Gustav Holst among his students. Stanford helped introduce unison hymn tunes, in contrast to the traditional four-part settings of the Victorian era.

562 Take My Gifts

Shirley Erena Murray (b. 1931) wrote this hymn for use during a stewardship campaign in a local church. The text reminds Christians that their offerings, pledges, and gifts are in response to love already given by God, love that never can be fully repaid.

Shirley Erena Murray has written hymns, poems, and satirical songs. Her fame as a hymnist is spreading, and her work has been published in Australia, Great Britain, and the United States. She is editor and executive secretary of the New Zealand Hymnbook Trust.

Colin Gibson (b. 1933) composed this tune "almost instantaneously" when given the text, according to a report by Shirley Erena Murray. The tune is named TALAVERA TERRACE for the Wellington, New Zealand, street where Murray lives.

Colin Gibson has served for forty-five years as organist and choir director at Mornington Methodist Church in New Zealand. In addition, he serves as a lay preacher at Dunedin Methodist parish. Gibson has traveled extensively around the world giving workshops on hymn writing.

563 We Cannot Own the Sunlit Sky

Ruth C. Duck (b. 1947) was inspired to write this text while she was on the corporate board of the United Church Board for World Ministries from 1975 to 1985. This text was suggested for use during the 1984 One Great Hour of Sharing all-church offering, which supports the board's work throughout the world.

Ruth Duck served as an interim pastor for three churches in Massachusetts from 1985 to 1989, while at the same time studying for her doctor of theology degree at Boston University. In 1989, she moved to Evanston, Illinois, where she has been a seminary professor for nearly a decade.

Robert Lowry (1826–1899) is believed to have written this tune, END-LESS SONG, since it appeared in his *Bright Jewels for the Sunday School*, published in New York City in 1869. Lowry served as president of the New Jersey Baptist Sunday School Convention for many years.

Robert Lowry was born in Philadelphia, Pennsylvania, and educated at Bucknell University in Lewisburg, Pennsylvania. He later moved to Crozer Theological Seminary of Bucknell as professor of rhetoric, served as a member of the board of curators, and later became chancellor there.

564 We Are Not Our Own

Brian Arthur Wren (b. 1936) was commissioned to write this text for the tenth anniversary of the Liturgical Studies Program of Drew University in New Jersey. The six-stanza hymn employs the poetic device "chiasmus," in which phrases (or themes) are repeated in subsequent stanzas to unifying effect.

Brian Wren published *Education for Justice* in 1977, reflecting on his work with the British Council of Churches, in which he sought to communicate to churches the tragedy and causes of world poverty. He was chair of the Council of War on Want in England.

Brian Arthur Wren (b. 1936) is known primarily as a hymn text writer, but he composed this tune, YARNTON, along with the poem in 1987. This melody came to him in the midst of writing the text and helped him to finish the words to the last stanzas. Fred Graham supplied the harmonization.

Brian Wren has published a number of collections of his works beginning with *Faith Looking Forward* in 1983. Wren revised thirty-three of the forty-nine hymns from that volume and reissued them twelve years later in *Faith Renewed* (1995). *Piece Together Praise* (1996) is an anthology of his work from three decades.

565 God, Whose Giving Knows No Ending

Robert Lansing Edwards (b. 1915) wrote this text in 1961 for a hymn contest on the theme of stewardship. Edwards wrote the hymn while vacationing in the White Mountains of New Hampshire during the summer months. The hymn was first published in *Ten New Stewardship Hymns* (1961).

Robert L. Edwards was educated at Princeton University, Harvard Divinity School, and Union Theological Seminary, New York. Ordained to the United Church of Christ ministry in 1949, he has served churches in the Connecticut conference.

Franz Joseph Haydn's (1732–1809) AUSTRIAN HYMN is one of only a few cases in which a classical composer has composed a piece to be used specifically as a hymn tune. It was first sung on February 12, 1797, for the emperor's birthday. Haydn later used the tune in the slow movement of his "Emperor" string quartet.

Franz Joseph Haydn was the oldest son of a wheelwright. He was educated in Roman Catholic schools in Vienna, Austria, and at age eighteen composed his first mass. While he was playing in a street band, he was "discovered" by a comedian, who asked him to set a farce to music.

566 Heaven and Earth, and Sea and Air

Joachim Neander (1650–1680) subtitled this text "Rejoicing in God's Creation" in his 1680 hymnbook. He also considered this as a hymn for travelers. The new translation of the original German, "Himmel, Erde, Luft, und Meer," was made by Madeleine Forell Marshall.

Joachim Neander, the greatest hymnwriter in the German Reformed Church, lived to be only thirty years old. Tuberculosis ended his life on May 21, 1680, at Bremen, Germany. Neander was a poet and musician and the author of sixty hymns. He worked as a headmaster at a church grammar school.

This anonymous German tune, GOTT SEI DANK, first appeared in Freylinghausen's *Geistreiches Gesangbuch*, published at Halle, Germany, in 1704. It accompanied Heinrich Held's hymn "Gott sei dank in aller Welt" in that two-volume collection for pietist churches. The hymnbook's influence spread, and the hymn became popular throughout Germany and Switzerland.

Johann Freylinghausen (1670–1739) has been cited as the "Charles Wesley of the pietist movement" in Germany because of his hymnbooks, which introduced a new, more personal style of hymn. Freylinghausen succeeded his mentor, August Herman Francke, at St. Ulrich's Church in Halle and married Francke's only daughter, Anastasia.

567 Stars and Planets Flung in Orbit

Herman G. Stuempfle Jr. (b. 1923) was inspired to write this text after reading Psalm 148. As with all his texts, he used Scripture as the starting point in the writing process. The hymn was published in 1993 in *The Word Goes Forth*, a collection of his hymns, songs, and carols.

Herman G. Stuempfle Jr. received his education at Susquehanna (Pennsylvania) University; Lutheran Theological Seminary in Gettysburg, Pennsylvania; Union Theological Seminary in New York City; and Southern California School of Theology at Claremont, where he earned his Th.D.

John Goss (1800–1880) composed the tune LAUDA ANIMA (Latin for "Praise, My Soul") for a text by H. F. Lyte which began with those words. It became one of the most widely sung Victorian hymn tunes in England and remains one of the most enduring of all Goss's compositions.

John Goss served as organist at a variety of English churches during his career. From 1827 until 1874, he was professor of harmony at the Royal Academy of Music. He was knighted when he retired, and in 1876 Cambridge University awarded him a doctor of music degree.

568 God Marked a Line and Told the Sea

Thomas H. Troeger (b. 1945) wrote this text in 1986 as a study on liberty and freedom. Having noticed that many people used liberty and freedom as license to do whatever they wanted, Troeger composed this poem to explain that God had set limits. The opening line is taken from Job 38:10–11.

Thomas H. Troeger (b. 1945) was born in Suffern, New York, on January 30, 1945. He served as associate pastor at New Hartford (Connecticut) Presbyterian Church from 1970 to 1977 and intended to stay in the parish ministry. However, in 1977, he shifted careers to become a seminary teacher.

Elkanah Kelsay Dare (1782–1826) is credited as the composer of KEDRON in the index of Amos Pilsbury's *United States Sacred Harmony*, a 1799 hymnal. Dare was only seventeen when the collection was published. This tune became one of the most popular tunes in the United States in the early nineteenth century.

Elkanah Kelsay Dare became a Methodist minister and edited the 1813 *Repository of Sacred Music, Part Second*, published by John Wyeth. He also contributed thirteen tunes to the collection. This hymnal set the tone for the vigorous singing tradition that thrived in the southern United States.

569 Touch the Earth Lightly

Shirley Erena Murray (b. 1931) based these words on a saying of the aboriginal people of Australia. She incorporated this saying into her text, which promotes an ecological land-use policy that encourages growth and renewal rather than destruction.

Shirley Erena Murray serves as the editor and executive secretary of the New Zealand Hymnbook Trust. Her experience writing hymn texts and poems, as well as her career as a church organist, prepared her well for this position in her native country.

Colin Gibson (b. 1933) created the tune TENDERNESS for these words by his New Zealand colleague Shirley Erena Murray. Although the hymn name does not appear in the text, it does reflect a Christian ethic of tenderness for the created order on the earth.

Colin Gibson was born in Dunedin, New Zealand. He has served as the head of the department of English and Donald Collie Professor of English at the University of Otago and has published a number of scholarly works, including editions of the plays of Shakespeare, Massinger, and Ford.

570 We Shall Overcome

This hymn has the ring of an African American spiritual, although its specific origins are a topic of some debate. These words developed during the civil-rights struggles in the United States in the 1950s and 1960s. Other published stanzas include: "We shall all be free" and "God is on our side."

This is more than a hymn of protest; it is a song of patriotic commitment to the ideals of equality for all people. It serves as a reminder that the struggles of the 1950s and 1960s have not been fully resolved. The hymn is now as much at home in the churches as it was on the streets during freedom rallies.

This anonymous tune, WE SHALL OVERCOME, was used as a rally song for striking southern tobacco workers as they fought for the right to unionize in the 1940s. Folk singer Pete Seeger included the song in his concerts in the 1950s and 1960s, contributing to its popularity.

This harmonization was composed by J. Jefferson Cleveland (1937–1986) for *Songs of Zion*, a compilation of African American spirituals, hymns, and gospel songs. Cleveland coedited this resource with Verolga Nix in 1981.

571 O God of Love, O God of Peace

Henry Williams Baker (1821–1877) wrote this hymn during the mid-nineteenth century when both England the United States were involved in or threatened by war. It was included in *Hymns Ancient and Modern*, which Baker edited in 1861.

Henry W. Baker, a High Church Anglican priest, remained celibate throughout his life. Aside from his pastoral duties, he compiled *Hymns Ancient and Modern*, which became the standard English hymnbook from 1861 into the twentieth century. The work took twenty years to complete.

Henry Williams Baker (1821–1877) called this tune WHITBURN for a small town in England where he wrote it in 1854. It was renamed HESPERUS, meaning "Evening Star," when set with the text "Sun of My Soul." Other names found in hymnals for this tune are ELIM, QUEBEC, and VENN.

Henry W. Baker was born in London, England, on May 27, 1821. A celibate High Churchman, he served only one parish during his career. He was the editor of the monumental work *Hymns Ancient and Modern*, which was the best-selling hymnal ever published. He died at Monkland, England, on February 12, 1877.

572 When Israel Was in Egypt's Land

This text, like many others of the spiritual tradition, kept hope alive for those African Americans living in slavery in the United States. It recalls the time of bondage endured by the nation of Israel, as recorded in the Hebrew Scriptures, and the promise of God's liberation.

African American spirituals were often based on the stories of the Hebrew people found in the Scriptures, as the enslaved saw in the Bible stories similarities between the bondage of the ancient Hebrews and their own slavery and persecution.

This tune, named GO DOWN MOSES, may be of African American or Hebrew origin. It was identified by people of both backgrounds as being a folk song called "Cain and Abel." Obviously, it is used here with words echoing freedom themes of the Hebrew Scriptures often used by black preachers.

In the late nineteenth century, some African Americans began to be afforded increased educational opportunities. This led to the preservation of songs and melodies that had been sung ever since the first slaves had been brought from Africa, when musicians began writing down traditional words and melodies.

573 Lead On Eternal Sovereign

Ernest Warburton Shurtleff (1862–1917), a member of the Andover (Massachusetts) Theological Seminary class of 1888, wrote this text for his class's graduation service. The hymn's imagery is of newly ordained soldiers being sent out to various fields of ministry to battle for Christ.

Ernest W. Shurtleff was born in Boston, Massachusetts, on April 4, 1862. He was ordained to the Congregational ministry and served churches in various states before moving to Germany and then France. Shurtleff was director of student activities at the Academy Vitti in Paris, France, when he died in 1917.

Henry Thomas Smart (1813–1879) composed the tune LANCASHIRE in 1836 while living and working at a church in that English county. The tune first became popular in Nonconformist churches in England and enjoyed wider use after publication in a Presbyterian hymnbook in 1867.

Henry T. Smart edited *The Presbyterian Hymnal* (1875) for the Church of Scotland and *The Chorale Book* (1856), which became the standard work on hymn tune harmonizations. His ability to improvise on the organ served him well after he lost his eyesight fifteen years before his death.

574 In Egypt under Pharaoh

M. Dosia Carlson (b. 1930) wrote this text as a contribution to the UCC celebration of the 150th anniversary of the Amistad event, in which rebelling slaves sought freedom and dignity. Stanza 2 is about this event. Stanza 1 is about a parallel freedom movement found in the book of Exodus.

Dosia Carlson transformed a life-altering illness, childhood polio, into an outreach ministry for others. As a United Church of Christ pastor at Church of the Beatitudes in Phoenix, Arizona, she works with the Beatitudes Center for Developing Older Adult Resources.

Henry Thomas Smart (1813–1879) composed LANCASHIRE as the setting for "From Greenland's Icy Mountains" by Reginald Heber. The hymn was sung for a missionary meeting in Blackburn, Lancashire, where Smart served as organist at the time.

Henry T. Smart composed a variety of church music, operas, cantatas, and more than two hundred part-songs during his lifetime. In 1835, he wrote an anthem for the tercentenary of the Reformation in England, which helped establish his reputation as a composer and church musician.

575 O for a World

Miriam Therese Winter (b. 1938) wrote this text for the Presbyterian Women's Triennial Conference in 1982 and revised it in 1987, when it was recorded by the Medical Mission Sisters. It was published in *The Presbyterian Hymnal* (1990) prior to its appearance in *The New Century Hymnal*.

Miriam Therese Winter has been writing biblical songs and hymns that have enriched the worship life of churches since Vatican II. Winter serves as professor of liturgy, worship, and spirituality at Hartford (Connecticut) Seminary, a historically related seminary of the United Church of Christ.

Carl Gotthelf Gläser (1784–1829) composed this tune in 1828. It was "discovered" in Germany by Lowell Mason, who was searching for new tunes for his 1839 hymnal, *Modern Psalmist*. Mason named the tune AZMON, a Hebrew word for "Fortress," found in Numbers 34:4–5.

Carl G. Gläser was born in Weissenfels, Germany, on May 4, 1784. He learned to play the violin from his father, which led to a career as a violinist, a teacher, and a choral conductor. In addition, he composed a number of works and operated a music store. Gläser died April 16, 1829, in Barmen, Germany.

576 For the Healing of the Nations

Frederik Herman Kaan (b. 1929) wrote this text in 1965 for a Human Rights Day service at Pilgrim Church, Plymouth, England, where he was serving as pastor. His most widely sung hymn, it was also used at the twenty-fifth anniversary of the United Nations.

Fred Kaan was born in Haarlem, The Netherlands, and became a minister of the Congregational Church Union of England and Wales (a forerunner of the United Reformed Church). He has written more than two hundred hymns, often using the themes of ecumenism and concern for the powerless. Kaan served on the staff of the World Alliance of Reformed Churches.

Henry Purcell (1659–1695) composed this melody as a choral anthem in the seventeenth century. Sydney Nicholson adapted it as a hymn tune and titled it WESTMINSTER ABBEY for the famous London church where Purcell was organist from 1679 until his death in 1695.

Henry Purcell is believed to have been born in London, England, in 1659. He died at Dean's Yard, Westminster, London, on November 21, 1695. Purcell had been organist at Westminster Abbey since 1679 and gained a reputation as one of England's greatest composers.

577 God the Omnipotent!

Henry Fothergill Chorley (1808–1872) wrote the first two stanzas of this hymn in 1842 as part of a text entitled "In Time of War." John Ellerton (1826–1893) wrote the last two stanzas in the style of Chorley's hymn nearly thirty years later, during the Franco-German War. This composite version appeared in *Church Hymns* (1871) and has been used in this combination ever since then.

Henry F. Chorley, an English Quaker, was born December 15, 1808, in Lancashire, England. He became a music and literary critic and wrote many librettos for English operas. Chorley died suddenly in London, England, on February 16, 1872.

Alexis Feodorovich Lvov (1798–1870) was commissioned in 1833 by Russian Emperor Nicholas I to write a new national hymn to replace the English tune that traditionally had been sung with Russian words. The tune, RUSSIAN HYMN, appeared with this text in *The Psaltery*, a Mason and Webb collection.

Alexis F. Lvov was born at Reval, Estonia, on June 5, 1798, and trained for a musical career with his father, director of the imperial court chapel at St. Petersburg. He succeeded his father in that post and became an acclaimed violinist, composer, and editor. He died at Kovno, Lithuania, in 1870.

578 Profetiza, Pueblo mío
(You Shall Prophesy, All My People)

Rosa Martha Zárate Macías (b. 20th century) wrote this song to express the need for the poor, oppressed, and suffering people of North and South America to unite in a call to free themselves from the yokes that imprison them. She feels that this prophetic work must come from within the Pueblo community itself.

Rosa Martha Zárate Macías traces her heritage to the Pueblo people who occupied this continent for centuries before it was called America. The Pueblos, now factionalized and called Apaches, Cahuilla, Yakis, Navajos, Mexicans, and Latinos (among others), called this continent Abya Yala.

Rosa Martha Zárate Macías (b. 20th century) composed the tune PROPHESY to accompany her text. It was so named to indicate the urgent need for oppressed communities to exercise their rights to be prophets, not only to their own cultures but to cultures that enslave them.

Rosa Martha Zárate Macías sees herself as a cantor/musician in the Mexican-Nahuatl tradition. It is the cantors' mission to accompany their people on the journey through time, keeping alive their stories and social history. In her culture, this is a religious calling.

579 Great God of Earth and Heaven

Shirley Erena Murray (b. 1931) attempted to cause comfortable Christians to think through this text, which deals with refugees, hunger, depression, and abused children. She wrote it for Refugee Sunday at St. Andrew's-on-the-Terrace Church, Wellington, New Zealand, in 1986.

Shirley Erena Murray brings a freshness to hymnwriting with her inclusive-language texts that address a range of contemporary social and theological issues. Murray usually writes with a particular hymn tune in mind and fits the words to the meter of the chosen tune.

This traditional English melody, KING'S LYNN, was collected by Ralph Vaughan Williams in a town by that name in Norfolk, England, in 1905. He adapted it as a hymn tune for *The English Hymnal* (1906), where it was the setting for "O God of Earth and Altar."

Ralph Vaughan Williams (1872–1958) studied with Maurice Ravel in Paris, France, and Max Bruch in Berlin, Germany. His first important choral composition was "Toward the Unknown Region" (1907), and his output over the next half-century included compositions of nearly every genre, constituting a major contribution to church music.

580 O Kou Aloha No (The Queen's Prayer)

Queen Liliuokalani (1838–1917) reflected the compassion of Christ in this hymn of forgiveness for those who jailed her following her overthrow from the leadership of Hawaii in 1893. An English translation given here respects the custom of Hawaiians and is not meant to be sung.

Queen Liliuokalani reigned as queen of Hawaii from 1891 to 1893. In 1893, wealthy settlers from the United States revolted when she sought to restore some of the power of the monarchy. Despite the efforts of President Grover Cleveland to restore her to the throne, Hawaii was annexed in 1898.

Queen Liliuokalani (1838–1917) wrote both the words and melody of this hymn. It is named LILIUOKALANI to honor her. At one time, Liliuokalani was the choir director and organist of the Kawaiahao Church, known as the "Westminster Abbey of Hawaii."

Queen Liliuokalani made two trips to the United States after having been deposed in 1893, but her work to regain the Hawaiian throne was in vain. Her most popular composition is "Aloha Oe," which has become the song traditionally sung to those departing the Hawaiian Islands.

581 Lead Us from Death to Life

Satish Kumar (dates unknown), a Jain monk, based the poem that serves as the refrain of this hymn on passages from the Hindu scriptures known as the *Upanishads*. This "World Peace Prayer" has been widely circulated by the Fellowship of Reconciliation, which asks that it be prayed daily at noon.

Marty Haugen (b. 1950) created the three stanzas of this hymn in 1985 while living at Holden Village Retreat Center Community in Chelan, Washington, as composer-in-residence. His stanzas continue the prayer of the refrain, petitioning God to show humankind the "way of compassion."

Marty Haugen (b. 1950) composed the tune WORLD PEACE PRAYER in 1983, incorporating one of the world's oldest prayers and his own stanzas. The World Peace Prayer of the refrain's text, was adapted from the *Upanishads*, Hindu scriptures probably written between 400 and 200 B.C.E.

Marty Haugen is a liturgical composer, workshop presenter, teacher, author, and recording artist, who works from his home in Eagan, Minnesota. He has recorded sixteen collections of music and published more than two hundred compositions, including *Mass of Remembrance* and *Mass of Creation*.

582 O God of Earth and Altar

Gilbert Keith Chesterton (1874–1936) wrote the poem on which this hymn was based, and it appeared in *The Commonwealth* and in *The English Hymnal* (1906). Jane Parker Huber (b. 1926) updated stanza 2 and added stanza 3 in the version provided here.

G. K. Chesterton is better known for his literary career than for his hymnwriting. A friend of George Bernard Shaw, Chesterton published more than one hundred volumes of stories, novels, plays, biographies, and verse. He converted to Roman Catholicism in 1922 and espoused a return to the trade practices of the Middle Ages as a cure for the ills of industrialization.

LLANGLOFFAN is a traditional Welsh melody. Its first publication has been traced to *Llwybrau Moliant* (1872), a Baptist tune collection. Some scholars believe that the tune may have spread from England to Wales in the eighteenth or nineteenth century. The title may refer to the "Church of St. Gloffan."

The harmonization of this popular Welsh folk melody should be attributed to *The English Hymnal* (1906) and may have been the work of Ralph Vaughan Williams. Welsh hymnbook editor and composer David Evans made a different arrangement of the tune for *The Church Hymnary* (1927).

583 Like a Mother Who Has Borne Us

Daniel Rodney Bechtel (b. 1932) was inspired for this text by the scriptural imagery of the Hebrew prophet Hosea. It was first sung as a solo on September 28, 1986, by an instructor of music at the Dickinson College Chapel in Carlisle, Pennsylvania, where Bechtel served on the religion faculty.

Daniel Bechtel was ordained to the ministry of the United Church of Christ in 1958. Beginning in 1964, he taught religion at Dickinson College, Carlisle, Pennsylvania. This college served as the first home of the German Reformed Theological Seminary when it was formed in 1825.

William Patrick Rowan (b. 1951) composed this tune, named AUSTIN, in 1992. Rowan's musical settings have been used at hymn festivals throughout the United States, Great Britain, and Europe, and his work has been included in most recent Roman Catholic and Protestant denominational hymnals.

William P. Rowan, in addition to serving as director of music ministries at St. Mary Cathedral in Lansing, Michigan, has served the diocese of Lansing as liturgical music consultant, reviewing and suggesting appropriate music for use during Roman Catholic worship.

584 I Am the Light of the World

Jim Strathdee (b. 1941) based this text on a Christmas poem by Howard Thurman. He used it during Epiphany at Temple United Methodist Church in Los Angeles. It was taken to Central America by a Methodist bishop who was visiting in Los Angeles and is widely sung in Nicaragua and Honduras.

Jim Strathdee was born in Sacramento, California, on May 9, 1941. His father was a United Methodist minister. By age fourteen, Strathdee was directing the choir at his home church. He received his musical training at California State University at Northridge and at the University of Redlands, California.

Jim Strathdee (b. 1941) wrote this song to meet the needs of an inner-city congregation in California. He named it LIGHT OF THE WORLD from the words of the refrain. The hymn was translated into Spanish and became popular in Panama and throughout Latin America.

Jim Strathdee and his wife, Jean, have traveled for more than twenty years, conducting workshops and leading conferences on church music. Strathdee continues to compose music for the wider church. In 1990, he became music director at St. Mark's United Methodist Church in Sacramento, California.

585 O God, We Bear the Imprint of Your Face

Shirley Erena Murray (b. 1931) wrote this text dealing with the themes of human rights and racism in 1981 when she was unable to find any hymns on these topics. It was published in her first hymn collection, *In Every Corner, Sing* (1987), where it was set with the tune SONG 1 by Orlando Gibbons.

Shirley Erena Murray once worked as the affairs coordinator for Amnesty International, an organization that monitors governments around the world for abuses to political prisoners, dissidents, and refugees. Her concern for human rights is often reflected in her hymns.

Bruce Neswick (b. 1956) was invited to compose a tune for Shirley Erena Murray's text when it was selected by the committee for *The New Century Hymnal*. Neswick, who serves as organist at Christ Church Episcopal Cathedral in Lexington, Kentucky, named the tune ROSEBERRY.

Bruce Neswick was born in Kennewick, Washington, and was educated at Pacific Lutheran University, Tacoma, Washington, and Yale Divinity School's Institute of Sacred Music. While there, he helped edit the Yale Divinity School supplemental hymnal *Laudamus*, published in 1980.

586 Come to Tend God's Garden

John A. Dalles (b. 1954) wrote this text for the 275th anniversary of the Presbyterian Synod of the Trinity in Pennsylvania. Using the imagery of the world as a garden, the hymn recalls God's command to be stewards of God's created order, as recorded in Genesis.

John A. Dalles was born in Pittsburgh, Pennsylvania, and received a degree in architecture from Penn State University. He then attended Lancaster (Pennsylvania) Theological Seminary. Ordained to the Presbyterian ministry in 1982, he has served churches in Indiana, Pennsylvania, and Florida.

Ralph Vaughan Williams (1872–1958) composed this tune in 1925 for the Ascension hymn "At the Name of Jesus." Vaughan Williams named the tune KING'S WESTON for the country home of a friend that overlooked the Bristol Channel, where he spent many weekends with other musicians.

Ralph Vaughan Williams was the son of an Anglican vicar and a descendant of Josiah Wedgwood, a cousin of Charles Darwin. He became the greatest English composer of his time and edited *The English Hymnal* (1906), *Songs of Praise* (1925 and 1931), and *The Oxford Book of Carols* (1928).

587 Through All the World, a Hungry Christ

Shirley Erena Murray (b. 1931) often uses her texts to shake up complacent congregations by reminding them of the hard truth of the Gospels. She interprets Christ's message for the modern age, as in this text which calls us to recognize "Christ's presence in the victims of the world."

Shirley Erena Murray became a language teacher following her graduation from Otago University in New Zealand, her native country. Her career led to positions with Amnesty International, her country's Parliament, and the New Zealand Hymnbook Trust.

Calvin Hampton (1938–1984) composed this tune in 1970, and it brought him international recognition. He named it DE TAR for his friend Vernon de Tar, who first performed the tune at a hymn festival at the Church of the Ascension in New York City. It was originally a setting for a text by Isaac Watts.

Calvin Hampton was born in Kittanning, Pennsylvania, and had a notable career as an interpreter of nineteenth-century music in recitals. He also served as organist and choirmaster at Calvary Church, New York, from 1963 to 1983. Hampton died at Port Charlotte, Florida, in 1984 at age forty-six.

588 Let Justice Flow like Streams

Jane Parker Huber (b. 1926) incorporated two verses from the Hebrew prophet Amos for this text: 5:24 and 7:8. She wanted to convey the idea of the necessity of "measuring up" to God's standards, setting a goal to inspire a community's progress in working toward God's justice.

Jane Parker Huber was born on October 24, 1926, in Jinan, China, the daughter of Presbyterian missionary parents stationed there. She grew up on the campus of Hanover College, Indiana, as her father served as president of that institution from 1929 until 1958.

This anonymous melody is named ST. THOMAS. It was part of a longer hymn tune called HOLBORN in Aaron Williams's *The Universal Psalmist* (1763) and appeared in the present version in Isaac Smith's *A Collection of Psalm Tunes* (1770) as a setting for Psalm 48. However, the composer responsible for the arrangement is unknown.

Aaron Williams (1731–1776) published *The Universal Psalmist* in 1763 and added various editions in later years, including *The New Universal Psalmist* (1770). Williams was a music engraver and publisher and was also a teacher in the city of London, England, where he was born and died.

589 Let There Be Light, O God of Hosts

William Merrill Vories (1880–1964) wrote this poem in 1908 after reading an account of the rise of German militarism. Published by the American Peace Society, it later was set to music and translated into Japanese. Vories was a lay missionary to Japan who devoted his life to nondenominational missions work.

William M. Vories was born October 28, 1880, in Leavenworth, Kansas. In college, he decided to enter the missionary field but did not want to work under the auspices of his own denomination (Congregational) or any other. He established the Omi Mission in Japan and spent the remainder of his life working for that cause.

William Boyd (1847–1928) composed the tune PENTECOST for his teacher Sabine Baring-Gould's text "Come, Holy Ghost, Our Souls Inspire" for use at the author's parish. Boyd was seventeen at the time. The tune was published in a small collection, *Thirty-Two Hymn Tunes* (1868), at Oxford University.

William Boyd was born in Montego Bay, Jamaica, but moved to England for his education at Worcester College, Oxford. In addition to his accomplishments as an organist, he studied for the ministry and was ordained in 1877 by the Church of England.

590 Spirit of Jesus, If I Love My Neighbor

Brian Arthur Wren (b. 1936) was inspired to write this text by the actions of nine white South Africans who in 1972 undertook a walk to draw attention to the injustice of their nation's migrant-labor laws. During this time, Wren was working with the British Council of Churches to alleviate world hunger.

Brian Wren began writing hymns while he was a student at Mansfield College, Oxford, England, with the encouragement of Erik Routley. By 1983 he had met with such success in this field that he took it on as his full-time ministry. Wren has published numerous collections of his work.

Jonathan McNair (b. 1959) composed the tune BENJAMIN in 1994 at the request of *New Century Hymnal* editor Arthur Clyde, who had been unable to find a folklike tune for this Wren text. McNair named the tune BENJAMIN to honor his firstborn son. The name is also a biblical one.

Jonathan McNair, a composer and music director, has taught music theory and composition at universities in Ohio and Tennessee. He served as assistant music editor for *The New Century Hymnal*, contributing two original tunes and several harmonizations.

591 This Is My Song

Lloyd Stone (b. 1912) wrote this text in 1934 during the brief period of international peace that was shattered by the start of World War II. It was published in *Sing a Tune* (1934). Georgia Harkness wrote a third stanza at the request of the Wesleyan Service Guild, and the hymn became a favorite in the Methodist Church.

Lloyd Stone was born at Coalinga, California, on June 29, 1912, and educated at the University of Southern California. In 1936 he moved to Hawaii and taught in public schools and at the University of Hawaii. Stone has written ten books of poetry as well as books for children.

Jean Sibelius (1865–1957) wrote the tone poem FINLANDIA, his most famous composition and the basis for this tune, in 1899. First performed in Helsinki, it received such a favorable response that the occupying Russian government refused to permit its performance.

Jean Sibelius, Finland's greatest composer, based much of his music on national myths and folk tales which instilled intense patriotic feelings in the Finnish people. Sibelius stopped composing in 1929 at age sixty-four, refusing to follow the trends of modern musical composition.

592 God of the Ages, Who with Sure Command

Daniel Crane Roberts (1841–1907) wrote this text in 1876 for Brandon, Vermont's, celebration of the centennial of the Declaration of Independence. It was used in 1894 in New York City to commemorate the centennial of the adoption of the U.S. Constitution.

Daniel C. Roberts, a graduate of Kenyon College, Gambier, Ohio, served as a soldier in the Civil War. He was ordained a priest in the Protestant Episcopal Church in 1866, serving first in Brandon, Vermont, and then, for twenty-nine years, in Concord, New Hampshire. Roberts is remembered now for this hymn alone.

George William Warren (1828–1902) composed NATIONAL HYMN for this text at the request of those planning New York City's 1894 centennial celebration of the adoption of the U.S. Constitution. The celebration was held at St. Thomas' Church, where Warren served as organist.

George W. Warren, a native of Albany, New York, and a self-taught musician, served as organist at churches in Albany and Brooklyn, New York, and then, for twenty years, at St. Thomas' Church in New York City. This is the only one of his tunes to survive the test of time.

593 Lift Every Voice and Sing

James Weldon Johnson (1871–1938) earned two degrees at Atlanta University and became a public-school teacher and principal in Jacksonville, Florida. He wrote this text for a celebration commemorating Abraham Lincoln's birthday on February 12, 1921, and it was performed by schoolchildren.

James Weldon Johnson, a multitalented poet, lawyer, and diplomat, served as the first national executive secretary of the National Association for the Advancement of Colored People (NAACP), and this anthem became that organization's official song. Johnson also founded the first African American newspaper, the *Daily American*.

John Rosamond Johnson (1873–1954) composed this tune, called LIFT EVERY VOICE, for his brother's text. He collected and published a number of important collections of African American songs and hymn tunes in addition to performing on the stage, composing, and directing musicals.

J. Rosamond Johnson was educated at the New England Conservatory of Music and studied further in Europe. From 1896 until 1908, he served as supervisor of music for the public school system of Jacksonville, Florida. Collecting African American music was his lifelong pursuit.

594 How Beautiful, Our Spacious Skies

Katharine Lee Bates (1859–1929) wrote stanza 1 of this patriotic hymn in Colorado Springs, Colorado, one evening in 1893 after having traveled to the top of Pike's Peak with a group of teachers. Miriam Therese Winter (b. 1938) adapted it and wrote the other stanzas in 1993 while serving as a member of the editorial panel for *The New Century Hymnal*.

Katharine Lee Bates was born in Falmouth, Massachusetts, the daughter of a Congregational minister. Trained as a teacher, she became head of the English Department of Wellesley College in Wellesley, Massachusetts. She was awarded honorary doctorates by Wellesley as well as Oberlin and Middlebury Colleges, in Ohio and Vermont, respectively.

Samuel Augustus Ward (1847–1903) composed this tune in 1882 for the hymn "O Mother Dear, Jerusalem." The tune was named MATERNA, meaning "mother" or "motherly." It first appeared in *The Parish Choir* (1888) and has been sung with Bates's text since World War I.

Samuel A. Ward was born December 28, 1847, in Newark, New Jersey, and earned his living in his hometown by selling musical instruments and supplies and sheet music. In addition, he conducted the Orpheus Club choir for fourteen years. Ward died in Newark on September 28, 1903.

595 Some Glad Morning (I'll Fly Away)

Albert Edward Brumley (1905–1977) was inspired to write this hymn by Vernon Dalhart's hit song "The Prisoner's Song." The text is based on Psalm 55:6: "O that I had wings like a dove! I would fly away and be at rest." The hymn anticipates the glories that follow death.

Albert E. Brumley, working from Powell, Missouri, became the most influential songwriter of the white gospel genre. He wrote more than seven hundred songs, many of which were recorded by artists such as Elvis Presley, Johnny Cash, and Red Foley. Brumley wrote his best work in the 1930s and 1940s.

Albert Edward Brumley (1905–1977) composed this tune for his own words, and it is named I'LL FLY AWAY from the repeated response to each phrase. This song has been recorded more than five hundred times by singers from diverse backgrounds. It is Brumley's most popular composition.

Albert E. Brumley was named to both the gospel-music and country-music halls of fame. Born at Spiro, Oklahoma, before the territory became a state, he studied music at the Hartford (Arkansas) Music Company and wrote songs for paperback songbooks sold at religious conventions and meetings.

596 Rock of Ages, Cleft for Me

Augustus Montague Toplady (1740–1778) published this hymn in 1776 in his *Psalms and Hymns for Publick and Private Worship*. For all its fame today, this hymn was overlooked for a half-century and not considered worthy to be used in churches.

Augustus M. Toplady was a vicar in the Church of England. He served in Devonshire, England, until ill health forced him to move to London. Toplady died of tuberculosis at age thirty-eight. An ardent supporter of Calvinist thought, he bitterly opposed the work of John Wesley.

Thomas Hastings (1784–1872) composed TOPLADY as the setting for this text in 1830. It was published in *Spiritual Songs for Social Worship* (1832), a collection edited by Hastings and Lowell Mason, where the tune was originally called ROCK OF AGES.

Thomas Hastings spent his early career in upstate New York but moved to New York City, where he served as music director at Bleeker Street Presbyterian Church for many years. Hastings composed some one thousand tunes, but this is one of the few to remain in current use.

597 Shall We Gather at the River

Robert Lowry (1826–1899) incorporated imagery from the book of Revelations in this text, published in *Happy Voices* (1865) under the title "Mutual Recognition in the Hereafter." It was written one hot summer day in 1864, when the Brooklyn pastor was preoccupied with questions raised by the deaths of many in his congregation due to an epidemic.

Robert Lowry became well known as the writer of the song "Where Is My Wandering Boy Tonight?" Although interest in this type of sentimental song has waned, Lowry's hymns remain popular.

Robert Lowry (1826–1899) composed both words and music for this gospel hymn in 1864. The tune was named HANSON PLACE nearly a century later by the committee that compiled the *Baptist Hymnal* (1956). Lowry, a Baptist preacher, became interested in hymnwriting during his pastorate at Hanson Place Baptist Church in Brooklyn.

Robert Lowry was born in Philadelphia, Pennsylvania, on March 12, 1826, was ordained, and worked as a Baptist minister, college professor, and church administrator. He died on November 25, 1899, in Plainfield, New Jersey, where he was serving a long pastorate at a Baptist church.

598 On River Jordan's Banks I Stand

Samuel Stennett (1727–1795) wrote this text, but the refrain was added by a later editor. The original eight-stanza hymn first appeared in John Rippon's English hymnal of 1787, *A Selection of Hymns from the Best Authors*, under the heading "The Promised Land."

Samuel Stennett could not attend a university in England because of his family's Nonconformist views. He received his education at an academy at Mile End and succeeded his father as pastor at a Seventh Day Baptist church.

This tune, PROMISED LAND, first appeared in *Southern Harmony* (1835) in a three-part setting. It was attributed to "Miss M. Durham" in that collection, but this citation has never been traced to a recognized individual.

Rigdon M. McIntosh (1836–1899), once head of the music department at Vanderbilt University, Nashville, Tennessee, prepared this arrangement for an 1874 collection published by the Methodist Episcopal Church South. McIntosh changed the key from F-sharp minor to the parallel major, as was the trend in Sunday-school music of the time.

599 Steal Away

This spiritual has been cited as one that was sung by slaves to notify others of a secret worship service. The site of the place of worship was sometimes indicated by breaking tree limbs so that they pointed in a certain direction.

The reference to the trumpet sound in this text may come from 1 Corinthians 15:52: "For the trumpet will sound, and the dead will be raised." To "steal away to Jesus" had a double meaning for slaves: escaping life's woes by death and escaping to freedom in the North.

This melody, called STEAL AWAY, may have been used as a call to a secret meeting or worship service. By singing the song, a leader could announce a secret meeting without raising the suspicions of the slave masters overseeing a work group.

In *Negro Slave Songs in the United States*, the writer Fisher maintains that the probable composer of this tune was Nat Turner. However, no absolute evidence has been discovered to verify this claim. The tune, like the words, is most likely to have evolved over a long period of time.

600 How Lovely Is Your Dwelling

Jean Wiebe Janzen (b. 1933) wrote this paraphrase of Psalm 84 at the request of the committee preparing a new hymnal for the Mennonite Church, and it was first published in that volume—*Hymnal: A Worship Book* (1992). This was one of Janzen's first works as a hymnwriter.

Jean Janzen received her master of arts degree from Fresno (California) State University in 1982 after raising her four children. She then began to teach poetry-writing in colleges and public schools. Janzen has published a number of collections of her work.

This tune, first printed in *Catholische Geistliche Kirchengesäng* (1599) in Cologne, Germany, was from an earlier manuscript found at St. Alban's Carthusian monastery in Trier, Germany. The tune name, ES IST EIN' ROS', derives from the German text with which it has long been used.

Michael Praetorius (1571–1621) arranged this tune for his 1609 collection, *Musae Sionae*. Born Michael Schulze, he latinized his name to Praetorius. He was the leading musician of the early baroque period, composing both secular and sacred music.

601 How Lovely Is Your Dwelling

Jean Wiebe Janzen (b. 1933) produced this text at the request of the Mennonite hymnal committee specifically for this tune by Heinrich Schütz. The committee desired to include the traditional pairing of the tune with Psalm 84 but wanted to replace the archaic translation with a more modern paraphrase.

Jean Janzen was born on December 5, 1933, at Langham, Saskatchewan, Canada. Her father was a schoolteacher, but when she was five he became a Mennonite minister. The family moved to southwestern Minnesota in 1939. Janzen's parents taught all six of their children to sing and play the piano.

Heinrich Schütz (1585–1672) composed this music as a setting for PSALM 84, hence the tune's name. The Psalms were a primary source of inspiration for Schütz, who supplied simple four-part settings for rhymed paraphrases by Cornelius Becker. They appeared in a collection known as the Becker Psalter, published in Freiberg (1628) and in Dresden (1661).

Heinrich Schütz spent time in Italy studying with Giovanni Gabrielli and later Claudio Monteverdi, and he introduced the Italian choral style in his native Germany. Schütz devoted his life to composing music for the church, culminating in three settings of the Passion story from Matthew, Luke, and John.

602 Savior God Above

Edward Kennedy "Duke" Ellington (1899–1974) added the lyrics to this instrumental jazz piece from his concert suite *Black, Brown, and Beige* in 1958, when it was recorded by gospel singer Mahalia Jackson. Ellington included "Come, Sunday" in his First Sacred Jazz Concert, which became an annual event in New York.

Duke Ellington was an innovative big-band leader, pianist, and composer. He founded a jazz concert series held annually at Carnegie Hall and instituted a series of sacred jazz concerts. Ellington was called "the Duke" because of his elegant and eloquent manner.

Edward Kennedy "Duke" Ellington (1899–1974) composed the original score for his jazz suite *Black, Brown, and Beige* in 1943 and reduced it into four movements for big band, solo saxophone, and jazz violin for a 1944 recording at Carnegie Hall. The arrangement for the excerpt known as COME SUNDAY is based on a vocal recording of the song by Mahalia Jackson.

Duke Ellington was awarded sixteen honorary doctorates, the President's Gold Medal, the Presidential Medal of Freedom, and the French Legion of Honor, all in recognition of contributions to jazz and to world understanding through his concert tours to every continent.

603 Giver of Life, Where'er They Be

Frederick Lucian Hosmer (1840–1929) wrote this text for an 1888 Easter service at Church of Unity (Unitarian) in Cleveland, Ohio, where he was the pastor. It was later printed in *Chicago Unity* and then in *The Thought of God in Hymns and Poems*, which Hosmer edited.

Frederick L. Hosmer was born in Framingham, Massachusetts, on October 16, 1840, and became a minister in the Unitarian Church. He served churches in Massachusetts, Illinois, Ohio, Missouri, and California. At one time, thirty of his hymns were being widely used in church hymnals.

Melchior Vulpius (c. 1560–1616) composed this tune, called GELOBT SEI GOTT after the opening words of the German text with which it was first used. An alternate name for the tune is VULPIUS, for the composer. The tune may have earlier roots than Vulpius's work.

Melchior Vulpius is believed to have been born at Wasungen, Henneberg, Thuringia, around 1560. By age forty, he was cantor at Weimar. Vulpius was renowned for his German chorales and published five books of church music. He died at Weimar on August 7, 1616.

604 Hush, Hush, Somebody's Calling My Name

This African American hymn sounds like a lullaby. The opening stanza presents an image of a person aware of the approach of death yet wishing to hide from it. However, the tone moves from one of dread to one of rejoicing when it is discovered that Jesus is the one who is calling.

Many African American spirituals do not picture death as disagreeable; instead they associate death with reward, deliverance, and the final step toward freedom. Often in spiritual songs about death, reunion with loved ones who have gone before is eagerly anticipated.

This African American tune was arranged for *The New Century Hymnal* by Jeffrey Radford (b. 1953), who served on the hymnal committee. Radford arranged eight African American spirituals for the hymnal, most of them in a gospel style.

Jeffrey Radford has provided a gentle, rocking arrangement for this syncopated melody, filling in the pauses between words with rhythmic patterns and "hallelujahs." To perform this song quickly would not do justice to its quiet intensity.

605 As Moses Raised the Serpent Up

This hymn text is a paraphrase of John 3:14–17, a scripture text prescribed for Holy Cross Day and Lent 4, year B. The text includes, in stanza 2, the words most children learn as their first Bible memory verse, John 3:16.

The tradition of paraphrasing Holy Scripture in meter and rhyme is as old as singing itself. In the earliest centuries of the Christian era, only the Psalms were versified, but later other canticles and selected verses became the basis for hymn settings. Singing a versified text is one of the easiest ways to memorize it.

The earliest source for this tune, MORNING SONG, was *Sixteen Tune Settings*, printed in 1812 by John Logan. There it was named CONSOLATION and presented in an unusual shape-note four-part arrangement. It subsequently appeared in more than three dozen similar tunebooks with a variety of texts.

This harmonization was composed by C. Winfred Douglas (1867–1944) for *The Hymnal 1940* (Episcopal), where it was first titled MORNING SONG to distinguish it from another tune which had shared the original title, CONSOLATION.

606 Nearer, My God, to You

Sarah Flower Adams (1805–1848) wrote this text and a dozen others for a London Unitarian hymnal compiled by her pastor, William J. Fox, in 1841. The hymn became widely popular and was a favorite of such dignitaries as Queen Victoria, King Edward VII, and U.S. presidents William McKinley and Theodore Roosevelt.

Sarah F. Adams showed promise as an actress when she portrayed Lady Macbeth in a London production, but ill health kept her from continuing a stage career. Adams died of tuberculosis in 1848, having contracted the disease while nursing her sister Eliza, who had died of the same illness twenty months earlier.

Lowell Mason (1792–1872) composed BETHANY for his *Sabbath Hymns and Tune Book* (1859) at the suggestion of his colleagues Edward A. Park and Austin Phelps. This tune came to him late one night, and he wrote it down the next morning.

Lowell Mason was a professor at Andover (Massachusetts) Theological Seminary late in his career. With other professors, he compiled two books of hymns for use in Congregational churches. Mason was born in Medfield, Massachusetts, and died in Orange, New Jersey.

607 We Would Be Building

Purd Eugene Deitz (1897–1987) wrote this text for a Philadelphia youth conference he was organizing when no suitable hymn could be found for the theme "Christian Youth Building a New World." He had heard the tune FINLANDIA while studying in Edinburgh, Scotland, and wrote the text specifically for it.

Purd E. Deitz was raised at Zion Reformed Church in York, Pennsylvania. Ordained to the Reformed ministry, he served churches in Dayton, Ohio, and Philadelphia, Pennsylvania. Deitz was professor at Eden Theological School and executive secretary of the Board of National Missions for the Evangelical and Reformed Church.

Jean Sibelius (1865–1957) composed FINLANDIA in 1899 for a series of historical tableaux performed in Helsinki, Finland. Sibelius's music accompanied the fourth of these tableaux titled "Finland Awakes." The tone poem was banned for a time in Finland and Russia by the Russian government.

Jean Sibelius was raised by his grandparents and began studies for a career in law. His musical talents prevailed, however, and he became Finland's greatest composer and something of a national hero. Sibelius first visited the United States in 1914 and conducted performances of his work, including "Finlandia," at the Norfolk Music Festival in Connecticut.

608 Christ Will Come Again

Brian Arthur Wren (b. 1936) attended a Seventh Day Adventist musicians convention in July 1987 and decided to write a hymn on the second coming of Christ (also known as the "Second Advent"), which Wren suggests may be understood literally or symbolically. The text was first printed in *Music Ministry*, a journal of the SDA Church.

Brian Wren was born in Romford, Essex, England, on June 3, 1936, and became a minister of what is now the United Reformed Church in Great Britain. Wren completed his doctorate in theology at Oxford University in 1968 with a dissertation on the "Language of Prophetic Eschatology in the Old Testament."

Joan Collier Fogg (b. 1949) composed this tune in 1987 at the request of Brian Wren. He knew of her ability to write a hymn tune in a short time without sacrificing quality. She named the tune IDA to honor a significant friend in her life.

Joan Collier Fogg was born July 30, 1949, in Easton, Maryland, and grew up there. She is a certified elementary-school principal and has worked as a church and school teacher and as a music teacher. Fogg received her master's degree in religious education from Pittsburgh (Pennsylvania) Theological Seminary.

609 Now Is the Time Approaching

Jane Laurie Borthwick (1813–1897) wrote this text as a poem in 1857. It was collected with other examples of her work in *Thoughts for Thoughtful Hours* (1859). Borthwick is remembered for both her original texts, such as this one, and for her work in translating hymns from German.

Jane Borthwick was born in Edinburgh, Scotland, on April 9, 1813, and died there eighty-four years later. She became one of the most prolific translators of German hymn texts into English and often worked with her sister, Sarah Findlater. She actively supported church missions.

George James Webb (1803–1887) composed this tune as a secular song in 1830 as he sailed from England to Boston, Massachusetts. It first appeared as a hymn setting for "The Morning Light Is Breaking" in *The Wesleyan Psalmist* (1842) but is best known for its association with "Stand Up, Stand Up for Jesus." It is called WEBB here for the composer.

George J. Webb was born in Wiltshire, near Salisbury, England, but emigrated to the United States when he was twenty-seven years old. He served as organist at Old South Church, Boston, Massachusetts, for forty years, taught at Boston Academy of Music, and was president of the Boston Handel and Haydn Society.

610 My Eyes Have Seen the Glory

Julia Ward Howe (1819–1910) followed the advice of her pastor and wrote this hymn for the familiar tune "John Brown's Body," after she heard it sung by Union troops in Washington, D.C., one evening in December 1861 and found herself wishing for a new set of words.

Julia Ward Howe was born in New York City in 1819. She often spoke from Unitarian Church pulpits on behalf of abolition and the end of war. Howe published three collections of her writings. She died in Newport, Rhode Island, in 1910.

An early form of the melody of the BATTLE HYMN OF THE REPUBLIC has been traced to a camp-meeting chorus in an 1851 songbook, *Songs of Zion*. The tune was used during the Civil War for numerous parodies about the abolitionist folk hero who was executed. African Americans serving in the Union army created their own adaptation which became a sort of unofficial theme song.

Although William Steffe (d. 1911) claimed to have written this tune around 1855 for the words "Say, bummers, will you meet us," scholars generally do not give him credit for it. The tune was used with numerous other texts and adaptations throughout the Civil War and Reconstruction era by a variety of groups.

611 O Day of God, Draw Near

Robert Balgarnie Young Scott (1899–1987) wrote this hymn in 1937 for the Fellowship for a Christian Social Order, which he served as the organization's president. The hymn was later published in *Hymns for Worship* (1939), *The Hymnal 1940,* and the *Pilgrim Hymnal* (1958).

R. B. Y. Scott was ordained in the United Church of Canada in 1926. He taught at McGill University in Montreal, Canada, and at Princeton University in New Jersey. During World War II, he served as a chaplain of the Canadian Air Force. Throughout his career, Scott was an advocate of social reform.

ST. MICHAEL is the name of this tune from the Genevan Psalter (1551). It was used as a setting for Psalm 134 in an English psalter, then fell into disuse until revived by William Crotch in 1836. He arranged it for his *Psalm Tunes* (1836) and named it for St. Michael's College, in Tenbury, England.

William Crotch (1775–1847) showed signs of his prodigious talent at eighteen months of age, when he began to pick out tunes on the piano. Crotch studied at Oxford and Cambridge Universities and became the first principal of the Royal Academy of Music in 1822. His later years were spent composing, writing, and sketching.

612 Strengthen All the Weary Hands

Martha E. McMane (b. 1943) wrote this hymn for a classroom assignment by opening her Bible, picking up her guitar, and improvising on the text in front of her. The words and music were written together. At the time, she was working on a creative project to present Hebrew Scripture verses in song.

Martie McMane experienced a life-changing conversion in 1973, and this led her to rejoin a church, learn to play the guitar, and later to attend seminary. She was ordained to the United Church of Christ at South Haven UCC, Bedford, Ohio, in 1983 and served there as pastor for eight years.

Martha E. McMane (b. 1943) composed this tune, which she named SONG OF REJOICING, for a class project on the Hebrew Scriptures at Ashland (Ohio) Theological Seminary. She first sang this hymn to her class along with one based on Ecclesiastes and several from the Psalms.

Martie McMane was born July 11, 1943, at Summit, New Jersey. She was encouraged in singing at the age of three by her father, who led a band that played for weddings and parties. Following high school, she earned a four-year voice scholarship to Douglass College, New Brunswick, New Jersey.

613 O Holy City, Seen of John

Walter Russell Bowie (1882–1969) based this text on the vision of John of Patmos described in Revelation, chapters 21 and 22. The text was written at the request of Henry Sloan Coffin, who was seeking new hymns for *Hymns of the Kingdom of God* (1910), which he helped edit.

W. Russell Bowie was a leader of the Protestant Episcopal Church in the United States. He was a hospital chaplain in France during World War I and served on the interdenominational Commission on Faith and Order of the World Council of Churches. Bowie died at Alexandria, Virginia, in 1969.

The Hymnal 1940 was the first publication to give this tune the name MORNING SONG, although it had appeared in numerous tunebooks and hymnals of the nineteenth and twentieth centuries. The tune had been used as a setting for Isaac Watts's text "Once More, My Soul, the Rising Day" in Wyeth's *Repository of Sacred Music, Part Second* (1813).

John Logan (dates unknown) was a singing-school teacher. In 1812, he compiled an eight-page leaflet, *Sixteen Tune Settings*, which included this tune. The publisher, Andrew Law, used his own four-shape shape-note system in this booklet and printed the notes in relation to one another as if on a staff but without staff lines.

614 Camina, Pueblo de Dios (Go Forth, O People of God)

Cesáreo Gabaráin (1936–1991) wrote this contemporary Spanish hymn in 1979, and its use has spread rapidly among Hispanic and other congregations. The English translation was done by George Lockwood (b. 1946) for *The United Methodist Hymnal* (1989).

George Lockwood served as a consultant for the Methodist supplement *Celebremos II* and *The United Methodist Hymnal* (1989). He has translated more than thirty Spanish hymn texts and presented workshops on this body of church song. Lockwood is an ordained minister in the United Methodist Church.

Cesáreo Gabaráin (1936–1991) wrote both music and words of this contemporary Hispanic hymn. The tune's name, NUEVA CREACION, appears throughout the hymn and reflects the primary theme of the text, that we are a "new creation" in Christ.

Cesáreo Gabaráin, born in Hernani, Spain, in 1936, became well known for his work in church music. In 1990, the year before his death, he toured the United States, stopping at twenty-two cities to present workshops. Many of his works have been recorded and are available from Oregon Catholic Press.

615 Enter in the Realm of God

Lavon Bayler (b. 1933) was asked to write a hymn on the theme of the realm of God to fill a need in this section of *The New Century Hymnal*. She quickly produced this text, based on passages from Mark, chapters 4 and 10. Bayler is a prolific writer of hymns, prayers, and other worship resources based on lectionary texts.

Lavon Bayler, the daughter and niece of Evangelical and Reformed pastors, planned to be a teaching missionary in Japan. In 1959, she was one of the first women ordained by the Evangelical and Reformed Church and spent twenty years in local church ministry before joining the Illinois Conference staff.

Vérne de la Peña (b. 1959) avoided use of a four-part harmonization, which he considers a "musical hegemonic device," and instead provided an arrangement of this Visayan folk melody, DANDANSOY, in a form more appropriate to its Philippine origins.

Vérne de la Peña and his wife, Gia, are Filipino musicians currently based in Hawaii who perform with choirs and Asian ensembles in Honolulu. A doctoral student, de la Peña also serves as director of music for a local UCC congregation.

616 I Want to Be Ready

This traditional African American spiritual is based on Revelation 21:1–4 (John's promise of a "new heaven and a new earth"), in contrast to many spirituals which use references to Hebrew Scriptures. The third stanza relates to Acts 2, the coming of the Holy Spirit to the church at Pentecost.

This African American spiritual is in the traditional call-and-response style, in which a leader sings the verse and the congregation responds with a repeated line or refrain. Stanzas 2 and 4 were added to include references to some of Jesus' women followers.

The music of I WANT TO BE READY was arranged by J. Jefferson Cleveland and Verolga Nix for *Songs of Zion* (1981), a collection of spirituals, evangelical hymns, and gospel songs. Cleveland and Nix were coeditors of that supplement published by the United Methodist Church.

J. Jefferson Cleveland (1937–1986) was born in Elberton, Georgia, and pursued studies at several institutions, earning a D.Ed. from Boston University. Verolga Nix-Allen (b. 1933) was born in Cleveland, Ohio, and received her music degrees from Oberlin Conservatory of Music. She is the founder of the Foundation for the Preservation of African American Music in Philadelphia.

617 Unite and Join Your Cheerful Songs

This text's author is not known, but it may have been James O'Kelly, who compiled *Hymns and Spiritual Songs* in Raleigh, North Carolina, in 1816. That collection, which included only texts to be sung to the familiar tunes of the day, was probably used in Christian churches in the South.

James O'Kelly (1736–1826) was a founder of one of the four major branches of the United Church of Christ. In 1794 he broke away from the Methodist Church to form an independent Christian Church. This body merged with the Congregational Church in 1931.

This tune, called AMAZING GRACE here but NEW BRITAIN in other hymnals, was first printed in *Columbian Harmony* (1829). Two versions of the tune were contained in that collection, one called ST. MARY's and the other GALLAHER. No composer's name was provided in this early hymnal.

Benjamin Shaw (dates unknown) and Charles H. Spilman (dates unknown) published *Columbian Harmony* in Cincinnati, Ohio, in 1829. It was one of a large group of hymnals that were widely used in the southern United States, especially in conjunction with the singing schools of the nineteenth century.

Bibliography to the Hymn Profiles

Bailey, Albert Edward. *The Gospel in Hymns*. New York: Charles Scribner's Sons, 1950.

Bell, John, and Graham Maule. *Enemy of Apathy*. Chicago: G.I.A. Publications, 1988.

Bonsall, Elizabeth Hubbard. *Famous Hymns with Stories and Pictures*. Philadelphia: Union Press, 1923, 1941.

Boyer, Horace Clarence. *How Sweet the Song: The Golden Age of Gospel*. Washington, D.C.: Elliott & Clark, 1995.

Brown, Robert K., and Mark R. Norton. *The One Year Book of Hymns*. Wheaton, Ill.: Tyndale House, 1995.

Bruce, Dickson D., Jr. *And They All Sang Hallelujah: Plain-Folk Camp-Meeting Religion, 1800–1845*. Knoxville: University of Tennessee Press, 1974.

Carlson, Dosia. *God's Glory*. Phoenix: The Beatitudes Center, 1986.

Chinese Christian Literature Council. *Hymns of Universal Praise*. English ed. Hong Kong: Chinese Christian Literature Council, 1981.

Christian Conference of Asia and the Asian Institute for Liturgy and Music. *Sound the Bamboo*. Manila: Asian Institute for Liturgy and Music, 1990.

Church, F. Forrester, and Terrence J. Mulry. *Earliest Christian Hymns*. New York: Macmillan, 1988.

Claghorn, Gene. *Women Composers and Hymnists: A Concise Biographical Dictionary*. Metuchen, N.J.: Scarecrow Press, 1984.

Cleveland, J. Jefferson, and Verolga Nix. *Song of Zion*. Nashville: Abingdon, 1981.

Colquhoun, Frank. *A Hymn Companion*. Wilton, Conn.: Morehouse Barlow, 1985.

Costen, Melva Wilson. *African American Christian Worship*. Nashville: Abingdon, 1993.

Damon, Dan. *Faith Will Sing*. Carol Stream, Ill.: Hope, 1993.

Daw, Carl B., Jr. *A Year of Grace: Hymns for the Church Year*. Carol Stream, Ill.: Hope, 1990.

Deming, Lynne M., ed. *The Feminine Mystic: Readings from Early Spiritual Writers*. Cleveland: Pilgrim Press, 1997.

Doran, Carol, and Thomas H. Troeger. *New Hymns for the Lectionary*. New York: Oxford University Press, 1986.

Duck, Ruth. *Dancing in the Universe*. Chicago: G.I.A. Publications, 1992.

Dunstan, Sylvia G. *In Search of Hope and Grace*. Chicago: G.I.A. Publications, 1991.

———. *Where the Promise Shines*. Chicago: G.I.A. Publications, 1995.

Ehret, Walter, et al. *The International Book of Sacred Song*. Englewood Cliffs, N.J.: Prentice-Hall, 1969.

Emurian, Ernest K. *Living Stories of Famous Hymns*. Grand Rapids, Mich.: Baker Book House, 1955, 1989.

Gibson, Colin. *Reading the Signature*. Carol Stream, Ill.: Hope, 1994.

Glover, Raymond. *A Commentary on New Hymns*. New York: Church Pension Fund, 1987.

———, ed. *The Hymnal 1982 Companion*. 3 vols. New York: Church Pension Fund, 1990, 1994.

Haeussler, Armin. *The Story of Our Hymns*. St. Louis: Eden, 1952.

Hawaii Conference United Church of Christ. *Na Himeni Haipule Hawaii*. Honolulu: Hawaii Conference, 1972.

Hope Publishing Co. *100 Hymns of Hope*. Carol Stream, Ill.: Hope, 1992.

Huber, Jane Parker. *A Singing Faith*. Philadelphia: Westminster Press, 1987.

Hughes, Charles W. *American Hymns Old and New*. New York: Columbia University Press, 1980.

Hurd, David. *The David Hurd Hymnary*. Chicago: G.I.A. Publications, 1983.

Hymn Society in the U.S. and Canada. *Holding in Trust*. Carol Stream, Ill.: Hope, 1992.

———. *The Hymn. Journal of The Hymn Society in the United States and Canada*, various issues.

Idle, Christopher. *Stories of Our Favorite Hymns*. Grand Rapids, Mich.: Eerdmans, 1980.

Jackson, George Pullen. *Down-East Spirituals and Others*. New York: J. J. Augustine, 1943.

———. *Spiritual Folk-Songs of Early America*. New York: J. J. Augustine, 1937; reprint 1964, New York: Dover..

James, Jacqui. *Between the Lines: Sources for Singing the Living Tradition*. Boston: Skinner House Books, 1995.

Julian, John. *A Dictionary of Hymnology*. 2 vols. New York: Dover, 1892, 1907.

Kondel, Wilber. *Living Hymn Stories*. Minneapolis: Bethany House, 1972, 1982.

Latourette, Kenneth Scott. *A History of Christianity*. New York: Harper & Row, 1953.

Loh, I-to. *Hymns from the Four Winds*. Nashville: Abingdon, 1983.

Long, Kenneth R. *The Music of the English Church*. New York: St. Martin's, 1971.

Lovell, John, Jr. *Black Song: The Forge and the Flame*. New York: Paragon House, 1986.

McClain, William B. *Come Sunday: The Liturgy of Zion*. Nashville: Abingdon, 1990.

McCutchan, Robert Guy. *Hymn Tune Names: Their Sources and Significance*. New York and Nashville: Abingdon, 1957.

McKim, LindaJo H. *The Presbyterian Hymnal Companion*. Louisville, Ky.: Westminster/John Knox Press, 1993.

Murray, Shirley Erena. *Every Day in Your Spirit*. Carol Stream, Ill.: Hope, 1996.

———. *In Every Corner Sing*. Carol Stream, Ill.: Hope, 1992.

Nyberg, Anders. *Freedom Is Coming*. Ft. Lauderdale, Fla.: Walton Music, 1984.

Osbeck, Kenneth W. *101 Hymn Stories*. Grand Rapids, Mich.: Kregel, 1982.

———. *101 More Hymn Stories*. Grand Rapids, Mich.: Kregel, 1985.

———. *Amazing Grace*. Grand Rapids, Mich.: Kregel, 1990.

Parry, K. L., ed. *Companion to Congregational Praise*. London: Independent Press, 1953.

Poston, Elizabeth, ed. *The Second Penguin Book of Christmas Carols*. Middlesex, England: Penguin, 1970.

Reagon, Bernice Johnson, ed. *We'll Understand It Better By and By*. Washington, D.C.: Smithsonian Institution Press, 1992.

Reynolds, William Jensen. *Hymns of Our Faith*. Nashville: Broadman Press, 1964.

Rizk, Helen Salem. *Stories of the Christian Hymns*. Nashville: Abingdon, 1986.

Ronander, Albert C., and Ethel K. Porter. *Guide to the Pilgrim Hymnal*. Philadelphia and Boston: United Church Press, 1966.

Routley, Erik. *A Panorama of Christian Hymnody*. Chicago: G.I.A. Publications, 1979.

———. *Our Lives Be Praise*. Carol Stream, Ill.: Hope, 1990.

———. *Twentieth Century Church Music*. Carol Stream, Ill.: Agape, 1964.

Sanchez, Diana, ed. *The Hymns of the United Methodist Hymnal*. Nashville: Abingdon, 1989.

Smith, Alfred B. *Hymn Histories*. Montrose, Pa.: Heritage Music Distributors, 1981.

Smith, C. Howard. *Scandinavian Hymnody from the Reformation to the Present*. Metuchen, N.J.: American Theological Library Association and Scarecrow Press, Inc., 1987.

Southern, Eileen. *The Music of Black Americans: A History*. New York: W. W. Norton, 1983.

Spencer, Jon Michael, ed. *Unsung Hymns by Black and Unknown Bards*. A special issue of *Black Sacred Music: A Journal of Theomusicology*, vol. 4, no. 1. Durham, N.C.: Duke University Press, 1990.

Stanislaw, Richard J., and Donald P. Hustad. *Companion to The Worshiping Church*. Carol Stream, Ill.: Hope, 1993.

Stuempfle, Herman. *The Word Goes Forth*. Chicago: G.I.A. Publications, 1993.

Stulken, Marilyn Kay. *Hymnal Companion to the Lutheran Book of Worship*. Philadelphia: Fortress Press, 1981.

Terry, Lindsay I. *Devotionals from Famous Hymn Stories*. Grand Rapids, Mich.: Baker Book House, 1974, 1986.

Thomson, Ronald W. *Who's Who of Hymn Writers*. London: Epworth Press, 1967.

United Church of Christ, Office of the Secretary. *Yearbook of the United Church of Christ*. Cleveland: UCC, various years.

Vajda, Jaroslav J. *Now the Joyful Celebration*. St. Louis: Morning Star Music Publishers, 1987.

VanDyke, Mary Louise, librarian/coordinator. Dictionary of American Hymnology Project.

Oberlin, Ohio: The Hymn Society in the U.S. and Canada.

Wake, Arthur N. *Companion to Hymnbook for Christian Worship.* St. Louis: Bethany Press, 1970.

Warren, James I., Jr. *O for a Thousand Tongues.* Grand Rapids, Mich.: Francis Asbury Press, 1988.

Westermeyer, Paul. *With Tongues of Fire: Profiles in Twentieth-Century Hymn Writing.* St. Louis: Concordia, 1995.

White, B. F., and E. J. King. *The Sacred Harp.* 3d ed. 1859. Reprint, Nashville: Broadman Press, 1968.

Winter, Miriam Therese. *Songlines.* New York: Crossroad, 1996.

Wren, Brian. *Faith Renewed.* Carol Stream, Ill.: Hope, 1995.

Ylvisaker, John Carl. *Borning Cry.* Waverly, Iowa: New Generations, 1992.

Young, Carlton R. Companion to the United Methodist Hymnal. Nashville: Abingdon, 1993.

About the Contributors

ROBERT L. ANDERSON is senior pastor of Zion United Church of Christ in York, Pennsylvania. He was ordained in 1971 after receiving a master of divinity degree from Andover Newton Theological School in Massachusetts. Anderson previously served churches in Wisconsin and Indiana, where he first began compiling background notes on hymns that later became the basis for his work in this volume.

EMILY R. BRINK is music and liturgy editor for CRC Publications, a ministry of the Christian Reformed Church in North America. She also serves as adjunct professor of church music and worship at Calvin Theological Seminary, Grand Rapids, Michigan. Brink edited the 1987 *Psalter Hymnal*, contributed to the *Psalter Hymnal Handbook*, and is editor of the quarterly journal *Reformed Worship*.

ARTHUR G. CLYDE is minister for worship, music, and liturgical arts on the staff of the United Church Board for Homeland Ministries. He edited *The New Century Hymnal* as well as other music resources for The Pilgrim Press. Clyde previously served as director of music at Zwingli United Church of Christ in Souderton, Pennsylvania, and was director of the Chamber Arts Guild, a Philadelphia-area choral and instrumental ensemble.

MELVA WILSON COSTEN is Helmar Nielson Professor of Worship and Music at the Interdenominational Theological Center, Atlanta, Georgia. She served as chairperson of the *Presbyterian Hymnal* committee and is the author of *African American Christian Worship* (Abingdon Press, 1993). Costen earned her Ph.D. from Georgia State University in 1978.

JAMES W. CRAWFORD has served as senior pastor of Old South Church in Boston, Massachusetts, since 1974. A graduate of Union Theological Seminary (M.Div.) and Andover Newton Theological School (D.D.), he has written numerous hymns and published a collection of sermons, *Worthy to Raise Issues* (The Pilgrim Press, 1991). Crawford was chairperson of the hymnal committee and a member of the editorial panel for *The New Century Hymnal*.

KRISTEN L. FORMAN served on the staff of the United Church Board for Homeland Ministries from 1991 to 1997. She was assistant editor of *The New Century Hymnal* and related publications. Her most recent project for The Pilgrim Press is *Bring the Feast*, a songbook compiled by the Re-

Imagining Community. She earned her music degree from Denison University, Granville, Ohio.

C. MICHAEL HAWN is associate professor of sacred music at Perkins School of Theology, Southern Methodist University, in Dallas, Texas. He has published articles and reviews in numerous periodicals and edited *Stepping Stones: An Ecumenical Children's Choir Curriculum* for the Choristers Guild. Hawn's graduate degrees, including the doctor of musical arts, are from Southern Baptist Theological Seminary.

DANIEL L. JOHNSON is senior pastor of Evangelical United Church of Christ in Godfrey, Illinois. He has taught UCC history and polity at Yale Divinity School and Eden Theological Seminary and is the author/editor of two books published by The Pilgrim Press, *Starting Right, and Staying Strong* (1983) and *Theology and Identity* (coeditor, 1990). Johnson served on the *New Century Hymnal* committee.

SWEE HONG LIM is director of worship and music at Paya Lebar Methodist Church, Singapore. An active composer, he cofounded the Methodist School of Music in that city, where he continues to teach church music. Swee Hong Lim is a graduate of the Asian Institute for Liturgy and Music in Manila and Perkins School of Music, Southern Methodist University, Dallas, Texas.

RAQUEL MORA MARTÍNEZ is editor of the Spanish United Methodist hymnal *Mil Voces Para Celebrar* (1996). She has served as church organist, choir director, and song leader for various events, including gatherings of United Methodist women. She was honored with an honorary doctor of music degree from Nebraska Wesleyan University, Lincoln, in 1997.

JONATHAN B. MCNAIR, assistant music editor of *The New Century Hymnal*, serves as director of music for Signal Crest United Methodist Church and adjunct professor of music at the University of Tennessee at Chattanooga. He holds a doctorate in composition from the Cleveland Institute of Music and is an active teacher, composer, and performer of twentieth-century music.

DAVID W. MUSIC is professor of church music at Southwestern Baptist Theological Seminary, Fort Worth, Texas. He is the compiler of *Hymnology: A Collection of Source Readings* (Scarecrow, 1996) and a former editor of *The Hymn*, the journal of the Hymn Society in the United States and Canada.

PAUL A. RICHARDSON is professor and assistant dean for graduate studies in the School of Music at Samford University, Birmingham, Alabama. He served on the editorial committee for *The Worshiping Church: A Hymnal* (Hope, 1990) and has contributed to several companions, including *Handbook to The Baptist Hymnal* (Convention, 1992). Richardson is joint author of *Singing Baptists: Studies in Baptist Hymnody in America* (Church Street, 1994).

MARILYN KAY STULKEN holds a doctor of musical arts degree from Eastman School of Music, Rochester, New York. She is author of the *Hymnal Companion to the Lutheran Book of Worship* (1981) as well as numerous other church music publications. Stulken lives in Racine, Wisconsin, where she is organist at historic St. Luke's Episcopal Church and maintains a private organ teaching studio.

MARY LOUISE VANDYKE is director of the Dictionary of American Hymnology project for the Hymn Society in the United States and Canada. She devotes countless volunteer hours to maintaining and cataloging this important collection housed at the Oberlin College Library, Oberlin, Ohio. VanDyke was an editorial consultant for the 1974 *Hymnal* of the United Church of Christ. She was named a Fellow of the Hymn Society in 1996.

VERNON WICKER is professor of music at Seattle Pacific University and editor of *The Hymnology Annual: An International Forum on the Hymn and Worship* (Selah). Wicker holds degrees from Biola University, Indiana University, and University of Oregon. He lectures and concertizes regularly in Europe and the United States.

MEL R. WILHOIT is chair of the Department of Music at Bryan College, Dayton, Tennessee. His work on church music has been published in numerous journals and reference works, including the *New Grove Dictionary of Music*, *The Hymn*, and the *American Dictionary of Biography*. Wilhoit received his doctorate in church music from Southern Baptist Theological Seminary.

INDEXES

Index to Survey of Christian Hymnody
(Numbers refer to pages in the present volume.)

Abbott, Lyman 127
Abelard, Peter 66
acculturation 151
Adams, Sarah Flower 103
African American music. *See* "African American Worship Music," 136–45
African American spirituals 122, 137–38, 141, 199
  performance of 141
African Methodist Episcopal Church 111
African music 136
Ahle, Johann Rudolph 77
Ainger, Geoffrey 186
Ainsworth, Henry 106
Alexander, Cecil Frances 103
Alexander, Charlie 129
Alford, Henry 103
Allen, Richard 111, 122
Ambrose 61, 62, 63
American Missionary Association 140
Anglo-Genevan Psalters 90–91
Aquinas, Thomas 67
Arias, Mortimer 157, 181, 186
Asian indigenous hymnody 147–50, 153
  historical overview 146
  stages of development 150
Asian Institute for Liturgy and Music 147–48
Auza, Antonio 157, 181, 186
Avila, Rubén Ruiz 159

Bach, Johann Sebastian 79
Bacon, Leonard 118
Badillo, Pablo Fernández 159, 183
Baker, Henry W. 102, 103
Baptists 107, 112

Baring-Gould, Sabine 103
Barnby, Joseph 104
Barton, William 95
Bates, Katharine Lee 131
Bay Psalm Book 107
Bayly, Albert 167, 168, 179
Beaumont, Geoffrey 168
Becker, Cornelius 76, 84
Bede, The Venerable 63, 64
Beecher, Henry Ward 119, 125
Beethoven, Ludwig van 82
Bell, John 174, 204
Bennard, George 130
Bernard of Clairvaux 66, 67
Berthier, Jacques 203
Beza, Theodore de 87
Billings, William 113
Bliss, Philip P. 128
blues, urban 137, 138–39
Boberg, Carl Gustaf 82, 183
Bonhoeffer, Dietrich 183
Borthwick, Jane Laurie 102
Bourgeois, Louis 87
Bowring, John 100
Bradbury, William B. 117–18, 128–29
Brady, Nicolas 93
Brandon, Don 188
Brébeuf, Jean de 110
Bridges, Matthew 101
Bridges, Robert 102, 164
British hymnody. *See* "Eighteenth and Nineteenth-Century British Hymnody," 95–104; "Twentieth-Century Hymnody in Great Britain," 163–74
Brorson, Hans Adolf 81
Burleigh, Harry T. 142
Bushnell, Horace 130
Byrd, Sidney 200

531

call-and-response 136, 138
Calvin, John 72, 83, 85–87, 91, 92
Cameron, Catherine 183
camp meetings 114
canons, Greek 61
Cantate Domino 167, 200
Canticles 59, 60, 61
  Canticle of the Three 59
  Song of Hannah 60
  Song of Mary 59, 60, 186
  Song of Simeon 59
  Song of Zechariah 59, 186
cantiones 72
Carter, Sydney 170
Caswell, Edward 101, 127
Catena, Osvaldo 157
Chapman, Wilbur 129
Chávez-Melo, Skinner 158
Chesterton, G. K. 166
Christian Church 116, 131
Christian Lyre, The 114–15
Church Hymnary, The 166
Clausnitzer, Tobias 77
Clephane, Elizabeth C. 103
Cleveland, J. Jefferson 143
Clyde, Arthur G. 189, 193
Cole-Turner, Ronald 181
Colom M., Alfredo 155
Congregational Church 119, 125–32
Congregational Praise 167
Consultation on Ecumenical Hymnody 199–200
contrafactum 73, 74
Coverdale, Miles 89
Cowper, William 97–98
Croft, William 93, 98
Crosby, Fanny 128–29
Crossman, Samuel 166
Crouch, Andraé 142, 183
Crüger, Johann 76–77, 88
Cutts, Peter 173, 189, 192, 195

Daily Office 63, 64, 72
Damon, Dan 184, 194, 198
Danish hymns 81
Dare, Elkanah Kelsay 114, 115
Darsane, Nyoman 149
Darwall, John 93, 99
Davenport, James 112
Davies, Samuel 111
Davisson, Ananias 115
Daw, Carl P., Jr. 181, 186
Day, John 92
Dearmer, Percy 164, 165
denominational hymnals, U.S. 118–20
Dett, R. Nathaniel 140
Diemer, Emma Lou 192, 195
Dix, William C. 103
Doane, George Washington 120
Doane, William H. 129
Doddridge, Philip 97
Doran, Carol 196
Dorsey, Thomas 139
Douroux, Margaret J. 186
Drese, Adam 79
Duck, Ruth C. 180, 181, 183, 185, 186
Dunblane consultations 169
Dunstan, Sylvia 181
Dutch Psalter 88, 107
Dutch Reformed Church 110, 111, 133
Dwight, Timothy 112, 127
Dykes, John B. 104

early Christian hymnody 59–60
East Asia Christian Conference 147
ecumenical hymnody 178. *See also* "Ecumenical and Global Congregational Song in the Late Twentieth Century," 199–206
Edwards, Jonathan 109, 127
Eliot, James 107
Ellerton, John 103
Ellington, Duke 139, 142

Elliott, Charlotte 103
Elvey, George J. 104
English Hymnal, The 164
Equiano, Olaudah 136
Escamilla, Roberto 159
Eslinger, Elise 159
Este, Thomas 106
Evangelical and Reformed Church 134
Evangelical hymnody 96–98, 101, 112
Evangelical Synod 80, 132–33
Evans, David 166
Everest, Charles W. 120

Faber, Frederick W. 101
family service movement 168
Fawcett, John 97
Finney, Charles G. 114, 127
Finnish hymns 81
Floríndez, Lorraine 157
Foley, Brian 169
folk music 169, 191
folk tunes 113, 165
Fortunatus 63, 64
Franck, Johann 75, 77
Francke, August Hermann 78
Franklin, Benjamin 109
Franklin, Kirk 142
Frazier, R. Philip 200
Frere, Walter Howard 164
Freylinghausen, Johann Anastasius 78
Fryson, Robert J. 142
fuging tunes 113
Funk, Joseph 116

Gabaráin, Cesáreo 161, 180, 182
Gabriel, Charles 129–30
Gardiner, William 100
Gastorius, Severus 77–78
Gay, Annabeth McClelland 189
Geistliche Lieder 84
Genevan Psalter 85–88, 106

Gerhardt, Paul 75
German hymnody. *See* "Hymnody from German, Scandinavian, and Finnish Sources," 72–82
German Reformed Church 110, 111, 121, 132–33
Gertmenian, James 189
Giardini, Felice de 99
Gibson, Colin 150, 188, 194
Gladden, Washington 131
Good, James 133
Good, Jeremiah H. 133
gospel, black 139, 142
gospel, contemporary 139, 142
gospel hymns 127–29
Goss, John 104
Goudimel, Claude 88
Grant, Robert 100
Great Awakening 109, 127
Greek hymns 60
Green, Fred Pratt 163, 167, 170, 171, 178–79, 182, 183, 185
Gregorian chant 83
Gregory I (the Great) 63, 64
Greitter, Matthais 87
Grieg, Edvard 81
Grindal, Gracia 183

Hampton, Calvin 196
Hanaoka, Nobuaki 201
Hancock, Eugene 142, 198
Handel G. F. 99–100
Hankey, Katherine 103, 128
Harbaugh, Henry 121, 133
Harkness, Georgia 182
Hastings, Thomas 115, 117
Haugen, Marty 191, 192
Havergal, Frances Ridley 103
Hawkins, Edwin 139
Haydn, Franz Joseph 82, 100, 167
Heber, Reginald 100
Hedge, Frederick H. 120
Heermann, Johann 76

Helmore, Thomas 102
Héloïse 66
Hendel, William 111
Herberger, Valerius 75
Herbert, George 165, 166
Hernaman, Claudia F. I. 103
Higbee, E. E. 133
Hildegard of Bingen 66
Hispanic hymnody. See "A Survey of Hispanic Hymnody," 154–62
Holbrook, Joseph P. 125
Holden, Oliver 99, 113
Hopkins, John 90
Hopkinson, Francis 111
Hopson, Hal 195
How, William Walsham 103
Howard, Samuel 93, 98
Howe, Julia Ward 125
Huber, Jane Parker 180, 187
Hungarian Psalter 88
Huntington, Ronald 189
Hurd, David 142, 192, 197, 198
Hus, Jan 79
Hymnal, The (UCC) 199, 200
Hymns Ancient and Modern 102–3, 163

inculturation 152
Iona Community 174, 199, 204–5

Janzen, Jean 180
Jewish traditional 60
John of Damascus 60
Johnson, Joyce Finch 141
Johnson, Samuel 120
Jones, William 99
jubilee songs 137, 141–42
Julian of Norwich 67
Juncas, Manuel Fernández 186
Jung, Chuang Chun 149

Kaan, Fred 163, 170, 171, 180, 182, 184, 201

Keach, Benjamin 95, 107
Keble, John 100–101, 163
Kelley, John 147
Kethe, William 91
King, E. J. 116
Knapp, William 99
Knecht, Justin Heinrich 80
Knox, John 92
Kocher, Conrad 80
König, Johann Balthasar 78

Latin hymnody. See "Early Christian, Hebrew, Greek, and Latin Hymns," 59–71
Law, Andrew 115
Leach, Richard 186
League of Arts 164
Leavitt, Joshua 114
Lew, Timothy Tingfang 201
Lewis, Freeman 116
Lindeman, Ludwig 81
lining out 95, 107, 110, 138
Lobwasser, Ambrosius 79
Lobwasser Psalmer 79
Logan, John 115
Loh, I-to 147, 149, 202
Longfellow, Samuel 120, 125, 165
Loperena Sotto, William 160
Lowry, Robert 129
Luther, Martin 72–74, 83–84
Lutheran hymnals 110, 121
Lyons, James 113
Lyte, Henry Francis 100

macaronic hymns 68, 72
Manley, James K. 191
Maquiso, Elena 201
March, Daniel 125
Marian exile 90–92
Marot, Clement 86–87
Marshall, Jane 189, 190, 198
Martínez, Nicolás 157, 186, 201
Martinez, Salvador 205
Mason, John 95, 112

Mason, Lowell 115, 117–118, 119
Mather, Cotton 108–9, 138
Matsumoto, Sogo 201
Maule, Graham 174, 204
Maurus, Rhabanus 63, 65
McGranahan, James 128
McLeod, George 204
McMane, Martie 188
McNair, Jonathan 192, 195
Mendelssohn, Felix 82
Mercersburg 121, 133
Methodist Episcopal Church 111
metrical psalmody 106–7. *See also* "Sixteenth and Seventeenth-Century Metrical Psalmody," 83–94
Miles, C. Austin 130
Miller, Edward 99
Milman, Henry Hart 100
Milton, John 89
Minchin, Jim 150
Misa Popular Nicaragüense 155, 181
Monk, W. H. 102
Montgomery, James 97
Moody, Dwight Lyman 127, 163
Moore, William 116
Moravians 79, 110
Morris, Sally Ann 189, 190, 192
Mozarabic tradition 66
Murray, Shirley Erena 150, 165, 182, 184, 185, 186
mysticism 74, 75

Nason, Elias 119
Native American 107, 110, 200
Neale, John Mason 70, 101–2, 127, 177
Neander, Joachim 80
Neswick, Bruce 195, 198
Nettleton, Asahel 114
Neumark, Georg 75
New England colonies 106
Newman, John 101, 163

Newton, John 97–98
"New Version" 93, 108, 113
Nicolai, Philip 75
Niedling, Johann 77
Niles, D. T. 147, 200
Nix, Verolga 143
North, Frank Mason 131
Norwegian hymns 81
Noyes, Charles 131

"O" antiphons 64
Occum, Samuel 110
O'Kelly, James 116
"Old Version" 93
Olearius, Johannes 77
Olivieri, Luis 161
Olney Hymns 97–98, 112
Oxford movement 70, 101, 133, 163

Palmer, Ray 115, 119, 127
parish communion movement 168
Park, Edward A. 119
Parker, Matthew 90
Peacey, John 184
Peña, Vérne de la 148
Perronet, Edward 97
Phelps, Austin 119
Phelps, Sylvanus Dryden 120
Piae Cantiones 81
Pierpoint, Folliott S. 103
pietism 74, 78, 80
Pilgrim Hymnal 131–32, 199
Pilgrims 106
Pilsbury, Amos 113
plainsong 73, 83, 102–3, 164
Plumptre, Edward 103
Potter, Doreen 180, 201
Praetorius, Michael 76
Praxis Pietatis Melica 76
Prentiss, Elizabeth Payson 120
Protestant Episcopal Church 111
Proulx, Richard 190

Prudentius 62, 63
Psalms, the 59, 83
Pulkingham, Betty Carr 169
Purcell, Henry 99
Puritans 106–7

Quinn, James 169

Radford, Jeffrey 141
Rambach, Johann Jakob 78
Rankin, Jeremiah 129
rationalism 80
Rauschenbusch, Walter 130
Reformation, Lutheran 72–74
Reformed hymnwriters 80
regular singing 108
Reimann, Balthasar 78
Renville, Joseph R. 110
revivalism 114, 127
Richards, C. H. 126
Rinkart, Martin 75
Rippon, John 97, 112
Rist, Johann 77
Roach, Hildred 140
Roberts, Leon C. 142
Robinson, Charles S. 125–26
Robinson, Robert 97
Rodeheaver, Homer 129
Rodigast, Samuel 77
Romanticism 100–101
Root, George W. 117
Rosas, Carlos 157
Rossetti, Christina 103
Routley, Erik 167, 200
Rowan, William 189, 192
Rowthorn, Jeffery 179, 180

Sacred Harp, The 116, 191
Samba Likhaan 148, 149
Sandell, Lina 82
Sankey, Ira D. 127, 163
Sarum breviary 69
Schaff, Philip 121, 132
Schalk, Carl 190, 194, 195

Schmidt, Vicki Vogel 192
Schop, Johann 77
Schumann, Robert 82
Schütz, Heinrich 76, 84
Schütz, Johann Jakob 78
Schwedler, Johann Christoph 78
Scottish psalters 92–93, 107
Sears, Edmund H. 120
Second Vatican Council 155, 169, 177, 200, 205–6
Sekolah Tinggi Teologi Jakarta 148
shape notes 115
Shaw, Benjamin 116
Shaw, Martin 164, 165, 166
Shurtleff, Ernest W. 131
Sibelius, Jean 82
Siena, Bianco da 70
singing schools 108, 115
Smart, Henry T. 104
social gospel 130
Songs of Praise 165
Sosa, Pablo 156, 186, 201, 202
South Africa 143
Southern Harmony, The 116, 191
Spener, Philip Jacob 78
Spilman, Charles H. 116
Srisuwan, Ruth and Inchai 148
Stainer, John 104
Stanford Charles V. 163
Stebbins, George C. 128
Stennett, Samuel 97
Sternhold and Hopkins Psalter 90–93, 106
Sternhold, Thomas 90
Stone, Samuel J. 103
Strathdee, Jim 143, 191
Stuempfle, Herman G., Jr. 185
Sullivan, Arthur 104
Sunday, Billy 129
Sunday schools 117
Swedish hymns 81–82
Sweelinck, Jan P. 88
Swift, Donald 142

Taizé Community 199, 202–3
Tallis, Thomas 90
Tate, William 93
Taulé, Alberto 186
Taylor, Cyril 167
Teresa of Avila 204
Teschner, Melchoir 75
Theodulph of Orléans 65
Thiman, Eric 167
Thirty Years' War 74
Threlfall, Jeannette 103
Thurman, Howard 143
Tindley, Charles S. 139, 142
Tisserand, Jean 70
Toplady, Augustus M. 97
Tractarians 101
traveling choruses 114
Troeger, Thomas 183, 187
twentieth-century hymnody
  texts (see "Theological Trends in Twentieth-Century Hymnody," 177–87)
  tunes (see "A Survey of Hymn Tunes of the Late Twentieth Century," 188–98)
Twentieth Century Light Music Group 168

United Church of Christ 134
U.S. hymnody. See "Hymnody in the U.S. through the Mid-Nineteenth Century," 106–22; "U.S. Hymnody from the Mid-Nineteenth to Late-Twentieth Centuries," 125–35

Vajda, Jaroslav J. 183
Van Dyke, Henry 131
Vaughan Williams, Ralph 163, 164–65
Victorian era 103–4, 163
Vulpius, Melchior 76

Wade, John Francis 70, 99

Walker, William 116
Walther, Johann 72
Warner, Anna 118
Watts, Isaac 93, 95–97, 98, 108, 112, 138
Weaver, John 190
Webb, George J. 117
Weissel, Georg 84
Weissel, Johann 77
Welsh hymns 104
Wesley, Charles 96–97, 99
Wesley, John 96, 99, 109, 111
Wesley, Samuel S. 104
White, Benjamin Franklin 116
Whitefield, George 109
Whittier, John Greenleaf 120, 125
Wilbur, Hervey 117
Wilhelm II, Duke of Saxe-Weimar 75
Williams, Aaron 93, 99
Williams, Thomas 93, 99
Willis, Richard S. 120
Wilson, John 173
Winkworth, Catherine 102, 127
Winter, Miriam Therese 186
Wolcott, Samuel 125
Wood, Charles 164
Woodbury, Isaac Baker 117, 121
Woodward, George 164
Wordsworth, Christopher 103
work songs 137
World Council of Churches 200
Wren, Brian 163, 170, 172, 180, 182, 183, 184, 185
Wyeth, John 115

Yamaguchi, Tokuo 184, 201
Ylvisaker, John 181
Young, Carlton 193

Zinzendorf, Nicolaus Ludwig von 79
Zundel, John 119, 125

AUTHOR, COMPOSER, AND SOURCE INDEX
(Numbers refer to hymns in *The New Century Hymnal*.)

Abe, Seigi (1890–1974) 162
Abelard, Peter (1079–1142) 385
Adams, Sarah Flower (1805–1848) 78, 606
The Agincourt Song, England, c. 1415 ... 184, 209, 259
Ahle, Johann R. (1625–1673) 74
Ainger, Geoffrey (b. 1925) 152
Airs sur les hymnes sacrez, Paris, 1623 244
Akers, Doris M. (b. 1923) 293
Albright, William H. (b. 1944) 411
Alexander, Cecil F. (1818–1895) 31, 145, 171, 172
Alexander, James W. (1804–1859) 226
Alford, Henry (1810–1871) 256, 422
Alford, Janie (1887–1986) 267
Ambrose of Milan (340–397) 87
Anderson, Boris (20th cent.) 33
Anderson, Clare (20th cent.) 33
Anglo-Genevan Psalter, 1556 316
Aquinas, Thomas (c. 1225–1274) 339
Arias, Mortimer (b. 1924) 246
Arnatt, Ronald (b. 1930) 274
Atkinson, Frederick C. (1841–1896) 290, 336
Auza, Antonio (1915–1981) 246
Avila, Rubén Ruíz (b. 1945) 214

B. C. M. (20th cent.) 499
Bach, J. S. (1685–1750) 37, 60, 112, 140, 158, 179, 202, 226, 375, 404, 480
Badillo, Pablo Fernández (b. 1919) 34
Bain, James Leith Macbeth (c. 1840–1925) 479
Baker, Henry W. (1821–1877) 248, 329, 469, 571
Baker, Theodore (1851–1934) 127, 421
Bancroft, Henry Hugh (1904–1988) 120
Barbauld, Anna Laetitia Aiken (1743–1825) 422
Baring-Gould, Sabine (1834–1924) 98
Barnby, Joseph (1838–1896) 58, 86, 98, 261
Barnes, Edward Shippen (1887–1958) 139
Batastini, Robert J. (b. 1942) 554
Bates, Katharine Lee (1859–1929) 594
Battersby, C. Maud (19th–20th cent.) 544
Bayler, Lavon (b. 1933) 170, 174, 215, 312, 421, 479, 615
Bayly, Albert F. (1901–1984) 64, 453
Beach, Curtis (1914–1993) 8, 558
Bechtel, Daniel (b. 1932) 583
Bede, The Venerable (673–735) 259
Beebe, David (b. 1931) 461
Beethoven, Ludwig van (1770–1827) 4
Bell, John (b. 1949) 150, 153, 515
Bello, Lois (b. 20th cent.) 142

Bennard, George (1873–1958) 195
Bennett, William S. (1816–1875) 22
Benoit, Paul (1893–1979) 396
Benson, Louis F. (1855–1930) 51
Bernard of Clairvaux (1090–1153) ... 226, 329
Biggs, E. Power (1906–1977) 259
Billings, William (1746–1800) 192
Birkland, Carol (b. 1946) 105, 353
Blanchard, Ferdinand Q. (1876–1968) 191
Bliss, Philip P. (1838–1876) 319, 438
Boberg, Carl (1859–1940) 35
Bode, John E. (1816–1874) 493
Bohemian Brethren's Kirchengesäng, 1566 6
Bonar, Horatius (1808–1889) 336, 489
Bonhoeffer, Dietrich (1906–1945) 413
Borthwick, Jane Laurie (1813–1897) ... 446, 488, 532, 609
Bortniansky, Dimitri (1752–1825) 50
Bourgeois, Louis (c. 1510–c. 1561) ... 7, 167
Bourne, George Hugh (1840–1925) 258
Bowie, Walter Russell (1882–1969) 613
Bowring, John (1792–1872) ... 103, 193, 194
Boyd, William (1847–1928) 328, 589
Bradbury, William B. (1816–1868) 207, 252, 327, 403, 505
Brandon, Don (b. 1956) 612
Brébeuf, Jean de (d. 1649) 151
Bridges, Matthew (1800–1894) 301, 352
Bridges, Robert (1844–1930) 218, 408
Bristol, Lee Hastings, Jr. (1923–1979) 168, 268
Brooks, Phillips (1835–1893) 133
Brorson, Hans A. (1694–1764) 296
Brumley, Albert E. (1905–1977) 595
Buchanan, Annabel Morris (1888–1983) 354, 378, 521
Buck, Percy C. (1871–1947) 221
Budry, Edmond L. (1854–1932) 253
Bunyan, John (1628–1688) 494
Burleigh, Harry T. (1866–1949) 394
Butler, Henry M. (1833–1918) 38
Byrd, Sidney H. (b. 1918) 341
Byrne, Mary E. (1880–1931) 451

Cameron, Catherine (b. 1927) 556
Campbell, John, Duke of Argyll (1845–1914) 466
Canitz, Friedrich R. L. von (1654–1699) 91
Cantate Domino, 1980 279
Cantionale Sacrum, Gotha, 1651 375
Carlson, Dosia (b. 1930) 179, 560, 574
Carmines, Al (b. 1936) 177
Carols Old and Carols New, Boston, 1916 125

AUTHOR, COMPOSER, AND SOURCE INDEX

Carr, Benjamin (1768–1831) 185
Carter, Sydney (b. 1915) 108, 210
Caswall, Edward (1814–1878) 86, 507
Catena, Osvaldo (20th cent.) 56
Catholische Geistliche Kirchengesäng,
 Cologne, 1559 .... 127, 600
Cawood, John (1775–1852) 318
Chambers, H. A. (1880–1946) 129, 422
Chao, Tzu-chen (1888–1979) 424, 470
Charles, Elizabeth R. (1828–1896) 259
Chávez-Melo, Skinner (1944–1992) 121,
 173, 174, 338, 528
Chesterton, Gilbert K. (1874–1936) 582
Chisholm, Thomas O. (1866–1960) 423
Chorley, Henry F. (1808–1872) 577
The Christian Harp, 1832 .... 354, 378
The Christian Lyre, 1831 397
Christierson, Frank von (b. 1900) 429, 520
Christmas Carols New and Old, 1871 39
Clark, Francis A. (1851–1933) 444, 447
Clausnitzer, Tobias (1618–1684) 74
Clephane, Elizabeth C. (1830–1869) 190
Cleveland, J. Jefferson (1937–1986) 284,
 490, 514, 570, 616
Clyde, Arthur G. (b. 1940) 112, 206,
 280, 287
Cober, Kenneth L. (b. 1902) 311
Coffin, Charles (1676–1749) 115
Coffin, Henry Sloane (1877–1954) 116
Cole-Turner, Ronald S. (b. 1948) 325
A Collection of Sacred Ballads, 1790
 .... 547, 548
Collections of Motets or Antiphons, 1792 135
Colom M., Alfredo (1904–1971) 88
Columbia Harmony, Cincinnati, 1829 ... 547,
 548, 617
Colvin, Thomas S. (b. 1925) 498
Conkey, Ithamar (1815–1867) 193
Converse, Charles C. (1832–1918) 506
Copes, V. Earle (b. 1921) 264
Corbett, Cecil (b. 20th cent.) 291
Cory, Julia C. (1882–1963) 420
Cowper, William (1731–1800) 250, 412, 450
Crawford, James W. (b. 1936) 47
Croft, William (1678–1727) 25, 263,
 278, 305, 359, 464
Croly, George (1780–1860) 290
Crosby, Fanny (1820–1915) 146, 197,
 455, 473, 551
Crossman, Samuel (c. 1624–1684) 222
Crotch, William (1775–1847) 611
Crouch, Andraé (b. 1945) 14
Crown of Jesus Music II, 1862 125
Crüger, Johann (1598–1662) ... 40, 218, 334,
 419, 480
Crull, August (1845–1923) 208
Crum, John M. C. (1872–1958) 238
Cummings, William H. (1831–1915).... 144
Cutts, Peter (b. 1937) 270, 399, 552, 555

Cyprian of Carthage (d. 258) 163

Dakota Odowan, 1842 327
Dalles, John A. (b. 1954) 265, 586
Damon, Dan (b. 1955) 201, 302, 398,
 406, 557
Dare, Elkanah Kelsay (1782–1826) 568
Darwall, John (1731–1789) 303
Das grosse Cantional, Darmstadt, 1687   74
Daw, Carl P., Jr. (b. 1944) 100, 167,
 182, 270, 332, 355, 367, 401, 530
Day's *The Whole Booke of Psalms,* 1562
 .... 211, 318, 342
Dearmer, Percy (1867–1936) 337
Deitz, Purd E. (1897–1987) 607
Diemer, Emma Lou (b. 1927) 227, 461
Dirksen, Richard Wayne (b. 1921) 71
Dix, William C. (1837–1898) 148, 159,
 257, 484
Doane, George W. (1799–1859) 40
Doane, William H. (1832–1915) 197,
 455, 456, 551
Doddridge, Philip (1702–1751) 491
Doran, Carol (b. 1936) 54, 176, 271
Dorsey, Thomas A. (1899–1993) 472
Douglas, C. Winfred (1867–1944) 89,
 118, 119, 494, 605, 613
Douroux, Margaret J. (b. 1941) 188
Doving, Carl (1867–1937) 296
Downing, Edith Sinclair (b. 1922)   196, 356
Drese, Adam (1620–1701) 446
Duck, Ruth (b. 1947) 30, 36, 106, 110,
 164, 168, 274, 343, 357, 376, 439,
 521, 554, 563
Duffield, S. W. (1843–1887) 385
Dunstan, Sylvia G. (1955–1993) 326,
 350, 380, 384, 504, 509
Dwight, Timothy (1725–1817) 312
Dykes, John B. (1823–1876) 215, 248,
 277, 281, 450, 507, 508

Edwards, Howard M., III (Rusty)
 (b. 1955) 180, 545
Edwards, John D. (1806–1885) 222, 426
Edwards, Robert L. (b. 1915) 565
Elderkin, George D. 160
Ellerton, John (1826–1893) 80, 95, 516, 577
Ellington, "Duke" (1899–1974) 602
Elliott, Charlotte (1789–1871) 207
Elvey, George J. (1816–1893) 8, 301,
 350, 422
Emerson, Luther O. (1820–1915) 425
The English Hymnal, 1906 .... 334, 582
Erneuerten Gesangbuch, Stralsund, 1665 22
Escamilla, Roberto (b. 1931)   34, 65, 246
Eschbach, Douglas C. (b. 1960) 280
Eslinger, Elise S. (b. 1942)   34, 65, 246, 499
Este's *Whole Book of Psalmes,* 1592 516
Etzler, Carole A. (b. 1944) 501

*The European Magazine and
   Review,* 1792 77
Evans, David (1874–1948) 212, 390,
   429, 451, 527
Everest, Charles W. (1814–1877) 204
Excell, Edwin O. (1851–1921) 547, 548, 617

F. B. P. (c. 16th cent.) 378
Faber, Frederick William
   (1814–1863) 23, 381
Fawcett, John (1739/40–1817) 77, 393
Fedak, Alfred V. (b. 1953) 431
Fellowship Hymn Book, 1910 418
Ferguson, John (b. 1941) 530
Ferguson, Manie Payne (b. 1850) 284
Fischer, William G. (1835–1912) 522
Fleischaker, Mary Frances (b. 1945) 123
Flemming, Friedrich F. (1778–1813) 518
Floríndez, Lorraine (b. 1926) 56
Fogg, Joan Collier (b. 1949) 608
Foley, Brian (b. 1919) 264
Fortunatus, Venantius Honorius
   (c. 535–c. 600) 220, 221, 262
Fosdick, Harry Emerson (1878–1969)   436
Foster, Frederick W. (1760–1835) 68
The Foundery Collection, 1742 430
Francis of Assisi (1182–1226) 17
Franck, Johann (1618–1677) 334, 480
Franklin, Kirk (b. 20th cent.) 523
Frazier, R. Philip (1892–1964) 3
Freedom Is Coming, 1984 526
Freylinghausen's *Geistreiches
   Gesangbuch,* Halle, 1704 566
French "Processional," 15th century .. 116
Friedell, Harold (1905–1958) 337
Frostenson, Anders (b. 1906) 163
Fryson, Robert J. (1944–1994) 53
Funk's *Genuine Church Music,* 1832 407

Gabaraín, Cesáreo (1936–1991) ... 173, 338,
   528, 614
Gabriel, Charles H. (1856–1932)   442, 475
Gannett, William C. (1840–1923) 430
García, Juan Luis (b. 1935) 614
William Gardiner's *Sacred
   Melodies,* 1815 .... 361, 543
Garrett, Les (b. 1943) 84
Gastorius, Severus (fl. 1675) 415
Gauntlett, Henry J. (1805–1876) 145
Gay, Annabeth McClelland (b. 1925) 320,
   435
Gay, William (b. 1920) 435
Geistliche Gesangbuchlein,
   Wittenberg, 1524 64
Geistliche Kirchengesäng,
   Cologne, 1623 .... 17, 27, 60
Geistreiches Gesangbuch,
   Darmstadt, 1698 446

Gerhardt, Paul (1607–1676) 94, 102, 226,
   269, 404
Gertmenian, James (b. 1947) 20, 464
*Gesangbuch der herzoglichen
   Wirtembergischen katholischen
   Hofkapelle,* 1784 .... 12, 104, 213
Giardini, Felice de (1716–1796) 275
Gibbons, Kendyl L. R. (b. 1955) 552
Gibson, Colin (b. 1933) 141, 562, 569
Gieseke, Richard (b. 1952) 175
Gill, Thomas H. (1819–1906) 374
Gillard, Richard (b. 1953) 364, 539
Gladden, Washington (1836–1918) 503
Gläser, Carl G. (1784–1829) 42, 383, 575
Glaubund Liebesübung, Bremen, 1680 68
Goss, John (1800–1880) 273, 567
Gottheil, Gustave (1827–1903) 10
Gottschalk, Louis Moreau (1829–1869)   63
Gould, John E. (1822–1875) 441
Graham, Fred (20th cent.) 564
Grant, Robert (1779–1838) 26, 185
Greatorex, Walter (1877–1949) 38
Green, Fred Pratt (b. 1903) 70, 140, 175,
   261, 306, 323, 365, 413,
   425, 529, 555, 561
Gregory, Paul R. (b. 1920) 317, 538
Gregory the Great (540–604) 90, 187
Grenoble Antiphoner, 1753 204
Grieg, Edvard (1843–1907) 296
Grindal, Gracia (b. 1943) 9, 545
Grubb, Edward (1854–1939) 37
Gruber, Franz (1787–1863) 134
Gutiérrez–Achon, Raquel (b. 1927) 528, 578

Haddix, James L. (b. 1946) 426
Haile, Elizabeth (b. 20th cent.) 291
Hall, Sara M. de 544
Hampton, Calvin (1938–1984) 587
Hanaoka, Nobuaki (b. 1944) 5
Hancock, Eugene W. (b. 1929) 462
Handel, G. F. (1685–1759) 253, 491
Hankey, Katherine (1834–1911) 522
Harbaugh, Henry (1817–1867) 457
Harding, James P. (1850–1911) 157
Harkness, Georgia (1891–1974) 46
Hartunian, Vartan (b. 1915) 327
Hassler, Hans Leo (1564–1612) ... 130, 179,
   202, 226
Hastings, Thomas (1784–1872) 19, 596
Hatch, Edwin (1835–1889) 292
Hatton, John (d. 1793) 300
Haugen, Marty (b. 1950) 107, 181, 581
Havergal, Frances Ridley
   (1836–1879) 448, 531
Havergal, William H. (1793–1870) 489
Haweis, Thomas (1734–1820) 36
Hawk, Jean Slates (b. 1925) 453
Hawkins, Ernest (1802–1868) ... 47, 308, 576
Hawks, Annie S. (1835–1918) 517

AUTHOR, COMPOSER, AND SOURCE INDEX

Haydn, Franz Joseph (1732–1809) 91, 307, 565
Haydn, J. Michael (1737–1806) 26
Heber, Reginald (1783–1826) 156, 157, 277, 346
Hedge, Frederick H. (1805–1890) 439, 512
Heermann, Johann (1585–1647) 513
Heiliges Lippen und Herzens Opfer,
   Stettin, 1778 208
Helmore, Thomas (1811–1890) 116
Hemy, Henri F. (1818–1888) 381
Herbert, George (1593–1633) 331
Herbst, Martin (1654–1681) 205
Hernaman, Claudia F. I. (1838–1898)   211
Hibbard, Esther (b. 1903) 203
Hildegard, Abbess of Bingen (12th cent.) 57
Himnario Metodista, 1968 327
Hobbs, Herbert G. (b. 1934) 413
Hodges, Edward (1796–1867) 4
Hodges, J. S. B. (1830–1915) 346
Hoffman, Elisha A. (1839–1929) 189, 471, 486
Hohu, Martha (b. 1907) 496
Holden, Oliver (1765–1844) 304
Holmes, Stephen W. (b. 20th cent.) 548
Holst, Gustav (1874–1934) 128
Hopkins, Edward J. (1818–1901) 80
Hopkins, John H. (1861–1945) 295
Hopp, Roy (b.1951) 313, 323, 529
Hopper, Edward (1818–1888) 441
Hopson, Hal H. (b. 1933) 186
Horvath, Theodore S. (b. 1919) 445
Hosmer, Frederick Lucian
   (1840–1929) 377, 603
How, William W. (1823–1897) 299, 315
Howard, Samuel (1710–1782) 483
Howe, Julia Ward (1819–1910) 610
Howells, Herbert (1892–1983) 408
Hu, Te-ngai (b. c. 1900) 470
Huber, Jane Parker (b. 1926) 21, 272, 278, 328, 371, 372, 495, 535, 582, 588
Hudson, Ralph E. (1843–1901) 199
Hughes, John (1873–1932) 18, 436
Hull, Eleanor H. (1860–1935) 451
Hunter, Tom (b. 1946) 359
Huntington, Ronald (1929–1994) 20
Hurd, David (b. 1950) 93, 169, 171, 330, 356, 357
Hussey, Jennie Evelyn (1874–1958) 228
Hymn of the Hungarian Galley
   Slaves, 1674 445
The Hymnal, 1933 .... 488, 591, 607
The Hymnal 1982 66
Hymnal: A Worship Book, 1992 327
Hymns for the Young, 1836 252

Imakoma, Yasushige (b. 1926) 317
The Iona Community 29, 150, 273, 344, 515
Irvine, Jesse Seymour (1836–1887) 468

Isaak, Heinrich (c. 1450–1517) 94
Iverson, Daniel (1890–1977) 283

Jackson, Robert (1840–1914) 292
Jacob, Gordon (1895–1984) 479
Janzen, Jean (b. 1933) 57, 467, 600, 601
Jastrow, Marcus (20th cent.) 10
Jeffrey, J. Albert (1855–1929) 46
Jenkins, William Vaughan (1868–1920) 363
Jennings, Carolyn (b. 1936) 88, 155, 235, 340, 389, 392
Jeszensky, Károly (b. c. 1674) 445
Joachim, Pauli (1636–1708) 445
John of Damascus (c. 696–c. 754)   230, 245
Johnson, J. Rosamond (1873–1954) 593
Johnson, James Weldon (1871–1938) ... 593
Johnson, Joyce Finch (b. 1935) 2, 41, 154, 229, 282, 409, 454, 497
Johnson, Nelsie T. (b. 1912) 161
Jones, Charles P. (1865–1949) 482
Jones, Joseph David (1827–1870) 260
Jones, William (1726–1800) 352
Judah, Daniel ben (b. c. 1400) 24
Jude, William H. (1851–1922) 172
Julian of Norwich (d. c. 1417) 467
Juncos, Manuel Fernández (1846–1928) 55

"K" in John Rippon's *Selection of*
   Hymns, 1787 407
Kaan, Fred (b. 1929) 347, 354, 388, 576
Katholisches Gesangbuch, 1828 86
Katholisches Gesangbuch, Vienna,
   c. 1774 .... 96, 276
Kawashima, Mas (20th cent.) 327
Keble, John (1792–1866) 96
Ken, Thomas (1637–1711) 100
Kennedy, Benjamin H. (1804–1889) 49
Kentucky Harmony, 1816 .... 89, 119
Kerr, Hugh T. (1872–1950) 366
Kethe, William (d. 1608) 7
Kirchengesäng, Psalmen und Geistlich
   Lieder, Nürnberg, 1608 130
Kirkland, Elaine (b. 1946) 335
Kirkland, Patrick M. (1857–1943) 255
Kirkpatrick, William J. (1838–1921) 228
Kitchin, George William (1827–1912)   198
Klug's *Geistliche Lieder,* 1535 374
Klug's *Geistliche Lieder,* 1543 187
Knapp, Phoebe P. (1839–1908) 473
Knapp, Shepherd (1873–1946) 534
Knapp, William (c. 1698–1768) 306
Knecht, Justin H. (1752–1817) 448
Kocher, Conrad (1786–1872) 28, 159
Koizumi, Isao (b. 1907) 72
Johann B. König, *Harmonischer*
   Liederschatz, 1738 324
Koyama, Shōzō (b. 1930) 317
Kremser, Edward (1838–1914) 421

Kumar, Satish 581
La Feillée's *Méthode de plain chant*, 1782 90
La Feillée's *Nouvelle Méthode de
  Plain Chant*, 1808 385
Laiana (Lorenzo Lyons)
  (1807–1886) 146, 252, 327
Landsberg, Max (1845–1928) 24
Lathbury, Mary A. (1841–1913) 321
Latin 111, 129, 135, 209, 241, 242, 268,
  396, 400, 507
Leach, Richard D. (b. 1953) 201, 206
LeCroy, Anne (b. 1930) 93
Leech, Bryan Jeffery (b. 1931) 285
Lew, Timothy Tingfang (1892–1947) 333, 387
Lewis, David (b. 1916) 163
Lewis, Freeman (1780–1859) 225
Lewis-Butts, Magnolia (d. 1949) 288
Liliuokalani, Queen (1838–1917) 580
Lincoln, C. Eric (b. 1924) 443
Lindsley, Phil V. S. 239
Littledale, Richard F. (1833–1890) 289
Liturgy of St. James, 4th cent 345
Lloyd, William (1786–1852) 484
Lockwood, George (b. 1946) 338, 614
Loh, I-to (b. 1936) 33, 72
Longfellow, Samuel (1819–1892) 63, 432, 463
Loperena, William (b. 1935) 389, 392
Lovelace, Austin (b. 1919) 349
Robert Lowry's *Bright Jewels for the
  Sunday School*, 1869 476
Lowry, Robert (1826–1899) 146, 382,
  452, 476, 517, 563, 597
Lowry, Somerset T. C. (1855–1932) 542
Luce, Allena (19th cent.) 149
Luff, Alan (b. 1928) 373
Lum, Maryette H. 477
Luther, Martin (1483–1546) 130, 374,
  439, 440
*The Lutheran Book of
  Worship*, 1978 .... 94, 130
Lvov, Alexis F. (1798–1870) 367, 577
Lynch, Thomas T. (1818–1871) 418
Lyon, Meyer (1751–1797) 24, 314, 373
Lyra Davidica, London, 1708 .... 233, 240
Lyte, Henry F. (1793–1847) 99

Macías, Rosa Martha Zárate
  (b. 20th cent.) 578
Maimonides, Moses (1130–1205) 24
Maker, Frederick C. (1844–1927) 190,
  191, 502
Malan, H. A. César (1787–1864) 49
Manley, James K. (b. 1940) 286
Mann, A. H. (1850–1929) 145, 493
Mann, Newton (1836–1926) 24
Mant, Richard (1776–1848) 298
Maquiso, Elena G. (b. 1914) 97, 279
Marsh, Simeon B. (1798–1875) 546

Marshall, Jane (b. 1924) 61, 180, 370,
  498, 512
Marshall, Madeleine Forell (b. 1946) 6, 22,
  44, 50, 60, 67, 74, 91, 173, 269,
  375, 404, 415, 440, 513, 566
Marshall, W. S. 284
Martin, Civilla D. (1869–1948)...... 460, 475
Martin, James F. D. (b. 1953) 114, 313
Martin, W. Stillman (1862–1935) 460
Martínez, Nicolás (1917–1972) 235
Martinez, Salvador T. (b. 1939) 29
Mason and Webb's *Cantica Laudis*, 1850 170
Mason, Lowell (1792–1872) 132, 224,
  393, 489, 606
Lowell Mason's *Modern
  Psalmody*, 1839 .... 42, 383, 575
Mathams, Walter J. (1853–1932) 350
Matheson, George (1842–1906) 485
Matney, Mary Bryan (b. 1955) 540
Matsumoto, Sogo (1840–1903) 203
Matson, William (1833–1906) 465
Maule, Graham (b. 1958) 153
Maurus, Rhabanus (d. 856).................... 268
May, Janet W. (b. 20th cent.) 544
McAllister, Louise (1913–1960) 225
McDougall, Alan (1875–1964) 93
McFarland, Samuel (fl. 1816) 256
McGuire, David Rutherford (1929–1971) 327
McIntosh, Rigdon M. (1836–1899) 598
McKinstry, Anne (b. 1937) 109
McMane, Martie (b. 1943) 612
McNair, Jonathan (b. 1959) 5, 143, 151, 156,
  254, 362, 363, 467, 590
Memmingen manuscript, 17th century 66
Mendelssohn, Felix (1809–1847) 144,
  272, 315, 419
Mercer's *Cluster*, 1836 223
Messiter, Arthur H. (1834–1916) 55
Meyer, Marion M. (b. 1923) 69
Middleton, Jesse Edgar (1872–1960) 151
Milano, Roberto (b. 1936) 65, 389, 392
Miles, C. Austin (1868–1946) 237
Miller, Anabel S. (b. 1921) 227
Miller, Edward (1731–1807) 208, 414, 465
Milligan, J. Lewis (1876–1961) 120
Milman, Henry H. (1791–1868) 215
Milton, John (1608–1674) 16
"Misa Popular Nicaragüense,"
  20th century 340
Miwa, Genzō (b. 19th cent.) 137
Mohr, Joseph (1792–1848) 134
Monk, William H. (1823–1889) 28, 99, 159, 242
Montgomery, James (1771–1854) 104,
  126, 219, 342, 508
Moore, William (19th cent.) 376, 556
Morales, F.S.C., Alfredo (20th cent.) 402
Morris, Kenneth (1917–1988) 41, 405
Morris, Sally Ann (b. 1952) ... 269, 540, 550
Morris, Stephen J. (b. 1956) 549

Morrow, J. T. 371
Moss, John (b. 1925) 137
Mote, Edward (1797–1874) 403
Moultrie, Gerard (1829–1885)............... 345
Münster Gesangbuch, 1677 44
Murray, James R. (1841–1905)... 3, 124, 341
Murray, Shirley Erena (b. 1931) 58, 141,
    231, 287, 297, 314, 562, 569, 579, 585, 587
Musical Relicks of the Welsh Bards,
    Dublin, 1784 425
Musikalisches Handbuch,
    Hamburg, 1690 115

Nägeli, Johann G. (1773–1836) 393
Nawahine, Robert (1868–1951) 496
Neale, John Mason (1818–1866)   116, 129,
    184, 216, 217, 230, 241, 244, 245, 385, 400
Neander, Joachim (1650–1680) 22, 67,
    68, 408, 566
Nebres, Fé (b. 1938) 97, 428
Neswick, Bruce (b. 1956) 194, 585
Neu Ordentlich Gesangbuch, 1646 37
Neumann, Gustav J. (b. 1888) 445
Neumark, Georg (1621–1681) 410
Neuvermehrtes Gesangbuch,
    Meiningen, 1693 .... 272, 315, 513
The New Century Hymnal, 1995 12, 17, 35,
    39, 45, 46, 56, 62, 69, 73, 76, 87, 90, 105,
    111, 115, 118, 149, 187, 209, 220, 221, 223,
    240, 249, 253, 262, 268, 286, 332, 339, 344,
    369, 391, 402, 487, 504, 578, 605, 739, 740
New England Psalm Singer 192
*The New Hymnal for American
    Youth*, 1930 439
The New Psalms and Hymns, 1901 157
Newbolt, Michael Robert (1874–1956) 198
Newton, John (1725–1807) 307, 547, 548
Ng, Greer Anne Wenh-In (b. 20th cent.) 333
Ni, Chi-pi (b. 1909) 477
Nichols, Kevin (b. 1929) 202
Nicholson, Sydney Hugo (1875–1947) 198
Nicolai, Philipp (1556–1608) 112, 158
Niedling, Johann (1602–1668) 60
Niedmann, Peter (b. 1960) 560
Niles, D. T. (1908–1970)......................... 279
Nix-Allen, Verolga (b. 1933) 284, 490,
    514, 616
Nixon, Darryl 163, 333
Noble, Thomas Tertius (1867–1953) 532
North, Frank Mason (1850–1935) 543

"O Antiphons," Latin,
    6th–7th century 740
James O'Kelly's (1735–1826) *Hymns
    and Spiritual Songs*, 1816 617
Oakeley, Frederick (1802–1880) 135
Oatman, Johnson, Jr. (1856–1922) 442
Olearius, Johannes (1611–1684) 101
Olivieri, Luis (b. 1937) 45, 389, 392

The 150 Psalms of David, Edinburgh,
    1615 412
J. Oudaen's *David's Psalmen*, 1685   231, 232
Owen, William (1813–1883) 258
Oxenham, John (1852–1941) 394, 395

Palestrina, Giovanni Perluigi da
    (c. 1525–1594) 242
Palmer, Ray (1808–1887) 329
The Parish Choir, 1850 .... 16, 537
Parker, Edwin (1836–1925) 63, 536
Parry, C. Hubert H. (1848–1918) 114
Parry, Joseph (1841–1903) 103
Patterson, Deborah (b. 1956) 368
Patterson, Joy F. (b. 1931) 108, 291
Peace, Albert L. (1844–1912) 485
Peacey, John R. (1896–1971) 266
Peek, Joseph Y. (1843–1911) 492
Peña, Vérne de la (b. 1959) 142, 217,
    428, 615
Pensum Sacrum, Görlitz, 1648 375
Perera, Homero (20th cent.) 246
Perronet, Edward (1726–1792) 304
Petri's *Piae Cantiones*, 1582 .... 57, 118
Phelps, Sylvanus Dryden (1816–1895) 452
Pierpoint, Folliott S. (1835–1917) 28
Amos Pilsbury's *United States
    Harmony*, 1799 568
Plainsong melody 64
Plainsong melody from *Processionalle*,
    Paris, 1697 339
Planas-Belfort, Dimas 39
Plenn, Doris (b. 20th cent.) 476
Plumptre, Edward H. (1821–1891) ... 55, 71
Porter, Phil (b. 1956) 335
Post, Marie J. (1919–1990) 364
Postlethwaite, R. Deane (20th cent.) 468
Pott, Francis (1832–1909) 242
Potter, Doreen (1925–1980) 347
Powell, Roger (b. 1914) 397
Praetorius, Michael (1571–1621) 57,
    127, 241
Prentiss, Elizabeth P. (1818–1869) 456
Price, Charles P. (b. 1920) 66
Price, Frank W. (1895–1974) 387, 424,
    470, 477
Prichard, Rowland H. (1811–1887) 182,
    257, 355
Pritchard, T. C. L. (1885–1960) 468
Proulx, Richard (b. 1938) 9, 256, 259
Prudentius, Marcus Aurelius
    Clemens (348–410) 118
Psalmen und Geistliche Lieder,
    Nürnberg, 1608 130
Psalmodia Sacra, Gotha, 1715   13, 122,
    325, 326
Psalter und Harfe, 1876 327
*Psalteriolum Cantionum
    Catholicarum*, 1710 116

Pulkingham, Betty Carr (b. 1928) 364, 539
Purcell, Henry (1659–1695) 47, 308, 576
Purday, Charles Henry (1799–1885) 366, 466

Quinn, James, S.J. (b. 1919) 92

Radford, Jeffrey (b. 1953) 85, 136,
   160, 322, 416, 458, 524, 604
Rambach, Johann J. (1694–1735) 324
Rankin, Jeremiah E. (1828–1904) 81
Rawson, George (1807–1889) 316
Redhead, Richard (1820–1901) 219, 250, 294
Redner, Lewis H. (1831–1908) 133
Rees, Timothy (1874–1939) 59
Reid, William W., Jr. (b. 1923) 390
Reimann's *Sammlung Alter und
   Neuer Melodien*, 1747 463
Reinagle, Alexander R. (1799–1877) 395
René, Nancy M. (b. 1942) 297
Joseph R. Renville's (1779–1846)
   Dakota Hymn 3, 341
Repp, Ray (b. 1942) 249
Rinkart, Martin (1586–1649) 419
Rippon, John (1751–1836) 304
Rist, Johann (1607–1667) 140
John Roberts' *Caniadaeth y
   Cysegr*, 1839 .... 1, 427
Roberts, Daniel Crane (1841–1907) 592
Roberts, John (1807–1876) 240
Roberts, Leon C. (b. 20th cent.) 348
Robinson, Robert (1735–1790) 459
Rodigast, Samuel (1649–1708) 415
Röntgen, Julius (1855–1932) 23, 558
Rosas, Carlos (b. 1939) 39
Rossetti, Christina G. (1830–1894) 128, 165
Rossman, Vern 162
Routley, Erik (1917–1982) 247
Rowan, William P. (b. 1951) 83, 353, 583
Rowthorn, Jeffery (b. 1934) 308, 462
Rufty, Hilton (b. 1909) 265
Runyan, William M. (1870–1957) 423
Rush, Julian (b. 1936) 391
Ruspini, Louise 73
Russell, Francis Albert Rollo (1849–1914) 537

The Sacred Harp, 1844 .... 254, 332
St. Francis of Assisi (1182–1226) 17
St. Patrick (372–466) 83
San, Lee Yu 557
Sandell, Lina (1832–1903) 487
Sarum Breviary, 1495 184
Sarum plainsong, mode I 87
Sarum plainsong, mode IV ... 111, 739, 740
Sateren, Leland (b. 1913) 76
Scagnelli, Peter J. (b. 1949) 187
Schalk, Carl F. (b. 1929) 32, 183, 220
Schicht, Johann Gottfried (1753–1823) 276
Schlegel, Katharina von (1697–?) 488
Schmidt, Vicki Vogel (b. 1945) 62

Schmolck, Benjamin (1672–1737) 67
Scholefield, Clement E. (1839–1904) 95
Schop, Johann (c. 1595–1667) 140
Schulz-Widmar, Russell (b. 1944) 361
Schumann, Robert (1810–1856) 531
Valentin Schumann's *Geistliche
   Lieder*, 1539 130
Schutmaat, Alvin (b. 1921) 214
Schütz, Johann J. (1640–1690) 6
Heinrich Schütz, (1585–1672)
   Psalter, 1628 601
Schwedler, Johann C. (1672–1730) 49
Scott, Lesbia (1898–1986) 295
Scott, R. B. Y. (1899–1987) 611
Scott-Gatty, Alfred (1847–1918) 533,
   534, 535
Scottish Psalter, 1650 479
Scriven, Joseph (1819–1886) 506
Sears, Edmund H. (1810–1876) 131
Seerveld, Calvin (b. 1930) 113
Sensmeier, Randall (b. 1948) 343
Shaw, Martin F. (1875–1958) ... 31, 113, 238
Sheppard, Franklin L. (1852–1930) 21
Sherwin, William F. (1826–1888) 321
Showalter, Anthony J. (1858–1924) 471
Shurtleff, Ernest W. (1862–1917) 573
Sibelius, Jean (1865–1957) 488, 591, 607
Siena, Bianco da (d. 1434) 289
Sixteen Tune Settings, 1812 .... 605, 613
Sleeth, Natalie (1930–1992) 433
Smallwood, Richard (b. 1948) 511
Smart, Henry T. (1813–1879) 126, 245, 400,
   573, 574
Smith, Alfred M. (1879–1971) 443, 520
Smith, Elizabeth L. (1817–1898) 251
Smith, Emerson C. (20th cent.) 580
Smith, H. Percy (1825–1898) 365, 503
Smith, Walter C. (1824–1908) 1
Smith, William Farley (b. 1941) 525
Smyttan, George Hunt (1822–1870) 205
Sonafrank, Russell E., II (b. 1947) 549
Song Book for Sunday School, 1871 487
Sosa, Pablo D. (b. 1933) 65, 235, 544
Sotto, Angel 142
Southern Harmony, 1835 .... 78, 156, 223,
   247, 349, 530, 598
Spafford, Horatio G. (1828–1888) 438
Stainer, John (1840–1901) 129
Stanford, Charles V. (1852–1924)   109, 561
Stennett, Samuel (1727–1795) 598
Sternhold, Thomas (d. 1549) 247
Stockton, John H. (1813–1877) 189
Stone, Lloyd (b. 1912) 591
Stone, Samuel J. (1839–1900) 386
Stookey, Laurence Hull (b. 1937)   394, 395
Stowe, Everett M. (20th cent.) 72
Strasbourg Psalter, 1545 251
Strathdee, Jim (b. 1941) 584
Studdert-Kennedy, Geoffrey A. (1883–1929) 89

AUTHOR, COMPOSER, AND SOURCE INDEX 545

Stuempfle, Herman G., Jr. (b. 1923) 550, 567
Su, Yin-Lan (1915–1937) 333
Sullivan, Arthur S. (1842–1900) 230,
377, 401, 538
Suppe, Gertrude C. (b. 1911) 121, 214
Swift, Donald (b. 1952) 147

Tabada, Grace R. (b. 1942) 428
Tabayoyong, Wesley Tactay (b. 1925) ... 234
Tallis, Thomas (c. 1505–1585) 100, 178, 509
Tarrant, William G. (1853–1928) 383
Nahum Tate and Nicholas Brady's
  *A New Version of the Psalms of
  David*, 1696 .... 481, 483
Taulé, Alberto V. (b. 1932) 121
Taylor, Cyril V. (1907–1991) 70, 266
Tennyson, Alfred (1809–1892) 414
Tersteegen, Gerhard (1697–1769) 50, 68
Teschner, Melchior (1584–1635) ... 102, 216
Tessier, Albert D. 188
Theodulph of Orléans (d. 821) 216, 217
Thompson, Mikkel (b. 20th cent.) 79
Thompson, Will L. (1847–1909) 449
Threlfall, Jennette (1821–1880) 213
Thring, Godfrey (1823–1903) 301
Thrupp, Dorothy A. (1779–1847) 252
Thurman, Howard (1899–1981) 584
Tindley, Charles Albert (1851–1933)
.... 444, 447
Tisserand, Jean (d. 1494) 244
Tochter Sion, Cologne, 1741 .... 243, 542
Tollefson, Paulette (b. 1950) 15
Tomer, William G. (1833–1896) 81
Toplady, Augustus M. (1740–1778) 596
Torii, Chūgorō (b. 1898) 137
Tóth, William (1905–1963) 445
Traditional
  African-American 2, 75, 85, 136, 154,
  161, 229, 239, 282, 310, 322, 330, 369,
  394, 409, 416, 454, 458, 474, 478, 490,
  497, 500, 501, 511, 514, 519, 524, 525,
  553, 572, 599, 604, 616
  Caribbean 236
  Chinese 470
  Confucian Dacheng 424
  Dutch 23, 421, 558
  English 1, 31, 51, 110, 135, 139,
  143, 148, 153, 275, 311, 362, 363,
  401, 432, 434, 579
  Finnish 390
  French 125, 138, 151, 238, 250, 294, 345
  German 105, 123, 127, 129, 241,
  276, 384, 510
  Ghanaian 498
  Greek 739
  Hebrew 10, 314
  Irish 109, 206, 451, 504
  Jamaican 347
  Japanese 5, 72, 203

Mexican 402, 499
Mozarabic 94
Native American 3, 341
Netherlands 421
Norwegian 56, 296
Philippine 234
Pi-po 33
Puerto Rican 45, 149, 155
Scottish 200, 344
Sicilian 77
Silesian 44
Slovak 431
South African 360, 437, 526
Swedish 35, 106, 487
Swiss 418
Taiwanese 33
United States 52, 124, 223, 407,
521, 570, 610
Urdu 48
Visayan 615
Welsh 1, 76, 82, 92, 425, 484, 582
Yigdal 24, 373
Trente quatre Pseaumes, Geneva, 1551
.... 7, 101, 167, 251, 358, 611
Trier Gesangbuch, 1695 384
Troeger, Thomas H. (b. 1945) ... 7, 16, 54,
169, 176, 178, 254, 271, 301,
400, 411, 427, 568
Troutbeck, John (1832–1899) 140
Turner, Jet (1928–1984) 337
Tuttiett, Lawrence (1825–1897) 469
Tweedy, Henry Hallam (1868–1953) ... 263

Union Harmony, 1836 265
United Presbyterian Book of Psalms, 1871 13

Vajda, Jaroslav J. (b. 1919)   32, 82, 183, 431
Valerius, *Nederlandtsch Gedenkclanck*, 1626 420
van Dyke, Henry (1852–1933) 4
Vaughan Williams, Ralph (1872–1958) 17, 27,
51, 110, 123, 138, 182, 255, 257, 262, 289,
299, 331, 345, 355, 432, 434, 510, 579, 586
Victor, János (1860–1937) 327
Vinluan, Vivincio L. (b. 1937) 234
Vories, William M. (1880–1964) 589
Vulpius, Melchior (c. 1560–1615) ... 64, 603

L. J. W., in *The Sunny Side*, 1875 518
John Francis Wade's *Cantus Diversi*,
  c. 1743 135
Walford, William (1772–1850) 505
Wallace, William V. (1812–1865) 166
Walter, Howard Arnold (1883–1918) ... 492
Walter, William (1825–1893) 164, 298
Walther, Johann (1496–1570) 64
Walton, James G. (1821–1905) 381
Walworth, Clarence Alphonsus
  (1820–1900) 276
Ward, Samuel A. (1847–1903) 594

Warner, Anna B. (1820–1915) 327
Warren, George W. (1828–1902) ... 372, 592
Watts, Isaac (1674–1748) 12, 25, 27,
    132, 199, 200, 224, 225, 247, 281,
    300, 379, 382, 511
Weaver, John (b. 1937) 559
Webb, Benjamin (1819–1885) 259
Webb, George J. (1803–1887) 609
Webster, Bradford Gray (1898–1991) ... 212
Weissel, Georg (1590–1635) 117
Welch, Celene (b. 1949) 196
Wesley, Charles (1707–1788) 42, 43, 122,
    144, 160, 233, 260, 303, 305, 546
Wesley, Samuel S. (1810–1876) 386, 387, 388
Wesson, Jan (b. 1925) 541
Westbrook, Francis B. (1903–1975) 48
Westendorf, Omer (b. 1916) 76, 396
Wetzel, Richard D. (b. 1935) 152
Whitfield, Frederick (1829–1904) 52
Whitney, Maurice C. (1909–1984) 165
Whitney, Rae (b. 1927) 510
Whittier, John Greenleaf (1807–1892) 166,
    502, 533
Wiant, Bliss (1895–1975) 470
Widestrand, Olle (b. 1906) 163
Wile, Frances W. (1878–1939) 434
Wilhelm, August, II 375
Williams, David McK. (1887–1978) 277
Williams, Peter (1722–1796) 18, 19
Williams, Robert (1781–1821) 240
Williams, Thomas J. (1869–1944) 267
Williams, William (1717–1791) 18, 19
Aaron Williams' *New Universal
    Psalmodist*, 1770 .... 312, 379, 588
Thomas Williams' *Psalmodia
    Evangelica*, 1789 117

Willis, Richard S. (1819–1900) 44, 131
Wilson, Hugh (1766–1824) 481
Wilson, John W. (1905–1991) 309
Winkworth, Catherine (1827–1878) 101,
    102, 117, 130, 158, 324, 334, 410, 419, 480
Winter, Miriam Therese (b. 1938) 15, 17,
    28, 119, 575, 594
Witt, Christian F. (c. 1660–1716) 13, 122,
    325, 326
Wong, W. H. (b. 1917) 424
Woodbury, Isaac B. (1819–1858) 457
Woodward, George R. (1848–1934) 66,
    232, 241
Wordsworth, Christopher
    (1807–1885) 61, 66, 243
Work, John W., II (b. 1901) 154
Wortman, Denis (1835–1922) 358
Wren, Brian (b. 1936) 11, 79, 186, 294,
    309, 320, 349, 362, 399, 417, 527,
    559, 564, 590, 608
Wubbena, Jan Helmut (b. 1947) 413
Wyeth's *Repository of Sacred
    Music*, 1813 .... 59, 459

Y Perl Cerddoral, 1852 258
Yamaguchi, Tokuo (20th cent.) 72
Ylvisaker, John (b. 1937) 351
Young, Carlton R. (b. 1926)   11, 30, 78, 417
Young, John F. (1820–1885) 134
Yūki, Kō (b. 1896) 162

Zinzendorf, Nicolaus Ludwig von
    (1700–1760) 446
Zundel, John (1815–1882) 43, 368, 495

Tune Index

(Numbers refer to hymns in *The New Century Hymnal.*)

ABBOT'S LEIGH 70
ABERYSTWYTH 103
ADESTE FIDELES 135
ADORO TE DEVOTE 339
AFTON WATER 344
ALABANZA 34
ALL IS WELL 311
AMAZING GRACE (NEW BRITAIN) 547, 548, 617
AMEN 161
AMSTEIN 559
ANCIENT OF DAYS 46
ANDERSON 61
ANDREW 467
ANGEL'S STORY 493
ANNIKA'S DANCE 180
ANNIVERSARY SONG 370
ANTIOCH 132
AR HYD Y NOS 82, 92, 425
ASCENSION 120
ASCENSIUS 239
ASSURANCE 473
AURELIA 386, 387, 388
AUSTIN 583
AUSTRIAN HYMN 307, 565
AUTHORITY 176
AVON 200
AWAY IN A MANGER (MÜLLER) 124
AZMON 42, 383, 575

BAHAY KUBO 234
BALM IN GILEAD 553
BATTLE HYMN OF THE REPUBLIC 610
BEACH SPRING 332
BEATITUDO 450
BEECHER 43, 368, 495
BEGINNINGS 417
BENJAMIN 590
BETHANY 606
BLESSED QUIETNESS 284
BONHOEFFER 413
BORNING CRY 351
BOUNDLESS MERCY 265
BOURBON 225
BRADBURY 252
BREAD OF LIFE 321
BRIDEGROOM 270, 552
BRING FORTH 181
BROTHER JAMES' AIR 479
BRYN CALFARIA 258
BY AND BY 444

CAMACUA 544
CAMANO 9

CANONBURY 531
CAROL 131
CAROL OF HOPE 435
CENTRAL 235
CHARLESTOWN 78
CHARTERHOUSE 212, 429, 527
CHATHAM 555
CHEREPONI 498
CHRISTE SANCTORUM 90
CHRISTIAN LOVE 396
CHRISTMAS 491
CHRISTOPHER 223
CHRISTPRAISE RAY 54
CHUQUISACA 246
COME SUNDAY 602
CONDITOR ALME SIDERUM 111, 739, 740
CONSOLATION 247
CONSTANTINE 20
CORONATION 304
CRANHAM 128
CRAVEN 196
CRIMOND 468
CRISTO ES LA PEÑA 45
CRUCIFER 198
CWM RHONDDA 18, 436
DANBY 432
DANDANSOY 615
DARMSTADT 513
DARWALL'S 148TH 303
DE COLORES 402
DE TAR 587
DEN STORE HVIDE FLOK 296
DENNIS 393
DEO GRACIAS 184, 209, 259
DEUS TUORUM MILITUM 204
DIADEMATA 8, 301, 350
DICKINSON COLLEGE 168, 268
DIFFERENT SONG 150
DISTRESS 254
DIVINUM MYSTERIUM 118
DIX 28, 159
DOMINUS REGIT ME 248
DOUROUX 188
DOVE OF PEACE 349
DOWN AMPNEY 289
DOWN AT THE CROSS 189
DUKE STREET 300
DUNCANNON 228
DUNDEE 412
DUNLAP'S CREEK 256
DUST AND ASHES 186

EASTER HYMN 233
EBENEZER (TON-Y-BOTEL) 267

TUNE INDEX

EIN' FESTE BURG (ISOMETRIC) 439
EIN' FESTE BURG (RHYTHMIC) 440
ELDERKIN 160
ELLACOMBE 12, 104, 213
ELLERS 80
EN SANTA HERMANDAD 392
ENDLESS SONG 476, 563
ENGELBERG 561
ENTER, REJOICE 73
ERHALT UNS, HERR 187
ERIE 506
ERMUNTRE DICH 140
ES FLOG EIN KLEINS WALDVÖGELEIN 66
ES IST EIN' ROS 127, 600
ESTE ES EL DIA 65
EUCHARISTIC HYMN 346
EULOGIA 217
EVAN 489
EVENTIDE 99

FAITHFULNESS 423
FALCONE 271
FENNVILLE 554
FESTAL SONG 164, 298
FINLANDIA 488, 591, 607
FLORINDEZ 56
FOR THE BREAD 264
FOREST GREEN 110, 434
FORTUNATUS NEW 220
FOUNDATION 407

GALILEE 172
GARDEN 237
GATHER 335
GELOBT SEI GOTT 603
GERMANY (GARDINER) 361, 543
GIVE ME JESUS 409
GLAD TIDINGS 146
GLORIA (LES ANGES DANS NOS CAMPAGNES) 125
GLORIOUS IS YOUR NAME 53
GLORY, GLORY 2
GO DOWN, MOSES 572
GOD BE WITH YOU 81
GONFALON ROYAL 221
GOTT SEI DANK 566
GRÄFENBERG 40
GRAND ISLE 295
GREENSLEEVES 148
GROSSER GOTT, WIR LOBEN DICH 276
GUIDE MY FEET 497
GWALCHMAI 260

HALAD 279
HALLELUJA 236
HAMBURG 224
HANCOCK 462
HANKEY 522
HANOVER 305

HANSON PLACE 597
HAYDN 91
HEINLEIN 205
HENDON 49
HERR JESU CHRIST, DICH ZU UNS WEND 375
HERZLICH TUT MICH VERLANGEN 179, 202, 226
HERZLIEBSTER JESU 218
HESPERUS 329, 469, 571
HIGHER GROUND 442
HOLY MANNA 376, 556
HOSANNA 214
HOUGHTON 30
HSUAN P'ING 424
HUDSON 199
HURSLEY 96
HYFRYDOL 182, 257, 355
HYMN TO JOY 4

I AM YOURS 455
I WANT TO BE A CHRISTIAN 454
I WANT TO BE READY 616
ICH HALTE TREULICH STILL 404
ID Y ENSEÑAD 528
IDA 608
I'LL FLY AWAY 595
I'M SO GLAD 474
IMAYO 203
IN BABILONE 23, 558
IN DULCI JUBILO 129
INNOCENTS 16, 537
INNSBRUCK 94
INTEGER VITAE 518
IRBY 145
ITALIAN HYMN 275
I'VE GOT A FEELING 458
IVERSON 283

JACOB'S LADDER 500, 501
JEFFERSON 530
JESU, MEINE FREUDE 480
JESUS IS HERE 348
JESUS LOVES ME 327
JOEL 269
JONES 482
JOSEPH LIEBER, JOSEPH MEIN 105
JUDAS AND MARY 108, 210
JUDAS MACCABEUS 253
JULION 356, 357

KASTAAK 291
KATHERINE 177
KEDRON 568
KEEP YOUR LAMPS 369
KENTRIDGE 175
KING'S LYNN 579
KING'S WESTON 255, 586
KINGSFOLD 51

TUNE INDEX

KŌRIN 137
KREMSER 420, 421

LACQUIPARLE 3, 341
LADUE CHAPEL 274
LAKE ENON 457
LANCASHIRE 245, 573, 574
LAND OF REST 354, 378, 521
LASST UNS ERFREUEN 17, 27
LATTIMER 525
LAUDA ANIMA (PRAISE MY SOUL) 273, 567
LAUDES DOMINI 86, 261
LE P'ING 470
LEANING 471
LEONI 24, 314, 373
LES ANGES DANS NOS CAMPAGNES 125
LET IT BREATHE 288
LET US BREAK BREAD 330
LET US HOPE 461
LIEBSTER JESU 74
LIFT EVERY VOICE 593
LIGHT OF THE WORLD 584
LIGHTBEAMS 163
LILIUOKALANI 580
LINSTEAD 347
LITTLE BABY 147
LLANFAIR 240
LLANGLOFFAN 582
LOBE DEN HERREN 22
LOPERENA 389
LORD, MAKE ME MORE HOLY 75
LOS MAGOS 155
LOVE'S OFFERING 536
LUX EOI 538
LYONS 26

MABUNE 162
MAGYAR 445
MANGLAKAT 142
MANTON 512
MAOZ TSUR 10
MARCHING TO ZION 382
MARIAS LOVSANG 106
MARION 55
MARTIN 460
MARTINEZ 29
MARTYN 546
MARTYRDOM (AVON) 200, 481
MARY'S CHILD 152
MARYTON 365, 503
MATERNA 594
MAUNDY THURSDAY 227
MCKEE 394
MEIRIONYDD 484
MENDELSSOHN 144
MERCY 63
MERRIAL 98

MICHAEL 408
MIGHTY SAVIOR 93
MIKOTOBA 317
MIT FREUDEN ZART 6
MONING 97
MORE LOVE TO YOU 456
MORECAMBE 290, 336
MORNING SONG 89, 119, 605, 613
MORNING STAR 157
MUNICH 272, 315
MURRAY 287
MY TRIBUTE 14

NATIONAL HYMN 372, 592
NAWAHINE 496
NEAR THE CROSS 197
NEED 517
NEED OF PRAYER 519
NEIGHBOR 541
NETTLETON 59, 459
NEUMARK 410
NEW BEGINNINGS 540
NEW BRITAIN 547, 548, 617
NEW DIMENSIONS 391
NEW HOPE 343
NEW REFORMATION 371
NICAEA 277
NOËL 401
NOËL NOUVELET 238
NU OLI (GLAD TIDINGS) 146
NUEVA CREACION 614
NUN DANKET 419
NUN DANKET ALL' (GRÄFENBERG) 40
NUN FREUT EUCH 374
NUN KOMM DER HEIDEN HEILAND 64
NUN RUHEN ALLE WÄLDER (INNSBRUCK) 94
NYLAND 390

O DASS ICH TAUSEND ZUNGEN HÄTTE 324
O FILII ET FILIAE 244
O GOD MY GOD 515
O GOTT, DU FROMMER GOTT (DARMSTADT) 513
O HEILIGER GEIST (O JESULEIN SÜSS) 60
O HOLY DOVE 285
O HOW I LOVE JESUS 52
O JESU 463
O JESULEIN SÜSS 60
O QUANTA QUALIA 385
O STORE GUD 35
O WALY WALY 362, 363
OFFERING 453
OGONTZ 560
OLD FIRST 69
OLD HUNDREDTH 7
OLD SHIP OF ZION 310
OLD 22ND 316

OMNI DIE 384
ONLY STARTED 437
OPEN DOOR 529
ORA LABORA 532
ORIENTIS PARTIBUS 138, 250, 294
ORWIGSBURG 486

PASS ME NOT 551
PASSION CHORALE (HERZLICH TUT MICH VERLANGEN) 179, 202, 226
PASTORES A BELEN 149
PEACE LIKE A RIVER 478
PEACE, MY FRIENDS 249
PEEK 492
PENTECOST 328, 589
PERFECT LOVE 58
PESCADOR DE HOMBRES 173
PICARDY 345
PILOT 441
PLEADING SAVIOR 397
POR LA MAÑANA 88
POST STREET 201
PRAISE MY SOUL 273, 567
PRECIOUS LORD 472
PROCESSION 411
PROMISE 433
PROMISED LAND 598
PROPHESY 578
PSALM 42 101
PSALM 84 601
PUER NOBIS NASCITUR 57, 241
PUES SI VIVIMOS 499

QUEM PASTORES 123, 510
RAQUEL 174
RATHBUN 193
REDHEAD NO. 76 219
REGENT SQUARE 126, 400
REJOICE, REJOICE 107
RELIANCE 280
RENDEZ À DIEU 167
REPTON 114
REST 502
REVERSI 141
RHOSYMEDRE 222, 426
RICHMOND 36
ROBINSON 297
ROCKINGHAM 208, 414, 465
ROEDER 32
ROLLINGBAY 79
ROSAS 39
ROSEBERRY 585
ROYAL OAK 31
RUSSIAN HYMN 367, 577

ST. AGNES 281, 507, 508
ST. ANDREW 171
ST. ANNE 25, 278, 359
ST. BRIDE 483

ST. CATHERINE 381
ST. CHRISTOPHER 190, 191
ST. CLEMENT 95
ST. COLUMBA 109
ST. DENIO 1, 427
ST. DROSTANE 215
ST. DUNSTAN'S 494
ST. FLAVIAN 211, 318, 342
ST. GEORGE'S WINDSOR 422
ST. GERTRUDE 377
ST. KEVIN 230
ST. LOUIS 133
ST. MARGARET 485
ST. MATTHEW 263, 464
ST. MICHAEL 611
ST. PETER 395
ST. PETERSBURG 50
ST. STEPHEN 352
ST. THEODULPH (VALET WILL ICH DIR GEBEN) 102, 216
ST. THOMAS 312, 379, 380, 588
SAIPAN 323
SAKURA 5
SALLEY GARDENS 504
SALVE FESTA DIES 262
SANDON 366, 466
SAVANNAH 430
SCARLET RIBBONS 153
SCHMÜCKE DICH 334
SCHÖNSTER HERR JESU 44
SCHUMANN 170
SEED OF LIFE 83
SEELENBRÄUTIGAM 446
SERENITY 166
SERVANT SONG 364, 539
SHARE THE SPIRIT 62
SHELDONIAN 266
SHENG EN 333
SHEPHERDS' PIPES 320
SICILIAN MARINERS 77
SILVER CREEK 313
SILVER SPRING 183
SINE NOMINE 299
SIXTH NIGHT 431
SIYAHAMBA 526
SLANE 451
SMALLWOOD 511
SOFTLY AND TENDERLY 449
SOLID ROCK 403
SOME DAY 447
SOMETHING FOR JESUS 452
SOMOS PUEBLO 340
SONG OF REJOICING 612
SPANISH HYMN 185
SPARROW 475
SPIRIT 286
SPLENDOR PATERNAE 87
SPRING WOODS 549
STEADFAST 37

STEAL AWAY 599
STILLE NACHT 134
STITELER 406
STUTTGART 13, 122, 325, 326
SURSUM CORDA 443, 520
SUSSEX CAROL 143
SWEET HOUR 505
SWEET, SWEET SPIRIT 293

TABADA 428
TALAVERA TERRACE 562
TALITHA CUMI 545
TALLIS' CANON 100
TALLIS' THIRD TUNE 178, 509
TAULE 121
TENDERNESS 569
TERRA BEATA 21
THANK YOU, JESUS 41
THE ASH GROVE 76
THE BROOK CHERITH 477
THE CALL 331
THE FIRST NOWELL 139
THE OLD RUGGED CROSS 195
THE STAFF OF FAITH 418
THIS IS THE DAY 84
THIS JOY 524
THROCKMORTON 302
THUMA MINA 360
TŌA-SĪA 33
TOKYO 72
TOLLEFSON 15
TOMTER 194
TOPLADY 596
TOULON 251, 358
TRENTHAM 292
TRINITY CAROL 399
TRURO 117
TRUST IN THE LORD 416
TRYGGARE KAN INGEN VARA 487
TWILIGHT 398

UNA ESPIGA 338
UNE JEUNE PUCELLE 151
UNION SEMINARY 337
UNSER HERRSCHER 67

VENI EMMANUEL 116
VERBUM DEI 353

VICTORY 242
VIENNA 448
VILLE DU HAVRE 438
VINEYARD HAVEN 71
VOM HIMMEL HOCH 130
VRUECHTEN 231, 232

WACHET AUF 112
WALKER 156
WAREHAM 306
WAS GOTT TUT 415
WATER OF BAPTISM 169
WE SHALL OVERCOME 570
WEBB 609
WEISSE FLAGGEN 243, 542
WELWYN 533, 534, 535
WERE YOU THERE 229
WESTCHASE 11
WESTMINSTER ABBEY 47, 308, 576
WESTRIDGE 113
WEXFORD CAROL 206
WHEN JESUS WEPT 192
WHITFIELD 309
WHITNEY 165
WHY WE SING 523
WIE SCHÖN LEUCHTET 158
WILDERNESS 557
WINCHESTER NEW 115
WINCHESTER OLD 516
WINSTON-SALEM 550
WOKE UP THIS MORNING 85
WONDERFUL CHILD 136
WONDROUS LOVE (CHRISTOPHER) 223
WOODLANDS 38
WOODWORTH 207
WORDS OF LIFE 319
WORLD PEACE PRAYER 581
WUNDERBARER KÖNIG 68

YARNTON 564
YES, GOD IS REAL 405
YISU NE KAHA 48

ZION 19

First Line Index

(Indention and italics are used to indicate a first line or name by which a hymn is also known, or a translation. Numbers refer to hymns in *The New Century Hymnal*.)

A hymn of glory let us sing 259
A mighty fortress is our God 439, 440
A toi la gloire, ô Ressuscité! 253
A woman came who did not count the cost 206
Abide with me 99
Adeste, fideles 135
Adoro te devote 339
Again we keep this solemn fast 187
Ah, holy Jesus 218
Ah, what shame I have to bear 203
Alabanza 34
Alas! and did my Savior bleed 199, 200
All beautiful the march of days 434
All creatures of our God and King 17
All earth is waiting 121
All glory, laud, and honor 216, 217
All hail the power of Jesus' name! 304
All my hope on God is founded 408
All people that on earth do dwell 7
All praise be yours, my God, this night 100
All things bright and beautiful 31
Alleluia! Alleluia! Hearts to heaven 243
Alleluia! Gracious Jesus! 257
Alleluia! Sing to Jesus! 257
Almighty God, your Word is cast 318
Amazing grace, how sweet the sound 547, 548
Amen, Amen 161
An outcast among outcasts 201
Angels, from the realms of glory 126
Angels we have heard on high 125
Arise, your light is come! 164
As Moses raised the serpent up 605
As pants the hart for cooling streams 481
As shepherds filled with joy 149
As the rain is falling 34
As we gather at your table 332
As with gladness those of old 159
Ask me what great thing I know 49
At early dawn 88
At the Cross 199
At the font we start our journey 308
Awake! awake, and greet the new morn 107
Awake, awake to love and work! 89
Awake, my soul, stretch every nerve .. 491
Away in a manger 124

Baptized into your name most holy 324
Be known to us in breaking bread 342

Be not dismayed 460
Be now my vision 451
Be still, my soul 488
Be thou my vision 451
Beams of heaven, as I go 447
Beautiful Jesus 44
Beautiful Savior 44
Because you live, O Christ 231
Before the cross of Jesus 191
Before your cross, O Jesus 191
Behold a host all robed in white 296
Behold the host all robed in light 296
Behold us, Lord, a little space 516
Beneath the cross of Jesus 190
Bless God, O my soul! 549
Blessed are the poor in spirit 180
Blessed assurance 473
Blessed be the tie that binds 393
Blessed Jesus, at thy word 74
Blessed Quietness 284
Born in the night, Mary's Child 152
Born of God, Eternal Savior 542
Bread of the world, in mercy broken   346
Break forth, O beauteous heavenly light 140
Break now the bread of life 321
Break thou the bread of life 321
Breath of the living God 56
Breathe on me, Breath of God 292
Brightest and best 156, 157
Bring many names 11
By gracious powers 413
By whatever name we call you 560

Called as partners in Christ's service   495
Camina, pueblo de Dios 614
Cantemos al Creador 39
Carol our Christmas 141
Child of blessing, child of promise 325
Children of God 533
Children of the heavenly Father 487
Christ at table, there with friends 227
Christ, enthroned in heavenly splendor 258
Christ is living 235
Christ is made the sure foundation 400
Christ is the Mountain of Horeb 45
Christ Jesus, please be by our side 375
Christ, mighty Savior 93
Christ rose up from the dead 239
Christ the Lord is risen today 233
Christ the Victorious 367
Christ will come again 608

FIRST LINE INDEX

Christian, rise and act your creed 537
Colorful Creator 30
  Come, celebrate with thanksgiving 246
  Come down, O Love divine 289
Come forth, O Love divine 289
Come, gather in this special place 335
Come, God, Creator, be our shield 69
  Come, Holy Ghost, our souls inspire 268
Come, Holy Spirit, heavenly Dove 281
Come, labor on 532
Come, let us join with faithful souls ... 383
  Come, my soul 91
Come, my Way, my Truth, my Life 331
Come now, Almighty God 275
Come, O Creator Spirit 268
Come, O Fount of every blessing 459
Come, O long-expected Jesus 122
Come, O Spirit, dwell among us 267
Come, O Spirit, with your sound 265
Come, O thankful people, come 422
Come, share the Spirit 62
Come, teach us, Spirit of our God 287
  Come, thou almighty King 275
  Come, thou fount of every blessing 459
  Come, thou long-expected Jesus 122
Come to tend God's garden 586
  Come unto me, ye weary 484
Come, we who love God's name   379, 382
  Come, we who love the Lord 379, 382
  Come ye thankful people, come 422
Come, you faithful, raise the strain 230
"Comfort, comfort O my people" 101
Community of Christ 314
Crashing waters at creation 326
Creating God, your fingers trace 462
Creator God, creating still 278
  Creator God we sing 39
  Creator of the stars of night 111
Creator Spirit, come, we pray 268
Cristo es la peña de Horeb 45
¡Cristo vive! 235
  Crown him with many crowns 301
Crown with your richest crowns 301

Day is done 92
De colores 402
  De tierra lejana venimos 155
Dear God, embracing humankind 502
  Dear Lord and Father of mankind 502
  Deck thyself, my soul, with gladness ... 334
Deep in the shadows of the past 320
Down at the cross 189
Draw us in the Spirit's tether 337
Dust and ashes touch our face 186

Each winter as the year grows older ... 435
Ekolu mea nui 496
En santa hermandad 392
Enter in the realm of God 615

Enter, rejoice, and come in 73
Es ist ein' Ros entsprungen 127
Este es el día 65
Eternal Christ, who, kneeling 390
Eternal Christ, you rule 302
Eternal Spirit of the living Christ 520
Every time I feel the Spirit 282

Fairest Lord Jesus 44
Faith of our fathers 381
Faith of the martyrs 381
Father almighty, bless us 518
  Father, we praise thee 90
  Filled with excitement 214
Filled with the Spirit's power 266
Fire of God, undying Flame 64
For all the saints 299
For the beauty of the earth 28
For the faithful who have answered ... 384
For the fruit of all creation 425
For the healing of the nations 576
Forty days and forty nights 205
Forward through the ages 377
From all that dwell below the skies 27
  "*From heaven above to earth
  I come*" 130
"From heaven unto earth I come" 130
From the crush of wealth and power ... 552

"Gentle Joseph, Joseph dear" 105
Give me a clean heart 188
Give thanks for life 297
  Give to the winds thy fears 404
Give up your anxious pains 404
Giver of life, where'er they be 603
  Glad tidings 146
Glorious is your name, O Jesus 53
Glorious things of you are spoken 307
Glory, glory hallelujah 2
  Go forth, O people of God 614
Go, my children, with my blessing 82
Go tell it on the mountain 154
  Go to dark Gethsemane 219
God be with you 81
God, bless our homes 429
God created heaven and earth 33
God, creation's great designer 371
  God himself is with us 68
God is here! As we your people meet ... 70
God is my shepherd 479
God is truly with us 68
God loved the world 208
God made from one blood 427
God marked a line and told the sea 568
God moves in a mysterious way 412
God of Abraham and Sarah 20
God of change and glory 177
God of grace and God of glory 436

God of our fathers, whose almighty hand 592
God of our life 366
God of the ages, who with sure command 592
God of the prophets 358
God of the sparrow God of the whale 32
God our Author and Creator 530
God reigns o'er all the earth! 21
God, speak to me, that I may speak 531
God the Omnipotent! 577
God the Spirit, guide and guardian 355
God, today bless this new marriage 364
God, we thank you for our people 376
God, when I came into this life 354
God, who stretched the spangled heavens 556
God, who summons through all ages 356
God, whose giving knows no ending 565
God Will Take Care of You 460
God, you have set us 372
God's actions, always good and just 415
God's Eye Is on the Sparrow 475
Golden breaks the dawn 470
Good Christian friends, rejoice 129
Graced with garments of great gladness 334
Gracious Spirit, Holy Ghost 61
Grant us wisdom to perceive you 510
Great God of earth and heaven 579
Great is your faithfulness 423
Great Spirit God 341
Great work has God begun in you 353
Guide me, O my great Redeemer 18, 19
Guide me, O thou great Jehovah 18, 19
Guide my feet 497

Hail, O festal day! 262
Hail the day that sees Christ rise 260
Hail thee festal day 262
Hail to the Lord's anointed 104
Halleluja 236
Hark! the herald angels sing 144
Hark! the herald angels sing (Jesus, the Light) 160
He arose 239
He who would valiant be 494
Hear the voice of God, so tender 174
Heaven and earth, and sea and air 566
Help us accept each other 388
Here, O God, Your Servants Gather 72
Here, O my Lord, I see you face to face 336
Here, Savior, in this quiet place 555
Higher Ground 442
His Eye Is on the Sparrow 475
Hitsuji wa nemureri 137
Holy Ghost, dispel our sadness 269
Holy God, we praise your name 276
Holy, holy, holy 277
Holy Spirit, come, confirm us 264

Holy Spirit, ever dwelling 59
Holy Spirit, truth divine 63
Hope of the world 46
"Hosanna, loud hosanna" 213
How beautiful, our spacious skies 594
How blessed are they who trust in Christ 365
How brightly beams the Morning Star 158
How Can I Keep from Singing 476
How can I say thanks 14
How deep the silence of the soul 509
How firm a foundation 407
How like a gentle spirit 443
How lovely is your dwelling 600, 601
Hoy celebramos con gozo al Dios 246
Humbly I adore thee 339
Hush, Hush, Somebody's calling my name 604

"I am the light of the world!" 584
I am yours, O Lord 455
I come to the garden alone 237
I come with joy 349
I greet thee, who my sure Redeemer 251
I greet you, sure Redeemer 251
I heard my mother say 409
I heard the voice of Jesus say 489
I look to you in every need 463
I love my God, who heard my cry 511
I love the Lord, who heard my cry 511
I love thy Kingdom, Lord 312
I love to tell the story 522
I must tell Jesus 486
I need you every hour 517
I sing a song of the saints of God 295
I sing as I arise today! 83
I sing the mighty power of God 12
I sing the praise of Love almighty 50
I sing the praise of love unbounded 50
I thank you, Jesus 41
I want Jesus to go with me 490
I want Jesus to walk with me 490
I want to be ready 616
I was there to hear your borning cry 351
I will lift the cloud of night 482
I will make the darkness light 482
I will trust in the Lord 416
I woke up this morning 85
I would be true 492
If I have been the source of pain, O God 544
If thou but suffer God to guide thee 410
If you but trust in God to guide you ... 410
I'll Fly Away 595
I'll shout the name of Christ who lives 234
I'm pressing on the upward way 442
I'm so glad, Jesus lifted me 474
Immortal, invisible, God only wise 1
Immortal Love, forever full 166
In a lowly manger born 162

FIRST LINE INDEX

In all our living 499
In Christ there is no East or West 394, 395
In Egypt under Pharaoh 574
In solitude, in solitude 521
In the bleak midwinter 128
In the bulb there is a flower 433
In the cross of Christ I glory 193, 194
In the Garden 237
In the midst of new dimensions 391
Incarnate God, immortal Love 414
Isaiah the prophet has written of old   108
It came upon the midnight clear 131
It Is Well with My Soul 438
It was a sad and solemn night 225
It's the old ship of Zion 310
I've got a feeling 458
I've got peace like a river 478

Jerusalem, my happy home 378
Jesu, Jesu, fill us with your love 498
*Jesus a new commandment has
   given us* 389
Jesus calls us, o'er the tumult 171, 172
Jesus Christ is risen today 240
Jesus, I live to thee 457
Jesus, I live to you 457
Jesus is here right now 348
Jesus, Jesus, oh, what a wonderful child 136
Jesus, keep me near the cross 197
Jesus, lead thou on 446
Jesus, lover of my soul 546
Jesus loves me! 327
Jesus, our brother, strong and good 138
Jesus, priceless treasure 480
Jesus, Savior, pilot me 441
Jesus shall reign 300
Jesus, Sovereign, Savior 255
Jesus, still lead on 446
Jesus, take us to the mountain 183
Jesus the Christ says 48
Jesus, the joy of loving hearts 329
Jesus, the Light of the World 160
Jesus, the very thought of thee 507
Jesus—the very thought to me 507
Jesus, thou joy of loving hearts 329
Jesus took the bread 343
Journey to Gethsemane 219
Joy dawned again on Easter Day 241
Joy to the world! 132
Joyful, joyful, we adore you 4
Joys are flowing like a river 284
Just as I am 207

Keep awake, be always ready 112
Keep your lamps trimmed and burning 369
King of my life, I crown thee now 228

Lead on eternal Sovereign 573
Lead on, O King eternal 573

Lead us from death to life 581
Leaning on the Everlasting Arms 471
Let all mortal flesh keep silence 345
Let every Christian pray 261
Let heaven your wonders proclaim 29
Let it breathe on me 288
Let justice flow like streams 588
Let me enter God's own dwelling 67
Let there be light, O God of hosts! 589
Let us break bread together 330
Let us even now go to Bethlehem 142
Let us hope when hope seems hopeless 461
Let us talents and tongues employ 347
Let us with a gladsome mind 16
Let us with a joyful mind 16
Lift every voice and sing 593
Lift high the cross 198
Lift thy head, O Zion, weeping 445
Lift up your heads, O mighty gates 117
"Lift up your hearts!" 38
Lift your heads, O martyrs, weeping   445
Like a mother who has borne us 583
Like a tree beside the waters 313
Like the murmur of the dove's song 270
Listen to your Savior call 250
Little Bethlehem of Judah 113
Little children, welcome! 323
Lo, how a Rose e'er blooming 127
Lord, bless our homes 429
Lord, dear Lord above 602
Lord, dismiss us with your blessing 77
Lord, enthroned in heavenly splendor   258
Lord God of hosts 534
Lord, I want to be a Christian 454
Lord Jesus Christ, be present now 375
Lord Jesus, who through forty days 211
Lord, make me more holy 75
Lord, speak to me, that I may speak 531
Lord, we thank thee for our brothers 397
Lord, when I came into this life 354
Lord, who throughout these
   forty days 211
Los magos que llegaron a Belén 155
Love came down at Christmas 165
Love divine, all loves excelling 43

Make a gift of your holy Word 317
Malipayong adlaw'ng natawhan 428
Manglakat na kita sa Belen 142
Mantos y Ramos 214
*Many and great, O God, are
   your works* 3
Many are the lightbeams 163
Many Gifts, One Spirit 177
Maoz tsur y'shuati 10
Mark how the Lamb of God's
   self-offering 167
Mary, woman of the promise 123
Master, no offering costly and sweet 536

May the Sending One defend you 79	O God of love 363
Mikotoba o kudasai 317	O God of love, O God of peace 571
Mine eyes have seen the glory 610	O God of strength 534
More love to you, O Christ 456	O God, our help in ages past 25
Mothering God, you gave me birth 467	O God, the Creator 291
My eyes have seen the glory 610	O God, we bear the imprint of
My faith, it is an oaken staff 418	your face 585
My God, accept my heart this day 352	O God, who teaches us to live 359
My heart is overflowing 15	O God, whose steadfast love 426
My heart sings out with joyful praise 106	O grant us, God, a little space 516
My hope is built on nothing less 403	O grant us light 469
My life flows on in endless song 476	O holy city, seen of John 613
My shepherd is the living God 247	O holy Dove of God descending 285
My shepherd will supply my need 247	O holy God, whose gracious power 535
My song is love unknown 222	O holy radiance, joyous light 739
My soul gives glory to my God 119	O Holy Spirit, Root of life 57
My Soul Overflows with Praise 88	O how glorious, full of wonder 558
	O How I Love Jesus 52
Nearer, my God, to you 606	O how shall I receive you 102
Not my brother, nor my sister 519	O Jesus Christ, may grateful hymns 212
Not with naked eye, not with human	O Jesus, I have promised 493
sense 406	O kou aloha no 580
Now all the woods are sleeping 94	O little town of Bethlehem 133
Now bless the God of Israel 110	*O Lord of life, where'er they be* 603
Now greet the swiftly changing year 431	*O Love, how deep, how broad,*
Now in the days of youth 350	*how high* 209
Now is the time approaching 609	O love, how vast, how flowing free 209
Now let us all, in hymns of praise 529	O Love that will not let me go 485
Now thank we all our God 419	O loving founder of the stars 111
Now the day is over 98	*O Master, let me walk with thee* 503
Now the green blade rises 238	O mighty God, when I survey in wonder 35
Now the sun is setting 97	O Morning Star, how clear and bright 158
Nu oli! 146	*O my soul, bless God, the Father* 13
Nun danket alle Gott 419	O my soul, bless your Creator 13
	O praise the gracious power 54
O beautiful for spacious skies 594	O radiant Christ, incarnate Word 168
O Bread of life 333	O sacred Head, now wounded 226
O brother man, fold to thy heart 533	O saints in splendor sing 380
O Christ Jesus, sent from heaven 47	*O Sapientia* 740
O Christ, the great foundation 387	O Savior, for the saints 298
O Christ, the healer, we have come 175	O Savior, let me walk with you 503
O come, all you faithful 135	O sing a song of Bethlehem 51
O come, O come, Emmanuel 116	O sons and daughters, let us sing 244
"O come to me, you weary" 484	O Source of all that is 513
O Day of God, draw near 611	O Spirit of God 60
O day of God, draw nigh 611	*O spirit of life* 60
O day of radiant gladness 66	O spirit of the living God 263
O day of rest and gladness 66	O splendor of God's glory bright 87
O for a closer bond with God 450	O Trinity, your face we see 280
O for a closer walk with God 450	O what their joy and their glory
O for a thousand tongues to sing 42	must be 385
O for a world 575	O Wisdom breathed from God 740
O God, as with a potter's hand 550	O wondrous sight, O vision fair 184
O God, how we have wandered 202	O Word of God incarnate 315
O God in heaven 279	*O worship the King* 26
O God in whom all life begins 401	*Of the Father's love begotten* 118
O God, my God 515	Of the Parent's heart begotten 118
O God of all your people past 374	On a hill far away 195
O God of earth and altar 582	On Christmas night all Christians sing 143

FIRST LINE INDEX

On Jordan's bank the Baptist's cry 115
On Jordan's stormy banks I stand 598
On Pentecost they gathered 272
On River Jordan's banks I stand 598
Once in royal David's city 145
Onuniyan tehanl waun 548
Open now thy gates of beauty 67
Our God, to whom we turn 37
Out of the depths I call 483
Out of the depths, O God, we call 554
Over my head 514

Part in peace! 78
Pass me not, O gentle Savior 551
Pastores a Belén 149
Peace I leave with you, my friends 249
Pero Queda Cristo 88
Por la mañana 88
Praise our God above 424
Praise the Source of faith and learning 411
Praise to God 5
Praise to God, your praises bring 430
Praise to the living God 8
Praise with joy the world's Creator 273
Praise ye the Lord, the Almighty 22
Pray for the wilderness 557
Prayer is the soul's sincere desire 508
Precious Lord, take my hand 472
Profetiza, Pueblo mío 578
Pues si vivimos 499

Rejoice, give thanks and sing 303
Rejoice, the Lord is King! 303
Rejoice, you pure in heart 55, 71
Renew your church 311
Return, my people 114
Ride on! Ride on in majesty! 215
Rising in darkness 90
Rock of ages, cleft for me 596
Rock of ages, let our song 10
Ruler of life, we crown you now 228

Said Judas to Mary 210
Salup na ang adlaw 97
Savior, again to your dear name 80
Savior, an offering costly and sweet 536
Savior God above 602
Savior, like a shepherd lead us 252
Savior, thy dying love 452
Savior, when in tears and dust 185
Savior, who dying gave 452
See the little baby 147
Sekai no tomo 72
Send Me, Lord 360
Sent forth by God's blessing 76
Shadow and substance 398
Shall we gather at the river 597
Sheaves of summer 338
Sheep fast asleep 137

Sheltered by God's loving Spirit 368
Si fui motivo de dolor, oh Dios 544
"Silence! Frenzied, unclean spirit" 176
Silent night, holy night 134
Sing a different song 150
Sing, my tongue 220
Sing of colors 402
Sing praise to God, our highest good 6
Sing praise to God, who has shaped 22
Sing praise to God who reigns above 6
Sing them over again to me 319
Siyahamb' ekukhanyen' kwenkhos' 526
Softly and tenderly 449
Sois la semilla 528
Some Day 447
Some glad morning 595
Someone asked the question 523
Somos pueblo que camina 340
Son of God, eternal Savior 542
Soplo de Dios viviente 56
Sovereign and transforming Grace 512
Spirit of God, descend upon my heart 290
Spirit of Jesus, if I love my neighbor ... 590
Spirit of love 58
Spirit of the living God 283
Spirit, spirit of gentleness 286
Standing at the future's threshold 538
Standing in the Need of Prayer 519
Stars and planets flung in orbit 567
Steal away 599
Strengthen all the weary hands 612
Strong Son of God, immortal Love 414
Such perfect love my shepherd shows 248
Sun of my soul, O Savior dear 96
Surely no one can be safer 487
Sweet delight, most lovely 269
Sweet hour of prayer! 505
Sweet, Sweet Spirit 293

Take me to the water 322
Take my gifts 562
Take my life and let it be 448
Take my life, God, let it be 448
"Take up your cross," the Savior said   204
Teach me, O Lord, your holy way 465
Thank our God for sisters, brothers 397
Thank you, God 559
The Baptist shouts on Jordan's shore ... 115
The care the eagle gives her young 468
The church of Christ, in every age 306
The church's one foundation 386
The day of resurrection! 245
The day thou gavest, Lord, is ended 95
The day you gave us, God, is ended 95
The duteous day now closeth 94
The first Nowell 139
The God of Abraham praise 24
The King of love my shepherd is 248
The magi who to Bethlehem did go 155

The Old Rugged Cross 195	*We come unto our fathers' God* 374
The Queen's Prayer 580	We gather together 421
The royal banners forward fly 221	We hail you God's anointed 104
The Song of Hannah 15	We have come at Christ's own bidding 182
The strife is o'er 242	We have gathered, Jesus dear 74
The time was early evening 344	We have the strength to lift and bear 178
The weaver's shuttle swiftly flies 464	We limit not the truth of God 316
There are some things I may not know 405	We live by faith and not by sight 256
There is a balm in Gilead 553	We love your realm, O God 312
There is a name I love to hear 52	We offer Christ 527
There was Jesus by the water 545	We plant a grain of mustard seed 540
There's a spirit in the air 294	We praise you, O God 420
There's a sweet, sweet Spirit 293	We shall not give up the fight 437
There's a voice in the wilderness 120	We shall overcome 570
There's a wideness in God's mercy 23	We sing to you, O God 9
These things did Thomas count 254	We who would valiant be 494
They asked, "Who's my neighbor?" 541	We worship you, God 26
They did not build in vain 373	We would be building 607
Thine is the glory 253	We yearn, O Christ, for wholeness 179
This is a day of new beginnings 417	*We'll Understand It Better By and By* 444
This is my song 591	Were you there 229
This is the day 84	What a covenant 471
This is the day 65	*What a fellowship* 471
This joy I have 524	What a friend we have in Jesus 506
This joyful Eastertide 232	*What a glad day* 428
This little light of mine 524, 525	What child is this 148
Thou art the way 40	What gift can we bring 370
Though falsely some revile or hate me 477	What ruler wades through
Three Greatest Things 496	murky streams 169
Through all the world, a hungry Christ 587	What wondrous love is this 223
Thuma mina 360	*Whate'er my God ordains is right* 415
'Tis the old ship of Zion 310	*When I, O Lord, behold thy vast*
'Tis winter now; the fallen snow 432	*creation* 35
To God compose a song of joy 36	When I survey the wondrous cross 224
To you, O God, all creatures sing 17	When in our music God is glorified ... 561
Toda la tierra 121	When Israel was in Egypt's land 572
Touch the earth lightly 569	When Jesus wept 192
Truth whom we adore 339	When, like the woman at the well 196
Tú has venido a la orilla 173	When love is found 362
'Twas in the moon of wintertime 151	When minds and bodies meet as one 399
'Twas on that dark and doleful night 225	When morning gilds the skies 86
	When peace, like a river 438
Un mandamiento nuevo 389	When the morning stars together 453
Una espiga 338	Where charity and love prevail 396
Unite and join your cheerful songs 617	Where cross the crowded ways of life 543
United by God's love 392	Who would think that what was needed 153
Unto the hills we lift our longing eyes 466	Why should I feel discouraged 475
	Why We Sing 523
Wakantanka taku nitawa 3	Wind who makes all winds that blow 271
Wake, my soul 91	With joy draw water 109
Watcher, tell us of the night 103	Womb of life, and source of being 274
We are climbing Jacob's ladder 500	Wonder of wonders, here revealed 328
We are dancing Sarah's circle 501	*Wonderful Words of Life* 319
We are marching in the light of God 526	Won't you let me be your servant? 539
We are not our own 564	
We are often tossed and driven 444	Ye servants of God, your Master
We are people on a journey 340	proclaim 305
We are your people 309	*Yes, God Is Real* 405
We cannot own the sunlit sky 563	Yigdal elohim chai 24

You are called to tell the story 357	*You shall prophesy, all my people* 578
You are salt for the earth, O people 181	You walk along our shoreline 504
You are the seed 528	Your love, O God, has called us here 361
You are the way 40	Your ways are not our own 170
You have come down to the lakeshore 173	*Yours is the glory, Resurrected One!* 253
You servants of God, your Sovereign proclaim 305